California Cannabis Laws and Regulations

2023 Edition

Omar Figueroa

California Cannabis Laws and Regulations

ISBN 979-8-9856826-6-3

Disclaimer

This publication has been created to provide you with accurate and authoritative information concerning California cannabis and hemp laws and regulations. It is sold with the understanding that the publisher is not engaged in rendering legal or other professional services. This publication is not a substitute for legal advice of an attorney. If you require legal or other expert advice, you should seek the services of a competent attorney or other professional.

The law is ever changing and sometimes errors happen even with careful attention to detail. If you find any errors, please email us the details at book@omarfigueroa.com with the phrase "Book Error: Confidential" in the subject line. Although this publication is designed to aid in the research and practice of cannabis law, it is recommended that you cross check the California Legislature website for any change in the law. The URL for the Legislature's website is:

http://leginfo.legislature.ca.gov/faces/codes.xhtml

Because California's cannabis and hemp regulations are also evolving, please check for the latest regulatory updates at the California Cannabis Portal and the CDFA's Industrial Hemp Program webpage:

http://cannabis.ca.gov and *http://www.cdfa.ca.gov/plant/industrialhemp/*

Also, please keep yourself informed by purchasing the most up-to-date edition of this publication as it comes available.

Colophon

Author: Omar Figueroa, Esq.

Legal and Research Assistant: Tina S. Smith, Esq.

Text Design: Jocelyn Bergen

Cover Design: Ophelia Chong

Cover Image: Ruth Frase

Typeface: PT Serif

Published by Lux Law Publishing

Preface

California cannabis law has continually evolved over the past few years. After California voters "legalized" cannabis for adults ages 21 and older with the passage of Proposition 64 in 2016, the Legislature merged adult use and medical cannabis laws to create the Medicinal and Adult-Use Cannabis Regulation and Safety Act (MAUCRSA) in 2017. The MAUCRSA regulatory framework created three regulatory agencies for different parts of the cannabis supply chain, and these agencies promulgated emergency regulations as an initial step in the regulatory rulemaking process. The process included public hearings, public comment, and review by the Office of Administrative Law. The final permanent regulations took effect in 2019. At the time, the regulatory framework felt settled and stable. Nevertheless, the heavily regulated cannabis market in California had numerous difficulties competing with the laissez faire "duty-free" market. Tax revenues fell far short of projections. In early 2020, Governor Newsom announced a proposal to simplify licensing and regulatory oversight by consolidating the three regulatory agencies into a new Department of Cannabis Control (DCC). Such a proposal would require amending the MAUCRSA regulatory framework and restarting the regulatory rulemaking process. On July 12, 2021, DCC was finally created. Three regulatory agencies merged into one to license, inspect, and regulate all cannabis activity in California. On November 7, 2022, DCC promulgated consolidated regulations allowing similar sections to be combined and conflicts between the separate regulations to be resolved.

Over the last few years, California's Industrial Hemp Program has also greatly evolved. The California Industrial Hemp Farming Act became effective on January 1, 2017, authorizing the commercial production of industrial hemp. Since then, there has been steady progress to develop and refine regulations. Governor Gavin Newsom signed Assembly Bill 45 on October 6, 2021, to include new hemp products in the regulatory framework and to incorporate hemp-derived cannabinoids into the cannabis supply chain. California's laws and regulations for industrial hemp products will continue to evolve to come in line with federal regulations.

This book fulfills a need for a carefully curated compendium designed to give the reader a deep understanding of California's laws and regulations relating to cannabis and hemp, updated for 2022. The relevant statutory law can be easily found with the annotated table of contents, with detailed section descriptors summarizing each code section. Similarly, the numerous regulations set forth in the California Code of Regulations are organized by Title. Finally, a handy Index makes it easy to pinpoint germane laws and regulations.

Why is such a book necessary in this day of free online access to California's codes and regulations? Because MAUCRSA did not create a legal tabula rasa by repealing all former cannabis laws and establishing a new legal order. Instead, MAUCRSA changed and augmented existing laws, making California cannabis laws even more byzantine than before.

It was not always this way. Cannabis was legal in California until 1913, when the Poison Act was amended to outlaw "narcotic preparations of hemp or loco-weed." (At that point, it was legal under federal law.) In the 1950s, possession was escalated to a felony with mandatory incarceration. The madness continued until 1976, when the Legislature decriminalized possession of small quantities of marijuana with the Moscone Act. Nevertheless, the cultivation of a single plant, and the sale or possession for sale of any amount, remained non-reducible felonies under California law for decades.

On November 5, 1996, California voters approved Proposition 215, the Compassionate Use Act (CUA), making California the first state in the United States to legalize the possession and cultivation of medical cannabis by patients and primary caregivers. For the first time in nearly a century, patients were allowed to use medical cannabis for the treatment of "cancer, anorexia, AIDS, chronic pain, spasticity, glaucoma, arthritis, migraine, or any other illness for which marijuana provides relief." Proposition 215 remains in effect and can be found at Health & Safety Code Section 11362.5.

Senate Bill 420 was passed in 2003, and became effective on January 1, 2004, establishing a voluntary program for the issuance of official identification cards to qualified medical cannabis patients and caregivers. SB 420 also purported to establish default limits of no more than eight ounces of dried processed flowers per qualified patient and no more than six mature or 12 immature marijuana plants per qualified patient; these "limits" were subsequently struck down by the California Supreme Court as unconstitutional legislative amendments to Proposition 215, to the extent that they burden an accused's defense. SB 420 also established a medical defense for qualified patients and caregivers who associate "in order collectively or cooperatively to cultivate cannabis for medical purposes." The era of collectives and cooperatives was born and lasted for approximately fifteen years, until January 9, 2019, when Health and Safety Code Section 11362.775 was repealed. The Legislature took away in 2019 what it had given in 2004.

In 2010, Governor Schwarzenegger signed Senate Bill 1449, which reclassified possession of up to 28.5 grams of marijuana from a no jail misdemeanor punishable by a $100 maximum fine, to an infraction with the same lenient penalties, but without the right to a jury trial afforded to misdemeanor defendants by the California Constitution. This helped defeat Proposition 19, the first adult legalization initiative to get on the ballot in the new millennium, in 2010.

The Medical Marijuana Regulation and Safety Act (with the unfortunate acronym MMRSA, which sounds just like the acronym for Methicillin-resistant Staphylococcus aureus) was passed on September 11, 2015, and went into effect on January 1, 2016. It first consisted of three bills: SB 643, AB 266, and AB 243. They established a new regulatory agency, the Bureau of Medical Marijuana Regulation (BMMR, pronounced "bummer"), created a regulatory framework with a dual licensing system requiring local permits and state licenses, and added a sunset clause to the collective and cooperative statute, Health and Safety Code Section 11362.775. Within the next year, more legislation was added, which resulted in numerous changes including a renamed Medical Cannabis Regulation and Safety Act (MCRSA) and Bureau of Medical Cannabis Regulation (BMCR).

On November 8, 2016, the California voters approved the Adult Use of Marijuana Act (AUMA), which officially went into effect the next day. AUMA partially legalized marijuana under state law by adults 21 and older, allowing adults to legally grow, possess, and use small quantities of marijuana for non-medical purposes. It also reduced the severity of, and penalties for, many cannabis-related offenses, and established a regulatory framework for non-medical adult-use cannabis similar to the MCRSA framework.

Subsequently, the laws governing medical and recreational cannabis were merged together by the Legislature to create the Medicinal and Adult-Use Cannabis Regulation and Safety Act (MAUCRSA). MAUCRSA set forth a comprehensive regulatory framework with different license types overseen by different regulatory agencies. First, cultivation activities are licensed and regulated by Cal Cannabis Cultivation Licensing within the California Department of Food and Agriculture. Second, manufacturing is licensed and regulated by the Manufactured Cannabis Safety Branch within the Department of Public Health. Finally, distribution, laboratory testing, retail (both storefront and delivery-only), microbusinesses, and cannabis events are overseen by the Bureau of Cannabis Control within the Department of Consumer Affairs.

These agencies promulgated emergency regulations which became effective on January 1, 2018, and evolved over time, until the final permanent regulations were approved by the Office of Administrative Law on January 16, 2019. 2019 was the second year of the regulated cannabis market. The regulated market struggled to compete with a legacy market unburdened by regulations, taxes, and restrictive local permitting. Tax revenues fell far short of projections.

On January 10, 2020, Governor Newsom announced a proposal to simplify licensing and regulatory oversight by consolidating the three regulatory agencies into a new Department of Cannabis Control, by July 2021. Such a proposal would require amending the MAUCRSA regulatory framework and restarting the regulatory rulemaking process, similar to 2017, when the regulatory frameworks established by MCRSA and Proposition 64 were consolidated into MAUCRSA, and the regulatory rulemaking process that had almost been completed with respect to medical cannabis had to be restarted to harmonize medicinal and adult-use regulations.

The COVID-19 global pandemic delayed progress for regulatory unification and created new challenges. The cannabis industry emerged stronger after it was deemed essential by the Governor, meaning licensed cannabis businesses were allowed to remain open when many other types of businesses were not. Notably, regulatory agencies were open to regulatory innovations, and allowed curbside pickup for storefront retailers and contactless delivery for retailers engaged in deliveries.

The long-anticipated creation of the Department of Cannabis Control (DCC) finally happened on July 12, 2021, when Gov. Gavin Newsom signed Assembly Bill 141 into law. Three regulatory agencies merged into one to license, inspect, and regulate all cannabis activity in California eliminating the complexity of determining which regulatory body to answer to, understanding how the various regulatory bodies play into vertical integration, and keeping track of each program's frequent updates. Three sets of regulations were then consolidated into Title 4, Division 19 of the California Code of Regulations combining similar sections and resolving conflicts between the separate regulations.

Regulations for the OCal comparable-to-organic certification and cannabis appellations were also finalized in late 2021. OCal is a statewide certification program that establishes and enforces comparable-to-organic cannabis standards. The OCal Program will ensure that cannabis products bearing the OCal seal have been certified to consistent, uniform standards comparable to the National Organic Program. The Cannabis Appellations Program helps prevent misrepresentation of the cannabis good's geographical origin and promotes regional collaboration around cannabis production.

In 2022, DCC launched the equity fee waiver program providing a way for businesses to apply for a waiver or deferral of their annual license or renewal fee depending on their gross revenues and status as an equity applicant. Major overhauls were also implemented to California's cultivation and excise tax. As of July 1, 2022, the cultivation tax was permanently eliminated. These changes are intended to help the smaller cannabis operations compete in the legal marketplace.

As of January 1, 2023, cultivators may now obtain a large cultivation license. As a result, licensees have more opportunity to hold licenses with more expansive cultivation areas on one premises, rather than several smaller cultivation licenses on different premises to equal the same size cultivation area. California has also implemented laws relating to interstate cannabis agreements in anticipation of future federal laws allowing commercial cannabis activity between California and out-of-state licensees.

On January 30, 2023, the California Office of Administrative Law (OAL) approved emergency regulations related to cannabis taxes that were proposed by the California Department of Tax and Fee Administration (CDTFA), including a new program for certain eligible retailers to retain a portion of the cannabis taxes collected as vendor compensation.

To provide a comprehensive research resource, this edition includes numerous regulations applicable to cannabis as well as the latest available version of California's hemp regulations. These selected regulations cover lake and streambed alterations for cannabis cultivation, cannabis tax, the use of natural water resources for cultivation, the waste discharge requirements, and the state's water quality policies on cannabis cultivation.

The goal of this publication is to provide a carefully curated compendium designed to give the reader a deep understanding of California's laws and regulations relating to cannabis and hemp, updated for 2022. It is a user-friendly guide that can be used by operators, professionals, and regulators. We hope you find California Cannabis Laws and Regulations to be an indispensable tool in your library.

Because California law is rapidly evolving, we suggest that readers check for the latest changes, amendments, and updates at the California Legislature's web site:

http://leginfo.legislature.ca.gov/faces/codes.xhtml

California's cannabis and hemp regulations are also evolving. Please check for the latest regulatory updates at the California Cannabis Portal and the CDFA's Industrial Hemp Program webpage:

http://cannabis.ca.gov and http://www.cdfa.ca.gov/plant/industrialhemp/

A Word About Legal Taxonomy

In order to get the most out of this resource, it's helpful to know the legal classification of California's laws. The California Codes are 29 legal codes enacted by the California State Legislature, which together form the general statutory law of California. The California Codes are organized by subject matter, such as the Business and Professions Code, the Health and Safety Code, and the Vehicle Code. Codes are divided into "Titles," which are numbered and cover a broad area of law within that subject matter. Titles are further broken down into numbered "Divisions" which cover a narrow area of law within that Title. Divisions are broken down into "Parts," followed by "Chapters," then "Articles," and finally into individual "Sections." A law is most typically referred to in the California Courts by its Code name and Section number (for example, Health and Safety Code Section 11362.5).

Changes to the 2023 Edition

PART 1: LAW CHANGES

AB 195	Amended Business and Professions Code sections 26038, 26051.5, 26067, 26068, and 26090 Added and repealed Business and Professions Code section 26203 Amended Fish and Game Code sections 5650, 5650.1, and 13103 Amended Government Code section 11552 Amended Revenue and Taxation Code sections 6479.3, 34010, 34011, 34012, 34012.5, 34013, 34014, and 34019 Amended, repealed, and added Revenue and Taxation Code section 34015 Added Revenue and Taxation Code sections 6369.6, 34011.01, 34011.1, 34011.2, 34012.3, 34014.1, 34015.1, 34015.2, 34019.01, and 34020.1 Added and repealed Revenue and Taxation Code sections 17053.64, 17053.82, 23664, 23682, and 34019.1 Amended Water Code section 1052
AB 960	Amended Penal Code section 1170
AB 1380	Amended Business and Professions Code sections 27, 26012.5, 26162 Amended Health and Safety Code section 111928
AB 1598	Amended Health and Safety Code sections 11014.5, 11364.5
AB 1706	Amended Health and Safety Code section 11361.9

AB 1885	Amended Business and Professions Code sections 4883, 4884, 26000, 26001, and 26130
AB 1894	Amended, repealed, and added Business and Professions Code section 26120 Added Business and Professions Code section 26152.1
AB 1954	Added Business and Professions Code section 2228.5
AB 2089	Amended Civil Code section 56.06
AB 2155	Amended Business and Professions Code section 26001
AB 2188	Added Government section 12954
AB 2568	Added Business and Professions Code section 26261
AB 2595	Added Welfare and Institutions Code section 328.2
AB 2685	Amended Business and Professions Code section 101
AB 2925	Amended Revenue and Taxation Code section 34019
SB 891	Amended Water Code section 13260
SB 988	Amended Health and Safety Code sections 1649.1, 1649.2, 1649.4, and 1649.5 Repeal and added Health and Safety Code section 1649.3
SB 1186	Amended Business and Professions Code section 26200 Added Business and Professions Code sections 26320 to 26325 (Chapter 26)
SB 1326	Amended Business and Professions Code sections 26080 and 26190 Added Business and Professions Code section 26300 to 26308 (Chapter 25)
SB 1496	Amended Penal Code section 830.11 Amended Revenue and Taxation Code sections 34016, 34018, 55044

PART 2: REGULATION CHANGES

Cannabis Tax	Title 18: Public Revenues; Division 2: California Department of Tax and Fee Administration; Chapter 8.7: Cannabis Tax Regulations Added sections 3703, 3800, 3805, 3810 Amended section 3700
Equity Fee Waivers	Title 4: Business Regulations; Division 19: Department of Cannabis Control Added section 15014.1
Industrial Hemp	Title 3: Food and Agriculture; Division 4: Plant Industry; Chapter 8: Industrial Hemp Cultivation Added sections 4890, 4934, 4936, 4951, 4952
Large Cultivation and Conversion to Large Cultivation	Title 4: Business Regulations; Division 19: Department of Cannabis Control Added sections 15014.2, 15027.1, 16201.1, 16300.1 Amended section 15006
Track and Trace	Title 4: Business Regulations; Division 19: Department of Cannabis Control Added section 15049.3 Amended section 15418

Contents at a Glance

PART 1: LAWS

PART 2: REGULATIONS

Table of Contents
Part 1: Laws

I. Business and Professions Code Sections

Chapter 2. Administration

Chapter 3. Enforcement

Chapter 4. Appeals

Chapter 5. Licensing

Chapter 6. Licensed Cultivation Sites

Chapter 6.5. Unique Identifiers and Track and Trace

Chapter 7. Retailers and Distributors

Chapter 8. Distribution and Transport

Chapter 9. Delivery

Chapter 10. Testing Laboratories

Chapter 11. Quality Assurance, Inspection, and Testing

Chapter 12. Packaging and Labeling

Chapter 13. Manufacturers and Cannabis Products

Chapter 14. Protection of Minors

Chapter 15. Advertising and Marketing Restrictions

Chapter 16. Records

Chapter 18. License Fees

Chapter 19. Annual Reports; Performance Audit

Chapter 20. Local Control

Chapter 21. Funding

Chapter 22. Cannabis Cooperative Associations

ARTICLE 1. DEFINITIONS

ARTICLE 2. GENERAL PROVISIONS

ARTICLE 3. PURPOSES

ARTICLE 4. ARTICLES OF INCORPORATION

ARTICLE 5. BYLAWS

ARTICLE 6. DIRECTORS AND MANAGEMENT

ARTICLE 7. POWERS

ARTICLE 8. FINANCIAL PROVISIONS

ARTICLE 9. MEMBERS

ARTICLE 10. MARKETING CONTRACTS

ARTICLE 11. REORGANIZATION OF CORPORATIONS ORGANIZED PURSUANT TO OTHER LAWS

Chapter 23. The California Cannabis Equity Act

Chapter 24. Information Sharing with Financial Institutions

Chapter 25. Interstate Cannabis Agreements

ARTICLE 1. DEFINITIONS

ARTICLE 2. AGREEMENTS

Chapter 26. Medicinal Cannabis Patients' Right of Access Act

II. Civil Code Sections

III. Education Code Sections

IV. Evidence Code Sections

V. Fish and Game Code Sections

VI. Food and Agricultural Code Sections

DIVISION 20. PROCESSORS, STORES, DEALERS, AND DISTRIBUTORS OF AGRICULTURAL PRODUCTS

Chapter 6. Processors of Farm Products

ARTICLE 9. PRODUCER'S LIEN

DIVISION 24. INDUSTRIAL HEMP

VII. Government Code Sections

VIII. Health and Safety Code Sections

Chapter 4.9. Compassionate Access to Medical Cannabis Act or Ryan's Law

Chapter 9. Industrial Hemp

ARTICLE 1. DEFINITIONS

ARTICLE 2. GENERAL PROVISIONS

ARTICLE 3. MANUFACTURE

ARTICLE 4. REGISTRATION AND FEES

ARTICLE 5. RECORDKEEPING

ARTICLE 6. TESTING REQUIREMENTS

ARTICLE 7. LABELING AND ADVERTISEMENT

ARTICLE 8. ENFORCEMENT

ARTICLE 9. AGENCY COORDINATION

ARTICLE 10. INHALABLE PRODUCTS

IX. Labor Code Sections

X. Penal Code Sections

XI. Revenue and Taxation Code Sections

XII. Vehicle Code Sections

XIII. Water Code Sections

XIV. Welfare and Institutions Code

Table of Contents Part 2: Regulations

Title 3. Food and Agriculture

DIVISION 4. PLANT INDUSTRY

Chapter 8. Industrial Hemp Cultivation

ARTICLE 1. REGISTRATION OF INDUSTRIAL HEMP GROWERS

ARTICLE 2. REGULATIONS FOR INDUSTRIAL HEMP CULTIVATION

ARTICLE 3. PETITION REVIEW PROCESS

Chapter 3. Ocal Program

ARTICLE 1. DEFINITIONS

ARTICLE 2. APPLICABILITY

ARTICLE 3. OCAL CULTIVATION AND DISTRIBUTION REQUIREMENTS

ARTICLE 4. LABELS, LABELING, AND MARKET INFORMATION

ARTICLE 5. ACCREDITATION AND REGISTRATION OF CERTIFYING AGENTS

ARTICLE 6. CERTIFICATION OF OPERATIONS

ARTICLE 7. FEES

ARTICLE 8. COMPLIANCE

Title 4. Business Regulations

DIVISION 19. DEPARTMENT OF CANNABIS CONTROL

Chapter 1. All Licensees

ARTICLE 1. DIVISION DEFINITIONS AND GENERAL REQUIREMENTS

ARTICLE 2. APPLICATIONS

ARTICLE 3. LICENSING

ARTICLE 4. POSTING AND ADVERTISING

ARTICLE 5. SECURITY MEASURES

ARTICLE 6. TRACK AND TRACE REQUIREMENTS

ARTICLE 7. ACCEPTANCE OR REJECTION OF SHIPMENTS

Chapter 2. Distributors

Chapter 3. Retailers

Chapter 4. Microbusiness

Chapter 5. Cannabis Events

Chapter 6. Testing Laboratories

ARTICLE 1. CHAPTER DEFINITIONS

ARTICLE 2. LABORATORY LICENSE

ARTICLE 3. SAMPLING CANNABIS AND CANNABIS PRODUCTS

ARTICLE 4. STANDARD OPERATING PROCEDURES

ARTICLE 5. LABORATORY TESTING AND REPORTING

ARTICLE 6. POST TESTING PROCEDURES

ARTICLE 7. LABORATORY QUALITY ASSURANCE AND QUALITY CONTROL

ARTICLE 8. LABORATORY EMPLOYEE QUALIFICATIONS

ARTICLE 9. RECORD RETENTION [REPEALED]

Chapter 7. Enforcement [Repealed]

Chapter 7. Cultivators

ARTICLE 1. GENERAL CULTIVATION REQUIREMENTS

ARTICLE 2. CULTIVATION SITE REQUIREMENTS

ARTICLE 2. SHARED-USE FACILITIES

ARTICLE 3. SOLVENT USE AND SAFETY

ARTICLE 4. GOOD MANUFACTURING PRACTICES

ARTICLE 5. SPECIAL MANUFACTURING

Chapter 9. Other Responsibilities

Chapter 10. Cannabis and Cannabis Products

ARTICLE 1. STANDARDS FOR MANUFACTURED CANNABIS PRODUCTS

ARTICLE 2. CANNABINOID CONCENTRATION LIMITS

ARTICLE 3. FAILED PRODUCT BATCHES

Chapter 11. Labeling and Packaging Requirements

ARTICLE 1. BULK CANNABIS OR CANNABIS PRODUCTS, IMMATURE PLANTS, AND SEEDS

ARTICLE 2. CANNABIS PRODUCTS RELEASED FROM MANUFACTURING

ARTICLE 3. LABELING REQUIREMENTS

ARTICLE 4. PACKAGING

Chapter 12. Enforcement

ARTICLE 1. AUTHORITY

ARTICLE 2. COMPLIANCE AND ENFORCEMENT ACTIONS

ARTICLE 3. DISCIPLINARY ACTIONS

ARTICLE 4. EMERGENCY DECISION AND ORDERS

ARTICLE 5. POSTING NOTICES OF SUSPENSION AND REVOCATION

Chapter 13. Other Provisions

ARTICLE 1. RESEARCH FUNDING

Title 14. Natural Resources

DIVISION 1. FISH AND GAME COMMISSION DEPARTMENT OF FISH AND GAME

SUBDIVISION 3. GENERAL REGULATIONS

Chapter 3. Miscellaneous

Title 16. Professional and Vocational Regulations

DIVISION 42. BUREAU OF CANNABIS CONTROL [RENUMBERED]

DIVISION 43. CANNABIS CONTROL APPEALS PANEL

ARTICLE 1. GENERAL

ARTICLE 2. FILING OF APPEAL

ARTICLE 3. RECORD ON APPEAL

ARTICLE 4. FILING BRIEFS

ARTICLE 5. HEARINGS

ARTICLE 6. NEWLY DISCOVERED EVIDENCE

ARTICLE 7. MOTIONS

DIVISION 2. CALIFORNIA DEPARTMENT OF TAX AND FEE ADMINISTRATION - BUSINESS TAXES

Chapter 8.7. Cannabis Tax Regulations

Title 23. Waters

DIVISION 3. STATE WATER RESOURCES CONTROL BOARD AND REGIONAL WATER QUALITY CONTROL BOARDS

Chapter 5. Fees.

Chapter 9. Waste Discharge Reports and Requirements.

Chapter 22. State Policy for Water Quality Control.

Part 3: Charts of California

Cannabis License Types

Index

Part 1: Laws

I. Business and Professions Code Sections

Business and Professions Code § 27

(Amended by Stats. 2022, Ch. 28, Sec. 1. (SB 1380) Effective January 1, 2023.)

(a) Each entity specified in subdivisions (c), (d), and (e) shall provide on the internet information regarding the status of every license issued by that entity in accordance with the California Public Records Act (Division 10 (commencing with Section 7920.000) of Title 1 of the Government Code) and the Information Practices Act of 1977 (Chapter 1 (commencing with Section 1798) of Title 1.8 of Part 4 of Division 3 of the Civil Code). The public information to be provided on the internet shall include information on suspensions and revocations of licenses issued by the entity and other related enforcement action, including accusations filed pursuant to the Administrative Procedure Act (Chapter 3.5 (commencing with Section 11340) of Part 1 of Division 3 of Title 2 of the Government Code) taken by the entity relative to persons, businesses, or facilities subject to licensure or regulation by the entity. The information may not include personal information, including home telephone number, date of birth, or social security number. Each entity shall disclose a licensee's address of record. However, each entity shall allow a licensee to provide a post office box number or other alternate address, instead of the licensee's home address, as the address of record. This section shall not preclude an entity from also requiring a licensee, who has provided a post office box number or other alternative mailing address as the licensee's address of record, to provide a physical business address or residence address only for the entity's internal administrative use and not for disclosure as the licensee's address of record or disclosure on the internet.

(b) In providing information on the internet, each entity specified in subdivisions (c) and (d) shall comply with the Department of Consumer Affairs' guidelines for access to public records.

(c) Each of the following entities within the Department of Consumer Affairs shall comply with the requirements of this section:

(1) The Board for Professional Engineers, Land Surveyors, and Geologists shall disclose information on its registrants and licensees.

(2) The Bureau of Automotive Repair shall disclose information on its licensees, including auto repair dealers, smog stations, lamp and brake stations, smog check technicians, and smog inspection certification stations.

(3) The Bureau of Household Goods and Services shall disclose information on its licensees, registrants, and permitholders.

(4) The Cemetery and Funeral Bureau shall disclose information on its licensees, including cemetery brokers, cemetery salespersons, cemetery managers, crematory managers, cemetery authorities, crematories, cremated remains disposers, embalmers, funeral establishments, and funeral directors.

(5) The Professional Fiduciaries Bureau shall disclose information on its licensees.

(6) The Contractors State License Board shall disclose information on its licensees and registrants in accordance with Chapter 9 (commencing with Section 7000) of Division 3. In addition to information related to licenses as specified in subdivision (a), the board shall also disclose information provided to the board by the Labor Commissioner pursuant to Section 98.9 of the Labor Code.

(7) The Bureau for Private Postsecondary Education shall disclose information on private postsecondary institutions under its jurisdiction, including disclosure of notices to comply issued pursuant to Section 94935 of the Education Code.

(8) The California Board of Accountancy shall disclose information on its licensees and registrants.

(9) The California Architects Board shall disclose information on its licensees, including architects and landscape architects.

(10) The State Athletic Commission shall disclose information on its licensees and registrants.

(11) The State Board of Barbering and Cosmetology shall disclose information on its licensees.

(12) The Acupuncture Board shall disclose information on its licensees.

(13) The Board of Behavioral Sciences shall disclose information on its licensees and registrants.

(14) The Dental Board of California shall disclose information on its licensees.

(15) The California State Board of Optometry shall disclose information on its licensees and registrants.

(16) The Board of Psychology shall disclose information on its licensees, including psychologists and registered psychological associates.

(17) The Veterinary Medical Board shall disclose information on its licensees, registrants, and permitholders.

(d) The State Board of Chiropractic Examiners shall disclose information on its licensees.

(e) The Structural Pest Control Board shall disclose information on its licensees, including applicators, field representatives, and operators in the areas of fumigation, general pest and wood destroying pests and organisms, and wood roof cleaning and treatment.

(f) "Internet" for the purposes of this section has the meaning set forth in paragraph (6) of subdivision (f) of Section 17538.

Business and Professions Code § 101

(Amended by Stats. 2022, Ch. 414, Sec. 1. (AB 2685) Effective January 1, 2023.)

The department is comprised of the following:

(a) The Dental Board of California.

(b) The Medical Board of California.

(c) The California State Board of Optometry.

(d) The California State Board of Pharmacy.

(e) The Veterinary Medical Board.

(f) The California Board of Accountancy.

(g) The California Architects Board.

(h) The State Board of Barbering and Cosmetology.

(i) The Board for Professional Engineers, Land Surveyors, and Geologists.

(j) The Contractors State License Board.

(k) The Bureau for Private Postsecondary Education.

(l) The Bureau of Household Goods and Services.

(m) The Board of Registered Nursing.

(n) The Board of Behavioral Sciences.

(o) The State Athletic Commission.

(p) The Cemetery and Funeral Bureau.

(q) The Bureau of Security and Investigative Services.

(r) The Court Reporters Board of California.

(s) The Board of Vocational Nursing and Psychiatric Technicians.

(t) The Landscape Architects Technical Committee.

(u) The Division of Investigation.

(v) The Bureau of Automotive Repair.

(w) The Respiratory Care Board of California.

(x) The Acupuncture Board.

(y) The Board of Psychology.

(z) The Podiatric Medical Board of California.

(aa) The Physical Therapy Board of California.

(ab) The Arbitration Review Program.

(ac) The Physician Assistant Board.

(ad) The Speech-Language Pathology and Audiology and Hearing Aid Dispensers Board.

(ae) The California Board of Occupational Therapy.

(af) The Osteopathic Medical Board of California.

(ag) The California Board of Naturopathic Medicine.

(ah) The Dental Hygiene Board of California.

(ai) The Professional Fiduciaries Bureau.

(aj) The State Board of Chiropractic Examiners.

(ak) The Bureau of Real Estate Appraisers.

(al) The Structural Pest Control Board.

(am) Any other boards, offices, or officers subject to its jurisdiction by law.

Business and Professions Code § 144

(Amended by Stats. 2021, Ch. 630, Sec. 4.5. (AB 1534) Effective January 1, 2022.)

(a) Notwithstanding any other law, an agency designated in subdivision (b) shall require an applicant to furnish to the agency a full set of fingerprints for purposes of conducting criminal history record checks. Any agency designated in subdivision (b) may obtain and receive, at its discretion, criminal history information from the Department of Justice and the United States Federal Bureau of Investigation.

(b) Subdivision (a) applies to the following:

(1) California Board of Accountancy.

(2) State Athletic Commission.

(3) Board of Behavioral Sciences.

(4) Court Reporters Board of California.

(5) Dental Board of California.

(6) California State Board of Pharmacy.

(7) Board of Registered Nursing.

(8) Veterinary Medical Board.

(9) Board of Vocational Nursing and Psychiatric Technicians of the State of California.

(10) Respiratory Care Board of California.

(11) Physical Therapy Board of California.

(12) Physician Assistant Board.

(13) Speech-Language Pathology and Audiology and Hearing Aid Dispensers Board.

(14) Medical Board of California.

(15) California State Board of Optometry.

(16) Acupuncture Board.

(17) Cemetery and Funeral Bureau.

(18) Bureau of Security and Investigative Services.

(19) Division of Investigation.

(20) Board of Psychology.

(21) California Board of Occupational Therapy.

(22) Structural Pest Control Board.

(23) Contractors State License Board.

(24) Naturopathic Medicine Committee.

(25) Professional Fiduciaries Bureau.

(26) Board for Professional Engineers, Land Surveyors, and Geologists.

(27) Podiatric Medical Board of California.

(28) Osteopathic Medical Board of California.

(29) California Architects Board, beginning January 1, 2021.

(30) Landscape Architects Technical Committee, beginning January 1, 2022.

(31) Bureau of Household Goods and Services with respect to household movers as described in Chapter 3.1 (commencing with Section 19225) of Division 8.

(c) For purposes of paragraph (26) of subdivision (b), the term "applicant" shall be limited to an initial applicant who has never been registered or licensed by the board or to an applicant for a new licensure or registration category.

Business and Professions Code § 205.1

(Amended by Stats. 2016, Ch. 32, Sec. 4. (SB 837) Effective June 27, 2016.)

Notwithstanding subdivision (a) of Section 205, the Medical Cannabis Regulation and Safety Act Fund is a special fund within the Professions and Vocations Fund, and is subject to subdivision (b) of Section 205.

Business and Professions Code § 2220.05

(Amended by Stats. 2017, Ch. 775, Sec. 72. (SB 798) Effective January 1, 2018.)

(a) In order to ensure that its resources are maximized for the protection of the public, the Medical Board of California and the California Board of Podiatric Medicine shall prioritize their investigative and prosecutorial resources to ensure that physicians and surgeons and doctors of podiatric medicine representing the greatest threat of harm are identified and disciplined expeditiously. Cases involving any of the following allegations shall be handled on a priority basis, as follows, with the highest priority being given to cases in the first paragraph:

(1) Gross negligence, incompetence, or repeated negligent acts that involve death or serious bodily injury to one or more patients, such that the physician and surgeon or the doctor of podiatric medicine represents a danger to the public.

(2) Drug or alcohol abuse by a physician and surgeon or a doctor of podiatric medicine involving death or serious bodily injury to a patient.

(3) Repeated acts of clearly excessive prescribing, furnishing, or administering of controlled substances, or repeated acts of prescribing, dispensing, or furnishing of controlled substances without a good faith prior examination of the patient and medical reason therefor. However, in no event shall a physician and surgeon prescribing, furnishing, or administering controlled substances for intractable pain consistent with lawful prescribing, including, but not limited to, Sections 725, 2241.5, and 2241.6 of this code and Sections 11159.2 and 124961 of the Health and Safety Code, be prosecuted for excessive prescribing and prompt review of the applicability of these provisions shall be made in any complaint that may implicate these provisions.

(4) Repeated acts of clearly excessive recommending of cannabis to patients for medical purposes, or repeated acts of recommending cannabis to patients for medical purposes without a good faith prior examination of the patient and a medical reason for the recommendation.

(5) Sexual misconduct with one or more patients during a course of treatment or an examination.

(6) Practicing medicine while under the influence of drugs or alcohol.

(7) Repeated acts of clearly excessive prescribing, furnishing, or administering psychotropic medications to a minor without a good faith prior examination of the patient and medical reason therefor.

(b) The board may by regulation prioritize cases involving an allegation of conduct that is not described in subdivision (a). Those cases prioritized by regulation shall not be assigned a priority equal to or higher than the priorities established in subdivision (a).

(c) The Medical Board of California shall indicate in its annual report mandated by Section 2312 the number of temporary restraining orders, interim suspension orders, and disciplinary actions that are taken in each priority category specified in subdivisions (a) and (b).

Business and Professions Code § 2228.5

(Added by Stats. 2022, Ch. 232, Sec. 1. (AB 1954) Effective January 1, 2023.)

(a) A physician and surgeon shall not automatically deny treatment or medication to a qualified patient based solely on a positive drug screen for tetrahydrocannabinol (THC) or report of medical cannabis use without first completing a case-by-case evaluation of the patient that includes, but is not limited to, a determination that the qualified patient's use of medical cannabis is medically significant to the treatment or medication.

(b) The use of medical cannabis that has been recommended by a licensed physician and surgeon shall not constitute the use of an illicit substance in the evaluation described in subdivision (a).

(c) No physician and surgeon shall be punished, or denied any right or privilege, for having administered treatment or medication to a qualified patient within the requirements of this section and consistent with the standard of care.

(d) For purposes of this section, the following terms have the following meanings:

(1) "Medically significant" means that a physician and surgeon has made a clinical determination that may include, but is not limited to, any of the following:

(A) The treatment or medication is contraindicated or is likely, or expected, to cause an adverse reaction or physical or mental harm to the qualified patient if administered or used in conjunction with THC or medical cannabis, based on the known clinical characteristics of the patient and the known characteristics and history of the patient's treatment or medication regimen.

(B) The treatment or medication is expected to be ineffective based on the known clinical characteristics of the qualified patient and the known characteristics and history of the patient's treatment or medication regimen.

(C) The treatment or medication, when administered or used in conjunction with THC or medical cannabis, is not clinically appropriate for the qualified patient because the treatment or medication is expected to do any of the following, as determined by a physician and surgeon:

(i) Worsen a comorbid condition.

(ii) Decrease the capacity to maintain a reasonable functional ability in performing daily activities.

(iii) Pose a significant barrier to adherence to, or compliance with, the qualified patient's drug regimen or plan of care.

(D) Any other clinically or medically relevant determination.

(2) "Qualified patient" has the same meaning as defined in Section 11362.7 of the Health and Safety Code.

Business and Professions Code § 2241.5

(Amended by Stats. 2015, Ch. 719, Sec. 3. (SB 643) Effective January 1, 2016.)

(a) A physician and surgeon may prescribe for, or dispense or administer to, a person under his or her treatment for a medical condition dangerous drugs or prescription controlled substances for the treatment of pain or a condition causing pain, including, but not limited to, intractable pain.

(b) No physician and surgeon shall be subject to disciplinary action for prescribing, dispensing, or administering dangerous drugs or prescription controlled substances in accordance with this section.

(c) This section shall not affect the power of the board to take any action described in Section 2227 against a physician and surgeon who does any of the following:

(1) Violates subdivision (b), (c), or (d) of Section 2234 regarding gross negligence, repeated negligent acts, or incompetence.

(2) Violates Section 2241 regarding treatment of an addict.

(3) Violates Section 2242 or 2525.3 regarding performing an appropriate prior examination and the existence of a medical indication for prescribing, dispensing, or furnishing dangerous drugs or recommending medical cannabis.

(4) Violates Section 2242.1 regarding prescribing on the Internet.

(5) Fails to keep complete and accurate records of purchases and disposals of substances listed in the California Uniform Controlled Substances Act (Division 10 (commencing with Section 11000) of the Health and Safety Code) or controlled substances scheduled in the federal Comprehensive Drug Abuse Prevention and Control Act of 1970 (21 U.S.C. Sec. 801 et seq.), or pursuant to the federal Comprehensive Drug Abuse Prevention and Control Act of 1970. A physician and surgeon shall keep records of his or her purchases and disposals of these controlled substances or dangerous drugs, including the date of purchase, the date and records of the sale or disposal of the drugs by the physician and surgeon, the name and address of the person receiving the drugs, and the reason for the disposal or the dispensing of the drugs to the person, and shall otherwise comply with all state recordkeeping requirements for controlled substances.

(6) Writes false or fictitious prescriptions for controlled substances listed in the California Uniform Controlled Substances Act or scheduled in the federal Comprehensive Drug Abuse Prevention and Control Act of 1970.

(7) Prescribes, administers, or dispenses in violation of this chapter, or in violation of Chapter 4 (commencing with Section 11150) or Chapter 5 (commencing with Section 11210) of Division 10 of the Health and Safety Code.

(d) A physician and surgeon shall exercise reasonable care in determining whether a particular patient or condition, or the complexity of a patient's treatment, including, but not limited to, a current or recent pattern of drug abuse, requires consultation with, or referral to, a more qualified specialist.

(e) Nothing in this section shall prohibit the governing body of a hospital from taking disciplinary actions against a physician and surgeon pursuant to Sections 809.05, 809.4, and 809.5.

Business and Professions Code § 2242.1

(Amended by Stats. 2015, Ch. 719, Sec. 4. (SB 643) Effective January 1, 2016.)

(a) No person or entity may prescribe, dispense, or furnish, or cause to be prescribed, dispensed, or furnished, dangerous drugs or dangerous devices, as defined in Section 4022, on the Internet for delivery to any person in this state, without an appropriate prior examination and medical indication, except as authorized by Section 2242.

(b) Notwithstanding any other provision of law, a violation of this section may subject the person or entity that has committed the violation to either a fine of up to twenty-five thousand dollars ($25,000) per occurrence pursuant to a citation issued by the board or a civil penalty of twenty-five thousand dollars ($25,000) per occurrence.

(c) The Attorney General may bring an action to enforce this section and to collect the fines or civil penalties authorized by subdivision (b).

(d) For notifications made on and after January 1, 2002, the Franchise Tax Board, upon notification by the Attorney

General or the board of a final judgment in an action brought under this section, shall subtract the amount of the fine or awarded civil penalties from any tax refunds or lottery winnings due to the person who is a defendant in the action using the offset authority under Section 12419.5 of the Government Code, as delegated by the Controller, and the processes as established by the Franchise Tax Board for this purpose. That amount shall be forwarded to the board for deposit in the Contingent Fund of the Medical Board of California.

(e) If the person or entity that is the subject of an action brought pursuant to this section is not a resident of this state, a violation of this section shall, if applicable, be reported to the person's or entity's appropriate professional licensing authority.

(f) Nothing in this section shall prohibit the board from commencing a disciplinary action against a physician and surgeon pursuant to Section 2242 or 2525.3.

Business and Professions Code § 2525

(Amended by Stats. 2018, Ch. 599, Sec. 3. (AB 3261) Effective January 1, 2019.)

(a) It is unlawful for a physician and surgeon who recommends cannabis to a patient for a medical purpose to accept, solicit, or offer any form of remuneration from or to a facility issued a state license pursuant to Division 10 (commencing with Section 26000), if the physician and surgeon or his or her immediate family have a financial interest in that facility.

(b) For the purposes of this section, "financial interest" shall have the same meaning as in Section 650.01.

(c) A violation of this section shall be a misdemeanor punishable by up to one year in county jail and a fine of up to five thousand dollars ($5,000) or by civil penalties of up to five thousand dollars ($5,000) and shall constitute unprofessional conduct.

Business and Professions Code § 2525.1

(Added by Stats. 2015, Ch. 719, Sec. 5. (SB 643) Effective January 1, 2016.)

The Medical Board of California shall consult with the California Marijuana Research Program, known as the Center for Medicinal Cannabis Research, authorized pursuant to Section 11362.9 of the Health and Safety Code, on developing and adopting medical guidelines for the appropriate administration and use of medical cannabis.

Business and Professions Code § 2525.2

(Amended by Stats. 2017, Ch. 775, Sec. 96. (SB 798) Effective January 1, 2018.)

An individual who possesses a license in good standing to practice medicine or osteopathy issued by the Medical Board of California, the California Board of Podiatric Medicine, or the Osteopathic Medical Board of California shall not recommend medical cannabis to a patient, unless that person is the patient's attending physician, as defined by subdivision (a) of Section 11362.7 of the Health and Safety Code.

Business and Professions Code § 2525.3

(Added by Stats. 2015, Ch. 719, Sec. 5. (SB 643) Effective January 1, 2016.)

Recommending medical cannabis to a patient for a medical purpose without an appropriate prior examination and a medical indication constitutes unprofessional conduct.

Business and Professions Code § 2525.4

(Added by Stats. 2015, Ch. 719, Sec. 5. (SB 643) Effective January 1, 2016.)

It is unprofessional conduct for any attending physician recommending medical cannabis to be employed by, or enter into any other agreement with, any person or entity dispensing medical cannabis.

Business and Professions Code § 2525.5

(Added by Stats. 2015, Ch. 719, Sec. 5. (SB 643) Effective January 1, 2016.)

(a) A person shall not distribute any form of advertising for physician recommendations for medical cannabis in California unless the advertisement bears the following notice to consumers:

NOTICE TO CONSUMERS: The Compassionate Use Act of 1996 ensures that seriously ill Californians have the right to obtain and use cannabis for medical purposes where medical use is deemed appropriate and has been recommended by a physician who has determined that the person's health would benefit from the use of medical cannabis. Recommendations must come from an attending physician as defined in Section 11362.7 of the Health and Safety Code. Cannabis is a Schedule I drug according to the federal Controlled Substances Act. Activity related to cannabis use is subject to federal prosecution, regardless of the protections provided by state law.

(b) Advertising for attending physician recommendations for medical cannabis shall meet all of the requirements in Section 651. Price advertising shall not be fraudulent, deceitful, or misleading, including statements or advertisements of bait, discounts, premiums, gifts, or statements of a similar nature.

Business and Professions Code § 2529

(Amended by Stats. 2021, Ch. 649, Sec. 30. (SB 806) Effective January 1, 2022.)

(a) Graduates of the Southern California Psychoanalytic Institute, the Los Angeles Psychoanalytic Society and Institute, the San Francisco Psychoanalytic Institute, the San Diego Psychoanalytic Center, or institutes deemed equivalent by the Medical Board of California who have completed clinical training in psychoanalysis may engage in psychoanalysis as an adjunct to teaching, training, or research and hold themselves out to the public as psychoanalysts, and students in those institutes may engage in psychoanalysis under supervision, if the students and graduates do not hold themselves out to the public by any title or description of services incorporating the words "psychological," "psychologist," "psychology," "psychometrists," "psychometrics," or "psychometry," or that they do not state or imply that they are licensed to practice psychology.

(b) Those students and graduates seeking to engage in psychoanalysis under this chapter shall register with the Medical Board of California, presenting evidence of their student or graduate status. The board may suspend or revoke the exemption of those persons for unprofessional conduct as defined in Sections 726, 2234, 2235, and 2529.1.

(c) Each application for registration as a research psychoanalyst or student research psychoanalyst shall be made upon an online electronic form, or other form, provided by the board, and each application form shall contain a legal verification by the applicant certifying under penalty of perjury that the information provided by the applicant is true and correct and that any information in supporting documents provided by the applicant is true and correct.

Business and Professions Code § 2529.1

(Amended by Stats. 2018, Ch. 571, Sec. 9. (SB 1480) Effective January 1, 2019.)

(a) The use of any controlled substance or the use of any of the dangerous drugs specified in Section 4022, or of alcoholic beverages, to the extent, or in such a manner as to be dangerous or injurious to the registrant, or to any other person or to the public, or to the extent that this use impairs the ability of the registrant to practice safely or more than one misdemeanor or any felony conviction involving the use, consumption, or self-administration of any of the substances referred to in this section, or any combination thereof, constitutes unprofessional conduct. The record of the conviction is conclusive evidence of this unprofessional conduct.

(b) A plea or verdict of guilty or a conviction following a plea of nolo contendere is deemed to be a conviction within the meaning of this section. The board may order discipline of the registrant in accordance with Section 2227 or may order the denial of the registration when the time for appeal has elapsed or the judgment of conviction has been affirmed on appeal or when an order granting probation is made suspending imposition of sentence, irrespective of a subsequent order under the provisions of Section 1203.4 of the Penal Code allowing this person to withdraw his or her plea of guilty and to enter a plea of not guilty, or setting aside the verdict of guilty, or dismissing the accusation, complaint, information, or indictment.

Business and Professions Code § 2529.5

(Amended by Stats. 2021, Ch. 649, Sec. 31. (SB 806) Effective January 1, 2022.)

(a) Each person to whom registration is granted under the provisions of this chapter shall pay into the Contingent Fund of the Medical Board of California a fee to be fixed by the Medical Board of California at a sum of one hundred fifty dollars ($150).

(b) The registration shall expire after two years. The registration may be renewed biennially. For registrations that expire on or after January 1, 2022, the fee shall be seventy-five dollars ($75). Students seeking to renew their registration shall present to the board evidence of their continuing student status.

(c) The money in the Contingent Fund of the Medical Board of California shall be used for the administration of this chapter.

Business and Professions Code § 2529.6

(Amended by Stats. 2018, Ch. 571, Sec. 11. (SB 1480) Effective January 1, 2019.)

(a) Except as provided in subdivisions (b) and (c), the board shall revoke the registration of any person who has been required to register as a sex offender pursuant to Section 290 of the Penal Code for conduct that occurred on or after January 1, 2017.

(b) This section shall not apply to a person who is required to register as a sex offender pursuant to Section 290 of the Penal Code solely because of a misdemeanor conviction under Section 314 of the Penal Code.

(c) This section shall not apply to a person who has been relieved under Section 290.5 of the Penal Code of his or her duty to register as a sex offender, or whose duty to register has otherwise been formally terminated under California law.

(d) A proceeding to revoke a registration pursuant to this section shall be conducted in accordance with Chapter 5 (commencing with Section 11500) of Part 1 of Division 3 of Title 2 of the Government Code.

Business and Professions Code § 4883

(Amended by Stats. 2022, Ch. 511, Sec. 26.1. (SB 1495) Effective January 1, 2023.)

The board may deny, revoke, or suspend a license or registration or assess a fine as provided in Section 4875 for any of the following:

(a) Conviction of a crime substantially related to the qualifications, functions, or duties of veterinary medicine, surgery, or dentistry, in which case the record of the conviction shall be conclusive evidence.

(b) For having professional connection with, or lending the licensee's or registrant's name to, any illegal practitioner of veterinary medicine and the various branches thereof.

(c) Violation or attempting to violate, directly or indirectly, any of the provisions of this chapter.

(d) Fraud or dishonesty in applying, treating, or reporting on tuberculin or other biological tests.

(e) Employment of anyone but a veterinarian licensed in the state to demonstrate the use of biologics in the treatment of animals.

(f) False or misleading advertising.

(g) Unprofessional conduct, that includes, but is not limited to, the following:

(1) Conviction of a charge of violating any federal statutes or rules or any statute or rule of this state regulating dangerous drugs or controlled substances. The record of the conviction is conclusive evidence thereof. A plea or verdict of guilty or a conviction following a plea of nolo contendere is deemed to be a conviction within the meaning of this section. The board may order the license or registration to be suspended or revoked, or assess a fine, or decline to issue a license or registration, when the time for appeal has elapsed, or the judgment of conviction has been affirmed on appeal or when an order granting probation is made suspending the imposition of sentence, irrespective of a subsequent order under Section 1203.4, 1210.1, or 3063.1 of the Penal Code allowing the person to withdraw a plea of guilty and to enter a plea of not guilty, or setting aside the verdict of guilty, or dismissing the accusation, information, or indictment.

(2) (A) The use of, or prescribing for or administering to oneself, any controlled substance.

(B) The use of any of the dangerous drugs specified in Section 4022, or of alcoholic beverages to the extent, or in any manner as to be dangerous or injurious to a person licensed or registered under this chapter, or to any other person or to the public, or to the extent that the use impairs the ability of the person so licensed or registered to conduct with safety the practice authorized by the license or registration.

(C) The conviction of more than one misdemeanor or any felony involving the use, consumption, or self-administration of any of the substances referred to in this section or any combination thereof, and the record of the conviction is conclusive evidence.

A plea or verdict of guilty or a conviction following a plea of nolo contendere is deemed to be a conviction within the meaning of this section. The board may order the license or registration to be suspended or revoked or assess a fine, or may decline to issue a license or registration, when the time for appeal has elapsed or the judgment of conviction has been affirmed on appeal or when an order granting probation is made suspending imposition of sentence, irrespective of a subsequent order under Section 1203.4, 1210.1, or 3063.1 of the Penal Code allowing the person to withdraw a plea of guilty and to enter a plea of not guilty, or setting aside the verdict of guilty, or dismissing the accusation, information, or indictment.

(3) A violation of any federal statute, rule, or regulation or any of the statutes, rules, or regulations of this state regulating dangerous drugs or controlled substances.

(h) Failure to keep the licensee's or registrant's premises and all equipment therein in a clean and sanitary condition.

(i) Fraud, deception, negligence, or incompetence in the practice of veterinary medicine.

(j) Aiding or abetting in any acts that are in violation of any of the provisions of this chapter.

(k) The employment of fraud, misrepresentation, or deception in obtaining the license or registration.

(l) The revocation, suspension, or other discipline by another state or territory of a license, certificate, or registration to practice veterinary medicine or as a veterinary technician in that state or territory.

(m) Cruelty to animals, conviction on a charge of cruelty to animals, or both.

(n) Disciplinary action taken by any public agency in any state or territory for any act substantially related to the practice of veterinary medicine or the practice of a veterinary technician.

(o) Violation, or the assisting or abetting violation, of any regulations adopted by the board pursuant to this chapter.

(p) Accepting, soliciting, or offering any form of remuneration from or to a cannabis licensee if the veterinarian or the veterinarian's immediate family have a financial interest with the cannabis licensee. For purposes of this subdivision, the following definitions shall apply:

(1) "Cannabis licensee" shall have the same meaning as "licensee" in Section 26001.

(2) "Financial interest" shall have the same meaning as in Section 650.01.

(q) Discussing or recommending cannabis for use with a client while the veterinarian is employed by, or has an agreement with, a cannabis licensee. For purposes of this subdivision, "cannabis licensee" shall have the same meaning as "licensee" in Section 26001.

(r) Distributing any form of advertising for cannabis in California.

(s) Making any statement, claim, or advertisement that the licensee or registrant is a veterinary specialist or board certified unless they are certified by an American Veterinary Medical Association-Recognized Veterinary Specialty Organization or a National Association of Veterinary Technicians in America-Recognized Veterinary Specialty Organization.

(t) Exercising control over, interfering with, or attempting to influence the professional judgment of another California-licensed veterinarian or registered veterinary technician through coercion, extortion, inducement, collusion, or intimidation through any means, including, but not limited to, compensation, in order to require the other California-licensed veterinarian or registered veterinary technician to perform veterinary services in a manner inconsistent with current veterinary medical practice in this state.

Business and Professions Code § 4884

(Amended by Stats. 2022, Ch. 389, Sec. 2. (AB 1885) Effective January 1, 2023.)

(a) A licensee shall not dispense or administer cannabis or cannabis products to an animal patient.

(b) Notwithstanding any other law and absent negligence or incompetence, a veterinarian licensed under this chapter shall not be disciplined by the board or have their license denied, revoked, or suspended solely for discussing or recommending the use of cannabis on an animal for potential therapeutic effect or health supplementation purposes.

(c) On or before January 1, 2020, the board shall adopt guidelines for veterinarians to follow when discussing cannabis within the veterinarian-client-patient relationship. The board shall post the guidelines on its internet website.

(d) By January 1, 2024, the board shall adopt guidelines for veterinarians to follow when recommending cannabis within the veterinarian-client-patient relationship. The board shall post the guidelines on its internet website.

DIVISION 6. BUSINESS RIGHTS

Chapter 3. Trade Names and Designations

ARTICLE 3. FARM NAMES

Business and Professions Code § 14460

(Added by Stats. 1941, Ch. 59.)

"Farm," as used in this article, includes ranch, estate and villa.

Business and Professions Code 14461

(Amended by Stats. 1999, Ch. 1000, Sec. 6. Effective January 1, 2000.)

Any farm owner or lessee in this state may register the name of his or her farm with the Secretary of State, and the Secretary of State shall issue a certificate setting forth the name and location of the farm and the name of the owner upon payment of the fee as set forth in subdivision (g) of Section 12193 of the Government Code.

Business and Professions Code § 14462

(Added by Stats. 1941, Ch. 59.)

Any person selling or marketing the products grown on a farm may use the name of the farm as a trade-mark on the products of the farm, in the same manner as provided for other trade-marks, and subject to the same rights and duties, as provided in this code.

Business and Professions Code § 14463

(Added by Stats. 1941, Ch. 59.)

Registration under this article shall have the same effect as the registration of a trade-mark.

Business and Professions Code § 14464

(Added by Stats. 1941, Ch. 59.)

When any name has been registered as the name of any farm, that name shall not be registered as the name of any other farm in this State, unless designating words have been prefixed or added thereto. The Secretary of State shall register such name only for the person entitled thereto.

Business and Professions Code § 14465

(Added by Stats. 1941, Ch. 59.)

Any person who registers as his own, any name already in use in this State, knowing that the name is already adopted as the name of a farm, or makes use of the name when regularly registered and in use by any other person entitled thereto under this article is guilty of a misdemeanor.

DIVISION 9. ALCOHOLIC BEVERAGES

Business and Professions Code § 25621.5

(Added by Stats. 2018, Ch. 827, Sec. 2. (AB 2914) Effective January 1, 2019.)

(a) A licensee shall not, at its licensed premises, sell, offer, or provide cannabis or cannabis products, as defined in Section 26001, including an alcoholic beverage that contains cannabis or a cannabis product, and no alcoholic beverage shall be manufactured, sold, or offered for sale if it contains tetrahydrocannabinol or cannabinoids, regardless of source.

(b) The department shall take disciplinary action against a licensee that violates this section, including, but not limited to, suspension or revocation of the license.

DIVISION 10. CANNABIS

Chapter 1. General Provisions and Definitions

Business and Professions Code § 26000

(Amended by Stats. 2022, Ch. 389, Sec. 3. (AB 1885) Effective January 1, 2023. Note: This section was added on Nov. 8, 2016, by initiative Prop. 64.)

(a) This division shall be known, and may be cited, as the Medicinal and Adult-Use Cannabis Regulation and Safety Act.

(b) The purpose and intent of this division is to establish a comprehensive system to control and regulate the cultivation, distribution, transport, storage, manufacturing, processing, and sale of both of the following:

> (1) Medicinal cannabis and medicinal cannabis products for patients with valid physician's recommendations.
>
> (2) Adult-use cannabis and adult-use cannabis products for adults 21 years of age and over and cannabis products intended for use on, or consumption by, animals.

(c) In the furtherance of subdivision (b), this division sets forth the power and duties of the state agencies responsible for controlling and regulating the commercial medicinal and adult-use cannabis industry.

(d) The Legislature may, by majority vote, enact laws to implement this division, provided those laws are consistent with the purposes and intent of the Control, Regulate and Tax Adult Use of Marijuana Act.

Business and Professions Code § 26001

(Amended (as amended by Stats. 2022, Ch. 33, Sec. 1) by Stats. 2022, Ch. 389, Sec. 4. (AB 1885) Effective January 1, 2023.)

For purposes of this division, the following definitions apply:

(a) "A-license" means a state license issued under this division for cannabis or cannabis products that are intended for adults who are 21 years of age and older and who do not possess a physician's recommendation, or are intended for use on, or consumption by, animals.

(b) "A-licensee" means any person holding a license under this division for cannabis or cannabis products that are intended for adults who are 21 years of age and older and who do not possess a physician's recommendation, or are intended for use on, or consumption by, animals.

(c) "Animal" does not include a food animal as defined in Section 4825.1 or livestock as defined in Section 14205 of the Food and Agricultural Code.

(d) "Applicant" means an owner applying for a state license pursuant to this division.

(e) "Batch" means a specific quantity of homogeneous cannabis or cannabis product that is one of the following types:

(1) Harvest batch. "Harvest batch" means a specifically identified quantity of dried flower or trim, leaves, and other cannabis plant matter that is harvested at the same time, and, if applicable, cultivated using the same pesticides and other agricultural chemicals.

(2) Manufactured cannabis batch. "Manufactured cannabis batch" means either of the following:

(A) An amount of cannabis concentrate or extract that is produced in one production cycle using the same extraction methods and standard operating procedures.

(B) An amount of a type of manufactured cannabis produced in one production cycle using the same formulation and standard operating procedures.

(f) "Cannabis" means all parts of the plant Cannabis sativa Linnaeus, Cannabis indica, or Cannabis ruderalis, whether growing or not; the seeds thereof; the resin, whether crude or purified, extracted from any part of the plant; and every compound, manufacture, salt, derivative, mixture, or preparation of the plant, its seeds, or resin. "Cannabis" also means the separated resin, whether crude or purified, obtained from cannabis. "Cannabis" does not include the mature stalks of the plant, fiber produced from the stalks, oil or cake made from the seeds of the plant, any other compound, manufacture, salt, derivative, mixture, or preparation of the mature stalks (except the resin extracted therefrom), fiber, oil, or cake, or the sterilized seed of the plant which is incapable of germination. For the purpose of this division, "cannabis" does not mean "industrial hemp" as defined by Section 11018.5 of the Health and Safety Code.

(g) "Cannabis accessories" has the same meaning as in Section 11018.2 of the Health and Safety Code.

(h) "Cannabis beverage" means a form of edible cannabis product that is intended to be consumed in its final state as a beverage.

(i) "Cannabis concentrate" means cannabis that has undergone a process to concentrate one or more active cannabinoids, thereby increasing the product's potency. Resin from glandular trichomes from a cannabis plant is a concentrate for purposes of this division. A cannabis concentrate is not considered food, as defined by Section 109935 of the Health and Safety Code, a processed pet food, as defined by Section 113025 of the Health and Safety Code, or a drug, as defined by Section 109925 of the Health and Safety Code.

(j) "Cannabis products" has the same meaning as in Section 11018.1 of the Health and Safety Code, and includes cannabis products intended for use on, or consumption by, an animal. Cannabis products are not considered food, as defined by Section 109935 of the Health and Safety Code, a drug, as defined by Section 109925 of the Health and Safety Code, or a cosmetic, as defined by Section 109900 of the Health and Safety Code.

(k) "Child resistant" means designed or constructed to be significantly difficult for children under five years of age to open, and not difficult for normal adults to use properly.

(l) "Commercial cannabis activity" includes the cultivation, possession, manufacture, distribution, processing, storing, laboratory testing, packaging, labeling, transportation, delivery, or sale of cannabis and cannabis products as provided for in this division, or acting as a cannabis event organizer for temporary cannabis events.

(m) "Cultivation" means any activity involving the planting, growing, harvesting, drying, curing, grading, or trimming of cannabis.

(n) "Cultivation site" means a location where cannabis is planted, grown, harvested, dried, cured, graded, or trimmed, or a location where any combination of those activities occurs.

(o) "Customer" means a natural person 21 years of age or older or a natural person 18 years of age or older who possesses a physician's recommendation, or a primary caregiver.

(p) "Daycare center" has the same meaning as in Section 1596.76 of the Health and Safety Code.

(q) "Delivery" means the commercial transfer of cannabis or cannabis products to a customer. "Delivery" also includes the use by a retailer of any technology platform.

(r) "Department" means the Department of Cannabis Control within the Business, Consumer Services, and Housing Agency.

(s) "Director" means the Director of the Department of Cannabis Control.

(t) "Distribution" means the procurement, sale, and transport of cannabis and cannabis products between licensees.

(u) "Distributor" means a licensee that is authorized to engage in the distribution of cannabis and cannabis products.

(v) "Dried flower" means all dead cannabis that has been harvested, dried, cured, or otherwise processed, excluding leaves and stems.

(w) "Edible cannabis product" means a cannabis product that is intended to be used, in whole or in part, for human or animal consumption, including, but not limited to, chewing gum, but excluding products set forth in Division 15 (commencing with Section 32501) of the Food and Agricultural Code. An edible cannabis product is not considered food, as defined by Section 109935 of the Health and Safety Code, a processed pet food, as defined by Section 113025 of the Health and Safety Code, or a drug, as defined by Section 109925 of the Health and Safety Code.

(x) "Fund" means the Cannabis Control Fund established pursuant to Section 26210.

(y) "Kind" means applicable type or designation regarding a particular cannabis variant, origin, or product type, including, but not limited to, strain name, trademark, or production area designation.

(z) "Labeling" means any label or other written, printed, or graphic matter upon a cannabis product, upon its container or wrapper, or that accompanies any cannabis product.

(aa) "Labor peace agreement" means an agreement between a licensee and any bona fide labor organization that, at a minimum, protects the state's proprietary interests by prohibiting labor organizations and members from engaging in picketing, work stoppages, boycotts, and any other economic interference with the applicant's business. This agreement means that the applicant has agreed not to disrupt efforts by the bona fide labor organization to communicate with, and attempt to organize and represent, the applicant's employees. The agreement shall provide a bona fide labor organization access at reasonable times to areas in which the applicant's employees work, for the purpose of meeting with employees to discuss their right to representation, employment rights under state law, and terms and conditions of employment. This type of agreement shall not mandate a particular method of election or certification of the bona fide labor organization.

(ab) "License" means a state license issued under this division, and includes both an A-license and an M-license, as well as a testing laboratory license.

(ac) "Licensee" means any person holding a license under this division, regardless of whether the license held is an A-license or an M-license, and includes the holder of a testing laboratory license.

(ad) "Licensing authority" means the department and any state agency currently or formerly responsible for the issuance, renewal, or reinstatement of the license, or the state agency authorized to take disciplinary action against the licensee.

(ae) “Live plants” means living cannabis flowers and plants, including seeds, immature plants, and vegetative stage plants.

(af) “Local jurisdiction” means a city, county, or city and county.

(ag) “Lot” means a batch or a specifically identified portion of a batch.

(ah) “M-license” means a state license issued under this division for commercial cannabis activity involving medicinal cannabis.

(ai) “M-licensee” means any person holding a license under this division for commercial cannabis activity involving medicinal cannabis.

(aj) “Manufacture” means to compound, blend, extract, infuse, package, label, or otherwise make or prepare a cannabis product.

(ak) (1) “Medicinal cannabis” or “medicinal cannabis product” means cannabis or a cannabis product, respectively, intended to be sold or donated for use pursuant to the Compassionate Use Act of 1996 (Proposition 215), found in Section 11362.5 of the Health and Safety Code, by a medicinal cannabis patient in California who possesses a physician’s recommendation, or in compliance with any compassionate use, equity, or other similar program administered by a local jurisdiction.

(2) The amendments made to this subdivision by the act adding this paragraph shall become operative upon completion of the necessary changes to the track and trace program in order to implement the act adding this paragraph, as determined by the Department of Food and Agriculture, or on March 1, 2020, whichever occurs first.

(al) “Microbusiness” means a licensee that is authorized to engage in cultivation of cannabis on an area less than 10,000 square feet and to act as a licensed distributor, Level 1 manufacturer, and retailer under this division, provided such licensee can demonstrate compliance with all requirements imposed by this division on licensed cultivators, distributors, Level 1 manufacturers, and retailers to the extent the licensee engages in such activities.

(am) “Nursery” means a licensee that produces only clones, immature plants, seeds, and other agricultural products used specifically for the propagation and cultivation of cannabis.

(an) “Operation” means any act for which licensure is required under the provisions of this division, or any commercial transfer of cannabis or cannabis products.

(ao) “Owner” means any of the following:

(1) A person with an aggregate ownership interest of 20 percent or more in the person applying for a license or a licensee, unless the interest is solely a security, lien, or encumbrance.

(2) The chief executive officer of a nonprofit or other entity.

(3) A member of the board of directors of a nonprofit.

(4) An individual who will be participating in the direction, control, or management of the person applying for a license.

(ap) “Package” means any container or receptacle used for holding cannabis or cannabis products.

(aq) “Person” includes any individual, firm, partnership, joint venture, association, corporation, limited liability company, estate, trust, business trust, receiver, syndicate, or any other group or combination acting as a unit, and the plural as well as the singular.

(ar) “Physician’s recommendation” means a recommendation by a physician and surgeon that a patient use cannabis provided in accordance with the Compassionate Use Act of 1996 (Proposition 215), found at Section 11362.5 of the Health and Safety Code.

(as) "Premises" means the designated structure or structures and land specified in the application that is owned, leased, or otherwise held under the control of the applicant or licensee where the commercial cannabis activity will be or is conducted. The premises shall be a contiguous area and shall only be occupied by one licensee.

(at) "Primary caregiver" has the same meaning as in Section 11362.7 of the Health and Safety Code.

(au) "Purchaser" means the customer who is engaged in a transaction with a licensee for purposes of obtaining cannabis or cannabis products.

(av) "Retailer" means a person authorized to engage in the retail sale and delivery of cannabis or cannabis products to customers.

(aw) "Sell," "sale," and "to sell" include any transaction whereby, for any consideration, title to cannabis or cannabis products is transferred from one person to another, and includes the delivery of cannabis or cannabis products pursuant to an order placed for the purchase of the same and soliciting or receiving an order for the same, but does not include the return of cannabis or cannabis products by a licensee to the licensee from whom the cannabis or cannabis product was purchased.

(ax) "Testing laboratory" means a laboratory, facility, or entity in the state that offers or performs tests of cannabis or cannabis products and that is both of the following:

(1) Accredited by an accrediting body that is independent from all other persons involved in commercial cannabis activity in the state.

(2) Licensed by the department.

(ay) "Unique identifier" means an alphanumeric code or designation issued pursuant to the track and trace program established by the department and used for reference to a specific plant on a licensed premises and any cannabis or cannabis product derived or manufactured from that plant.

(az) "Youth center" has the same meaning as in Section 11353.1 of the Health and Safety Code.

Business and Professions Code § 26002

(Amended by Stats. 2021, Ch. 157, Sec. 1. (AB 1305) Effective January 1, 2022.)

(a) This division does not apply to any product containing cannabinoids that has been approved by the federal Food and Drug Administration that has either been placed on a schedule of the federal Controlled Substances Act other than Schedule I or has been exempted from one or more provisions of that act, and that is intended for prescribed use for the treatment of a medical condition.

(b) This division does not apply to activity performed pursuant to a registration with the United States Drug Enforcement Administration pursuant to Part 1318 (commencing with Section 1318.01) of Chapter 2 of Title 21 of the Code of Federal Regulations, as it read on January 19, 2021, provided that the person engaging in the activity provides the licensing authority valid documentation of their registration with the United States Drug Enforcement Administration and the location where the activity will be performed prior to engaging in the activity.

Chapter 2. Administration

Business and Professions Code § 26010

(Amended by Stats. 2021, Ch. 70, Sec. 6. (AB 141) Effective July 12, 2021.)

There is in the Business, Consumer Services, and Housing Agency, the Department of Cannabis Control under the supervision and control of a director. The director shall administer and enforce the provisions of this division related to the department.

Business and Professions Code § 26010.5

(Amended by Stats. 2021, Ch. 70, Sec. 7. (AB 141) Effective July 12, 2021.)

(a) The Governor shall appoint the director of the department, subject to confirmation by the Senate. The director shall serve under the direction and supervision of the Secretary of the Business, Consumer Services, and Housing Agency and at the pleasure of the Governor.

(b) Every power granted to or duty imposed upon the director under this division may be exercised or performed in the name of the director by a deputy or assistant director or by a chief, subject to conditions and limitations that the director may prescribe.

(c) (1) The director may employ and appoint all employees necessary to properly administer the work of the department, in accordance with civil service laws and regulations.

(2) The Governor may also appoint a chief deputy director, a deputy director of equity and inclusion, and either a deputy director of legal affairs or a chief counsel to the department. These positions shall serve under the direction and supervision of the director and hold office at the pleasure of the Governor.

(d) The department has the power, duty, purpose, responsibility, and jurisdiction to regulate commercial cannabis activity as provided in this division.

(e) Upon the effective date of this section, whenever any reference to the "Medical Cannabis Regulation and Safety Act," "Medical Marijuana Regulation and Safety Act," or former Chapter 3.5 (commencing with Section 19300) of Division 8 appears in any statute, regulation, contract, or in any other code, it shall be construed to refer to this division as it relates to medicinal cannabis and medicinal cannabis products.

Business and Professions Code § 26010.7

(Added by Stats. 2021, Ch. 70, Sec. 8. (AB 141) Effective July 12, 2021.)

(a) Except as provided in Sections 26062 and 26063 and Chapter 23 (commencing with Section 26240), on and after the operative date of this section, the Department of Cannabis Control and the director shall succeed to and be vested with all the duties, powers, purposes, functions, responsibilities, and jurisdiction of the Bureau of Cannabis Control, also formerly known as the Bureau of Medical Cannabis Regulation and the Bureau of Medical Marijuana Regulation under the former Medical Cannabis Regulation and Safety Act (former Chapter 3.5 commencing with Section 19300 of Division 8), the State Department of Public Health, and the Department of Food and Agriculture, as provided for pursuant to this division as it read on the day before the operative date of this section.

(b) Except as provided in Sections 26062 and 26063 and Chapter 23 (commencing with Section 26240), on and after the operative date of this section, both of the following shall apply:

(1) Whenever "Bureau of Marijuana Control," "Bureau of Medical Cannabis Regulation," or "Bureau of Medical Marijuana Regulation" appears in any statute, regulation, or contract, or in any other code, it shall be construed to refer to the Department of Cannabis Control.

(2) Unless the context clearly requires otherwise, whenever "Department of Public Health," "State Department of Public Health," "Department of Food and Agriculture," or "California Department of Food and Agriculture"

appears in this division, or any statute, regulation, or contract, related to regulation of cannabis pursuant to this division, it shall be construed to refer to the Department of Cannabis Control.

(c) Any regulation, order, or other action adopted, prescribed, taken, or performed by the Bureau of Cannabis Control, the State Department of Public Health, or the Department of Food and Agriculture under this division in effect immediately preceding the operative date of this section shall remain in effect and shall be fully enforceable unless and until readopted, amended, or repealed, or until they expire by their own terms, and shall be deemed to be a regulation, order, or action of the Department of Cannabis Control. On and after the operative date of this section, any proposed regulation noticed by, or submitted to the Office of Administrative Law by, the Bureau of Cannabis Control, the State Department of Public Health, or the Department of Food and Agriculture under this division, shall be deemed to be a regulation noticed by or submitted by the Department of Cannabis Control.

(d) Any action by or against the Bureau of Cannabis Control, the State Department of Public Health, or the Department of Food and Agriculture pertaining to matters vested in the Department of Cannabis Control by this section shall not abate but shall continue in the name of the Department of Cannabis Control, and the Department of Cannabis Control shall be substituted for the Bureau of Cannabis Control, the State Department of Public Health, and the Department of Food and Agriculture by the court wherein the action is pending. The substitution shall not in any way affect the rights of the parties to the action.

(e) On and after the operative date of this section, all books, documents, forms, records, data systems, and property of the Bureau of Cannabis Control, the Department of Consumer Affairs, the State Department of Public Health, and the Department of Food and Agriculture pertaining to functions transferred to the Department of Cannabis Control shall be transferred to the Department of Cannabis Control.

(f) On and after the operative date of this section, positions filled by appointment by the Governor in the Bureau of Cannabis Control, the State Department of Public Health, and the Department of Food and Agriculture whose principal assignment was to perform functions transferred pursuant to this section shall be transferred to the Department of Cannabis Control. Individuals in positions transferred pursuant to this subdivision shall serve at the pleasure of the Governor. Salaries of positions transferred shall remain at the level established pursuant to law unless otherwise provided. Individuals in positions transferred pursuant to this subdivision who have been previously confirmed by the Senate shall not be required to undergo a new confirmation as a result of this transfer. Titles of positions transferred pursuant to this subdivision shall be determined by the director with the approval of the Governor.

(g) On and after the operative date of this section, every officer and employee of the Bureau of Cannabis Control, the State Department of Public Health, the Department of Food and Agriculture, and the Department of Consumer Affairs who is performing a function transferred to the Department of Cannabis Control and who is serving in the state civil service, including an excluded or temporary employee, shall be transferred to the Department of Cannabis Control pursuant to the provisions of Section 19050.9 of the Government Code. The status, position, and rights of any officer or employee of the Bureau of Cannabis Control, the State Department of Public Health, the Department of Food and Agriculture, and the Department of Consumer Affairs shall not be affected by the transfer and shall be retained by the person as an officer or employee of the Department of Cannabis Control, as applicable, pursuant to the State Civil Service Act (Part 2 (commencing with Section 18500) of Division 5 of Title 2 of the Government Code), except for a position that is exempt from civil service. The personnel records of all transferred employees shall be transferred to the Department of Cannabis Control.

(h) A contract, lease, license, or any other agreement to which the Bureau of Cannabis Control, the Department of Consumer Affairs, the State Department of Public Health, or the Department of Food and Agriculture is a party shall not be void or voidable by reason of this section, and shall continue in full force and effect, with the Department of Cannabis Control assuming all of the rights, obligations, liabilities, and duties of the Bureau of Cannabis Control, the State Department of Public Health, and the Department of Food and Agriculture relating to the transfer of duties, powers, purposes, functions, responsibilities, and jurisdiction made pursuant to this section. The assumption by the Department of Cannabis Control shall not in any way affect the rights of the parties to any contract, lease, license, or agreement.

(i) This section shall become operative on and after July 1, 2021, or the operative date of the act adding this section, whichever is later.

Business and Professions Code § 26011

(Amended by Stats. 2021, Ch. 70, Sec. 9. (AB 141) Effective July 12, 2021. Note: This section was added on Nov. 8, 2016, by initiative Prop. 64.)

Neither the director nor any member of the Cannabis Control Appeals Panel established under Section 26040 shall do any of the following:

(a) Receive any commission or profit whatsoever, directly or indirectly, from any person applying for or receiving any license or permit under this division.

(b) Engage or have any interest in the sale or any insurance covering a licensee's business or premises.

(c) Engage or have any interest in the sale of equipment for use upon the premises of a licensee engaged in commercial cannabis activity.

(d) Knowingly solicit any licensee for the purchase of tickets for benefits or contributions for benefits.

(e) Knowingly request any licensee to donate or receive money, or any other thing of value, for the benefit of any person whatsoever.

Business and Professions Code § 26011.5

(Amended by Stats. 2021, Ch. 70, Sec. 10. (AB 141) Effective July 12, 2021.)

The protection of the public shall be the highest priority for the department in exercising licensing, regulatory, and disciplinary functions under this division. Whenever the protection of the public is inconsistent with other interests sought to be promoted, the protection of the public shall be paramount.

Business and Professions Code § 26012

(Amended (as amended by Stats. 2021, Ch. 70, Sec. 11) by Stats. 2021, Ch. 87, Sec. 2. (SB 160) Effective July 16, 2021. Note: This section was added on Nov. 8, 2016, by initiative Prop. 64.)

(a) It being a matter of statewide concern, except as otherwise authorized in this division, the department shall have the sole authority to create, issue, deny, renew, discipline, condition, suspend, or revoke licenses for commercial cannabis activity.

(b) The department shall have the authority to collect fees in connection with activities it regulates concerning cannabis. The department may create licenses in addition to those identified in this division that the department deems necessary to effectuate its duties under this division.

(c) For the performance of its duties, the department has the power conferred by Sections 11180 to 11191, inclusive, of the Government Code.

Business and Professions Code § 26012.5

(Amended by Stats. 2022, Ch. 28, Sec. 17. (SB 1380) Effective January 1, 2023.)

(a) The department shall provide on its internet website information regarding the status of every license issued by the department in accordance with the California Public Records Act (Division 10 (commencing with Section 7920.000) of Title 1 of the Government Code) and the Information Practices Act of 1977 (Chapter 1 (commencing with Section 1798) of Title 1.8 of Part 4 of Division 3 of the Civil Code).

(b) Beginning January 1, 2022, the information provided on the department's internet website pursuant to subdivision (a) shall include information on suspensions and revocations of licenses and final decisions adopted by the department pursuant to the Administrative Procedure Act (Chapter 3.5 (commencing with Section 11340) of Part 1 of Division 3 of Title 2 of the Government Code) relating to persons or businesses licensed or regulated by the department.

(c) The information provided shall not include personal information, including home addresses, home telephone numbers, dates of birth, or social security numbers. The department shall disclose the county of a licensee's address of record.

Business and Professions Code § 26013

(Amended by Stats. 2021, Ch. 70, Sec. 13. (AB 141) Effective July 12, 2021. Note: This section was added on Nov. 8, 2016, by initiative Prop. 64.)

(a) The department shall make and prescribe reasonable rules and regulations as may be necessary to implement, administer, and enforce its duties under this division in accordance with Chapter 3.5 (commencing with Section 11340) of Part 1 of Division 3 of Title 2 of the Government Code. Those rules and regulations shall be consistent with the purposes and intent of the Control, Regulate and Tax Adult Use of Marijuana Act.

(b) (1) The department may adopt emergency regulations to consolidate, clarify, or make consistent regulations, including emergency regulations adopted before or in place as of July 1, 2021, or to implement Section 26010.7.

(2) The department may readopt any emergency regulation authorized by this section that is the same as, or substantially equivalent to, an emergency regulation previously adopted as authorized by this section. Any such readoption shall be limited to one time for each regulation.

(3) Notwithstanding any other law, the adoption of emergency regulations and the readoption of emergency regulations authorized by this section shall be deemed an emergency and necessary for the immediate preservation of the public peace, health, safety, or general welfare. The emergency regulations and the readopted emergency regulations authorized by this section shall be each submitted to the Office of Administrative Law for filing with the Secretary of State and shall remain in effect for no more than 180 days, by which time final regulations may be adopted.

(c) Regulations issued under this division shall be necessary to achieve the purposes of this division, based on best available evidence, and shall mandate only commercially feasible procedures, technology, or other requirements, and shall not unreasonably restrain or inhibit the development of alternative procedures or technology to achieve the same substantive requirements, nor shall the regulations make compliance so onerous that the operation under a cannabis license is not worthy of being carried out in practice by a reasonably prudent businessperson.

Business and Professions Code § 26013.2

(Added by Stats. 2021, Ch. 576, Sec. 1. (AB 45) Effective October 6, 2021. Repealed as of January 1, 2025, by its own provisions.)

(a) On or before July 1, 2022, the department shall prepare a report to the Governor and the Legislature outlining the steps necessary to allow for the incorporation of hemp cannabinoids into the cannabis supply chain. The report shall include, but not be limited to, the incorporation of hemp cannabinoids into manufactured cannabis products and the sale of hemp products at cannabis retailers.

(b) (1) The report to be submitted pursuant to subdivision (a) shall be submitted in compliance with Section 9795 of the Government Code.

(2) Pursuant to Section 10231.5 of the Government Code, this section is repealed on January 1, 2025.

(c) It is the intent of the Legislature to consider, in light of the report submitted pursuant to subdivision (a), whether and how to take legislative action concerning the incorporation of hemp into the cannabis supply chain no later than the 2023–24 legislative session.

Business and Professions Code § 26013 .5

(Amended by Stats. 2021, Ch. 70, Sec. 14. (AB 141) Effective July 12, 2021.)

(a) Notice of any action of the department required by this division to be given may be signed and given by the director or an authorized employee of the department and may be made personally or in the manner prescribed by Section 1013 of the Code of Civil Procedure, or in the manner prescribed by Section 124 of this code.

(b) Notwithstanding subdivision (c) of Section 11505 of the Government Code, whenever written notice, including a notice, order, or document served pursuant to Chapter 3.5 (commencing with Section 11340), Chapter 4 (commencing with Section 11370), or Chapter 5 (commencing with Section 11500), of Part 1 of Division 3 of Title 2 of the Government Code, is required to be given by the department, the notice may be given by regular mail addressed to the last known address of the licensee or by personal service, at the option of the department.

Business and Professions Code § 26014

(Amended by Stats. 2021, Ch. 70, Sec. 15. (AB 141) Effective July 12, 2021. Note: This section was added on Nov. 8, 2016, by initiative Prop. 64.)

(a) The department shall convene an advisory committee to advise the department on the development of standards and regulations pursuant to this division, including best practices and guidelines that protect public health and safety while ensuring a regulated environment for commercial cannabis activity that does not impose such barriers so as to perpetuate, rather than reduce and eliminate, the illicit market for cannabis.

(b) The advisory committee members shall include, but not be limited to, representatives of the cannabis industry, including medicinal cannabis, representatives of labor organizations, appropriate state and local agencies, persons who work directly with racially, ethnically, and economically diverse populations, public health experts, and other subject matter experts, including representatives from the Department of Alcoholic Beverage Control, with expertise in regulating commercial activity for adult-use intoxicating substances. The advisory committee members shall be determined by the director.

(c) Commencing on January 1, 2019, the advisory committee shall publish an annual public report describing its activities including, but not limited to, the recommendations the advisory committee made to the department during the immediately preceding calendar year and whether those recommendations were implemented by the department.

(d) Each member of the advisory committee shall be reimbursed for traveling and other expenses necessarily incurred in the performance of official duties. The payments in each instance shall be made only from the fund and shall be subject to the availability of money.

Business and Professions Code § 26015

(Amended by Stats. 2021, Ch. 70, Sec. 16. (AB 141) Effective July 12, 2021.)

(a) The department may make or cause to be made such investigation as it deems necessary to carry out its duties under this division.

(b) The chief of enforcement and all investigators, inspectors, and deputies of the department identified by the director have the authority of peace officers while engaged in exercising the powers granted or performing the duties imposed upon them in investigating the laws administered by the department or commencing directly or indirectly any criminal prosecution arising from any investigation conducted under these laws. All persons herein referred to shall be deemed to be acting within the scope of employment with respect to all acts and matters set forth in this section.

(c) The department may employ individuals, who are not peace officers, to provide investigative services.

(d) Notwithstanding any other law, the department may employ peace officers and shall be exempt from the requirements of Section 13540 of the Penal Code.

Business and Professions Code § 26016

(Amended by Stats. 2021, Ch. 70, Sec. 17. (AB 141) Effective July 12, 2021.)

For any hearing held pursuant to this division, except a hearing held under Chapter 4 (commencing with Section 26040), the department may delegate the power to hear and decide to an administrative law judge. Any hearing before an administrative law judge shall be pursuant to the procedures, rules, and limitations prescribed in Chapter 5 (commencing with Section 11500) of Part 1 of Division 3 of Title 2 of the Government Code.

Business and Professions Code § 26017

(Amended by Stats. 2021, Ch. 70, Sec. 18. (AB 141) Effective July 12, 2021.)

In any hearing before the department pursuant to this division, the department may pay any person appearing as a witness at the hearing at the request of the department pursuant to a subpoena, the person's actual, necessary, and reasonable travel, food, and lodging expenses, not to exceed the amount authorized for state employees.

Business and Professions Code § 26018

(Amended by Stats. 2021, Ch. 70, Sec. 19. (AB 141) Effective July 12, 2021.)

The department may on its own motion at any time before a penalty assessment is placed into effect, and without any further proceedings, review the penalty, but such review shall be limited to its reduction.

Chapter 3. Enforcement

Business and Professions Code § 26030

(Amended by Stats. 2021, Ch. 70, Sec. 20. (AB 141) Effective July 12, 2021. Note: This section was added on Nov. 8, 2016, by initiative Prop. 64.)

Grounds for disciplinary action include, but are not limited to, all of the following:

(a) Failure to comply with the provisions of this division or any rule or regulation adopted pursuant to this division.

(b) Conduct that constitutes grounds for denial of licensure pursuant to Chapter 2 (commencing with Section 480) of Division 1.5 or discipline of a license pursuant to Chapter 3 (commencing with Section 490) of Division 1.5.

(c) Any other grounds contained in regulations adopted by the department pursuant to this division.

(d) Failure to comply with any state law including, but not limited to, the payment of taxes as required under the Revenue and Taxation Code, except as provided for in this division or other California law.

(e) Knowing violations of any state or local law, ordinance, or regulation conferring worker protections or legal rights on the employees of a licensee.

(f) Failure to comply with the requirement of a local ordinance regulating commercial cannabis activity.

(g) The intentional and knowing sale of cannabis or cannabis products by an A-licensee to a person under 21 years of age.

(h) The intentional and knowing sale of medicinal cannabis or medicinal cannabis products by an M-licensee to a person without a physician's recommendation.

(i) Failure to maintain safe conditions for inspection by the department.

(j) Failure to comply with any operating procedure submitted to the department pursuant to subdivision (b) of Section 26051.5.

(k) Failure to comply with license conditions established pursuant to subdivision (b) of Section 26060.1.

Business and Professions Code § 26031

(Amended by Stats. 2021, Ch. 70, Sec. 21. (AB 141) Effective July 12, 2021. Note: This section was added on Nov. 8, 2016, by initiative Prop. 64.)

(a) The department may suspend, revoke, place on probation with terms and conditions, or otherwise discipline licenses issued by the department and fine a licensee, after proper notice and hearing to the licensee, except as provided in Section 26031.01, if the licensee is found to have committed any of the acts or omissions constituting grounds for disciplinary action. The disciplinary proceedings under this chapter shall be conducted in accordance with Chapter 5 (commencing with Section 11500) of Part 1 of Division 3 of Title 2 of the Government Code, and the director shall have all the powers granted therein.

(b) The department may suspend or revoke a license when a local agency has notified the department that a licensee within its jurisdiction is in violation of state rules and regulations relating to commercial cannabis activities, and the department, through an investigation, has determined that the violation is grounds for suspension or revocation of the license.

(c) The department may take disciplinary action against a licensee for any violation of this division when the violation was committed by the licensee's officers, directors, owners, agents, or employees while acting on behalf of the licensee or engaged in commercial cannabis activity.

(d) The suspension or expiration of a license issued by the department, or its suspension, forfeiture, or cancellation by order of the department or by order of a court of law, or its surrender without the written consent of the department, shall not, during any period in which it may be renewed, restored, reissued, or reinstated, deprive the department of its authority to institute or continue a disciplinary proceeding against the licensee upon any ground provided by law or to enter an order suspending or revoking the license or otherwise taking disciplinary action against the licensee on any such ground.

Business and Professions Code § 26031.01

(Added by Stats. 2021, Ch. 70, Sec. 22. (AB 141) Effective July 12, 2021.)

(a) Notwithstanding Section 26031, the department may, before a hearing, suspend the license of a person who procured the issuance of the license by fraud, misrepresentation, deceit, or by the making of any material misstatement of fact in the application for such license.

(b) The department shall not order the suspension of a license pursuant to subdivision (a) 90 days after the date of issuance of the license.

(c) An order of suspension pursuant to subdivision (a) shall expire on the effective date of a decision of the department after a hearing conducted pursuant to this section.

(d) (1) The department shall file and serve a person whose license is suspended pursuant to subdivision (a) the order of suspension and a statement of issues as defined in Section 11504 of the Government Code. The department may serve the person by regular mail addressed to the last known address of the person or by personal service.

(2) A person whose license is suspended pursuant to subdivision (a) shall have 30 days after service of the order of suspension and statement of issues in which to file with the department a written request for a hearing on the statement of issues filed against them.

(3) (A) The department shall hold a hearing within 30 days after receipt of a request pursuant to paragraph (2) unless the person requests or agrees to a continuance. If the person does not request or agree to a continuance and a hearing is not commenced within 30 days after receipt of the request for a hearing, the order of suspension shall be vacated and set aside unless the person requests or agrees to a continuance.

(B) If the person requests or agrees to a continuance, the department shall hold a hearing on the date to which the department and the person agreed. If a hearing is not commenced on that date, the order of suspension shall be vacated and set aside.

(4) If the department does not render a decision within 30 days after completion of the hearing, the order of suspension shall be vacated and set aside.

(e) A hearing conducted pursuant to this section shall in all respects, except as otherwise expressly provided herein, conform to the substantive and procedural provisions of Chapter 5 (commencing with Section 11500) of Part 1 of Division 3 of Title 2 of the Government Code applicable to a hearing on a statement of issues.

Business and Professions Code § 26031.1

(Added by Stats. 2021, Ch. 70, Sec. 23. (AB 141) Effective July 12, 2021.)

(a) Except as otherwise provided by law, in an order issued in resolution of a disciplinary proceeding before the department, the administrative law judge, upon request, may direct a licensee found to have committed a violation to pay a sum not to exceed the reasonable costs of the investigation and enforcement of the case.

(b) A certified copy of the actual costs, or a good faith estimate of costs where actual costs are not available, signed by the department or its designated representative shall be prima facie evidence of reasonable costs of investigation and prosecution of the case. The costs shall include the amount of investigative and enforcement costs up to the date of the hearing, including, but not limited to, charges imposed by the Attorney General.

(c) The administrative law judge shall make a proposed finding of the amount of reasonable costs of investigation and prosecution of the case when requested pursuant to subdivision (a). The finding of the administrative law judge with regard to costs shall not be reviewable by the department to increase the cost award. The department may reduce or eliminate the cost award, or remand to the administrative law judge if the proposed decision fails to make a finding on costs requested pursuant to subdivision (a).

(d) If an order for recovery of costs is made and timely payment is not made as directed in the department's decision, the department may enforce the order for repayment in any appropriate court. This right of enforcement shall be in addition to any other rights the department may have as to any licensee to pay costs.

(e) In any action for recovery of costs, proof of the department's decision shall be conclusive proof of the validity of the order of payment and the terms for payment.

(f) (1) Except as provided in paragraph (2), the department shall not renew or reinstate the license of any licensee who has failed to pay all of the costs ordered under this section.

(2) Notwithstanding paragraph (1), the department may, in its discretion, conditionally renew or reinstate for a maximum of one year the license of any licensee who demonstrates financial hardship and who enters into a formal agreement with the department to reimburse the department within that one-year period for the unpaid costs.

(g) All costs recovered under this section shall be considered a reimbursement for costs incurred and shall be deposited into the Cannabis Control Fund to be available upon appropriation by the Legislature.

(h) Nothing in this section shall preclude the department from including the recovery of the costs of investigation and enforcement of a case in any stipulated settlement.

Business and Professions Code § 26031.2

(Added by Stats. 2021, Ch. 70, Sec. 24. (AB 141) Effective July 12, 2021.)

(a) The superior court for the county in which any person has engaged or is about to engage in any act which constitutes a violation of this division may, upon a petition filed by the department with the approval of the director, issue an injunction or other appropriate order restraining such conduct. The proceedings under this section shall be governed by Chapter 3 (commencing with Section 525) of Title 7 of Part 2 of the Code of Civil Procedure.

(b) The superior court for the county in which any person has engaged in any act which constitutes a violation of this division may, upon a petition filed by the department with the approval of the director, order such person to make restitution to persons injured as a result of such violation.

(c) The court may order a person subject to an injunction or restraining order, provided for in subdivision (a), or subject to an order requiring restitution pursuant to subdivision (b), to reimburse the department for expenses incurred by the department in its investigation related to its petition.

(d) The remedy provided for by this section shall be in addition to, and not a limitation on, the authority provided for in any other section of this division.

Business and Professions Code § 26031.5

(Amended by Stats. 2021, Ch. 70, Sec. 25. (AB 141) Effective July 12, 2021.)

(a) The department may issue a citation to a licensee or unlicensed person for any act or omission that violates or has violated any provision of this division or any regulation adopted pursuant thereto. The department shall issue the citation in writing, and shall describe with particularity the basis of the citation and the notification described in subdivision (c). The department may include in each citation an order of abatement and fix a reasonable time for abatement of the violation. The department may, as part of each citation, assess an administrative fine not to exceed five thousand dollars ($5,000) per violation by a licensee and thirty thousand dollars ($30,000) per violation by an unlicensed person. Each day of violation shall constitute a separate violation. In assessing a fine, the department shall give due consideration to the appropriateness of the amount of the fine with respect to factors the department determines to be relevant, including the following:

(1) The gravity of the violation by the licensee or person.

(2) The good faith of the licensee or person.

(3) The history of previous violations.

(b) The sanctions authorized under this section shall be separate from, and in addition to, all other administrative, civil, or criminal remedies.

(c) A citation issued pursuant to this section shall include a provision that notifies the licensee or person that a hearing may be requested to contest the finding of a violation by submitting a written request within 30 days from service of the citation. The hearing shall be held pursuant to the Administrative Procedure Act (Chapter 5 (commencing with Section 11500) of Part 1 of Division 3 of Title 2 of the Government Code), unless held in accordance with the provisions of Chapter 4.5 (commencing with Section 11400) as authorized by regulation of the department. If the licensee or person cited fails to submit a written request for a hearing within 30 days from the date of service of the citation, the right to a hearing is waived and the citation shall be deemed a final order of the department and is not subject to review by any court.

(d) After the exhaustion of the administrative and judicial review procedures, the department may apply to the appropriate superior court for a judgment in the amount of the administrative fine and an order compelling the cited person to comply with the order of the department. The application, which shall include a certified copy of the final order of the department, shall constitute a sufficient showing to warrant the issuance of the judgment and order.

(e) The department may recover from the licensee or person who was the subject of the citation costs of investigation and enforcement, which may include reasonable attorney's fees for the services rendered. If the department recovers costs from a licensee, the department shall recover the costs pursuant to Section 26031.1.

(f) Fines shall be paid within 30 days of service of a citation by the department. Failure to pay a fine assessed pursuant to this section within 30 days of the date of service of the citation, unless the citation is being appealed, shall constitute a separate violation under this division subject to additional action by the department. The department shall not renew or grant a license to a person who was the subject of the fine until that person pays the fine.

(g) All moneys collected pursuant to this section associated with the recovery of investigation and enforcement costs shall be deposited into the Cannabis Control Fund. Any administrative fine amount shall be deposited directly into the Cannabis Fines and Penalties Account and shall be distributed pursuant to subdivision (d) of Section 26210.

Business and Professions Code § 26032

(Repealed and added by Stats. 2017, Ch. 27, Sec. 18. (SB 94) Effective June 27, 2017.)

(a) The actions of a licensee, its employees, and its agents are not unlawful under state law and shall not be an offense subject to arrest, prosecution, or other sanction under state law, or be subject to a civil fine or be a basis for seizure or forfeiture of assets under state law if they are all of the following:

(1) Permitted pursuant to a state license.

(2) Permitted pursuant to a local authorization, license, or permit issued by the local jurisdiction, if any.

(3) Conducted in accordance with the requirements of this division and regulations adopted pursuant to this division.

(b) The actions of a person who, in good faith, allows his or her property to be used by a licensee, its employees, and its agents, as permitted pursuant to a state license and, if required by the applicable local ordinances, a local license or permit, are not unlawful under state law and shall not be an offense subject to arrest, prosecution, or other sanction under state law, or be subject to a civil fine or be a basis for seizure or forfeiture of assets under state law.

Business and Professions Code § 26033

(Repealed and added by Stats. 2017, Ch. 27, Sec. 20. (SB 94) Effective June 27, 2017.)

(a) A qualified patient, as defined in Section 11362.7 of the Health and Safety Code, who cultivates, possesses, stores, manufactures, or transports cannabis exclusively for his or her personal medical use but who does not provide, donate, sell, or distribute cannabis to any other person is not thereby engaged in commercial cannabis activity and is therefore exempt from the licensure requirements of this division.

(b) A primary caregiver who cultivates, possesses, stores, manufactures, transports, donates, or provides cannabis exclusively for the personal medical purposes of no more than five specified qualified patients for whom he or she is the primary caregiver within the meaning of Section 11362.7 of the Health and Safety Code, but who does not receive remuneration for these activities except for compensation in full compliance with subdivision (c) of Section 11362.765 of the Health and Safety Code, is exempt from the licensure requirements of this division.

Business and Professions Code § 26034

(Amended by Stats. 2021, Ch. 70, Sec. 26. (AB 141) Effective July 12, 2021.)

All accusations against licensees shall be filed by the department within five years after the performance of the act or omission alleged as the ground for disciplinary action; provided, however, that the foregoing provision shall not constitute a defense to an accusation alleging fraud or misrepresentation as a ground for disciplinary action. The cause for disciplinary action in that case shall not be deemed to have accrued until discovery, by the department, of the facts constituting the fraud or misrepresentation, and, in that case, the accusation shall be filed within five years after that discovery.

Business and Professions Code § 26035

(Amended by Stats. 2021, Ch. 70, Sec. 27. (AB 141) Effective July 12, 2021.)

The director shall designate the persons employed by the department for purposes of the administration and enforcement of this division. The director shall ensure that a sufficient number of employees are qualified peace officers for purposes of enforcing this division.

Business and Professions Code § 26036

(Added November 8, 2016, by initiative Proposition 64, Sec. 6.1.)

Nothing in this division shall be interpreted to supersede or limit state agencies from exercising their existing enforcement authority, including, but not limited to, under the Fish and Game Code, the Food and Agricultural Code, the Government Code, the Health and Safety Code, the Public Resources Code, the Water Code, or the application of those laws.

Business and Professions Code § 26037

(Added November 8, 2016, by initiative Proposition 64, Sec. 6.1.)

(a) The actions of a licensee, its employees, and its agents that are:

(1) permitted under a license issued under this division and any applicable local ordinances; and

(2) conducted in accordance with the requirements of this division and regulations adopted pursuant to this division, are not unlawful under state law and shall not be an offense subject to arrest, prosecution, or other sanction under state law, or be subject to a civil fine or be a basis for seizure or forfeiture of assets under state law.

(b) The actions of a person who, in good faith, allows his or her property to be used by a licensee, its employees, and its agents, as permitted pursuant to a state license and any applicable local ordinances, are not unlawful under state law and shall not be an offense subject to arrest, prosecution, or other sanction under state law, or be subject to a civil fine or be a basis for seizure or forfeiture of assets under state law.

Business and Professions Code § 26037.5

(Added by Stats. 2021, Ch. 70, Sec. 28. (AB 141) Effective July 12, 2021.)

(a) A person or entity shall not engage in commercial cannabis activity without a state license issued by the department pursuant to this division.

(b) The requirement to obtain a state license for the cultivation of cannabis pursuant to this division does not apply to the cultivation of cannabis in accordance with Section 11362.1 of the Health and Safety Code or the Compassionate Use Act or to persons or entities licensed under subdivision (b) of Section 26070.5.

Business and Professions Code § 26038

(Amended by Stats. 2022, Ch. 56, Sec. 2. (AB 195) Effective June 30, 2022. Note: This section was added on Nov. 8, 2016, by initiative Prop. 64.)

(a) (1) A person engaging in commercial cannabis activity without a license as required by this division shall be subject to civil penalties of up to three times the amount of the license fee for each violation. Each day of operation shall constitute a separate violation of this section.

(2) A person aiding and abetting unlicensed commercial cannabis activity shall be subject to civil penalties of up to three times the amount of the license fee for each violation, but in no case shall the penalty exceed thirty thousand dollars ($30,000) for each violation. Each day of operation of unlicensed commercial cannabis activity that a person is found to have aided and abetted shall constitute a separate violation of this section.

(3) A person who has management or control of a commercial property, or a commercial building, room, space, or enclosure, either as an owner, lessee, agent, employee, or mortgagee, who knowingly rents, leases, or makes available for use, with or without compensation, the commercial property, building, room, space, or enclosure for the purpose of the unlicensed commercial cultivation, manufacture, storage, sale, or distribution of cannabis shall be subject to civil penalties of up to ten thousand dollars ($10,000) for each violation. Each day of violation shall constitute a separate violation of this section.

(4) In assessing a penalty, a court shall give due consideration to the appropriateness of the amount of the civil penalty with respect to factors the court determines to be relevant, including the following:

(A) The gravity of the violation by the licensee or person.

(B) The good faith of the licensee or person.

(C) The licensee's or person's history of previous violations.

(D) Whether, and to what extent, the licensee or person profited from the unlicensed cannabis activity.

(5) Cannabis associated with a violation described in this subdivision may be destroyed in accordance with Section

11479 of the Health and Safety Code. The person in violation shall be responsible for the cost of the destruction of cannabis associated with their violation.

(b) An action for civil penalties brought against a person pursuant to this division shall not be commenced unless the action is filed within three years from the date of the violation.

(c) All civil penalties imposed and collected pursuant to this section by a court shall be deposited into the General Fund except as provided in subdivision (e).

(d) For the purposes of this section, in order to prove that a person aided and abetted an unlicensed cannabis activity all of the following must be demonstrated:

(1) The person was an owner, officer, controlling shareholder, or in a similar position of authority allowing them to make command or control decisions regarding the operations and management of the unlicensed cannabis activity or the property in which the activity is taking place.

(2) The person had actual knowledge that the cannabis activity was unlicensed and that the cannabis activity required a license.

(3) The person provided substantial assistance or encouragement to the unlicensed cannabis activity.

(4) The person's conduct was a substantial factor in furthering the unlicensed cannabis activity.

(e) (1) If an action for civil penalties is brought against a person pursuant to this division by the Attorney General on behalf of the people or on behalf of the department or a participating agency, the penalty shall first be used to reimburse the Attorney General and the department or the participating agency for the costs of investigating and prosecuting the action, including expert fees and reasonable attorney's fees, with the remainder, if any, to be deposited into the General Fund.

(2) If the action is brought by a county counsel, the penalty shall first be used to reimburse the county counsel for the costs of bringing the action for civil penalties, with the remainder, if any, to be deposited into the General Fund.

(3) If the action is brought by a city attorney or city prosecutor, the penalty collected shall first be used to reimburse the city attorney or city prosecutor for the costs of bringing the action for civil penalties, with the remainder, if any, to be deposited into the General Fund.

(4) Actions for civil penalties pursuant to paragraph (2) of subdivision (a) shall be brought exclusively by the Attorney General on behalf of the people, on behalf of the department, or on behalf of the participating agency, or by a city or county counsel or city prosecutor in a city or county having a population in excess of 750,000.

(5) Actions for civil penalties pursuant to paragraph (3) of subdivision (a) shall be brought exclusively by the Attorney General on behalf of the people, on behalf of the department, or on behalf of the participating agency, or by a city or county counsel, or city prosecutor.

(f) For purposes of paragraph (3) of subdivision (a), in order to prove that a person knowingly rented, leased, or made available the commercial property for unlawful commercial cannabis activity, it shall be demonstrated that the person had actual knowledge that the cannabis-related activity was for commercial purposes, required a license, and was unlicensed. The presence of a lawful amount of cannabis, cannabis products, or cannabis plants, subject to Sections 11362.1 and 11362.45 of the Health and Safety Code, shall not be evidence of actual knowledge.

(g) Notwithstanding subdivision (a), criminal penalties shall continue to apply to an unlicensed person engaging in commercial cannabis activity in violation of this division.

(h) (1) This section does not limit, preempt, or otherwise affect any other state or local law, rule, regulation, or ordinance applicable to the conduct described in subdivision (a), or otherwise relating to commercial cannabis activities.

(2) This section is meant to further the intent of the Control, Regulate and Tax Adult Use of Marijuana Act of 2016 (AUMA), which allows local governments to reasonably regulate the cultivation of nonmedical cannabis for personal use by adults 21 years of age and older through zoning and other local laws.

Business and Professions Code § 26039.1

(Added by renumbering Section 26132 by Stats. 2021, Ch. 70, Sec. 70. (AB 141) Effective July 12, 2021.)

(a) When the department has evidence that cannabis or a cannabis product is adulterated or misbranded, the department shall notify the licensee. The licensee may conduct a voluntary recall of the affected cannabis or cannabis product and may remediate the cannabis or cannabis product, if approved by the department, or shall destroy the affected cannabis or cannabis product under the supervision of the department.

(b) The department may issue a mandatory recall order and require the licensee to immediately cease distribution of cannabis or a cannabis product and recall the cannabis or cannabis product if the department determines both of the following:

(1) The cultivation, manufacture, distribution, or sale of the cannabis or cannabis product creates or poses an immediate and serious threat to human life or health.

(2) Other procedures available to the department to remedy or prevent the occurrence of the situation would result in an unreasonable delay.

(c) The department shall provide the licensee an opportunity for an informal proceeding on the matter, as determined by the department, within five days, on the actions required by the order and on why the cannabis or cannabis product should not be recalled. Following the proceeding, the order shall be affirmed, modified, or set aside as determined appropriate by the department.

(d) The department's powers set forth in this section expressly include the power to order movement, segregation, isolation, or destruction of cannabis or cannabis products, as well as the power to hold cannabis or cannabis products in place.

(e) If the department determines it is necessary, it may issue the mandatory recall order, may conduct the recall, and may use all appropriate measures to obtain reimbursement from the licensee for any and all costs associated with these orders. All funds obtained by the department from these efforts shall be deposited in the Cannabis Control Fund, and shall be available for use by the department upon appropriation by the Legislature.

(f) It is unlawful to move or allow to be moved cannabis or a cannabis product subject to an order issued pursuant to this section unless that person has first obtained written authorization from the department.

Business and Professions Code § 26039.3

(Added by renumbering Section 26133 by Stats. 2021, Ch. 70, Sec. 71. (AB 141) Effective July 12, 2021.)

(a) If the department finds or has probable cause to believe that cannabis or a cannabis product is adulterated or misbranded within the meaning of this division, or the sale of the cannabis or cannabis product would be in violation of this division, the department shall affix to the cannabis or cannabis product, or component thereof, a tag or other appropriate marking. The department shall give notice that the cannabis or cannabis product is, or is suspected of being, adulterated or misbranded, or the sale of the cannabis or cannabis product would be in violation of this division and has been embargoed and that the cannabis or cannabis product shall not be removed or disposed of by sale or otherwise until permission for removal or disposal is given by the department or a court.

(b) (1) It is unlawful to remove, sell, or dispose of embargoed cannabis or an embargoed cannabis product without written permission of the department or a court. The removal, sale, or disposal of each item of embargoed cannabis or cannabis product without written permission of the department constitutes a violation of this subdivision. A violation of this subdivision is subject to a citation and fine of not more than ten thousand dollars ($10,000).

(2) Notwithstanding paragraph (1), a licensed cultivator may request permission for the continued cultivation or harvesting of the cannabis subject to embargo. The department may authorize, and may impose conditions on, the continued cultivation or harvesting of the cannabis subject to embargo.

(c) If the adulteration or misbranding can be corrected by proper labeling or additional processing of the cannabis or cannabis product and all of the provisions of this division can be complied with, the licensee may request that the department remove the tag or other marking to permit correction. If, under the supervision of the department, the adulteration or misbranding has been corrected, the department may remove the tag or other marking. Cannabis and cannabis products found at an unlicensed location, or cultivated, processed, produced, or manufactured at an unlicensed location, or derived from an unlicensed source, cannot be corrected and shall be destroyed.

(d) If the department finds that cannabis or a cannabis product that is embargoed is not adulterated or misbranded, or that its sale is not otherwise in violation of this division, the department may remove the tag or other marking.

(e) The cannabis or cannabis product may be destroyed by the licensee or product owner pursuant to a corrective action plan approved by the department and under the supervision of the department. The cannabis or cannabis product shall be destroyed at the expense of the licensee or product owner.

(f) The department may condemn cannabis or a cannabis product under the provisions of this section. A proceeding for condemnation shall be subject to appropriate notice to, and the opportunity for a hearing with regard to, the person or licensee affected in accordance with Chapter 5 (commencing with Section 11500) of Part 1 of Division 3 of Title 2 of the Government Code.

> (1) Upon a finding by the administrative law judge that the cannabis or cannabis product is adulterated or misbranded, or that its sale is otherwise in violation of this division, the administrative law judge may direct the cannabis or cannabis product to be destroyed at the expense of the licensee or product owner and under the supervision of the department. The licensee or owner of the affected cannabis or cannabis product shall pay fees and reasonable costs, including the costs of storage, testing, and supervision, incurred by the department in investigating and prosecuting the action taken pursuant to this section.
>
> (2) Upon a finding by the administrative law judge that the adulteration or misbranding can be corrected by proper labeling or additional processing of the cannabis or cannabis product and that all provisions of this division can be complied with, the administrative law judge may direct the cannabis or cannabis products to be brought into compliance under the department's supervision. The licensee shall pay fees and reasonable costs, including the costs of storage, testing, and supervision, incurred by the department in investigating and prosecuting the action. After the costs, fees, and expenses have been paid, the department may release the embargo and remove the tag or other marking and supervise the corrective action.

Business and Professions Code § 26039.4

(Added by renumbering Section 26135 by Stats. 2021, Ch. 70, Sec. 73. (AB 141) Effective July 12, 2021.)

A peace officer, including a peace officer with the department, may seize cannabis and cannabis products in any of the following circumstances:

(a) The cannabis or cannabis product is subject to recall or embargo by the department.

(b) The cannabis or cannabis product is subject to destruction pursuant to this division.

(c) The cannabis or cannabis product is seized related to an investigation or disciplinary action for violation of this division.

Business and Professions Code § 26039.5

(Added by renumbering Section 26121 by Stats. 2021, Ch. 70, Sec. 67. (AB 141) Effective July 12, 2021.)

(a) Cannabis or a cannabis product is misbranded if it is any of the following:

(1) Cultivated, processed, manufactured, packed, or held in a location not duly licensed as provided in this division.

(2) Consists of cannabis or cannabis product that was cultivated, processed, manufactured, packed, or held in a location not duly licensed as provided in this division.

(3) Its labeling is false or misleading in any particular.

(4) Its labeling or packaging does not conform to the requirements of Section 26120 or any other labeling or packaging requirement established pursuant to this division.

(b) It is unlawful to cultivate, process, manufacture, sell, deliver, hold, or offer for sale cannabis or a cannabis product that is misbranded.

(c) It is unlawful to misbrand cannabis or a cannabis product.

(d) It is unlawful to receive in commerce cannabis or a cannabis product that is misbranded or to distribute, deliver, or offer for delivery any such cannabis or cannabis product.

Business and Professions Code § 26039.6

(Added by renumbering Section 26131 by Stats. 2021, Ch. 70, Sec. 69. (AB 141) Effective July 12, 2021.)

(a) Cannabis or a cannabis product is adulterated if it is any of the following:

(1) It has been produced, prepared, packed, or held under unsanitary conditions in which it may have become contaminated with filth or in which it may have been rendered injurious.

(2) It consists, in whole or in part, of any filthy, putrid, or decomposed substance.

(3) It bears or contains any poisonous or deleterious substance that may render it injurious to users under the conditions of use suggested in the labeling or under conditions that are customary or usual.

(4) It bears or contains a substance that is restricted or limited under this division or regulations promulgated pursuant to this division and the level of substance in the product exceeds the limits specified pursuant to this division or in regulation.

(5) Its concentrations differ from, or its purity or quality is below, that which it is represented to possess.

(6) The methods, facilities, or controls used for its cultivation, manufacture, packing, or holding do not conform to, or are not operated or administered in conformity with, practices established by regulations adopted under this division to ensure that the cannabis or cannabis product meets the requirements of this division as to safety and has the concentrations it purports to have and meets the quality and purity characteristics that it purports or is represented to possess.

(7) Its container is composed, in whole or in part, of any poisonous or deleterious substance that may render the contents injurious to health.

(8) It is an edible cannabis product and a substance has been mixed or packed with it after testing by a testing laboratory so as to reduce its quality or concentration or if a substance has been substituted, wholly or in part,

for the edible cannabis product.

(b) It is unlawful to cultivate, manufacture, distribute, sell, deliver, hold, or offer for sale cannabis or a cannabis product that is adulterated.

(c) It is unlawful to adulterate cannabis or a cannabis product.

(d) It is unlawful to receive in commerce cannabis or a cannabis product that is adulterated or to distribute, deliver, or proffer for delivery any such cannabis or cannabis product.

Chapter 4. Appeals

Business and Professions Code § 26040

(Amended by Stats. 2020, Ch. 93, Sec. 1. (AB 1872) Effective September 18, 2020. Note: This section was added on Nov. 8, 2016, by initiative Prop. 64.)

(a) (1) There is established in state government, in the Business, Consumer Services, and Housing Agency, a Cannabis Control Appeals Panel which shall consist of the following members:

(A) One member appointed by the Senate Committee on Rules.

(B) One member appointed by the Speaker of the Assembly.

(C) Three members appointed by the Governor and subject to confirmation by a majority vote of all of the members elected to the Senate.

(2) Each member appointed by the Governor, at the time of their initial appointment, shall be a resident of a different county from the one in which either of the other members appointed by the Governor resides. Members of the panel shall receive an annual salary as provided for by Chapter 6 (commencing with Section 11550) of Part 1 of Division 3 of Title 2 of the Government Code.

(b) The members of the panel may be removed from office by their appointing authority.

Business and Professions Code § 26041

(Amended by Stats. 2021, Ch. 70, Sec. 30. (AB 141) Effective July 12, 2021.)

All personnel of the panel shall be appointed, employed, directed, and controlled by the panel consistent with state civil service requirements. The Executive Director of the panel shall furnish the equipment, supplies, and housing necessary for the authorized activities of the panel and shall perform such other mechanics of administration as determined by the panel.

Business and Professions Code § 26042

(Added November 8, 2016, by initiative Proposition 64, Sec. 6.1.)

The panel shall adopt procedures for appeals similar to the procedures used in Articles 3 and 4 in Chapter 1.5 in Division 9 of the Business and Professions Code. Such procedures shall be adopted in accordance with the Administrative Procedure Act (Government Code, Title 2, Division 3, section 11340 et seq.).

Business and Professions Code § 26043

(Amended by Stats. 2021, Ch. 70, Sec. 31. (AB 141) Effective July 12, 2021. Note: This section was added on Nov. 8, 2016, by initiative Prop. 64.)

(a) After proceedings pursuant to Section 26031, 26031.5, or 26058 or Chapter 2 (commencing with Section 480) or Chapter 3 (commencing with Section 490) of Division 1.5, any person aggrieved by the decision of the department denying the person's application for any license, denying the person's renewal of any license, placing any license on probation, imposing any condition on any license, imposing any fine on any license or licensee, assessing any penalty on any license, or canceling, suspending, revoking, or otherwise disciplining any license as provided for under this division, may appeal the department's written decision to the panel.

(b) The panel shall review the decision subject to such limitations as may be imposed by the Legislature. In such cases, the panel shall not receive evidence in addition to that considered by the department.

(c) Review by the panel of a decision of the department shall be limited to the following questions:

(1) Whether the department has proceeded without or in excess of its jurisdiction.

(2) Whether the department has proceeded in the manner required by law.

(3) Whether the decision is supported by the findings.

(4) Whether the findings are supported by substantial evidence in the light of the whole record.

Business and Professions Code § 26044

(Amended by Stats. 2021, Ch. 70, Sec. 32. (AB 141) Effective July 12, 2021. Note: This section was added on Nov. 8, 2016, by initiative Prop. 64.)

(a) In appeals where the panel finds that there is relevant evidence which, in the exercise of reasonable diligence, could not have been produced or which was improperly excluded at the hearing before the department, it may enter an order remanding the matter to the department for reconsideration in the light of that evidence.

(b) Except as provided in subdivision (a), in all appeals, the panel shall enter an order either affirming or reversing the decision of the department. When the order reverses the decision of the department, the panel may direct the reconsideration of the matter in the light of its order and may direct the department to take such further action as is specially enjoined upon it by law, but the order shall not limit or control in any way the discretion vested by law in the department

Business and Professions Code § 26045

(Amended by Stats. 2021, Ch. 70, Sec. 33. (AB 141) Effective July 12, 2021.)

(a) No court of this state, except the Supreme Court and the courts of appeal to the extent specified in this chapter, shall have jurisdiction to review, affirm, reverse, correct, or annul any order, rule, or decision of the department or to suspend, stay, or delay the operation or execution thereof, or to restrain, enjoin, or interfere with the department in the performance of its duties, but a writ of mandate shall lie from the Supreme Court or the courts of appeal in any proper case.

(b) Any person affected by a final order of the panel, including the department, may apply to the Supreme Court or to the court of appeal for the appellate district in which the proceeding arose, for a writ of review of that final order.

(c) The application for writ of review shall be made within 30 days after filing of the final order.

(d) The provisions of the Code of Civil Procedure relating to writs of review shall, insofar as applicable, apply to proceedings in the courts as provided by this chapter. A copy of every pleading filed pursuant to this chapter shall be served on the panel, the department, and on each party who entered an appearance before the panel.

(e) No decision of the department that has been appealed to the panel and no final order of the panel shall become effective during the period in which application may be made for a writ of review, as provided by subdivision (c).

(f) The filing of a petition for, or the pendency of, a writ of review shall not of itself stay or suspend the operation of any order, rule, or decision of the department, but the court before which the petition is filed may stay or suspend, in whole or in part, the operation of the order, rule, or decision of the department subject to review, upon the terms and conditions which it by order directs.

Business and Professions Code § 26046

(Amended by Stats. 2021, Ch. 70, Sec. 34. (AB 141) Effective July 12, 2021.)

(a) The review by the court shall not extend further than to determine, based on the whole record of the department as certified by the panel, whether:

(1) The department has proceeded without or in excess of its jurisdiction.

(2) The department has proceeded in the manner required by law.

(3) The decision of the department is supported by the findings.

(4) The findings in the department's decision are supported by substantial evidence in the light of the whole record.

(5) There is relevant evidence which, in the exercise of reasonable diligence, could not have been produced or which was improperly excluded at the hearing before the department.

(b) Nothing in this chapter shall permit the court to hold a trial de novo, to take evidence, or to exercise its independent judgment on the evidence.

Business and Professions Code § 26047

(Amended by Stats. 2021, Ch. 70, Sec. 35. (AB 141) Effective July 12, 2021.)

The findings and conclusions of the department on questions of fact are conclusive and final and are not subject to review. Those questions of fact shall include ultimate facts and the findings and conclusions of the department. The panel, the department, and each party to the action or proceeding before the panel shall have the right to appear in the review proceeding. Following the hearing, the court shall enter judgment either affirming or reversing the decision of the department, or the court may remand the case for further proceedings before or reconsideration by the department.

Chapter 5. Licensing

Business and Professions Code § 26050

(Amended by Stats. 2021, Ch. 70, Sec. 36. (AB 141) Effective July 12, 2021. Note: This section was added on Nov. 8, 2016, by initiative Prop. 64.)

(a) The license classification pursuant to this division shall, at a minimum, be as follows:

(1) Type 1—Cultivation; Specialty outdoor; Small.

(2) Type 1A—Cultivation; Specialty indoor; Small.

(3) Type 1B—Cultivation; Specialty mixed-light; Small.

(4) Type 1C—Cultivation; Specialty cottage; Small.

(5) Type 2—Cultivation; Outdoor; Small.

(6) Type 2A—Cultivation; Indoor; Small.

(7) Type 2B—Cultivation; Mixed-light; Small.

(8) Type 3—Cultivation; Outdoor; Medium.

(9) Type 3A—Cultivation; Indoor; Medium.

(10) Type 3B—Cultivation; Mixed-light; Medium.

(11) Type 4—Cultivation; Nursery.

(12) Type 5—Cultivation; Outdoor; Large.

(13) Type 5A—Cultivation; Indoor; Large.

(14) Type 5B—Cultivation; Mixed-light; Large.

(15) Type 6—Manufacturer 1.

(16) Type 7—Manufacturer 2.

(17) Type 8—Testing laboratory.

(18) Type 10—Retailer.

(19) Type 11—Distributor.

(20) Type 12—Microbusiness.

(b) With the exception of testing laboratory licenses, which may be used to test cannabis and cannabis products regardless of whether they are intended for use by individuals who possesses a physician's recommendation, all licenses issued under this division shall bear a clear designation indicating whether the license is for commercial adult-use cannabis activity as distinct from commercial medicinal cannabis activity by prominently affixing an "A" or "M," respectively. Examples of such a designation include, but are not limited to, "A-Type 1" or "M-Type 1." Except as specifically specified in this division, the requirements for A-licenses and M-licenses shall be the same. For testing laboratories, the department shall create a license that indicates a testing laboratory may test both adult-use and medicinal cannabis.

(c) A license issued pursuant to this division shall be valid for 12 months from the date of issuance. The license may be renewed annually.

(d) The department shall establish procedures for the issuance and renewal of licenses.

Business and Professions Code § 26050.2

(Amended by Stats. 2021, Ch. 260, Sec. 1. (SB 166) Effective September 23, 2021. Repealed as of January 1, 2026, by its own provisions.)

(a) (1) Until June 30, 2022, except as provided in paragraphs (3) and (4), the department may, in its sole discretion, issue a provisional license to an applicant if the applicant has submitted a completed license application to the department, including the following, if applicable:

(A) If compliance with the California Environmental Quality Act (Division 13 (commencing with Section 21000) of the Public Resources Code) is not complete, evidence that compliance is underway.

(B) If compliance with local ordinances enacted pursuant to Section 26200 is not complete, evidence that compliance is underway.

(C) Compliance with paragraphs (5) and (11) of subdivision (a) of Section 26051.5.

(D) For a license application that includes cultivation activities, any of the following documents:

(i) A final streambed alteration agreement.

(ii) A draft streambed alteration agreement provided by the Department of Fish and Wildlife and signed and returned to the Department of Fish and Wildlife.

(iii) Written verification by the Department of Fish and Wildlife that a streambed alteration agreement is not needed.

(iv) Written verification by the Department of Fish and Wildlife that the applicant has submitted a notification described in Section 1602 of the Fish and Game Code, submitted payment of applicable fees pursuant to Section 1609 of the Fish and Game Code, and is responsive to the Department of Fish and Wildlife. For purposes of this subparagraph, an applicant is not responsive to the Department of Fish and Wildlife if either of the following apply:

(I) The notification has been deemed incomplete a second time.

(II) After a notification has been deemed incomplete once, the Department of Fish and Wildlife has not received requested information from the applicant for more than 60 days.

(E) The application is submitted to the department on or before March 31, 2022.

(2) If an application for a cultivation license is submitted on or after January 1, 2022, the department shall not issue a provisional license pursuant to this section if issuing the provisional license would cause a licensee to hold multiple cultivation licenses on contiguous premises to exceed one acre of total canopy for outdoor cultivation, or 22,000 square feet for mixed-light or indoor cultivation.

(3) Until June 30, 2023, the department may, in its sole discretion, issue a provisional license for a local equity license application, provided that the applicant meets the following requirements:

(A) The local equity applicant is not a cultivation license applicant for a premises that exceeds one acre of total canopy for outdoor cultivation, or 22,000 square feet for mixed-light or indoor cultivation.

(B) Issuing the license would not cause the applicant to hold multiple cultivation licenses on contiguous premises to exceed one acre of total canopy for outdoor cultivation, or 22,000 square feet for mixed-light or indoor cultivation.

(C) The local equity applicant satisfies all of the requirements in subparagraphs (A) to (D), inclusive, of paragraph (1).

(D) The local equity applicant submits an application to the department on or before March 31, 2023.

(4) Until September 30, 2022, the department may, in its sole discretion, issue a provisional license to a cultivation

license applicant, provided that the applicant meets the following requirements:

(A) The applicant is not a cultivation license applicant for a premises that exceeds 20,000 square feet of total canopy for outdoor cultivation.

(B) Issuing the license would not cause the applicant to hold multiple cultivation licenses on contiguous premises to exceed one acre of total canopy for outdoor cultivation, or 22,000 square feet for mixed-light or indoor cultivation.

(C) The cultivation license applicant satisfies all of the requirements in subparagraphs (A) to (D), inclusive, of paragraph (1).

(D) The cultivation license applicant submits an application to the department on or before June 30, 2022.

(b) A provisional license issued pursuant to this section shall be valid for no more than 12 months from the date it was issued or renewed. If the department issues or renews a provisional license, it shall include the outstanding items needed to qualify for an annual license specific to the licensee.

(c) The department may, in its sole discretion, renew a provisional license until it issues or denies the provisional licensee's annual license, subject to the requirements of this section.

(d) For a renewal of a provisional license beginning July 1, 2022, through June 30, 2023, the department shall not renew a provisional license unless the following criteria are met:

(1) For cultivation licenses, to illustrate progress with compliance with Chapter 6 (commencing with Section 1600) of Division 2 of the Fish and Game Code, one of the following documents:

(A) A final streambed alteration agreement issued by the Department of Fish and Wildlife.

(B) A draft streambed alteration agreement provided by the Department of Fish and Wildlife and signed and returned to the Department of Fish and Wildlife by the provisional licensee.

(C) Written verification by the Department of Fish and Wildlife that the provisional licensee has submitted a complete notification described in Section 1602 of the Fish and Game Code.

(D) Written verification by the Department of Fish and Wildlife that a streambed alteration agreement is not needed.

(2) If compliance with the California Environmental Quality Act (Division 13 (commencing with Section 21000) of the Public Resources Code) is not yet complete, a determination from the department that one of the following requirements has been met:

(A) The lead agency is in the process of preparing a site-specific initial study, addendum, or checklist pursuant to Section 15063, 15164, 15168, or 15183 of Title 14 of the California Code of Regulations to demonstrate whether it is consistent with a previously circulated and adopted negative declaration, mitigated negative declaration, or environmental impact report.

(B) If a local jurisdiction is the lead agency, the lead agency has made substantial progress during the previous 12-month licensure term toward completing project-specific environmental review by drafting, preparing, or circulating for public review an environmental document pursuant to the California Environmental Quality Act (Division 13 (commencing with Section 21000) of the Public Resources Code).

(C) If the department is the lead agency, information requested by the department of the provisional licensee that demonstrates the furtherance of environmental review.

(D) Information submitted to the department by the provisional licensee applicant that demonstrates evidence of substantial progress toward compliance with the California Environmental Quality Act (Division 13 (commencing with Section 21000) of the Public Resources Code) during the previous

12-month licensure term.

(e) On or after July 1, 2023, the department shall not renew a provisional license unless the following criteria are met:

(1) For cultivation licenses, to illustrate progress with compliance with Chapter 6 (commencing with Section 1600) of Division 2 of the Fish and Game Code, one of the following documents:

(A) A final streambed alteration agreement issued by the Department of Fish and Wildlife.

(B) A draft streambed alteration agreement provided by the Department of Fish and Wildlife and signed and returned to the Department of Fish and Wildlife by the provisional licensee.

(C) Written verification from the Department of Fish and Wildlife that a streambed alteration agreement is not needed.

(2) If compliance with the California Environmental Quality Act (Division 13 (commencing with Section 21000) of the Public Resources Code) is not yet complete, to illustrate progress with compliance, a determination from the department that one of the following has been met:

(A) The lead agency for the license has prepared and circulated for public review a negative declaration or a mitigated negative declaration.

(B) The lead agency for the license has determined that an environmental impact report is required pursuant to Section 21157 of the Public Resources Code and has either made substantial progress in preparing that environmental impact report or has a contract or contracts with consultants in place for the preparation of that environmental impact report.

(C) The lead agency has certified to the department that it has conducted a reasonably comprehensive site-specific review and has reviewed, prepared, and deemed complete an initial study, addendum, or checklist pursuant to Section 15063, 15164, 15168, or 15183 of Title 14 of the California Code of Regulations, which demonstrates consistency with a previously circulated and adopted negative declaration, mitigated negative declaration, or environmental impact report, in preparation for approval of an annual license.

(D) The lead agency for the license has reviewed, prepared, and deemed complete a notice of exemption pursuant to Section 21108 or 21152 of the Public Resources Code, except for ministerial projects not subject to the California Environmental Quality Act pursuant to paragraph (1) of subdivision (b) of Section 21080 of the Public Resources Code.

(f) A provisional license authorizing cultivation activities shall not be renewed if the department is notified of either or both of the following:

(1) The State Water Resources Control Board has notified the department that the provisional licensee is not in compliance with subdivision (a) or (b) of Section 26060.1 or the principles, guidelines, and requirements established pursuant to Section 13149 of the Water Code.

(2) The Department of Fish and Wildlife has notified the department that the provisional licensee is not in compliance with any final streambed alteration agreement, any conditions set forth in a signed draft streambed alteration agreement, or a condition established pursuant to subdivision (a) or paragraphs (1) and (2) of subdivision (b) of Section 26060.1.

(g) (1) After January 1, 2023, the department shall not renew a license pursuant to this section for cultivation activities if renewing the license would cause a licensee to hold multiple cultivation licenses on contiguous premises to exceed one acre of total canopy for outdoor cultivation or 22,000 square feet for mixed-light or indoor cultivation.

(2) After January 1, 2024, no provisional license that causes a licensee to hold multiple cultivation licenses on contiguous premises to exceed one acre of total canopy for outdoor cultivation or 22,000 square feet for mixed-light

or indoor cultivation shall be in effect.

(h) The department, in its sole discretion, may allow a provisional licensee to move locations after the date provisional licenses can no longer be issued provided that the new location is approved in compliance with California Environmental Quality Act, and Chapter 6 (commencing with Section 1600) of Division 2 of the Fish and Game Code. If all other renewal requirements are satisfied, the department may also renew the license at the new location.

(i) The department may, in its sole discretion, revoke or suspend a provisional license if it determines the licensee failed to actively and diligently pursue requirements for the annual license. The department shall adopt regulations clarifying what constitutes actively and diligently pursuing requirements for the annual license.

(j) The department shall cancel a provisional license upon issuance of an annual license, denial of an annual license, abandonment of an application for licensure, or withdrawal of an application for licensure.

(k) Except as specified in this section, the provisions of this division shall apply to a provisional license in the same manner as to an annual license.

(l) Without limiting any other statutory exemption or categorical exemption, Division 13 (commencing with Section 21000) of the Public Resources Code does not apply to the issuance of a license pursuant to this section by the department, except as otherwise provided in this section.

(m) Refusal by the department to issue a license pursuant to this section or revocation or suspension by the department of a license issued pursuant to this section shall not entitle the applicant or licensee to a hearing or an appeal of the decision. Chapter 2 (commencing with Section 480) of Division 1.5 and Chapter 4 (commencing with Section 26040) of this division and Sections 26031 and 26058 shall not apply to licenses issued pursuant to this section.

(n) For purposes of this section, "streambed alteration agreement" has the same meaning as the term "agreement" is defined in Section 1601 of the Fish and Game Code, which includes both individual agreements and general agreements under Section 1617 of the Fish and Game Code.

(o) The Department may not renew a provisional license after January 1, 2025 and no provisional license shall be effective after January 1, 2026.

(p) This section shall remain in effect only until January 1, 2026, and as of that date is repealed.

(q) It is the intent of the Legislature that no further exemptions from annual licenses be adopted and that any licenses issued under this division after January 1, 2025, be issued in compliance with all relevant environmental laws.

(r) It is the intent of the Legislature that funds appropriated in Item 1115-101-0001 of the Budget Act of 2021 shall be promptly deployed to allow local jurisdictions to meet the deadlines in this Act.

Business and Professions Code § 26051

(Amended by Stats. 2021, Ch. 70, Sec. 38. (AB 141) Effective July 12, 2021.)

(a) The Cartwright Act, the Unfair Practices Act, the Unfair Competition Law, and the other provisions of Part 2 (commencing with Section 16600) of Division 7 apply to all licensees regulated under this division.

(b) It shall be unlawful for any person to monopolize, attempt to monopolize, or combine or conspire with any person or persons to monopolize, any part of the trade or commerce related to cannabis. The Attorney General shall have the sole authority to enforce the provisions of this subdivision.

(c) In determining whether to grant, deny, or renew a retail license, microbusiness license, or a license issued under Section 26070.5, the department shall consider if an excessive concentration exists in the area where the licensee will operate. For purposes of this section "excessive concentration" applies when either of the following conditions exist:

(1) The ratio of licensees to population in the census tract or census division in which the applicant premises is located exceeds the ratio of licensees to population in the county in which the applicant premises is located, unless denial of the application would unduly limit the development of the legal market so as to perpetuate the illegal market for cannabis or cannabis products.

(2) The ratio of retail licenses, microbusiness licenses, or licenses under Section 26070.5 to the population in the census tract, census division, or jurisdiction exceeds that allowable by local ordinance adopted under Section 26200.

Business and Professions Code § 26051.5

(Amended by Stats. 2022, Ch. 56, Sec. 3. (AB 195) Effective June 30, 2022.)

(a) An applicant for a state license issued pursuant to this division to conduct commercial cannabis activity, as defined in Section 26001, shall do all of the following:

(1) Require that each owner electronically submit to the Department of Justice fingerprint images and related information required by the Department of Justice for the purpose of obtaining information as to the existence and content of a record of state or federal convictions and state and federal arrests, and also information as to the existence and content of a record of state or federal convictions and arrests for which the Department of Justice establishes that the person is free on bail or on their own recognizance pending trial or appeal.

(A) Notwithstanding any other law, the Bureau of Cannabis Control, the Department of Food and Agriculture, the State Department of Public Health, and the department, as defined in Section 26001, may obtain criminal history information from the Department of Justice and the Federal Bureau of Investigation for an applicant for any state license under this division, including any license established by a licensing authority, as defined in Section 26001, by regulation pursuant to subdivision (b) of Section 26012.

(B) When received, the Department of Justice shall transmit fingerprint images and related information received pursuant to this section to the Federal Bureau of Investigation for the purpose of obtaining a federal criminal history records check. The Department of Justice shall review the information returned from the Federal Bureau of Investigation and compile and disseminate a response to the licensing authority.

(C) The Department of Justice shall provide a response to the licensing authority pursuant to paragraph (1) of subdivision (p) of Section 11105 of the Penal Code.

(D) The licensing authority shall request from the Department of Justice subsequent notification service, as provided pursuant to Section 11105.2 of the Penal Code, for applicants.

(E) The Department of Justice shall charge the applicant a fee sufficient to cover the reasonable cost of processing the requests described in this paragraph.

(F) Employees of a licensing authority, as defined in Section 26001, acting on behalf of the department may receive criminal history information pursuant to this section. This subparagraph shall become inoperative on July 1, 2023.

(G) Notwithstanding any other law, a licensing authority may request and receive from a local or state agency certified records of all arrests and convictions, certified records regarding probation, and any and all other related documentation needed to complete an applicant or licensee investigation. A local or state agency may provide those records to a licensing authority upon request.

(2) Provide evidence of the legal right to occupy and use the proposed location and provide a statement from the landowner of real property or that landowner's agent where the commercial cannabis activity will occur, as proof to demonstrate the landowner has acknowledged and consented to permit commercial cannabis activities to be conducted on the property by the tenant applicant.

(3) Provide evidence that the proposed location is in compliance with subdivision (b) of Section 26054.

(4) Provide a statement, signed by the applicant under penalty of perjury, that the information provided is complete, true, and accurate.

(5) (A) (i) For an applicant with 20 or more employees, or an applicant with 10 or more employees that submits an application on or after July 1, 2024, provide a notarized statement that the applicant will enter into, or demonstrate that it has already entered into, and will abide by the terms of a labor peace agreement. On and after July 1, 2024, the department shall not renew a license for a licensee with 10 or more employees unless the licensee provides a statement that the licensee has already entered into and will abide by the terms of a labor peace agreement.

(ii) For an applicant with 10 or more employees but less than 20 employees that has not yet entered into a labor peace agreement, provide a notarized statement as a part of its application indicating that the applicant will enter into and abide by the terms of a labor peace agreement within 60 days of employing its 20th employee, or on or before July 1, 2024, whichever is earlier.

(iii) For an applicant with less than 10 employees that has not yet entered into a labor peace agreement, provide a notarized statement as a part of its application indicating that the applicant will enter into and abide by the terms of a labor peace agreement within 60 days of employing its 10th employee or on or before July 1, 2024, whichever is later.

(iv) Nothing in this paragraph shall be construed to limit the authority of the department to revoke or suspend a license for a violation of this paragraph.

(B) Compliance with the terms of an applicable labor peace agreement is a condition of licensure. A licensee seeking renewal of any license shall attest to the department that it remains in compliance with the terms of any applicable labor peace agreement.

(C) Any labor organization, or any current or former employee of the relevant licensee, may report to the department that a licensee has failed to provide a truthful attestation of compliance with subparagraph (B).

(i) The reporting party shall provide documentation, in a form and manner required by the department, to substantiate their allegation before the department considers it. The department shall collaborate with such agencies as it deems relevant to evaluate the report.

(ii) If the department substantiates the validity of a report made pursuant to this subparagraph, the department may suspend, revoke, place on probation with terms and conditions, or otherwise discipline the license and fine the licensee.

(D) (i) Any labor organization, or any current or former employee of the relevant licensee, may file a complaint with the Agricultural Labor Relations Board that an organization with which a licensee has entered into a labor peace agreement is not a bona fide labor organization.

(ii) The Agricultural Labor Relations Board shall consider all relevant evidence provided or obtained in rendering a decision on whether the entity is a bona fide labor organization and issue a report with its findings no later than ninety (90) days from receiving the complaint.

(iii) If the Agricultural Labor Relations Board determines that the entity is not a bona fide labor organization, the labor peace agreement shall be null and void. The department shall promptly notify all licensees that have signed labor peace agreements with the entity that the entity was found not to be a bona fide labor organization and offer those licensees a reasonable time period, not to exceed 180 days, to enter into a labor peace agreement with a bona fide labor organization. Failure to enter into a labor peace agreement with a bona fide labor organization after that reasonable time period shall be a violation of this section.

(E) For the purposes of this paragraph, all of the following shall apply:

(i) "Employee" does not include a supervisor.

(ii) "Labor organization" means any organization of any kind, or any agency or employee representation committee or plan, in which employees participate and which exists, in whole or in part, for the purpose of dealing with employers concerning grievances, labor disputes, wages, rates of pay, hours of employment, or conditions of work for employees.

(iii) "Supervisor" means an individual having authority, in the interest of the applicant, to hire, transfer, suspend, lay off, recall, promote, discharge, assign, reward, or discipline other employees, or responsibility to direct them or to adjust their grievances, or effectively to recommend such action, if, in connection with the foregoing, the exercise of that authority is not of a merely routine or clerical nature, but requires the use of independent judgment.

(6) Provide the applicant's valid seller's permit number issued pursuant to Part 1 (commencing with Section 6001) of Division 2 of the Revenue and Taxation Code or indicate that the applicant is currently applying for a seller's permit.

(7) Provide any other information required by the department.

(8) For an applicant seeking a cultivation license, provide a statement declaring the applicant is an "agricultural employer," as defined in the Alatorre-Zenovich-Dunlap-Berman Agricultural Labor Relations Act of 1975 (Part 3.5 (commencing with Section 1140) of Division 2 of the Labor Code), to the extent not prohibited by law.

(9) Pay all applicable fees required for licensure by the department.

(10) Provide proof of a bond to cover the costs of destruction of cannabis or cannabis products if necessitated by a violation of licensing requirements.

(11) (A) Provide a statement, upon initial application and application for renewal, that the applicant employs, or will employ within one year of receiving or renewing a license, one supervisor and one employee who have successfully completed a Cal-OSHA 30-hour general industry outreach course offered by a training provider that is authorized by an OSHA Training Institute Education Center to provide the course. This paragraph shall not be construed to alter or amend existing requirements for employers to provide occupational safety and health training to employees.

(B) An applicant with only one employee shall not be subject to subparagraph (A).

(C) For purposes of this paragraph "employee" has the same meaning as provided in subparagraph (B) of paragraph (5) and "supervisor" has the same meaning as provided in subparagraph (C) of paragraph (5).

(b) An applicant shall also include in the application a detailed description of the applicant's operating procedures for all of the following, as required by the department:

(1) Cultivation.

(2) Extraction and infusion methods.

(3) The transportation process.

(4) Inventory procedures.

(5) Quality control procedures.

(6) Security protocols.

(7) For applicants seeking licensure to cultivate, the source or sources of water the applicant will use for cultivation, as provided in subdivisions (a) to (c), inclusive, of Section 26060.1. For purposes of this paragraph, "cultivation" as used in Section 26060.1 shall have the same meaning as defined in Section 26001. The department shall consult with the State Water Resources Control Board and the Department of Fish and Wildlife in the implementation of this paragraph.

(c) The applicant shall also provide a complete detailed diagram of the proposed premises wherein the license privileges will be exercised, with sufficient particularity to enable ready determination of the bounds of the premises, showing all boundaries, dimensions, entrances and exits, interior partitions, walls, rooms, and common or shared entryways, and include a brief statement or description of the principal activity to be conducted therein, and, for licenses permitting cultivation, measurements of the planned canopy, including aggregate square footage and individual square footage of separate cultivation areas, if any, roads, water crossings, points of diversion, water storage, and all other facilities and infrastructure related to the cultivation.

(d) Provide a complete list of every person with a financial interest in the person applying for the license as required by the department. For purposes of this subdivision, "persons with a financial interest" does not include persons whose only interest in a licensee is an interest in a diversified mutual fund, blind trust, or similar instrument.

Business and Professions Code § 26052

(Amended by Stats. 2017, Ch. 27, Sec. 36. (SB 94) Effective June 27, 2017. Note: This section was added on Nov. 8, 2016, by initiative Prop. 64.)

(a) A licensee shall not perform any of the following acts, or permit any of the following acts to be performed by any employee, agent, or contractor of the licensee:

(1) Make any contract in restraint of trade in violation of Section 16600.

(2) Form a trust or other prohibited organization in restraint of trade in violation of Section 16720.

(3) Make a sale or contract for the sale of cannabis or cannabis products, or to fix a price charged therefor, or discount from, or rebate upon, that price, on the condition, agreement, or understanding that the consumer or purchaser thereof shall not use or deal in the goods, merchandise, machinery, supplies, commodities, or services of a competitor or competitors of the seller, where the effect of that sale, contract, condition, agreement, or understanding may be to substantially lessen competition or tend to create a monopoly in any line of trade or commerce.

(4) Sell any cannabis or cannabis products at less than cost for the purpose of injuring competitors, destroying competition, or misleading or deceiving purchasers or prospective purchasers.

(5) Discriminate between different sections, communities, or cities or portions thereof, or between different locations in those sections, communities, or cities or portions thereof in this state, by selling or furnishing cannabis or cannabis products at a lower price in one section, community, or city or any portion thereof, or in one location in that section, community, or city or any portion thereof, than in another, for the purpose of injuring competitors or destroying competition.

(6) Sell any cannabis or cannabis products at less than the cost thereof to such vendor, or to give away any article or product for the purpose of injuring competitors or destroying competition.

(b) Any person who, either as director, officer, or agent of any firm or corporation, or as agent of any person, violates the provisions of this chapter, or assists or aids, directly or indirectly, in that violation is responsible therefor equally with the person, firm, or corporation for which that person acts.

(c) Any person or trade association may bring an action to enjoin and restrain any violation of this section for the recovery of damages.

Business and Professions Code § 26053

(Amended by Stats. 2021, Ch. 70, Sec. 40. (AB 141) Effective July 12, 2021. Note: This section was added on Nov. 8, 2016, by initiative Prop. 64.)

(a) All commercial cannabis activity shall be conducted between licensees, except as otherwise provided in this division.

(b) (1) A person that holds a state testing laboratory license under this division is prohibited from licensure for any other activity, except testing, as authorized under this division. A person that holds a state testing laboratory license shall not employ an individual who is also employed by any other licensee that does not hold a state testing laboratory license.

(2) A person with a financial interest in a state testing laboratory license under this division is prohibited from holding a financial interest in any other type of cannabis license.

(c) Except as provided in subdivision (b), a person may apply for and be issued more than one license under this division.

(d) Each applicant or licensee shall apply for, and if approved, shall obtain, a separate license for each location where it engages in commercial cannabis activity.

Business and Professions Code § 26054

(Amended by Stats. 2021, Ch. 70, Sec. 41. (AB 141) Effective July 12, 2021. Note: This section was added on Nov. 8, 2016, by initiative Prop. 64.)

(a) A licensee shall not sell alcoholic beverages or tobacco products on or at any premises licensed under this division.

(b) A premises licensed under this division shall not be located within a 600-foot radius of a school providing instruction in kindergarten or any grades 1 through 12, daycare center, or youth center that is in existence at the time the license is issued, unless the department or a local jurisdiction specifies a different radius. The distance specified in this section shall be measured in the same manner as provided in subdivision (c) of Section 11362.768 of the Health and Safety Code unless otherwise provided by law.

(c) It shall not be a violation of state or local law for a business engaged in the manufacture of cannabis accessories to possess, transport, purchase, or otherwise obtain small amounts of cannabis or cannabis products as necessary to conduct research and development related to the cannabis accessories, provided the cannabis and cannabis products are obtained from a person licensed under this division permitted to provide or deliver the cannabis or cannabis products.

(d) It shall not be a violation of state or local law for an agent of the department to possess, transport, or obtain cannabis or cannabis products as necessary to conduct activities reasonably related to the duties of the department.

(e) It shall not be a violation of state or local law for an agent of a state agency, as defined in Section 1100 of the Government Code, or a local agency, as defined in Section 50001 of the Government Code, to possess, transport, or obtain cannabis or cannabis products as necessary to conduct activities reasonably related to the duties of the state or local agency.

Business and Professions Code § 26055

(Amended by Stats. 2021, Ch. 70, Sec. 43. (AB 141) Effective July 12, 2021. Note: This section was added on Nov. 8, 2016, by initiative Prop. 64.)

(a) The department may issue state licenses only to qualified applicants.

(b) Revocation of a state license issued under this division shall terminate the ability of the licensee to operate pursuant to that license within California until a new license is obtained.

(c) A licensee shall not change or alter the premises in a manner which materially or substantially alters the premises, the usage of the premises, or the mode or character of business operation conducted from the premises, from the plan contained in the diagram on file with the application, unless and until written approval by the department has been obtained. For purposes of this section, material or substantial physical changes of the premises, or in the usage of the premises, shall include, but not be limited to, a substantial increase or decrease in the total area of the licensed premises previously diagrammed, or any other physical modification resulting in substantial change in the mode or character of business operation.

(d) The department shall not approve an application for a state license under this division if approval of the state license will violate the provisions of any local ordinance or regulation adopted in accordance with Section 26200.

(e) An applicant may voluntarily provide proof of a license, permit, or other authorization from the local jurisdiction verifying that the applicant is in compliance with the local jurisdiction. An applicant that voluntarily submits a valid, unexpired license, permit, or other authorization from the local jurisdiction shall be presumed to be in compliance with all local ordinances unless the department is notified otherwise by the local jurisdiction. The department shall notify the contact person for the local jurisdiction of any applicant that voluntarily submits a valid, unexpired license, permit, or other authorization from the local jurisdiction.

(f) (1) A local jurisdiction shall provide to the department a copy of any ordinance or regulation related to commercial cannabis activity and the name and contact information for the person who will serve as the contact for the department regarding commercial cannabis activity within the jurisdiction. If a local jurisdiction does not provide a contact person, the department shall assume that the clerk of the legislative body of the local jurisdiction is the contact person.

(2) Whenever there is a change in a local ordinance or regulation adopted pursuant to Section 26200 or a change in the contact person for the jurisdiction, the local jurisdiction shall provide that information to the department.

(g) (1) The department shall deny an application for a license under this division for a commercial cannabis activity that the local jurisdiction has notified the department is prohibited in accordance with subdivision (f). The department shall notify the contact person for the local jurisdiction of each application denied due to the local jurisdiction's indication that the commercial cannabis activity for which a license is sought is prohibited by a local ordinance or regulation.

(2) Prior to issuing a state license under this division for any commercial cannabis activity, if an applicant has not provided adequate proof of compliance with local laws pursuant to subdivision (e):

> (A) The department shall notify the contact person for the local jurisdiction of the receipt of an application for commercial cannabis activity within their jurisdiction.
>
> (B) A local jurisdiction may notify the department that the applicant is not in compliance with a local ordinance or regulation. In this instance, the department shall deny the application.
>
> (C) A local jurisdiction may notify the department that the applicant is in compliance with all applicable local ordinances and regulations. In this instance, the department may proceed with the licensing process.
>
> (D) If the local jurisdiction does not provide notification of compliance or noncompliance with applicable local

ordinances or regulations, or otherwise does not provide notification indicating that the completion of the local permitting process is still pending, within 60 business days of receiving the inquiry from the department submitted pursuant to subparagraph (A), the department shall make a rebuttable presumption that the applicant is in compliance with all local ordinances and regulations adopted in accordance with Section 26200, except as provided in subparagraphs (E) and (F).

(E) At any time after expiration of the 60-business-day period set forth in subparagraph (D), the local jurisdiction may provide written notification to the department that the applicant or licensee is not in compliance with a local ordinance or regulation adopted in accordance with Section 26200. Upon receiving this notification, the department shall not presume that the applicant or licensee has complied with all local ordinances and regulations adopted in accordance with Section 26200, and may commence disciplinary action in accordance with Chapter 3 (commencing with Section 26030). If the department does not take action against the licensee before the time of the renewal of the license, the license shall not be renewed until and unless the local jurisdiction notifies the department that the licensee is once again in compliance with local ordinances.

(F) A presumption by the department pursuant to this paragraph that an applicant has complied with all local ordinances and regulations adopted in accordance with Section 26200 shall not prevent, impair, or preempt the local government from enforcing all applicable local ordinances or regulations against the applicant, nor shall the presumption confer any right, vested or otherwise, upon the applicant to commence or continue operating in any local jurisdiction except in accordance with all local ordinances or regulations.

(3) For purposes of this section, "notification" includes written notification or access by the department to a local jurisdiction's registry, database, or other platform designated by a local jurisdiction, containing information specified by the department, on applicants to determine local compliance.

(h) Without limiting any other statutory exemption or categorical exemption, Division 13 (commencing with Section 21000) of the Public Resources Code does not apply to the adoption of an ordinance, rule, or regulation by a local jurisdiction that requires discretionary review and approval of permits, licenses, or other authorizations to engage in commercial cannabis activity. To qualify for this exemption, the discretionary review in any such law, ordinance, rule, or regulation shall include any applicable environmental review pursuant to Division 13 (commencing with Section 21000) of the Public Resources Code. This subdivision shall become inoperative on July 1, 2021.

(i) A local or state public agency may charge and collect a fee from a person proposing a project pursuant to subdivision (a) of Section 21089 of the Public Resources Code.

Business and Professions Code § 26056

(Repealed and added by Stats. 2017, Ch. 27, Sec. 44. (SB 94) Effective June 27, 2017.)

The requirements of Sections 13143.9, 13145, and 13146 of the Health and Safety Code shall apply to all licensees.

Business and Professions Code § 26057

(Amended by Stats. 2021, Ch. 70, Sec. 44. (AB 141) Effective July 12, 2021. Note: This section was added on Nov. 8, 2016, by initiative Prop. 64.)

(a) The department shall deny an application if either the applicant, or the premises for which a state license is applied, do not qualify for licensure under this division.

(b) The department may deny the application for licensure or renewal of a state license if any of the following conditions apply:

(1) Failure or inability to comply with the provisions of this division, any rule or regulation adopted pursuant

to this division, or any requirement imposed to protect natural resources, including, but not limited to, protections for instream flow, water quality, and fish and wildlife.

(2) Conduct that constitutes grounds for denial of licensure under Chapter 2 (commencing with Section 480) of Division 1.5, except as otherwise specified in this section and Section 26059.

(3) Failure to provide information required by the department.

(4) The applicant, owner, or licensee has been convicted of an offense that is substantially related to the qualifications, functions, or duties of the business or profession for which the application is made, except that if the department determines that the applicant, owner, or licensee is otherwise suitable to be issued a license, and granting the license would not compromise public safety, the department shall conduct a thorough review of the nature of the crime, conviction, circumstances, and evidence of rehabilitation of the applicant or owner, and shall evaluate the suitability of the applicant, owner, or licensee to be issued a license based on the evidence found through the review. In determining which offenses are substantially related to the qualifications, functions, or duties of the business or profession for which the application is made, the department shall include, but not be limited to, the following:

(A) A violent felony conviction, as specified in subdivision (c) of Section 667.5 of the Penal Code.

(B) A serious felony conviction, as specified in subdivision (c) of Section 1192.7 of the Penal Code.

(C) A felony conviction involving fraud, deceit, or embezzlement.

(D) A felony conviction for hiring, employing, or using a minor in transporting, carrying, selling, giving away, preparing for sale, or peddling, any controlled substance to a minor; or selling, offering to sell, furnishing, offering to furnish, administering, or giving any controlled substance to a minor.

(E) A felony conviction for drug trafficking with enhancements pursuant to Section 11370.4 or 11379.8 of the Health and Safety Code.

(5) Except as provided in subparagraphs (D) and (E) of paragraph (4) and notwithstanding Chapter 2 (commencing with Section 480) of Division 1.5, a prior conviction, where the sentence, including any term of probation, incarceration, or supervised release, is completed, for possession, possession for sale, sale, manufacture, transportation, or cultivation of a controlled substance is not considered substantially related, and shall not be the sole ground for denial of a license. Conviction for any controlled substance felony subsequent to licensure shall be grounds for revocation of a license or denial of the renewal of a license.

(6) The applicant, or any of its officers, directors, or owners, has been subject to fines, penalties, or otherwise been sanctioned for cultivation or production of a controlled substance on public or private lands pursuant to Section 12025 or 12025.1 of the Fish and Game Code.

(7) The applicant, or any of its officers, directors, or owners, has been sanctioned by the department, the Bureau of Cannabis Control, the Department of Food and Agriculture, or the State Department of Public Health or a city, county, or city and county for unauthorized commercial cannabis activities, has had a license suspended or revoked under this division in the three years immediately preceding the date the application is filed with the department.

(8) Failure to obtain and maintain a valid seller's permit required pursuant to Part 1 (commencing with Section 6001) of Division 2 of the Revenue and Taxation Code.

(9) Any other condition specified in law.

(c) The withdrawal of an application for a license after it has been filed with the department shall not deprive the department of its authority to institute or continue a proceeding against the applicant for the denial of the license upon any ground provided by law or to enter an order denying the license upon any ground.

Business and Professions Code § 26058

(Amended by Stats. 2021, Ch. 70, Sec. 45. (AB 141) Effective July 12, 2021. Note: This section was added on Nov. 8, 2016, by initiative Prop. 64.)

Upon the denial of any application for a license, the department shall notify the applicant in writing. Within 30 days of service of the notice, the applicant may file a written petition for a license with the department. Upon receipt of a timely filed petition, the department shall set the petition for hearing. The hearing shall be conducted in accordance with Chapter 5 (commencing with Section 11500) of Part 1 of Division 3 of Title 2 of the Government Code, and the director shall have all the powers granted therein. Any appeal from a final decision of the department shall be conducted in accordance with Chapter 4 (commencing with Section 26040).

Business and Professions Code § 26059

(Added November 8, 2016, by initiative Proposition 64, Sec. 6.1.)

An applicant shall not be denied a state license if the denial is based solely on any of the following:

(a) A conviction or act that is substantially related to the qualifications, functions, or duties of the business or profession for which the application is made for which the applicant or licensee has obtained a certificate of rehabilitation pursuant to Chapter 3.5 (commencing with Section 4852.0l) of Title 6 of Part 3 of the Penal Code.

(b) A conviction that was subsequently dismissed pursuant to Sections 1203.4, l203.4a, or 1203.41 of the Penal Code or any other provision allowing for dismissal of a conviction.

Chapter 6. Licensed Cultivation Sites

Business and Professions Code § 26060

(Amended by Stats. 2021, Ch. 70, Sec. 46. (AB 141) Effective July 12, 2021. Note: This section was added on Nov. 8, 2016, by initiative Prop. 64.)

(a) (1) For the purposes of this division, cannabis is an agricultural product.

(2) In issuing cannabis cultivation licenses, the department shall consider issues, including, but not limited to, water use and environmental impacts. If the State Water Resources Control Board or the Department of Fish and Wildlife finds, based on substantial evidence, that cannabis cultivation is causing significant adverse impacts on the environment in a watershed or other geographic area, the department shall not issue new licenses or increase the total number of plant identifiers within that watershed or area.

(b) The regulations related to cannabis cultivation shall do all of the following:

(1) Provide that weighing or measuring devices used in connection with the sale or distribution of cannabis are required to meet standards equivalent to Division 5 (commencing with Section 12001).

(2) Require that cannabis cultivation by licensees is conducted in accordance with state and local laws.

(3) Establish procedures for the issuance and revocation of unique identifiers for activities associated with a cannabis cultivation license, pursuant to Chapter 6.5 (commencing with Section 26067). All cannabis shall be labeled with the unique identifier issued by the department.

(4) Prescribe standards for the reporting of information as necessary related to unique identifiers pursuant to Chapter 6.5 (commencing with Section 26067).

(c) The Department of Pesticide Regulation shall develop guidelines for the use of pesticides in the cultivation of cannabis and residue in harvested cannabis.

(d) A cannabis cultivator shall not use any pesticide that has been banned for use in the state.

(e) The regulations adopted by the department under this division shall implement the requirements of subdivision (b) of Section 26060.1.

(f) The Department of Pesticide Regulation shall require that the application of pesticides or other pest control in connection with the indoor, outdoor, nursery, specialty cottage, or mixed-light cultivation of cannabis complies with Division 6 (commencing with Section 11401) of the Food and Agricultural Code and its implementing regulations.

Business and Professions Code § 26060.1

(Amended by Stats. 2021, Ch. 70, Sec. 47. (AB 141) Effective July 12, 2021.)

(a) An application for a license for cultivation issued by the department shall identify the source of water supply as follows:

(1) (A) If water will be supplied by a retail water supplier, as defined in Section 13575 of the Water Code, the application shall identify the retail water supplier.

(B) Paragraphs (2) and (3) do not apply to any water subject to subparagraph (A) unless the retail water supplier has 10 or fewer customers, the applicant receives 10 percent or more of the water supplied by the retail water supplier, 25 percent or more of the water delivered by the retail water supplier is used for cannabis cultivation, or the applicant and the retail water supplier are affiliates, as defined in Section 2814.20 of Title 23 of the California Code of Regulations.

(2) If the water supply includes a diversion within the meaning of Section 5100 of the Water Code, the application shall identify the point of diversion and the maximum amount to be diverted as follows:

(A) For an application submitted before January 1, 2019, the application shall include a copy of one of the following:

(i) A small irrigation use registration certificate, permit, or license issued pursuant to Part 2 (commencing with Section 1200) of Division 2 of the Water Code that covers the diversion.

(ii) A statement of water diversion and use filed with the State Water Resources Control Board on or before October 31, 2017, that covers the diversion and specifies the amount of water used for cannabis cultivation.

(iii) A pending application for a permit to appropriate water, filed with the State Water Resources Control Board on or before October 31, 2017.

(iv) Documentation submitted to the State Water Resources Control Board on or before January 1, 2019, demonstrating that the diversion is subject to subdivision (a), (c), (d), or (e) of Section 5101 of the Water Code.

(v) Documentation submitted to the State Water Resources Control Board on or before October 31, 2017, demonstrating that the diversion is authorized under a riparian right and that no diversion occurred after January 1, 2010, and before January 1, 2017. The documentation shall be submitted on or accompany a form provided by the State Water Resources Control Board and shall include all of the information outlined in subdivisions (a) to (d), inclusive, and (e) of Section 5103 of the Water Code. The documentation shall also include a general description of the area in which the water will be used in accordance with subdivision (g) of Section 5103 of the Water Code and the year in which the diversion is planned to commence.

(B) For an application submitted after December 31, 2018, the application shall include a copy of one of the following:

(i) A small irrigation use registration certificate, permit, or license issued pursuant to Part 2 (commencing with Section 1200) of Division 2 of the Water Code that covers the diversion.

(ii) A statement of water diversion and use filed with the State Water Resources Control Board that covers the diversion and specifies the amount of water used for cannabis cultivation.

(iii) Documentation submitted to the State Water Resources Control Board demonstrating that the diversion is subject to subdivision (a), (c), (d), or (e) of Section 5101 of the Water Code.

(iv) Documentation submitted to the State Water Resources Control Board demonstrating that the diversion is authorized under a riparian right and that no diversion occurred after January 1, 2010, and in the calendar year in which the application is submitted. The documentation shall be submitted on or accompany a form provided by the State Water Resources Control Board and shall include all of the information outlined in subdivisions (a) to (d), inclusive, and (e) of Section 5103 of the Water Code. The documentation shall also include a general description of the area in which the water will be used in accordance with subdivision (g) of Section 5103 of the Water Code and the year in which the diversion is planned to commence.

(3) If water will be supplied from a groundwater extraction not subject to paragraph (2), the application shall identify the location of the extraction and the maximum amount to be diverted for cannabis cultivation in any year.

(b) The department shall include in any license for cultivation all of the following:

(1) Conditions requested by the Department of Fish and Wildlife and the State Water Resources Control Board to: (A) ensure that individual and cumulative effects of water diversion and discharge associated with cultivation do not affect the instream flows needed for fish spawning, migration, and rearing, and the flows needed to maintain natural flow variability; (B) ensure that cultivation does not negatively impact springs, riparian habitat, wetlands, or aquatic habitat; and (C) otherwise protect fish, wildlife, fish and wildlife habitat, and water quality. The conditions shall include, but not be limited to, the principles, guidelines, and requirements established pursuant to Section 13149 of the Water Code.

(2) Any relevant mitigation requirements the department identifies as part of its approval of the final environmental documentation for the cannabis cultivation licensing program as requirements that should be included in a license for cultivation. Chapter 3.5 (commencing with Section 11340) of Part 1 of Division 3 of Title 2 of the Government Code does not apply to the identification of these mitigation measures. This paragraph does not reduce any requirements established pursuant to Division 13 (commencing with Section 21000) of the Public Resources Code.

(3) A condition that the license shall not be effective until the licensee has demonstrated compliance with Section 1602 of the Fish and Game Code or receives written verification from the Department of Fish and Wildlife that a streambed alteration agreement is not required.

(c) The department shall consult with the State Water Resources Control Board and the Department of Fish and Wildlife in the implementation of this section.

(d) Notwithstanding paragraph (1) of subdivision (b), the department is not responsible for verifying compliance with the conditions requested or imposed by the Department of Fish and Wildlife or the State Water Resources Control Board. The Department of Fish and Wildlife or the State Water Resources Control Board, upon finding and making the final determination of a violation of a condition included pursuant to paragraph (1) of subdivision (b), shall notify the department, which may take appropriate action with respect to the licensee in accordance with Chapter 3 (commencing with Section 26030).

Business and Professions Code § 26061

(Amended by Stats. 2021, Ch. 70, Sec. 48. (AB 141) Effective July 12, 2021. Note: This section was added on Nov. 8, 2016, by initiative Prop. 64.)

(a) The state cultivator license types to be issued by the department under this division shall include all of the following:

(1) Type 1, or "specialty outdoor," for outdoor cultivation using no artificial lighting of less than or equal to 5,000 square feet of total canopy size on one premises, or up to 50 mature plants on noncontiguous plots.

(2) Type 1A, or "specialty indoor," for indoor cultivation using exclusively artificial lighting of between 501 and 5,000 square feet of total canopy size on one premises.

(3) Type 1B, or "specialty mixed-light," for cultivation using a combination of natural and supplemental artificial lighting at a maximum threshold to be determined by the department of between 2,501 and 5,000 square feet of total canopy size on one premises.

(4) Type 1C, or "specialty cottage," for cultivation using a combination of natural and supplemental artificial lighting at a maximum threshold to be determined by the department, of 2,500 square feet or less of total canopy size for mixed-light cultivation, 2,500 square feet or less of total canopy size for outdoor cultivation with the option to meet an alternative maximum threshold to be determined by the department of up to 25 mature plants for outdoor cultivation, or 500 square feet or less of total canopy size for indoor cultivation, on one premises.

(5) Type 2, or "small outdoor," for outdoor cultivation using no artificial lighting between 5,001 and 10,000 square feet, inclusive, of total canopy size on one premises.

(6) Type 2A, or "small indoor," for indoor cultivation using exclusively artificial lighting between 5,001 and 10,000 square feet, inclusive, of total canopy size on one premises.

(7) Type 2B, or "small mixed-light," for cultivation using a combination of natural and supplemental artificial lighting at a maximum threshold to be determined by the department, between 5,001 and 10,000 square feet, inclusive, of total canopy size on one premises.

(8) Type 3, or "outdoor," for outdoor cultivation using no artificial lighting from 10,001 square feet to one acre, inclusive, of total canopy size on one premises. The department shall limit the number of licenses allowed of this type.

(9) Type 3A, or "indoor," for indoor cultivation using exclusively artificial lighting between 10,001 and 22,000 square feet, inclusive, of total canopy size on one premises. The department shall limit the number of licenses allowed of this type.

(10) Type 3B, or "mixed-light," for cultivation using a combination of natural and supplemental artificial lighting at a maximum threshold to be determined by the department between 10,001 and 22,000 square feet, inclusive, of total canopy size on one premises. The department shall limit the number of licenses allowed of this type.

(11) Type 4, or "nursery," for cultivation of cannabis solely as a nursery.

(b) Except as otherwise provided by law:

(1) Type 5, or "outdoor," means for outdoor cultivation using no artificial lighting greater than one acre, inclusive, of total canopy size on one premises.

(2) Type 5A, or "indoor," means for indoor cultivation using exclusively artificial lighting greater than 22,000 square feet, inclusive, of total canopy size on one premises.

(3) Type 5B, or "mixed-light," means for cultivation using a combination of natural and supplemental artificial lighting at a maximum threshold to be determined by the department greater than 22,000 square feet, inclusive, of total canopy size on one premises.

(c) No Type 5, Type 5A, or Type 5B cultivation licenses may be issued before January 1, 2023.

(d) Commencing on January 1, 2023, a Type 5, Type 5A, or Type 5B licensee may apply for and hold a Type 6 or Type 7 license and apply for and hold a Type 10 license. A Type 5, Type 5A, or Type 5B licensee shall not be eligible to apply for or hold a Type 8, Type 11, or Type 12 license.

Business and Professions Code § 26062

(Amended (as amended by Stats. 2021, Ch. 70, Sec. 49) by Stats. 2021, Ch. 87, Sec. 4. (SB 160) Effective July 16, 2021. Conditionally inoperative as prescribed by its own provisions. Repealed, by its own provisions, on January 1 following inoperative date.)

(a) (1) (A) No later than July 1, 2021, the Department of Food and Agriculture shall establish a program for cannabis that is comparable to the National Organic Program (Section 6517 of the federal Organic Foods Production Act of 1990 (7 U.S.C. Sec. 6501 et seq.)), and the California Organic Food and Farming Act (Chapter 10 (commencing with Section 46000) of Division 17 of the Food and Agricultural Code) and Article 7 (commencing with Section 110810) of Chapter 5 of Part 5 of Division 104 of the Health and Safety Code. For purposes of administrating this paragraph, the Department of Food and Agriculture shall be exempt from the Administrative Procedure Act (Chapter 3.5 (commencing with Section 11340) of Part 1 of Division 3 of Title 2 of the Government Code).

(B) The Department of Food and Agriculture may collect fees to cover the reasonable regulatory costs of performing duties pursuant to this paragraph. The Department of Food and Agriculture may deny, suspend, or revoke a registration or certification issued under the program established pursuant to this paragraph for a violation of the program or Section 26062.5. A violation of the program established pursuant to this paragraph or Section 26062.5 may also be subject to a civil penalty in an amount not to exceed thirty thousand dollars ($30,000) for each individual violation.

(C) A person may request a hearing to contest a denial, suspension, revocation, or civil penalty levied pursuant to this paragraph by submitting a written request within 30 days of service. The hearing shall be held pursuant to the provisions of Chapter 4.5 (commencing with Section 11400) of Part 1 of Division 3 of Title 2 of the Government Code and any informal hearing regulations adopted by the Department of Food and Agriculture.

(D) After the exhaustion of the administrative and judicial review procedures, the Department of Food and Agriculture may apply to the appropriate superior court for a judgment in the amount of the administrative penalty and an order compelling the person to comply with the order of the Department of Food and Agriculture. The application, which shall include a certified copy of the final order of the Department of Food and Agriculture, shall constitute a sufficient showing to warrant the issuance of the judgment and order.

(E) Any penalties or fees collected by the Department of Food and Agriculture pursuant to this paragraph shall be deposited in the Department of Food and Agriculture Fund.

(2) (A) No later than July 1, 2021, the State Department of Public Health shall establish a certification program for manufactured cannabis products that is comparable to the National Organic Program (Section 6517 of the federal Organic Foods Production Act of 1990 (7 U.S.C. Sec. 6501 et seq.)), the California Organic Food and Farming Act (Chapter 10 (commencing with Section 46000) of Division 17 of the Food and Agricultural Code), and Article 7 (commencing with Section 110810) of Chapter 5 of Part 5 of Division 104 of the Health and Safety Code. For purposes of administrating this paragraph, the State Department of Public Health shall be exempt from the Administrative

Procedure Act (Chapter 3.5 (commencing with Section 11340) of Part 1 of Division 3 of Title 2 of the Government Code).

(B) For the purposes of enforcement of this paragraph, any authorized agent of the State Department of Public Health, including those defined in Section 109945 of the Health and Safety Code, may examine records and inspect the premises of a cannabis manufacturer and embargo cannabis products in that premises as necessary to perform the duties pursuant to this paragraph.

(C) The State Department of Public Health may collect fees to cover the reasonable regulatory costs of performing duties pursuant to this paragraph. The State Department of Public Health may deny, suspend, or revoke a registration or certification issued pursuant to this paragraph for a violation of the certification program or for a violation of Section 26062.5, consistent with Section 110875 of the Health and Safety Code. The State Department of Public Health may levy a civil penalty for a violation of the certification program or Section 26062.5. The amount of any penalty imposed pursuant to this paragraph shall be consistent with Section 110915 of the Health and Safety Code. A person subject to a penalty shall have the right to an informal hearing, consistent with Section 110915 of the Health and Safety Code. Any penalties or fees collected by the State Department of Public Health pursuant to this paragraph shall be deposited in the Food Safety Fund established pursuant to Section 110050 of the Health and Safety Code for use by the State Department of Public Health, upon appropriation by the Legislature, for the purpose of administering the certification program.

(b) If at any time preceding or following the establishment of a program pursuant to subdivision (a), the National Organic Program (Section 6517 of the federal Organic Foods Production Act of 1990 (7 U.S.C. Sec. 6501 et seq.)) authorizes organic designation and certification for cannabis, this section shall become inoperative and, as of January 1, of the following year, is repealed.

Business and Professions Code § 26062.5

(Amended by Stats. 2019, Ch. 40, Sec. 8. (AB 97) Effective July 1, 2019.)

A person shall not represent, sell, or offer for sale any cannabis or cannabis product as organic except in accordance with the National Organic Program (Section 6517 of the federal Organic Foods Production Act of 1990 (7 U.S.C. Sec. 6501 et seq.)), if applicable. A person shall not represent, sell, or offer for sale any cannabis or cannabis product with the designation or certification established by the Department of Food and Agriculture or the State Department of Public Health pursuant to subdivision (a) of Section 26062 except in accordance with that subdivision.

Business and Professions Code § 26063

(Amended (as amended by Stats. 2021, Ch. 70, Sec. 50) by Stats. 2021, Ch. 87, Sec. 5. (SB 160) Effective July 16, 2021. Note: This section was added on Nov. 8, 2016, by initiative Prop. 64.)

(a) (1) No later than January 1, 2018, the department shall establish standards by which a licensed cultivator may designate a county, city, or city and county of origin for cannabis. To be eligible for the designation, 100 percent of the cannabis shall be produced within the designated county, city, or city and county, as defined by finite political boundaries.

(2) Cannabis shall not be advertised, marketed, labeled, or sold as produced in a California county, city, or city and county, including any similar name that is likely to mislead consumers as to the kind of cannabis, when the cannabis was not produced in that county, city, or city and county.

(3) The name of a California county, city, or city and county, including any similar name that is likely to mislead consumers as to the kind of cannabis contained in the product, shall not be used in the advertising, labeling, marketing, or packaging of cannabis products unless 100 percent of the cannabis contained in the product was

produced in that county, city, or city and county.

(b) (1) No later than January 1, 2022, the Department of Food and Agriculture shall establish a process by which licensed cultivators may establish appellations of origin, including standards, practices, and cultivars applicable to cannabis produced in a certain geographical area in California, not otherwise specified in subdivision (a).

(2) Cannabis shall not be advertised, marketed, labeled, or sold using an appellation of origin established pursuant to paragraph (1), including any similar name that is likely to mislead consumers as to the kind of cannabis, unless the cannabis meets the appellation of origin requirements for, and was produced in, the geographical area.

(3) An appellation of origin established pursuant to this subdivision, including any similar name that is likely to mislead consumers as to the kind of cannabis contained in a product, shall not be used in the advertising, labeling, marketing, or packaging of a cannabis product unless 100 percent of the cannabis contained in the product meets the appellation of origin requirements and was produced in the geographical area.

(4) The Department of Food and Agriculture may collect fees to cover the reasonable regulatory costs of performing duties pursuant to this section. Any fees collected by the Department of Food and Agriculture pursuant to this section shall be deposited in the Department of Food and Agriculture Fund.

(c) An appellation of origin shall not be approved unless it requires the practice of planting in the ground in the canopy area and excludes the practices of using structures, including a greenhouse, hoop house, glasshouse, conservatory, hothouse, and any similar structure, and any artificial light in the canopy area.

Business and Professions Code § 26065

(Amended by Stats. 2017, Ch. 27, Sec. 55. (SB 94) Effective June 27, 2017. Note: This section was added on Nov. 8, 2016, by initiative Prop. 64.)

An employee engaged in the cultivation of cannabis under this division shall be subject to Wage Order No. 4-2001 of the Industrial Welfare Commission.

Business and Professions Code § 26066

(Amended by Stats. 2017, Ch. 27, Sec. 56. (SB 94) Effective June 27, 2017. Note: This section was added on Nov. 8, 2016, by initiative Prop. 64.)

Indoor and outdoor cannabis cultivation by persons and entities licensed under this division shall be conducted in accordance with state and local laws related to land conversion, current building and fire standards, grading, electricity usage, water usage, water quality, woodland and riparian habitat protection, agricultural discharges, and similar matters. State agencies, including, but not limited to, the State Board of Forestry and Fire Protection, the Department of Fish and Wildlife, the State Water Resources Control Board, the California regional water quality control boards, and traditional state law enforcement agencies, shall address environmental impacts of cannabis cultivation and shall coordinate when appropriate with cities and counties and their law enforcement agencies in enforcement efforts.

Business and Professions Code § 26066.1

(Added by renumbering Section 26069.1 by Stats. 2021, Ch. 70, Sec. 54. (AB 141) Effective July 12, 2021.)

The department may enter into a cooperative agreement with a county agricultural commissioner or other state or local agency to assist the department in implementing the provisions of this division related to administration, investigation, inspection, fee collection, document management, education and outreach, distribution of individual licenses approved by the department, and technical assistance pertaining to the cultivation of cannabis. The department shall pay compensation under a cooperative agreement from fees collected and deposited pursuant to this division and shall provide reimbursement to a county agricultural commissioner, state, or local agency for associated costs. The department shall not delegate through a cooperative agreement, or otherwise, its authority to issue cultivation licenses to a county agricultural commissioner, local agency, or another state agency. The department shall provide notice of any cooperative agreement entered into pursuant to this section to other relevant state agencies involved in the regulation of cannabis cultivation. No cooperative agreement under this section shall relieve the department of its obligations under subdivision (a) of Section 26012 to administer the provisions of this division related to, and associated with, the cultivation of cannabis.

Business and Professions Code § 26066.2

(Added by renumbering Section 26069.5 by Stats. 2021, Ch. 70, Sec. 55. (AB 141) Effective July 12, 2021.)

(a) A county agricultural commissioner may report to the director on the condition, acreage, production, and value of cannabis produced in the commissioner's county under a cultivation license issued pursuant to this division. The cannabis data may be submitted in a separate report that is similar to those reports required for agricultural products pursuant to Section 2279 of the Food and Agricultural Code. This section does not require the department to publish this report.

(b) Data on cannabis production that is included in a report pursuant to this section may be organized by categories including, but not limited to, the following:

(1) State cultivator license type, as set forth in Chapter 5 (commencing with Section 26050), and regulations adopted pursuant to that chapter.

(2) Local license, permit, or other authorization type, as described in Section 26200.

(3) Price tier, including for different strains of cannabis, different production methods, or different parts of a plant, such as flowers or leaves.

(c) A county agricultural commissioner shall not seek reimbursement for expenses incurred in making a report pursuant to this section from either of the following sources:

(1) The Department of Food and Agriculture Fund.

(2) Funding that may otherwise be available for the purposes of this section from a cooperative agreement entered into pursuant to Section 2222 of the Food and Agricultural Code.

Chapter 6.5. Unique Identifiers and Track and Trace

Business and Professions Code § 26067

(Amended by Stats. 2022, Ch. 56, Sec. 4. (AB 195) Effective June 30, 2022.)

(a) The department shall establish a track and trace program for reporting the movement of cannabis and cannabis products throughout the distribution chain that utilizes a unique identifier and is capable of providing information that captures, at a minimum, all of the following:

(1) The licensee from which the product originates and the licensee receiving the product.

(2) The transaction date.

(3) The unique identifier or identifiers for the cannabis or cannabis product.

(4) The date of retail sale to a customer and whether the sale is conducted on the retail premises or by delivery.

(5) Information relating to cannabis and cannabis products leaving the licensed premises in a delivery vehicle as determined by regulations adopted pursuant to subdivision (d) of Section 26068.

(b) (1) The department, in consultation with the California Department of Tax and Fee Administration, shall create an electronic database containing the electronic shipping manifests to facilitate the administration of the track and trace program, which shall include, but not be limited to, the following information:

(A) The variety and quantity or weight of cannabis or cannabis products shipped.

(B) The estimated times of departure and arrival.

(C) The variety and quantity or weight of cannabis or cannabis products received.

(D) The actual time of departure and arrival.

(E) A categorization and the unique identifier of the cannabis or cannabis product.

(F) The license number issued by the department for all licensees involved in the shipping process, including, but not limited to, cultivators, manufacturers, distributors, and retailers.

(2) The database shall be designed to flag irregularities for the department to investigate.

(3) The department and state and local agencies may, at any time, inspect shipments and request documentation for current inventory.

(4) The California Department of Tax and Fee Administration shall have read access to the electronic database for the purpose of taxation and regulation of cannabis and cannabis products.

(5) Information received and contained in records kept by the department for the purposes of administering this chapter are confidential and shall not be disclosed pursuant to the California Public Records Act (Chapter 3.5 (commencing with Section 6250) of Division 7 of Title 1 of the Government Code), except as necessary for authorized employees of the State of California or any city, county, or city and county to perform official duties pursuant to this division or a local ordinance.

(6) Upon the request of a state or local law enforcement agency, the department shall allow access to or provide information contained within the database to assist law enforcement in their duties and responsibilities pursuant to this division.

Business and Professions Code § 26068

(Amended by Stats. 2022, Ch. 56, Sec. 5. (AB 195) Effective June 30, 2022.)

(a) The department, in consultation with the California Department of Tax and Fee Administration, shall ensure that the track and trace program can also track and trace the amount of the cultivation tax due pursuant to Part 14.5 (commencing with Section 34010) of Division 2 of the Revenue and Taxation Code. The track and trace program shall include an electronic seed to sale software tracking system with data points for the different stages of commercial activity, including, but not limited to, cultivation, harvest, processing, manufacturing, distribution, inventory, sale, and delivery.

(b) The department shall ensure that licensees under this division are allowed to use third-party applications, programs, and information technology systems to comply with the requirements of the expanded track and trace program described in subdivision (a) to report the movement of cannabis and cannabis products throughout the distribution chain and communicate the information to licensing agencies as required by law.

(c) Any software, database, or other information technology system utilized by the department to implement the expanded track and trace program shall support interoperability with third-party cannabis business software applications and allow all licensee-facing system activities to be performed through a secure application programming interface (API) or comparable technology that is well documented, bi-directional, and accessible to any third-party application that has been validated and has appropriate credentials. The API or comparable technology shall have version control and provide adequate notice of updates to third-party applications. The system should provide a test environment for third-party applications to access that mirrors the production environment.

(d) (1) The department shall incorporate delivery into the track and trace program no later than January 1, 2023.

(2) Notwithstanding any other law, provisions related to inclusion of information related to delivery in the track and trace system in Sections 26067 and 26090 shall only become effective after the department incorporates delivery into the track and trace program as required by this subdivision.

(3) Notwithstanding any other law, the department may adopt and readopt emergency regulations to implement this subdivision. The provisions of Section 26013 shall be applicable to emergency regulations adopted or readopted pursuant to this section. The emergency regulations authorized by this paragraph shall be deemed an emergency and necessary for the immediate preservation of public peace, health, safety, or general welfare.

Business and Professions Code § 26069

(Amended by Stats. 2021, Ch. 70, Sec. 53. (AB 141) Effective July 12, 2021.)

(a)(1) The department shall implement a unique identification program for cannabis and cannabis products.

(2) The unique identification program shall include the identification of permitted cannabis plants at a cultivation site during the cultivation period. A unique identifier shall be issued for each cannabis plant. The department shall ensure that unique identifiers are issued as quickly as possible to ensure the implementation of this division. The unique identifier shall be attached at the base of each plant or as otherwise required by law or regulation.

(b) Unique identifiers shall only be issued to those persons appropriately licensed by this division.

(c) Information associated with the assigned unique identifier and licensee shall be included in the trace and track program specified in Section 26067.

(d) The department may charge a fee to cover the reasonable costs of issuing the unique identifier and monitoring, tracking, and inspecting each cannabis plant.

(e) The department shall take adequate steps to establish protections against fraudulent unique identifiers and limit illegal diversion of unique identifiers to unlicensed persons.

(f) A city, county, or city and county may administer unique identifiers and associated identifying information but a city, county, or city and county's identifiers shall not supplant the department's track and trace program.

(g) This section does not apply to the cultivation of cannabis in accordance with Section 11362.1 of the Health and Safety Code or the Compassionate Use Act.

Chapter 7. Retailers and Distributors

Business and Professions Code § 26070

(Amended by Stats. 2021, Ch. 70, Sec. 57. (AB 141) Effective July 12, 2021. Note: This section was added on Nov. 8, 2016, by initiative Prop. 64.)

Retailers, Distributors, and Microbusinesses.

(a) State licenses to be issued by the department related to the sale and distribution of cannabis and cannabis products are as follows:

(1) A retailer shall have a licensed premises which is a physical location from which commercial cannabis activities are conducted. A retailer's premises may be closed to the public. A retailer may conduct sales exclusively by delivery.

(2) A distributor licensee shall be bonded and insured at a minimum level established by the department.

(3) (A) Microbusiness licenses that authorize cultivation of cannabis shall include the license conditions described in subdivision (b) of Section 26060.1.

(B) The department shall establish a process by which an applicant for a microbusiness license can demonstrate compliance with all the requirements under this division for the activities that will be conducted under the license.

(b) The department shall establish minimum security and transportation safety requirements for the commercial distribution and delivery of cannabis and cannabis products. Except as provided in subdivision (d) of Section 26110, the transportation of cannabis and cannabis products shall only be conducted by persons holding a distributor license under this division or employees of those persons. Transportation safety standards established by the department shall include, but not be limited to, minimum standards governing the types of vehicles in which cannabis and cannabis products may be distributed and delivered and minimum qualifications for persons eligible to operate such vehicles.

(c) The driver of a vehicle transporting or transferring cannabis or cannabis products shall be directly employed by a licensee authorized to transport or transfer cannabis or cannabis products.

(d) Notwithstanding any other law, all vehicles transporting cannabis and cannabis products for hire shall be required to have a valid motor carrier permit pursuant to Chapter 2 (commencing with Section 34620) of Division 14.85 of the Vehicle Code. The Department of the California Highway Patrol shall have authority over the safe operation of these vehicles, including, but not limited to, requiring licensees engaged in the transportation of cannabis or cannabis products to participate in the Basic Inspection of Terminals (BIT) program pursuant to Section 34501.12 of the Vehicle Code.

(e) Prior to transporting cannabis or cannabis products, a licensed distributor shall do both of the following:

(1) Complete an electronic shipping manifest as prescribed by the department. The shipping manifest shall include the unique identifier, pursuant to Section 26067, issued by the department for the cannabis product.

(2) Securely transmit the manifest to the department and the licensee that will receive the cannabis product.

(f) During transportation, the licensed distributor shall maintain a physical copy of the shipping manifest and make it available upon request to agents of the department and law enforcement officers.

(g) The licensee receiving the shipment shall maintain each electronic shipping manifest and shall make it available upon request to the department and any law enforcement officers.

(h) Upon receipt of the transported shipment, the licensee receiving the shipment shall submit to the department a record verifying receipt of the shipment and the details of the shipment.

(i) Transporting, or arranging for or facilitating the transport of, cannabis or cannabis products in violation of this chapter is grounds for disciplinary action against the license.

(j) Licensed retailers and microbusinesses, and licensed nonprofits under Section 26070.5, shall implement security measures reasonably designed to prevent unauthorized entrance into areas containing cannabis or cannabis products and theft of cannabis or cannabis products from the premises. These security measures shall include, but not be limited to, all of the following:

(1) Prohibiting individuals from remaining on the licensee's premises if they are not engaging in activity expressly related to the operations of the retailer.

(2) Establishing limited access areas accessible only to authorized personnel.

(3) Other than limited amounts of cannabis used for display purposes, samples, or immediate sale, storing all finished cannabis and cannabis products in a secured and locked room, safe, or vault, and in a manner reasonably designed to prevent diversion, theft, and loss.

(k) A retailer shall notify the department and the appropriate law enforcement authorities within 24 hours after discovering any of the following:

(1) Significant discrepancies identified during inventory. The level of significance shall be determined by the department.

(2) Diversion, theft, loss, or any criminal activity pertaining to the operation of the retailer.

(3) Diversion, theft, loss, or any criminal activity by any agent or employee of the retailer pertaining to the operation of the retailer.

(4) The loss or unauthorized alteration of records related to cannabis or cannabis products, registered qualifying patients, primary caregivers, or retailer employees or agents.

(5) Any other breach of security.

Business and Professions Code § 26070.1

(Added by Stats. 2017, Ch. 27, Sec. 60. (SB 94) Effective June 27, 2017.)

Cannabis or cannabis products purchased by a customer shall not leave a licensed retail premises unless they are placed in an opaque package.

Business and Professions Code § 26070.2

(Added by Stats. 2018, Ch. 827, Sec. 2. (AB 2914) Effective January 1, 2019.)

A licensee shall not sell, offer, or provide a cannabis product that is an alcoholic beverage, including, but not limited to, an infusion of cannabis or cannabinoids derived from industrial hemp into an alcoholic beverage.

Business and Professions Code § 26070.5

(Amended by Stats. 2021, Ch. 70, Sec. 58. (AB 141) Effective July 12, 2021. Note: This section was added on Nov. 8, 2016, by initiative Prop. 64.)

(a) The Bureau of Cannabis Control shall, by January 1, 2020, investigate the feasibility of creating one or more classifications of nonprofit licenses under this section. The feasibility determination shall be made in consultation with the relevant licensing agencies and representatives of local jurisdictions which issue temporary licenses pursuant to subdivision (b). The Bureau of Cannabis Control shall consider factors including, but not limited to, the following:

(1) Should nonprofit licensees be exempted from any or all state taxes, licensing fees, and regulatory provisions applicable to other licenses in this division?

(2) Should funding incentives be created to encourage others licensed under this division to provide professional services at reduced or no cost to nonprofit licensees?

(3) Should nonprofit licenses be limited to, or prioritize those, entities previously operating on a not-for-profit basis primarily providing whole-plant cannabis and cannabis products and a diversity of cannabis strains and seed stock to low-income persons?

(b) Any local jurisdiction may issue temporary local licenses to nonprofit entities primarily providing whole-plant cannabis and cannabis products and a diversity of cannabis strains and seed stock to low-income persons so long as the local jurisdiction does all of the following:

(1) Confirms the license applicant's status as a nonprofit entity registered with the California Attorney General's Registry of Charitable Trusts and that the applicant is in good standing with all state requirements governing nonprofit entities.

(2) Licenses and regulates any such entity to protect public health and safety, and so as to require compliance with all environmental requirements in this division.

(3) Provides notice to the department of any such local licenses issued, including the name and location of any such licensed entity and all local regulations governing the licensed entity's operation.

(4) Certifies to the department that any such licensed entity will not generate annual gross revenues in excess of two million dollars ($2,000,000).

(c) Temporary local licenses authorized under subdivision (b) shall expire after 12 months unless renewed by the local jurisdiction.

(d) The department may impose reasonable additional requirements on the local licenses authorized under subdivision (b).

(e) (1) New temporary local licenses shall not be issued pursuant to this section after the date the Bureau of Cannabis Control determines that creation of nonprofit licenses under this division is not feasible, or if the Bureau of Cannabis Control determines that creation of nonprofit licenses under this division is feasible, after the date a licensing agency commences issuing state nonprofit licenses.

(2) If the Bureau of Cannabis Control determines that creation of nonprofit licenses under this division is feasible, no temporary license issued under subdivision (b) shall be renewed or extended after the date on which a licensing agency commences issuing state nonprofit licenses.

(3) If the Bureau of Cannabis Control determines that creation of nonprofit licenses under this division is not feasible, the Bureau of Cannabis Control shall provide notice of this determination to all local jurisdictions that have issued temporary licenses under subdivision (b). The department may, in its discretion, permit any such local jurisdiction to renew or extend on an annual basis any temporary license previously issued under subdivision (b).

Business and Professions Code § 26071

(Added by Stats. 2019, Ch. 837, Sec. 4. (SB 34) Effective January 1, 2020. Operative on or before March 1, 2020, as prescribed by its own provisions.)

(a) To provide access to medicinal cannabis patients who have difficulty accessing cannabis or cannabis products, a licensee that is authorized to make retail sales may provide free cannabis or cannabis products if all of the following criteria are met:

(1) Free cannabis or cannabis products are provided only to a medicinal cannabis patient or the patient's primary caregiver. For purposes of this section, "medicinal cannabis patient" includes a qualified patient, as defined under Section 11362.7 of the Health and Safety Code, or a person in possession of a valid identification card issued under Section 11362.71 of the Health and Safety Code.

(2) (A) A licensed retailer providing medicinal cannabis or medicinal cannabis products pursuant to this section to a qualified patient, as defined under Section 11362.7 of the Health and Safety Code, that possesses a valid physician's recommendation, shall ensure that the physician is in good standing by following the procedures described in subparagraph (B) before providing the qualified patient with any medicinal cannabis or medicinal cannabis products that a cultivator certified were for donation pursuant to Section 34012.1 of the Revenue and Taxation Code or that are exempt from the use tax pursuant to Section 6414 of the Revenue and Taxation Code.

(B) In order to verify the physician's recommendation, the licensed retailer shall do all of the following:

(i) Verify with the Medical Board of California, the Osteopathic Medical Board of California, and the California Board of Podiatric Medicine that the attending physician has a license in good standing to practice medicine or osteopathy in the state.

(ii) Keep a copy of the patient's or primary caregiver's driver's license or other government issued identification.

(3) Except as provided for under Section 34012.1 of the Revenue and Taxation Code, the cannabis or cannabis products comply with all applicable requirements for cultivation, manufacture, distribution, processing, storing, laboratory testing, packaging, labeling, transportation, delivery, or donation under this division.

(4) A licensee intending to donate the cannabis or cannabis products shall designate the cannabis or cannabis products for donation in the track and trace system. If a cultivator certified that the cannabis or cannabis products are designated for donation to medicinal cannabis patients pursuant to Section 34012.1 of the Revenue and Taxation Code, a licensee shall not change that designation pursuant to subdivision (b) of Section 34012.1 of the Revenue and Taxation Code.

(5) Before being provided to the patient or primary caregiver, the cannabis or cannabis products have been properly recorded in the track and trace system as belonging to the retailer.

(6) The cannabis or cannabis products provided to a medicinal cannabis patient or the primary caregiver of the patient in a single day shall not exceed the possession limits prescribed by Section 11362.77 of the Health and Safety Code.

(7) The event shall be properly recorded in the retailer's inventory records and the track and trace system. The retailer shall include in its inventory records for each medicinal cannabis patient the number of an identification card issued pursuant to Article 2.5 (commencing with Section 11362.7) of Chapter 6 of Division 10 of the Health and Safety Code or a copy of the physician's recommendation for no less than four years. If the medicinal cannabis patient is a qualified patient, as defined under Section 11362.7 of the Health and Safety Code, that possesses a valid physician's recommendation, the retailer shall certify in writing that they verified the recommendation pursuant to paragraph (2) and shall keep a copy of that certification for no less than seven years.

(8) A licensed retailer that donates medicinal cannabis or medicinal cannabis products shall note the donation in their sales invoice or receipt pursuant to Section 26161 of the Business and Professions Code.

(b) In addition to the provision of free cannabis or cannabis products in subdivision (a), a licensee that is authorized to make retail sales may donate cannabis or cannabis products and the use of equipment in compliance with any compassionate use, equity, or other similar program administered by a local jurisdiction.

(c) A licensee that is authorized to make retail sales may contract with an individual or organization to coordinate the provision of free medicinal cannabis or medicinal cannabis products on the retailer's premises. Licensed retailers that are solely authorized to engage in retail sales by means of delivery may provide free medicinal cannabis or medicinal cannabis products by means of delivery.

(d) This section shall become operative upon completion of the necessary changes to the track and trace program in order to implement the act adding this section, as determined by the Department of Food and Agriculture, or on March 1, 2020, whichever occurs first.

Chapter 8. Distribution and Transport

Business and Professions Code § 26080

(Amended by Stats. 2022, Ch. 396, Sec. 1. (SB 1326) Effective January 1, 2023. Note: This section was added on Nov. 8, 2016, by initiative Prop. 64.)

(a) Except as provided in Chapter 25 (commencing with Section 26300), this division does not authorize or permit a licensee to transport or distribute, or cause to be transported or distributed, cannabis or cannabis products outside the state.

(b) A local jurisdiction shall not prevent transportation of cannabis or cannabis products on public roads by a licensee transporting cannabis or cannabis products in compliance with this division.

Chapter 9. Delivery

Business and Professions Code § 26090

(Amended by Stats. 2022, Ch. 56, Sec. 6. (AB 195) Effective June 30, 2022. Note: This section was added on Nov. 8, 2016, by initiative Prop. 64.)

(a) Deliveries, as defined in this division, may only be made by a licensed retailer or microbusiness, or a licensed nonprofit under Section 26070.5.

(b) All employees of a retailer, microbusiness, or nonprofit delivering cannabis or cannabis products shall carry a copy of the licensee's current license and a government-issued identification with a photo of the employee, such as a driver's license. The employee shall present that license and identification upon request to state and local law enforcement, employees of the department and other state and local agencies enforcing this division.

(c) Before cannabis or a cannabis product leaves the licensed premises in a delivery vehicle, the retailer shall enter into the track and trace system all information required by the department and shall update the information as required by the department.

(d) During delivery, the licensee shall maintain a copy of the delivery request and shall make it available upon request of the department and law enforcement officers. The delivery request documentation shall comply with state and federal law regarding the protection of confidential medical information.

(e) A customer requesting delivery shall maintain a physical or electronic copy of the delivery request and shall make it available upon request by the department and law enforcement officers.

(f) A local jurisdiction shall not prevent delivery of cannabis or cannabis products on public roads by a licensee acting in compliance with this division and local law as adopted under Section 26200.

Chapter 10. Testing Laboratories

Business and Professions Code § 26100

(Amended by Stats. 2021, Ch. 547, Sec. 1. (SB 544) Effective January 1, 2022. Note: This section was added (as Section 26101) on Nov. 8, 2016, by initiative Prop. 64.)

(a) Except as otherwise provided by law, cannabis or cannabis products shall not be sold pursuant to a license provided for under this division unless a representative sample of the cannabis or cannabis products has been tested by a licensed testing laboratory.

(b) The department shall develop criteria to determine which batches shall be tested. All testing of the samples shall be performed on the final form in which the cannabis or cannabis product will be consumed or used.

(c) Testing of batches to meet the requirements of this division shall only be conducted by a licensed testing laboratory.

(d) For each batch tested, the testing laboratory shall issue a certificate of analysis for selected lots at a frequency determined by the department with supporting data, to report both of the following:

(1) Whether the chemical profile of the sample conforms to the labeled content of compounds, including, but not limited to, all of the following, unless limited through regulation by the department:

(A) Tetrahydrocannabinol (THC).

(B) Tetrahydrocannabinolic Acid (THCA).

(C) Cannabidiol (CBD).

(D) Cannabidiolic Acid (CBDA).

(E) The terpenes required by the department in regulation.

(F) Cannabigerol (CBG).

(G) Cannabinol (CBN).

(H) Other compounds or contaminants required by the department.

(2) That the presence of contaminants does not exceed the levels established by the department. In establishing the levels, the department shall consider the American Herbal Pharmacopoeia monograph, guidelines set by the Department of Pesticide Regulation pursuant to subdivision (c) of Section 26060, and any other relevant sources. For purposes of this paragraph, “contaminants” includes, but is not limited to, all of the following:

(A) Residual solvent or processing chemicals.

(B) Foreign material, including, but not limited to, hair, insects, or similar or related adulterant.

(C) Microbiological impurities as identified by the department in regulation.

(3) For edible cannabis products, that the milligrams per serving of THC does not exceed 10 milligrams per serving, plus or minus 12 percent. After January 1, 2022, the milligrams of THC per serving shall not deviate from 10 milligrams by more than 10 percent.

(e) A testing laboratory may amend a certificate of analysis to correct minor errors, as defined by the department.

(f) (1) Standards for residual levels of volatile organic compounds shall be established by the department.

(2) On or before January 1, 2023, the department shall establish a standard cannabinoids test method, including standardized operating procedures, that shall be utilized by all testing laboratories. The department may establish more than one method for use by testing laboratories and these standards may be developed through a reference laboratory.

(g) The testing laboratory shall conduct all testing required by this section in a manner consistent with general requirements for the competence of testing and calibrations activities, including sampling and using verified methods.

(h) All testing laboratories performing tests pursuant to this section shall obtain and maintain ISO/IEC 17025 accreditation as required by the department in regulation.

(i) (1) If a test result falls outside the specifications authorized by law or regulation, the testing laboratory shall follow a standard operating procedure to confirm or refute the original result.

(2) If a test result falls outside the specifications authorized by law or regulation, the testing laboratory may retest the sample if both of the following occur:

(A) The testing laboratory notifies the department, in writing, that the test was compromised due to equipment malfunction, staff error, or other circumstances allowed by the department.

(B) The department authorizes the testing laboratory to retest the sample.

(j) A testing laboratory shall destroy the remains of the sample of cannabis or cannabis product upon completion of the analysis, as determined by the department through regulations.

(k) Presale inspection, testing transfer, or transportation of cannabis or cannabis products pursuant to this section shall conform to a specified chain of custody protocol and any other requirements imposed under this division.

(l) This division does not prohibit a licensee from performing testing on the licensee's premises for the purposes of quality control of the product in conjunction with reasonable business operations. This division also does not prohibit a licensee from performing testing on the licensee's premises of cannabis or cannabis products obtained from another licensee. Onsite testing by the licensee shall not be certified by the department and does not exempt the licensee from the requirements of compliance testing at a testing laboratory pursuant to this section.

Business and Professions Code § 26102

(Amended by Stats. 2021, Ch. 70, Sec. 61. (AB 141) Effective July 12, 2021.)

A testing laboratory shall not be licensed by the department unless the laboratory meets all of the following:

(a) Complies with any other requirements specified by the department.

(b) Notifies the department within one business day after the receipt of notice of any kind that its accreditation has been denied, suspended, or revoked.

(c) Has established standard operating procedures that provide for adequate chain of custody controls for samples transferred to the testing laboratory for testing.

Business and Professions Code § 26104

(Amended by Stats. 2021, Ch. 70, Sec. 62. (AB 141) Effective July 12, 2021. Note: This section was added on Nov. 8, 2016, by initiative Prop. 64.)

(a) A licensed testing laboratory shall, in performing activities concerning cannabis and cannabis products, comply with the requirements and restrictions set forth in applicable law and regulations.

(b) The department shall develop procedures to do all of the following:

(1) Ensure that testing of cannabis and cannabis products occurs prior to distribution to retailers, microbusinesses, or nonprofits licensed under Section 26070.5.

(2) Specify how often licensees shall test cannabis and cannabis products, and that the cost of testing cannabis shall be borne by the licensed cultivators and the cost of testing cannabis products shall be borne by the licensed manufacturer, and that the costs of testing cannabis and cannabis products shall be borne by a nonprofit licensed under Section 26070.5.

(3) Require destruction of harvested batches whose testing samples indicate noncompliance with health and safety standards required by the department, unless remedial measures can bring the cannabis or cannabis products into compliance with quality assurance standards as specified by law and implemented by the department.

(4) Ensure that a testing laboratory employee takes the sample of cannabis or cannabis products from the distributor's premises for testing required by this division and that the testing laboratory employee transports the sample to the testing laboratory. The driver transporting the sample pursuant to this requirement shall be directly employed by the testing laboratory.

(c) (1) Except as provided in this division, a testing laboratory shall not acquire or receive cannabis or cannabis products except from a licensee in accordance with this division, and shall not distribute, sell, or dispense cannabis or cannabis products, from the licensed premises from which the cannabis or cannabis products were acquired or received. All transfer or transportation shall be performed pursuant to a specified chain of custody protocol.

(2) A testing laboratory may receive and test samples of cannabis or cannabis products from a state or local law enforcement, or a prosecuting or regulatory agency in order to test the cannabis or cannabis products. For purposes of this section, testing conducted by a testing laboratory for state or local law enforcement, a prosecuting agency, or a regulatory agency is not commercial cannabis activity and shall not be arranged or overseen by the department.

(d) A testing laboratory may receive and test samples of cannabis or cannabis products from a licensed manufacturer or licensed cultivator for quality control purposes. A testing laboratory shall not certify samples from a licensed manufacturer or licensed cultivator for retail sale. All tests performed by a testing laboratory for a licensed manufacturer or licensed cultivator shall be recorded with the name of the licensee and the amount of cannabis or cannabis product received.

(e) A testing laboratory may receive and test samples of cannabis or cannabis products from a qualified patient or primary caregiver with a valid physician's recommendation for cannabis for medicinal purposes. A testing laboratory shall not certify samples from a qualified patient or primary caregiver for resale or transfer to another person or licensee. All tests performed by a testing laboratory for a qualified patient or primary caregiver shall be recorded with the name of the qualified patient or primary caregiver and the amount of cannabis or cannabis product received.

(f) A testing laboratory may receive and test samples of cannabis or cannabis products from a person over 21 years of age when the cannabis has been grown by that person and will be used solely for that person's use, as authorized pursuant to Section 11362.1 of the Health and Safety Code. A testing laboratory shall not certify samples from the person over 21 years of age for resale or transfer to another person or licensee. All tests recorded pursuant to this subdivision shall be recorded with the name of the person submitting the sample and the amount of cannabis or cannabis product received.

Chapter 11. Quality Assurance, Inspection, and Testing

Business and Professions Code § 26110

(Amended by Stats. 2021, Ch. 70, Sec. 65. (AB 141) Effective July 12, 2021.)

(a) Cannabis batches are subject to quality assurance standards and testing prior to sale at a retailer, microbusiness, or nonprofit licensed under Section 26070.5, except for immature cannabis plants and seeds, as provided for in this division.

(b) A licensee that holds a valid distributor license may act as the distributor for the licensee's cannabis and cannabis products.

(c) The distributor shall store, as determined by the department, the cannabis batches on the premises of the distributor before testing and continuously until either of the following occurs:

> (1) The cannabis batch passes the testing requirements pursuant to this division and is transported to a licensed retailer or to another licensed distributor.
>
> (2) The cannabis batch fails the testing requirements pursuant to this division and is destroyed or transported to a manufacturer for remediation as allowed by the department.

(d) The distributor shall arrange for a testing laboratory to obtain a representative sample of each cannabis batch at the distributor's licensed premises. After obtaining the sample, the testing laboratory representative shall maintain custody of the sample and transport it to the testing laboratory.

(e) Upon issuance of a certificate of analysis by the testing laboratory that the cannabis batch has passed the testing requirements pursuant to this division, the distributor shall conduct a quality assurance review before distribution to ensure the labeling and packaging of the cannabis and cannabis products conform to the requirements of this division.

(f) (1) There shall be a quality assurance compliance monitor who is an employee or contractor of the department and who shall not hold a license in any category or own or have an ownership interest in a licensee or the premises of a licensee.

(2) The quality assurance compliance monitor shall conduct random quality assurance reviews at a distributor's licensed premises before distribution to ensure the labeling and packaging of the cannabis and cannabis products conform to the requirements of this division.

(3) The quality assurance compliance monitor shall have access to all records and test results required of a licensee by law in order to conduct quality assurance analysis and to confirm test results. All records of inspection and verification by the quality assurance compliance monitor shall be provided to the department. Failure to comply shall be noted by the quality assurance compliance monitor for further investigation. Violations shall be reported to the department. The quality assurance compliance monitor shall also verify the tax payments collected and paid under Sections 34011 and 34012 of the Revenue and Taxation Code are accurate. The monitor shall also have access to the inputs and assumptions in the track and trace system and shall be able to verify their accuracy and that they are commensurate with the tax payments.

(g) After testing, all cannabis and cannabis products fit for sale may be transported only from the distributor's premises to the premises of another licensed distributor for further distribution, or to a licensed retailer, microbusiness, or nonprofit for retail sale.

(h) A licensee is not required to sell cannabis or cannabis products to a distributor and may directly contract for sale with a licensee authorized to sell cannabis and cannabis products to purchasers.

(i) A distributor performing services pursuant to this section may collect a fee from the licensee for the services provided. The fee may include, but is not limited to, the costs incurred for laboratory testing. A distributor may also collect applicable state or local taxes and fees.

(j) This section does not prohibit a licensee from performing testing on the licensee's premises for the purposes of quality control of the product in conjunction with reasonable business operations. The testing conducted on the licensee's premises by the licensee does not meet the testing requirements pursuant to this division.

Chapter 12. Packaging and Labeling

Business and Professions Code § 26120

(Amended by Stats. 2022, Ch. 390, Sec. 1.5. (AB 1894) Effective January 1, 2023. Repealed July 1, 2024, by its own provisions. See later operative version as added by Sec. 2.5 of Stats. 2022, Ch. 390. Note: This section was added on Nov. 8, 2016, by initiative Prop. 64.)

(a) Prior to delivery or sale at a retailer, cannabis and cannabis products shall be labeled and placed in a tamper-evident, child-resistant package, and shall include a unique identifier for the purposes of identifying and tracking cannabis and cannabis products. If the cannabis or cannabis product contains multiple servings, the package shall also be resealable.

(b) Packages and labels shall not be made to be attractive to children.

(c) All cannabis and cannabis product labels and inserts shall include the following information prominently displayed in a clear and legible fashion in accordance with the requirements, including font size, prescribed by the department:

(1) The following statements, in bold print:

(A) For cannabis: "GOVERNMENT WARNING: THIS PACKAGE CONTAINS CANNABIS, A SCHEDULE I CONTROLLED SUBSTANCE. KEEP OUT OF REACH OF CHILDREN AND ANIMALS. CANNABIS MAY ONLY BE POSSESSED OR CONSUMED BY PERSONS 21 YEARS OF AGE OR OLDER UNLESS THE PERSON IS A QUALIFIED PATIENT. CANNABIS USE WHILE PREGNANT OR BREASTFEEDING MAY BE HARMFUL. CONSUMPTION OF CANNABIS IMPAIRS YOUR ABILITY TO DRIVE AND OPERATE MACHINERY. PLEASE USE EXTREME CAUTION."

(B) For cannabis products: "GOVERNMENT WARNING: THIS PRODUCT CONTAINS CANNABIS, A SCHEDULE I CONTROLLED SUBSTANCE. KEEP OUT OF REACH OF CHILDREN AND ANIMALS. CANNABIS PRODUCTS MAY ONLY BE POSSESSED OR CONSUMED BY PERSONS 21 YEARS OF AGE OR OLDER UNLESS THE PERSON IS A QUALIFIED PATIENT. THE INTOXICATING EFFECTS OF CANNABIS PRODUCTS MAY BE DELAYED UP TO TWO HOURS. CANNABIS USE WHILE PREGNANT OR BREASTFEEDING MAY BE HARMFUL. CONSUMPTION OF CANNABIS PRODUCTS IMPAIRS YOUR ABILITY TO DRIVE AND OPERATE MACHINERY. PLEASE USE EXTREME CAUTION."

(2) For packages containing only dried flower, the net weight of cannabis in the package.

(3) Identification of the type of cannabis or cannabis product and the date of packaging.

(4) The appellation of origin, if any.

(5) List of pharmacologically active ingredients, including, but not limited to, tetrahydrocannabinol (THC), cannabidiol (CBD), and other cannabinoid content, the THC and other cannabinoid amount in milligrams per serving, servings per package, and the THC and other cannabinoid amount in milligrams for the package total.

(6) A warning if nuts or other known allergens are used.

(7) Information associated with the unique identifier issued by the department.

(8) For a medicinal cannabis product sold at a retailer, the statement "FOR MEDICAL USE ONLY."

(9) Any other requirement set by the department.

(d) Only generic food names may be used to describe the ingredients in edible cannabis products.

(e) Cannabis beverages may be packaged in containers that are clear or any color.

(f) In the event the Attorney General determines that cannabis is no longer a Schedule I controlled substance under federal law, the label prescribed in subdivision (c) shall no longer require a statement that cannabis is a Schedule I controlled substance.

(g) This section shall remain in effect only until July 1, 2024, and as of that date is repealed.

Business and Professions Code § 26120

(Repealed (in Sec. 1.5) and added by Stats. 2022, Ch. 390, Sec. 2.5. (AB 1894) Effective January 1, 2023. Operative July 1, 2024, by its own provisions.)

(a) Prior to delivery or sale at a retailer, cannabis and cannabis products shall be labeled and placed in a tamper-evident, child-resistant package and shall include a unique identifier for the purposes of identifying and tracking cannabis and cannabis products. If the cannabis or cannabis product contains multiple servings, the package shall also be resealable.

(b) Packages and labels shall not be made to be attractive to children.

(c) All cannabis and cannabis product labels and inserts shall include the following information prominently displayed in a clear and legible fashion in accordance with the requirements, including font size, prescribed by the department:

(1) The following statements, in bold print:

(A) For cannabis: "GOVERNMENT WARNING: THIS PACKAGE CONTAINS CANNABIS, A SCHEDULE I CONTROLLED SUBSTANCE. KEEP OUT OF REACH OF CHILDREN AND ANIMALS. CANNABIS MAY ONLY BE POSSESSED OR CONSUMED BY PERSONS 21 YEARS OF AGE OR OLDER UNLESS THE PERSON IS A QUALIFIED PATIENT. CANNABIS USE WHILE PREGNANT OR BREASTFEEDING MAY BE HARMFUL. CONSUMPTION OF CANNABIS IMPAIRS YOUR ABILITY TO DRIVE AND OPERATE MACHINERY. PLEASE USE EXTREME CAUTION."

(B) For cannabis products: "GOVERNMENT WARNING: THIS PRODUCT CONTAINS CANNABIS, A SCHEDULE I CONTROLLED SUBSTANCE. KEEP OUT OF REACH OF CHILDREN AND ANIMALS. CANNABIS PRODUCTS MAY ONLY BE POSSESSED OR CONSUMED BY PERSONS 21 YEARS OF AGE OR OLDER UNLESS THE PERSON IS A QUALIFIED PATIENT. THE INTOXICATING EFFECTS OF CANNABIS PRODUCTS MAY BE DELAYED UP TO TWO HOURS. CANNABIS USE WHILE PREGNANT OR BREASTFEEDING MAY BE HARMFUL. CONSUMPTION OF CANNABIS PRODUCTS IMPAIRS YOUR ABILITY TO DRIVE AND OPERATE MACHINERY. PLEASE USE EXTREME CAUTION."

(2) For packages containing only dried flower, the net weight of cannabis in the package.

(3) Identification of the type of cannabis or cannabis product and the date of packaging.

(4) The appellation of origin, if any.

(5) List of pharmacologically active ingredients, including, but not limited to, tetrahydrocannabinol (THC), cannabidiol (CBD), and other cannabinoid content, the THC and other cannabinoid amount in milligrams per serving, servings per package, and the THC and other cannabinoid amount in milligrams for the package total.

(6) A warning if nuts or other known allergens are used.

(7) Information associated with the unique identifier issued by the department.

(8) For a medicinal cannabis product sold at a retailer, the statement "FOR MEDICAL USE ONLY."

(9) Any other requirement set by the department.

(d) Only generic food names may be used to describe the ingredients in edible cannabis products.

(e) Cannabis beverages may be packaged in containers that are clear or any color.

(f) The package and label of a cannabis cartridge and an integrated cannabis vaporizer shall not indicate that the cannabis cartridge or integrated cannabis vaporizer is disposable nor imply that it may be thrown in the trash or recycling streams.

(g) In the event the Attorney General determines that cannabis is no longer a Schedule I controlled substance under federal law, the label prescribed in subdivision (c) shall no longer require a statement that cannabis is a Schedule I controlled substance.

(h) This section shall become operative on July 1, 2024.

Business and Professions Code § 26122

(Added by Stats. 2019, Ch. 830, Sec. 1. (AB 1529) Effective October 12, 2019.)

(a) A cannabis cartridge or integrated cannabis vaporizer that contains cannabis or a cannabis product shall bear the universal symbol described in paragraph (7) of subdivision (c) of Section 26130. The universal symbol shall be visible on the cannabis cartridge or integrated cannabis vaporizer and shall not be smaller than one-quarter inch wide by one-quarter inch high. The universal symbol shall be engraved, affixed with a sticker, or printed in black or white.

(b) For purposes of this section, the following definitions shall apply:

(1) "Cannabis cartridge" means a cartridge containing cannabis oil that is intended to be affixed to an electronic device that heats the oil and creates an aerosol or vapor.

(2) "Integrated cannabis vaporizer" means a singular device that contains both cannabis oil and an integrated electronic device that creates an aerosol or vapor.

Chapter 13. Manufacturers and Cannabis Products

Business and Professions Code § 26130

(Amended by Stats. 2022, Ch. 389, Sec. 5. (AB 1885) Effective January 1, 2023. Note: This section was added on Nov. 8, 2016, by initiative Prop. 64.)

(a) The department shall promulgate regulations governing the licensing of cannabis manufacturers and standards for the manufacturing, packaging, and labeling of all manufactured cannabis products. Licenses to be issued are as follows:

(1) "Manufacturing Level 1," for sites that manufacture cannabis products using nonvolatile solvents, or no solvents.

(2) "Manufacturing Level 2," for sites that manufacture cannabis products using volatile solvents.

(b) For purposes of this section, "volatile solvents" shall have the same meaning as in paragraph (3) of subdivision (b) of Section 11362.3 of the Health and Safety Code, unless otherwise provided by law or regulation.

(c) Edible cannabis products shall be:

(1) Not designed to be appealing to children or easily confused with commercially sold candy or foods that do not contain cannabis.

(2) Produced and sold with a standardized concentration of cannabinoids not to exceed 10 milligrams tetrahydrocannabinol (THC) per serving.

(3) Delineated or scored into standardized serving sizes if the cannabis product contains more than one serving and is an edible cannabis product in solid form.

(4) Homogenized to ensure uniform disbursement of cannabinoids throughout the product.

(5) Manufactured and sold under sanitation standards established by the department that are similar to the standards for preparation, storage, handling, and sale of food products.

(6) Provided to customers with sufficient information to enable the informed consumption of the product, including the potential effects of the cannabis product and directions as to how to consume the cannabis product, as necessary.

(7) Marked with a universal symbol, as determined by the department through regulation.

(d) Cannabis, including concentrated cannabis, included in a cannabis product manufactured in compliance with law is not considered an adulterant under state law.

(e) (1) If the cannabis product is intended for therapeutic effect or health supplementation use on, or for consumption by, an animal, the cannabis product shall also conform with any additional relevant standards, including, but not limited to, an alternative standardized concentration, established by the department through regulations.

(2) The department shall promulgate regulations for animal product standards no later than July 1, 2025. Cannabis products shall not be marketed or sold for use on, or consumption by, animals before these regulations for animal standards take effect.

Business and Professions Code § 26131

(Added by renumbering Section 26106 by Stats. 2021, Ch. 70, Sec. 64. (AB 141) Effective July 12, 2021. Note: This section was added on Nov. 8, 2016, by initiative Prop. 64.)

Standards for the production, packaging, and labeling of all cannabis products developed by the department apply to all licensed manufacturers and microbusinesses, and nonprofits licensed under Section 26070.5, unless otherwise specified by the department.

Business and Professions Code § 26132

(Added by renumbering Section 26105 by Stats. 2021, Ch. 70, Sec. 63. (AB 141) Effective July 12, 2021.)

Manufacturing Level 2 licensees shall enact sufficient methods or procedures to capture or otherwise limit risk of explosion, combustion, or any other unreasonably dangerous risk to public safety created by volatile solvents. The department shall establish minimum standards concerning such methods and procedures for Level 2 licensees.

Chapter 14. Protection of Minors

Business and Professions Code § 26140

(Amended by Stats. 2021, Ch. 70, Sec. 74. (AB 141) Effective July 12, 2021. Note: This section was added on Nov. 8, 2016, by initiative Prop. 64.)

(a) An A-licensee shall not:

(1) Sell cannabis or cannabis products to persons under 21 years of age.

(2) Allow any person under 21 years of age on its premises, unless the A-licensee holds an M-license and the licensed premises for the A-license and M-license are the same.

(3) Employ or retain persons under 21 years of age.

(4) Sell or transfer cannabis or cannabis products unless the person to whom the cannabis or cannabis product is to be sold first presents documentation that reasonably appears to be a valid government-issued identification card showing that the person is 21 years of age or older.

(b) Persons under 21 years of age may be used by peace officers in the enforcement of this division and to apprehend licensees, or employees or agents of licensees, or other persons who sell or furnish cannabis to minors. Notwithstanding any other law, a person under 21 years of age who purchases or attempts to purchase cannabis or cannabis products while under the direction of a peace officer is immune from prosecution for that purchase or attempt to purchase cannabis or cannabis products. Guidelines with respect to the use of persons under 21 years of age as decoys shall be adopted and published by the department in accordance with the rulemaking portion of the Administrative Procedure Act (Chapter 3.5 (commencing with Section 11340) of Part 1 of Division 3 of Title 2 of the Government Code).

(c) Notwithstanding subdivision (a), an M-licensee may:

(1) Allow on the premises a person 18 years of age or older who possesses a valid government-issued identification card, and either a valid county-issued identification card under Section 11362.712 of the Health and Safety Code or a valid physician's recommendation for themselves or for a person for whom that person is a primary caregiver.

(2) Allow a person 21 years of age or older on its premises if the M-licensee holds an A-license and the licensed premises for the M-license and A-license are the same.

(3) Sell cannabis, cannabis products, and cannabis accessories to a person 18 years of age or older who possesses a valid government-issued identification card and either a valid county-issued identification card under Section 11362.712 of the Health and Safety Code or a valid physician's recommendation for themselves or for a person for whom the person is a primary caregiver.

(4) The department may establish requirements for the purchase of cannabis, cannabis products, or cannabis accessories by a primary caregiver for a patient to ensure that the status of a person as a primary caregiver is verified.

Chapter 15. Advertising and Marketing Restrictions

Business and Professions Code § 26150

(Amended by Stats. 2017, Ch. 27, Sec. 84. (SB 94) Effective June 27, 2017. Note: This section was added on Nov. 8, 2016, by initiative Prop. 64.)

For purposes of this chapter:

(a) "Advertise" means the publication or dissemination of an advertisement.

(b) "Advertisement" includes any written or verbal statement, illustration, or depiction which is calculated to induce sales of cannabis or cannabis products, including any written, printed, graphic, or other material, billboard, sign, or other outdoor display, public transit card, other periodical literature, publication, or in a radio or television broadcast, or in any other media; except that such term shall not include:

(1) Any label affixed to any cannabis or cannabis products, or any individual covering, carton, or other wrapper of that container that constitutes a part of the labeling under provisions of this division.

(2) Any editorial or other reading material, such as a news release, in any periodical or publication or newspaper for the publication of which no money or valuable consideration is paid or promised, directly or indirectly, by any licensee, and which is not written by or at the direction of the licensee.

(c) "Advertising sign" is any sign, poster, display, billboard, or any other stationary or permanently affixed advertisement promoting the sale of cannabis or cannabis products which are not cultivated, manufactured, distributed, or sold on the same lot.

(d) "Health-related statement" means any statement related to health, and includes statements of a curative or therapeutic nature that, expressly or by implication, suggest a relationship between the consumption of cannabis or cannabis products and health benefits, or effects on health.

(e) "Market" or "Marketing" means any act or process of promoting or selling cannabis or cannabis products, including, but not limited to, sponsorship of sporting events, point-of-sale advertising, and development of products specifically designed to appeal to certain demographics.

Business and Professions Code § 26151

(Amended by Stats. 2017, Ch. 27, Sec. 85. (SB 94) Effective June 27, 2017. Note: This section was added on Nov. 8, 2016, by initiative Prop. 64.)

(a) (1) All advertisements and marketing shall accurately and legibly identify the licensee responsible for its content, by adding, at a minimum, the licensee's license number.

(2) A technology platform shall not display an advertisement by a licensee on an Internet Web page unless the advertisement displays the license number of the licensee.

(3) An outdoor advertising company subject to the Outdoor Advertising Act (Chapter 2 (commencing with Section 5200) of Division 3) shall not display an advertisement by a licensee unless the advertisement displays the license number of the licensee.

(b) Any advertising or marketing placed in broadcast, cable, radio, print, and digital communications shall only be displayed where at least 71.6 percent of the audience is reasonably expected to be 21 years of age or older, as determined by reliable, up-to-date audience composition data.

(c) Any advertising or marketing involving direct, individualized communication or dialogue controlled by the licensee shall utilize a method of age affirmation to verify that the recipient is 21 years of age or older before engaging in that communication or dialogue controlled by the licensee. For purposes of this section, that method of age affirmation may include user confirmation, birth date disclosure, or other similar registration method.

(d) All advertising shall be truthful and appropriately substantiated.

Business and Professions Code § 26152

(Amended by Stats. 2018, Ch. 923, Sec. 1. (AB 2899) Effective January 1, 2019. Note: This section was added on Nov. 8, 2016, by initiative Prop. 64.)

A licensee shall not do any of the following:

(a) Advertise or market in a manner that is false or untrue in any material particular, or that, irrespective of falsity, directly, or by ambiguity, omission, or inference, or by the addition of irrelevant, scientific, or technical matter, tends to create a misleading impression.

(b) Publish or disseminate advertising or marketing containing any statement concerning a brand or product that is inconsistent with any statement on the labeling thereof.

(c) Publish or disseminate advertising or marketing containing any statement, design, device, or representation which tends to create the impression that the cannabis originated in a particular place or region, unless the label of the advertised product bears an appellation of origin, and such appellation of origin appears in the advertisement.

(d) Advertise or market on a billboard or similar advertising device located on an Interstate Highway or on a State Highway which crosses the California border.

(e) Advertise or market cannabis or cannabis products in a manner intended to encourage persons under 21 years of age to consume cannabis or cannabis products.

(f) Publish or disseminate advertising or marketing that is attractive to children.

(g) Advertise or market cannabis or cannabis products on an advertising sign within 1,000 feet of a day care center, school providing instruction in kindergarten or any grades 1 to 12, inclusive, playground, or youth center.

(h) Publish or disseminate advertising or marketing while the licensee's license is suspended.

Business and Professions Code § 26152.1

(Added by Stats. 2022, Ch. 390, Sec. 3. (AB 1894) Effective January 1, 2023. Operative July 1, 2024, by its own provisions.)

(a) (1) Advertisement and marketing of an integrated cannabis vaporizer, as defined in Section 26122, shall prominently provide in a clear and legible fashion: "An empty integrated cannabis vaporizer shall be properly disposed of as hazardous waste at a household hazardous waste collection facility or other approved facility."

(2) Advertisement and marketing of a cannabis cartridge shall prominently provide in a clear and legible fashion: "A spent cannabis cartridge shall be properly disposed of as hazardous waste at a household hazardous waste collection facility or other approved facility."

(3) For the purposes of this subdivision, "authorized facility" means a facility authorized under the hazardous waste control laws under Chapter 6.5 (commencing with Section 25100) of Division 20 of the Health and Safety Code.

(b) Advertisement and marketing of a cannabis cartridge and an integrated cannabis vaporizer shall not indicate that a cannabis cartridge or an integrated cannabis vaporizer is disposable nor imply that it may be thrown in the trash or recycling streams.

(c) This section shall become operative on July 1, 2024.

Business and Professions Code § 26153

(Amended by Stats. 2021, Ch. 70, Sec. 75. (AB 141) Effective July 12, 2021. Note: This section was added on Nov. 8, 2016, by initiative Prop. 64.)

(a) A licensee shall not give away any amount of cannabis or cannabis products, or any cannabis accessories, as part of a business promotion or other commercial activity.

(b) For purposes of this section, the donation of cannabis or cannabis products by a licensee to a patient or the primary caregiver of a patient pursuant to Section 26071 shall not be considered a business promotion or other commercial activity.

(c) For purposes of this section, the provision of cannabis or cannabis products by a licensee pursuant to Section 26153.1 shall not be considered a business promotion or other commercial activity.

Business and Professions Code § 26153.1

(Amended (as added by Stats. 2021, Ch. 70, Sec. 76) by Stats. 2021, Ch. 87, Sec. 6. (SB 160) Effective July 16, 2021. Operative on or before January 1, 2023, by its own provisions.)

(a) The Department of Cannabis Control shall adopt regulations to establish a process authorizing licensees to designate cannabis or cannabis products as a trade sample at any time while the cannabis or cannabis product is in the possession of the licensee.

(b) The department shall adopt regulations to establish a definition of trade sample, the quantity of cannabis and cannabis products that may be designated as trade samples, the amount of trade samples that may be provided to a licensee, and any other provisions necessary to implement this section.

(c) Cannabis or cannabis products designated as trade samples shall be subject to quality assurance and testing pursuant to Section 26110, and may be returned to cultivators and manufacturers following quality assurance and testing pursuant to Section 26110.

(d) Cannabis or cannabis products designated as trade samples shall be recorded into the track and trace program established pursuant to Section 26067.

(e) Cannabis or cannabis products designated as trade samples shall be labeled with the following: “TRADE SAMPLE. NOT FOR RESALE OR DONATION.”

(f) Cannabis or cannabis products designated as trade samples shall only be given for targeted advertising to licensees about new or existing cannabis or cannabis products. The department may adopt regulations specifying additional purposes of trade samples.

(g) Cannabis or cannabis products designated as trade samples may be transported between any two licensees by an employee of a licensed distributor or microbusiness authorized to engage in distribution, or by a licensee authorized to engage in transportation of cannabis, including a distributor transport-only licensee as established by the department in regulation. Employees transporting trade samples pursuant to this subdivision but outside of a registered vehicle of the licensed distributor or microbusiness shall be subject to possession limits established in Section 11357 of the Health and Safety Code.

(h) Cannabis and cannabis products designated as trade samples shall not be provided for any form of payment, consideration, cost, or compensation.

(i) Except as otherwise provided in this section, cannabis and cannabis products designated as trade samples shall comply with all applicable requirements for cultivation, manufacturing, distribution, processing, storing, laboratory testing, quality assurance, packaging, or labeling under this division.

(j) This section shall become effective upon adoption of regulations by the department and no later than January 1,

2023.

(k) Notwithstanding any other law, the department may adopt and readopt emergency regulations to implement this section. The provisions of Section 26013 shall be applicable to emergency regulations adopted or readopted pursuant to this section. The emergency regulations authorized by this section shall be deemed an emergency and necessary for the immediate preservation of public peace, health, safety or general welfare.

Business and Professions Code § 26154

(Amended by Stats. 2017, Ch. 27, Sec. 88. (SB 94) Effective June 27, 2017. Note: This section was added on Nov. 8, 2016, by initiative Prop. 64.)

A licensee shall not include on the label of any cannabis or cannabis product or publish or disseminate advertising or marketing containing any health-related statement that is untrue in any particular manner or tends to create a misleading impression as to the effects on health of cannabis consumption.

Business and Professions Code § 26155

(Amended by Stats. 2017, Ch. 27, Sec. 89. (SB 94) Effective June 27, 2017. Note: This section was added on Nov. 8, 2016, by initiative Prop. 64.)

(a) The provisions of subdivision (g) of Section 26152 shall not apply to the placement of advertising signs inside a licensed premises and which are not visible by normal unaided vision from a public place, provided that such advertising signs do not advertise cannabis or cannabis products in a manner intended to encourage persons under 21 years of age to consume cannabis or cannabis products.

(b) This chapter does not apply to any noncommercial speech.

Business and Professions Code § 26156

(Added by Stats. 2017, Ch. 27, Sec. 90. (SB 94) Effective June 27, 2017.)

The requirements of Section 5272 apply to this division.

Chapter 16. Records

Business and Professions Code § 26160

(Amended by Stats. 2021, Ch. 70, Sec. 77. (AB 141) Effective July 12, 2021. Note: This section was added on Nov. 8, 2016, by initiative Prop. 64.)

(a) A licensee shall keep accurate records of commercial cannabis activity.

(b) All records related to commercial cannabis activity as defined by the department shall be maintained for a minimum of seven years.

(c) The department may examine the records of a licensee and inspect the premises of a licensee as the department, or a state or local agency, deems necessary to perform its duties under this division. All inspections and examinations of records shall be conducted during standard business hours of the licensed facility or at any other reasonable time. Licensees shall provide and deliver records to the department upon request.

(d) Licensees shall keep records identified by the department on the premises of the location licensed. The department may make any examination of the records of any licensee. Licensees shall also provide and deliver copies of documents to the department upon request.

(e) A licensee, or its agent or employee, that refuses, impedes, obstructs, or interferes with an inspection of the premises or records of the licensee pursuant to this section, has engaged in a violation of this division.

(f) If a licensee, or an agent or employee of a licensee, fails to maintain or provide the records required pursuant to this section, the licensee shall be subject to a citation and fine of up to thirty thousand dollars ($30,000) per individual violation.

Business and Professions Code § 26161

(Amended by Stats. 2021, Ch. 70, Sec. 78. (AB 141) Effective July 12, 2021. Note: This section was added on Nov. 8, 2016, by initiative Prop. 64.)

(a) Every sale or transport of cannabis or cannabis products from one licensee to another licensee must be recorded on a sales invoice or receipt. Sales invoices and receipts may be maintained electronically and must be filed in such manner as to be readily accessible for examination by employees of the department or California Department of Tax and Fee Administration and shall not be commingled with invoices covering other commodities.

(b) Each sales invoice required by subdivision (a) shall include the name and address of the seller and shall include the following information:

(1) Name and address of the purchaser.

(2) Date of sale and invoice number.

(3) Kind, quantity, size, and capacity of packages of cannabis or cannabis products sold.

(4) The cost to the purchaser, together with any discount applied to the price as shown on the invoice.

(5) The place from which transport of the cannabis or cannabis product was made unless transport was made from the premises of the licensee.

(6) Whether the cannabis or cannabis products are designated for donation to a medicinal cannabis patient.

(7) Any other information specified by the department.

Business and Professions Code § 26161.5

(Added by Stats. 2018, Ch. 583, Sec. 1. (AB 2402) Effective January 1, 2019.)

(a) A licensee shall not disclose a consumer's personal information to a third party, except to the extent necessary to allow responsibility for payment to be determined and payment to be made or if the consumer has consented to the licensee's disclosure of the personal information. This section does not prohibit the disclosure of nonpublic personal information to the State of California or a city, county, or city and county to perform official duties pursuant to this division or a local ordinance.

(b) A licensee shall not discriminate against a consumer, or deny a consumer a product or service, because the consumer has not provided consent, pursuant to subdivision (a), to authorize the licensee to disclose the consumer's nonpublic personal information to a third party not directly related to the transaction.

(c) For purposes of this section, "personal information" has the same meaning as defined in subdivision (d) of Section 1798.81.5 of the Civil Code.

(d) For the purposes of this section, "third party" does not include a contractor providing software services to a licensee for the purpose of conducting a transaction or verifying eligibility, provided that the contractor does not use or retain a consumer's personal information for any other purpose or share a consumer's personal information with any party other than the contracting licensee.

(e) This section provides greater protection to personal information than that provided by Section 1798.81.5 of the Civil Code, which does not apply to licensees under this division pursuant to paragraph (5) of subdivision (e) of Section 1798.81.5 of the Civil Code.

Business and Professions Code § 26162

(Amended by Stats. 2022, Ch. 28, Sec. 19. (SB 1380) Effective January 1, 2023.)

(a) Information identifying the names of patients, their medical conditions, or the names of their primary caregivers received and contained in records kept by the office or the department for the purposes of administering this chapter are confidential and shall not be disclosed pursuant to the California Public Records Act (Division 10 (commencing with Section 7920.000) of Title 1 of the Government Code), except as necessary for authorized employees of the State of California or any city, county, or city and county to perform official duties pursuant to this chapter, or a local ordinance.

(b) Information identifying the names of patients, their medical conditions, or the names of their primary caregivers received and contained in records kept by the department for the purposes of administering this chapter shall be maintained in accordance with Chapter 1 (commencing with Section 123100) of Part 1 of Division 106 of the Health and Safety Code, Part 2.6 (commencing with Section 56) of Division 1 of the Civil Code, and other state and federal laws relating to confidential patient information.

(c) Nothing in this section precludes the following:

(1) Employees of the department notifying state or local agencies about information submitted to the agency that the employee suspects is falsified or fraudulent.

(2) Notifications from the department to state or local agencies about apparent violations of this division or applicable local ordinance.

(3) Verification of requests by state or local agencies to confirm licenses and certificates issued by the department or other state agency.

(4) Provision of information requested pursuant to a court order or subpoena issued by a court or an administrative agency or local governing body authorized by law to issue subpoenas.

(d) Information shall not be disclosed by any state or local agency beyond what is necessary to achieve the goals of a specific investigation, notification, or the parameters of a specific court order or subpoena.

Business and Professions Code § 26162.5

(Amended by Stats. 2019, Ch. 837, Sec. 7. (SB 34) Effective January 1, 2020.)

(a) Identification cards issued pursuant to Section 11362.71 of the Health and Safety Code are hereby deemed "medical information" within the meaning of the Confidentiality of Medical Information Act (Part 2.6 (commencing with Section 56) of Division 1 of the Civil Code) and shall not be disclosed by a licensee except as (1) necessary for the State of California or any city, county, or city and county to perform official duties pursuant to this chapter, Part 1 (commencing with Section 6001) and Part 14.5 (commencing with Section 34010) of Division 2 of the Revenue and Taxation Code, or a local ordinance, or (2) to a contractor providing software services to a licensee for the purpose of conducting a transaction or verifying eligibility, provided that the contractor does not use or retain medical information for any other purpose or share information with any party other than the contracting licensee.

(b) Information contained in a physician's recommendation issued in accordance with Article 25 (commencing with Section 2525) of Chapter 5 of Division 2 and received by a licensee, including, but not limited to, the name, address, or social security number of the patient, the patient's medical condition, or the name of the patient's primary caregiver is hereby deemed "medical information" within the meaning of the Confidentiality of Medical Information Act (Part 2.6 (commencing with Section 56) of Division 1 of the Civil Code) and shall not be disclosed by a licensee except as (1) necessary for the State of California or any city, county, or city and county to perform official duties pursuant to this chapter, Part 1 (commencing with Section 6001) and Part 14.5 (commencing with Section 34010) of Division 2 of the Revenue and Taxation Code, or a local ordinance, or (2) to a contractor providing software services to a licensee for the purpose of conducting a transaction or verifying eligibility, provided that the contractor does not use or retain medical information for any other purpose or share information with any party other than the contracting licensee.

Business and Professions Code § 26163

(Amended by Stats. 2021, Ch. 70, Sec. 80. (AB 141) Effective July 12, 2021.)

(a) The department shall, upon the request of the CalSavers Retirement Savings Board, furnish to the board, as applicable, the following information with respect to every licensee:

(1) Licensee.

(2) Licensee's physical and mailing addresses.

(3) Federal employer identification number if the licensee is a partnership, or the licensee's individual taxpayer identification number or social security number for all other licensees.

(4) Type of license.

(5) Effective date of license or a renewal.

(6) Expiration date of license.

(7) Whether license is active or inactive, if known.

(b) Information shared with the CalSavers Retirement Savings Board shall be used only for the purposes of administering the CalSavers Retirement Program.

Chapter 18. License Fees

Business and Professions Code § 26180

(Amended by Stats. 2021, Ch. 70, Sec. 81. (AB 141) Effective July 12, 2021. Note: This section was added on Nov. 8, 2016, by initiative Prop. 64.)

The department shall establish a scale of application, licensing, and renewal fees, based upon the cost of enforcing this division, as follows:

(a) The department shall charge each licensee a licensure and renewal fee, as applicable. The licensure and renewal fee shall be calculated to cover the costs of administering this division. The licensure fee may vary depending upon the varying costs associated with administering the various regulatory requirements of this division as they relate to the nature and scope of the different licensure activities, including, but not limited to, the track and trace program required pursuant to Section 26067, but shall not exceed the reasonable regulatory costs to the department.

(b) The total fees assessed pursuant to this division shall be set at an amount that will fairly and proportionately generate sufficient total revenue to fully cover the total costs of administering this division.

(c) All license fees shall be set on a scaled basis by the department, dependent on the size of the business.

(d) The department shall deposit all fees collected in a fee account to be established in the Cannabis Control Fund. Moneys in the fee account shall be used, upon appropriation by the Legislature, by the department for the administration of this division.

Business and Professions Code § 26180.5

(Added by Stats. 2017, Ch. 27, Sec. 97. (SB 94) Effective June 27, 2017.)

No later than January 1, 2018, the Secretary of Business, Consumer Services, and Housing or his or her designee shall initiate work with the Legislature, the Department of Consumer Affairs, the Department of Food and Agriculture, the State Department of Public Health, and any other related departments to ensure that there is a safe and viable way to collect cash payments for taxes and fees related to the regulation of cannabis activity throughout the state.

Business and Professions Code § 26181

(Amended by Stats. 2017, Ch. 27, Sec. 98. (SB 94) Effective June 27, 2017. Note: This section was added on Nov. 8, 2016, by initiative Prop. 64.)

The State Water Resources Control Board, the Department of Fish and Wildlife, and other agencies may establish fees to cover the costs of their cannabis programs.

Chapter 19. Annual Reports; Performance Audit

Business and Professions Code § 26190

(Amended by Stats. 2022, Ch. 396, Sec. 2. (SB 1326) Effective January 1, 2023. Note: This section was added on Nov. 8, 2016, by initiative Prop. 64.)

Beginning on March 1, 2023, and on or before March 1 of each year thereafter, the department shall prepare and submit to the Legislature an annual report on the department's activities, in compliance with Section 9795 of the Government Code, and post the report on the department's internet website. The report shall include, but not be limited to, the following information for the previous fiscal year:

(a) The amount of funds allocated and spent by the department for cannabis licensing, enforcement, and administration.

(b) The number of state licenses issued, renewed, denied, suspended, and revoked, by state license category.

(c) The average time for processing state license applications, by state license category.

(d) The number of appeals from the denial of state licenses or other disciplinary actions taken by the department and the average time spent on these appeals.

(e) The number of complaints submitted by citizens or representatives of cities or counties regarding licensees, provided as both a comprehensive statewide number and by geographical region.

(f) The number and type of enforcement activities conducted by the department and by local law enforcement agencies in conjunction with the department.

(g) The number, type, and amount of penalties, fines, and other disciplinary actions taken by the department.

(h) The number of licenses on which the department imposed conditions and the categories of conditions imposed on licenses.

(i) A detailed list of the petitions for regulatory relief or rulemaking changes received by the department from licensees requesting modifications of the enforcement of rules under this division.

(j) A list of interstate cannabis agreements entered into pursuant to Chapter 25 (commencing with Section 26300), including information regarding the terms and conditions of each agreement, the activities undertaken by state agencies to implement the agreement, and the effects of the agreement on California's cannabis industry.

(k) (1) For the first publication of the reports, the department shall provide a joint report to the Legislature regarding the state of the cannabis market in California. This report shall identify any statutory or regulatory changes necessary to ensure that the implementation of this division does not do any of the following:

(A) Allow unreasonable restraints on competition by creation or maintenance of unlawful monopoly power.

(B) Perpetuate the presence of an illegal market for cannabis or cannabis products in the state or out of the state.

(C) Encourage underage use or adult abuse of cannabis or cannabis products, or illegal diversion of cannabis or cannabis products out of the state.

(D) Result in an excessive concentration of licensees in a given city, county, or both.

(E) Present an unreasonable risk of minors being exposed to cannabis or cannabis products.

(F) Result in violations of any environmental protection laws.

(2) For purposes of this subdivision, "excessive concentration" means when the premises for a retail license, microbusiness license, or a license issued under Section 26070.5 is located in an area where either of the following conditions exist:

(A) The ratio of licensees to population in a census tract or census division exceeds the ratio of licensees to population in the county in which the census tract or census division is located, unless reduction of that ratio would unduly limit the development of the legal market so as to perpetuate the illegal market for cannabis or cannabis products.

(B) The ratio of retail licenses, microbusiness licenses, or licenses under Section 26070.5 to population in the census tract, division, or jurisdiction exceeds that allowable by local ordinance adopted under Section 26200.

Business and Professions Code § 26190.5

(Amended by Stats. 2021, Ch. 70, Sec. 83. (AB 141) Effective July 12, 2021.)

The department shall contract with the California Cannabis Research Program, known as the Center for Medicinal Cannabis Research, and formerly known as the California Marijuana Research Program, authorized pursuant to Section 11362.9 of the Health and Safety Code, to develop a study that identifies the impact that cannabis has on motor skills.

Business and Professions Code § 26191

(Amended by Stats. 2021, Ch. 70, Sec. 84. (AB 141) Effective July 12, 2021. Note: This section was added on Nov. 8, 2016, by initiative Prop. 64.)

(a) Commencing January 1, 2022, and by January 1 triennially thereafter, the Office of State Audits and Evaluations within the Department of Finance shall conduct a performance audit of the department's activities under this division, and shall report its findings to the department and the Legislature by July 1 of that same year. The report shall include, but not be limited to, the following:

(1) The actual costs of the program.

(2) The overall effectiveness of enforcement programs.

(3) Any report submitted pursuant to this section shall be submitted in compliance with Section 9795 of the Government Code.

(b) The Legislature shall provide sufficient funds to the Department of Finance to conduct the triennial audit required by this section.

Chapter 20. Local Control

Business and Professions Code § 26200

(Amended by Stats. 2022, Ch. 395, Sec. 1.5. (SB 1186) Effective January 1, 2023. Note: This section was added on Nov. 8, 2016, by initiative Prop. 64.)

(a) (1) Except as set forth in the Medicinal Cannabis Patients' Right of Access Act (Chapter 26 (commencing with Section 26320)), this division shall not be interpreted to supersede or limit the authority of a local jurisdiction to adopt and enforce local ordinances to regulate businesses licensed under this division, including, but not limited to, local zoning and land use requirements, business license requirements, and requirements related to reducing exposure to secondhand smoke, or to completely prohibit the establishment or operation of one or more types of businesses licensed under this division within the local jurisdiction.

(2) Except as set forth in the Medicinal Cannabis Patients' Right of Access Act (Chapter 26 (commencing with Section 26320)), this division shall not be interpreted to supersede or limit existing local authority for law enforcement activity, enforcement of local zoning requirements or local ordinances, or enforcement of local license, permit, or other authorization requirements.

(b) This division shall not be interpreted to require the department to undertake local law enforcement responsibilities, enforce local zoning requirements, or enforce local licensing, permitting, or other authorization requirements.

(c) A local jurisdiction shall notify the department upon revocation of any local license, permit, or authorization for a licensee to engage in commercial cannabis activity within the local jurisdiction. Within 60 days of being so informed, the department shall begin the process to determine whether a license issued to the licensee should be suspended or revoked pursuant to Chapter 3 (commencing with Section 26030).

(d) For facilities issued a state license that are located within the incorporated area of a city, the city shall have full power and authority to enforce this division and the regulations promulgated by the department, if delegated by the state. Notwithstanding Sections 101375, 101400, and 101405 of the Health and Safety Code or any contract entered into pursuant thereto, or any other law, the city shall assume complete responsibility for any regulatory function pursuant to this division within the city limits that would otherwise be performed by the county or any county officer or employee, including a county health officer, without liability, cost, or expense to the county.

(e) (1) This division does not prohibit the issuance of a state temporary event license to a licensee authorizing onsite cannabis sales to, and consumption by, persons 21 years of age or older at a county fair event, district agricultural association event, or at another venue expressly approved by a local jurisdiction for the purpose of holding temporary events of this nature, provided that the activities, at a minimum, comply with all the following:

(A) The requirements of paragraphs (1) to (3), inclusive, of subdivision (g).

(B) All participants who are engaged in the onsite retail sale of cannabis or cannabis products at the event are licensed under this division to engage in that activity.

(C) The activities are otherwise consistent with regulations promulgated and adopted by the department governing state temporary event licenses, except as otherwise provided in paragraphs (6), (7), and (8).

(D) A state temporary event license shall only be issued in local jurisdictions that authorize such events.

(E) A licensee who submits an application for a state temporary event license shall, 60 days before the event, provide to the department a list of all licensees that will be providing onsite sales of cannabis or cannabis products at the event. If any changes occur in that list, the licensee shall provide the department with a final updated list to reflect those changes. A person shall not engage in the onsite retail sale of cannabis or cannabis products, or in any way participate in the event, who is not included in the list, including any updates, provided to the department.

(2) The department may impose a civil penalty on any person who violates this subdivision, or any regulations adopted by the department governing state temporary event licenses, in an amount up to three times the amount of the license fee for each violation, consistent with Sections 26018 and 26038.

(3) The department may require the event and all participants to cease operations without delay if in the opinion of the department or local law enforcement it is necessary to protect the immediate public health and safety of the people of the state. The department may also require the event organizer to immediately expel from the event any participant selling cannabis or cannabis products without a license from the department that authorizes the participant to sell cannabis or cannabis products. If the unlicensed participant does not leave the event, the department may require the event and all participants to cease operations immediately.

(4) The order by the department for the event to cease operations pursuant to paragraph (3) does not entitle the event organizer or any participant in the event to a hearing or an appeal of the decision. Chapter 3 (commencing with Section 490) of Division 1.5 and Chapter 4 (commencing with Section 26040) of this division shall not apply to the order by the department for the event to cease operations pursuant to paragraph (3).

(5) The smoking of cannabis or cannabis products at temporary events authorized pursuant to this subdivision is prohibited in locations where smoking is prohibited. For purposes of this section, "smoking" has the same meaning as defined in subdivision (c) of Section 22950.5.

(6) (A) All licensees who are issued a state temporary event license allowed pursuant to this subdivision may, upon completion or cessation of the temporary event, reconcile unsold inventory of cannabis or cannabis products and return it to the licensee's retail premises.

(B) All unsold inventory of cannabis or cannabis products from the temporary event shall be noted in track and trace prior to transport.

(C) All unsold inventory of cannabis or cannabis products from the temporary event shall be in its original packaging in which it was placed pursuant to Chapter 12 (commencing with Section 26120).

(7) The inventory of cannabis or cannabis products authorized to be sold by a state temporary event license pursuant to this subdivision shall only be transported to and from the temporary event by a licensed distributor or licensed microbusiness.

(8) The department shall not deny an application for a state temporary event license pursuant to this subdivision solely on the basis that there is a license issued pursuant to the Alcoholic Beverage Control Act (Division 9 (commencing with Section 23000)) for the proposed premises of the event. Furthermore, the Department of Alcoholic Beverage Control shall not take any disciplinary action against a person licensed pursuant to the Alcoholic Beverage Control Act on the basis of a state temporary event license issued by the department to a licensee pursuant to this subdivision that utilizes the same premises as the person licensed pursuant to the Alcoholic Beverage Control Act.

(A) All on- and off-sale privileges of alcoholic beverages at the venue shall be suspended for the day of the event and shall not resume until 6 a.m. on the day after the event has ended.

(B) Alcohol consumption on the venue premises shall be strictly prohibited for the day of the event and shall not resume until 6 a.m. on the day after the event has ended.

(f) This division, or any regulations promulgated thereunder, shall not be deemed to limit the authority or remedies of a city, county, or city and county under any provision of law, including, but not limited to, Section 7 of Article XI of the California Constitution.

(g) Notwithstanding paragraph (1) of subdivision (a) of Section 11362.3 of the Health and Safety Code, a local jurisdiction may allow for the smoking, vaporizing, and ingesting of cannabis or cannabis products on the premises of a retailer or microbusiness licensed under this division if all of the following are met:

(1) Access to the area where cannabis consumption is allowed is restricted to persons 21 years of age or older.

(2) Cannabis consumption is not visible from any public place or nonage-restricted area.

(3) Sale or consumption of alcohol or tobacco is not allowed on the premises.

(h) This division shall not be interpreted to supersede Section 6404.5 of the Labor Code.

(i) This section does not alter or affect the prohibition on the sale of alcoholic beverages by a licensee, as provided in Section 26054, on or at a venue premises licensed under this division.

Business and Professions Code § 26201

(Added November 8, 2016, by initiative Proposition 64, Sec. 6.1.)

Any standards, requirements, and regulations regarding health and safety, environmental protection, testing, security, food safety, and worker protections established by the state shall be the minimum standards for all licensees under this division statewide. A local jurisdiction may establish additional standards, requirements, and regulations.

Business and Professions Code § 26202

(Amended by Stats. 2021, Ch. 70, Sec. 86. (AB 141) Effective July 12, 2021. Note: This section was added on Nov. 8, 2016, by initiative Prop. 64.)

(a) A local jurisdiction may enforce this division and the regulations promulgated by the department if delegated the power to do so by the department.

(b) The department shall implement the delegation of enforcement authority in subdivision (a) through an agreement between the department and the local jurisdiction to which enforcement authority is to be delegated.

Business and Professions Code § 26203

(Added by Stats. 2022, Ch. 56, Sec. 7. (AB 195) Effective June 30, 2022. Repealed as of January 1, 2025, by its own provisions.)

(a) There is hereby established a task force on state and local regulation of commercial cannabis activity. The purpose of the task force is to promote communication between state and local entities engaged in the regulation of commercial cannabis activity and facilitate cooperation to enforce applicable state and local laws.

(b) The task force shall be composed of representatives from all of the following:

(1) The Department of Cannabis Control.

(2) The California Department of Tax and Fee Administration.

(3) The Department of Fish and Wildlife.

(4) The State Water Resources Control Board.

(5) The Department of the California Highway Patrol.

(6) The Labor and Workforce Development Agency.

(7) The Department of Justice.

(8) All local jurisdictions regulating commercial cannabis activity that opt to participate in the task force, which may send representatives from one or more of the following:

(A) The contact person designated pursuant to subdivision (f) of Section 26055.

(B) A county sheriff's office or municipal police department.

(C) A district attorney's office or city attorney's office.

(c) Beginning July 1, 2023, the task force shall meet twice each fiscal year, through teleconference or similar means to facilitate remote participation, for discussions to be convened and led by the Department of Cannabis Control. Discussion topics may include, but need not be limited to, enforcement against the illicit market, social equity programs, state licensing requirements, and labor and workforce compliance.

(d) The task force shall not be subject to the requirements of the Bagley-Keene Open Meeting Act (Article 9 (commencing with Section 11120) of Chapter 1 of Part 1 of Division 3 of Title 2 of the Government Code) or the Ralph M. Brown Act (Chapter 9 (commencing with Section 54950) of Part 1 of Division 2 of Title 5 of the Government Code).

(e) This section shall remain in effect only until January 1, 2025, and as of that date is repealed.

Chapter 21. Funding

Business and Professions Code § 26210

(Amended by Stats. 2021, Ch. 70, Sec. 87. (AB 141) Effective July 12, 2021. Note: This section was added on Nov. 8, 2016, by initiative Prop. 64.)

(a) The Marijuana Control Fund, formerly known as the Medical Cannabis Regulation and Safety Act Fund and the Medical Marijuana Regulation and Safety Act Fund, is hereby renamed the Cannabis Control Fund. Notwithstanding Section 16305.7 of the Government Code, the fund shall include any interest and dividends earned on moneys in the fund.

(b) Upon the effective date of this section, whenever "Marijuana Control Fund," "Medical Cannabis Regulation and

Safety Act Fund," or "Medical Marijuana Regulation and Safety Act Fund" appears in any statute, regulation, or contract, or in any other code, it shall be construed to refer to the Cannabis Control Fund.

(c) Any General Fund or special fund loan that was used to establish and support the regulatory activities of the state licensing entities pursuant to former Section 19351 shall be repaid by the initial proceeds from fees collected pursuant to this division or any rule or regulation adopted pursuant to this division, by January 1, 2022. Should the initial proceeds from fees not be sufficient to repay the loan, moneys from the Cannabis Fines and Penalties Account shall be made available to the department, by appropriation of the Legislature, to repay the loan.

(d) Except as otherwise provided, all moneys collected pursuant to this division as a result of fines or penalties imposed under this division shall be deposited directly into the Cannabis Fines and Penalties Account, which is hereby continued in existence, and shall be available, upon appropriation by the Legislature.

Business and Professions Code § 26210.5

(Amended by Stats. 2021, Ch. 70, Sec. 88. (AB 141) Effective July 12, 2021.)

By July 1, 2018, the Bureau of Cannabis Control, in coordination with the Department of General Services, shall establish an office to collect fees and taxes in the County of Humboldt, County of Trinity, or County of Mendocino in order to ensure the safe payment and collection of cash in those counties.

Business and Professions Code § 26211

(Amended by Stats. 2021, Ch. 70, Sec. 89. (AB 141) Effective July 12, 2021. Note: This section was added on Nov. 8, 2016, by initiative Prop. 64.)

(a) Funds for the initial establishment and support of the regulatory activities under this division, including the public information program described in subdivision (c), and for the activities of the California Department of Tax and Fee Administration under Part 14.5 (commencing with Section 34010) of Division 2 of the Revenue and Taxation Code until July 1, 2017, or until the 2017 Budget Act is enacted, whichever occurs later, shall be advanced from the General Fund and shall be repaid by the initial proceeds from fees collected pursuant to this division, any rule or regulation adopted pursuant to this division, or revenues collected from the tax imposed by Sections 34011 and 34012 of the Revenue and Taxation Code, by January 1, 2025.

> (1) Funds advanced pursuant to this subdivision shall be appropriated to the department as necessary to implement the provisions of this division, and to the California Department of Tax and Fee Administration, as necessary, to implement the provisions of Part 14.5 (commencing with Section 34010) of Division 2 of the Revenue and Taxation Code.
>
> (2) Within 45 days of November 9, 2016, the date this section became operative:
>
> > (A) The Director of Finance shall determine an amount of the initial advance from the General Fund to the Cannabis Control Fund that does not exceed thirty million dollars ($30,000,000); and
> >
> > (B) There shall be advanced a sum of five million dollars ($5,000,000) from the General Fund to the State Department of Health Care Services to provide for the public information program described in subdivision (c).

(b) Notwithstanding subdivision (a), the Legislature shall provide sufficient funds to the Cannabis Control Fund to support the activities of the department under this division, and the California Department of Tax and Fee Administration to support its activities under Part 14.5 (commencing with Section 34010) of Division 2 of the Revenue and Taxation Code. It is anticipated that this funding will be provided annually beginning on July 1, 2017.

(c) The State Department of Health Care Services shall establish and implement a public information program no later than September 1, 2017. This public information program shall, at a minimum, describe the provisions of the Control, Regulate and Tax Adult Use of Marijuana Act of 2016, the scientific basis for restricting access of cannabis and cannabis products to persons under the age of 21 years, describe the penalties for providing access to cannabis and cannabis products to persons under the age of 21 years, provide information regarding the dangers of driving a motor vehicle, boat, vessel, aircraft, or other vehicle used for transportation while impaired from cannabis use, the potential harms of using cannabis while pregnant or breastfeeding, and the potential harms of overusing cannabis or cannabis products.

Chapter 22. Cannabis Cooperative Associations

ARTICLE 1. DEFINITIONS

Business and Professions Code § 26220

(Added by Stats. 2017, Ch. 27, Sec. 107. (SB 94) Effective June 27, 2017.)

Unless the context otherwise requires, the definitions in this article govern the construction of this chapter.

Business and Professions Code § 26220.1

(Added by Stats. 2017, Ch. 27, Sec. 107. (SB 94) Effective June 27, 2017.)

"Association" means any cannabis cooperative that is organized pursuant to this chapter. An association shall be deemed incorporated pursuant to this chapter, or organized pursuant to this chapter and shall be deemed a cultivator of a cannabis product within the meaning of this chapter, if it is functioning under, or is subject to, the provisions of this chapter, irrespective of whether it was originally incorporated pursuant to those provisions or was incorporated under other provisions.

Business and Professions Code § 26220.2

(Added by Stats. 2017, Ch. 27, Sec. 107. (SB 94) Effective June 27, 2017.)

"Member" includes members of associations without capital stock and holders of common stock in associations that are organized with shares of stock.

Business and Professions Code § 26220.3

(Added by Stats. 2017, Ch. 27, Sec. 107. (SB 94) Effective June 27, 2017.)

"Cannabis product" includes any cannabis associated with a licensed cultivator.

ARTICLE 2. GENERAL PROVISIONS

Business and Professions Code § 26222

(Added by Stats. 2017, Ch. 27, Sec. 107. (SB 94) Effective June 27, 2017.)

The purpose of this chapter is to do all of the following:

(a) Promote, foster, and encourage the intelligent and orderly marketing of cannabis product through cooperation.

(b) Eliminate speculation and waste.

(c) Make the distribution of cannabis product as direct as can be efficiently done.

(d) Stabilize the marketing of cannabis product.

(e) Satisfy the conditions of Section 26052.

Business and Professions Code § 26222.1

(Added by Stats. 2017, Ch. 27, Sec. 107. (SB 94) Effective June 27, 2017.)

An exemption under law that applies to a cannabis product in the possession, or under the control, of the individual cultivator, shall apply similarly and completely to the cannabis product that is delivered by its cultivator members that are in the possession, or under the control, of the association.

Business and Professions Code § 26222.2

(Added by Stats. 2017, Ch. 27, Sec. 107. (SB 94) Effective June 27, 2017.)

A person, firm, corporation, or association, that is hereafter organized or doing business in this state, may not use the word "cannabis cooperative" as part of its corporate name or other business name or title for producers' cooperative marketing activities, unless it has complied with this chapter.

Business and Professions Code § 26222.3

(Added by Stats. 2017, Ch. 27, Sec. 107. (SB 94) Effective June 27, 2017.)

An association that is organized pursuant to this chapter shall not conspire in restraint of trade, or serve as an illegal monopoly, attempt to lessen competition, or to fix prices in violation of law of this state.

Business and Professions Code § 26222.4

(Added by Stats. 2017, Ch. 27, Sec. 107. (SB 94) Effective June 27, 2017.)

The marketing contracts and agreements between an association that is organized pursuant to this chapter and its members and any agreements authorized in this chapter shall not result in restraint of trade, or violation of law of this state.

Business and Professions Code § 26222.5

(Added by Stats. 2017, Ch. 27, Sec. 107. (SB 94) Effective June 27, 2017.)

The General Corporation Law (Division 1 (commencing with Section 100) of Title 1 of the Corporations Code) applies to each association that is organized pursuant to this chapter, except where those provisions are in conflict with or inconsistent with the express provisions of this chapter. For the purpose of associations organized without shares of stock, the members shall be deemed to be "shareholders" as the term is used in the General Corporation Law.

Business and Professions Code § 26222.6

(Added by Stats. 2017, Ch. 27, Sec. 107. (SB 94) Effective June 27, 2017.)

(a) Except as provided in subdivision (c), Chapter 7 (commencing with Section 1500) of Title 10 of Part 3 of the Code of Civil Procedure does not apply to a proprietary interest in an association organized in accordance with this chapter. A proprietary interest that would otherwise escheat to the state pursuant to Chapter 7 (commencing with Section 1500) of Title 10 of Part 3 of the Code of Civil Procedure shall instead become the property of the association.

(b) Notwithstanding subdivision (a), no proprietary interest shall become the property of the association under this section unless all of the following requirements are satisfied:

(1) At least 60 days' prior notice of the proposed transfer of the proprietary interest to the association is given to the affected member by first-class or certified mail to the last address of the member shown on the association's records, and by publication in a newspaper of general circulation in the county in which the member last resided as shown on the association's records. Notice given pursuant to this paragraph constitutes actual notice.

(2) No written notice objecting to the transfer is received by the association from the affected member or, if the member is deceased, from the member's heirs or the executor or executrix of the estate, prior to the date of the proposed transfer.

(c) "Proprietary interest" means and includes any membership, membership certificate, membership share, share certificate, or equity or dividend certificate of any class representing a proprietary interest in, and issued by, the association together with all accrued and unpaid earnings, dividends, and patronage distributions relating thereto.

ARTICLE 3. PURPOSES

Business and Professions Code § 26223

(Amended by Stats. 2021, Ch. 70, Sec. 90. (AB 141) Effective July 12, 2021.)

(a) Three or more natural persons, who are engaged in the cultivation of any cannabis product, may form an association pursuant to this chapter for the purpose of engaging in any activity in connection with any of the following:

(1) The cultivation, marketing, or selling of the cannabis products of its members.

(2) The growing, harvesting, curing, drying, trimming, packing, grading, storing, or handling of any product of its members.

(3) The manufacturing, selling, or supplying to its members of machinery, equipment, or supplies.

(4) The financing of the activities that are specified by this section.

(b) Members of a cannabis cooperative shall be disclosed to the department before the application is processed.

(c) Members of a cannabis cooperative formed pursuant to this chapter shall be limited to cultivators who only hold a single Type 1 or Type 2 license.

(d) Collectively, members of a cannabis cooperative shall not grow more than four acres of total canopy size of cultivation throughout the state during the period that the respective licensees are valid.

(e) No member of a cooperative formed pursuant to this section shall be licensed to operate a cannabis business in another state or country.

ARTICLE 4. ARTICLES OF INCORPORATION

Business and Professions Code § 26224

(Added by Stats. 2017, Ch. 27, Sec. 107. (SB 94) Effective June 27, 2017.)

The articles of incorporation of an association shall show that the signers of the articles of incorporation are engaged in the cultivation of cannabis products, and that they propose to incorporate an association pursuant to this chapter, and shall state all of the following:

(a) The name of the association.

(b) The purposes for which it is formed.

(c) The city, county, or city and county where the principal office for the transaction of business of the association is to be located.

(d) The number of directors of the association, which shall not be less than three, and the names and addresses of the persons who are to serve as first directors. If it is desired that the first directors shall serve for terms of different lengths, the term for which each person so named to serve shall also be stated.

(e) If organized without shares of stock, whether the voting power and the property rights and interest of each member are equal or unequal. If voting power and property rights and interest of each member are unequal, the general rule or rules that are applicable to all members by which the voting power and the property rights and interests, respectively, of each member may be and are determined and fixed shall also be stated.

(f) (1) If organized with shares of stock, the number of shares that may be issued and if the shares are to have a par value, the par value of each share, and the aggregate par value of all shares. If the shares are to be without par value, it shall be so stated.

(2) If the shares of stock are to be classified, a description of the classes of shares and a statement of the number of shares of each kind or class and the nature and extent of the preferences, rights, privileges, and restrictions that are granted to or imposed upon the holders of the respective classes of stock. Except as to the matters and things so stated, no distinction shall exist between the classes of stock or the holders of them. One class of stock shall always be known as common stock, and voting power may be restricted to holders of common stock.

Business and Professions Code § 26224.1

(Added by Stats. 2017, Ch. 27, Sec. 107. (SB 94) Effective June 27, 2017.)

Articles of incorporation shall be signed, acknowledged, and filed in the manner that is prescribed by the general laws of this state for domestic corporations.

Business and Professions Code § 26224.2

(Added by Stats. 2017, Ch. 27, Sec. 107. (SB 94) Effective June 27, 2017.)

The articles of incorporation of any association may be amended in the manner and for the purposes which are authorized by the General Corporation Law, Division 1 (commencing with Section 100) of Title 1 of the Corporations Code.

ARTICLE 5. BYLAWS

Business and Professions Code § 26225

(Added by Stats. 2017, Ch. 27, Sec. 107. (SB 94) Effective June 27, 2017.)

Each association shall, within 30 days after its incorporation, adopt for its government and management, a code of bylaws, consistent with this chapter. The vote or written assent of shareholders or members that hold at least a majority of the voting power is necessary to adopt the bylaws and is effectual to repeal or amend a bylaw, or to adopt an additional bylaw. The power to repeal and amend the bylaws, and adopt new bylaws, may, by a similar vote, or similar written assent, be delegated to the board of directors, which authority may, by a similar vote, or similar written assent, be revoked.

Business and Professions Code § 26225.1

(Added by Stats. 2017, Ch. 27, Sec. 107. (SB 94) Effective June 27, 2017.)

The bylaws may prescribe the time, place, and manner of calling and conducting its meetings. Meetings of members or stockholders shall be held at the place as provided in the bylaws, or, if no provision is made, in the city, county, or city and county where the principal place of business is located at a place designated by the board of directors. Meetings of the board of directors may be held at any place within or without the state that is fixed by a quorum of the board of directors unless otherwise provided in the articles of incorporation or bylaws.

Business and Professions Code § 26225.2

(Added by Stats. 2017, Ch. 27, Sec. 107. (SB 94) Effective June 27, 2017.)

The bylaws may prescribe the number of stockholders, directors, or members that constitutes a quorum.

Business and Professions Code § 26225.3

(Added by Stats. 2017, Ch. 27, Sec. 107. (SB 94) Effective June 27, 2017.)

The bylaws may prescribe the following:

(a) The right of members or stockholders to vote by proxy or by mail or both, and the conditions, manner, form, and effects of those votes.

(b) The right of members or stockholders to cumulate their votes and the prohibition, if any, of cumulative voting.

Business and Professions Code § 26225.4

(Added by Stats. 2017, Ch. 27, Sec. 107. (SB 94) Effective June 27, 2017.)

(a) The bylaws may prescribe the qualifications, compensation, duties, and term of office of directors and officers and the time of their election.

(b) The number of directors set forth in the articles of incorporation shall be either a fixed number or a variable number. If a fixed number, it shall not be less than three, and if a variable number, the stated minimum shall not be less than three and the stated maximum shall not be greater than two times the stated minimum minus one.

(c) The number of directors may also be set forth in the bylaws either as a fixed number or as a variable number subject to the same limitations as in subdivision (b). After shares have been issued or members have been admitted, any adoption or amendment of the bylaw provision shall be approved by the outstanding shares as provided in Section 152 of the Corporations Code.

(d) In the event of an inconsistency between an article provision referred to in subdivision (b) and a bylaw provision referred to in subdivision (c), the provision more recently adopted or amended shall prevail.

(e) If a variable number of directors is set forth in the articles of incorporation or the bylaws, the exact number of directors shall be fixed, within the limits specified, by approval of the board of directors or the shareholders as provided in Section 153 of the Corporations Code in the manner designated in the bylaws.

Business and Professions Code § 26225.5

(Added by Stats. 2017, Ch. 27, Sec. 107. (SB 94) Effective June 27, 2017.)

The bylaws may prescribe penalties for violations of the bylaws.

Business and Professions Code § 26225.6

(Added by Stats. 2017, Ch. 27, Sec. 107. (SB 94) Effective June 27, 2017.)

The bylaws may prescribe the amount of entrance, organization, and membership fees, if any, the manner and method of collection of the fees, and the purposes for which they may be used.

Business and Professions Code § 26225.7

(Added by Stats. 2017, Ch. 27, Sec. 107. (SB 94) Effective June 27, 2017.)

The bylaws may prescribe the amount that each member or stockholder shall be required to pay annually, or from time to time, if at all, to carry on the business of the association, the charge, if any, to be paid by each member or stockholder for services that are rendered by the association to him, the time of payment and the manner of collection, and the marketing contract between the association and its members or stockholders that every member or stockholder may be required to sign.

Business and Professions Code § 26225.8

(Added by Stats. 2017, Ch. 27, Sec. 107. (SB 94) Effective June 27, 2017.)

The bylaws may prescribe the amount of dividends, if any, that may be declared on the stock or membership capital. To the extent that dividends are payable out of the excess of association income over association expenses attributable to business transacted with or for members, dividends shall not exceed 8 percent per annum.

Business and Professions Code § 26225.9

(Added by Stats. 2017, Ch. 27, Sec. 107. (SB 94) Effective June 27, 2017.)

The bylaws may prescribe any of the following:

(a) The number and qualification of members or stockholders of the association and the conditions precedent to membership or ownership of common stock.

(b) The method, time, and manner of permitting members to withdraw or the holders of common stock to transfer their stock.

(c) The manner of assignment and transfer of the interest of members, and of the shares of common stock.

(d) The conditions under which, and time when, membership of a member shall cease.

(e) The automatic suspension of the rights of a member when he or she ceases to be eligible to membership in the association.

(f) The mode, manner, and effect of the expulsion of a member.

Business and Professions Code § 26225.95

(Added by Stats. 2017, Ch. 27, Sec. 107. (SB 94) Effective June 27, 2017.)

(a) The bylaws may prescribe any of the following:

(1) The manner of determining the value of a member's interest and provision for its purchase by the association upon the death or withdrawal of a member or upon the expulsion of a member or forfeiture of his or her membership, or at the option of the association, the purchase at a price fixed by conclusive appraisal by the board of directors.

(2) The conditions and terms for the repurchase by the association from its stockholders of their stock upon their disqualification as stockholders.

(b) If a member is expelled and the bylaws do not provide any procedure or penalty for expulsion, the board of directors shall equitably and conclusively appraise his or her property interest in the association and shall fix the amount of his or her property interest in money, which shall be paid to him or her within one year after such expulsion.

ARTICLE 6. DIRECTORS AND MANAGEMENT

Business and Professions Code § 26226

(Added by Stats. 2017, Ch. 27, Sec. 107. (SB 94) Effective June 27, 2017.)

The affairs of the association shall be managed by a board of not less than three directors who are elected by the members or stockholders.

Business and Professions Code § 26226.1

(Added by Stats. 2017, Ch. 27, Sec. 107. (SB 94) Effective June 27, 2017.)

The bylaws may provide that the territory in which the association has members shall be divided into districts and that directors shall be elected from the several districts. If the bylaws divides the territory into districts for the election of directors, the bylaws shall specify the number of directors to be elected by each district and the manner and method of reapportioning the directors and of redistricting the territory covered by the association.

Business and Professions Code § 26226.2

(Added by Stats. 2017, Ch. 27, Sec. 107. (SB 94) Effective June 27, 2017.)

The bylaws may provide that primary elections shall be held to nominate directors. If the bylaws provide that the territory in which the association has members shall be divided into districts, the bylaws may also provide that the results of the primary elections in the various districts shall be final and shall be ratified at the annual meeting of the association.

Business and Professions Code § 26226.3

(Added by Stats. 2017, Ch. 27, Sec. 107. (SB 94) Effective June 27, 2017.)

The bylaws may provide that the territory in which the association has members shall be divided into districts, and that the directors shall be elected by representatives or advisers, who themselves have been elected by the members or stockholders from the several territorial districts. If the bylaws divide the territory into districts for the election of representatives or advisers who elect the directors, the bylaws shall specify the number of representatives or advisers to be elected by each district and the manner and method of reapportioning the representatives or advisers and of redistricting the territory that is covered by the association.

Business and Professions Code § 26226.4

(Added by Stats. 2017, Ch. 27, Sec. 107. (SB 94) Effective June 27, 2017.)

The bylaws may provide that one or more directors may be chosen by a public official or commission or by the other directors selected by the members. The director shall represent primarily the interest of the general public in the association. The director shall have the same powers and rights as other directors. These directors shall not number more than one-fifth of the entire number of directors.

Business and Professions Code § 26226.5

(Added by Stats. 2017, Ch. 27, Sec. 107. (SB 94) Effective June 27, 2017.)

The bylaws may provide for an executive committee and may allot to the committee all the functions and powers of the board of directors, subject to the general direction and control of the board.

Business and Professions Code § 26226.6

(Added by Stats. 2017, Ch. 27, Sec. 107. (SB 94) Effective June 27, 2017.)

An association may provide a fair remuneration for the time that is actually spent by its officers and directors in its service and for the service of the members of its executive committee.

Business and Professions Code § 26226.7

(Added by Stats. 2017, Ch. 27, Sec. 107. (SB 94) Effective June 27, 2017.)

If a vacancy on the board of directors occurs, except by expiration of term, the remaining members of the board, by a majority vote, shall fill the vacancy, unless the bylaws provide for an election of directors by districts. If the bylaws provide for an election of directors by districts, the vacancy shall be filled either by the election of a director from the district in which the vacancy occurs or by the board of directors calling a special meeting of the members or stockholders in that district to fill the vacancy.

Business and Professions Code § 26226.8

(Added by Stats. 2017, Ch. 27, Sec. 107. (SB 94) Effective June 27, 2017.)

(a) The directors shall elect a president, one or more vice presidents, a secretary, a treasurer, and such other officers as may be prescribed by the bylaws. Any two or more offices, except those of president and secretary, may be held by the same person.

(b) The treasurer may be a bank or a depository and, as such, shall not be considered as an officer, but as a function of the board of directors. In such case, the secretary shall perform the usual accounting duties of the treasurer, except that the funds shall be deposited only as and where authorized by the board of directors.

Business and Professions Code § 26226.9

(Added by Stats. 2017, Ch. 27, Sec. 107. (SB 94) Effective June 27, 2017.)

(a) A member may bring charges against an officer or director by filing them in writing with the secretary of the association, together with a petition that is signed by 5 percent of the members, which requests the removal of the officer or director in question. The removal shall be voted upon at the next regular or special meeting of the association and, by a vote of a majority of the members, the association may remove the officer or director and fill the vacancy. The director or officer, against whom the charges have been brought, shall be informed in writing of the charges previous to the meeting and shall have an opportunity at the meeting to be heard in person or by counsel and to present witnesses. The person bringing the charges against him or her shall have the same opportunity.

(b) If the bylaws provide for election of directors by districts with primary elections in each district, the petition for removal of a director shall be signed by 20 percent of the members that reside in the district from which the director was elected. The board of directors shall call a special meeting of the members who reside in that district to consider the removal of the director. By a vote of the majority of the members of that district at the special meeting, the director in question shall be removed from office.

ARTICLE 7. POWERS

Business and Professions Code § 26227

(Added by Stats. 2017, Ch. 27, Sec. 107. (SB 94) Effective June 27, 2017.)

An association may engage in any activity in connection with the growing, harvesting, curing, drying, trimming, packing, grading, storing, or handling of any cannabis product that is produced or delivered to it by its members; or any activity in connection with the purchase, hiring, or use by its members of supplies, machinery, or equipment, or in the financing of any such activities; or in any one or more of the activities that are specified in this section with a valid license.

Business and Professions Code § 26227.1

(Added by Stats. 2017, Ch. 27, Sec. 107. (SB 94) Effective June 27, 2017.)

An association may borrow without limitation as to the amount of corporate indebtedness or liability and may make advances to members.

Business and Professions Code § 26227.2

(Added by Stats. 2017, Ch. 27, Sec. 107. (SB 94) Effective June 27, 2017.)

An association may act as the agent or representative of any member or members in any of the activities specified in Section 26226.2 or 26226.3.

Business and Professions Code § 26227.3

(Added by Stats. 2017, Ch. 27, Sec. 107. (SB 94) Effective June 27, 2017.)

An association may purchase or otherwise acquire, hold, own, and exercise all rights of ownership in, sell, transfer, pledge, or guarantee the payment of dividends or interest on, or the retirement or redemption of, shares of the capital stock or bonds of an association that is engaged in any related activity or in the growing, harvesting, curing, drying, trimming, packing, grading, storing, or handling of a cannabis product that is handled by the association.

Business and Professions Code § 26227.4

(Added by Stats. 2017, Ch. 27, Sec. 107. (SB 94) Effective June 27, 2017.)

An association may establish reserves and invest the funds of the reserves in bonds or in other property as may be provided in the bylaws.

Business and Professions Code § 26227.5

(Added by Stats. 2017, Ch. 27, Sec. 107. (SB 94) Effective June 27, 2017.)

An association may buy, hold, and exercise all privileges of ownership over such real or personal property as may be necessary or convenient for the conduct and operation of, or incidental to, the business of the association.

Business and Professions Code § 26227.6

(Added by Stats. 2017, Ch. 27, Sec. 107. (SB 94) Effective June 27, 2017.)

An association may levy assessments in the manner and in the amount as may be provided in its bylaws.

Business and Professions Code § 26227.7

(Added by Stats. 2017, Ch. 27, Sec. 107. (SB 94) Effective June 27, 2017.)

An association may do any of the following anywhere:

(a) That which is what is necessary, suitable, or proper for the accomplishment of a purpose, or the attainment of an object, that is enumerated in this article.

(b) That which is conducive to, or expedient for, the interest or benefit of the association.

(c) Contract accordingly.

(d) Exercise and possess all powers, rights, and privileges that are necessary or incidental to the purposes for which the association is organized or to the activities in which it is engaged.

(e) Exercise any other rights, powers, and privileges that are granted by the laws of this state to ordinary corporations, except such as are inconsistent with the express provisions of this chapter.

Business and Professions Code § 26227.75

(Added by Stats. 2017, Ch. 27, Sec. 107. (SB 94) Effective June 27, 2017.)

An association may use or employ any of its facilities for any purpose, provided the proceeds that arise from such use and employment shall go to reduce the cost of operation for its members. The cannabis products that are handled for, or the services, machinery, equipment, or supplies or facilities that are furnished to, nonmembers shall not, however, exceed in value the cannabis products that are handled for, or the services, merchandise, or facilities that are supplied to, members during the same period.

Business and Professions Code § 26227.8

(Added by Stats. 2017, Ch. 27, Sec. 107. (SB 94) Effective June 27, 2017.)

(a) An association may organize, form, operate, own, control, have an interest in, own stock of, or be a member of any other association, with or without capital stock, that is engaged in growing, harvesting, curing, drying, trimming, packing, grading, storing, or handling of any cannabis product that is handled by the association, or the byproducts of the cannabis product.

(b) Any two or more associations that are organized pursuant to this section may be merged into one constituent association or consolidated into a new association. The merger or consolidation shall be made in the manner that is prescribed by the general laws of the state that cover domestic corporations.

Business and Professions Code § 26227.9

(Amended by Stats. 2017, Ch. 253, Sec. 12. (AB 133) Effective September 16, 2017.)

(a) Any association may, upon resolution adopted by its board of directors, enter into all necessary and proper contracts and agreements and make all necessary and proper stipulations and arrangements with another cannabis cooperative or association that is formed in this state for the cannabis cooperative and more economical carrying on of its business or any part of its business.

(b) Any two or more associations may, by agreement between them, unite in employing and using, or may separately employ and use, the same personnel, methods, means, and agencies for carrying on and conducting their respective business.

ARTICLE 8. FINANCIAL PROVISIONS

Business and Professions Code § 26228

(Added by Stats. 2017, Ch. 27, Sec. 107. (SB 94) Effective June 27, 2017.)

An association is not subject in any manner to the terms of the Corporate Securities Law (Division 1 (commencing with Section 25000) of Title 4 of the Corporations Code), and any association may issue its membership certificates or stock or other securities as provided in this chapter without the necessity of any qualification under that law.

Business and Professions Code § 26228.1

(Added by Stats. 2017, Ch. 27, Sec. 107. (SB 94) Effective June 27, 2017.)

If an association issues nonpar value stock, the issuance of the stock shall be governed by the terms of all general laws that cover the issuance of nonpar value stock in domestic corporations.

Business and Professions Code § 26228.2

(Added by Stats. 2017, Ch. 27, Sec. 107. (SB 94) Effective June 27, 2017.)

If an association with preferred shares of stock purchases the stock or any property, or any interest in any property of any person, it may discharge the obligations that are so incurred, wholly or in part, by exchanging for the acquired interest, shares of its preferred stock to an amount that at par value would equal the fair market value of the stock or interest so purchased, as determined by the board of directors. In that case, the transfer to the association of the stock or interest that is purchased is equivalent to payment in cash for the shares of stock that are issued.

Business and Professions Code § 26228.3

(Added by Stats. 2017, Ch. 27, Sec. 107. (SB 94) Effective June 27, 2017.)

The board of directors of every association shall cause to be sent to the members of the association not later than 120 days after the close of the fiscal or calendar year an annual report of the operations of the association, unless the report is expressly dispensed with in the bylaws. If required by the bylaws, interim reports of the operations of the association for the three-month, six-month, or nine-month periods of the current fiscal year of the association shall be furnished to the members of the association. Such annual report and any such interim reports shall include a balance sheet as of such closing date. Such financial statement shall be prepared from, and be in accordance with, the books. It shall be prepared in a form that is sanctioned by sound accounting practice for the association or approved by a duly certified public accountant or a public accountant.

ARTICLE 9. MEMBERS

Business and Professions Code § 26229

(Added by Stats. 2017, Ch. 27, Sec. 107. (SB 94) Effective June 27, 2017.)

Under the terms and conditions that are prescribed in the bylaws adopted by it, an association may admit as members or issue common stock only to persons engaged in the cultivation of a cannabis product that is to be handled by or through the association.

Business and Professions Code § 26229.1

(Added by Stats. 2017, Ch. 27, Sec. 107. (SB 94) Effective June 27, 2017.)

If a member of a nonstock association is other than a natural person, the member may be represented by any individual, associate, officer, or manager or member of it, who is duly authorized in writing.

Business and Professions Code § 26229.2

(Added by Stats. 2017, Ch. 27, Sec. 107. (SB 94) Effective June 27, 2017.)

Any association may become a member or stockholder of any other association.

Business and Professions Code § 26229.3

(Added by Stats. 2017, Ch. 27, Sec. 107. (SB 94) Effective June 27, 2017.)

If a member of an association that is established without shares of stock has paid his membership fee in full, he or she shall receive a certificate of membership.

Business and Professions Code § 26229.4

(Added by Stats. 2017, Ch. 27, Sec. 107. (SB 94) Effective June 27, 2017.)

An association shall not issue a certificate for stock to a member until it has been fully paid for. The promissory notes of the members may be accepted by the association as full or partial payment. The association shall hold the stock as security for the payment of the note, but the retention as security does not affect the member's right to vote.

Business and Professions Code § 26229.5

(Added by Stats. 2017, Ch. 27, Sec. 107. (SB 94) Effective June 27, 2017.)

An association, in its bylaws, may limit the amount of common stock that any member may own.

Business and Professions Code § 26229.6

(Added by Stats. 2017, Ch. 27, Sec. 107. (SB 94) Effective June 27, 2017.)

The bylaws shall prohibit the transfer of the common stock or membership certificates of the associations to a person that is not qualified to be a shareholder or member as specified in this chapter. These restrictions shall be printed upon every certificate of stock or membership that is subject to them.

Business and Professions Code § 26229.7

(Added by Stats. 2017, Ch. 27, Sec. 107. (SB 94) Effective June 27, 2017.)

The association may, at any time, as specified in the bylaws, except when the debts of the association exceed 50 percent of its assets, buy in or purchase its common stock at the book value of the common stock, as conclusively determined by the board of directors, and pay for it in cash within one year thereafter.

Business and Professions Code § 26229.8

(Added by Stats. 2017, Ch. 27, Sec. 107. (SB 94) Effective June 27, 2017.)

A member or stockholder is not liable for the debts of the association to an amount that exceeds the sum that remains unpaid on his membership fee or his subscription to the capital stock, including any unpaid balance on any promissory note that is given in payment of the membership fee or the subscription to the capital stock.

ARTICLE 10. MARKETING CONTRACTS

Business and Professions Code § 26230

(Added by Stats. 2017, Ch. 27, Sec. 107. (SB 94) Effective June 27, 2017.)

The association and its members may make and execute marketing contracts that require the members to sell, for any period of time, but not over 15 years, all or a specified part of a cannabis product exclusively to or through the association, or a facility that is created by the association. If the members contract a sale to the association, title to the cannabis product passes absolutely and unreservedly, except for recorded liens, to the association upon delivery or at another specified time that is expressly and definitely agreed in the contract.

Business and Professions Code § 26230.1

(Added by Stats. 2017, Ch. 27, Sec. 107. (SB 94) Effective June 27, 2017.)

Notwithstanding any provisions of the Civil Code, a contract that is entered into by a member or stockholder of an association that provides for the delivery to the association of a cannabis product that is produced or acquired by the member or stockholder may be specifically enforced by the association to secure the delivery to it of the cannabis product.

Business and Professions Code § 26230.2

(Added by Stats. 2017, Ch. 27, Sec. 107. (SB 94) Effective June 27, 2017.)

The bylaws or a marketing contract may fix, as liquidated damages, specific sums to be paid by the member or stockholder to the association upon the breach by him or her of any provision of the marketing contract regarding the sale or delivery or withholding of a cannabis product and may provide that the member will pay all costs, premiums for bonds, expenses, and fees, if any action is brought upon the contract by the association. These provisions are valid and enforceable in the courts of this state. The clauses that provide for liquidated damages are enforceable as such and shall not be regarded as penalties.

Business and Professions Code § 26230.3

(Added by Stats. 2017, Ch. 27, Sec. 107. (SB 94) Effective June 27, 2017.)

If there is a breach or threatened breach of a marketing contract by a member, the association shall be entitled to an injunction to prevent the further breach of the contract and to a decree of specific performance of the contract.

Pending the adjudication of the action and upon filing a verified complaint that shows the breach or threatened breach, and upon filing a sufficient bond, the association shall be entitled to a temporary restraining order and preliminary injunction against the member.

ARTICLE 11. REORGANIZATION OF CORPORATIONS ORGANIZED PURSUANT TO OTHER LAWS

Business and Professions Code § 26231

(Amended by Stats. 2018, Ch. 92, Sec. 32. (SB 1289) Effective January 1, 2019.)

A corporation that is organized or existing pursuant to any law except Part 12 (commencing with Section 14550) of Division 3 of Title 1 of the Corporations Code may be brought under the provisions of this chapter by amending its articles of incorporation, in the manner that is prescribed by the general corporation laws, to conform to this chapter. If a corporation amends its articles of incorporation to conform to this chapter, it shall be deemed to be organized and existing pursuant to, and entitled to the benefit of, and subject to this chapter for all purposes and as fully as though it had been originally organized pursuant to this chapter.

Business and Professions Code § 26231.1

(Added by Stats. 2017, Ch. 27, Sec. 107. (SB 94) Effective June 27, 2017.)

Articles of incorporation shall be deemed to conform to this chapter within the meaning of Section 26231 if it clearly appears from the articles of incorporation that the corporation desires to be subject to, and to be organized, exist, and function pursuant to this chapter.

Business and Professions Code § 26231.2

(Added by Stats. 2017, Ch. 27, Sec. 107. (SB 94) Effective June 27, 2017.)

If the amended articles conform, as provided in Section 26231.1, provisions in the articles of incorporation that appeared in the original articles or some previous amended articles, are ineffective if, and to the extent that, they are inapplicable to, or inconsistent with, this chapter.

Chapter 23. The California Cannabis Equity Act

Business and Professions Code § 26240

(Amended by Stats. 2021, Ch. 70, Sec. 91. (AB 141) Effective July 12, 2021.)

For purposes of this chapter, the following definitions apply:

(a) “Eligible local jurisdiction” means a local jurisdiction that demonstrates an intent to develop a local program or that has adopted or operates a local equity program.

(b) “Equity assessment” means an assessment conducted by the local jurisdiction that was used to inform the creation of a local equity program, and that assessment may include the following:

(1) Reference to local historical rates of arrests or convictions for cannabis law violations.

(2) Identification of the impacts that cannabis-related policies have had historically on communities and populations within that local jurisdiction.

(3) Other information that demonstrates how individuals and communities within the local jurisdiction have been disproportionately or negatively impacted by the War on Drugs.

(c) "Local equity applicant" means an applicant who has submitted, or will submit, an application to a local jurisdiction to engage in commercial cannabis activity within the jurisdictional boundaries of that jurisdiction and who meets the requirements of that jurisdiction's local equity program.

(d) "Local equity licensee" means a person who has obtained a license from a local jurisdiction to engage in commercial cannabis activity within the jurisdictional boundaries of that jurisdiction and who meets the requirements of that jurisdiction's local equity program.

(e) "Local equity program" means a program adopted or operated by a local jurisdiction that focuses on inclusion and support of individuals and communities in California's cannabis industry who are linked to populations or neighborhoods that were negatively or disproportionately impacted by cannabis criminalization as evidenced by the local jurisdiction's equity assessment. Local equity programs may include, but are not limited to, the following types of services:

(1) Small business support services offering technical assistance or professional and mentorship services to those persons from economically disadvantaged communities that experience high rates of poverty or communities most harmed by cannabis prohibition, determined by historically high rates of arrests or convictions for cannabis law violations.

(2) Tiered fees or fee waivers for cannabis-related permits and licenses.

(3) Assistance in paying state regulatory and licensing fees.

(4) Assistance securing business locations prior to or during the application process.

(5) Assistance securing capital investments or direct access to capital.

(6) Assistance with regulatory compliance.

(7) Assistance in recruitment, training, and retention of a qualified and diverse workforce, including transitional workers.

(8) Other services deemed by the Governor's Office of Business and Economic Development to be consistent with the intent of this chapter.

(f) "Transitional worker" means a person who, at the time of starting employment at the business premises, resides in a ZIP Code or census track area with higher than average unemployment, crime, or child death rates, and faces at least one of the following barriers to employment: (1) is homeless; (2) is a custodial single parent; (3) is receiving public assistance; (4) lacks a GED or high school diploma; (5) has a criminal record or other involvement with the criminal justice system; (6) suffers from chronic unemployment; (7) is emancipated from the foster care system; (8) is a veteran; or (9) is over 65 years of age and is financially compromised.

Business and Professions Code § 26242

(Amended by Stats. 2021, Ch. 70, Sec. 92. (AB 141) Effective July 12, 2021.)

(a) The department may provide technical assistance to a local equity program that helps local equity applicants or local equity licensees. When determining whether to provide technical assistance, the department shall make individual determinations based on the reasonableness of the request and available resources.

(b) "Technical assistance" includes providing training and educational sessions regarding state cannabis licensing and regulatory processes and requirements to equity applicants or equity licensees that are coordinated with the local equity program.

Business and Professions Code § 26244

(Amended by Stats. 2021, Ch. 70, Sec. 93. (AB 141) Effective July 12, 2021.)

(a) (1) An eligible local jurisdiction may, in the form and manner prescribed by the Governor's Office of Business and Economic Development, submit an application to the Governor's Office of Business and Economic Development for a grant to assist with the development of an equity program or to assist local equity applicants and local equity licensees through that local jurisdiction's equity program.

(2) An eligible local jurisdiction that has a local equity program shall include in its application submitted pursuant to paragraph (1) the equity assessment that was used to inform the creation of the local equity program.

(3) The Governor's Office of Business and Economic Development shall consider the following factors when reviewing an application:

(A) Whether the local jurisdiction is an eligible local jurisdiction.

(B) Whether the local jurisdiction has identified communities and populations within that local jurisdiction that have been disproportionately or negatively impacted by arrests and convictions for cannabis law violations and has demonstrated a nexus between the individuals served through the local equity program and the communities and populations identified by the local jurisdiction.

(C) Whether the local jurisdiction has adopted or operates a local equity program, and, if so, the Governor's Office of Business and Economic Development shall consider the following:

(i) How long the local jurisdiction has operated the program.

(ii) The outcomes of the program.

(D) Whether the local jurisdiction has demonstrated the ability to provide, or created a plan to provide, the services identified in subdivision (b).

(E) Whether the local jurisdiction has demonstrated a financial commitment to the implementation and administration of the program.

(F) Whether the local jurisdiction has demonstrated a commitment to remove, or has taken steps to remove, local barriers to entering the legal cannabis market for local equity applicants and local equity licensees, including, but not limited to, developing a local regulatory framework that facilitates an equitable and economically just industry.

(G) The number of existing and potential local equity applicants and local equity licensees in the local jurisdiction.

(H) Any additional relevant and reasonable criteria the Governor's Office of Business and Economic Development deems necessary.

(4) The Governor's Office of Business and Economic Development shall grant funding to an eligible local jurisdiction based on the eligible local jurisdiction's compliance with paragraph (2), if applicable, and its review of the factors in paragraph (3).

(b) (1) An eligible local jurisdiction that receives a grant pursuant to subdivision (a) shall use grant funds to do either of the following:

(A) Assist the local jurisdiction in the development of a local equity program.

(B) Assist local equity applicants or local equity licensees in that local jurisdiction to gain entry to, and to successfully operate in, the state's regulated cannabis marketplace.

(2) For purposes of this subdivision, "assist" includes, but is not limited to, any of the following methods:

(A) To provide a low-interest or no-interest loan or a grant to a local equity applicant or local equity licensee to assist the applicant or licensee with startup and ongoing costs. For purposes of this paragraph, "startup and ongoing costs" include, but are not limited to, the following:

(i) Rent.

(ii) Leases.

(iii) Local and state application, licensing, and regulatory fees.

(iv) Legal assistance.

(v) Regulatory compliance.

(vi) Testing of cannabis.

(vii) Furniture.

(viii) Fixtures and equipment.

(ix) Capital improvements.

(x) Training and retention of a qualified and diverse workforce.

(B) To support local equity program efforts to provide sources of capital to local equity applicants and local equity licensees.

(C) To provide or fund direct technical assistance to local equity applicants and local equity licensees.

(D) To assist in the development or administration of local equity programs.

(E) To fund the creation of an equity assessment to inform the development of a local equity program.

(c) An eligible local jurisdiction that receives a grant pursuant to subdivision (a) shall, on or before January 1 of the year following receipt of the grant and annually thereafter for each year that grant funds are expended, submit an annual report to the Governor's Office of Business and Economic Development that includes all of the following information:

(1) How the local jurisdiction disbursed grant funds.

(2) How the local jurisdiction identified local equity applicants or local equity licensees, including how the local jurisdiction determines who qualifies as a local equity applicant or local equity licensee.

(3) The number of local equity applicants and local equity licensees that were served by the grant funds.

(4) Aggregate demographic data on equity applicants, equity licensees, and all other applicants and licensees in the jurisdiction, including, but not limited to, race, ethnicity, gender, sexual orientation, income level, education level, prior convictions, and veteran status. This information will be consolidated and reported without the individual's identifying information.

(5) If the local jurisdiction requires equity applicants to become eligible through specific ownership percentages, a breakdown of equity applicants' and equity licensees' business ownership types and percentages of ownership.

(6) Other information that the Governor's Office of Business and Economic Development deems necessary to evaluate the outcomes of the program consistent with the intent of this chapter and that was specified in the grant agreement between the Governor's Office of Business and Economic Development and the local jurisdiction.

(d) An eligible local jurisdiction that receives a grant pursuant to this section shall use no more than 10 percent of the state grant for administration, including employing staff or hiring consultants to administer grants and the program.

(e) The Governor's Office of Business and Economic Development may review, adopt, amend, and repeal guidelines to implement uniform standards, criteria, requirements, or forms that supplement or clarify the terms, references, or standards set forth in this section and Section 26240. The adoption, amendment, or repeal of a guideline, term, or standard authorized by this subdivision is hereby exempted from the rulemaking provisions of the Administrative Procedure Act (Chapter 3.5 (commencing with Section 11340) of Part 1 of Division 3 of Title 2 of the Government Code).

Business and Professions Code § 26246

(Amended by Stats. 2021, Ch. 70, Sec. 94. (AB 141) Effective July 12, 2021.)

(a) To facilitate greater equity in business ownership and employment in the cannabis market, the department shall serve as a point of contact for local equity programs.

(b) On or before January 1, 2022, the Governor's Office of Business and Economic Development shall publish on its internet website local equity ordinances that have been enacted by the legislative body of the respective local jurisdiction, and model local equity ordinances created by advocacy groups and experts. Advocacy groups and experts may include, but are not limited to, minority business owners and entrepreneurs, organizations with expertise in addressing barriers to employment and licensure for low-income communities or persons with prior arrests or convictions, and unions representing cannabis workers.

(c) To the extent feasible, the department and the Governor's Office of Business and Economic Development shall coordinate with the relevant local jurisdictions to carry out the responsibilities described in this section.

Business and Professions Code § 26248

(Amended by Stats. 2021, Ch. 70, Sec. 95. (AB 141) Effective July 12, 2021.)

(a) On or before July 1, 2021, and annually thereafter, the Governor's Office of Business and Economic Development shall submit a report to the Legislature regarding the progress of local equity programs that have received funding pursuant to Section 26244.

(b) The report shall include, but is not limited to, the following information:

(1) The local jurisdictions that have enacted local equity programs.

(2) A copy of the equity assessment and equity program description of each local jurisdiction that applied for grant funding pursuant to Section 26244.

(3) The number of local equity applicants and general applicants applying for and receiving licenses in the jurisdictions that received grants pursuant to Section 26244.

(4) Information collected pursuant to subdivision (c) of Section 26244.

(c) The Governor's Office of Business and Economic Development shall post the report required by this section on its internet website.

(d) The report required by this section shall be submitted in compliance with Section 9795 of the Government Code, and shall apply notwithstanding Section 10231.5 of the Government Code.

Business and Professions Code § 26249

(Amended by Stats. 2021, Ch. 260, Sec. 2. (SB 166) Effective September 23, 2021.)

(a) Notwithstanding Sections 26012 and 26180:

(1) On or before January 1, 2022, the department shall develop and implement a program to provide waivers for application fees, licensing fees, and renewal fees required by this division.

(2) On or before January 1, 2023, the department shall develop and implement a program to provide deferrals for application fees, licensing fees, and renewal fees required by this division.

(b) (1) At least 60 percent of the total dollar amount of deferrals of fees pursuant to the program developed and implemented by the department pursuant to subdivision (a) shall be allocated to the deferral of fees for equity applicants and licensees.

(2) At least 60 percent of the total dollar amount of waivers of fees pursuant to the program developed and implemented by the department pursuant to subdivision (a) shall be allocated to the waiver of fees for equity applicants and licensees.

(c) For purposes of this section, "equity applicants and licensees" means applicants and licensees that demonstrate all of the following:

(1) (A) For applicants and licensees in local jurisdictions with local equity programs, that they are locally verified equity applicants and licensees; or

(B) For applicants and licensees in local jurisdictions without local equity programs, that they are local applicants and licensees.

(2) That they, either individually or in combination with other persons who qualify as equity applicants or licensees pursuant to this section, own no less than 50 percent of the business that is in the process of being licensed or is licensed.

(3) That they satisfy one of the following:

(A) They have previously been convicted of an offense related to the sale, possession, use, manufacture, or cultivation of cannabis, under past criminal justice policies implementing cannabis prohibition.

(B) They have previously been arrested for an offense related to the sale, possession, use, manufacture, or cultivation of cannabis, under past criminal justice policies implementing cannabis prohibition.

(C) Residence in a household with a household income less than or equal to 60 percent of the area median income for the applicable local jurisdiction.

(D) Residence in an area with a population disproportionately impacted by past criminal justice policies implementing cannabis prohibition.

(4) The eligibility for those that qualify pursuant to the criteria listed under subparagraphs (A) to (D), inclusive, of paragraph (3) may be further refined by the department through regulations, including, but not limited to, regulations regarding the following:

(A) Criteria regarding the license or licenses an applicant or licensee may seek or hold.

(B) Criteria regarding the time period or length of time in which an applicant or licensee resided in a low-income household for purposes of subparagraph (C) of paragraph (3), or in an area with a population disproportionately impacted by past criminal justice policies implementing cannabis prohibition for purposes of subparagraph (D) of paragraph (3).

(d) The department may adopt regulations, including emergency regulations to implement this section. The adoption, amendment, repeal, or readoption of a regulation authorized by this section is deemed to address an emergency, for purposes of Sections 11346.1 and 11349.6 of the Government Code, and the department is hereby exempted from the requirements of subdivision (b) of Section 11346.1 of the Government Code.

(e) The operation of this section is contingent upon an appropriation in the annual Budget Act or another statute for purposes of this section.

Business and Professions Code § 26250

(Added by Stats. 2018, Ch. 794, Sec. 3. (SB 1294) Effective January 1, 2019.)

The provisions of this chapter are severable. If any provision of this chapter or its application is held invalid, that invalidity shall not affect other provisions or applications that can be given effect without the invalid provision or application.

Chapter 24. Information Sharing with Financial Institutions

Business and Professions Code § 26260

(Amended by Stats. 2021, Ch. 70, Sec. 97. (AB 141) Effective July 12, 2021.)

(a) An entity that receives deposits, extends credit, conducts fund transfers, transports cash or financial instruments, or provides other financial services does not commit a crime under any California law, including Chapter 10 (commencing with Section 186.9) of Title 7 of Part 1 of the Penal Code, solely by virtue of the fact that the person receiving the benefit of any of those services engages in commercial cannabis activity as a licensee pursuant to this division.

(b) (1) A person licensed to engage in commercial cannabis activity pursuant to this division may request in writing that the department, a local licensing authority, a state or local agency, or a joint powers authority share the person's application, license, and other regulatory and financial information with a financial institution of the person's designation. The person shall include in that written request a waiver authorizing the transfer of that information and waiving any confidentiality or privilege that applies to that information.

(2) Notwithstanding any other law that might proscribe the disclosure of application, licensee, and other regulatory and financial information, upon receipt of a written request and waiver pursuant to paragraph (1), the department, a local licensing authority, a state or local agency, or a joint powers authority may share application, licensee, and other regulatory and financial information with the financial institution designated by the licensee in that request for the purpose of facilitating the provision of financial services for that licensee.

(3) A person who provides a waiver may withdraw that waiver at any time. Upon receipt of the withdrawal, the department, local licensing authority, state or local agency, or joint powers authority shall cease to share application, licensee, or other regulatory or financial information with the financial institution.

(c) For purposes of this section, all of the following definitions apply:

(1) "Application, licensee, and other regulatory and financial information" includes, but is not limited to, information in the track and trace system established pursuant to Sections 26067 and 26068.

(2) “Entity” means a financial institution as defined in this section, an armored car service licensed by the Department of the California Highway Patrol pursuant to Section 2510 of the Vehicle Code that has been contracted by a financial institution, or a person providing financial services to persons licensed to engage in commercial cannabis activity pursuant to this division.

(3) “Financial institutions” means a licensee defined in Section 185 of the Financial Code.

(4) “Firm” has the same meaning as in Section 5035.1.

(5) “Joint powers authority” is one formed pursuant to Chapter 5 (commencing with Section 6500) of Division 7 of Title 1 of the Government Code.

(6) “State or local agency” has the same meaning as in Section 50001 of the Government Code.

(d) An individual or firm, that practices public accounting pursuant to Chapter 1 (commencing with Section 5000) of Division 3, does not commit a crime under California law solely for providing professional accounting services as specified to persons licensed to engage in commercial cannabis activity pursuant to this division.

(e) This section shall be construed to refer only to the disclosure of information by the department, a local licensing authority, a state or local agency, or a joint powers authority reasonably necessary to facilitate the provision of financial services for the licensee making a request pursuant to this section. Nothing in this section shall be construed to authorize the disclosure of confidential or privileged information, nor waive a licensee’s rights to assert confidentiality or privilege, except to a financial institution as provided herein and except as reasonably necessary to facilitate the provision of financial services for the licensee making the request.

Business and Professions Code § 26261

(Added by Stats. 2022, Ch. 393, Sec. 1. (AB 2568) Effective January 1, 2023.)

An individual or firm, that is licensed by the Department of Insurance pursuant to Chapter 5 (commencing with Section 1621), Chapter 6 (commencing with Section 1760), or Chapter 8 (commencing with Section 1831) of Part 2 of Division 1 of the Insurance Code, does not commit a crime under California law solely for providing insurance or related services to persons licensed to engage in commercial cannabis activity pursuant to this division.

Chapter 25. Interstate Cannabis Agreements

ARTICLE 1. DEFINITIONS

Business and Professions Code § 26300

(Added by Stats. 2022, Ch. 396, Sec. 3. (SB 1326) Effective January 1, 2023.)

As used in this chapter, the following definitions apply:

(a) “Agreement” means an agreement relating to commercial cannabis authorized under this chapter and entered into between this state and another state or states.

(b) “Contracting state” means a state of the United States, including a district, commonwealth, territory, or possession subject to the legislative authority of the United States, with which the Governor has entered into an agreement pursuant to this chapter.

(c) “Foreign license” means a commercial cannabis license issued under the laws of another state that has entered into an agreement pursuant to this chapter.

(d) "State license" means a commercial cannabis license issued by a licensing authority pursuant to this division.

ARTICLE 2. AGREEMENTS

Business and Professions Code § 26301

(Added by Stats. 2022, Ch. 396, Sec. 3. (SB 1326) Effective January 1, 2023.)

(a) The Governor may enter into an agreement with another state or states authorizing medicinal or adult-use commercial cannabis activity, or both, between entities licensed under the laws of the contracting state and entities operating with a state license, provided that both of the following criteria are met:

(1) The commercial cannabis activities are lawful and subject to licensure under the laws of the contracting state.

(2) With respect to the interstate transportation of cannabis or cannabis products, the agreement prohibits both of the following:

(A) The transportation of cannabis and cannabis products by any means other than those authorized under both the laws of the contracting state and the regulations of the department.

(B) The transportation of cannabis and cannabis products through the jurisdiction of a state, district, commonwealth, territory, or possession of the United States that does not authorize that transportation.

(b) Notwithstanding any other law, the execution of, and compliance with the terms of, an agreement does not constitute a project for purposes of the California Environmental Quality Act (Division 13 (commencing with Section 21000) of the Public Resources Code).

Business and Professions Code § 26302

(Added by Stats. 2022, Ch. 396, Sec. 3. (SB 1326) Effective January 1, 2023.)

(a) Notwithstanding any other law, a foreign licensee may engage in commercial cannabis activity with a state licensee and a state licensee may engage in commercial cannabis activity with a foreign licensee, subject to the requirements and limitations set forth in this chapter.

(b) A foreign licensee shall not engage in commercial cannabis activity within the boundaries of this state without a state license, or engage in commercial cannabis activity within a local jurisdiction without a license, permit, or other authorization issued by the local jurisdiction.

(c) A foreign licensee shall be subject to the jurisdiction of this state for the purpose of actions taken for violation of California commercial cannabis laws and regulations.

Business and Professions Code § 26303

(Added by Stats. 2022, Ch. 396, Sec. 3. (SB 1326) Effective January 1, 2023.)

(a) An agreement shall require that the contracting state impose requirements on foreign licensees with regard to cannabis and cannabis products to be sold or otherwise transferred or distributed within this state that meet or exceed the requirements applicable to state licensees, including all of the following:

(1) Enforceable public health and safety standards that are equivalent to the requirements of this division.

(2) Mandatory participation in a system administered by the state to regulate and track the cultivation, manufacturing, distribution, transportation, sale, and destruction of cannabis and cannabis products from seed to sale.

(3) Standards for the testing of cannabis or cannabis products that meet or exceed the standards applicable to testing laboratories licensed under this division.

(4) Requirements for the packaging and labeling of cannabis and cannabis products that meet or exceed the packaging and labeling requirements established pursuant to Chapter 12 (commencing with Section 26120).

(5) Requirements for quality assurance and inspection of cannabis or cannabis products that meet or exceed the requirements applicable to cannabis or cannabis products cultivated, manufactured, or sold by state licensees.

(6) Restrictions on marketing, labeling, and advertising within this state by foreign licensees that meet or exceed the restrictions on state licensees established in Section 26063 and Chapter 15 (commencing with Section 26150).

(7) A process for the identification of adulterated or misbranded cannabis products, and the destruction of those products, using standards that meet or exceed the standards and procedures established pursuant to this division.

(b) An agreement shall require that the contracting state impose restrictions upon advertising, marketing, labeling, or sale within the contracting state that meet or exceed the restrictions established in Section 26063.

Business and Professions Code § 26304

(Added by Stats. 2022, Ch. 396, Sec. 3. (SB 1326) Effective January 1, 2023.)

(a) An agreement shall include provisions requiring the department and the appropriate regulatory authorities of the contracting state to address public health and welfare emergencies concerning cannabis or cannabis products that are sold or intended for sale within this state, including for the prompt recall or embargo of adulterated or misbranded cannabis or cannabis products.

(b) An agreement shall include provisions requiring the appropriate regulatory authorities of each state to investigate instances of alleged noncompliance with the commercial cannabis regulatory programs upon request by the other state and in accordance with mutually agreed-upon procedures. An agreement shall include provisions requiring the contracting state to reasonably cooperate with California investigations concerning foreign licensees, and requiring the department to reasonably cooperate with investigations by the contracting state concerning persons or entities holding state licenses.

Business and Professions Code § 26305

(Added by Stats. 2022, Ch. 396, Sec. 3. (SB 1326) Effective January 1, 2023.)

An agreement shall include provisions determined by the Governor to promote the inclusion and support of individuals and communities in the cannabis industry who are linked to populations or neighborhoods that were negatively or disproportionately impacted by cannabis criminalization.

Business and Professions Code § 26306

(Added by Stats. 2022, Ch. 396, Sec. 3. (SB 1326) Effective January 1, 2023.)

An agreement shall provide for collection of all applicable taxes.

Business and Professions Code § 26307

(Added by Stats. 2022, Ch. 396, Sec. 3. (SB 1326) Effective January 1, 2023.)

The Governor is exempt from the rulemaking procedures and requirements of the Administrative Procedure Act (Chapter 3.5 (commencing with Section 11340) of Part 1 of Division 3 of Title 2 of the Government Code) when entering into agreements or amendments to agreements, provided that prior to execution of an agreement or amendment to an agreement, the Governor shall do both of the following:

(a) Submit the proposed agreement or amendment to the Joint Legislative Budget Committee for review and comment. The committee shall have 60 days to review the proposed agreement or amendment and to submit written recommendations to the Governor. The committee shall only submit a recommendation to the Governor if a majority of the members agree to that recommendation. The Governor shall consider all recommendations submitted by the committee and may revise the proposed agreement or amendment to incorporate the recommendations. If the Governor does not incorporate any recommendation submitted by the committee, the Governor shall set forth, in writing, the reasons for not incorporating that recommendation.

(b) Post the proposed agreement or amendment on the department's internet website for public comment for 30 days. The comments received shall be considered by the Governor.

Business and Professions Code § 26308

(Added by Stats. 2022, Ch. 396, Sec. 3. (SB 1326) Effective January 1, 2023.)

(a) An agreement entered into pursuant to this chapter shall not take effect unless one of the following occurs:

(1) Federal law is amended to allow for the interstate transfer of cannabis or cannabis products between authorized commercial cannabis businesses.

(2) Federal law is enacted that specifically prohibits the expenditure of federal funds to prevent the interstate transfer of cannabis or cannabis products between authorized commercial cannabis businesses.

(3) The United States Department of Justice issues an opinion or memorandum allowing or tolerating the interstate transfer of cannabis or cannabis products between authorized commercial cannabis businesses.

(4) The Attorney General issues a written opinion, through the process established pursuant to Section 12519 of the Government Code, that state law authorization, under an agreement pursuant to this chapter, for medicinal or adult-use commercial cannabis activity, or both, between foreign licensees and state licensees will not result in significant legal risk to the State of California under the federal Controlled Substances Act, based on review of applicable law, including federal judicial decisions and administrative actions.

(b) The department shall notify the Governor and the appropriate policy committees of the Legislature upon the occurrence of an event described in subdivision (a), and shall post the notification on the department's internet website.

Chapter 26. Medicinal Cannabis Patients' Right of Access Act

Business and Professions Code § 26320

(Added by Stats. 2022, Ch. 395, Sec. 2. (SB 1186) Effective January 1, 2023.)

The Legislature finds and declares as follows:

(a) Access to medicinal cannabis is an integral aspect of access to health care, and eliminating barriers to medicinal cannabis access is essential to promoting and preserving the health of Californians for whom physicians have recommended the use of cannabis or cannabis products.

(b) It is the policy of the state and the intent of the Legislature to ensure that Californians throughout the state have timely and convenient access to safe, effective, and affordable medicinal cannabis.

Business and Professions Code § 26321

(Added by Stats. 2022, Ch. 395, Sec. 2. (SB 1186) Effective January 1, 2023.)

(a) This act shall be known, and may be cited, as the Medicinal Cannabis Patients' Right of Access Act.

(b) For purposes of this chapter:

(1) "Medicinal cannabis" means medicinal cannabis or medicinal cannabis products, as those terms are defined in paragraph (1) of subdivision (ai) of Section 26001.

(2) "Medicinal cannabis business" means a retailer authorized to engage in the retail sale by delivery of medicinal cannabis to medicinal cannabis patients pursuant to an M-license.

(3) "Medicinal cannabis patient" means a qualified patient, as defined in Section 11362.7 of the Health and Safety Code, who possesses a physician's recommendation that complies with Article 25 (commencing with Section 2525) of Chapter 5 of Division 2, or a qualified patient or primary caregiver for a qualified patient issued a valid identification card pursuant to Section 11362.71 of the Health and Safety Code.

(4) "Regulation" means a local ordinance, regulation, policy, or practice.

Business and Professions Code § 26322

(Added by Stats. 2022, Ch. 395, Sec. 2. (SB 1186) Effective January 1, 2023. Operative January 1, 2024, by its own provisions.)

(a) A local jurisdiction shall not adopt or enforce any regulation that prohibits the retail sale by delivery within the local jurisdiction of medicinal cannabis to medicinal cannabis patients or their primary caregivers, or that otherwise has the effect of prohibiting the retail sale by delivery within the local jurisdiction of medicinal cannabis to medicinal cannabis patients or their primary caregivers by licensed medicinal cannabis businesses in a timely and readily accessible manner, and in types and quantities that are sufficient to meet demand from medicinal cannabis patients within the local jurisdiction, including, but not limited to, regulation of any of the following that has the effect of prohibiting the retail sale by delivery of medicinal cannabis:

(1) The number of medicinal cannabis businesses authorized to deliver medicinal cannabis in the local jurisdiction.

(2) The operating hours of medicinal cannabis businesses.

(3) The number or frequency of sales by delivery of medicinal cannabis.

(4) The types or quantities of medicinal cannabis authorized to be sold by delivery.

(5) The establishment of physical premises from which retail sale by delivery of medicinal cannabis within the

jurisdiction is conducted by a licensed nonstorefront retailer, except that this paragraph shall not be construed to require the establishment of additional physical premises in a local jurisdiction that allowed medicinal cannabis retail as of January 1, 2022, and in which at least one physical premises engaged in the retail sale of medicinal cannabis, whether storefront or delivery, is already established.

(b) Nothing in this chapter shall be construed to prohibit the adoption or enforcement of reasonable regulations on retail sale by delivery of medicinal cannabis, including, but not limited to, reasonable regulations related to:

(1) Zoning requirements that are not inconsistent with subdivision (a). If compliance with subdivision (a) would otherwise require a local jurisdiction to authorize a physical premises from which retail sale by delivery of medicinal cannabis within the jurisdiction is conducted, this paragraph shall not be construed to alter that requirement.

(2) Security or public health and safety requirements.

(3) Licensing requirements.

(4) The imposition, collection, and remittance of any applicable state or local taxes upon retail sales occurring within the local jurisdiction.

(5) Regulations consistent with requirements or restrictions imposed on cannabis businesses by this division or regulations issued under this division.

(c) Nothing in this chapter shall be construed to limit or otherwise affect the ability of a local jurisdiction to adopt or enforce any regulations on commercial cannabis operations other than retail sale by delivery of medicinal cannabis in the local jurisdiction.

(d) This section shall become operative on January 1, 2024.

Business and Professions Code § 26323

(Added by Stats. 2022, Ch. 395, Sec. 2. (SB 1186) Effective January 1, 2023. Operative January 1, 2024, by its own provisions.)

(a) This chapter may be enforced by an action brought pursuant to Chapter 2 (commencing with Section 1084) of Title 1 of Part 3 of the Code of Civil Procedure by any of the following parties, who shall be beneficially interested within the meaning of Section 1086 of the Code of Civil Procedure:

(1) A medicinal cannabis patient or their primary caregiver who seeks to purchase medicinal cannabis or medicinal cannabis products within the local jurisdiction.

(2) A medicinal cannabis business that seeks to offer medicinal cannabis for sale within the local jurisdiction.

(3) The Attorney General.

(4) Any other party otherwise authorized by law.

(b) This section shall not be construed to limit the availability of any other remedy otherwise available to enforce this chapter. The existence of any other remedy shall not restrict the availability of relief to enforce this chapter under Chapter 2 (commencing with Section 1084) of Title 1 of Part 3 of the Code of Civil Procedure.

(c) This section shall become operative on January 1, 2024.

Business and Professions Code § 26324

(Added by Stats. 2022, Ch. 395, Sec. 2. (SB 1186) Effective January 1, 2023.)

(a) Nothing in this chapter shall be construed to limit or otherwise affect the ability or right of a local jurisdiction to regulate adult-use cannabis pursuant to Section 26200.

Business and Professions Code § 26325

(Added by Stats. 2022, Ch. 395, Sec. 2. (SB 1186) Effective January 1, 2023.)

(a) This chapter addresses a matter of statewide concern and not a municipal affair, as that term is used in Section 5 of Article XI of the California Constitution.

II. Civil Code Sections

Civil Code § 56.06

(Amended by Stats. 2022, Ch. 690, Sec. 2. (AB 2089) Effective January 1, 2023.)

(a) Any business organized for the purpose of maintaining medical information in order to make the information available to an individual or to a provider of health care at the request of the individual or a provider of health care, for purposes of allowing the individual to manage their information, or for the diagnosis and treatment of the individual, shall be deemed to be a provider of health care subject to the requirements of this part. However, this section shall not be construed to make a business specified in this subdivision a provider of health care for purposes of any law other than this part, including laws that specifically incorporate by reference the definitions of this part.

(b) Any business that offers software or hardware to consumers, including a mobile application or other related device that is designed to maintain medical information in order to make the information available to an individual or a provider of health care at the request of the individual or a provider of health care, for purposes of allowing the individual to manage their information, or for the diagnosis, treatment, or management of a medical condition of the individual, shall be deemed to be a provider of health care subject to the requirements of this part. However, this section shall not be construed to make a business specified in this subdivision a provider of health care for purposes of any law other than this part, including laws that specifically incorporate by reference the definitions of this part.

(c) Any business that is licensed pursuant to Division 10 (commencing with Section 26000) of the Business and Professions Code that is authorized to receive or receives identification cards issued pursuant to Section 11362.71 of the Health and Safety Code or information contained in a physician's recommendation issued in accordance with Article 25 (commencing with Section 2525) of Chapter 5 of Division 2 of the Business and Professions Code shall be deemed to be a provider of health care subject to the requirements of this part. However, this section shall not be construed to make a business specified in this subdivision a provider of health care for purposes of any law other than this part, including laws that specifically incorporate by reference the definitions of this part.

(d) Any business that offers a mental health digital service to a consumer for the purpose of allowing the individual to manage the individual's information, or for the diagnosis, treatment, or management of a medical condition of the individual, shall be deemed to be a provider of health care subject to the requirements of this part. However, this section shall not be construed to make a business specified in this subdivision a provider of health care for purposes of any law other than this part, including laws that specifically incorporate by reference the definitions of this part.

(e) Any business described in this section shall maintain the same standards of confidentiality required of a provider of health care with respect to medical information disclosed to the business.

(f) Any business described in this section is subject to the penalties for improper use and disclosure of medical information prescribed in this part.

Civil Code § 1550.5

(Amended by Stats. 2018, Ch. 92, Sec. 35. (SB 1289) Effective January 1, 2019.)

(a) The Legislature finds and declares all of the following:

(1) The Compassionate Use Act of 1996, an initiative measure enacted by the approval of Proposition 215 at the November 5, 1996, statewide general election, authorized the use of marijuana for medical purposes in this state.

(2) The Legislature passed the Medical Cannabis Regulation and Safety Act, formerly Chapter 3.5 (commencing with Section 19300) of Division 8 of the Business and Professions Code, to regulate and license medical cannabis in the state.

(3) The Control, Regulate and Tax Adult Use of Marijuana Act (AUMA), an initiative measure enacted by the approval of Proposition 64 at the November 8, 2016, statewide general election, authorized the consumption of nonmedical marijuana by persons over 21 years of age and provided for the licensure and regulation of certain commercial nonmedical marijuana activities in this state.

(4) The Legislature passed the Medicinal and Adult-Use Cannabis Regulation and Safety Act (Division 10 (commencing with Section 26000) of the Business and Professions Code) to consolidate the licensure and regulation of certain commercial activities with respect to medicinal cannabis and nonmedical marijuana, now known as adult-use cannabis.

(b) Notwithstanding any law, including, but not limited to, Sections 1550, 1667, and 1668 and federal law, commercial activity relating to medicinal cannabis or adult-use cannabis conducted in compliance with California law and any applicable local standards, requirements, and regulations shall be deemed to be all of the following:

(1) A lawful object of a contract.

(2) Not contrary to, an express provision of law, any policy of express law, or good morals.

(3) Not against public policy.

III. Education Code Sections

Education Code § 49414.1

(Amended by Stats. 2020, Ch. 370, Sec. 80. (SB 1371) Effective January 1, 2021.)

(a) For purposes of this section, the following apply:

(1) "Cannabis" has the same meaning as in Section 11018 of the Health and Safety Code. "Cannabis" includes cannabis products.

(2) "Cannabis products" has the same meaning as in Section 11018.1 of the Health and Safety Code.

(3) "Medicinal cannabis" excludes medicinal cannabis or cannabis products in a smokeable or vapeable form.

(b) Notwithstanding Sections 11357 and 11361 of the Health and Safety Code, the governing board of a school district, a county board of education, or the governing body of a charter school maintaining kindergarten or any of grades 1 to 12, inclusive, may adopt, at a regularly scheduled meeting of the governing board or body, a policy that allows a parent or guardian of a pupil to possess and administer medicinal cannabis at a schoolsite to the pupil who is a qualified patient pursuant to Article 2.5 (commencing with Section 11362.7) of Chapter 6 of Division 10 of the Health and Safety Code.

(c) The policy shall include, at a minimum, all of the following elements:

(1) The parent or guardian shall not administer the medicinal cannabis in a manner that disrupts the educational environment or exposes other pupils.

(2) After the parent or guardian administers the medicinal cannabis, the parent or guardian shall remove any remaining medicinal cannabis from the schoolsite.

(3) The parent or guardian shall sign in at the schoolsite before administering the medicinal cannabis.

(4) Before administering the medicinal cannabis, the parent or guardian shall provide to an employee of the school a valid written medical recommendation for medicinal cannabis for the pupil to be kept on file at the school.

(d) For purposes of confidentiality and disclosure, pupil records collected in accordance with a policy adopted pursuant to subdivision (b) for the purpose of administering medicinal cannabis to a pupil shall be treated as medical records and shall be subject to all provisions of state and federal law that govern the confidentiality and disclosure of medical records.

(e) The governing board of a school district, a county board of education, or the governing body of a charter school that adopts a policy pursuant to subdivision (b) may amend or rescind the policy at a regularly scheduled meeting of the governing board or body for any reason, including, but not limited to, if the school district, county office of education, or charter school is at risk of, or has lost, federal funding as a result of the policy.

(f) The governing board of a school district, a county board of education, or the governing body of a charter school that adopts a policy pursuant to subdivision (b) may amend or rescind the policy at a special meeting in compliance with Section 54956 of the Government Code if both of the following conditions are met:

(1) Exigent circumstances necessitate an immediate change to the policy adopted pursuant to subdivision (b).

(2) At the meeting the governing board or body will address the intent to amend or rescind the policy adopted pursuant to subdivision (b).

(g) This section does not require the staff of a school district, county office of education, or charter school to administer medicinal cannabis.

IV. Evidence Code Sections

Evidence Code § 956

(Amended by Stats. 2017, Ch. 530, Sec. 2. (AB 1159) Effective January 1, 2018.)

(a) There is no privilege under this article if the services of the lawyer were sought or obtained to enable or aid anyone to commit or plan to commit a crime or a fraud.

(b) This exception to the privilege granted by this article shall not apply to legal services rendered in compliance with state and local laws on medicinal cannabis or adult-use cannabis, and confidential communications provided for the purpose of rendering those services are confidential communications between client and lawyer, as defined in Section 952, provided the lawyer also advises the client on conflicts with respect to federal law.

V. Fish and Game Code Sections

Fish and Game Code § 1602

(Amended by Stats. 2021, Ch. 70, Sec. 98. (AB 141) Effective July 12, 2021.)

(a) An entity shall not substantially divert or obstruct the natural flow of, or substantially change or use any material from the bed, channel, or bank of, any river, stream, or lake, or deposit or dispose of debris, waste, or other material containing crumbled, flaked, or ground pavement where it may pass into any river, stream, or lake, unless all of the following occur:

(1) The department receives written notification regarding the activity in the manner prescribed by the department. The notification shall include, but is not limited to, all of the following:

(A) A detailed description of the project's location and a map.

(B) The name, if any, of the river, stream, or lake affected.

(C) A detailed project description, including, but not limited to, construction plans and drawings, if applicable.

(D) A copy of any document prepared pursuant to Division 13 (commencing with Section 21000) of the Public Resources Code.

(E) A copy of any other applicable local, state, or federal permit or agreement already issued.

(F) Any other information required by the department.

(2) The department determines the notification is complete in accordance with Chapter 4.5 (commencing with Section 65920) of Division 1 of Title 7 of the Government Code, irrespective of whether the activity constitutes a development project for the purposes of that chapter.

(3) The entity pays the applicable fees, pursuant to Section 1609.

(4) One of the following occurs:

(A) (i) The department informs the entity, in writing, that the activity will not substantially adversely affect an existing fish or wildlife resource, and that the entity may commence the activity without an agreement, if the entity conducts the activity as described in the notification, including any measures in the notification that are intended to protect fish and wildlife resources.

(ii) Each region of the department shall log the notifications of activities where no agreement is required. The log shall list the date the notification was received by the department, a brief description of the proposed activity, and the location of the activity. Each item shall remain on the log for one year. Upon written request by any person, a regional office shall send the log to that person monthly for one year. A request made pursuant to this clause may be renewed annually.

(B) The department determines that the activity may substantially adversely affect an existing fish or wildlife resource and issues a final agreement to the entity that includes reasonable measures necessary to protect the resource, and the entity conducts the activity in accordance with the agreement.

(C) A panel of arbitrators issues a final agreement to the entity in accordance with subdivision (b) of Section 1603, and the entity conducts the activity in accordance with the agreement.

(D) The department does not issue a draft agreement to the entity within 60 days from the date notification is complete, and the entity conducts the activity as described in the notification, including any measures in the notification that are intended to protect fish and wildlife resources.

(b) (1) If an activity involves the routine maintenance and operation of water supply, drainage, flood control, or waste treatment and disposal facilities, notice to and agreement with the department shall not be required after the initial notification and agreement, unless the department determines either of the following:

(A) The work described in the agreement has substantially changed.

(B) Conditions affecting fish and wildlife resources have substantially changed, and those resources are adversely affected by the activity conducted under the agreement.

(2) This subdivision applies only if notice to, and agreement with, the department was attained prior to January 1, 1977, and the department has been provided a copy of the agreement or other proof of the existence of the agreement that satisfies the department, if requested.

(c) Notwithstanding subdivision (a), the department is not required to determine whether the notification is complete or otherwise process the notification until the department has received the applicable fees.

(d) (1) Notwithstanding subdivision (a), an entity shall not be required to obtain an agreement with the department pursuant to this chapter for activities authorized by a license or renewed license for cannabis cultivation issued by the Department of Cannabis Control for the term of the license or renewed license if all of the following occur:

(A) The entity submits all of the following to the department:

(i) The written notification described in paragraph (1) of subdivision (a).

(ii) A copy of the license or renewed license for cannabis cultivation issued by the Department of Cannabis Control that includes the requirements specified in Section 26060.1 of the Business and Professions Code.

(iii) The fee specified in paragraph (3) of subdivision (a).

(B) The department determines in its sole discretion that compliance with the requirements specified in Section 26060.1 of the Business and Professions Code that are included in the license will adequately protect existing fish and wildlife resources that may be substantially adversely affected by the cultivation without the need for additional measures that the department would include in a draft streambed alteration agreement in accordance with Section 1603.

(C) The department notifies the entity in writing that the exemption applies to the cultivation authorized by the license or renewed license.

(2) The department shall notify the entity in writing whether the exemption in paragraph (1) applies to the cultivation authorized by the license or renewed license within 60 days from the date that the notification is complete and the fee has been paid.

(3) If an entity receives an exemption pursuant to this subdivision and fails to comply with any of the requirements described in Section 26060.1 of the Business and Professions Code that are included in the license, the failure shall constitute a violation under this section, and the department shall notify the Department of Cannabis Control of any enforcement action taken.

(e) It is unlawful for any entity to violate this chapter.

Fish and Game Code § 1617

(Amended by Stats. 2017, Ch. 27, Sec. 109. (SB 94) Effective June 27, 2017.)

(a) The department may adopt general agreements for the cultivation of cannabis.

(b) Any general agreement adopted by the department subsequent to adoption of regulations under this section shall be in lieu of an individual agreement described in subparagraph (B) of paragraph (4) of subdivision (a) of Section 1602.

(c) Subparagraph (D) of paragraph (4) of subdivision (a) of Section 1602 and all other time periods to process agreements specified in this chapter do not apply to the issuance of a general agreement adopted by the department pursuant to this section.

(d) Any general agreement issued by the department pursuant to this section is a final agreement and is not subject to Section 1603 or 1604.

(e) The department shall charge a fee for a general agreement adopted by the department under this section in accordance with Section 1609.

(f) If the department adopts or amends a general agreement under this section, it shall do so as an emergency regulation. An emergency regulation adopted pursuant to this section, and any amendments to it, shall be adopted by the department in accordance with Chapter 3.5 (commencing with Section 11340) of Part 1 of Division 3 of Title 2 of the Government Code. The adoption of these regulations is an emergency and shall be considered by the Office of Administrative Law as necessary for the immediate preservation of the public peace, health and safety, and general welfare. Notwithstanding Chapter 3.5 (commencing with Section 11340) of Part 1 of Division 3 of Title 2 of the Government Code, an emergency regulation adopted by the department, or any amendments to it made by the department pursuant to this section, shall stay in effect until revised by the department.

(g) Regulations adopted pursuant to this section, and any amendment thereto, shall not be subject to Division 13 (commencing with Section 21000) of the Public Resources Code.

Fish and Game Code § 2080

(Amended by Stats. 2018, Ch. 329, Sec. 9. (SB 473) Effective January 1, 2019.)

No person or public agency shall import into this state, export out of this state, or take, possess, purchase, or sell within this state, any species, or any part or product thereof, that the commission determines to be an endangered species or a threatened species, or attempt any of those acts, except as otherwise provided in this chapter, the Native Plant Protection Act (Chapter 10 (commencing with Section 1900) of this code), or the California Desert Native Plants Act (Division 23 (commencing with Section 80001) of the Food and Agricultural Code).

Fish and Game Code § 3513

(Repealed (in Sec. 2) and added by Stats. 2019, Ch. 349, Sec. 3. (AB 454) Effective January 1, 2020. Operative January 20, 2025, by its own provisions.)

(a) It is unlawful to take or possess any migratory nongame bird as designated in the federal Migratory Bird Treaty Act (16 U.S.C. Sec. 703 et seq.), or any part of a migratory nongame bird described in this section, except as provided by rules and regulations adopted by the United States Secretary of the Interior under that federal act.

(b) This section shall become operative on January 20, 2025.

Fish and Game Code § 5650

(Amended by Stats. 2022, Ch. 56, Sec. 8. (AB 195) Effective June 30, 2022.)

(a) Except as provided in subdivision (b), it is unlawful to deposit in, permit to pass into, or place where it can pass into the waters of this state any of the following:

(1) Any petroleum, acid, coal or oil tar, lampblack, aniline, asphalt, bitumen, or residuary product of petroleum, or carbonaceous material or substance.

(2) Any refuse, liquid or solid, from any refinery, gas house, tannery, distillery, chemical works, mill, or factory of any kind.

(3) Any sawdust, shavings, slabs, or edgings.

(4) Any factory refuse, lime, or slag.

(5) Any cocculus indicus.

(6) Any substance or material deleterious to fish, plant life, mammals, or bird life.

(b) This section does not apply to a discharge or a release that is expressly authorized pursuant to, and in compliance with, the terms and conditions of a waste discharge requirement pursuant to Section 13263 of the Water Code or a waiver issued pursuant to subdivision (a) of Section 13269 of the Water Code issued by the State Water Resources Control Board or a California regional water quality control board after a public hearing, or that is expressly authorized pursuant to, and in compliance with, the terms and conditions of a federal permit for which the State Water Resources Control Board or a California regional water quality control board has, after a public hearing, issued a water quality certification pursuant to Section 13160 of the Water Code. This section does not confer additional authority on the State Water Resources Control Board, a California regional water quality control board, or any other entity.

(c) It shall be an affirmative defense to a violation of this section if the defendant proves, by a preponderance of the evidence, all of the following:

(1) The defendant complied with all applicable state and federal laws and regulations requiring that the discharge or release be reported to a government agency.

(2) The substance or material did not enter the waters of the state or a storm drain that discharges into the waters of the state.

(3) The defendant took reasonable and appropriate measures to effectively mitigate the discharge or release in a timely manner.

(d) The affirmative defense in subdivision (c) does not apply and may not be raised in an action for civil penalties or injunctive relief pursuant to Section 5650.1, or in any other civil action that alleges a violation of this section resulting from unlicensed cannabis cultivation.

(e) The affirmative defense in subdivision (c) does not apply and may not be raised by any defendant who has on two prior occasions in the preceding five years, in any combination within the same county in which the case is prosecuted, either pleaded nolo contendere, been convicted of a violation of this section, or suffered a judgment for a violation of this section or Section 5650.1. This subdivision shall apply only to cases filed on or after January 1, 1997.

(f) The affirmative defense in subdivision (c) does not apply and may not be raised by the defendant in any case in which a district attorney, city attorney, or Attorney General alleges, and the court finds, that the defendant acted willfully.

Fish and Game Code § 5650.1

(Amended by Stats. 2022, Ch. 56, Sec. 8. (AB 195) Effective June 30, 2022.)

(a) A person who violates Section 5650 is subject to a civil penalty of not more than twenty-five thousand dollars ($25,000) for each violation.

(b) The civil penalty imposed for each separate violation pursuant to this section is separate, and in addition to, any other civil penalty imposed for a separate violation pursuant to this section or any other provision of law, except as provided in subdivision (j).

(c) In determining the amount of a civil penalty imposed pursuant to this section, the court shall take into consideration all relevant circumstances, including, but not limited to, the nature, circumstance, extent, and gravity of the violation. In making this determination, the court shall consider the degree of toxicity and volume of the discharge, the extent of harm caused by the violation, whether the effects of the violation may be reversed or mitigated, and with respect to the defendant, the ability to pay, the effect of any civil penalty on the ability to continue in business, any voluntary cleanup efforts undertaken, any prior history of violations, the gravity of the behavior, the economic benefit, if any, resulting from the violation, and any other matters the court determines justice may require.

(d) (1) Every civil action brought under this section shall be brought by the Attorney General, district attorney, or city attorney in the name of the people of the State of California, and any actions relating to the same violation may be joined or consolidated.

(2) A civil action alleging a violation resulting from unlicensed cannabis cultivation may be brought by a county counsel in the name of the people of the State of California.

(e) In a civil action brought pursuant to this chapter in which a temporary restraining order, preliminary injunction, or permanent injunction is sought, it is not necessary to allege or prove at any stage of the proceeding that irreparable damage will occur if the temporary restraining order, preliminary injunction, or permanent injunction is not issued, or that the remedy at law is inadequate.

(f) After the party seeking the injunction has met its burden of proof, the court shall determine whether to issue a temporary restraining order, preliminary injunction, or permanent injunction without requiring the defendant to prove that it will suffer grave or irreparable harm. The court shall make the determination whether to issue a temporary restraining order, preliminary injunction, or permanent injunction by taking into consideration, among other things, the nature, circumstance, extent, and gravity of the violation, the quantity and characteristics of the substance or material involved, the extent of environmental harm caused by the violation, measures taken by the defendant to remedy the violation, the relative likelihood that the material or substance involved may pass into waters of the state, and the harm likely to be caused to the defendant.

(g) The court, to the maximum extent possible, shall tailor a temporary restraining order, preliminary injunction, or permanent injunction narrowly to address the violation in a manner that will otherwise allow the defendant to continue business operations in a lawful manner.

(h) All civil penalties collected pursuant to this section shall not be considered fines or forfeitures as defined in Section 13003 and shall be apportioned in the following manner:

(1) Fifty percent shall be distributed to the county treasurer of the county in which the action is prosecuted. Amounts paid to the county treasurer shall be deposited in the county fish and wildlife propagation fund established pursuant to Section 13100.

(2) Fifty percent shall be distributed to the department for deposit in the Fish and Game Preservation Fund. These funds may be expended to cover the costs of legal actions or for any other law enforcement purpose consistent with Section 9 of Article XVI of the California Constitution.

(i) Except as provided in subdivision (j), in addition to any other penalty provided by law, a person who violates Section 5650 is subject to a civil penalty of not more than ten dollars ($10) for each gallon or pound of material discharged. The total amount of the civil penalty shall be reduced for every gallon or pound of the illegally discharged material that is recovered and properly disposed of by the responsible party.

(j) A person shall not be subject to a civil penalty imposed under this section and to a civil penalty imposed pursuant to Article 9 (commencing with Section 8670.57) of Chapter 7.4 of Division 1 of Title 2 of the Government Code for the same act or failure to act.

Fish and Game Code § 5652

(Amended by Stats. 2007, Ch. 285, Sec. 107. Effective January 1, 2008.)

(a) It is unlawful to deposit, permit to pass into, or place where it can pass into the waters of the state, or to abandon, dispose of, or throw away, within 150 feet of the high water mark of the waters of the state, any cans, bottles, garbage, motor vehicle or parts thereof, rubbish, litter, refuse, waste, debris, or the viscera or carcass of any dead mammal, or the carcass of any dead bird.

(b) The abandonment of any motor vehicle in any manner that violates this section shall constitute a rebuttable presumption affecting the burden of producing evidence that the last registered owner of record, not having complied with Section 5900 of the Vehicle Code, is responsible for that abandonment and is thereby liable for the cost of removal and disposition of the vehicle. This section prohibits the placement of a vehicle body on privately owned property along a streambank by the property owner or tenant for the purpose of preventing erosion of the streambank.

(c) This section does not apply to a refuse disposal site that is authorized by the appropriate local agency having jurisdiction or to the depositing of those materials in a container from which the materials are routinely removed to a legal point of disposal.

(d) This section shall be enforced by all law enforcement officers of this state.

Fish and Game Code § 12025.2

(Amended by Stats. 2016, Ch. 32, Sec. 60. (SB 837) Effective June 27, 2016.)

The director or his or her designee may issue a complaint to any person or entity in accordance with Section 1055 of the Water Code alleging a violation for which liability may be imposed under Section 1052 or 1847 of the Water Code that harms fish and wildlife resources. The complaint is subject to the substantive and procedural requirements set forth in Section 1055 of the Water Code, and the department shall be designated a party to any proceeding before the State Water Resources Control Board regarding a complaint filed pursuant to this section.

Fish and Game Code § 12029

(Amended by Stats. 2021, Ch. 70, Sec. 99. (AB 141) Effective July 12, 2021.)

(a) The Legislature finds and declares all of the following:

(1) The environmental impacts associated with cannabis cultivation have increased, and unlawful water diversions for cannabis irrigation have a detrimental effect on fish and wildlife and their habitat, which are held in trust by the state for the benefit of the people of the state.

(2) The remediation of existing cannabis cultivation sites is often complex and the permitting of these sites

requires greater department staff time and personnel expenditures. The potential for cannabis cultivation sites to significantly impact the state's fish and wildlife resources requires immediate action on the part of the department's lake and streambed alteration permitting staff.

(b) In order to address unlawful water diversions and other violations of the Fish and Game Code associated with cannabis cultivation, the department shall establish the watershed enforcement program to facilitate the investigation, enforcement, and prosecution of these offenses.

(c) The department, in coordination with the State Water Resources Control Board and the Department of Cannabis Control, shall establish a permanent multiagency task force to address the environmental impacts of cannabis cultivation. The multiagency task force, to the extent feasible and subject to available resources, shall expand its enforcement efforts on a statewide level to ensure the reduction of adverse impacts of cannabis cultivation on fish and wildlife and their habitats throughout the state.

(d) In order to facilitate the remediation and permitting of cannabis cultivation sites, the department may adopt regulations to enhance the fees on any entity subject to Section 1602 for cannabis cultivation sites that require remediation. The fee schedule established pursuant to this subdivision shall not exceed the fee limits in Section 1609.

Fish and Game Code § 13103

(Amended by Stats. 2022, Ch. 56, Sec. 10. (AB 195) Effective June 30, 2022.)

Expenditures from the fish and wildlife propagation fund of any county may be made only for the following purposes:

(a) Public education relating to the scientific principles of fish and wildlife conservation, consisting of supervised formal instruction carried out pursuant to a planned curriculum and aids to education such as literature, audio and video recordings, training models, and nature study facilities.

(b) Temporary emergency treatment and care of injured or orphaned wildlife.

(c) Temporary treatment and care of wildlife confiscated by the department as evidence.

(d) Breeding, raising, purchasing, or releasing fish or wildlife that are to be released upon approval of the department pursuant to Sections 6400 and 6401 onto land or into waters of local, state, or federal agencies or onto land or into waters open to the public.

(e) Improvement of fish and wildlife habitat, including, but not limited to, construction of fish screens, weirs, and ladders; drainage or other watershed improvements; gravel and rock removal or placement; construction of irrigation and water distribution systems; earthwork and grading; fencing; planting trees and other vegetation management; and removal of barriers to the migration of fish and wildlife.

(f) Construction, maintenance, and operation of public hatchery facilities.

(g) Purchase and maintain materials, supplies, or equipment for either the department's ownership and use or the department's use in the normal performance of the department's responsibilities.

(h) Predator control actions for the benefit of fish or wildlife following certification in writing by the department that the proposed actions will significantly benefit a particular wildlife species.

(i) Scientific fish and wildlife research conducted by institutions of higher learning, qualified researchers, or governmental agencies, if approved by the department.

(j) Reasonable administrative costs, excluding the costs of audits required by Section 13104, for secretarial service, travel, and postage by the county fish and wildlife commission when authorized by the county board of supervisors. For purposes of this subdivision, "reasonable cost" means an amount that does not exceed 15 percent of the average amount received by the fund during the previous three-year period, or ten thousand dollars ($10,000) annually, whichever is greater, excluding any funds carried over from a previous fiscal year.

(k) Contributions to a secret witness program for the purpose of facilitating enforcement of this code and regulations adopted pursuant to this code.

(l) Costs incurred by the district attorney or city attorney in investigating and prosecuting civil and criminal actions for violations of this code, as approved by the department.

(m) Costs incurred by a county counsel in investigating and prosecuting an action for civil penalties, injunctive relief, or civil penalties and injunctive relief pursuant to Section 5650.1 resulting from unlicensed cannabis cultivation.

(n) Other expenditures, approved by the department, for the purpose of protecting, conserving, propagating, and preserving fish and wildlife.

VI. Food and Agricultural Code Sections

Food and Agricultural Code § 37104

(Amended by Stats. 2017, Ch. 27, Sec. 110. (SB 94) Effective June 27, 2017.)

Notwithstanding Section 26001 of the Business and Professions Code, butter purchased from a licensed milk products plant or retail location that is subsequently infused or mixed with medicinal or adult-use cannabis at the premises or location that is not subject to licensing as a milk product plant is exempt from the provisions of this division.

Food and Agricultural Code § 52452

(Amended by Stats. 2021, Ch. 70, Sec. 100. (AB 141) Effective July 12, 2021.)

(a) Except as otherwise provided in Section 52454, each container of agricultural seed that is for sale or sold within this state for sowing purposes shall bear upon it or have attached to it in a conspicuous place a plainly written or printed label or tag in the English language that includes all of the following information:

(1) The commonly accepted name of the kind, kind and variety, or kind and type of each agricultural seed component in excess of 5 percent of the whole, and the percentage by weight of each. If the aggregate of agricultural seed components, each present in an amount not exceeding 5 percent of the whole, exceeds 10 percent of the whole, each component in excess of 1 percent of the whole shall be named together with the percentage by weight of each. If more than one component is required to be named, the names of all components shall be shown in letters of the same type and size.

(2) The lot number or other lot identification.

(3) The percentage by weight of all weed seeds.

(4) The name and approximate number of each kind of restricted noxious weed seed per pound.

(5) The percentage by weight of any agricultural seed except that which is required to be named on the label.

(6) The percentage by weight of inert matter. If a percentage by weight is required to be shown by any provision of this section, that percentage shall be exclusive of any substance that is added to the seed as a coating and shown on the label as such.

(7) For each agricultural seed in excess of 5 percent of the whole, stated in accordance with paragraph (1), the percentage of germination exclusive of hard seed, the percentage of hard seed, if present, and the calendar month and year the test was completed to determine the percentages. Following the statement of those percentages, the additional statement "total germination and hard seed" may be stated.

(8) The name and address of the person who labeled the seed or of the person who sells the seed within this state.

(b) Subdivision (a) does not apply in the following instances:

(1) The sale is an occasional sale of seed grain by the producer of the seed grain to their neighbor for use by the purchaser within the county of production.

(2) Any cannabis seed, as defined in Section 26001 of the Business and Professions Code, sold or offered for sale in the state.

(c) All determinations of noxious weed seeds are subject to tolerances and methods of determination prescribed in the regulations that are adopted pursuant to this chapter.

(d) For purposes of this section, "neighbor" means a person who lives in close proximity, not to exceed three miles, to another.

Food and Agricultural Code § 54036

(Amended by Stats. 2017, Ch. 27, Sec. 111. (SB 94) Effective June 27, 2017.)

A person, firm, corporation, or association, that is hereafter organized or doing business in this state, may not use the word "cooperative" as part of its corporate name or other business name or title for producers' cooperative marketing activities, unless it has complied with this chapter or is otherwise authorized by Chapter 22 (commencing with Section 26220) of Division 10 of the Business and Professions Code.

Food and Agricultural Code § 55403

(Amended by Stats. 1997, Ch. 696, Sec. 2. Effective January 1, 1998.)

"Farm product" includes every agricultural, horticultural, viticultural, or vegetable product of the soil, honey and beeswax, oilseeds, poultry, poultry product, livestock product, and livestock for immediate slaughter. It does not include timber or any timber product, milk or any milk product, any aquacultural product, or cattle sold to any person who is bonded under the federal Packers and Stockyards Act, 1921 (7 U.S.C. Sec. 181, et seq.).

Food and Agricultural Code § 55407

(Amended by Stats. 1967, Ch. 807.)

"Processor" means any person that is engaged in the business of processing or manufacturing any farm product, that solicits, buys, contracts to buy, or otherwise takes title to, or possession or control of, any farm product from the producer of the farm product for the purpose of processing or manufacturing it and selling, reselling, or redelivering it in any dried, canned, extracted, fermented, distilled, frozen, eviscerated, or other preserved or processed form. It does not, however, include any retail merchant that has a fixed or established place of business in this state and does not sell at wholesale any farm product which is processed or manufactured by him.

Food and Agricultural Code § 55408

(Enacted by Stats. 1967, Ch. 15.)

"Producer" means any person that is engaged in the business of growing or producing any farm product.

DIVISION 20. PROCESSORS, STORES, DEALERS, AND DISTRIBUTORS OF AGRICULTURAL PRODUCTS

Chapter 6. Processors of Farm Products

ARTICLE 9. PRODUCER'S LIEN

Food and Agricultural Code § 55631

(Amended by Stats. 2016, Ch. 86, Sec. 144. (SB 1171) Effective January 1, 2017.)

(a) Every producer of any farm product that sells any product that is grown by him or her to any processor under contract, express or implied, in addition to all other rights and remedies that are provided for by law, has a lien upon that product and upon all processed or manufactured forms of that farm product for his or her labor, care, and expense in growing and harvesting that product. The lien shall be to the extent of the agreed price, if any, for that product so sold. If there is no agreed price or a method for determining the price that is agreed upon, the extent of the lien is the value of the farm product as of the date of the delivery. Any portion of that product or the processed or manufactured forms of that product, in excess of the amount necessary to satisfy the total amount owed to producers under contract, shall be free and clear of that lien.

(b) Every producer of a flower, agricultural, or vegetable seed that sells seed that is grown by him or her, when the seed was purchased or supplied by the grower and not supplied by the dealer or an independent third party who paid for the seed, to any seed dealer under contract, express or implied, in addition to all other rights and remedies that are provided for by law, has a lien upon that product and upon all processed or manufactured forms of that product for his or her labor, care, and expense in growing and harvesting that product. The lien shall be to the extent of the agreed price, if any, for that product so sold. If there is no agreed price or a method for determining the price that is agreed upon, the extent of the lien is the value of that product as of the date of the delivery. Any portion of that product or the processed or manufactured forms of that product, in excess of the amount necessary to satisfy the total amount owed to producers under contract, shall be free and clear of that lien.

Food and Agricultural Code § 55631.5

(Added by Stats. 1986, Ch. 1109, Sec. 2.)

Notwithstanding Section 55461, a nonprofit cooperative association acting as a producer bargaining association may assert producer's lien rights for, or on behalf of, its members.

Food and Agricultural Code § 55632

(Enacted by Stats. 1967, Ch. 15.)

This producer's lien attaches on all of such delivered product from the date of delivery of such farm product or any portion of it by a producer to any processor.

Food and Agricultural Code § 55633

(Amended by Stats. 1979, Ch. 969.)

The producer's lien is a preferred lien prior in dignity to all other liens, claims, or encumbrances except the following:

(a) Labor claims for wages and salaries for personal services which are rendered by any person to any processor in connection with such processing business after the delivery of any such product for processing.

(b) The lien of a warehouseman as provided by Division 7 (commencing with Section 7101) of the Uniform Commercial Code.

Food and Agricultural Code § 55634

(Amended by Stats. 1986, Ch. 1109, Sec. 3.)

Every lien which is provided for in this article is on every farm product and any processed form of the farm product which is in the possession of the processor without segregation of the product. For purposes of this chapter, any and all farm products or processed form of farm products deposited by a processor with a warehouse, whether or not warehouse receipts are given as security to a lender, shall be considered as being in the possession of the processor and subject to the lien.

Food and Agricultural Code § 55635

(Amended by Stats. 1986, Ch. 1109, Sec. 4.)

The lien of a producer, unless sooner released by payment or by security which is given for the payment as provided in this article, attaches from the date of delivery of the product, or if there is a series of deliveries, it attaches from the date of the last delivery.

Food and Agricultural Code § 55636

(Amended by Stats. 1979, Ch. 969.)

If suit is commenced by any such producer to enforce any lien, such lien shall remain in effect until one of the following occurs:

(a) The payment of the agreed price or the value of such product.

(b) Deposit of the amount of the lien or claims with the clerk of the court in which any such action is pending.

(c) The final determination of such court proceeding.

Food and Agricultural Code § 55637

(Enacted by Stats. 1967, Ch. 15.)

Any lien on any product or processed product may, however, be released, to the extent the value of the claim upon such product is secured, by a surety bond or a cash deposit or other security given as provided in this article. Any producer may also release any lien which is possessed by him upon payment being made to him for the agreed or reasonable value of the product which is so sold and delivered, or upon arrangements being made for such payment which are satisfactory to the producer.

Food and Agricultural Code § 55638

(Amended by Stats. 1979, Ch. 969.)

It is unlawful for any processor to remove, from this state or beyond his ownership or control, any farm product which is delivered to him, or any processed form of the farm product, to which any of the liens provided for in this chapter has attached, except for any of such product or processed product as may be in excess of a quantity on hand which is of a value that is sufficient to satisfy all existing liens. Furthermore, this section shall not prohibit the sale of any farm product or processed form of the product to which such a lien has attached, so long as the total proceeds of the sale are used to satisfy obligations to producers which are secured by a lien established pursuant to this chapter.

Food and Agricultural Code § 55638.5

(Added by Stats. 1986, Ch. 1109, Sec. 5.)

The director, within 15 days of the filing of a verified complaint by a producer, shall investigate any charge that a purchaser of a farm product to which a lien has attached has removed any farm product, or any processed form of a farm product, in violation of Section 55638.

Food and Agricultural Code § 55639

(Enacted by Stats. 1967, Ch. 15.)

Any processor that desires to secure a release of any or all of such liens on any product or processed product may do so in any of the following ways:

(a) By paying the agreed or actual value of any farm product which is purchased by such processor within 20 days from the date of delivery of the farm product unless the date of payment is otherwise agreed upon in writing or such payment is secured other than by lien.

(b) By depositing with the director a surety bond which is executed by such processor as principal and by a surety company which is qualified and authorized to do business in this state as surety in an amount which equals the current market value of the product or processed product which is intended by such processor to be sold or otherwise disposed of, as such value may appear by the sworn statement of such processor in accordance with quotations from the federal-state market news service or other evidence which is satisfactory to the director. The bond shall be conditioned that if the processor fails to pay up to the amount of such bond the lawful claims of all producers whose liens have been released by the bond, within 35 days after date of the bond, the surety shall be liable to and shall pay to the state on behalf of such claimants all such lawful claims as may be covered by the amount of the bond, together with costs of suit if an action is filed on the bond.

(c) By depositing with the director a cash sum in lawful money of the United States which is expressly set apart by an instrument in writing that is signed by the processor for the purpose of guaranteeing to the extent of such sum, payment of all existing claims of producers whose liens are released by the deposit, within 35 days from the date of such deposit. The director shall be named in such instrument as trustee to carry out the purpose and intent of the instrument.

(d) By designating, setting apart, and depositing in a public warehouse a quantity of any processed farm products and indorsing over to the director and delivering to him the warehouse receipt for such products for the purpose of guaranteeing to the extent of the value of such deposit, payment within 35 days from the date of such deposit, all existing claims of producers and labor claimants whose liens are released by it.

(e) By securing a release from the director after payment in full for such farm product.

Food and Agricultural Code § 55640

(Enacted by Stats. 1967, Ch. 15.)

If all lawful claims of the producers have been paid in accordance with this article by any processor, any product which is released by such action may be sold, transported, or otherwise disposed of.

Food and Agricultural Code § 55641

(Enacted by Stats. 1967, Ch. 15.)

If a bond, cash deposit, or security is given to the director by any processor as provided in this article, such processor may sell, transport, or otherwise dispose of the product or processed product to the value which is represented by such security as such value may appear by the sworn statement of such processor in accordance with quotations from the federal-state market news service or other evidence satisfactory to the director.

Food and Agricultural Code § 55642

(Enacted by Stats. 1967, Ch. 15.)

The director may accept such bond, if approved by him, and such other security. If the claims or any of them are not paid in accordance with the condition of such security, the director may, on proof being made to his satisfaction of the amounts which are due such claimants, pay all such unpaid claims insofar as possible out of the deposit money, or proceeds from any sale made by him of any securities or processed products which are given as security.

Food and Agricultural Code § 55643

(Enacted by Stats. 1967, Ch. 15.)

If a bond has been given as security, the director shall notify the principal and surety of any default on the part of the principal under the bond, and make demand for payment on behalf of such unpaid claimants. If payment is not made, the director may take any legal action he may deem necessary to enforce payment under such bond.

Food and Agricultural Code § 55644

(Enacted by Stats. 1967, Ch. 15.)

If the director has received warehouse receipts for any processed product as security, and the processor giving them has failed to pay the claims in accordance with the terms of such security, the director may sell such security with or without notice, and in such manner as he shall determine.

Food and Agricultural Code § 55645

(Enacted by Stats. 1967, Ch. 15.)

All claims in relation to payment shall have equal standing and payment shall be prorated if necessary among the claimants.

Food and Agricultural Code § 55646

(Enacted by Stats. 1967, Ch. 15.)

This article does not prevent the director if in his opinion the rights of all of the claimants are fully protected, as provided for in this article, from issuing a certificate in the name of the department and signed by him which releases any specific lot or quantity of any product or processed product from all liens of the claimants. No security which is held by the director shall, however, be released by him to any processor unless and until it is made to appear to his satisfaction that all claims have been fully paid, or that the rights of all of the claimants are fully protected.

A fee of five dollars ($5) shall be paid to the director for issuing any certificate or release which is provided for in this section.

Food and Agricultural Code § 55647

(Enacted by Stats. 1967, Ch. 15.)

This article does not impair or affect the right of any claimant that possesses a lien to maintain a personal action to recover such debt against a processor, either in an action to foreclose his lien or in a separate action. He is not required to state in his affidavit to procure an attachment that his demand is not secured by a lien.

Food and Agricultural Code § 55648

(Enacted by Stats. 1967, Ch. 15.)

The judgment, if any, which is obtained by the plaintiff in such personal action, or personal judgment which is obtained in such lien action, does not impair or merge any lien right or claim which is held by such plaintiff. Any money, however, which is collected on the judgment shall be credited on the amount of such lien or claims in any action which is brought to enforce the lien or in any action which is filed pursuant to this article by the director.

Food and Agricultural Code § 55649

(Amended by Stats. 1982, Ch. 517, Sec. 234.)

In an action that is filed by any such lien claimant, the defendant processor may file with the court in which the action is pending a surety bond in an amount that is sufficient to cover the demand of plaintiff's complaint, including the costs, whereupon the court may order the release of a portion or the whole of any product or processed product upon which the lien of plaintiff has attached.

Food and Agricultural Code § 55650

(Enacted by Stats. 1967, Ch. 15.)

Such processor may also, on motion duly noticed, introduce evidence to the court before whom any such action is pending to the effect that he has sufficient security or money on deposit with the director to protect the lien or other rights of plaintiff. If he does so, the court may order the release of a portion or the whole of such product upon which the lien of plaintiff is attached, and deny to plaintiff any recovery in such action. Such action by the court does not, however, prejudice any other rights or remedies which are possessed by the plaintiff.

Food and Agricultural Code § 55651

(Enacted by Stats. 1967, Ch. 15.)

The plaintiff in an action which is brought to foreclose any of the liens which are provided for in this article may, in a proper case, and upon proper allegations, secure an injunction against the processor in accordance with the provisions of Chapter 3 (commencing with Section 525), Title 7, Part 2 of the Code of Civil Procedure to restrain the doing of any acts on the part of such processor which are designed to or which would, in effect, remove any processed product in his possession or under his control and upon which valid liens exist, beyond the process of the court, to plaintiff's injury.

Food and Agricultural Code § 55652

(Enacted by Stats. 1967, Ch. 15.)

If in a court proceeding to foreclose such lien, it is found and determined by the court that there is no cash, bond, or other deposit placed with the director as security for the payment of any of the lien claims as set out in the complaint, the judgment of foreclosure shall be against a sufficient quantity in value of such farm product or processed product in the possession or under the control of the defendant processor, as may be necessary to satisfy such claim or render judgment and declare forfeited any bond which is deposited in the court by such processor to secure the lawful claims of the plaintiff as determined by the court.

Food and Agricultural Code § 55653

(Enacted by Stats. 1967, Ch. 15.)

All actions filed by the director or producers against any processor for the foreclosure of the liens or other security which are provided for in this article may be consolidated by the court and all persons that are necessary to a determination of such action may be made parties to such actions. Any judgment which is rendered shall determine the lawfulness of the amount of each claim as represented by the pleadings.

DIVISION 24. INDUSTRIAL HEMP

Food and Agricultural Code § 81000

(Amended (as amended by Stats. 2019, Ch. 838, Sec. 2) by Stats. 2021, Ch. 485, Sec. 1. (SB 292) Effective January 1, 2022. Repealed on the date prescribed by its own provisions. See later operative version amended by Sec. 2 of Stats. 2021, Ch. 485.)

(a) For purposes of this division, the following terms have the following meanings:

(1) "Approved state plan" means a state plan for California that is approved pursuant to Section 297B of the federal Agricultural Marketing Act of 1946 (added by Section 10113 of the federal Agriculture Improvement Act

of 2018 (Public Law 115-334)) and in effect.

(2) "Board" means the Industrial Hemp Advisory Board.

(3) "Cultivar" means a variety of industrial hemp.

(4) "Disposal" has the same meaning as defined in Section 990.1 of Title 7 of the Code of Federal Regulations.

(5) "Established agricultural research institution" means an institution that is either of the following:

(A) A public or private institution or organization that maintains land or facilities for agricultural research, including colleges, universities, agricultural research centers, and conservation research centers.

(B) An institution of higher education, as defined in Section 101 of the federal Higher Education Act of 1965 (20 U.S.C. Sec. 1001), that grows, cultivates, or manufactures industrial hemp for purposes of research conducted under an agricultural pilot program or other agricultural or academic research.

(6) "Hemp breeder" means an individual or a public or private institution or organization that is registered with the commissioner to develop cultivars intended for sale or research.

(7) "Industrial hemp" or "hemp" means an agricultural product, whether growing or not, that is limited to types of the plant Cannabis sativa L. and any part of that plant, including the seeds of the plant and all derivatives, extracts, the resin extracted from any part of the plant, cannabinoids, isomers, acids, salts, and salts of isomers, with a delta-9 tetrahydrocannabinol concentration of no more than 0.3 percent on a dry weight basis.

(8) "Industrial hemp program" means growth of industrial hemp pursuant to this division and, if in effect, an approved state plan.

(9) "Measurement of uncertainty" means the parameter associated with the result of a measurement that characterizes the dispersion of the values that could reasonably be attributed to the particular quantity subject to measurement.

(10) "Premises" has the same meaning as defined in subdivision (ap) of Section 26001 of the Business and Professions Code.

(11) "THC" means delta-9 tetrahydrocannabinol.

(12) "Variety development plan" means a strategy devised by a hemp breeder, or applicant hemp breeder, detailing their planned approach to growing and developing a new cultivar for industrial hemp.

(b) This section shall remain operative only until the date on which a state plan for California is approved pursuant to Section 297B of the federal Agricultural Marketing Act of 1946 (added by Section 10113 of the federal Agriculture Improvement Act of 2018 (Public Law 115-334)), and as of January 1 of the following year is repealed.

(Amended (as amended by Stats. 2019, Ch. 838, Sec. 2) by Stats. 2021, Ch. 485, Sec. 1. (SB 292) Effective January 1, 2022. Repealed on the date prescribed by its own provisions. See later operative version amended by Sec. 2 of Stats. 2021, Ch. 485.)

Food and Agricultural Code § 81000

(Amended (as added by Stats. 2019, Ch. 838, Sec. 3) by Stats. 2021, Ch. 485, Sec. 2. (SB 292) Effective January 1, 2022. Operative on the date prescribed by its own provisions.)

Definitions.

(a) For purposes of this division, the following terms have the following meanings:

(1) “Approved state plan” means a state plan for California that is approved pursuant to Section 297B of the federal Agricultural Marketing Act of 1946 (added by Section 10113 of the federal Agriculture Improvement Act of 2018 (Public Law 115-334)) and in effect.

(2) “Board” means the Industrial Hemp Advisory Board.

(3) “Cultivar” means a variety of industrial hemp.

(4) “Disposal” has the same meaning as defined in Section 990.1 of Title 7 of the Code of Federal Regulations.

(5) “Established agricultural research institution” means an institution of higher education, as defined in Section 101 of the federal Higher Education Act of 1965 (20 U.S.C. Sec. 1001), that grows, cultivates, or manufactures industrial hemp for purposes of agricultural or academic research.

(6) “Hemp breeder” means an individual or a public or private institution or organization that is registered with the commissioner to develop cultivars intended for sale or research.

(7) “Industrial hemp” or “hemp” means an agricultural product, whether growing or not, that is limited to types of the plant Cannabis sativa L. and any part of that plant, including the seeds of the plant and all derivatives, extracts, the resin extracted from any part of the plant, cannabinoids, isomers, acids, salts, and salts of isomers, with a delta-9 tetrahydrocannabinol concentration of no more than 0.3 percent on a dry weight basis.

(8) “Industrial hemp program” means growth of industrial hemp pursuant to this division and, if in effect, an approved state plan.

(9) “Measurement of uncertainty” means the parameter associated with the result of a measurement that characterizes the dispersion of the values that could reasonably be attributed to the particular quantity subject to measurement.

(10) “Premises” has the same meaning as defined in subdivision (ap) of Section 26001 of the Business and Professions Code.

(11) “Research plan” means a strategy devised by an established agricultural research institution, or applicant established agricultural research institution, detailing its planned approach to growing or cultivating hemp for academic or agricultural research.

(12) “THC” means delta-9 tetrahydrocannabinol.

(13) “Variety development plan” means a strategy devised by a hemp breeder, or applicant hemp breeder, detailing their planned approach to growing and developing a new cultivar for industrial hemp.

(b) This section shall become operative as of the date on which a state plan for California is approved pursuant to Section 297B of the federal Agricultural Marketing Act of 1946 (added by Section 10113 of the federal Agriculture Improvement Act of 2018 (Public Law 115-334)).

Food and Agriculture Code § 81001

(Amended by Stats. 2021, Ch. 485, Sec. 3. (SB 292) Effective January 1, 2022.)

(a) There is in the department an Industrial Hemp Advisory Board. The board shall consist of 13 members, appointed by the secretary as follows:

(1) Six of the board members shall be growers of industrial hemp that are registered pursuant to the provisions of this division.

(2) Two of the board members shall be members of an established agricultural research institution.

(3) One member of the board shall be a representative as provided by the California State Sheriffs' Association and approved by the secretary.

(4) One member of the board shall be a county agricultural commissioner.

(5) Two members of the board shall be representatives of businesses that sell industrial hemp products.

(6) One member of the board shall be a member of the public.

(b) It is hereby declared, as a matter of legislative determination, that growers and representatives of industrial hemp product manufacturers and businesses appointed to the board pursuant to this division are intended to represent and further the interest of a particular agricultural industry, and that the representation and furtherance is intended to serve the public interest. Accordingly, the Legislature finds that persons who are appointed to the board shall be subject to the conflict-of-interest provisions described in Sections 87100 and 87103 of the Government Code.

(c) The term of office for a member of the board is three years. If a vacancy exists, the secretary shall, consistent with the membership requirements described in subdivision (a), appoint a replacement member to the board for the duration of the term.

(d) A member of the board shall not receive a salary but may be reimbursed by the department for attendance at meetings and other board activities authorized by the board and approved by the secretary.

(e) The board shall advise the secretary and may make recommendations on all matters pertaining to this division, including, but not limited to, industrial hemp seed law and regulations, enforcement, annual budgets required to accomplish the purposes of this division, and the setting of an appropriate assessment rate necessary for the administration of this division.

(f) The board shall annually elect a chair from its membership and, from time to time, other officers as it deems necessary.

(g) The board shall meet at the call of its chair or the secretary, or at the request of any four members of the board. The board shall meet at least once a year to review budget proposals and fiscal matters related to the proposals.

Food and Agriculture Code § 81002

(Amended by Stats. 2021, Ch. 485, Sec. 4. (SB 292) Effective January 1, 2022.)

(a) Except when grown by a registered established agricultural research institution or by a registered hemp breeder developing a new cultivar, industrial hemp shall be grown only if it is on the list of approved cultivars, or produced by clonal propagation of industrial hemp that is on the list of approved cultivars.

(b) The list of approved cultivars shall include all of the following:

(1) Industrial hemp cultivars that have been certified by member organizations of the Association of Official Seed Certifying Agencies, including, but not limited to, the Canadian Seed Growers' Association.

(2) Industrial hemp cultivars that have been certified by the Organization of Economic Cooperation and Development.

(3) California varieties of industrial hemp cultivars that have been certified by a seed-certifying agency pursuant to Article 6.5 (commencing with Section 52401) of Chapter 2 of Division 18.

(c) (1) Upon recommendation by the board or the department, the secretary may update the list of approved cultivars by adding, amending, or removing cultivars.

(2) The adoption, amendment, or repeal of the list of approved cultivars, and the adoption of a methodology and

procedure to add, amend, or remove a cultivar from the list of approved cultivars, pursuant to this section shall not be subject to the requirements of the Administrative Procedure Act (Chapter 3.5 (commencing with Section 11340) of Part 1 of Division 3 of Title 2 of the Government Code).

(3) The department, in consultation with the board, shall hold at least one public hearing with public comment to determine the methodology and procedure by which a cultivar is added, amended, or removed from the list of approved cultivars.

(4) The department shall finalize the methodology and procedure to add, amend, or remove a cultivar from the list of approved cultivars and send the methodology and procedure to the Office of Administrative Law. The Office of Administrative Law shall file the methodology and procedure promptly with the Secretary of State without further review pursuant to Article 6 (commencing with Section 11349) of Chapter 3.5 of Part 1 of Division 3 of Title 2 of the Government Code. The methodology and procedure shall do all of the following:

(A) Indicate that the methodology and procedure are adopted pursuant to this division.

(B) State that the methodology and procedure are being transmitted for filing.

(C) Request that the Office of Administrative Law publish a notice of the filing of the methodology and procedure and print an appropriate reference in Title 3 of the California Code of Regulations.

(d) The department, in consultation with the board, may determine the manner in which the public is given notice of the list of approved cultivars, and any addition, amendment, or removal from that list.

Food and Agriculture Code § 81003

(Amended by Stats. 2021, Ch. 485, Sec. 5. (SB 292) Effective January 1, 2022.)

(a) (1) Except for an established agricultural research institution subject to Section 81004.5 or a hemp breeder subject to Section 81004, and before cultivation, a grower of industrial hemp shall register with the commissioner of the county in which the grower intends to engage in industrial hemp cultivation.

(2) The application shall include all of the following:

(A) The name, physical address, and mailing address of the applicant.

(B) The legal description, Global Positioning System coordinates, and map of the land area on which the applicant plans to engage in industrial hemp cultivation, storage, or both.

(C) The approved cultivar to be grown, including the state or country of origin.

(3) The application shall be accompanied by a registration fee, as determined pursuant to Section 81005.

(4) A registration issued pursuant to this section shall be valid for one year, after which the registrant shall renew the registration and pay an accompanying renewal fee, as determined pursuant to Section 81005.

(b) If the commissioner determines that the requirements for registration pursuant to this division are met and that the applicant is eligible to participate in the industrial hemp program, in accordance with Sections 81012 to 81014, inclusive, the commissioner shall issue a registration to the applicant.

(c) A registrant that wishes to change or alter the land area on which the registrant conducts industrial hemp cultivation or storage, or both, shall, before any alteration or change, submit to the commissioner an updated registration with the legal description, Global Positioning System coordinates, and map specifying the proposed land change or alteration. Once the commissioner has received the change to the registration and the commissioner determines that the requirements pursuant to this division are met, the commissioner shall notify the registrant that it may cultivate industrial hemp on the changed or altered land area.

(d) A registrant that wishes to change the cultivar grown shall submit to the commissioner the name of the new, approved cultivar to be grown. Once the commissioner has received the change to the registration and the commissioner determines that the requirements pursuant to this division are met, the commissioner shall notify the registrant that it may cultivate the new cultivar.

(e) (1) The commissioner shall transmit information collected under this section to the department no more than 10 business days after the date on which it is collected or the date of a change in registration status occurred.

(2) The department shall submit the information described in paragraph (a) of Section 990.70 of Title 7 of the Code of Federal Regulations to the United States Department of Agriculture no more than 30 business days after the date on which it is collected or the date of a change in registration status occurred.

(f) The department and the commissioner shall retain information collected under this section for at least three years after collecting or receiving it.

Food and Agriculture Code § 81004

(Amended by Stats. 2021, Ch. 485, Sec. 6. (SB 292) Effective January 1, 2022.)

(a) (1) Except when grown by an established agricultural research institution subject to Section 81004.5, and before cultivation, a hemp breeder shall register with the commissioner of the county in which the hemp breeder intends to engage in industrial hemp cultivation.

(2) The application shall include all of the following:

(A) The name, physical address, and mailing address of the applicant.

(B) The legal description, Global Positioning System coordinates, and map of the land area on which the applicant plans to engage in industrial hemp cultivation, storage, or both.

(C) A variety development plan, which shall include all of the following:

(i) If a new cultivar is to be certified by a seed-certifying agency, the name of the seed-certifying agency that will be conducting the certification.

(ii) The industrial hemp varieties that will be used and, if applicable, how those varieties will be used in the development of a new cultivar.

(iii) A plan for testing a representative sample of the plants grown.

(iv) The measures that will be taken to destroy or dispose of any plants with THC concentrations that test above 0.3 percent.

(v) The measures that will be taken to prevent the unlawful use of industrial hemp under this division.

(vi) A procedure for the maintenance of records documenting the development of the new cultivar.

(3) The application shall be accompanied by a registration fee, as determined pursuant to Section 81005.

(4) A registration issued pursuant to this section shall be valid for one year, after which the registrant shall renew its registration and pay an accompanying renewal fee, as determined pursuant to Section 81005.

(b) If the commissioner determines that the requirements for registration pursuant to this division are met and that the applicant is eligible to participate in the industrial hemp program, in accordance with Sections 81012 to 81014, inclusive, the commissioner shall issue a hemp breeder registration to the applicant.

(c) A registrant that wishes to change or alter the land area on which the registrant conducts industrial hemp cultivation or storage, or both, shall, before any alteration or change, submit to the commissioner an updated registration with the legal description, Global Positioning System coordinates, and map specifying the proposed land change or alteration. Once the commissioner has received the change to the registration and the commissioner determines that the requirements pursuant to this division are met, the commissioner shall notify the registrant that it may cultivate industrial hemp on the changed or altered land area.

(d) A registrant that wishes to change the cultivar grown shall submit to the commissioner the name of the new, approved cultivar to be grown. Once the commissioner has received the change to the registration and the commissioner determines that the requirements pursuant to this division are met, the commissioner shall notify the registrant that it may cultivate the new cultivar.

(e) A registrant developing a new cultivar who wishes to change any provision of the variety development plan shall submit to the commissioner the revised variety development plan. Once the commissioner has received the change to the registration and the commissioner determines that the requirements pursuant to this division are met, the commissioner shall notify the registrant that the registrant may cultivate under the revised variety development plan.

(f) All records pertaining to the variety development plan shall be kept and maintained by the hemp breeder and be available upon request by the commissioner, a law enforcement agency, or a seed certifying agency.

(g) (1) The commissioner shall transmit information collected under this section to the department no more than 10 business days after the date on which it is collected or the date of a change in registration status occurred.

(2) The department shall submit the information described in paragraph (a) of Section 990.70 of Title 7 of the Code of Federal Regulations to the United States Department of Agriculture no more than 30 business days after the date on which it is collected or the date of a change in registration status occurred.

(h) The department and the commissioner shall retain information collected under this section for at least three years after collecting or receiving it.

Food and Agriculture Code § 81004.5

(Amended by Stats. 2021, Ch. 485, Sec. 7. (SB 292) Effective January 1, 2022. Operative on the date prescribed by its own provisions.)

(a) (1) Before cultivating hemp for agricultural or academic research, an established agricultural research institution shall register with the commissioner of the county in which it intends to cultivate.

(2) The registration application shall include all of the following:

(A) The name, physical address, and mailing address of the applicant.

(B) The legal description, Global Positioning System coordinates, and map of the geographic area where the applicant plans to engage in hemp cultivation or storage, or both.

(C) A research plan that shall include all of the following:

(i) The hemp varieties that will be used and, if applicable, how those varieties will be used for purposes of agricultural or academic research.

(ii) A plan for testing a representative sample of the plants cultivated.

(iii) The measures that will be taken to destroy or dispose of any plants with THC concentrations that test above 0.3 percent.

(iv) A procedure for the maintenance of records documenting the agricultural or academic research.

(3) A registration issued pursuant to this section shall be valid for one year, after which the registrant shall renew its registration if it will continue cultivating hemp beyond that term.

(b) If the commissioner determines that the requirements for registration pursuant to this division are met and that the applicant is eligible to participate in the hemp program, in accordance with Sections 81012 to 81014, inclusive, the commissioner shall issue an established agricultural research institution registration to the applicant.

(c) A registrant that wishes to change or alter the land area on which the registrant conducts hemp cultivation or storage, or both, shall, before any alteration or change, submit to the commissioner an updated registration with the legal description, Global Positioning System coordinates, and map specifying the proposed land change or alteration. Once the commissioner has received the change to the registration and the commissioner determines that the requirements pursuant to this division are met, the commissioner shall notify the registrant that it may cultivate hemp on the changed or altered land area.

(d) A registrant conducting agricultural or academic research who wishes to change any provision of the research plan shall submit to the commissioner a revised research plan. Once the commissioner has received the revised research plan, and the commissioner determines that the requirements of this division are met, the commissioner shall notify the registrant that it may cultivate under the revised research plan.

(e) All records pertaining to the research plan shall be kept and maintained by the established agricultural research institution and be available upon request by the commissioner or a law enforcement agency.

(f) (1) The commissioner shall transmit information collected under this section to the department no more than 10 business days after the date on which it is collected or the date of a change in registration status occurred.

(2) The department shall submit the information described in paragraph (a) of Section 990.70 of Title 7 of the Code of Federal Regulations to the United States Department of Agriculture no more than 30 business days after the date on which it is collected or the date of a change in registration status occurred.

(g) The department and the commissioner shall retain information collected under this section for at least three years after collecting or receiving it.

(h) This section shall become operative as of the date on which a state plan for California is approved pursuant to Section 297B of the federal Agricultural Marketing Act of 1946 (added by Section 10113 of the federal Agriculture Improvement Act of 2018 (Public Law 115-334)).

Food and Agriculture Code § 81004.6

(Added by Stats. 2021, Ch. 485, Sec. 8. (SB 292) Effective January 1, 2022.)

Each registered established agricultural research institution, registered grower of industrial hemp, and registered hemp breeder shall report on its hemp production in the state and any changes to the location where it will produce hemp to the Farm Service Agency of the United States Department of Agriculture and shall provide, at minimum, all of the following information:

(a) Street address and, to the extent practicable, geospatial location of the lot, parcel, greenhouse, building, or site of all locations in the state where hemp will be produced.

(b) The acreage dedicated to the production of hemp, or greenhouse or indoor square footage dedicated to the production of hemp, for each location in the state where hemp will be produced.

(c) The license or registration number associated with each location in the state where hemp will be produced.

Food and Agriculture Code § 81005

(Amended by Stats. 2019, Ch. 838, Sec. 9. (SB 153) Effective January 1, 2020.)

(a) The department shall establish a registration fee and appropriate renewal fee to be paid by growers of industrial hemp and hemp breeders, not including an established agricultural research institution, to cover the actual costs of implementing, administering, and enforcing the provisions of this division.

(b) Fees established pursuant to subdivision (a) that are collected by the commissioners upon registration or renewal pursuant to Section 81003 or 81004, except for amounts retained pursuant to this subdivision, shall be forwarded, according to procedures set by the department, to the department for deposit into the Department of Food and Agriculture Fund to be used for the administration and enforcement of this division. A commissioner or the county, as appropriate, may retain the amount of a fee necessary to reimburse direct costs incurred by the commissioner in the collection of the fee.

(c) The board of supervisors of a county may establish a reasonable fee, in an amount necessary to cover the actual costs of the commissioner and the county of implementing, administering, and enforcing the provisions of this division, except for costs that are otherwise reimbursed pursuant to subdivision (b), to be charged and collected by the commissioner upon registrations or renewals required pursuant to Section 81003 or 81004 and retained by the commissioner or the county, as appropriate.

Food and Agriculture Code § 81006

(Amended (as amended by Stats. 2021, Ch. 70, Sec. 101) by Stats. 2021, Ch. 485, Sec. 9. (SB 292) Effective January 1, 2022.)

Industrial Hemp Growth Limitations; Prohibitions; Imports; Laboratory Testing.

(a) Except when grown by a registered established agricultural research institution or a registered hemp breeder, industrial hemp shall be grown in acreages of not less than one-tenth of an acre at the same time.

(b) Clandestine cultivation of industrial hemp is prohibited. All plots shall have adequate signage indicating they are industrial hemp.

(c) Industrial hemp shall not be cultivated on a premises licensed by the Department of Cannabis Control to cultivate or process cannabis. Industrial hemp, regardless of its THC content, that is cultivated on a premises licensed by the Department of Cannabis Control for cannabis cultivation shall be considered cannabis as defined in Section 26001 of the Business and Professions Code and subject to licensing and regulatory requirements for cannabis pursuant to Division 10 (commencing with Section 26000) of the Business and Professions Code.

(d) Industrial hemp shall include products imported under the Harmonized Tariff Schedule of the United States (2013) of the United States International Trade Commission, including, but not limited to, hemp seed, per subheading 1207.99.03, hemp oil, per subheading 1515.90.80, oilcake, per subheading 2306.90.01, true hemp, per heading 5302, true hemp yarn, per subheading 5308.20.00, and woven fabrics of true hemp fibers, per subheading 5311.00.40.

(e) (1) Except when industrial hemp is grown by a registered established agricultural research institution and tested in accordance with an approved research plan or by a registered hemp breeder and tested in accordance with an approved variety development plan, a registrant that grows industrial hemp under this section shall, before the harvest of each crop and as provided below, obtain a laboratory test report indicating the THC levels of a random sampling of the dried flowering tops of the industrial hemp grown.

(2) Sampling shall occur within the timeframe established by the department.

(3) The sample collected for THC testing shall be taken with the grower or hemp breeder present. The department shall establish, by regulation, the sampling procedures, including all of the following:

(A) The number of plants to be sampled per field, and any compositing of samples.

(B) The portions of the plant to be sampled.

(C) The plant parts to be included in a sample.

(D) Additional procedures as necessary to ensure accuracy and the sanitation of samples and fields.

(4) The sample collected for THC testing shall be accompanied by the registrant's proof of registration.

(5) The laboratory test report shall be issued by a laboratory approved by the department, using a department-approved testing method. The testing method shall use postdecarboxylation or similarly reliable methods for determining THC concentration levels. The laboratory test report shall indicate the percentage concentration of THC on a dry-weight basis, indicate the date and location of samples taken, and state the Global Positioning System coordinates and total acreage of the crop. If the laboratory test report indicates a percentage concentration of THC that is equal to or less than 0.3 percent, the words "PASSED AS CALIFORNIA INDUSTRIAL HEMP" shall appear at or near the top of the laboratory test report. If the laboratory test report indicates a percentage concentration of THC that is greater than 0.3 percent, the words "FAILED AS CALIFORNIA INDUSTRIAL HEMP" shall appear at or near the top of the laboratory test report. The laboratory test report shall also include an estimate of the measurement of uncertainty associated with the test results. A laboratory shall use appropriate, validated methods and procedures for all testing activities and estimates of the measurement of uncertainty.

(6) If the laboratory test report indicates a percentage concentration of THC that is equal to or less than 0.3 percent, the laboratory shall provide the person who requested the testing not less than 10 original copies signed by an employee authorized by the laboratory and shall retain one or more original copies of the laboratory test report for a minimum of two years from its date of sampling.

(7) If the laboratory test report indicates a percentage concentration of THC that is greater than 0.3 percent and does not exceed 1 percent, the registrant that grows industrial hemp shall submit additional samples for testing of the industrial hemp grown.

(8) A registrant that grows industrial hemp shall destroy or dispose of the industrial hemp grown upon receipt of a first laboratory test report indicating a percentage concentration of THC that exceeds 1 percent or a second laboratory test report pursuant to paragraph (7) indicating a percentage concentration of THC that exceeds 0.3 percent but is less than 1 percent. If the percentage concentration of THC exceeds 1 percent, the destruction or disposal shall begin within 48 hours, and be completed within seven days, after receipt of the laboratory test report. If the percentage concentration of THC in the second laboratory test report exceeds 0.3 percent but is less than 1 percent, the destruction or disposal shall take place as soon as practicable, but no later than 45 days after receipt of the second test report.

(9) A registrant that intends to grow industrial hemp and who complies with this section shall not be prosecuted for the cultivation or possession of marijuana as a result of a laboratory test report that indicates a percentage concentration of THC that is greater than 0.3 percent but does not exceed 1 percent.

(10) A registered established agricultural research institution or a registered hemp breeder shall obtain laboratory results in accordance with its approved research plan or variety development plan. The secretary may authorize a registered established agricultural research institution or hemp breeder to cultivate or possess industrial hemp with a laboratory test report that indicates a percentage concentration of THC that is greater than 0.3 percent in accordance with its approved research plan or variety development plan if that cultivation or possession contributes to the development of types of industrial hemp that will comply with the 0.3 percent THC limit established in this division.

(11) A registrant that grows industrial hemp shall retain an original signed copy of the laboratory test report for two years from its date of sampling, make an original signed copy of the laboratory test report available to the department, the commissioner, or law enforcement officials or their designees upon request, and shall provide an original copy of the laboratory test report to each person purchasing, transporting, or otherwise obtaining from the registrant that grows industrial hemp the fiber, oil, cake, or seed, or any component of the seed, of the plant.

Food and Agriculture Code § 81007

(Amended by Stats. 2021, Ch. 485, Sec. 10. (SB 292) Effective January 1, 2022. Conditionally inoperative as prescribed by its own provisions. Repealed January 1 following the inoperative date.)

(a) As part of the registration program established pursuant to this division, the department may establish and carry out, by regulation, an agricultural pilot program pursuant to Section 7606 of the federal Agricultural Act of 2014 (7 U.S.C. Sec. 5940) in accordance with the purposes of that section.

(b) This section shall remain operative only until the date on which a state plan for California is approved pursuant to Section 297B of the federal Agricultural Marketing Act of 1946 (added by Section 10113 of the federal Agriculture Improvement Act of 2018 (Public Law 115-334)), and as of January 1 of the following year is repealed.

Food and Agricultural Code § 81008 (Repealed)

Food and Agricultural Code § 81009

(Added by Stats. 2013, Ch. 398, Sec. 4. (SB 566) Effective January 1, 2014. Section operative January 1, 2017, pursuant to Section 81010.)

Not later than January 1, 2019, or five years after the provisions of this division are authorized under federal law, whichever is later, the board, in consultation with the Hemp Industries Association, or its successor industry association, shall report the following to the Assembly and Senate Committees on Agriculture and the Assembly and Senate Committees on Public Safety:

(a) The economic impacts of industrial hemp cultivation, processing, and product manufacturing in California.

(b) The economic impacts of industrial hemp cultivation, processing, and product manufacturing in other states that may have permitted industrial hemp cultivation.

Food and Agricultural Code § 81010

(Amended by Stats. 2017, Ch. 27, Sec. 112. (SB 94) Effective June 27, 2017. Note: This section was amended on Nov. 8, 2016, by initiative Prop. 64, making Division 24 (commencing with Section 81000) operative on January 1, 2017.)

This division, and Section 221 shall become operative on January 1, 2017.

Food and Agriculture Code § 81011

(Amended by Stats. 2021, Ch. 485, Sec. 12. (SB 292) Effective January 1, 2022. Conditionally inoperative as prescribed by its own provisions. Repealed January 1 following the inoperative date.)

(a) Before cultivating industrial hemp, an established agricultural research institution shall provide the Global Positioning System coordinates of the planned cultivation site to the commissioner of the county in which the site is located.

(b) This section shall remain operative only until the date on which a state plan for California is approved pursuant to Section 297B of the federal Agricultural Marketing Act of 1946 (added by Section 10113 of the federal Agriculture Improvement Act of 2018 (Public Law 115-334)), and as of January 1 of the following year is repealed.

Food and Agriculture Code § 81012

(Amended by Stats. 2021, Ch. 485, Sec. 13. (SB 292) Effective January 1, 2022. Operative on the date prescribed by its own provisions.)

(a) Enforcement of the approved state plan shall comply with subsection (e) of Section 297B of the federal Agricultural Marketing Act of 1946 (added by Section 10113 of the federal Agriculture Improvement Act of 2018 (Public Law 115-334)).

(b) A grower of industrial hemp, established agricultural research institution, or hemp breeder that the secretary determines has violated a provision of this division listed in the approved state plan or an additional requirement listed pursuant to subdivision (b) of Section 81015, including, but not limited to, by failing to provide a legal description of the land on which industrial hemp is grown, failing to register as required, or exceeding the 0.3 percent THC limit established in this division, shall be subject to the following consequences:

(1) For a negligent violation, as determined by the secretary, the consequences under state laws for a violation of this division shall be as follows:

(A) If the violation is not a repeat violation subject to subparagraph (B), the grower of industrial hemp, established agricultural research institution, or hemp breeder shall comply with a corrective action plan, to be established by the secretary, that includes both of the following:

(i) A reasonable date by which the grower of industrial hemp, established agricultural research institution, or hemp breeder shall correct the negligent violation.

(ii) A requirement that the grower of industrial hemp, established agricultural research institution, or hemp breeder shall periodically report to the secretary, for a period of at least the next two calendar years, on its compliance with this division or the approved state plan.

(B) A grower of industrial hemp, established agricultural research institution, or hemp breeder that commits a negligent violation three times in a five-year period shall be ineligible to participate in the industrial hemp program for a period of five years beginning on the date of the finding of the third violation.

(C) A grower of industrial hemp, established research institution, or hemp breeder shall not, as a result of a negligent violation, be subject to any criminal enforcement action by the state or a local government.

(2) For a violation committed intentionally, or with recklessness or gross negligence, the secretary shall immediately report the grower of industrial hemp, established agricultural research institution, or hemp breeder to the Attorney General of the United States and the Attorney General of this state, as applicable.

(c) This section shall become operative as of the date on which a state plan for California is approved pursuant to Section 297B of the federal Agricultural Marketing Act of 1946 (added by Section 10113 of the federal Agriculture Improvement Act of 2018 (Public Law 115-334)).

Food and Agriculture Code § 81013

(Added by Stats. 2019, Ch. 838, Sec. 12. (SB 153) Effective January 1, 2020.)

Any person convicted of a felony relating to a controlled substance under state or federal law before, on, or after January 1, 2020, shall be ineligible, during the 10-year period following the date of the conviction, to participate in the industrial hemp program.

Food and Agriculture Code § 81014

(Added by Stats. 2019, Ch. 838, Sec. 13. (SB 153) Effective January 1, 2020.)

A person that materially falsifies any information contained in an application or registration under Section 81003 or 81004, or other application to participate in the industrial hemp program, shall be ineligible to participate in the industrial hemp program.

Food and Agriculture Code § 81015

(Added by Stats. 2019, Ch. 838, Sec. 14. (SB 153) Effective January 1, 2020.)

(a) On or before May 1, 2020, the secretary, in consultation with the Governor and the Attorney General, shall develop and submit to the United States Secretary of Agriculture a state plan, consistent with this division, pursuant to Section 297B of the federal Agricultural Marketing Act of 1946 (added by Section 10113 of the federal Agriculture Improvement Act of 2018 (Public Law 115-334)), including a certification that the state has the resources and personnel to carry out the practices and procedures described in clauses (i) to (iv), inclusive, of subparagraph (A) of paragraph (2) of subsection (a) of that section.

(b) In an annex to the state plan, the secretary shall list the provisions of this division that are included in the state plan, and any additional requirements in the state plan, that shall be subject to enforcement pursuant to Section 81012.

VII. Government Code Sections

Government Code § 9147.7

(Amended by Stats. 2021, Ch. 70, Sec. 102. (AB 141) Effective July 12, 2021.)

(a) For the purpose of this section, "eligible agency" means any agency, authority, board, bureau, commission, conservancy, council, department, division, or office of state government, however denominated, excluding an agency that is constitutionally created or an agency related to postsecondary education, for which a date for repeal has been established by statute on or after January 1, 2011.

(b) The Joint Sunset Review Committee is hereby created to identify and eliminate waste, duplication, and inefficiency in government agencies. The purpose of the committee is to conduct a comprehensive analysis over 15 years, and on a periodic basis thereafter, of every eligible agency to determine if the agency is still necessary and cost effective.

(c) Each eligible agency scheduled for repeal shall submit to the committee, on or before December 1 before the year it is set to be repealed, a complete agency report covering the entire period since last reviewed, including, but not limited to, the following:

(1) The purpose and necessity of the agency.

(2) A description of the agency budget, priorities, and job descriptions of employees of the agency.

(3) Programs and projects under the direction of the agency.

(4) Measures of the success or failures of the agency and justifications for the metrics used to evaluate successes and failures.

(5) Recommendations of the agency for changes or reorganization in order to better fulfill its purpose.

(d) The committee shall take public testimony and evaluate the eligible agency before the date the agency is scheduled to be repealed. An eligible agency shall be eliminated unless the Legislature enacts a law to extend, consolidate, or reorganize the eligible agency. An eligible agency shall not be extended in perpetuity unless specifically exempted from the provisions of this section. The committee may recommend that the Legislature extend the statutory sunset date for no more than one year to allow the committee more time to evaluate the eligible agency.

(e) The committee shall be comprised of 10 members of the Legislature. The Senate Committee on Rules shall appoint five members of the Senate to the committee, not more than three of whom shall be members of the same political party. The Speaker of the Assembly shall appoint five members of the Assembly to the committee, not more than three of whom shall be members of the same political party. Members shall be appointed within 15 days after the commencement of the regular session. Each member of the committee who is appointed by the Senate Committee on Rules or the Speaker of the Assembly shall serve during that committee member's term of office or until that committee member no longer is a Member of the Senate or the Assembly, whichever is applicable. A vacancy on the committee shall be filled in the same manner as the original appointment. Three Assembly Members and three Senators who are members of the committee shall constitute a quorum for the conduct of committee business. Members of the committee shall receive no compensation for their work with the committee.

(f) The committee shall meet not later than 30 days after the first day of the regular session to choose a chairperson and to establish the schedule for eligible agency review provided for in the statutes governing the eligible agencies. The chairperson of the committee shall alternate every two years between a Member of the Senate and a Member of the Assembly, and the vice chairperson of the committee shall be a member of the opposite house as the chairperson.

(g) This section shall not be construed to change the existing jurisdiction of the budget or policy committees of the Legislature.

(h) This section does not apply to the Department of Cannabis Control.

Government Code § 11552

(Amended by Stats. 2022, Ch. 56, Sec. 11. (AB 195) Effective June 30, 2022.)

(a) Effective January 1, 1988, an annual salary of eighty-five thousand four hundred two dollars ($85,402) shall be paid to each of the following:

(1) Commissioner of Financial Protection and Innovation.

(2) Director of Transportation.

(3) Real Estate Commissioner.

(4) Director of Social Services.

(5) Director of Water Resources.

(6) Director of General Services.

(7) Director of Motor Vehicles.

(8) Executive Officer of the Franchise Tax Board.

(9) Director of Employment Development.

(10) Director of Alcoholic Beverage Control.

(11) Director of Housing and Community Development.

(12) Director of Alcohol and Drug Programs.

(13) Director of Statewide Health Planning and Development.

(14) Director of the Department of Human Resources.

(15) Director of Health Care Services.

(16) Director of State Hospitals.

(17) Director of Developmental Services.

(18) State Public Defender.

(19) Director of the California State Lottery.

(20) Director of Fish and Wildlife.

(21) Director of Parks and Recreation.

(22) Director of Rehabilitation.

(23) Director of the Office of Administrative Law.

(24) Director of Consumer Affairs.

(25) Director of Forestry and Fire Protection.

(26) The Inspector General pursuant to Section 6125 of the Penal Code.

(27) Director of Child Support Services.

(28) Director of Industrial Relations.

(29) Director of Toxic Substances Control.

(30) Director of Pesticide Regulation.

(31) Director of Managed Health Care.

(32) Director of Environmental Health Hazard Assessment.

(33) Director of California Bay-Delta Authority.

(34) Director of California Conservation Corps.

(35) Director of Technology.

(36) Director of Emergency Services.

(37) Director of the Office of Energy Infrastructure Safety.

(38) Director of Cannabis Control.

(b) The annual compensation provided by this section shall be increased in any fiscal year in which a general salary increase is provided for state employees. The amount of the increase provided by this section shall be comparable to, but shall not exceed, the percentage of the general salary increases provided for state employees during that fiscal year.

Government Code § 11553

(Repealed (in Sec. 89) and added by Stats. 2019, Ch. 29, Sec. 90. (SB 82) Effective June 27, 2019. Section operative July 1, 2019, by its own provisions.)

(a) Effective January 1, 1988, an annual salary of eighty-one thousand six hundred thirty-five dollars ($81,635) shall be paid to each of the following:

(1) Chairperson of the Unemployment Insurance Appeals Board.

(2) Chairperson of the Agricultural Labor Relations Board.

(3) Chairperson of the Fair Political Practices Commission.

(4) Chairperson of the Energy Resources Conservation and Development Commission.

(5) Chairperson of the Public Employment Relations Board.

(6) Chairperson of the Workers' Compensation Appeals Board.

(7) Administrative Director of the Division of Industrial Accidents.

(8) Chairperson of the State Water Resources Control Board.

(9) Chairperson of the Cannabis Control Appeals Panel.

(b) The annual compensation provided by this section shall be increased in any fiscal year in which a general salary increase is provided for state employees. The amount of the increase provided by this section shall be comparable to, but shall not exceed, the percentage of the general salary increases provided for state employees during that fiscal year.

(c) Notwithstanding subdivision (b), any salary increase is subject to Section 11565.5.

(d) This section shall be operative on July 1, 2019.

Government Code § 11553.5

(Amended by Stats. 2021, Ch. 258, Sec. 2. (SB 155) Effective September 23, 2021.)

(a) Effective January 1, 1988, an annual salary of seventy-nine thousand one hundred twenty-two dollars ($79,122) shall be paid to the following:

(1) Member of the Agricultural Labor Relations Board.

(2) Member of the State Energy Resources Conservation and Development Commission.

(3) Member of the Public Utilities Commission.

(4) Member of the Public Employment Relations Board.

(5) Member of the Unemployment Insurance Appeals Board.

(6) Member of the Workers' Compensation Appeals Board.

(7) Member of the State Water Resources Control Board.

(8) Member of the Cannabis Control Appeals Panel.

(b) (1) The annual compensation provided by this section shall be increased in any fiscal year in which a general salary increase is provided for state employees. The amount of the increase provided by this section shall be comparable to, but shall not exceed, the percentage of the general cost-of-living salary increases provided for state employees during that fiscal year.

(2) In addition to the annual increase provided in paragraph (1), the members of the Public Utilities Commission shall receive an annual salary increase of 5 percent in each of the 2021–22, 2022–23, and 2023–24 fiscal years.

(c) Notwithstanding subdivision (b), any salary increase pursuant to paragraph (1) of subdivision (b) is subject to Section 11565.5.

Government Code § 12954

(Added by Stats. 2022, Ch. 392, Sec. 2. (AB 2188) Effective January 1, 2023. Operative January 1, 2024, by its own provisions.)

(a) It is unlawful for an employer to discriminate against a person in hiring, termination, or any term or condition of employment, or otherwise penalizing a person, if the discrimination is based upon any of the following:

(1) The person's use of cannabis off the job and away from the workplace. This paragraph does not prohibit an employer from discriminating in hiring, or any term or condition of employment, or otherwise penalize a person based on scientifically valid preemployment drug screening conducted through methods that do not screen for nonpsychoactive cannabis metabolites.

(2) An employer-required drug screening test that has found the person to have nonpsychoactive cannabis metabolites in their hair, blood, urine, or other bodily fluids.

(b) Nothing in this section permits an employee to possess, to be impaired by, or to use, cannabis on the job, or affects the rights or obligations of an employer to maintain a drug- and alcohol-free workplace, as specified in Section 11362.45 of the Health and Safety Code, or any other rights or obligations of an employer specified by federal law or regulation.

(c) This section does not apply to an employee in the building and construction trades.

(d) This section does not apply to applicants or employees hired for positions that require a federal government background investigation or security clearance in accordance with regulations issued by the United States Department of Defense pursuant to Part 117 of Title 32 of the Code of Federal Regulations, or equivalent regulations applicable to other agencies.

(e) This section does not preempt state or federal laws requiring applicants or employees to be tested for controlled substances, including laws and regulations requiring applicants or employees to be tested, or the manner in which they are tested, as a condition of employment, receiving federal funding or federal licensing-related benefits, or entering into a federal contract.

(f) This section shall become operative on January 1, 2024.

Government Code § 53069.4

(Amended by Stats. 2018, Ch. 316, Sec. 1. (AB 2164) Effective January 1, 2019.)

(a)(1) The legislative body of a local agency, as the term "local agency" is defined in Section 54951, may by ordinance make any violation of any ordinance enacted by the local agency subject to an administrative fine or penalty. The local agency shall set forth by ordinance the administrative procedures that shall govern the imposition, enforcement, collection, and administrative review by the local agency of those administrative fines or penalties. Where the violation would otherwise be an infraction, the administrative fine or penalty shall not exceed the maximum fine or penalty amounts for infractions set forth in Section 25132 and subdivision (b) of Section 36900.

(2)(A) The administrative procedures set forth by ordinance adopted by the local agency pursuant to this subdivision shall provide for a reasonable period of time, as specified in the ordinance, for a person responsible for a continuing violation to correct or otherwise remedy the violation prior to the imposition of administrative fines or penalties, when the violation pertains to building, plumbing, electrical, or other similar structural or zoning issues, that do not create an immediate danger to health or safety.

(B) Notwithstanding subparagraph (A), the ordinance adopted by the local agency pursuant to this subdivision may provide for the immediate imposition of administrative fines or penalties for the violation of building, plumbing, electrical, or other similar structural, health and safety, or zoning requirements if the violation exists as a result of, or to facilitate, the illegal cultivation of cannabis. This subparagraph shall not be construed to apply to cannabis cultivation that is lawfully undertaken pursuant to Section 11362.1 of the Health and Safety Code.

(C) If a local agency adopts an ordinance that provides for the immediate imposition of administrative fines or penalties as allowed in subparagraph (B), that ordinance shall provide for a reasonable period of time for the correction or remedy of the violation prior to the imposition of administrative fines or penalties as required in subparagraph (A) if all of the following are true:

(i) A tenant is in possession of the property that is the subject of the administrative action.

(ii) The rental property owner or agent can provide evidence that the rental or lease agreement prohibits the cultivation of cannabis.

(iii) The rental property owner or agent did not know the tenant was illegally cultivating cannabis and no complaint, property inspection, or other information caused the rental property owner or agent to have actual notice of the illegal cannabis cultivation.

(b) (1) Notwithstanding Section 1094.5 or 1094.6 of the Code of Civil Procedure, within 20 days after service of the final administrative order or decision of the local agency is made pursuant to an ordinance enacted in accordance with this section regarding the imposition, enforcement, or collection of the administrative fines or penalties, a person contesting that final administrative order or decision may seek review by filing an appeal to be heard by the superior court, where the same shall be heard de novo, except that the contents of the local agency's file in the case shall be received in evidence. A proceeding under this subdivision is a limited civil case. A copy of the document or instrument of the local agency providing notice of the violation and imposition of the administrative fine or penalty shall be admitted into evidence as prima facie evidence of the facts stated therein. A copy of the notice of appeal shall be served in person or by first-class mail upon the local agency by the contestant.

(2) The fee for filing the notice of appeal shall be as specified in Section 70615. The court shall request that the local agency's file on the case be forwarded to the court, to be received within 15 days of the request. The court shall retain the fee specified in Section 70615 regardless of the outcome of the appeal. If the court finds in favor of the contestant, the amount of the fee shall be reimbursed to the contestant by the local agency. Any deposit of the fine or penalty shall be refunded by the local agency in accordance with the judgment of the court.

(3) The conduct of the appeal under this section is a subordinate judicial duty that may be performed by traffic trial commissioners and other subordinate judicial officials at the direction of the presiding judge of the court.

(c) If no notice of appeal of the local agency's final administrative order or decision is filed within the period set forth in this section, the order or decision shall be deemed confirmed.

(d) If the fine or penalty has not been deposited and the decision of the court is against the contestant, the local agency may proceed to collect the penalty pursuant to the procedures set forth in its ordinance.

Government Code § 68152

(Amended by Stats. 2018, Ch. 423, Sec. 31. (SB 1494) Effective January 1, 2019.)

The trial court clerk may destroy court records under Section 68153 after notice of destruction, and if there is no request and order for transfer of the records, except the comprehensive historical and sample superior court records preserved for research under the California Rules of Court, when the following times have expired after the date of final disposition of the case in the categories listed:

(a) Civil actions and proceedings, as follows:

(1) Except as otherwise specified: retain 10 years.

(2) Civil unlimited cases, limited cases, and small claims cases, including after trial de novo, if any, except as otherwise specified: retain for 10 years.

(3) Civil judgments for unlimited civil cases: retain permanently.

(4) Civil judgments for limited and small claims cases: retain for 10 years, unless judgment is renewed. If judgment is renewed, retain judgment for length of renewal pursuant to Article 2 (commencing with Section 683.110) of Chapter 3 of Division 1 of Title 9 of Part 2 of the Code of Civil Procedure.

(5) If a party in a civil case appears by a guardian ad litem: retain for 10 years after termination of the court's jurisdiction.

(6) Civil harassment, domestic violence, elder and dependent adult abuse, private postsecondary school violence, gun violence, and workplace violence cases: retain for the same period of time as the duration of the restraining or other orders and any renewals thereof, then retain the restraining or other orders permanently as a judgment; 60 days after expiration of the temporary restraining or other temporary orders; retain judgments establishing paternity under Section 6323 of the Family Code permanently.

(7) Family law, except as otherwise specified: retain for 30 years.

(8) Adoption: retain permanently.

(9) Parentage: retain permanently.

(10) Change of name, gender, or name and gender: retain permanently.

(11) Probate:

(A) Decedent estates: retain permanently all orders, judgments, and decrees of the court, all inventories and appraisals, and all wills and codicils of the decedent filed in the case, including those not admitted to probate. All other records: retain for five years after final disposition of the estate proceeding.

(B) Wills and codicils transferred or delivered to the court pursuant to Section 732, 734, or 8203 of the Probate Code: retain permanently. For wills and codicils delivered to the clerk of the court under Section 8200 of the Probate Code, retain the original documents as provided in Section 26810.

(C) Substitutes for decedent estate administration:

(i) Affidavit procedures for real property of small value under Chapter 3 (commencing with Section 13100) of Part 1 of Division 8 of the Probate Code: retain permanently.

(ii) Proceedings for determining succession to property under Chapter 4 (commencing with Section 13150) of Part 1 of Division 8 of the Probate Code: retain permanently all inventories and appraisals and court orders. Other records: retain for five years after final disposition of the proceeding.

(iii) Proceedings for determination of property passing or belonging to surviving spouse under

Chapter 5 (commencing with Section 13650) of Part 2 of Division 8 of the Probate Code: retain permanently all inventories and appraisals and court orders. Other records: retain for five years after final disposition of the proceeding.

(D) Conservatorships: retain permanently all court orders. Documents of trusts established under substituted judgment pursuant to Section 2580 of the Probate Code: retain as provided in clause (iii) of subparagraph (G). Other records: retain for five years after the later of either (i) the final disposition of the conservatorship proceeding, or (ii) the date of the conservatee's death, if that date is disclosed in the court's file.

(E) Guardianships: retain permanently orders terminating the guardianship, if any, and court orders settling final account and ordering distribution of the estate. Other records: retain for five years after the later of (i) the final disposition of the guardianship proceeding, or (ii) the earlier of the date of the ward's death, if that date is disclosed in the court's file, or the date the ward reaches 23 years of age.

(F) Compromise of minor's or disabled person's claim or action, and disposition of judgment for minors and disabled persons under Section 372 of the Code of Civil Procedure and Chapter 4 (commencing with Section 3600) of Part 8 of Division 4 of the Probate Code:

(i) Retain permanently judgments in favor of minors or disabled persons, orders approving compromises of claims and actions and disposition of the proceeds of judgments, orders directing payment of expenses, costs, and fees, orders directing deposits into blocked accounts and receipts and acknowledgments of those orders, and orders for the withdrawal of funds from blocked accounts.

(ii) Retain other records for the same retention period as for records in the underlying case. If there is no underlying case, retain for five years after the later of either (I) the date the order for payment or delivery of the final balance of the money or property is entered, or (II) the earlier of the date of the minor's death, if that date is disclosed in the court's file, or the date the minor reaches 23 years of age.

(G) Trusts:

(i) Proceedings under Part 5 (commencing with Section 17000) of Division 9 of the Probate Code: retain permanently.

(ii) Trusts created by substituted judgment under Section 2580 of the Probate Code: retain permanently all trust instruments and court orders. Other records: retain as long as the underlying conservatorship file is retained.

(iii) Special needs trusts: retain permanently all trust instruments and court orders. Other records: retain until the later of either (I) the retention date of "other records" in the beneficiary's conservatorship or guardianship file under subparagraph (D) or (E), if any, or (II) five years after the date of the beneficiary's death, if that date is disclosed in the court's file.

(H) All other proceedings under the Probate Code: retain as provided for civil cases.

(12) Mental health:

(A) Lanterman Developmental Disabilities Services Act: retain for 10 years.

(B) Lanterman-Petris-Short Act: retain for 20 years.

(C) Riese (capacity) hearings under Sections 5333 and 5334 of the Welfare and Institutions Code: retain for the later of either (i) 20 years after the date of the capacity determination order, or (ii) the court records retention date of the underlying involuntary treatment or commitment proceeding, if any.

(D) Petitions under Chapter 3 (commencing with Section 8100) of Division 8 of the Welfare and Institutions Code for the return of firearms to petitioners who relinquished them to law enforcement while detained in a mental health facility: retain for 10 years.

(13) Eminent domain: retain permanently.

(14) Real property other than unlawful detainer: retain permanently if the action affects title or an interest in real property.

(15) Unlawful detainer: retain for one year if judgment is only for possession of the premises; retain for 10 years if judgment is for money, or money and possession.

(b) Notwithstanding subdivision (a), any civil or small claims case in the trial court:

(1) Involuntarily dismissed by the court for delay in prosecution or failure to comply with state or local rules: retain for one year.

(2) Voluntarily dismissed by a party without entry of judgment: retain for one year.

(c) Criminal actions and proceedings, as follows:

(1) Capital felony in which the defendant is sentenced to death, and any felony resulting in a sentence of life or life without the possibility of parole: retain permanently, including records of the cases of any codefendants and any related cases, regardless of the disposition. For the purpose of this paragraph, "capital felony" means murder with special circumstances when the prosecution seeks the death penalty. Records of the cases of codefendants and related cases required to be retained under this paragraph shall be limited to those cases that are factually linked or related to the charged offense, that are identified in the courtroom, and that are placed on the record. If a capital felony is disposed of by a sentence less than death, or imprisonment for life or life without the possibility of parole, the judgment shall be retained permanently, and the record shall be retained for 50 years or for 10 years after the official written notification of the death of the defendant. If a capital felony is disposed of by an acquittal, the record shall be retained for 10 years.

(2) Felony, except as otherwise specified, and in any felony or misdemeanor case resulting in a requirement that the defendant register as a sex offender under Section 290 of the Penal Code: retain judgment permanently. For all other documents: retain for 50 years or the maximum term of the sentence, whichever is longer. However, any record other than the judgment may be destroyed 10 years after the death of the defendant. Felony case files that do not include final sentencing or other final disposition because the case was bound over from a former municipal court to the superior court and not already consolidated with the superior court felony case file: retain for 10 years from the disposition of the superior court case.

(3) Felony reduced to a misdemeanor: retain in accordance with the retention period for the relevant misdemeanor.

(4) Felony, if the charge is dismissed, except as provided in paragraph (6): retain for three years.

(5) Misdemeanor, if the charge is dismissed, except as provided in paragraph (6): retain for one year.

(6) Dismissal under Section 1203.4 or 1203.4a of the Penal Code: retain for the same retention period as for records of the underlying case. If the records in the underlying case have been destroyed, retain for five years after dismissal.

(7) Misdemeanor, except as otherwise specified: retain for five years. For misdemeanors alleging a violation of Section 23103, 23152, or 23153 of the Vehicle Code: retain for 10 years.

(8) Misdemeanor alleging a marijuana violation under subdivision (b) or (c) of Section 11357 of the Health and Safety Code, or subdivision (b) of Section 11360 of the Health and Safety Code: records shall be destroyed, or redacted in accordance with subdivision (c) of Section 11361.5 of the Health and Safety Code, two years from

the date of conviction, or from the date of arrest if no conviction, if the case is no longer subject to review on appeal, all applicable fines and fees have been paid, and the defendant has complied with all terms and conditions of the sentence or grant of probation. As provided in subdivision (a) of Section 11361.5 of the Health and Safety Code and paragraph (5) of subdivision (e) of this section, records of an infraction alleging a marijuana violation under subdivision (d) of Section 11357 of the Health and Safety Code shall be retained until the offender attains 18 years of age, at which time the records shall be destroyed as provided in subdivision (c) of Section 11361.5 of the Health and Safety Code.

(9) Misdemeanor reduced to an infraction: retain in accordance with the retention period for the relevant infraction.

(10) Infraction, except as otherwise specified: retain for one year. Vehicle Code infraction: retain for three years. Infraction alleging a marijuana violation under subdivision (a) of Section 11357 of the Health and Safety Code: if records are retained past the one-year minimum retention period, the records shall be destroyed or redacted in accordance with subdivision (c) of Section 11361.5 of the Health and Safety Code two years from the date of conviction, or from the date of arrest if no conviction, if the case is no longer subject to review on appeal, all applicable fines and fees have been paid, and the defendant has complied with all terms and conditions of the sentence or grant of probation.

(11) Criminal protective order: retain until the order expires or is terminated.

(12) Arrest warrant: retain for the same retention period as for records in the underlying case. If there is no underlying case, retain for one year from the date of issue.

(13) Search warrant:

(A) If there is no underlying case, retain for five years from the date of issue.

(B) If there is any underlying case, retain for 10 years from the date of issue or, if the retention period for records in the underlying case is less than 10 years or if the underlying case is a capital felony described in paragraph (1) of subdivision (c), retain for the same retention period as for records in the underlying case.

(14) Probable cause declarations: retain for the same retention period as for records in the underlying case. If there is no underlying case, retain for one year from the date of declaration.

(15) Proceedings for revocation of postrelease community supervision or postrelease parole supervision: retain for five years after the period of supervision expires or is terminated.

(d) Habeas corpus:

(1) Habeas corpus in criminal and family law matters: retain for the same retention period as for records in the underlying case, whether granted or denied.

(2) Habeas corpus in mental health matters: retain all records for the same retention period as for records in the underlying case, whether granted or denied. If there is no underlying case, retain records for 20 years.

(e) Juveniles:

(1) Dependent pursuant to Section 300 of the Welfare and Institutions Code: upon reaching 28 years of age, or on written request, shall be released to the juvenile five years after jurisdiction over the person has terminated under subdivision (a) of Section 826 of the Welfare and Institutions Code. Sealed records shall be destroyed upon court order five years after the records have been sealed pursuant to subdivision (c) of Section 389 of the Welfare and Institutions Code.

(2) Ward pursuant to Section 601 of the Welfare and Institutions Code: upon reaching 21 years of age, or on written request, shall be released to the juvenile five years after jurisdiction over the person has terminated

under subdivision (a) of Section 826 of the Welfare and Institutions Code. Sealed records shall be destroyed upon court order five years after the records have been sealed under subdivision (d) of Section 781 of the Welfare and Institutions Code.

(3) Ward pursuant to Section 602 of the Welfare and Institutions Code: upon reaching 38 years of age under subdivision (a) of Section 826 of the Welfare and Institutions Code. Sealed records shall be destroyed upon court order when the subject of the record reaches 38 years of age under subdivision (d) of Section 781 of the Welfare and Institutions Code.

(4) Traffic and some nontraffic misdemeanors and infractions pursuant to Section 601 of the Welfare and Institutions Code: upon reaching 21 years of age, or five years after jurisdiction over the person has terminated under subdivision (c) of Section 826 of the Welfare and Institutions Code. Records may be microfilmed or photocopied.

(5) Marijuana infraction under subdivision (d) of Section 11357 of the Health and Safety Code in accordance with procedures specified in subdivision (a) of Section 11361.5 of the Health and Safety Code: upon reaching 18 years of age, the records shall be destroyed.

(f) Court records of the appellate division of the superior court: retain for five years.

(g) Other records:

(1) Bench warrant: retain for the same retention period as for records in the underlying case. For a bench warrant issued for a misdemeanor, retain records for the same retention period as for records in the underlying misdemeanor following issuance. If there is no return on the warrant, the court may dismiss on its own motion and immediately destroy the records.

(2) Body attachment: retain for same retention period as for records in the underlying case.

(3) Bond: retain for three years after exoneration and release.

(4) Court reporter notes:

(A) Criminal and juvenile proceedings: retain notes for 10 years, except as otherwise specified. Notes reporting proceedings in capital felony cases (murder with special circumstances when the prosecution seeks the death penalty and the sentence is death), including notes reporting the preliminary hearing, shall be retained permanently, unless the Supreme Court on request of the court clerk authorizes the destruction.

(B) Civil and all other proceedings: retain notes for five years.

(5) Electronic recordings made as the official record of the oral proceedings under the California Rules of Court may be destroyed or deleted as follows:

(A) Any time after final disposition of the case in infraction and misdemeanor proceedings.

(B) After 10 years in all other criminal proceedings.

(C) After five years in all other proceedings.

(6) Electronic recordings not made as the official record of the oral proceedings under the California Rules of Court may be destroyed at any time at the discretion of the court.

(7) Fee waiver applications: retain for the same retention period as for records in the underlying case.

(8) Judgments within the jurisdiction of the superior court other than in a limited civil case, misdemeanor case, or infraction case: retain permanently.

(9) Judgments in misdemeanor cases, infraction cases, and limited civil cases: retain for the same retention period as for records in the underlying case.

(10) Juror proceedings, including sanctions: retain for one year.

(11) Minutes: retain for the same retention period as for records in the underlying case.

(12) Orders not associated with an underlying case, such as orders for the destruction of court records for telephone taps, orders to destroy drugs, and other miscellaneous court orders: retain for one year.

(13) Naturalization index: retain permanently.

(14) Index for cases alleging traffic violations: retain for the same retention period as for records in the underlying case.

(15) Index, except as otherwise specified: retain permanently.

(16) Register of actions or docket: retain for the same retention period as for records in the underlying case, but in no event less than 10 years for civil and small claims cases.

(h) Retention of the court records under this section shall be extended by order of the court on its own motion, or on application of a party or an interested member of the public for good cause shown and on those terms as are just. A fee shall not be charged for making the application.

(i) The record retention periods provided in this section, as amended effective January 1, 2014, apply to all court records in existence prior to that date as well as to records created on or after that date.

VIII. Health and Safety Code Sections

Chapter 4.9. Compassionate Access to Medical Cannabis Act or Ryan's Law

Health and Safety Code § 1649

(Added by Stats. 2021, Ch. 384, Sec. 1. (SB 311) Effective January 1, 2022.)

(a) This chapter shall be known, and may be cited, as the "Compassionate Access to Medical Cannabis Act" or "Ryan's Law."

(b) It is the intent of the Legislature in enacting this chapter to support the ability of a terminally ill patient to safely use medicinal cannabis within specified health care facilities in compliance with the Compassionate Use Act of 1996 and Article 2.5 (commencing with Section 11362.7) of Chapter 6 of Division 10.

Health and Safety Code § 1649.1

(Amended by Stats. 2022, Ch. 242, Sec. 1. (SB 988) Effective January 1, 2023.)

Unless the context requires otherwise, the following definitions shall apply to this chapter:

(a) "Compassionate Use Act of 1996" means the initiative measure enacted by the approval of Proposition 215 at the November 5, 1996, statewide general election and found at Section 11362.5, and any amendments to that act.

(b) (1) Except as provided in paragraph (2), "health care facility" means a health facility specified in subdivision (a), (c), (f), (i), or (n) of Section 1250.

(2) The meaning of "health care facility" shall not include any of the following:

(A) A chemical dependency recovery hospital.

(B) A state hospital.

(C) An emergency department of a health care facility, as specified in subdivision (a) of Section 1250, while the patient is receiving emergency services and care.

(c) "Medicinal cannabis" means cannabis or a cannabis product used in compliance with the Compassionate Use Act of 1996 and Article 2.5 (commencing with Section 11362.7) of Chapter 6 of Division 10.

(d) "Patient" means an individual who is terminally ill. "Patient" does not include an individual receiving emergency services and care, as defined in Section 1317.1.

(e) "Terminally ill" means a medical condition resulting in a prognosis of life of one year or less, if the disease follows its natural course.

Health and Safety Code § 1649.2

(Amended by Stats. 2022, Ch. 242, Sec. 2. (SB 988) Effective January 1, 2023.)

A health care facility shall permit patient use of medical cannabis and shall do all of the following:

(a) Prohibit smoking or vaping as methods to use medicinal cannabis.

(b) Include the use of medicinal cannabis within the patient's medical records.

(c) Require a patient to provide a copy of the patient's valid identification card, as described in Section 11362.715, or a copy of that patient's written documentation as defined in Section 11362.7.

(d) Require a patient or a primary caregiver, as defined in Section 11362.7, to be responsible for acquiring, retrieving, administering, and removing medicinal cannabis.

(e) Require medicinal cannabis to be stored securely at all times in a locked container in the patient's room, other designated area, or with the patient's primary caregiver.

(f) Prohibit health care professionals and facility staff, including, but not limited to, physicians, nurses, and pharmacists, from administering medicinal cannabis or retrieving medicinal cannabis from storage.

(g) Develop and disseminate written guidelines for the use and disposal of medicinal cannabis within the health care facility pursuant to this chapter.

Health and Safety Code § 1649.3

(Repealed and added by Stats. 2022, Ch. 242, Sec. 4. (SB 988) Effective January 1, 2023.)

Upon discharge, all remaining medicinal cannabis shall be removed by the patient or patient's primary caregiver. If a patient cannot remove the medicinal cannabis and does not have a primary caregiver that is available to remove the medicinal cannabis, the product shall be stored in a locked container until it is disposed of in accordance with the health facility policy and procedure governing medicinal cannabis.

Health and Safety Code § 1649.4

(Amended by Stats. 2022, Ch. 242, Sec. 5. (SB 988) Effective January 1, 2023.)

This chapter does not require a health care facility to provide or furnish a patient with a recommendation to use medicinal cannabis in compliance with the Compassionate Use Act of 1996 and Article 2.5 (commencing with Section 11362.7) of Chapter 6 of Division 10 or include medicinal cannabis in a patient's discharge plan.

Health and Safety Code § 1649.5

(Amended by Stats. 2022, Ch. 242, Sec. 6. (SB 988) Effective January 1, 2023.)

(a) This chapter shall be enforced by the State Department of Public Health.

(b) Compliance with this chapter shall not be a condition for obtaining, retaining , or renewing a license as a health care facility.

(c) This chapter does not reduce, expand, or otherwise modify the laws restricting the cultivation, possession, distribution, or use of cannabis that may be otherwise applicable, including, but not limited to, the Control, Regulate and Tax Adult Use of Marijuana Act, an initiative measure enacted by the approval of Proposition 64 at the November 8, 2016, statewide general election, and any amendments to that act.

Health and Safety Code § 1649.6

(Added by Stats. 2021, Ch. 384, Sec. 1. (SB 311) Effective January 1, 2022.)

(a) If a federal regulatory agency, the United States Department of Justice (US DOJ), or the federal Centers for Medicare and Medicaid Services (CMS) takes one of the following actions, a health care facility may suspend compliance with Section 1649.2 until the regulatory agency, the US DOJ, or CMS notifies the health care facility that it may resume permitting the use of medicinal cannabis within the facility:

> (1) A federal regulatory agency or the US DOJ initiates enforcement action against a health care facility related to the facility's compliance with a state-regulated medical marijuana program.
>
> (2) A federal regulatory agency, the US DOJ, or CMS issues a rule or otherwise provides notification to the health care facility that expressly prohibits the use of medical marijuana in health care facilities or otherwise prohibits compliance with a state-regulated medical marijuana program.

(b) This section does not permit a health care facility to prohibit patient use of medicinal cannabis due solely to the fact that cannabis is a Schedule I drug pursuant to the federal Uniform Controlled Substances Act, or other federal constraints on the use of medicinal cannabis that were in existence prior to the enactment of this chapter.

Health and Safety Code § 7151.36

(Added by Stats. 2015, Ch. 51, Sec. 1. (AB 258) Effective January 1, 2016.)

(a) A hospital, physician and surgeon, procurement organization, or other person shall not determine the ultimate recipient of an anatomical gift based solely upon a potential recipient's status as a qualified patient, as defined in Section 11362.7, or based solely upon a positive test for the use of medical marijuana by a potential recipient who is a qualified patient, as defined in Section 11362.7, except to the extent that the qualified patient's use of medical marijuana has been found by a physician and surgeon, following a case-by-case evaluation of the potential recipient, to be medically significant to the provision of the anatomical gift.

(b) Subdivision (a) shall apply to each part of the organ transplant process. The organ transplant process includes, but is not limited to, all of the following:

(1) The referral from a primary care provider to a specialist.

(2) The referral from a specialist to a transplant center.

(3) The evaluation of the patient for the transplant by the transplant center.

(4) The consideration of the patient for placement on the official waiting list.

(c) The court shall accord priority on its calendar and handle expeditiously any action brought to seek any remedy authorized by law for purposes of enforcing compliance with this section.

(d) This section shall not be deemed to require referrals or recommendations for, or the performance of, medically inappropriate organ transplants.

Health and Safety Code § 11006.5

(Amended by Stats. 2017, Ch. 27, Sec. 113. (SB 94) Effective June 27, 2017.)

"Concentrated cannabis" means the separated resin, whether crude or purified, obtained from cannabis.

Health and Safety Code § 11007

(Added by Stats. 1987, Ch. 1174, Sec. 1. Effective September 26, 1987.)

"Controlled substance," unless otherwise specified, means a drug, substance, or immediate precursor which is listed in any schedule in Section 11054, 11055, 11056, 11057, or 11058.

Health and Safety Code § 11014.5

(Amended by Stats. 2022, Ch. 201, Sec. 1. (AB 1598) Effective January 1, 2023.)

(a) "Drug paraphernalia" means all equipment, products and materials of any kind which are designed for use or marketed for use, in planting, propagating, cultivating, growing, harvesting, manufacturing, compounding, converting, producing, processing, preparing, testing, analyzing, packaging, repackaging, storing, containing, concealing, injecting, ingesting, inhaling, or otherwise introducing into the human body a controlled substance in violation of this division. It includes, but is not limited to:

(1) Kits designed for use or marketed for use in planting, propagating, cultivating, growing, or harvesting of any species of plant which is a controlled substance or from which a controlled substance can be derived.

(2) Kits designed for use or marketed for use in manufacturing, compounding, converting, producing, processing, or preparing controlled substances.

(3) Isomerization devices designed for use or marketed for use in increasing the potency of any species of plant which is a controlled substance.

(4) Testing equipment designed for use or marketed for use in identifying, or in analyzing the strength, effectiveness, or purity of controlled substances, except as otherwise provided in subdivision (d).

(5) Scales and balances designed for use or marketed for use in weighing or measuring controlled substances.

(6) Containers and other objects designed for use or marketed for use in storing or concealing controlled substances.

(7) Hypodermic syringes, needles, and other objects designed for use or marketed for use in parenterally injecting controlled substances into the human body.

(8) Objects designed for use or marketed for use in ingesting, inhaling, or otherwise introducing cannabis, cocaine, hashish, or hashish oil into the human body, such as:

(A) Carburetion tubes and devices.

(B) Smoking and carburetion masks.

(C) Roach clips, meaning objects used to hold burning material, such as a cannabis cigarette, that has become too small or too short to be held in the hand.

(D) Miniature cocaine spoons, and cocaine vials.

(E) Chamber pipes.

(F) Carburetor pipes.

(G) Electric pipes.

(H) Air-driven pipes.

(I) Chillums.

(J) Bongs.

(K) Ice pipes or chillers.

(b) For the purposes of this section, the phrase "marketed for use" means advertising, distributing, offering for sale, displaying for sale, or selling in a manner which promotes the use of equipment, products, or materials with controlled substances.

(c) In determining whether an object is drug paraphernalia, a court or other authority may consider, in addition to all other logically relevant factors, the following:

(1) Statements by an owner or by anyone in control of the object concerning its use.

(2) Instructions, oral or written, provided with the object concerning its use for ingesting, inhaling, or otherwise introducing a controlled substance into the human body.

(3) Descriptive materials accompanying the object which explain or depict its use.

(4) National and local advertising concerning its use.

(5) The manner in which the object is displayed for sale.

(6) Whether the owner, or anyone in control of the object, is a legitimate supplier of like or related items to the community, such as a licensed distributor or dealer of tobacco products.

(7) Expert testimony concerning its use.

(d) Notwithstanding paragraph (4) of subdivision (a), "drug paraphernalia" does not include any testing equipment designed, marketed, intended to be used, or used, to test a substance for the presence of fentanyl, ketamine, gamma hydroxybutyric acid, or any analog of fentanyl.

(e) If any provision of this section or the application thereof to any person or circumstance is held invalid, it is the intent of the Legislature that the invalidity shall not affect other provisions or applications of the section which can be given effect without the invalid provision or application and to this end the provisions of this section are severable.

Health and Safety Code § 11018

(Amended by Stats. 2017, Ch. 27, Sec. 115. (SB 94) Effective June 27, 2017. Note: This section was amended on Nov. 8, 2016, by initiative Prop. 64.)

"Cannabis" means all parts of the plant Cannabis sativa L., whether growing or not; the seeds thereof; the resin extracted from any part of the plant; and every compound, manufacture, salt, derivative, mixture, or preparation of the plant, its seeds or resin. It does not include either of the following:

(a) Industrial hemp, as defined in Section 11018.5; or

(b) The weight of any other ingredient combined with cannabis to prepare topical or oral administrations, food, drink, or other product.

Health and Safety Code § 11018.1

(Amended by Stats. 2017, Ch. 27, Sec. 116. (SB 94) Effective June 27, 2017. Note: This section was added on Nov. 8, 2016, by initiative Prop. 64.)

"Cannabis products" means cannabis that has undergone a process whereby the plant material has been transformed into a concentrate, including, but not limited to, concentrated cannabis, or an edible or topical product containing cannabis or concentrated cannabis and other ingredients.

Health and Safety Code § 11018.2

(Amended by Stats. 2017, Ch. 27, Sec. 117. (SB 94) Effective June 27, 2017. Note: This section was added on Nov. 8, 2016, by initiative Prop. 64.)

"Cannabis accessories" means any equipment, products or materials of any kind which are used, intended for use, or designed for use in planting, propagating, cultivating, growing, harvesting, manufacturing, compounding, converting, producing, processing, preparing, testing, analyzing, packaging, repackaging, storing, smoking, vaporizing, or containing cannabis, or for ingesting, inhaling, or otherwise introducing cannabis or cannabis products into the human body.

Health & Safety Code § 11018.5

(Amended by Stats. 2021, Ch. 576, Sec. 2. (AB 45) Effective October 6, 2021. Note: This section was amended on Nov. 8, 2016, by initiative Prop. 64.)

(a) "Industrial hemp" or "hemp" means an agricultural product, whether growing or not, that is limited to types of the plant Cannabis sativa L. and any part of that plant, including the seeds of the plant and all derivatives, extracts, the resin extracted from any part of the plant, cannabinoids, isomers, acids, salts, and salts of isomers, with a delta-9 tetrahydrocannabinol concentration of no more than 0.3 percent on a dry weight basis.

(b) Industrial hemp shall not be subject to the provisions of this division or of Division 10 (commencing with Section 26000) of the Business and Professions Code, but instead shall be regulated by the Department of Food and

Agriculture in accordance with the provisions of Division 24 (commencing with Section 81000) of the Food and Agricultural Code, inclusive.

Health and Safety Code § 11032

(Amended by Stats. 2017, Ch. 27, Sec. 119. (SB 94) Effective June 27, 2017.)

If reference is made to the term "narcotics" in any law not in this division, unless otherwise expressly provided, it means those controlled substances classified in Schedules I and II, as defined in this division. If reference is made to "restricted dangerous drugs" not in this division, unless otherwise expressly provided, it means those controlled substances classified in Schedules III and IV. If reference is made to the term "marijuana" in any law not in this division, unless otherwise expressly provided, it means cannabis as defined in this division.

Health and Safety Code § 11054

(Amended by Stats. 2017, Ch. 27, Sec. 120. (SB 94) Effective June 27, 2017.)

(a) The controlled substances listed in this section are included in Schedule I.

(b) Opiates. Unless specifically excepted or unless listed in another schedule, any of the following opiates, including their isomers, esters, ethers, salts, and salts of isomers, esters, and ethers whenever the existence of those isomers, esters, ethers, and salts is possible within the specific chemical designation:

(1) Acetylmethadol.

(2) Allylprodine.

(3) Alphacetylmethadol (except levoalphacetylmethadol, also known as levo-alpha- acetylmethadol, levomethadyl acetate, or LAAM).

(4) Alphameprodine.

(5) Alphamethadol.

(6) Benzethidine.

(7) Betacetylmethadol.

(8) Betameprodine.

(9) Betamethadol.

(10) Betaprodine.

(11) Clonitazene.

(12) Dextromoramide.

(13) Diampromide.

(14) Diethylthiambutene.

(15) Difenoxin.

(16) Dimenoxadol.

(17) Dimepheptanol.

(18) Dimethylthiambutene.

(19) Dioxaphetyl butyrate.

(20) Dipipanone.

(21) Ethylmethylthiambutene.

(22) Etonitazene.

(23) Etoxeridine.

(24) Furethidine.

(25) Hydroxypethidine.

(26) Ketobemidone.

(27) Levomoramide.

(28) Levophenacylmorphan.

(29) Morpheridine.

(30) Noracymethadol.

(31) Norlevorphanol.

(32) Normethadone.

(33) Norpipanone.

(34) Phenadoxone.

(35) Phenampromide.

(36) Phenomorphan.

(37) Phenoperidine.

(38) Piritramide.

(39) Proheptazine.

(40) Properidine.

(41) Propiram.

(42) Racemoramide.

(43) Tilidine.

(44) Trimeperidine.

(45) Any substance which contains any quantity of acetylfentanyl (N-[1-phenethyl-4-piperidinyl] acetanilide) or a derivative thereof.

(46) Any substance which contains any quantity of the thiophene analog of acetylfentanyl (N-[1-[2-(2-thienyl) ethyl]-4-piperidinyl] acetanilide) or a derivative thereof.

(47) 1-Methyl-4-Phenyl-4-Propionoxypiperidine (MPPP).

(48) 1-(2-Phenethyl)-4-Phenyl-4-Acetyloxypiperidine (PEPAP).

(c) Opium derivatives. Unless specifically excepted or unless listed in another schedule, any of the following opium derivatives, its salts, isomers, and salts of isomers whenever the existence of those salts, isomers, and salts of isomers is possible within the specific chemical designation:

(1) Acetorphine.

(2) Acetyldihydrocodeine.

(3) Benzylmorphine.

(4) Codeine methylbromide.

(5) Codeine-N-Oxide.

(6) Cyprenorphine.

(7) Desomorphine.

(8) Dihydromorphine.

(9) Drotebanol.

(10) Etorphine (except hydrochloride salt).

(11) Heroin.

(12) Hydromorphinol.

(13) Methyldesorphine.

(14) Methyldihydromorphine.

(15) Morphine methylbromide.

(16) Morphine methylsulfonate.

(17) Morphine-N-Oxide.

(18) Myrophine.

(19) Nicocodeine.

(20) Nicomorphine.

(21) Normorphine.

(22) Pholcodine.

(23) Thebacon.

(d) Hallucinogenic substances. Unless specifically excepted or unless listed in another schedule, any material, compound, mixture, or preparation, which contains any quantity of the following hallucinogenic substances, or which contains any of its salts, isomers, and salts of isomers whenever the existence of those salts, isomers, and salts of isomers is possible within the specific chemical designation (for purposes of this subdivision only, the term "isomer" includes the optical, position, and geometric isomers):

(1) 4-bromo-2,5-dimethoxy-amphetamine—Some trade or other names: 4-bromo-2,5-dimethoxy-alphamethylphenethylamine; 4-bromo-2,5-DMA.

(2) 2,5-dimethoxyamphetamine—Some trade or other names: 2,5-dimethoxy-alpha-methylphenethylamine; 2,5-DMA.

(3) 4-methoxyamphetamine—Some trade or other names: 4-methoxy-alpha-methylphenethylamine, paramethoxyamphetamine, PMA.

(4) 5-methoxy-3,4-methylenedioxy-amphetamine.

(5) 4-methyl-2,5-dimethoxy-amphetamine—Some trade or other names: 4-methyl-2,5-dimethoxy-alphamethylphenethylamine; "DOM"; and "STP."

(6) 3,4-methylenedioxy amphetamine.

(7) 3,4,5-trimethoxy amphetamine.

(8) Bufotenine—Some trade or other names: 3-(beta-dimethylaminoethyl)-5-hydroxyindole; 3-(2-dimethylaminoethyl)-5 indolol; N,N-dimethylserolonin, 5-hydroxy-N,N-dimethyltryptamine; mappine.

(9) Diethyltryptamine—Some trade or other names: N,N-Diethyltryptamine; DET.

(10) Dimethyltryptamine—Some trade or other names: DMT.

(11) Ibogaine—Some trade or other names: 7-Ethyl-6,6beta, 7,8,9,10,12,13-octahydro-2-methoxy-6,9-methano-5H-pyrido [1',2':1,2] azepino [5,4-b] indole; Tabernantheiboga.

(12) Lysergic acid diethylamide.

(13) Cannabis.

(14) Mescaline.

(15) Peyote—Meaning all parts of the plant presently classified botanically as Lophophora williamsii Lemaire, whether growing or not, the seeds thereof, any extract from any part of the plant, and every compound, manufacture, salts, derivative, mixture, or preparation of the plant, its seeds or extracts (interprets 21 U.S.C. Sec. 812(c), Schedule 1(c)(12)).

(16) N-ethyl-3-piperidyl benzilate.

(17) N-methyl-3-piperidyl benzilate.

(18) Psilocybin.

(19) Psilocyn.

(20) Tetrahydrocannabinols. Synthetic equivalents of the substances contained in the plant, or in the resinous extractives of Cannabis, sp. and/or synthetic substances, derivatives, and their isomers with similar chemical structure and pharmacological activity such as the following: delta 1 cis or trans tetrahydrocannabinol, and their optical isomers; delta 6 cis or trans tetrahydrocannabinol, and their optical isomers; delta 3,4 cis or trans tetrahydrocannabinol, and its optical isomers.

Because nomenclature of these substances is not internationally standardized, compounds of these structures, regardless of numerical designation of atomic positions covered.

(21) Ethylamine analog of phencyclidine—Some trade or other names: N-ethyl-1-phenylcyclohexylamine, (1-phenylcyclohexyl) ethylamine, N-(1-phenylcyclohexyl) ethylamine, cyclohexamine, PCE.

(22) Pyrrolidine analog of phencyclidine—Some trade or other names: 1-(1-phenylcyclohexyl)-pyrrolidine, PCP, PHP.

(23) Thiophene analog of phencyclidine—Some trade or other names: 1-[1-(2 thienyl)-cyclohexyl]-piperidine, 2-thienyl analog of phencyclidine, TPCP, TCP.

(e) Depressants. Unless specifically excepted or unless listed in another schedule, any material, compound, mixture, or preparation which contains any quantity of the following substances having a depressant effect on the central nervous system, including its salts, isomers, and salts of isomers whenever the existence of those salts, isomers, and salts of isomers is possible within the specific chemical designation:

(1) Mecloqualone.

(2) Methaqualone.

(3) Gamma hydroxybutyric acid (also known by other names such as GHB; gamma hydroxy butyrate; 4-hydroxybutyrate; 4-hydroxybutanoic acid; sodium oxybate; sodium oxybutyrate), including its immediate precursors, isomers, esters, ethers, salts, and salts of isomers, esters, and ethers, including, but not limited to, gammabutyrolactone, for which an application has not been approved under Section 505 of the Federal Food, Drug, and Cosmetic Act (21 U.S.C. Sec. 355).

(f) Unless specifically excepted or unless listed in another schedule, any material, compound, mixture, or preparation which contains any quantity of the following substances having a stimulant effect on the central nervous system, including its isomers:

(1) Cocaine base.

(2) Fenethylline, including its salts.

(3) N-Ethylamphetamine, including its salts.

Health and Safety Code § 11107.2

(Added by Stats. 2018, Ch. 595, Sec. 1. (AB 3112) Effective January 1, 2019. Section operative July 1, 2019, by its own provisions.)

(a) Except as otherwise provided in subdivision (b), it is unlawful for a manufacturer, wholesaler, reseller, retailer, or other person or entity to sell to any customer any quantity of nonodorized butane.

(b) The limitations in subdivisions (a) shall not apply to any of the following transactions:

(1) Butane sold to manufacturers, wholesalers, resellers, or retailers solely for the purpose of resale.

(2) Butane sold to a person for use in a lawful commercial enterprise, including, but not limited to, a volatile solvent extraction activity licensed under Division 10 (commencing with Section 26000) of the Business and Professions Code or a medical cannabis collective or cooperative described in subdivision (b) of Section 11362.775 of this code, operating in compliance with all applicable state licensing requirements and local regulations governing that type of business.

(3) The sale of pocket lighters, utility lighters, grill lighters, torch lighters, butane gas appliances, refill canisters, gas cartridges, or other products that contain or use nonodorized butane and contain less than 150 milliliters of butane.

(4) The sale of any product in which butane is used as an aerosol propellant.

(c) (1) Any person or business that violates subdivision (a) is subject to a civil penalty of two thousand five hundred dollars ($2,500).

(2) The Attorney General, a city attorney, a county counsel, or a district attorney may bring a civil action to

enforce this section.

(3) The civil penalty shall be deposited into the General Fund if the action is brought by the Attorney General. If the action is brought by a city attorney, the civil penalty shall be paid to the treasurer of the city in which the judgment is entered. If the action is brought by a county counsel or district attorney, the civil penalty shall be paid to the treasurer of the county in which the judgment is entered.

(d) As used in this section, the following definitions shall apply:

(1) "Customer" means any person or entity other than those described in paragraphs (1) and (2) of subdivision (b) that purchases or acquires nonodorized butane from a seller during a transaction.

(2) "Nonodorized butane" means iso-butane, n-butane, butane, or a mixture of butane and propane of any power that may also use the words "refined," "pure," "purified," "premium," or "filtered," to describe the butane or butane mixture, which does not contain ethyl mercaptan or a similar odorant.

(3) "Sell" or "sale" means to furnish, give away, exchange, transfer, deliver, surrender, distribute, or supply, in exchange for money or any other consideration.

(4) "Seller" means any person, business entity, or employee thereof that sells nonodorized butane to any customer within this state.

(e) This section shall become operative on July 1, 2019.

Health and Safety Code § 11357

(Amended by Stats. 2017, Ch. 253, Sec. 15. (AB 133) Effective September 16, 2017. Note: This section was amended on Nov. 4, 2014, by initiative Prop. 47, and on Nov. 8, 2016, by initiative Prop. 64.)

(a) Except as authorized by law, possession of not more than 28.5 grams of cannabis, or not more than eight grams of concentrated cannabis, or both, shall be punished or adjudicated as follows:

(1) Persons under 18 years of age are guilty of an infraction and shall be required to:

(A) Upon a finding that a first offense has been committed, complete four hours of drug education or counseling and up to 10 hours of community service over a period not to exceed 60 days.

(B) Upon a finding that a second offense or subsequent offense has been committed, complete six hours of drug education or counseling and up to 20 hours of community service over a period not to exceed 90 days.

(2) Persons at least 18 years of age but less than 21 years of age are guilty of an infraction and punishable by a fine of not more than one hundred dollars ($100).

(b) Except as authorized by law, possession of more than 28.5 grams of cannabis, or more than eight grams of concentrated cannabis, shall be punished as follows:

(1) Persons under 18 years of age who possess more than 28.5 grams of cannabis or more than eight grams of concentrated cannabis, or both, are guilty of an infraction and shall be required to:

(A) Upon a finding that a first offense has been committed, complete eight hours of drug education or counseling and up to 40 hours of community service over a period not to exceed 90 days.

(B) Upon a finding that a second or subsequent offense has been committed, complete 10 hours of drug education or counseling and up to 60 hours of community service over a period not to exceed 120 days.

(2) Persons 18 years of age or older who possess more than 28.5 grams of cannabis, or more than eight grams

of concentrated cannabis, or both, shall be punished by imprisonment in a county jail for a period of not more than six months or by a fine of not more than five hundred dollars ($500), or by both that fine and imprisonment.

(c) Except as authorized by law, a person 18 years of age or older who possesses not more than 28.5 grams of cannabis, or not more than eight grams of concentrated cannabis, upon the grounds of, or within, any school providing instruction in kindergarten or any of grades 1 to 12, inclusive, during hours the school is open for classes or school-related programs is guilty of a misdemeanor and shall be punished as follows:

(1) A fine of not more than two hundred fifty dollars ($250), upon a finding that a first offense has been committed.

(2) A fine of not more than five hundred dollars ($500), or by imprisonment in a county jail for a period of not more than 10 days, or both, upon a finding that a second or subsequent offense has been committed.

(d) Except as authorized by law, a person under 18 years of age who possesses not more than 28.5 grams of cannabis, or not more than eight grams of concentrated cannabis, upon the grounds of, or within, any school providing instruction in kindergarten or any of grades 1 to 12, inclusive, during hours the school is open for classes or school-related programs is guilty of an infraction and shall be punished in the same manner provided in paragraph (1) of subdivision (b).

Health and Safety Code § 11357.5

(Amended by Stats. 2016, Ch. 624, Sec. 2. (SB 139) Effective September 25, 2016.)

(a) Every person who sells, dispenses, distributes, furnishes, administers, or gives, or offers to sell, dispense, distribute, furnish, administer, or give, or possesses for sale any synthetic cannabinoid compound, or any synthetic cannabinoid derivative, to any person, is guilty of a misdemeanor, punishable by imprisonment in a county jail not to exceed six months, or by a fine not to exceed one thousand dollars ($1,000), or by both that fine and imprisonment.

(b) Every person who uses or possesses any synthetic cannabinoid compound, or any synthetic cannabinoid derivative, is guilty of a public offense, punishable as follows:

(1) A first offense is an infraction punishable by a fine not exceeding two hundred fifty dollars ($250).

(2) A second offense is an infraction punishable by a fine not exceeding two hundred fifty dollars ($250) or a misdemeanor punishable by imprisonment in a county jail not exceeding six months, a fine not exceeding five hundred dollars ($500), or by both that fine and imprisonment.

(3) A third or subsequent offense is a misdemeanor punishable by imprisonment in a county jail not exceeding six months, or by a fine not exceeding one thousand dollars ($1,000), or by both that fine and imprisonment.

(c) As used in this section, the term “synthetic cannabinoid compound” refers to any of the following substances or an analog of any of the following substances:

(1) Adamantoylindoles or adamantoylindazoles, which includes adamantyl carboxamide indoles and adamantyl carboxamide indazoles, or any compound structurally derived from 3-(1-adamantoyl)indole, 3-(1-adamantoyl) indazole, 3-(2-adamantoyl)indole, N-(1-adamantyl)-1H-indole-3-carboxamide, or N-(1-adamantyl)-1H-indazole-3-carboxamide by substitution at the nitrogen atom of the indole or indazole ring with alkyl, haloalkyl, alkenyl, cyanoalkyl, hydroxyalkyl, cycloalkylmethyl, cycloalkylethyl, 1-(N-methyl-2-piperidinyl) methyl, 2-(4-morpholinyl)ethyl, or 1-(N-methyl-2-pyrrolidinyl)methyl, 1-(N-methyl-3-morpholinyl)methyl, or (tetrahydropyran-4-yl)methyl group, whether or not further substituted in the indole or indazole ring to any extent and whether or not substituted in the adamantyl ring to any extent, including, but not limited to, 2NE1, 5F-AKB-48, AB-001, AKB-48, AM-1248, JWH-018 adamantyl carboxamide, STS-135.

(2) Benzoylindoles, which includes any compound structurally derived from a 3-(benzoyl)indole structure with substitution at the nitrogen atom of the indole ring with alkyl, haloalkyl, cyanoalkyl, hydroxyalkyl, alkenyl, cycloalkylmethyl, cycloalkylethyl, 1-(N-methyl-2-piperidinyl)methyl, 2-(4-morpholinyl)ethyl, or 1-(N-methyl-2-pyrrolidinyl)methyl, 1-(N-methyl-3-morpholinyl)methyl, or (tetrahydropyran-4-yl)methyl group, whether or not further substituted in the indole ring to any extent and whether or not substituted in the phenyl ring to any extent, including, but not limited to, AM-630, AM-661, AM-679, AM-694, AM-1241, AM-2233, RCS-4, WIN 48,098 (Pravadoline).

(3) Cyclohexylphenols, which includes any compound structurally derived from 2-(3-hydroxycyclohexyl)phenol by substitution at the 5-position of the phenolic ring by alkyl, haloalkyl, cyanoalkyl, hydroxyalkyl, alkenyl, cycloalkylmethyl, cycloalkylethyl, 1-(N-methyl-2-piperidinyl)methyl, 2-(4-morpholinyl)ethyl, or 1-(N-methyl-2-pyrrolidinyl)methyl, 1-(N-methyl-3-morpholinyl)methyl, or tetrahydropyran-4-yl)methyl group, whether or not further substituted in the cyclohexyl ring to any extent, including, but not limited to, CP 47,497, CP 55,490, CP 55,940, CP 56,667, cannabicyclohexanol.

(4) Cyclopropanoylindoles, which includes any compound structurally derived from 3-(cyclopropylmethanoyl) indole, 3-(cyclopropylmethanone)indole, 3-(cyclobutylmethanone)indole or 3-(cyclopentylmethanone)indole by substitution at the nitrogen atom of the indole ring, whether or not further substituted in the indole ring to any extent, whether or not substituted on the cyclopropyl, cyclobutyl, or cyclopentyl rings to any extent.

(5) Naphthoylindoles, which includes any compound structurally derived from 3-(1-naphthoyl)indole or 1H-indol-3-yl-(1-naphthyl)methane by substitution at the nitrogen atom of the indole ring by alkyl, haloalkyl, cyanoalkyl, hydroxyalkyl, alkenyl, cycloalkylmethyl, cycloalkylethyl, 1-(N-methyl-2-piperidinyl)methyl, 2-(4-morpholinyl)ethyl group, 1-(N-methyl-2-pyrrolidinyl)methyl, 1-(N-methyl-3-morpholinyl)methyl, or (tetrahydropyran-4-yl)methyl group, whether or not further substituted in the naphthyl ring to any extent, including, but not limited to, AM-678, AM-1220, AM-1221, AM-1235, AM-2201, AM-2232, EAM-2201, JWH-004, JWH-007, JWH-009, JWH-011, JWH-015, JWH-016, JWH-018, JWH-019, JWH-020, JWH-022, JWH-046, JWH-047, JWH-048, JWH-049, JWH-050, JWH-070, JWH-071, JWH-072, JWH-073, JWH-076, JWH-079, JWH-080, JWH-081, JWH-082, JWH-094, JWH-096, JWH-098, JWH-116, JWH-120, JWH-122, JWH-148, JWH-149, JWH-164, JWH-166, JWH-180, JWH-181, JWH-182, JWH-189, JWH-193, JWH-198, JWH-200, JWH-210, JWH-211, JWH-212, JWH-213, JWH-234, JWH-235, JWH-236, JWH-239, JWH-240, JWH-241, JWH-242, JWH-258, JWH-262, JWH-386, JWH-387, JWH-394, JWH-395, JWH-397, JWH-398, JWH-399, JWH-400, JWH-412, JWH-413, JWH-414, JWH-415, JWH-424, MAM-2201, WIN 55,212.

(6) Naphthoylnaphthalenes, which includes any compound structurally derived from naphthalene-1-yl-(naphthalene-1-yl) methanone with substitutions on either of the naphthalene rings to any extent, including, but not limited to, CB-13.

(7) Naphthoylpyrroles, which includes any compound structurally derived from 3-(1-naphthoyl)pyrrole by substitution at the nitrogen atom of the pyrrole ring by alkyl, haloalkyl, cyanoalkyl, hydroxyalkyl, alkenyl, cycloalkylmethyl, cycloalkylethyl, 1-(N-methyl-2-piperidinyl)methyl, 2-(4-morpholinyl)ethyl, or 1-N-methyl-2-pyrrolidinyl)methyl, 1-(N-methyl-3-morpholinyl)methyl, or (tetrahydropyran-4-yl)methyl group, whether or not further substituted in the pyrrole ring to any extent and whether or not substituted in the naphthyl ring to any extent, including, but not limited to, JWH-030, JWH-031, JWH-145, JWH-146, JWH-147, JWH-150, JWH-156, JWH-243, JWH-244, JWH-245, JWH-246, JWH-292, JWH-293, JWH-307, JWH-308, JWH-309, JWH-346, JWH-348, JWH-363, JWH-364, JWH-365, JWH-367, JWH-368, JWH-369, JWH-370, JWH-371, JWH-373, JWH-392.

(8) Naphthylmethylindenes, which includes any compound containing a naphthylideneindene structure or which is structurally derived from 1-(1-naphthylmethyl)indene with substitution at the 3-position of the indene ring by alkyl, haloalkyl, cyanoalkyl, hydroxyalkyl, alkenyl, cycloalkylmethyl, cycloalkylethyl, 1-(N-methyl-2-piperidinyl)methyl, 2-(4-morpholinyl)ethyl, or 1-(N-methyl-2-pyrrolidinyl)methyl, 1-(N-methyl-3-morpholinyl)methyl, or (tetrahydropyran-4-yl)methyl group, whether or not further substituted in the indene ring to any extent and whether or not substituted in the naphthyl ring to any extent, including, but not limited to, JWH-171, JWH-176, JWH-220.

(9) Naphthylmethylindoles, which includes any compound structurally derived from an H-indol-3-yl-(1-naphthyl) methane by substitution at the nitrogen atom of the indole ring by alkyl, haloalkyl, cyanoalkyl, hydroxyalkyl, alkenyl, cycloalkylmethyl, cycloalkylethyl, 1-(N-methyl-2-piperidinyl)methyl, 2-(4-morpholinyl) ethyl, or 1-(N-methyl-2-pyrrolidinyl)methyl, 1-(N-methyl-3-morpholinyl)methyl, or (tetrahydropyran-4-yl)methyl group, whether or not further substituted in the indole ring to any extent and whether or not substituted in the naphthyl ring to any extent, including, but not limited to, JWH-175, JWH-184, JWH-185, JWH-192, JWH-194, JWH-195, JWH-196, JWH-197, JWH-199.

(10) Phenylacetylindoles, which includes any compound structurally derived from 3-phenylacetylindole by substitution at the nitrogen atom of the indole ring with alkyl, haloalkyl, cyanoalkyl, hydroxyalkyl, alkenyl, cycloalkylmethyl, cycloalkylethyl, 1-(N-methyl-2-piperidinyl)methyl, 2-(4-morpholinyl)ethyl, or 1-N-methyl-2-pyrrolidinyl)methyl, 1-(N-methyl-3-morpholinyl)methyl, or (tetrahydropyran-4-yl)methyl group, whether or not further substituted in the indole ring to any extent and whether or not substituted in the phenyl ring to any extent, including, but not limited to, cannabipiperidiethanone, JWH-167, JWH-201, JWH-202, JWH-203, JWH-204, JWH-205, JWH-206, JWH-207, JWH-208, JWH-209, JWH-237, JWH-248, JWH-249, JWH-250, JWH-251, JWH-253, JWH-302, JWH-303, JWH-304, JWH-305, JWH-306, JWH-311, JWH-312, JWH-313, JWH-314, JWH-315, JWH-316, RCS-8.

(11) Quinolinylindolecarboxylates, which includes any compound structurally derived from quinolin-8-yl-1H-indole-3-carboxylate by substitution at the nitrogen atom of the indole ring with alkyl, haloalkyl, benzyl, halobenzyl, alkenyl, haloalkenyl, alkoxy, cyanoalkyl, hydroxyalkyl, cycloalkylmethyl, cycloalkylethyl, (N-methylpiperidin-2-yl)alkyl, (4-tetrahydropyran)alkyl, or 2-(4-morpholinyl)alkyl, whether or not further substituted in the indole ring to any extent, whether or not substituted in the quinoline ring to any extent, including, but not limited to, BB-22, 5-Fluoro-PB-22, PB-22.

(12) Tetramethylcyclopropanoylindoles, which includes any compound structurally derived from 3-tetramethylcyclopropanoylindole, 3-(1- tetramethylcyclopropyl)indole, 3-(2,2,3,3-tetramethylcyclopropyl) indole or 3-(2,2,3,3-tetramethylcyclopropylcarbonyl)indole with substitution at the nitrogen atom of the indole ring by an alkyl, haloalkyl, cyanoalkyl, hydroxyalkyl, alkenyl, cycloalkylmethyl, cycloalkylethyl, 1-(N-methyl-2-piperidinyl)methyl, 2-(4-morpholinyl)ethyl, 1-(N-methyl-2-pyrrolidinyl)methyl, 1-(N-methyl-3-morpholinyl)methyl, or (tetrahydropyran-4-yl)methyl group whether or not further substituted in the indole ring to any extent and whether or not substituted in the tetramethylcyclopropanoyl ring to any extent, including, but not limited to, 5-bromo-UR-144, 5-chloro-UR-144, 5-fluoro-UR-144, A-796,260, A-834,735, AB-034, UR-144, XLR11.

(13) Tetramethylcyclopropane-thiazole carboxamides, which includes any compound structurally derived from 2,2,3,3-tetramethyl-N-(thiazol-2-ylidene)cyclopropanecarboxamide by substitution at the nitrogen atom of the thiazole ring by alkyl, haloalkyl, benzyl, halobenzyl, alkenyl, haloalkenyl, alkoxy, cyanoalkyl, hydroxyalkyl, cycloalkylmethyl, cycloalkylethyl, (N-methylpiperidin-2-yl)alkyl, (4-tetrahydropyran)alkyl, or 2-(4-morpholinyl)alkyl, whether or not further substituted in the thiazole ring to any extent, whether or not substituted in the tetramethylcyclopropyl ring to any extent, including, but not limited to, A-836,339.

(14) Unclassified synthetic cannabinoids, which includes all of the following:

(A) AM-087, (6aR,10aR)-3-(2-methyl-6-bromohex-2-yl)-6,6,9-t rimethyl-6a,7,10,10a-tetrahydrobenzo[c] chromen-1-ol.

(B) AM-356, methanandamide, including (5Z,8Z,11Z,14Z)--[(1R)-2-hydroxy-1-methylethyl]icosa-5,8,11,14-tetraenamide and arachidonyl-1'-hydroxy-2'-propylamide.

(C) AM-411, (6aR,10aR)-3-(1-adamantyl)-6,6,9-trimethyl-6 a,7,10,10a-tetrahydrobenzo[c]chromen-1-ol.

(D) AM-855, (4aR,12bR)-8-hexyl-2,5,5-trimethyl-1 ,4,4a,8,9,10,11,12b-octahydronaphtho[3,2-c] isochromen-12-ol.

(E) AM-905, (6aR,9R,10aR)-3-[(E)-hept-1-enyl]-9-(hydroxymethyl)-6,6-dimethyl-6a,7,8,9,10,10a-hexahydrobenzo[c]chromen-1-ol.

(F) AM-906, (6aR,9R,10aR)-3-[(Z)-hept-1-enyl]-9-(hydroxymethyl)-6,6-dimethyl-6a,7,8,9,10,10a-hexahydrobenzo[c]chromen-1-ol.

(G) AM-2389, (6aR,9R,10aR)-3-(1-hexyl-cyclobut-1-yl)-6 a,7,8,9,10,10a-hexahydro-6,6-dimethyl-6H-dibenzo[b,d]pyran-1 ,9 diol.

(H) BAY 38-7271, (-)-(R)-3-(2-Hydroxymethylindanyl-4-o xy)phenyl-4,4,4-trifluorobutyl-1-sulfonate.

(I) CP 50,556-1, Levonantradol, including 9-hydroxy-6-methyl-3 -[5-phenylpentan-2-yl]oxy-5,6,6a,7,8,9,10,10a-octahydrophenant hridin-1-yl]acetate; [(6S,6aR,9R, 10aR)-9-hydroxy-6-methyl-3-[(2R)-5-phenylpentan-2-yl]oxy-5,6,6a,7,8,9,10,10a-octahydrophenanthridin-1-yl]acetate; and [9-hydroxy-6-methyl-3-[5-phenylpentan-2-yl]oxy-5,6,6a,7,8,9,10,10a-octahydrophenanthridin-1-yl] acetate.

(J) HU-210, including (6aR,10aR)-9-(hydroxymethyl)-6,6-d imethyl-3-(2-methyloctan-2-yl)-6a,7,10,10a-tetrahydrobenzo[c] chromen-1-ol; [(6aR,10aR)-9-(hydroxymethyl)-6,6-dimethyl-3-(2-methyl octan-2-yl)-6a,7,10,10a-tetrahydrobenzo[c]chromen-1-o l and 1,1-Dimethylheptyl-11-hydroxytetrahydrocannabinol.

(K) HU-211, Dexanabinol, including (6aS, 10aS)-9-(hydroxy methyl)-6,6-dimethyl-3-(2-methyloctan-2-yl)-6a,7,10,10a-tetrahydrobenzo[c]chromen-1-ol and (6aS, 10aS)-9-(hydroxy methyl)-6,6-dimethyl-3-(2-methyloctan-2-yl)-6a,7,10,10a-tetrahydrobenzo[c]chromen-1-ol.

(L) HU-243, 3-dimethylheptyl-11-hydroxyhexahydrocannabinol.

(M) HU-308, [(91R,2R,5R)-2-[2,6-dimethoxy-4-(2-methyloctan-2 - yl)phenyl]-7,7-dimethyl-4-bicyclo[3.1.1]hept-3-enyl]methanol.

(N) HU-331, 3-hydroxy-2-[(1R,6R)-3-methyl-6-(1-m ethylethenyl)-2-cyclohexen-1-yl]-5-pentyl-2,5-cyclohexadiene-1 ,4-dione.

(O) HU-336, (6aR,10aR)-6,6,9-trimethyl-3-pentyl-6a,7,10,10a-tetrahydro-1H-benzo[c]chromene-1,4(6H)-dione.

(P) JTE-907, N-(benzol[1,3]dioxol-5-ylmethyl)-7-methoxy-2-o xo-8-pentyloxy-1,2-dihydroquinoline-3-carboxamide.

(Q) JWH-051, ((6aR,10aR)-6,6-dimethyl-3-(2-methyloctan-2-y l)-6a,7,10,10a-tetrahydrobenzo[c] chromen-9-yl)methanol.

(R) JWH-057 (6aR,10aR)-3-(1,1-dimethylheptyl)-6a,7,10,10a-t etrahydro-6,6,9-trimethyl-6H-Dibenzo[b,d]pyran.

(S) JWH-133 (6aR,10aR)-3-(1,1-Dimethylbutyl)-6a,7,10,10a-t etrahydro -6,6,9-trimethyl-6H-dibenzo[b,d] pyran.

(T) JWH-359, (6aR,10aR)- 1-methoxy- 6,6,9-trimethyl- 3-[(2R)-1 ,1,2-trimethylbutyl]- 6a,7,10,10a-tetrahydrobenzo[c]chromene.

(U) URB-597 [3-(3-carbamoylphenyl)phenyl]-N-cyclohexylcarb amate.

(V) URB-602 [1,1'-Biphenyl]-3-yl-carbamic acid, cyclohexyl ester; OR cyclohexyl [1,1'-biphenyl]-3-ylcarbamate.

(W) URB-754 6-methyl-2-[(4-methylphenyl)amino]-4H-3,1-b enzoxazin-4-one.

(X) URB-937 3'-carbamoyl-6-hydroxy-[1,1'-biphenyl]-3-yl cyclohexylcarbamate.

(Y) WIN 55,212-2, including (R)-(+)-[2,3-dihydro-5-methyl-3 -(4-morpholinylmethyl)pyrrolo[1,2,3-de]-1,4-benzoxazin-6-yl]-1 -napthalenylmethanone and [2,3-Dihydro-5-methyl-3-(4-morpholinylmethyl) pyrrolo[(1,2,3-de)-1,4-benzoxazin-6-yl]-1-napthalenylmethanone.

(d) The substances or analogs of substances identified in subdivision (c) may be lawfully obtained and used for bona fide research, instruction, or analysis if that possession and use does not violate federal law.

(e) As used in this section, "synthetic cannabinoid compound" does not include either of the following:

(1) Any substance for which there is an approved new drug application, as defined in Section 505 of the federal Food, Drug, and Cosmetic Act (21 U.S.C. Sec. 355) or which is generally recognized as safe and effective for use pursuant to Section 501, 502, and 503 of the federal Food, Drug, and Cosmetic Act and Title 21 of the Code of Federal Regulations.

(2) With respect to a particular person, any substance for which an exemption is in effect for investigational use for that person pursuant to Section 505 of the federal Food, Drug, and Cosmetic Act (21 U.S.C. Sec. 355), to the extent that the conduct with respect to that substance is pursuant to the exemption.

Health and Safety Code § 11358

(Amended by Stats. 2017, Ch. 27, Sec. 123. (SB 94) Effective June 27, 2017. Note: This section was amended on Nov. 8, 2016, by initiative Prop. 64.)

Every person who plants, cultivates, harvests, dries, or processes cannabis plants, or any part thereof, except as otherwise provided by law, shall be punished as follows:

(a) Every person under the age of 18 who plants, cultivates, harvests, dries, or processes any cannabis plants shall be punished in the same manner provided in paragraph (1) of subdivision (b) of section 11357.

(b) Every person at least 18 years of age but less than 21 years of age who plants, cultivates, harvests, dries, or processes not more than six living cannabis plants shall be guilty of an infraction and a fine of not more than one hundred dollars ($100).

(c) Every person 18 years of age or over who plants, cultivates, harvests, dries, or processes more than six living cannabis plants shall be punished by imprisonment in a county jail for a period of not more than six months or by a fine of not more than five hundred dollars ($500), or by both such fine and imprisonment.

(d) Notwithstanding subdivision (c), a person 18 years of age or over who plants, cultivates, harvests, dries, or processes more than six living cannabis plants, or any part thereof, except as otherwise provided by law, may be punished by imprisonment pursuant to subdivision (h) of Section 1170 of the Penal Code if any of the following conditions exist:

(1) the person has one or more prior convictions for an offense specified in clause (iv) of subparagraph (C) of paragraph (2) of subdivision (e) of Section 667 of the Penal Code or for an offense requiring registration pursuant to subdivision (c) of Section 290 of the Penal Code.

(2) the person has two or more prior convictions under subdivision (c).

(3) the offense resulted in any of the following:

(A) Violation of Section 1052 of the Water Code relating to illegal diversion of water.

(B) Violation of Section 13260, 13264, 13272, or 13387 of the Water Code relating to discharge of water.

(C) Violation of Section 5650 or Section 5652 of the Fish and Game Code relating to waters of the state.

(D) Violation of Section 1602 of the Fish and Game Code relating to rivers, streams and lakes.

(E) Violation of Section 374.8 of the Penal Code relating to hazardous substances or Sections 25189.5, 25189.6, or 25189.7 of the Health and Safety Code relating to hazardous waste.

(F) Violation of Section 2080 of the Fish and Game Code relating to endangered and threatened species or Section 3513 of the Fish and Game Code relating to the Migratory Bird Treaty Act, or Section 2000 of the Fish and Game Code relating to the unlawful taking of fish and wildlife.

(G) Intentionally or with gross negligence causing substantial environmental harm to public lands or other public resources.

Health and Safety Code § 11359

(Amended by Stats. 2017, Ch. 27, Sec. 124. (SB 94) Effective June 27, 2017. Note: This section was amended on Nov. 8, 2016, by initiative Prop. 64.)

Every person who possesses for sale any cannabis, except as otherwise provided by law, shall be punished as follows:

(a) Every person under the age of 18 who possesses cannabis for sale shall be punished in the same manner provided in paragraph (1) of subdivision (b) of Section 11357.

(b) Every person 18 years of age or over who possesses cannabis for sale shall be punished by imprisonment in a county jail for a period of not more than six months or by a fine of not more than five hundred dollars ($500), or by both such fine and imprisonment.

(c) Notwithstanding subdivision (b), a person 18 years of age or over who possesses cannabis for sale may be punished by imprisonment pursuant to subdivision (h) of Section 1170 of the Penal Code if:

(1) the person has one or more prior convictions for an offense specified in clause (iv) of subparagraph (C) of paragraph (2) of subdivision (e) of Section 667 of the Penal Code or for an offense requiring registration pursuant to subdivision (c) of Section 290 of the Penal Code;

(2) the person has two or more prior convictions under subdivision (b); or

(3) the offense occurred in connection with the knowing sale or attempted sale of cannabis to a person under the age of 18 years.

(d) Notwithstanding subdivision (b), a person 21 years of age or over who possesses cannabis for sale may be punished by imprisonment pursuant to subdivision (h) of Section 1170 of the Penal Code if the offense involves knowingly hiring, employing, or using a person 20 years of age or younger in unlawfully cultivating, transporting, carrying, selling, offering to sell, giving away, preparing for sale, or peddling any cannabis.

Health and Safety Code § 11360

(Amended by Stats. 2017, Ch. 27, Sec. 125. (SB 94) Effective June 27, 2017. Note: This section was amended on Nov. 8, 2016, by initiative Prop. 64.)

(a) Except as otherwise provided by this section or as authorized by law, every person who transports, imports into this state, sells, furnishes, administers, or gives away, or offers to transport, import into this state, sell, furnish, administer, or give away, or attempts to import into this state or transport any cannabis shall be punished as follows:

(1) Persons under the age of 18 years shall be punished in the same manner as provided in paragraph (1) of

subdivision (b) of section 11357.

(2) Persons 18 years of age or over shall be punished by imprisonment in a county jail for a period of not more than six months or by a fine of not more than five hundred dollars ($500), or by both such fine and imprisonment.

(3) Notwithstanding paragraph (2), a person 18 years of age or over may be punished by imprisonment pursuant to subdivision (h) of Section 1170 of the Penal Code for a period two, three, or four years if:

(A) The person has one or more prior convictions for an offense specified in clause (iv) of subparagraph (C) of paragraph (2) of subdivision (e) of Section 667 of the Penal Code or for an offense requiring registration pursuant to subdivision (c) of Section 290 of the Penal Code;

(B) The person has two or more prior convictions under paragraph (2);

(C) The offense involved the knowing sale, attempted sale, or the knowing offer to sell, furnish, administer or give away cannabis to a person under the age of 18 years; or

(D) The offense involved the import, offer to import; or attempted import into this state, or the transport for sale, offer to transport for sale, or attempted transport for sale out of this state, of more than 28.5 grams of cannabis or more than four grams of concentrated cannabis.

(b) Except as authorized by law, every person who gives away, offers to give away, transports, offers to transport, or attempts to transport not more than 28.5 grams of cannabis, other than concentrated cannabis, is guilty of an infraction and shall be punished by a fine of not more than one hundred dollars ($100). In any case in which a person is arrested for a violation of this subdivision and does not demand to be taken before a magistrate, such person shall be released by the arresting officer upon presentation of satisfactory evidence of identity and giving his or her written promise to appear in court, as provided in Section 853.6 of the Penal Code, and shall not be subjected to booking.

(c) For purposes of this section, "transport" means to transport for sale.

(d) This section does not preclude or limit prosecution for any aiding and abetting or conspiracy offenses.

Health & Safety Code § 11361

(Amended by Stats. 2017, Ch. 27, Sec. 126. (SB 94) Effective June 27, 2017.)

(a) A person 18 years of age or over who hires, employs, or uses a minor in unlawfully transporting, carrying, selling, giving away, preparing for sale, or peddling any cannabis, who unlawfully sells, or offers to sell, any cannabis to a minor, or who furnishes, administers, or gives, or offers to furnish, administer, or give any cannabis to a minor under 14 years of age, or who induces a minor to use cannabis in violation of law shall be punished by imprisonment in the state prison for a period of three, five, or seven years.

(b) A person 18 years of age or over who furnishes, administers, or gives, or offers to furnish, administer, or give, any cannabis to a minor 14 years of age or older in violation of law shall be punished by imprisonment in the state prison for a period of three, four, or five years.

Health and Safety Code § 11361.1

(Amended by Stats. 2017, Ch. 27, Sec. 127. (SB 94) Effective June 27, 2017. Note: This section was added on Nov. 8, 2016, by initiative Prop. 64.)

(a) The drug education and counseling requirements under sections 11357, 11358, 11359, and 11360 shall be:

(1) Mandatory, unless the court finds that such drug education or counseling is unnecessary for the person, or that a drug education or counseling program is unavailable;

(2) Free to participants, and shall consist of at least four hours of group discussion or instruction based on science and evidence-based principles and practices specific to the use and abuse of cannabis and other controlled substances.

(b) For good cause, the court may grant an extension of time not to exceed 30 days for a person to complete the drug education and counseling required under sections 11357, 11358, 11359, and 11360.

Health and Safety Code § 11361.5

(Amended by Stats. 2018, Ch. 92, Sec. 140. (SB 1289) Effective January 1, 2019. Note: This section was amended on Nov. 8, 2016, by initiative Prop. 64.)

(a) Records of any court of this state, any public or private agency that provides services upon referral under Section 1000.2 of the Penal Code, or of any state agency pertaining to the arrest or conviction of any person for a violation of Section 11357 or subdivision (b) of Section 11360, or pertaining to the arrest or conviction of any person under the age of 18 for a violation of any provision of this article except Section 11357.5, shall not be kept beyond two years from the date of the conviction, or from the date of the arrest if there was no conviction, except with respect to a violation of subdivision (d) of Section 11357, or any other violation by a person under the age of 18 occurring upon the grounds of, or within, any school providing instruction in kindergarten or any of grades 1 to 12, inclusive, during hours the school is open for classes or school-related programs, the records shall be retained until the offender attains the age of 18 years at which time the records shall be destroyed as provided in this section. A court or agency having custody of the records, including the statewide criminal databases, shall provide for the timely destruction of the records in accordance with subdivision (c), and those records shall also be purged from the statewide criminal databases. As used in this subdivision, "records pertaining to the arrest or conviction" shall include records of arrests resulting in the criminal proceeding and records relating to other offenses charged in the accusatory pleading, whether the defendant was acquitted or charges were dismissed. The two-year period beyond which records shall not be kept pursuant to this subdivision does not apply to any person who is, at the time at which this subdivision would otherwise require record destruction, incarcerated for an offense subject to this subdivision. For such persons, the two-year period shall commence from the date the person is released from custody. The requirements of this subdivision do not apply to records of any conviction occurring before January 1, 1976, or records of any arrest not followed by a conviction occurring before that date, or records of any arrest for an offense specified in subdivision (c) of Section 1192.7, or subdivision (c) of Section 667.5, of the Penal Code.

(b) This subdivision applies only to records of convictions and arrests not followed by conviction occurring before January 1, 1976, for any of the following offenses:

(1) A violation of Section 11357 or a statutory predecessor thereof.

(2) Unlawful possession of a device, contrivance, instrument, or paraphernalia used for unlawfully smoking cannabis, in violation of Section 11364, as it existed before January 1, 1976, or a statutory predecessor thereof.

(3) Unlawful visitation or presence in a room or place in which cannabis is being unlawfully smoked or used, in violation of Section 11365, as it existed before January 1, 1976, or a statutory predecessor thereof.

(4) Unlawfully using or being under the influence of cannabis, in violation of Section 11550, as it existed before January 1, 1976, or a statutory predecessor thereof.

(A) A person subject to an arrest or conviction for those offenses may apply to the Department of Justice for destruction of records pertaining to the arrest or conviction if two or more years have elapsed since the date of the conviction, or since the date of the arrest if not followed by a conviction. The application shall be submitted upon a form supplied by the Department of Justice and shall be accompanied by a fee, which shall be established by the department in an amount which will defray the cost of administering this subdivision and costs incurred by the state under subdivision (c), but which shall not exceed thirty-seven dollars and fifty cents ($37.50). The application form may be made available at every local police or sheriff's department and from the Department of Justice and may require that information which the department determines is necessary for purposes of identification.

(B) The department may request, but not require, the applicant to include a self-administered fingerprint upon the application. If the department is unable to sufficiently identify the applicant for purposes of this subdivision without the fingerprint or without additional fingerprints, it shall so notify the applicant and shall request the applicant to submit any fingerprints which may be required to effect identification, including a complete set if necessary, or, alternatively, to abandon the application and request a refund of all or a portion of the fee submitted with the application, as provided in this section. If the applicant fails or refuses to submit fingerprints in accordance with the department's request within a reasonable time which shall be established by the department, or if the applicant requests a refund of the fee, the department shall promptly mail a refund to the applicant at the address specified in the application or at any other address which may be specified by the applicant. However, if the department has notified the applicant that election to abandon the application will result in forfeiture of a specified amount which is a portion of the fee, the department may retain a portion of the fee which the department determines will defray the actual costs of processing the application, provided the amount of the portion retained shall not exceed ten dollars ($10).

(C) Upon receipt of a sufficient application, the Department of Justice shall destroy records of the department, if any, pertaining to the arrest or conviction in the manner prescribed by subdivision (c) and shall notify the Federal Bureau of Investigation, the law enforcement agency which arrested the applicant, and, if the applicant was convicted, the probation department which investigated the applicant and the Department of Motor Vehicles, of the application.

(c) Destruction of records of arrest or conviction pursuant to subdivision (a) or (b) shall be accomplished by permanent obliteration of all entries or notations upon the records pertaining to the arrest or conviction, and the record shall be prepared again so that it appears that the arrest or conviction never occurred. However, where (1) the only entries upon the record pertain to the arrest or conviction and (2) the record can be destroyed without necessarily effecting the destruction of other records, then the document constituting the record shall be physically destroyed.

(d) Notwithstanding subdivision (a) or (b), written transcriptions of oral testimony in court proceedings and published judicial appellate reports are not subject to this section. Additionally, no records shall be destroyed pursuant to subdivision (a) if the defendant or a codefendant has filed a civil action against the peace officers or law enforcement jurisdiction which made the arrest or instituted the prosecution and if the agency which is the custodian of those records has received a certified copy of the complaint in the civil action, until the civil action has finally been resolved. Immediately following the final resolution of the civil action, records subject to subdivision (a) shall be destroyed pursuant to subdivision (c) if more than two years have elapsed from the date of the conviction or arrest without conviction.

Health and Safety Code § 11361.7

(Added by Stats. 1976, Ch. 952.)

(a) Any record subject to destruction or permanent obliteration pursuant to Section 11361.5, or more than two years of age, or a record of a conviction for an offense specified in subdivision (a) or (b) of Section 11361.5 which became final more than two years previously, shall not be considered to be accurate, relevant, timely, or complete for any purposes by any agency or person. The provisions of this subdivision shall be applicable for purposes of the Privacy Act of 1974 (5 U.S.C. Section 552a) to the fullest extent permissible by law, whenever any information or record subject to destruction or permanent obliteration under Section 11361.5 was obtained by any state agency, local public agency, or any public or private agency that provides services upon referral under Section 1000.2 of the Penal Code, and is thereafter shared with or disseminated to any agency of the federal government.

(b) No public agency shall alter, amend, assess, condition, deny, limit, postpone, qualify, revoke, surcharge, or suspend any certificate, franchise, incident, interest, license, opportunity, permit, privilege, right, or title of any person because of an arrest or conviction for an offense specified in subdivision (a) or (b) of Section 11361.5, or because of the facts or events leading to such an arrest or conviction, on or after the date the records of such arrest or conviction are required to be destroyed by subdivision (a) of Section 11361.5, or two years from the date of such conviction or arrest without conviction with respect to arrests and convictions occurring prior to January 1, 1976. As used in this subdivision, "public agency" includes, but is not limited to, any state, county, city and county, city, public or constitutional corporation or entity, district, local or regional political subdivision, or any department, division, bureau, office, board, commission or other agency thereof.

(c) Any person arrested or convicted for an offense specified in subdivision (a) or (b) of Section 11361.5 may, two years from the date of such a conviction, or from the date of the arrest if there was no conviction, indicate in response to any question concerning his prior criminal record that he was not arrested or convicted for such offense.

(d) The provisions of this section shall be applicable without regard to whether destruction or obliteration of records has actually been implemented pursuant to Section 11361.5.

Health and Safety Code § 11361.8

(Amended by Stats. 2021, Ch. 434, Sec. 2. (SB 827) Effective January 1, 2022.)

(a) A person currently serving a sentence for a conviction, whether by trial or by open or negotiated plea, who would not have been guilty of an offense, or who would have been guilty of a lesser offense under the Control, Regulate and Tax Adult Use of Marijuana Act had that act been in effect at the time of the offense may petition for a recall or dismissal of sentence before the trial court that entered the judgment of conviction in their case to request resentencing or dismissal in accordance with Sections 11357, 11358, 11359, 11360, 11362.1, 11362.2, 11362.3, and 11362.4 as those sections have been amended or added by that act.

(b) Upon receiving a petition under subdivision (a), the court shall presume the petitioner satisfies the criteria in subdivision (a) unless the party opposing the petition proves by clear and convincing evidence that the petitioner does not satisfy the criteria. If the petitioner satisfies the criteria in subdivision (a), the court shall grant the petition to recall the sentence or dismiss the sentence because it is legally invalid unless the court determines that granting the petition would pose an unreasonable risk of danger to public safety.

> (1) In exercising its discretion, the court may consider, but shall not be limited to evidence provided for in subdivision (b) of Section 1170.18 of the Penal Code.
>
> (2) As used in this section, "unreasonable risk of danger to public safety" has the same meaning as provided in subdivision (c) of Section 1170.18 of the Penal Code.

(c) A person who is serving a sentence and is resentenced pursuant to subdivision (b) shall be given credit for any time already served and shall be subject to supervision for one year following completion of their time in custody or shall be subject to whatever supervision time they would have otherwise been subject to after release, whichever is shorter, unless the court, in its discretion, as part of its resentencing order, releases the person from supervision. Such person is subject to parole supervision under Section 3000.08 of the Penal Code or postrelease community supervision under subdivision (a) of Section 3451 of the Penal Code by the designated agency and the jurisdiction of the court in the county in which the offender is released or resides, or in which an alleged violation of supervision has occurred, for the purpose of hearing petitions to revoke supervision and impose a term of custody.

(d) Under no circumstances may resentencing under this section result in the imposition of a term longer than the original sentence, or the reinstatement of charges dismissed pursuant to a negotiated plea agreement.

(e) A person who has completed their sentence whether by trial or open or negotiated plea, who would not have been guilty of the conviction offense under the Control, Regulate and Tax Adult Use of Marijuana Act had that act been in effect at the time of the offense, may file an application before the trial court that entered the judgment of conviction in their case to have the conviction dismissed and sealed because the prior conviction is now legally invalid or redesignated as a misdemeanor or infraction in accordance with Sections 11357, 11358, 11359, 11360, 11362.1, 11362.2, 11362.3, and 11362.4 as those sections have been amended or added by that act.

(f) The court shall presume the petitioner satisfies the criteria in subdivision (e) unless the party opposing the application proves by clear and convincing evidence that the petitioner does not satisfy the criteria in subdivision (e). Once the applicant satisfies the criteria in subdivision (e), the court shall redesignate the conviction as a misdemeanor or infraction or dismiss and seal the conviction as legally invalid as now established under the Control, Regulate and Tax Adult Use of Marijuana Act.

(g) Unless requested by the applicant, no hearing is necessary to grant or deny an application filed under subdivision (e).

(h) Any felony conviction that is recalled and resentenced under subdivision (b) or designated as a misdemeanor or infraction under subdivision (f) shall be considered a misdemeanor or infraction for all purposes. Any misdemeanor conviction that is recalled and resentenced under subdivision (b) or designated as an infraction under subdivision (f) shall be considered an infraction for all purposes.

(i) If the court that originally sentenced the petitioner is not available, the presiding judge shall designate another judge to rule on the petition or application.

(j) Nothing in this section is intended to diminish or abrogate any rights or remedies otherwise available to the petitioner or applicant.

(k) Nothing in this and related sections is intended to diminish or abrogate the finality of judgments in any case not falling within the purview of the Control, Regulate and Tax Adult Use of Marijuana Act.

(l) A resentencing hearing ordered under the Control, Regulate and Tax Adult Use of Marijuana Act shall constitute a "post-conviction release proceeding" under paragraph (7) of subdivision (b) of Section 28 of Article I of the California Constitution (Marsy's Law).

(m) The provisions of this section shall apply equally to juvenile delinquency adjudications and dispositions under Section 602 of the Welfare and Institutions Code if the juvenile would not have been guilty of an offense or would have been guilty of a lesser offense under the Control, Regulate and Tax Adult Use of Marijuana Act.

(n) The Judicial Council shall promulgate and make available all necessary forms to enable the filing of the petitions and applications provided in this section.

Health & Safety Code § 11361.9

(Amended by Stats. 2022, Ch. 387, Sec. 1. (AB 1706) Effective January 1, 2023.)

(a) On or before July 1, 2019, the Department of Justice shall review the records in the state summary criminal history information database and shall identify past convictions that are potentially eligible for recall or dismissal of sentence, dismissal and sealing, or redesignation pursuant to Section 11361.8. The department shall notify the prosecution of all cases in their jurisdiction that are eligible for recall or dismissal of sentence, dismissal and sealing, or redesignation.

(b) The prosecution shall have until July 1, 2020, to review all cases and determine whether to challenge the recall or dismissal of sentence, dismissal and sealing, or redesignation.

(c) (1) The prosecution may challenge the resentencing of a person who is still serving a sentence pursuant to this section when the person does not meet the criteria established in Section 11361.8.

(2) The prosecution may challenge the dismissal and sealing or redesignation of a person pursuant to this section who has completed their sentence for a conviction when the person does not meet the criteria established in Section 11361.8.

(3) On or before July 1, 2020, the prosecution shall inform the court and the public defender's office in their county when they are challenging a particular recall or dismissal of sentence, dismissal and sealing, or redesignation. The prosecution shall inform the court when they are not challenging a particular recall or dismissal of sentence, dismissal and sealing, or redesignation.

(4) The public defender's office, upon receiving notice from the prosecution pursuant to paragraph (3), shall make a reasonable effort to notify the person whose resentencing or dismissal is being challenged.

(d) (1) If the prosecution did not challenge the recall or dismissal of sentence, dismissal and sealing, or redesignation of a conviction on or before July 1, 2020, the conviction shall be deemed unchallenged, recalled, dismissed, and redesignated, as applicable, and the court shall issue an order, recalling or dismissing the sentence, dismissing and sealing, or redesignating the conviction in each case pursuant to Section 11361.8 no later than March 1, 2023.

(2) On or before March 1, 2023, the court shall update its records in accordance with this section, and shall report all convictions that have been recalled, dismissed, redesignated, or sealed to the Department of Justice for adjustment of the state summary criminal history information database.

(3) On or before July 1, 2023, the Department of Justice shall ensure that all of the records in the state summary criminal history information database that have been recalled, dismissed, sealed, or redesignated pursuant to this section have been updated, and shall ensure that inaccurate state summary criminal history is not disseminated. For those individuals whose state summary criminal history information was disseminated pursuant to Section 11105 of the Penal Code in the 30 days prior to an update based on this section, and the requesting entity is still entitled to receive the state summary criminal history information, the Department of Justice shall provide a subsequent notice to the entity.

(e) The Department of Justice shall post general information on its internet website about the recall or dismissal of sentences, dismissal and sealing, or redesignation authorized in this section. The department shall conduct an awareness campaign about the recall or dismissal of sentences, dismissal and sealing, or redesignation authorized in this section, so that individuals that may be impacted by this process are informed of the process pursuant to Article 5 (commencing with Section 11120) of Chapter 1 of Title 1 of Part 4 of the Penal Code, to request their criminal history information to verify the updates or how to contact the courts, prosecution, or public defenders' offices to assist in verifying the updates. If an individual requests their criminal history information to verify updates to their criminal history made pursuant to this section, the department may provide a one-time fee waiver of its fees under Section 11123 of the Penal Code for processing and responding to the request.

(f) A conviction, arrest, or other proceeding that has been ordered sealed pursuant to Section 11361.8, is deemed never to have occurred, and the person may reply accordingly to any inquiry about the events.

(g) Courts that have previously eliminated court records covered by this article pursuant to Sections 68152 and 68153 of the Government Code are compliant with the provisions of subdivision (c) of Section 11361.5. Courts that have previously eliminated court records covered by this article pursuant to Sections 68152 and 68153 of the Government Code shall report to the Department of Justice, in a manner prescribed by the Department of Justice, that the relevant records have been destroyed and that the record are otherwise reduced, dismissed, or sealed in accordance with this section.

(h) Beginning March 1, 2023, and until June 1, 2024, the Department of Justice, in consultation with the Judicial Council, shall submit quarterly joint progress reports to the Legislature that include, but are not limited to, all of following information:

(1) Total number of cases recalled, dismissed, resentenced, sealed, and redesignated in each county, and the

status of the department's update to the state summary criminal history database.

(2) Status of cases challenged by the prosecution, and all relevant statistical information regarding the disposition of the challenged cases in each county.

(3) The number of past convictions in the state summary criminal history database that are potentially eligible for recall or dismissal of sentence, dismissal and sealing, or redesignation pursuant to Section 11361.8.

(4) The status of the department's public awareness campaign to provide notification to impacted individuals.

(i) It is the intent of the Legislature that persons who are currently serving a sentence or who proactively petition for a recall or dismissal of sentence, dismissal and sealing, or redesignation pursuant to Section 11361.8 be prioritized for review.

Health and Safety Code § 11362

(Amended by Stats. 2011, Ch. 15, Sec. 163. (AB 109) Effective April 4, 2011. Operative October 1, 2011, by Sec. 636 of Ch. 15, as amended by Stats. 2011, Ch. 39, Sec. 68.)

As used in this article "felony offense," and offense "punishable as a felony" refer to an offense prior to July 1, 2011, for which the law prescribes imprisonment in the state prison, or for an offense on or after July 1, 2011, imprisonment in either the state prison or pursuant to subdivision (h) of Section 1170 of the Penal Code, as either an alternative or the sole penalty, regardless of the sentence the particular defendant received.

Health and Safety Code § 11362.1

(Amended by Stats. 2017, Ch. 27, Sec. 129. (SB 94) Effective June 27, 2017. Note: This section was added on Nov. 8, 2016, by initiative Prop. 64.)

(a) Subject to Sections 11362.2, 11362.3, 11362.4, and 11362.45, but notwithstanding any other provision of law, it shall be lawful under state and local law, and shall not be a violation of state or local law, for persons 21 years of age or older to:

(1) Possess, process, transport, purchase, obtain, or give away to persons 21 years of age or older without any compensation whatsoever, not more than 28.5 grams of cannabis not in the form of concentrated cannabis;

(2) Possess, process, transport, purchase, obtain, or give away to persons 21 years of age or older without any compensation whatsoever, not more than eight grams of cannabis in the form of concentrated cannabis, including as contained in cannabis products;

(3) Possess, plant, cultivate, harvest, dry, or process not more than six living cannabis plants and possess the cannabis produced by the plants;

(4) Smoke or ingest cannabis or cannabis products; and

(5) Possess, transport, purchase, obtain, use, manufacture, or give away cannabis accessories to persons 21 years of age or older without any compensation whatsoever.

(b) Paragraph (5) of subdivision (a) is intended to meet the requirements of subdivision (f) of Section 863 a/Title 21 of the United States Code (21 US.C. § 863(f)) by authorizing, under state law, any person in compliance with this section to manufacture, possess, or distribute cannabis accessories.

(c) Cannabis and cannabis products involved in any way with conduct deemed lawful by this section are not contraband nor subject to seizure, and no conduct deemed lawful by this section shall constitute the basis for detention, search, or arrest.

Health and Safety Code § 11362.2

(Amended by Stats. 2017, Ch. 27, Sec. 130. (SB 94) Effective June 27, 2017. Note: This section was added on Nov. 8, 2016, by initiative Prop. 64.)

(a) Personal cultivation of cannabis under paragraph (3) of subdivision (a) of Section 11362.1 is subject to the following restrictions:

(1) A person shall plant, cultivate, harvest, dry, or process plants in accordance with local ordinances, if any, adopted in accordance with subdivision (b).

(2) The living plants and any cannabis produced by the plants in excess of 28.5 grams are kept within the person's private residence, or upon the grounds of that private residence (e.g., in an outdoor garden area), are in a locked space, and are not visible by normal unaided vision from a public place.

(3) Not more than six living plants may be planted, cultivated, harvested, dried, or processed within a single private residence, or upon the grounds of that private residence, at one time.

(b)(1) A city, county, or city and county may enact and enforce reasonable regulations to regulate the actions and conduct in paragraph (3) of subdivision (a) of Section 11362.1.

(2) Notwithstanding paragraph (1), a city, county, or city and county shall not completely prohibit persons engaging in the actions and conduct under paragraph (3) of subdivision (a) of Section 11362.1 inside a private residence, or inside an accessory structure to a private residence located upon the grounds of a private residence that is fully enclosed and secure.

(3) Notwithstanding paragraph (3) of subdivision (a) of Section 11362.1, a city, county, or city and county may completely prohibit persons from engaging in actions and conduct under paragraph (3) of subdivision (a) of Section 11362.1 outdoors upon the grounds of a private residence.

(4) Paragraph (3) shall become inoperable upon a determination by the California Attorney General that adult use of cannabis is lawful in the State of California under federal law, and an act taken by a city, county, or city and county under paragraph (3) is unenforceable upon the date of that determination by the Attorney General.

(5) For purposes of this section, ''private residence" means a house, an apartment unit, a mobile home, or other similar dwelling.

Health and Safety Code § 11362.3

(Amended by Stats. 2017, Ch. 27, Sec. 131. (SB 94) Effective June 27, 2017. Note: This section was added on November 8, 2016, by initiative Proposition 64.)

(a) Section 11362.1 does not permit any person to:

(1) Smoke or ingest cannabis or cannabis products in a public place, except in accordance with Section 26200 of the Business and Professions Code.

(2) Smoke cannabis or cannabis products in a location where smoking tobacco is prohibited.

(3) Smoke cannabis or cannabis products within 1,000 feet of a school, day care center, or youth center while children are present at the school, day care center, or youth center, except in or upon the grounds of a private residence or in accordance with Section 26200 of the Business and Professions Code and only if such smoking

is not detectable by others on the grounds of the school, day care center, or youth center while children are present.

(4) Possess an open container or open package of cannabis or cannabis products while driving, operating, or riding in the passenger seat or compartment of a motor vehicle, boat, vessel, aircraft, or other vehicle used for transportation.

(5) Possess, smoke or ingest cannabis or cannabis products in or upon the grounds of a school, day care center, or youth center while children are present.

(6) Manufacture concentrated cannabis using a volatile solvent, unless done in accordance with a license under Division 10 (commencing with section 26000) of the Business and Professions Code.

(7) Smoke or ingest cannabis or cannabis products while driving, operating a motor vehicle, boat, vessel, aircraft, or other vehicle used for transportation.

(8) Smoke or ingest cannabis or cannabis products while riding in the passenger seat or compartment of a motor vehicle, boat, vessel, aircraft, or other vehicle used for transportation except as permitted on a motor vehicle, boat, vessel, aircraft, or other vehicle used for transportation that is operated in accordance with Section 26200 of the Business and Professions Code and while no persons under the age of 21 years are present.

(b) For purposes of this section, the following definitions apply:

(1) "Day care center" has the same meaning as in Section 1596.76.

(2) "Smoke" means to inhale, exhale, burn, or carry any lighted or heated device or pipe, or any other lighted or heated cannabis or cannabis product intended for inhalation, whether natural or synthetic, in any manner or in any form. "Smoke" includes the use of an electronic smoking device that creates an aerosol or vapor, in any manner or in any form, or the use of any oral smoking device for the purpose of circumventing the prohibition of smoking in a place.

(3) "Volatile solvent" means a solvent that is or produces a flammable gas or vapor that, when present in the air in sufficient quantities, will create explosive or ignitable mixtures.

(4) "Youth center" has the same meaning as in Section 11353.1.

(c) Nothing in this section shall be construed or interpreted to amend, repeal, affect, restrict, or preempt laws pertaining to the Compassionate Use Act of 1996.

Health and Safety Code § 11362.4

(Amended by Stats. 2018, Ch. 92, Sec. 141. (SB 1289) Effective January 1, 2019. Note: This section was added on Nov. 8, 2016, by initiative Prop. 64.)

(a) A person who engages in the conduct described in paragraph (1) of subdivision (a) of Section 11362.3 is guilty of an infraction punishable by no more than a one-hundred-dollar ($100) fine; provided, however, that persons under 18 years of age shall instead be required to complete four hours of a drug education program or counseling, and up to 10 hours of community service, over a period not to exceed 60 days once the drug education program or counseling and community service opportunity are made available to the person.

(b) A person who engages in the conduct described in paragraph (2), (3), or (4) of subdivision (a) of Section 11362.3 is guilty of an infraction punishable by no more than a two-hundred-fifty-dollar ($250) fine, unless that activity is otherwise permitted by state and local law; provided, however, that a person under 18 years of age shall instead be required to complete four hours of drug education or counseling, and up to 20 hours of community service, over a period not to exceed 90 days once the drug education program or counseling and community service opportunity are made available to the person.

(c) A person who engages in the conduct described in paragraph (5) of subdivision (a) of Section 11362.3 is subject to the same punishment as provided under subdivision (c) or (d) of Section 11357.

(d) A person who engages in the conduct described in paragraph (6) of subdivision (a) of Section 11362.3 is subject to punishment under Section 11379.6.

(e) A person who violates the restrictions in subdivision (a) of Section 11362.2 is guilty of an infraction punishable by no more than a two-hundred-fifty-dollar ($250) fine.

(f) Notwithstanding subdivision (e), a person under 18 years of age who violates the restrictions in subdivision (a) of Section 11362.2 shall be punished under paragraph (1) of subdivision (b) of Section 11357.

(g) (1) The drug education program or counseling hours required by this section shall be mandatory unless the court makes a finding that the program or counseling is unnecessary for the person or that a drug education program or counseling is unavailable.

(2) The drug education program required by this section for persons under 18 years of age shall be free to participants and provide at least four hours of group discussion or instruction based on science and evidence-based principles and practices specific to the use and abuse of cannabis and other controlled substances.

(h) Upon a finding of good cause, the court may extend the time for a person to complete the drug education or counseling, and community service required under this section.

Health and Safety Code § 11362.45

(Amended by Stats. 2017, Ch. 27, Sec. 133. (SB 94) Effective June 27, 2017. Note: This section was added on Nov. 8, 2016, by initiative Prop. 64.)

Section 11362.1 does not amend, repeal, affect, restrict, or preempt:

(a) Laws making it unlawful to drive or operate a vehicle, boat, vessel, or aircraft, while smoking, ingesting, or impaired by, cannabis or cannabis products, including, but not limited to, subdivision (e) of Section 23152 of the Vehicle Code, or the penalties prescribed for violating those laws.

(b) Laws prohibiting the sale, administering, furnishing, or giving away of cannabis, cannabis products, or cannabis accessories, or the offering to sell, administer, furnish, or give away cannabis, cannabis products, or cannabis accessories to a person younger than 21 years of age.

(c) Laws prohibiting a person younger than 21 years of age from engaging in any of the actions or conduct otherwise permitted under Section 11362.1.

(d) Laws pertaining to smoking or ingesting cannabis or cannabis products on the grounds of, or within, any facility or institution under the jurisdiction of the Department of Corrections and Rehabilitation or the Division of Juvenile Justice, or on the grounds of, or within, any other facility or institution referenced in Section 4573 of the Penal Code.

(e) Laws providing that it would constitute negligence or professional malpractice to undertake any task while impaired from smoking or ingesting cannabis or cannabis products.

(f) The rights and obligations of public and private employers to maintain a drug and alcohol free workplace or require an employer to permit or accommodate the use, consumption, possession, transfer, display, transportation, sale, or growth of cannabis in the workplace, or affect the ability of employers to have policies prohibiting the use of cannabis by employees and prospective employees, or prevent employers from complying with state or federal law.

(g) The ability of a state or local government agency to prohibit or restrict any of the actions or conduct otherwise permitted under Section 11362.1 within a building owned, leased, or occupied by the state or local government agency.

(h) The ability of an individual or private entity to prohibit or restrict any of the actions or conduct otherwise permitted under Section 11362.1 on the individual's or entity's privately owned property.

(i) Laws pertaining to the Compassionate Use Act of 1996.

Health And Safety Code § 11362.5

(Added November 5, 1996, by initiative Proposition 215, Sec. 1.)

(a) This section shall be known and may be cited as the Compassionate Use Act of 1996.

(b)(1) The people of the State of California hereby find and declare that the purposes of the Compassionate Use Act of 1996 are as follows:

> (A) To ensure that seriously ill Californians have the right to obtain and use marijuana for medical purposes where that medical use is deemed appropriate and has been recommended by a physician who has determined that the person's health would benefit from the use of marijuana in the treatment of cancer, anorexia, AIDS, chronic pain, spasticity, glaucoma, arthritis, migraine, or any other illness for which marijuana provides relief.
>
> (B) To ensure that patients and their primary caregivers who obtain and use marijuana for medical purposes upon the recommendation of a physician are not subject to criminal prosecution or sanction.
>
> (C) To encourage the federal and state governments to implement a plan to provide for the safe and affordable distribution of marijuana to all patients in medical need of marijuana.

(b)(2) Nothing in this section shall be construed to supersede legislation prohibiting persons from engaging in conduct that endangers others, nor to condone the diversion of marijuana for nonmedical purposes.

(c) Notwithstanding any other provision of law, no physician in this state shall be punished, or denied any right or privilege, for having recommended marijuana to a patient for medical purposes.

(d) Section 11357, relating to the possession of marijuana, and Section 11358, relating to the cultivation of marijuana, shall not apply to a patient, or to a patient's primary caregiver, who possesses or cultivates marijuana for the personal medical purposes of the patient upon the written or oral recommendation or approval of a physician.

(e) For the purposes of this section, "primary caregiver" means the individual designated by the person exempted under this section who has consistently assumed responsibility for the housing, health, or safety of that person.

SEC. 2.

If any provision of this measure or the application thereof to any person or circumstance is held invalid, that invalidity shall not affect other provisions or applications of the measure that can be given effect without the invalid provision or application, and to this end the provisions of this measure are severable.

Heath and Safety Code § 11362.7

(Amended by Stats. 2017, Ch. 775, Sec. 112. (SB 798) Effective January 1, 2018.)

For purposes of this article, the following definitions shall apply:

(a) "Attending physician" means an individual who possesses a license in good standing to practice medicine, podiatry, or osteopathy issued by the Medical Board of California, the California Board of Podiatric Medicine, or the Osteopathic Medical Board of California and who has taken responsibility for an aspect of the medical care, treatment, diagnosis, counseling, or referral of a patient and who has conducted a medical examination of that patient before recording in the patient's medical record the physician's assessment of whether the patient has a serious medical condition and whether the medical use of cannabis is appropriate.

(b) "Department" means the State Department of Public Health.

(c) "Person with an identification card" means an individual who is a qualified patient who has applied for and received a valid identification card pursuant to this article.

(d) "Primary caregiver" means the individual, designated by a qualified patient, who has consistently assumed responsibility for the housing, health, or safety of that patient, and may include any of the following:

(1) In a case in which a qualified patient or person with an identification card receives medical care or supportive services, or both, from a clinic licensed pursuant to Chapter 1 (commencing with Section 1200) of Division 2, a health care facility licensed pursuant to Chapter 2 (commencing with Section 1250) of Division 2, a residential care facility for persons with chronic life-threatening illness licensed pursuant to Chapter 3.01 (commencing with Section 1568.01) of Division 2, a residential care facility for the elderly licensed pursuant to Chapter 3.2 (commencing with Section 1569) of Division 2, a hospice, or a home health agency licensed pursuant to Chapter 8 (commencing with Section 1725) of Division 2, the owner or operator, or no more than three employees who are designated by the owner or operator, of the clinic, facility, hospice, or home health agency, if designated as a primary caregiver by that qualified patient or person with an identification card.

(2) An individual who has been designated as a primary caregiver by more than one qualified patient or person with an identification card, if every qualified patient or person with an identification card who has designated that individual as a primary caregiver resides in the same city or county as the primary caregiver.

(3) An individual who has been designated as a primary caregiver by a qualified patient or person with an identification card who resides in a city or county other than that of the primary caregiver, if the individual has not been designated as a primary caregiver by any other qualified patient or person with an identification card.

(e) A primary caregiver shall be at least 18 years of age, unless the primary caregiver is the parent of a minor child who is a qualified patient or a person with an identification card or the primary caregiver is a person otherwise entitled to make medical decisions under state law pursuant to Section 6922, 7002, 7050, or 7120 of the Family Code.

(f) "Qualified patient" means a person who is entitled to the protections of Section 11362.5, but who does not have an identification card issued pursuant to this article.

(g) "Identification card" means a document issued by the department that identifies a person authorized to engage in the medical use of cannabis and the person's designated primary caregiver, if any.

(h) "Serious medical condition" means all of the following medical conditions:

(1) Acquired immune deficiency syndrome (AIDS).

(2) Anorexia.

(3) Arthritis.

(4) Cachexia.

(5) Cancer.

(6) Chronic pain.

(7) Glaucoma.

(8) Migraine.

(9) Persistent muscle spasms, including, but not limited to, spasms associated with multiple sclerosis.

(10) Seizures, including, but not limited to, seizures associated with epilepsy.

(11) Severe nausea.

(12) Any other chronic or persistent medical symptom that either:

(A) Substantially limits the ability of the person to conduct one or more major life activities as defined in the federal Americans with Disabilities Act of 1990 (Public Law 101-336).

(B) If not alleviated, may cause serious harm to the patient's safety or physical or mental health.

(i) "Written documentation" means accurate reproductions of those portions of a patient's medical records that have been created by the attending physician, that contain the information required by paragraph (2) of subdivision (a) of Section 11362.715, and that the patient may submit as part of an application for an identification card.

Health and Safety Code § 11362.71

(Amended by Stats. 2017, Ch. 27, Sec. 135. (SB 94) Effective June 27, 2017.)

(a) (1) The department shall establish and maintain a voluntary program for the issuance of identification cards to qualified patients who satisfy the requirements of this article and voluntarily apply to the identification card program.

(2) The department shall establish and maintain a 24-hour, toll-free telephone number that will enable state and local law enforcement officers to have immediate access to information necessary to verify the validity of an identification card issued by the department, until a cost-effective Internet Web-based system can be developed for this purpose.

(b) Every county health department, or the county's designee, shall do all of the following:

(1) Provide applications upon request to individuals seeking to join the identification card program.

(2) Receive and process completed applications in accordance with Section 11362.72.

(3) Maintain records of identification card programs.

(4) Utilize protocols developed by the department pursuant to paragraph (1) of subdivision (d).

(5) Issue identification cards developed by the department to approved applicants and designated primary caregivers.

(c) The county board of supervisors may designate another health-related governmental or nongovernmental entity or organization to perform the functions described in subdivision (b), except for an entity or organization that cultivates or distributes cannabis.

(d) The department shall develop all of the following:

(1) Protocols that shall be used by a county health department or the county's designee to implement the responsibilities described in subdivision (b), including, but not limited to, protocols to confirm the accuracy of information contained in an application and to protect the confidentiality of program records.

(2) Application forms that shall be issued to requesting applicants.

(3) An identification card that identifies a person authorized to engage in the medical use of cannabis and an

identification card that identifies the person's designated primary caregiver, if any. The two identification cards developed pursuant to this paragraph shall be easily distinguishable from each other.

(e) No person or designated primary caregiver in possession of a valid identification card shall be subject to arrest for possession, transportation, delivery, or cultivation of medicinal cannabis in an amount established pursuant to this article, unless there is probable cause to believe that the information contained in the card is false or falsified, the card has been obtained by means of fraud, or the person is otherwise in violation of the provisions of this article.

(f) It shall not be necessary for a person to obtain an identification card in order to claim the protections of Section 11362.5.

Health and Safety Code § 11362.712

(Added November 8, 2016, by initiative Proposition 64, Sec. 5.1.)

(a) Commencing on January 1, 2018, a qualified patient must possess a physician's recommendation that complies with Article 25 (commencing with Section 2525) of Chapter 5 of Division 2 of the Business and Professions Code. Failure to comply with this requirement shall not, however, affect any of the protections provided to patients or their primary caregivers by Section 11362.5.

(b) A county health department or the county's designee shall develop protocols to ensure that, commencing upon January 1, 2018, all identification cards issued pursuant to Section 11362.71 are supported by a physician's recommendation that complies with Article 25 (commencing with Section 2525) of Chapter 5 of Division 2 of the Business and Professions Code.

Health and Safety Code § 11362.713

(Added November 8, 2016, by initiative Proposition 64, Sec. 5.2.)

(a) Information identifying the names, addresses, or social security numbers of patients, their medical conditions, or the names of their primary caregivers, received and contained in the records of the Department of Public Health and by any county public health department are hereby deemed "medical information" within the meaning of the Confidentiality of Medical Information Act (Civil Code§ 56, et seq.) and shall not be disclosed by the Department or by any county public health department except in accordance with the restrictions on disclosure of individually identifiable information under the Confidentiality of Medical Information Act.

(b) Within 24 hours of receiving any request to disclose the name, address, or social security number of a patient, their medical condition, or the name of their primary caregiver, the Department of Public Health or any county public health agency shall contact the patient and inform the patient of the request and if the request was made in writing, a copy of the request.

(c) Notwithstanding Section 56.10 of the Civil Code, neither the Department of Public Health, nor any county public health agency, shall disclose, nor shall they be ordered by agency or court to disclose, the names, addresses, or social security numbers of patients, their medical conditions, or the names of their primary caregivers, sooner than the 10th day after which the patient whose records are sought to be disclosed has been contacted.

(d) No identification card application system or database used or maintained by the Department of Public Health or by any county department of public health or the county's designee as provided in Section 11362.71 shall contain any personal information of any qualified patient, including but not limited to, the patient's name, address, social security number, medical conditions, or the names of their primary caregivers. Such an application system or database may only contain a unique user identification number, and when that number is entered, the only information that may be provided is whether the card is valid or invalid.

Health and Safety Code § 11362.715

(Amended by Stats. 2017, Ch. 27, Sec. 136. (SB 94) Effective June 27, 2017.)

(a) A person who seeks an identification card shall pay the fee, as provided in Section 11362.755, and provide all of the following to the county health department or the county's designee on a form developed and provided by the department:

(1) The name of the person and proof of his or her residency within the county.

(2) Written documentation by the attending physician in the person's medical records stating that the person has been diagnosed with a serious medical condition and that the medicinal use of cannabis is appropriate.

(3) The name, office address, office telephone number, and California medical license number of the person's attending physician.

(4) The name and the duties of the primary caregiver.

(5) A government-issued photo identification card of the person and of the designated primary caregiver, if any. If the applicant is a person under 18 years of age, a certified copy of a birth certificate shall be deemed sufficient proof of identity.

(b) If the person applying for an identification card lacks the capacity to make medical decisions, the application may be made by the person's legal representative, including, but not limited to, any of the following:

(1) A conservator with authority to make medical decisions.

(2) An attorney-in-fact under a durable power of attorney for health care or surrogate decisionmaker authorized under another advanced health care directive.

(3) Any other individual authorized by statutory or decisional law to make medical decisions for the person.

(c) The legal representative described in subdivision (b) may also designate in the application an individual, including himself or herself, to serve as a primary caregiver for the person, provided that the individual meets the definition of a primary caregiver.

(d) The person or legal representative submitting the written information and documentation described in subdivision (a) shall retain a copy thereof.

Health and Safety Code § 11362.72

(Added by Stats. 2003, Ch. 875, Sec. 2. Effective January 1, 2004.)

(a) Within 30 days of receipt of an application for an identification card, a county health department or the county's designee shall do all of the following:

(1) For purposes of processing the application, verify that the information contained in the application is accurate. If the person is less than 18 years of age, the county health department or its designee shall also contact the parent with legal authority to make medical decisions, legal guardian, or other person or entity with legal authority to make medical decisions, to verify the information.

(2) Verify with the Medical Board of California or the Osteopathic Medical Board of California that the attending physician has a license in good standing to practice medicine or osteopathy in the state.

(3) Contact the attending physician by facsimile, telephone, or mail to confirm that the medical records submitted by the patient are a true and correct copy of those contained in the physician's office records. When

contacted by a county health department or the county' s designee, the attending physician shall confirm or deny that the contents of the medical records are accurate.

(4) Take a photograph or otherwise obtain an electronically transmissible image of the applicant and of the designated primary caregiver, if any.

(5) Approve or deny the application. If an applicant who meets the requirements of Section 11362.715 can establish that an identification card is needed on an emergency basis, the county or its designee shall issue a temporary identification card that shall be valid for 30 days from the date of issuance. The county, or its designee, may extend the temporary identification card for no more than 30 days at a time, so long as the applicant continues to meet the requirements of this paragraph.

(b) If the county health department or the county's designee approves the application, it shall, within 24 hours, or by the end of the next working day of approving the application, electronically transmit the following information to the department:

(1) A unique user identification number of the applicant.

(2) The date of expiration of the identification card.

(3) The name and telephone number of the county health department or the county's designee that has approved the application.

(c) The county health department or the county's designee shall issue an identification card to the applicant and to his or her designated primary caregiver, if any, within five working days of approving the application.

(d) In any case involving an incomplete application, the applicant shall assume responsibility for rectifying the deficiency. The county shall have 14 days from the receipt of information from the applicant pursuant to this subdivision to approve or deny the application.

Health and Safety Code § 11362.735

(Added by Stats. 2003, Ch. 875, Sec. 2. Effective January 1, 2004.)

(a) An identification card issued by the county health department shall be serially numbered and shall contain all of the following:

(1) A unique user identification number of the cardholder.

(2) The date of expiration of the identification card.

(3) The name and telephone number of the county health department or the county's designee that has approved the application.

(4) A 24-hour, toll-free telephone number, to be maintained by the department, that will enable state and local law enforcement officers to have immediate access to information necessary to verify the validity of the card.

(5) Photo identification of the cardholder.

(b) A separate identification card shall be issued to the person's designated primary caregiver, if any, and shall include a photo identification of the caregiver.

Health and Safety Code § 11362.74

(Added by Stats. 2003, Ch. 875, Sec. 2. Effective January 1, 2004.)

(a) The county health department or the county's designee may deny an application only for any of the following reasons:

(1) The applicant did not provide the information required by Section 11362.715, and upon notice of the deficiency pursuant to subdivision (d) of Section 11362.72, did not provide the information within 30 days.

(2) The county health department or the county's designee determines that the information provided was false.

(3) The applicant does not meet the criteria set forth in this article.

(b) Any person whose application has been denied pursuant to subdivision (a) may not reapply for six months from the date of denial unless otherwise authorized by the county health department or the county's designee or by a court of competent jurisdiction.

(c) Any person whose application has been denied pursuant to subdivision (a) may appeal that decision to the department. The county health department or the county's designee shall make available a telephone number or address to which the denied applicant can direct an appeal.

Health and Safety Code § 11362.745

(Added by Stats. 2003, Ch. 875, Sec. 2. Effective January 1, 2004.)

(a) An identification card shall be valid for a period of one year.

(b) Upon annual renewal of an identification card, the county health department or its designee shall verify all new information and may verify any other information that has not changed.

(c) The county health department or the county's designee shall transmit its determination of approval or denial of a renewal to the department.

Health and Safety Code § 11362.755

(Amended November 8, 2016, by initiative Proposition 64, Sec. 5.3.)

(a) Each county health department or the county's designee may charge a fee for all costs incurred by the county or the county's designee for administering the program pursuant to this article.

(b) In no event shall the amount of the fee charged by a county health department exceed $100 per application or renewal.

(c) Upon satisfactory proof of participation and eligibility in the Medi-Cal program, a Medi-Cal beneficiary shall receive a 50 percent reduction in the fees established pursuant to this section.

(d) Upon satisfactory proof that a qualified patient, or the legal guardian of a qualified patient under the age of 18, is a medically indigent adult who is eligible for and participates in the County Medical Services Program, the fee established pursuant to this section shall be waived.

(e) In the event the fees charged and collected by a county health department are not sufficient to pay for the administrative costs incurred in discharging the county health department's duties with respect to the mandatory identification card system, the Legislature, upon request by the county health department, shall reimburse the county health department for those reasonable administrative costs in excess of the fees charged and collected by the county health department.

Health and Safety Code § 11362.76

(Added by Stats. 2003, Ch. 875, Sec. 2. Effective January 1, 2004.)

(a) A person who possesses an identification card shall:

(1) Within seven days, notify the county health department or the county's designee of any change in the person's attending physician or designated primary caregiver, if any.

(2) Annually submit to the county health department or the county' s designee the following:

(A) Updated written documentation of the person's serious medical condition.

(B) The name and duties of the person's designated primary caregiver, if any, for the forthcoming year.

(b) If a person who possesses an identification card fails to comply with this section, the card shall be deemed expired. If an identification card expires, the identification card of any designated primary caregiver of the person shall also expire.

(c) If the designated primary caregiver has been changed, the previous primary caregiver shall return his or her identification card to the department or to the county health department or the county's designee.

(d) If the owner or operator or an employee of the owner or operator of a provider has been designated as a primary caregiver pursuant to paragraph (1) of subdivision (d) of Section 11362.7, of the qualified patient or person with an identification card, the owner or operator shall notify the county health department or the county's designee, pursuant to Section 11362.715, if a change in the designated primary caregiver has occurred.

Health and Safety Code § 11362.765

(Amended by Stats. 2017, Ch. 27, Sec. 137. (SB 94) Effective June 27, 2017.)

(a) Subject to the requirements of this article, the individuals specified in subdivision (b) shall not be subject, on that sole basis, to criminal liability under Section 11357, 11358, 11359, 11360, 11366, 11366.5, or 11570. This section does not authorize the individual to smoke or otherwise consume cannabis unless otherwise authorized by this article, nor shall anything in this section authorize any individual or group to cultivate or distribute cannabis for profit.

(b) Subdivision (a) shall apply to all of the following:

(1) A qualified patient or a person with an identification card who transports or processes cannabis for his or her own personal medical use.

(2) A designated primary caregiver who transports, processes, administers, delivers, or gives away cannabis for medical purposes, in amounts not exceeding those established in subdivision (a) of Section 11362.77, only to the qualified patient of the primary caregiver, or to the person with an identification card who has designated the individual as a primary caregiver.

(3) An individual who provides assistance to a qualified patient or a person with an identification card, or his or her designated primary caregiver, in administering medicinal cannabis to the qualified patient or person or acquiring the skills necessary to cultivate or administer cannabis for medical purposes to the qualified patient or person.

(c) A primary caregiver who receives compensation for actual expenses, including reasonable compensation incurred for services provided to an eligible qualified patient or person with an identification card to enable that person to use cannabis under this article, or for payment for out-of-pocket expenses incurred in providing those services, or both, shall not, on the sole basis of that fact, be subject to prosecution or punishment under Section 11359 or 11360.

Health and Safety Code § 11362.768

(Amended by Stats. 2017, Ch. 27, Sec. 138. (SB 94) Effective June 27, 2017.)

(a) This section shall apply to individuals specified in subdivision (b) of Section 11362.765.

(b) No medicinal cannabis cooperative, collective, dispensary, operator, establishment, or provider who possesses, cultivates, or distributes medicinal cannabis pursuant to this article shall be located within a 600-foot radius of a school.

(c) The distance specified in this section shall be the horizontal distance measured in a straight line from the property line of the school to the closest property line of the lot on which the medicinal cannabis cooperative, collective, dispensary, operator, establishment, or provider is to be located without regard to intervening structures.

(d) This section shall not apply to a medicinal cannabis cooperative, collective, dispensary, operator, establishment, or provider that is also a licensed residential medical or elder care facility.

(e) This section shall apply only to a medicinal cannabis cooperative, collective, dispensary, operator, establishment, or provider that is authorized by law to possess, cultivate, or distribute medicinal cannabis and that has a storefront or mobile retail outlet which ordinarily requires a local business license.

(f) Nothing in this section shall prohibit a city, county, or city and county from adopting ordinances or policies that further restrict the location or establishment of a medicinal cannabis cooperative, collective, dispensary, operator, establishment, or provider.

(g) This section does not preempt local ordinances, adopted prior to January 1, 2011, that regulate the location or establishment of a medicinal cannabis cooperative, collective, dispensary, operator, establishment, or provider.

(h) For the purposes of this section, "school" means any public or private school providing instruction in kindergarten or any of grades 1 to 12, inclusive, but does not include any private school in which education is primarily conducted in private homes.

Health and Safety Code § 11362.769

(Amended by Stats. 2016, Ch. 32, Sec. 66. (SB 837) Effective June 27, 2016.)

Indoor and outdoor medical cannabis cultivation shall be conducted in accordance with state and local laws. State agencies, including, but not limited to, the Department of Food and Agriculture, the State Board of Forestry and Fire Protection, the Department of Fish and Wildlife, the State Water Resources Control Board, the California regional water quality control boards, and traditional state law enforcement agencies shall address environmental impacts of medical cannabis cultivation and shall coordinate, when appropriate, with cities and counties and their law enforcement agencies in enforcement efforts.

Health and Safety Code § 11362.77

(Amended by Stats. 2017, Ch. 27, Sec. 139. (SB 94) Effective June 27, 2017.)

(a) A qualified patient or primary caregiver may possess no more than eight ounces of dried cannabis per qualified patient. In addition, a qualified patient or primary caregiver may also maintain no more than six mature or 12 immature cannabis plants per qualified patient.

(b) If a qualified patient or primary caregiver has a physician's recommendation that this quantity does not meet the qualified patient's medical needs, the qualified patient or primary caregiver may possess an amount of cannabis consistent with the patient's needs.

(c) Counties and cities may retain or enact medicinal cannabis guidelines allowing qualified patients or primary caregivers to exceed the state limits set forth in subdivision (a).

(d) Only the dried mature processed flowers of female cannabis plant or the plant conversion shall be considered when determining allowable quantities of cannabis under this section.

(e) A qualified patient or a person holding a valid identification card, or the designated primary caregiver of that qualified patient or person, may possess amounts of cannabis consistent with this article.

Health and Safety Code § 11362.78

(Amended by Stats. 2017, Ch. 27, Sec. 142. (SB 94) Effective June 27, 2017.)

A state or local law enforcement agency or officer shall not refuse to accept an identification card issued pursuant to this article unless the state or local law enforcement agency or officer has probable cause to believe that the information contained in the card is false or fraudulent, or the card is being used fraudulently.

Health and Safety Code § 11362.785

(Amended by Stats. 2017, Ch. 27, Sec. 143. (SB 94) Effective June 27, 2017.)

(a) Nothing in this article shall require any accommodation of medicinal use of cannabis on the property or premises of a place of employment or during the hours of employment or on the property or premises of a jail, correctional facility, or other type of penal institution in which prisoners reside or persons under arrest are detained.

(b) Notwithstanding subdivision (a), a person shall not be prohibited or prevented from obtaining and submitting the written information and documentation necessary to apply for an identification card on the basis that the person is incarcerated in a jail, correctional facility, or other penal institution in which prisoners reside or persons under arrest are detained.

(c) This article does not prohibit a jail, correctional facility, or other penal institution in which prisoners reside or persons under arrest are detained, from permitting a prisoner or a person under arrest who has an identification card, to use cannabis for medicinal purposes under circumstances that will not endanger the health or safety of other prisoners or the security of the facility.

(d) This article does not require a governmental, private, or any other health insurance provider or health care service plan to be liable for a claim for reimbursement for the medicinal use of cannabis.

Health and Safety Code § 11362.79

(Amended by Stats. 2017, Ch. 27, Sec. 144. (SB 94) Effective June 27, 2017.)

This article does not authorize a qualified patient or person with an identification card to engage in the smoking of medicinal cannabis under any of the following circumstances:

(a) In a place where smoking is prohibited by law.

(b) In or within 1,000 feet of the grounds of a school, recreation center, or youth center, unless the medicinal use occurs within a residence.

(c) On a schoolbus.

(d) While in a motor vehicle that is being operated.

(e) While operating a boat.

Health and Safety Code § 11362.795

(Amended by Stats. 2017, Ch. 27, Sec. 145. (SB 94) Effective June 27, 2017.)

(a) (1) Any criminal defendant who is eligible to use cannabis pursuant to Section 11362.5 may request that the court confirm that he or she is allowed to use medicinal cannabis while he or she is on probation or released on bail.

(2) The court's decision and the reasons for the decision shall be stated on the record and an entry stating those reasons shall be made in the minutes of the court.

(3) During the period of probation or release on bail, if a physician recommends that the probationer or defendant use medicinal cannabis, the probationer or defendant may request a modification of the conditions of probation or bail to authorize the use of medicinal cannabis.

(4) The court's consideration of the modification request authorized by this subdivision shall comply with the requirements of this section.

(b) (1) Any person who is to be released on parole from a jail, state prison, school, road camp, or other state or local institution of confinement and who is eligible to use medicinal cannabis pursuant to Section 11362.5 may request that he or she be allowed to use medicinal cannabis during the period he or she is released on parole. A parolee's written conditions of parole shall reflect whether or not a request for a modification of the conditions of his or her parole to use medicinal cannabis was made, and whether the request was granted or denied.

(2) During the period of the parole, where a physician recommends that the parolee use medicinal cannabis, the parolee may request a modification of the conditions of the parole to authorize the use of medicinal cannabis.

(3) Any parolee whose request to use medicinal cannabis while on parole was denied may pursue an administrative appeal of the decision. Any decision on the appeal shall be in writing and shall reflect the reasons for the decision.

(4) The administrative consideration of the modification request authorized by this subdivision shall comply with the requirements of this section.

Health and Safety Code § 11362.8

(Amended by Stats. 2017, Ch. 27, Sec. 146. (SB 94) Effective June 27, 2017.)

A professional licensing board shall not impose a civil penalty or take other disciplinary action against a licensee based solely on the fact that the licensee has performed acts that are necessary or appropriate to carry out the licensee's role as a designated primary caregiver to a person who is a qualified patient or who possesses a lawful identification card issued pursuant to Section 11362.72. However, this section shall not apply to acts performed by a physician relating to the discussion or recommendation of the medical use of cannabis to a patient. These discussions or recommendations, or both, shall be governed by Section 11362.5.

Health and Safey Code § 11362.81

(Amended by Stats. 2017, Ch. 27, Sec. 147. (SB 94) Effective June 27, 2017.)

(a) A person specified in subdivision (b) shall be subject to the following penalties:

(1) For the first offense, imprisonment in the county jail for no more than six months or a fine not to exceed one thousand dollars ($1,000), or both.

(2) For a second or subsequent offense, imprisonment in the county jail for no more than one year, or a fine not to exceed one thousand dollars ($1,000), or both.

(b) Subdivision (a) applies to any of the following:

(1) A person who fraudulently represents a medical condition or fraudulently provides any material misinformation to a physician, county health department or the county's designee, or state or local law enforcement agency or officer, for the purpose of falsely obtaining an identification card.

(2) A person who steals or fraudulently uses any person's identification card in order to acquire, possess, cultivate, transport, use, produce, or distribute cannabis.

(3) A person who counterfeits, tampers with, or fraudulently produces an identification card.

(4) A person who breaches the confidentiality requirements of this article to information provided to, or contained in the records of, the department or of a county health department or the county's designee pertaining to an identification card program.

(c) In addition to the penalties prescribed in subdivision (a), a person described in subdivision (b) may be precluded from attempting to obtain, or obtaining or using, an identification card for a period of up to six months at the discretion of the court.

(d) In addition to the requirements of this article, the Attorney General shall develop and adopt appropriate guidelines to ensure the security and nondiversion of cannabis grown for medicinal use by patients qualified under the Compassionate Use Act of 1996.

Health and Safety Code § 11362.82

(Added by Stats. 2003, Ch. 875, Sec. 2. Effective January 1, 2004.)

If any section, subdivision, sentence, clause, phrase, or portion of this article is for any reason held invalid or unconstitutional by any court of competent jurisdiction, that portion shall be deemed a separate, distinct, and independent provision, and that holding shall not affect the validity of the remaining portion thereof.

Health and Safety Code § 11362.83

(Amended by Stats. 2017, Ch. 27, Sec. 148. (SB 94) Effective June 27, 2017.)

Nothing in this article shall prevent a city or other local governing body from adopting and enforcing any of the following:

(a) Adopting local ordinances that regulate the location, operation, or establishment of a medicinal cannabis cooperative or collective.

(b) The civil and criminal enforcement of local ordinances described in subdivision (a).

(c) Enacting other laws consistent with this article.

Health and Safety Code § 11362.84

(Added November 8, 2016, by initiative Proposition 64, Sec. 5.4.)

The status and conduct of a qualified patient who acts in accordance with the Compassionate Use Act shall not, by itself, be used to restrict or abridge custodial or parental rights to minor children in any action or proceeding under the jurisdiction of family or juvenile court.

Health and Safety Code § 11362.85

(Amended by Stats. 2017, Ch. 27, Sec. 149. (SB 94) Effective June 27, 2017. Note: Section 11362.9 is in Article 2, following Section 11362.5. Note: This section was added on Nov. 8, 2016, by initiative Prop. 64.)

Upon a determination by the California Attorney General that the federal schedule of controlled substances has been amended to reclassify or declassify cannabis, the Legislature may amend or repeal the provisions of this code, as necessary, to conform state law to such changes in federal law.

Health and Safety Code § 11362.9

(Amended by Stats. 2019, Ch. 802, Sec. 1. (AB 420) Effective October 12, 2019.)

(a) (1) It is the intent of the Legislature that the state commission objective scientific research by the premier research institute of the world, the University of California, regarding the efficacy and safety of administering cannabis, its naturally occurring constituents, and synthetic compounds, as part of medical treatment. If the Regents of the University of California, by appropriate resolution, accept this responsibility, the University of California shall create a program, to be known as the California Cannabis Research Program, hosted by the Center for Medicinal Cannabis Research. Whenever "California Marijuana Research Program" appears in any statute, regulation, or contract, or in any other code, it shall be construed to refer to the California Cannabis Research Program.

(2) The program shall develop and conduct studies intended to ascertain the general medical safety and efficacy of cannabis and, if found valuable, shall develop medical guidelines for the appropriate administration and use of cannabis. The studies may examine the effect of cannabis on motor skills, the health and safety effects of cannabis, cannabinoids, and other related constituents, and other behavioral and health outcomes.

(b) The program may immediately solicit proposals for research projects to be included in the cannabis studies. Program requirements to be used when evaluating responses to its solicitation for proposals shall include, but not be limited to, all of the following:

(1) Proposals shall demonstrate the use of key personnel, including clinicians or scientists and support personnel, who are prepared to develop a program of research regarding the general medical efficacy and safety of cannabis.

(2) Proposals shall contain procedures for outreach to patients with various medical conditions who may be suitable participants in research on cannabis.

(3) Proposals shall contain provisions for a patient registry.

(4) Proposals shall contain provisions for an information system that is designed to record information about possible study participants, investigators, and clinicians, and deposit and analyze data that accrues as part of clinical trials.

(5) Proposals shall contain protocols suitable for research on cannabis, addressing patients diagnosed with acquired immunodeficiency syndrome (AIDS) or human immunodeficiency virus (HIV), cancer, glaucoma, or seizures or muscle spasms associated with a chronic, debilitating condition. The proposal may also include research on other serious illnesses, provided that resources are available and medical information justifies the

research.

(6) Proposals shall demonstrate the use of a specimen laboratory capable of housing plasma, urine, and other specimens necessary to study the concentration of cannabinoids in various tissues, as well as housing specimens for studies of toxic effects of cannabis.

(7) Proposals shall demonstrate the use of a laboratory capable of analyzing cannabis, provided to the program under this section, for purity and cannabinoid content and the capacity to detect contaminants.

(c) In order to ensure objectivity in evaluating proposals, the program shall use a peer review process that is modeled on the process used by the National Institutes of Health, and that guards against funding research that is biased in favor of or against particular outcomes. Peer reviewers shall be selected for their expertise in the scientific substance and methods of the proposed research, and their lack of bias or conflict of interest regarding the applicants or the topic of an approach taken in the proposed research. Peer reviewers shall judge research proposals on several criteria, foremost among which shall be both of the following:

(1) The scientific merit of the research plan, including whether the research design and experimental procedures are potentially biased for or against a particular outcome.

(2) Researchers' expertise in the scientific substance and methods of the proposed research, and their lack of bias or conflict of interest regarding the topic of, and the approach taken in, the proposed research.

(d) If the program is administered by the Regents of the University of California, any grant research proposals approved by the program shall also require review and approval by the research advisory panel.

(e) It is the intent of the Legislature that the program be established as follows:

(1) The program shall be located at one or more University of California campuses that have a core of faculty experienced in organizing multidisciplinary scientific endeavors and, in particular, strong experience in clinical trials involving psychopharmacologic agents. The campuses at which research under the auspices of the program is to take place shall accommodate the administrative offices, including the director of the program, as well as a data management unit, and facilities for detection and analysis of various naturally occurring and synthetic cannabinoids, as well as storage of specimens.

(2) When awarding grants under this section, the program shall utilize principles and parameters of the other well-tested statewide research programs administered by the University of California, modeled after programs administered by the National Institutes of Health, including peer review evaluation of the scientific merit of applications.

(3) The scientific and clinical operations of the program shall occur partly at University of California campuses and partly at other postsecondary institutions that have clinicians or scientists with expertise to conduct the required studies. Criteria for selection of research locations shall include the elements listed in subdivision (b) and, additionally, shall give particular weight to the organizational plan, leadership qualities of the program director, and plans to involve investigators and patient populations from multiple sites.

(4) The funds received by the program shall be allocated to various research studies in accordance with a scientific plan developed by the Scientific Advisory Council. As the first wave of studies is completed, it is anticipated that the program will receive requests for funding of additional studies. These requests shall be reviewed by the Scientific Advisory Council.

(5) The size, scope, and number of studies funded shall be commensurate with the amount of appropriated and available program funding.

(f) All personnel involved in implementing approved proposals shall be authorized as required by Section 11604.

(g) Studies conducted pursuant to this section shall include the greatest amount of new scientific research possible on the medical uses of, and medical hazards associated with, cannabis. The program shall consult with the Research

Advisory Panel analogous agencies in other states, and appropriate federal agencies in an attempt to avoid duplicative research and the wasting of research dollars.

(h) The program shall make every effort to recruit qualified patients and qualified physicians from throughout the state.

(i) The cannabis studies shall employ state-of-the-art research methodologies.

(j) The program shall ensure that all cannabis used in the studies is of the appropriate medicinal quality. Cannabis used by the program may be obtained from the National Institute on Drug Abuse or any other entity authorized by the appropriate federal agencies, the Attorney General pursuant to Section 11478, or may be cultivated by the program pursuant to applicable federal and state laws and regulations.

(k) The program may review, approve, or incorporate studies and research by independent groups presenting scientifically valid protocols for medical research, regardless of whether the areas of study are being researched by the committee.

(l) (1) To enhance understanding of the efficacy and adverse effects of cannabis as a pharmacological agent, the program shall conduct focused controlled clinical trials on the usefulness of cannabis in patients diagnosed with AIDS or HIV, cancer, glaucoma, or seizures or muscle spasms associated with a chronic, debilitating condition. The program may add research on other serious illnesses, provided that resources are available and medical information justifies the research. The studies shall focus on comparisons of both the efficacy and safety of methods of administering the drug to patients, including inhalational, tinctural, and oral, evaluate possible uses of cannabis as a primary or adjunctive treatment, and develop further information on optimal dosage, timing, mode of administration, and variations in the effects of different cannabinoids and varieties of cannabis or synthetic compounds that simulate the effects of naturally occurring cannabinoids. The studies may also focus on examining testing methods for detecting harmful contaminants in cannabis, including, but not limited to, mold, bacteria, and mycotoxins that could cause harm to patients.

(2) The program shall examine the safety of cannabis in patients with various medical disorders, including the interaction of cannabis with other drugs, relative safety of inhalation versus oral forms, and the effects on mental function in medically ill persons.

(3) The program shall be limited to providing for objective scientific research to ascertain the efficacy and safety of cannabis as part of medical treatment, and should not be construed as encouraging or sanctioning the social or recreational use of cannabis.

(m) (1) Subject to paragraph (2), the program shall, prior to approving proposals, seek to obtain research protocol guidelines from the National Institutes of Health and shall, if the National Institutes of Health issues research protocol guidelines, comply with those guidelines.

(2) If, after a reasonable period of time of not less than six months and not more than a year has elapsed from the date the program seeks to obtain guidelines pursuant to paragraph (1), no guidelines have been approved, the program may proceed using the research protocol guidelines it develops.

(n) In order to maximize the scope and size of the cannabis studies, the program may do any of the following:

(1) Solicit, apply for, and accept funds from foundations, private individuals, and all other funding sources that can be used to expand the scope or timeframe of the cannabis studies that are authorized under this section. The program shall not expend more than 5 percent of its General Fund allocation in efforts to obtain money from outside sources.

(2) Include within the scope of the cannabis studies other cannabis research projects that are independently funded and that meet the requirements set forth in subdivisions (a) to (c), inclusive. In no case shall the program accept funds that are offered with any conditions other than that the funds be used to study the efficacy and safety of cannabis as part of medical treatment.

(o) (1) Within six months of the effective date of this section, the program shall report to the Legislature, the Governor, and the Attorney General on the progress of the cannabis studies.

(2) Thereafter, the program shall issue a report to the Legislature every 24 months detailing the progress of the studies. The interim reports required under this paragraph shall include, but not be limited to, data on all of the following:

(A) The names and number of diseases or conditions under study.

(B) The number of patients enrolled in each study, by disease.

(C) Any scientifically valid preliminary findings.

(p) If the Regents of the University of California implement this section, the President of the University of California, or the president's designee, shall appoint a multidisciplinary Scientific Advisory Council, not to exceed 15 members, to provide policy guidance in the creation and implementation of the program. Members shall be chosen on the basis of scientific expertise. Members of the council shall serve on a voluntary basis, with reimbursement for expenses incurred in the course of their participation. The members shall be reimbursed for travel and other necessary expenses incurred in their performance of the duties of the council.

(q) No more than 10 percent of the total funds appropriated may be used for all aspects of the administration of this section.

(r) This section shall be implemented only to the extent that funding for its purposes is appropriated by the Legislature.

(s) Money appropriated to the program pursuant to subdivision (e) of Section 34019 of the Revenue and Taxation Code shall only be used as authorized by the Control, Regulate and Tax Adult Use of Marijuana Act (AUMA).

(t) This section does not limit or preclude cannabis-related research activities at any campus of the University of California.

Health & Safety Code § 11364.5

(Amended by Stats. 2022, Ch. 201, Sec. 2. (AB 1598) Effective January 1, 2023.)

(a) Except as authorized by law, no person shall maintain or operate any place of business in which drug paraphernalia is kept, displayed or offered in any manner, sold, furnished, transferred or given away unless such drug paraphernalia is completely and wholly kept, displayed or offered within a separate room or enclosure to which persons under the age of 18 years not accompanied by a parent or legal guardian are excluded. Each entrance to such a room or enclosure shall be signposted in reasonably visible and legible words to the effect that drug paraphernalia is kept, displayed or offered in such room or enclosure and that minors, unless accompanied by a parent or legal guardian, are excluded.

(b) Except as authorized by law, no owner, manager, proprietor or other person in charge of any room or enclosure, within any place of business, in which drug paraphernalia is kept, displayed or offered in any manner, sold, furnished, transferred or given away shall permit or allow any person under the age of 18 years to enter, be in, remain in or visit such room or enclosure unless that minor person is accompanied by their parent or legal guardian.

(c) Unless authorized by law, no person under the age of 18 years shall enter, be in, remain in, or visit any room or enclosure in any place of business in which drug paraphernalia is kept, displayed or offered in any manner, sold, furnished, transferred, or given away unless accompanied by their parent or legal guardian.

(d) As used in this section, "drug paraphernalia" means all equipment, products, and materials of any kind which are intended for use or designed for use, in planting, propagating, cultivating, growing, harvesting, manufacturing, compounding, converting, producing, processing, preparing, testing, analyzing, packaging, repackaging, storing, containing, concealing, injecting, ingesting, inhaling, or otherwise introducing into the human body a controlled substance. "Drug paraphernalia" includes, but is not limited to, all of the following:

(1) Kits intended for use or designed for use in planting, propagating, cultivating, growing, or harvesting of any species of plant which is a controlled substance or from which a controlled substance can be derived.

(2) Kits intended for use or designed for use in manufacturing, compounding, converting, producing, processing, or preparing controlled substances.

(3) Isomerization devices intended for use or designed for use in increasing the potency of any species of plant which is a controlled substance.

(4) Testing equipment intended for use or designed for use in identifying, or in analyzing the strength, effectiveness, or purity of controlled substances, except as otherwise provided in subdivision (g).

(5) Scales and balances intended for use or designed for use in weighing or measuring controlled substances.

(6) Diluents and adulterants, such as quinine hydrochloride, mannitol, mannite, dextrose, and lactose, intended for use or designed for use in cutting controlled substances.

(7) Separation gins and sifters intended for use or designed for use in removing twigs and seeds from, or in otherwise cleaning or refining, cannabis.

(8) Blenders, bowls, containers, spoons, and mixing devices intended for use or designed for use in compounding controlled substances.

(9) Capsules, balloons, envelopes, and other containers intended for use or designed for use in packaging small quantities of controlled substances.

(10) Containers and other objects intended for use or designed for use in storing or concealing controlled substances.

(11) Hypodermic syringes, needles, and other objects intended for use or designed for use in parenterally injecting controlled substances into the human body.

(12) Objects intended for use or designed for use in ingesting, inhaling, or otherwise introducing cannabis, cocaine, hashish, or hashish oil into the human body, such as the following:

(A) Metal, wooden, acrylic, glass, stone, plastic, or ceramic pipes with or without screens, permanent screens, hashish heads, or punctured metal bowls.

(B) Water pipes.

(C) Carburetion tubes and devices.

(D) Smoking and carburetion masks.

(E) Roach clips, meaning objects used to hold burning material, such as a cannabis cigarette that has become too small or too short to be held in the hand.

(F) Miniature cocaine spoons, and cocaine vials.

(G) Chamber pipes.

(H) Carburetor pipes.

(I) Electric pipes.

(J) Air-driven pipes.

(K) Chillums.

(L) Bongs.

(M) Ice pipes or chillers.

(e) In determining whether an object is drug paraphernalia, a court or other authority may consider, in addition to all other logically relevant factors, the following:

(1) Statements by an owner or by anyone in control of the object concerning its use.

(2) Prior convictions, if any, of an owner, or of anyone in control of the object, under any state or federal law relating to any controlled substance.

(3) Direct or circumstantial evidence of the intent of an owner, or of anyone in control of the object, to deliver it to persons whom they know, or should reasonably know, intend to use the object to facilitate a violation of this section. The innocence of an owner, or of anyone in control of the object, as to a direct violation of this section shall not prevent a finding that the object is intended for use, or designed for use, as drug paraphernalia.

(4) Instructions, oral or written, provided with the object concerning its use.

(5) Descriptive materials, accompanying the object which explain or depict its use.

(6) National and local advertising concerning its use.

(7) The manner in which the object is displayed for sale.

(8) Whether the owner, or anyone in control of the object, is a legitimate supplier of like or related items to the community, such as a licensed distributor or dealer of tobacco products.

(9) The existence and scope of legitimate uses for the object in the community.

(10) Expert testimony concerning its use.

(f) This section shall not apply to any of the following:

(1) Any pharmacist or other authorized person who sells or furnishes drug paraphernalia described in paragraph (11) of subdivision (d) upon the prescription of a physician, dentist, podiatrist, or veterinarian.

(2) Any physician, dentist, podiatrist, or veterinarian who furnishes or prescribes drug paraphernalia described in paragraph (11) of subdivision (d) to a patient.

(3) Any manufacturer, wholesaler, or retailer licensed by the California State Board of Pharmacy to sell or transfer drug paraphernalia described in paragraph (11) of subdivision (d).

(g) Notwithstanding paragraph (4) of subdivision (d), "drug paraphernalia" does not include any testing equipment designed, marketed, intended to be used, or used, to test a substance for the presence of fentanyl, ketamine, gamma hydroxybutyric acid, or any analog of fentanyl.

(h) Notwithstanding any other provision of law, including Section 11374, violation of this section shall not constitute a criminal offense, but operation of a business in violation of the provisions of this section shall be grounds for revocation or nonrenewal of any license, permit, or other entitlement previously issued by a city, county, or city and county for the privilege of engaging in such business and shall be grounds for denial of any future license, permit, or other entitlement authorizing the conduct of such business or any other business, if the business includes the sale of drug paraphernalia.

Health & Safety Code § 11366

(Amended by Stats. 1991, Ch. 492, Sec. 1.)

Every person who opens or maintains any place for the purpose of unlawfully selling, giving away, or using any controlled substance which is

(1) specified in subdivision (b), (c), or (e), or paragraph (1) of subdivision (f) of Section 11054, specified in paragraph (13), (14), (15), or (20) of subdivision (d) of Section 11054, or specified in subdivision (b), (c), paragraph (1) or (2) of subdivision (d), or paragraph (3) of subdivision (e) of Section 11055, or

(2) which is a narcotic drug classified in Schedule III, IV, or V, shall be punished by imprisonment in the county jail for a period of not more than one year or the state prison.

Health & Safety Code § 11366.5

(Amended by Stats. 2011, Ch. 15, Sec. 164. (AB 109) Effective April 4, 2011. Operative October 1, 2011, by Sec. 636 of Ch. 15, as amended by Stats. 2011, Ch. 39, Sec. 68.)

(a) Any person who has under his or her management or control any building, room, space, or enclosure, either as an owner, lessee, agent, employee, or mortgagee, who knowingly rents, leases, or makes available for use, with or without compensation, the building, room, space, or enclosure for the purpose of unlawfully manufacturing, storing, or distributing any controlled substance for sale or distribution shall be punished by imprisonment in the county jail for not more than one year, or pursuant to subdivision (h) of Section 1170 of the Penal Code.

(b) Any person who has under his or her management or control any building, room, space, or enclosure, either as an owner, lessee, agent, employee, or mortgagee, who knowingly allows the building, room, space, or enclosure to be fortified to suppress law enforcement entry in order to further the sale of any amount of cocaine base as specified in paragraph (1) of subdivision (f) of Section 11054, cocaine as specified in paragraph (6) of subdivision (b) of Section 11055, heroin, phencyclidine, amphetamine, methamphetamine, or lysergic acid diethylamide and who obtains excessive profits from the use of the building, room, space, or enclosure shall be punished by imprisonment pursuant to subdivision (h) of Section 1170 of the Penal Code for two, three, or four years.

(c) Any person who violates subdivision (a) after previously being convicted of a violation of subdivision (a) shall be punished by imprisonment pursuant to subdivision (h) of Section 1170 of the Penal Code for two, three, or four years.

(d) For the purposes of this section, excessive profits means the receipt of consideration of a value substantially higher than fair market value.

Health & Safety Code § 11379.6

(Amended by Stats. 2015, Ch. 141, Sec. 1. (SB 212) Effective January 1, 2016.)

(a) Except as otherwise provided by law, every person who manufactures, compounds, converts, produces, derives, processes, or prepares, either directly or indirectly by chemical extraction or independently by means of chemical synthesis, any controlled substance specified in Section 11054, 11055, 11056, 11057, or 11058 shall be punished by imprisonment pursuant to subdivision (h) of Section 1170 of the Penal Code for three, five, or seven years and by a fine not exceeding fifty thousand dollars ($50,000).

(b) Except when an enhancement pursuant to Section 11379.7 is pled and proved, the fact that a person under 16 years of age resided in a structure in which a violation of this section involving methamphetamine occurred shall be considered a factor in aggravation by the sentencing court.

(c) Except when an enhancement pursuant to Section 11379.7 is pled and proved, the fact that a violation of this section involving methamphetamine occurred within 200 feet of an occupied residence or any structure where another person was present at the time the offense was committed may be considered a factor in aggravation by the sentencing court.

(d) The fact that a violation of this section involving the use of a volatile solvent to chemically extract concentrated cannabis occurred within 300 feet of an occupied residence or any structure where another person was present at the time the offense was committed may be considered a factor in aggravation by the sentencing court.

(e) Except as otherwise provided by law, every person who offers to perform an act which is punishable under subdivision (a) shall be punished by imprisonment pursuant to subdivision (h) of Section 1170 of the Penal Code for three, four, or five years.

(f) All fines collected pursuant to subdivision (a) shall be transferred to the State Treasury for deposit in the Clandestine Drug Lab Clean-up Account, as established by Section 5 of Chapter 1295 of the Statutes of 1987. The transmission to the State Treasury shall be carried out in the same manner as fines collected for the state by the county.

Health and Safety Code § 11470

(Amended by Stats. 2017, Ch. 27, Sec. 152. (SB 94) Effective June 27, 2017.)

The following are subject to forfeiture:

(a) All controlled substances which have been manufactured, distributed, dispensed, or acquired in violation of this division.

(b) All raw materials, products, and equipment of any kind which are used, or intended for use, in manufacturing, compounding, processing, delivering, importing, or exporting any controlled substance in violation of this division.

(c) All property except real property or a boat, airplane, or any vehicle which is used, or intended for use, as a container for property described in subdivision (a) or (b).

(d) All books, records, and research products and materials, including formulas, microfilm, tapes, and data which are used, or intended for use, in violation of this division.

(e) The interest of any registered owner of a boat, airplane, or any vehicle other than an implement of husbandry, as defined in Section 36000 of the Vehicle Code, which has been used as an instrument to facilitate the manufacture of, or possession for sale or sale of 14.25 grams or more of heroin, or a substance containing 14.25 grams or more of heroin, or 14.25 grams or more of a substance containing heroin, or 28.5 grams or more of Schedule I controlled substances except cannabis, peyote, or psilocybin; 10 pounds dry weight or more of cannabis, peyote, or psilocybin; or 28.5 grams or more of cocaine, as specified in paragraph (6) of subdivision (b) of Section 11055, cocaine base as specified in paragraph (1) of subdivision (f) of Section 11054, or methamphetamine; or a substance containing 28.5 grams or more of cocaine, as specified in paragraph (6) of subdivision (b) of Section 11055, cocaine base as specified in paragraph (1) of subdivision (f) of Section 11054, or methamphetamine; or 57 grams or more of a substance containing cocaine, as specified in paragraph (6) of subdivision (b) of Section 11055, cocaine base as specified in paragraph (1) of subdivision (f) of Section 11054, or methamphetamine; or 28.5 grams or more of Schedule II controlled substances. An interest in a vehicle which may be lawfully driven on the highway with a class C, class M1, or class M2 license, as prescribed in Section 12804.9 of the Vehicle Code, shall not be forfeited under this subdivision if there is a community property interest in the vehicle by a person other than the defendant and the vehicle is the sole class C, class M1, or class M2 vehicle available to the defendant's immediate family.

(f) All moneys, negotiable instruments, securities, or other things of value furnished or intended to be furnished by any person in exchange for a controlled substance, all proceeds traceable to such an exchange, and all moneys, negotiable instruments, or securities used or intended to be used to facilitate any violation of Section 11351, 11351.5, 11352, 11355, 11359, 11360, 11378, 11378.5, 11379, 11379.5, 11379.6, 11380, 11382, or 11383 of this code, or Section 182 of the Penal Code, or a felony violation of Section 11366.8 of this code, insofar as the offense involves manufacture, sale, possession for sale, offer for sale, or offer to manufacture, or conspiracy to commit at least one of those offenses, if the exchange, violation, or other conduct which is the basis for the forfeiture occurred within five years of the seizure of the property, or the filing of a petition under this chapter, or the issuance of an order of forfeiture of the property, whichever comes first.

(g) The real property of any property owner who is convicted of violating Section 11366, 11366.5, or 11366.6 with respect to that property. However, property which is used as a family residence or for other lawful purposes, or which is owned by two or more persons, one of whom had no knowledge of its unlawful use, shall not be subject to forfeiture.

(h) (1) Subject to the requirements of Section 11488.5 and except as further limited by this subdivision to protect innocent parties who claim a property interest acquired from a defendant, all right, title, and interest in any personal property described in this section shall vest in the state upon commission of the act giving rise to forfeiture under this chapter, if the state or local governmental entity proves a violation of Section 11351, 11351.5, 11352, 11355, 11359, 11360, 11378, 11378.5, 11379, 11379.5, 11379.6, 11380, 11382, or 11383 of this code, or Section 182 of the Penal Code, or a felony violation of Section 11366.8 of this code, insofar as the offense involves the manufacture, sale, possession for sale, offer for sale, offer to manufacture, or conspiracy to commit at least one of those offenses, in accordance with the burden of proof set forth in paragraph (1) of subdivision (i) of Section 11488.4 or, in the case of cash or negotiable instruments in excess of twenty-five thousand dollars ($25,000), paragraph (4) of subdivision (i) of Section 11488.4.

(2) The operation of the special vesting rule established by this subdivision shall be limited to circumstances where its application will not defeat the claim of any person, including a bona fide purchaser or encumbrancer who, pursuant to Section 11488.5, 11488.6, or 11489, claims an interest in the property seized, notwithstanding that the interest in the property being claimed was acquired from a defendant whose property interest would otherwise have been subject to divestment pursuant to this subdivision.

Health and Safety Code § 11470.1

(Amended by Stats. 2016, Ch. 831, Sec. 1. (SB 443) Effective January 1, 2017.)

(a) The expenses of seizing, eradicating, destroying, or taking remedial action with respect to, any controlled substance or its precursors shall be recoverable from:

(1) Any person who manufactures or cultivates a controlled substance or its precursors in violation of this division.

(2) Any person who aids and abets or who knowingly profits in any manner from the manufacture or cultivation of a controlled substance or its precursors on property owned, leased, or possessed by the defendant, in violation of this division.

(b) The expenses of taking remedial action with respect to any controlled substance or its precursors shall also be recoverable from any person liable for the costs of that remedial action under Chapter 6.8 (commencing with Section 25300) of Division 20 of the Health and Safety Code.

(c) It shall be necessary to seek or obtain a criminal conviction for the unlawful manufacture or cultivation of any controlled substance or its precursors prior to the entry of judgment for the recovery of expenses. If criminal charges are pending against the defendant for the unlawful manufacture or cultivation of any controlled substance or its precursors, an action brought pursuant to this section shall, upon a defendant's request, be continued while the criminal charges are pending.

(d) The action may be brought by the district attorney, county counsel, city attorney, the State Department of Health Care Services, or Attorney General. All expenses recovered pursuant to this section shall be remitted to the law enforcement agency which incurred them.

(e) (1) The burden of proof as to liability shall be on the plaintiff and shall be by a preponderance of the evidence in an action alleging that the defendant is liable for expenses pursuant to paragraph (1) of subdivision (a). The burden of proof as to liability shall be on the plaintiff and shall be by clear and convincing evidence in an action alleging that the defendant is liable for expenses pursuant to paragraph (2) of subdivision (a). The burden of proof as to the amount of expenses recoverable shall be on the plaintiff and shall be by a preponderance of the evidence in any action brought pursuant to subdivision (a).

(2) Notwithstanding paragraph (1), for any person convicted of a criminal charge of the manufacture or cultivation of a controlled substance or its precursors there shall be a presumption affecting the burden of proof that the person is liable.

(f) Only expenses which meet the following requirements shall be recoverable under this section:

(1) The expenses were incurred in seizing, eradicating, or destroying the controlled substance or its precursors or in taking remedial action with respect to a hazardous substance. These expenses may not include any costs incurred in use of the herbicide paraquat.

(2) The expenses were incurred as a proximate result of the defendant's manufacture or cultivation of a controlled substance in violation of this division.

(3) The expenses were reasonably incurred.

(g) For purposes of this section, "remedial action" shall have the meaning set forth in Section 25322.

(h) For the purpose of discharge in bankruptcy, a judgment for recovery of expenses under this section shall be deemed to be a debt for willful and malicious injury by the defendant to another entity or to the property of another entity.

(i) Notwithstanding Section 526 of the Code of Civil Procedure, the plaintiff may be granted a temporary restraining order or a preliminary injunction, pending or during trial, to restrain the defendant from transferring, encumbering, hypothecating, or otherwise disposing of any assets specified by the court, if it appears by the complaint that the plaintiff is entitled to the relief demanded and it appears that the defendant may dispose of those assets to thwart enforcement of the judgment.

(j) The Legislature finds and declares that civil penalties for the recovery of expenses incurred in enforcing the provisions of this division shall not supplant criminal prosecution for violation of those provisions, but shall be a supplemental remedy to criminal enforcement.

(k) Any testimony, admission, or any other statement made by the defendant in any proceeding brought pursuant to this section, or any evidence derived from the testimony, admission, or other statement, shall not be admitted or otherwise used in any criminal proceeding arising out of the same conduct.

(l) No action shall be brought or maintained pursuant to this section against a person who has been acquitted of criminal charges for conduct that is the basis for an action under this section.

Health & Safety Code § 11472

(Added by renumbering Section 11473 by Stats. 1980, Ch. 1019.)

Controlled substances and any device, contrivance, instrument, or paraphernalia used for unlawfully using or administering a controlled substance, which are possessed in violation of this division, may be seized by any peace officer and in the aid of such seizure a search warrant may be issued as prescribed by law.

Health and Safety Code § 11473

(Amended by Stats. 1994, Ch. 979, Sec. 2. Effective January 1, 1995.)

(a) All seizures under provisions of this chapter, except seizures of vehicles, boats, or airplanes, as specified in subdivision (e) of Section 11470, or seizures of moneys, negotiable instruments, securities, or other things of value as specified in subdivision (f) of Section 11470, shall, upon conviction of the owner or defendant, be ordered destroyed by the court in which conviction was had.

(b) Law enforcement may request of the court that certain uncontaminated science equipment be relinquished to a school or school district for science classroom education in lieu of destruction.

Health and Safety Code § 11473.5

(Amended by Stats. 1994, Ch. 979, Sec. 3. Effective January 1, 1995.)

(a) All seizures of controlled substances, instruments, or paraphernalia used for unlawfully using or administering a controlled substance which are in possession of any city, county, or state official as found property, or as the result of a case in which no trial was had or which has been disposed of by way of dismissal or otherwise than by way of conviction, shall be destroyed by order of the court, unless the court finds that the controlled substances, instruments, or paraphernalia were lawfully possessed by the defendant.

(b) If the court finds that the property was not lawfully possessed by the defendant, law enforcement may request of the court that certain uncontaminated instruments or paraphernalia be relinquished to a school or school district for science classroom education in lieu of destruction.

Health and Safety Code § 11474

(Amended by Stats. 2021, Ch. 70, Sec. 105. (AB 141) Effective July 12, 2021.)

A court order for the destruction of controlled substances, instruments, or paraphernalia pursuant to the provisions of Section 11473 or 11473.5 may be carried out by a police or sheriff's department, the Department of Justice, the Department of the California Highway Patrol, the Department of Cannabis Control, or the Department of Alcoholic Beverage Control. The court order shall specify the agency responsible for the destruction. Controlled substances, instruments, or paraphernalia not in the possession of the designated agency at the time the order of the court is issued shall be delivered to the designated agency for destruction in compliance with the order.

Health and Safety Code § 11476

(Added by Stats. 1972, Ch. 1407.)

Species of plants from which controlled substances in Schedules I and II may be derived which have been planted or cultivated in violation of this division, or of which the owners or cultivators are unknown, or which are wild growths, may be seized and summarily forfeited to the state.

Health and Safety Code § 11477

(Amended by Stats. 1980, Ch. 1019.)

The failure, upon demand by a peace officer of the person in occupancy or in control of land or premises upon which the species of plants are growing or being stored, to produce an appropriate registration, or proof that he is the holder thereof, constitutes authority for the seizure and forfeiture of the plants.

Health & Safety Code § 11478

(Amended by Stats. 2017, Ch. 27, Sec. 153. (SB 94) Effective June 27, 2017.)

Cannabis may be provided by the Attorney General to the heads of research projects which have been registered by the Attorney General, and which have been approved by the research advisory panel pursuant to Section 11480.

The head of the approved research project shall personally receipt for such quantities of cannabis and shall make a record of their disposition. The receipt and record shall be retained by the Attorney General. The head of the approved research project shall also, at intervals and in the manner required by the research advisory panel, report the progress or conclusions of the research project.

Health & Safety Code § 11479

(Amended by Stats. 2017, Ch. 27, Sec. 154. (SB 94) Effective June 27, 2017.)

Notwithstanding Sections 11473 and 11473.5, at any time after seizure by a law enforcement agency of a suspected controlled substance, except in the case of growing or harvested cannabis, that amount in excess of 10 pounds in gross weight may be destroyed without a court order by the chief of the law enforcement agency or a designated subordinate. In the case of growing or harvested cannabis, that amount in excess of two pounds, or the amount of cannabis a medicinal cannabis patient or designated caregiver is authorized to possess by ordinance in the city or county where the cannabis was seized, whichever is greater, may be destroyed without a court order by the chief of the law enforcement agency or a designated subordinate. Destruction shall not take place pursuant to this section until all of the following requirements are satisfied:

(a) At least five random and representative samples have been taken, for evidentiary purposes, from the total amount of suspected controlled substances to be destroyed. These samples shall be in addition to the 10 pounds required above. When the suspected controlled substance consists of growing or harvested cannabis plants, at least one 2-pound sample or a sample in the amount of medicinal cannabis a medicinal cannabis patient or designated caregiver is authorized to possess by ordinance in the city or county where the cannabis was seized, whichever is greater, shall be retained. This sample may include stalks, branches, or leaves. In addition, five representative samples of leaves or buds shall be retained for evidentiary purposes from the total amount of suspected controlled substances to be destroyed.

(b) Photographs and videos have been taken that reasonably and accurately demonstrate the total amount of the suspected controlled substance to be destroyed.

(c) The gross weight of the suspected controlled substance has been determined, either by actually weighing the suspected controlled substance or by estimating that weight after dimensional measurement of the total suspected controlled substance.

(d) The chief of the law enforcement agency has determined that it is not reasonably possible to preserve the suspected controlled substance in place, or to remove the suspected controlled substance to another location. In making this determination, the difficulty of transporting and storing the suspected controlled substance to another site and the storage facilities may be taken into consideration.

Subsequent to any destruction of a suspected controlled substance pursuant to this section, an affidavit shall be filed within 30 days in the court that has jurisdiction over any pending criminal proceedings pertaining to that suspected controlled substance, reciting the applicable information required by subdivisions (a), (b), (c), and (d) together with information establishing the location of the suspected controlled substance, and specifying the date and time of the destruction. In the event that there are no criminal proceedings pending that pertain to that suspected controlled substance, the affidavit may be filed in any court within the county that would have jurisdiction over a person against whom those criminal charges might be filed.

Health & Safety Code § 11479.2

(Amended by Stats. 2017, Ch. 27, Sec. 155. (SB 94) Effective June 27, 2017.)

Notwithstanding the provisions of Sections 11473, 11473.5, 11474, 11479, and 11479.1, at any time after seizure by a law enforcement agency of a suspected controlled substance, except cannabis, any amount, as determined by the court, in excess of 57 grams may, by court order, be destroyed by the chief of a law enforcement agency or a designated subordinate. Destruction shall not take place pursuant to this section until all of the following requirements are satisfied:

(a) At least five random and representative samples have been taken, for evidentiary purposes, from the total amount of suspected controlled substances to be destroyed. Those samples shall be in addition to the 57 grams required above and each sample shall weigh not less than one gram at the time the sample is collected.

(b) Photographs have been taken which reasonably demonstrate the total amount of the suspected controlled substance to be destroyed.

(c) The gross weight of the suspected controlled substance has been determined, either by actually weighing the suspected controlled substance or by estimating such weight after dimensional measurement of the total suspected controlled substance.

(d) In cases involving controlled substances suspected of containing cocaine or methamphetamine, an analysis has determined the qualitative and quantitative nature of the suspected controlled substance.

(e) The law enforcement agency with custody of the controlled substance sought to be destroyed has filed a written motion for the order of destruction in the court which has jurisdiction over any pending criminal proceeding in which a defendant is charged by accusatory pleading with a crime specifically involving the suspected controlled substance sought to be destroyed. The motion shall, by affidavit of the chief of the law enforcement agency or designated subordinate, recite the applicable information required by subdivisions (a), (b), (c), and (d), together with information establishing the location of the suspected controlled substance and the title of any pending criminal proceeding as defined in this subdivision. The motion shall bear proof of service upon all parties to any pending criminal proceeding. No motion shall be made when a defendant is without counsel until the defendant has entered his or her plea to the charges.

(f) The order for destruction shall issue pursuant to this section upon the motion and affidavit in support of the order, unless within 20 days after application for the order, a defendant has requested, in writing, a hearing on the motion. Within 10 days after the filing of that request, or a longer period of time upon good cause shown by either party, the court shall conduct a hearing on the motion in which each party to the motion for destruction shall be permitted to call and examine witnesses. The hearing shall be recorded. Upon conclusion of the hearing, if the court finds that the defendant would not be prejudiced by the destruction, it shall grant the motion and make an order for destruction. In making the order, the court shall ensure that the representative samples to be retained are of sufficient quantities to allow for qualitative analyses by both the prosecution and the defense. Any order for destruction pursuant to this section shall include the applicable information required by subdivisions (a), (b), (c), (d), and (e) and the name of the agency responsible for the destruction. Unless waived, the order shall provide for a 10-day delay prior to destruction in order to allow expert analysis of the controlled substance by the defense.

Subsequent to any destruction of a suspected controlled substance pursuant to this section, an affidavit shall be filed within 30 days in the court which ordered destruction stating the location of the retained, suspected controlled substance and specifying the date and time of destruction.

This section does not apply to seizures involving hazardous chemicals or controlled substances in mixture or combination with hazardous chemicals.

Health and Safety Code § 11480

(Amended by Stats. 2017, Ch. 27, Sec. 156. (SB 94) Effective June 27, 2017.)

(a) The Legislature finds that there is a need to encourage further research into the nature and effects of cannabis and hallucinogenic drugs and to coordinate research efforts on such subjects.

(b) There is a Research Advisory Panel that consists of a representative of the State Department of Health Services, a representative of the California State Board of Pharmacy, the State Public Health Officer, a representative of the Attorney General, a representative of the University of California who shall be a pharmacologist, a physician, or a person holding a doctorate degree in the health sciences, a representative of a private university in this state who shall be a pharmacologist, a physician, or a person holding a doctorate degree in the health sciences, a representative of a statewide professional medical society in this state who shall be engaged in the private practice of medicine and shall be experienced in treating controlled substance dependency, a representative appointed by and serving at the pleasure of the Governor who shall have experience in drug abuse, cancer, or controlled substance research and who is either a registered nurse, licensed pursuant to Chapter 6 (commencing with Section 2700) of Division 2 of the Business and Professions Code, or other health professional. The Governor shall annually designate the private university and the professional medical society represented on the panel. Members of the panel shall be appointed by the heads of the entities to be represented, and they shall serve at the pleasure of the appointing power.

(c) The Research Advisory Panel shall appoint two special members to the Research Advisory Panel, who shall serve at the pleasure of the Research Advisory Panel only during the period Article 6 (commencing with Section 11260) of Chapter 5 remains effective. The additional members shall be physicians and surgeons, and who are board certified in oncology, ophthalmology, or psychiatry.

(d) The panel shall annually select a chairperson from among its members.

(e) The panel may hold hearings on, and in other ways study, research projects concerning cannabis or hallucinogenic drugs in this state. Members of the panel shall serve without compensation, but shall be reimbursed for any actual and necessary expenses incurred in connection with the performance of their duties.

(f) The panel may approve research projects, which have been registered by the Attorney General, into the nature and effects of cannabis or hallucinogenic drugs, and shall inform the Attorney General of the head of the approved research projects that are entitled to receive quantities of cannabis pursuant to Section 11478.

(g) The panel may withdraw approval of a research project at any time, and when approval is withdrawn shall notify the head of the research project to return any quantities of cannabis to the Attorney General.

(h) The panel shall report annually to the Legislature and the Governor those research projects approved by the panel, the nature of each research project, and, where available, the conclusions of the research project.

Health and Safety Code § 11485

(Amended by Stats. 2017, Ch. 27, Sec. 157. (SB 94) Effective June 27, 2017.)

Any peace officer of this state who, incident to a search under a search warrant issued for a violation of Section 11358 with respect to which no prosecution of a defendant results, seizes personal property suspected of being used in the planting, cultivation, harvesting, drying, processing, or transporting of cannabis, shall, if the seized personal property is not being held for evidence or destroyed as contraband, and if the owner of the property is unknown or has not claimed the property, provide notice regarding the seizure and manner of reclamation of the property to any owner or tenant of real property on which the property was seized. In addition, this notice shall be posted at the location of seizure and shall be published at least once in a newspaper of general circulation in the county in which the property was seized. If, after 90 days following the first publication of the notice, no owner appears and proves his or her ownership, the seized personal property shall be deemed to be abandoned and may be disposed of by sale to the public at public auction as set forth in Article 1 (commencing with Section 2080) of Chapter 4 of Title 6 of Part 4 of Division 3 of the Civil Code, or may be disposed of by transfer to a government agency or community service organization. Any profit from the sale or transfer of the property shall be expended for investigative services with respect to crimes involving cannabis.

Health and Safety Code § 11532

(Amended by Stats. 2017, Ch. 27, Sec. 158. (SB 94) Effective June 27, 2017.)

(a) It is unlawful for any person to loiter in any public place in a manner and under circumstances manifesting the purpose and with the intent to commit an offense specified in Chapter 6 (commencing with Section 11350) and Chapter 6.5 (commencing with Section 11400).

(b) Among circumstances that may be considered in determining whether a person has the requisite intent to engage in drug-related activity are that the person:

(1) Acts as a "look-out."

(2) Transfers small objects or packages for currency in a furtive fashion.

(3) Tries to conceal himself or herself or any object that reasonably could be involved in an unlawful drug-related activity.

(4) Uses signals or language indicative of summoning purchasers of illegal drugs.

(5) Repeatedly beckons to, stops, attempts to stop, or engages in conversations with passersby, whether on foot or in a motor vehicle, indicative of summoning purchasers of illegal drugs.

(6) Repeatedly passes to or receives from passersby, whether on foot or in a motor vehicle, money or small objects.

(7) Is under the influence of a controlled substance or possesses narcotic or drug paraphernalia. For the purposes of this paragraph, "narcotic or drug paraphernalia" means any device, contrivance, instrument, or apparatus designed or marketed for the use of smoking, injecting, ingesting, or consuming cannabis, hashish, PCP, or any controlled substance, including, but not limited to, roach clips, cigarette papers, and rollers designed or marketed for use in smoking a controlled substance.

(8) Has been convicted in any court within this state, within five years prior to the arrest under this chapter, of any violation involving the use, possession, or sale of any of the substances referred to in Chapter 6 (commencing with Section 11350) or Chapter 6.5 (commencing with Section 11400), or has been convicted of any violation of those provisions or substantially similar laws of any political subdivision of this state or of any other state.

(9) Is currently subject to any order prohibiting his or her presence in any high drug activity geographic area.

(10) Has engaged, within six months prior to the date of arrest under this section, in any behavior described in this subdivision, with the exception of paragraph (8), or in any other behavior indicative of illegal drug-related activity.

(c) The list of circumstances set forth in subdivision (b) is not exclusive. The circumstances set forth in subdivision (b) should be considered particularly salient if they occur in an area that is known for unlawful drug use and trafficking, or if they occur on or in premises that have been reported to law enforcement as a place suspected of unlawful drug activity. Any other relevant circumstances may be considered in determining whether a person has the requisite intent. Moreover, no one circumstance or combination of circumstances is in itself determinative of intent. Intent must be determined based on an evaluation of the particular circumstances of each case.

Health and Safety Code § 11553

(Amended by Stats. 2017, Ch. 27, Sec. 159. (SB 94) Effective June 27, 2017.)

The fact that a person is or has been, or is suspected of being, a user of cannabis is not alone sufficient grounds upon which to invoke Section 11551 or 11552.

This section shall not be construed to limit the discretion of a judge to invoke Section 11551 or 11552 if the court has reason to believe a person is or has been a user of narcotics or drugs other than cannabis.

Health & Safety Code § 11570

(Amended by Stats. 1986, Ch. 1043, Sec. 1.5.)

Every building or place used for the purpose of unlawfully selling, serving, storing, keeping, manufacturing, or giving away any controlled substance, precursor, or analog specified in this division, and every building or place wherein or upon which those acts take place, is a nuisance which shall be enjoined, abated, and prevented, and for which damages may be recovered, whether it is a public or private nuisance.

Health & Safety Code § 25189.5

(Amended by Stats. 2011, Ch. 15, Sec. 188. (AB 109) Effective April 4, 2011. Operative October 1, 2011, by Sec. 636 of Ch. 15, as amended by Stats. 2011, Ch. 39, Sec. 68. Note: Provisions now in subd. (e), but which had been in subd. (d) before Oct. 2, 1989, were amended on Nov. 4, 1986, by initiative Prop. 65.)

(a) The disposal of any hazardous waste, or the causing thereof, is prohibited when the disposal is at a facility which does not have a permit from the department issued pursuant to this chapter, or at any point which is not authorized according to this chapter.

(b) Any person who is convicted of knowingly disposing or causing the disposal of any hazardous waste, or who reasonably should have known that he or she was disposing or causing the disposal of any hazardous waste, at a facility which does not have a permit from the department issued pursuant to this chapter, or at any point which is not authorized according to this chapter shall, upon conviction, be punished by imprisonment in a county jail for not more than one year or by imprisonment pursuant to subdivision (h) of Section 1170 of the Penal Code.

(c) Any person who knowingly transports or causes the transportation of hazardous waste, or who reasonably should have known that he or she was causing the transportation of any hazardous waste, to a facility which does not have a permit from the department issued pursuant to this chapter, or at any point which is not authorized according to this chapter, shall, upon conviction, be punished by imprisonment in a county jail for not more than one year or by imprisonment pursuant to subdivision (h) of Section 1170 of the Penal Code.

(d) Any person who knowingly treats or stores any hazardous waste at a facility which does not have a permit from the department issued pursuant to this chapter, or at any point which is not authorized according to this chapter, shall, upon conviction, be punished by imprisonment in a county jail for not more than one year or by imprisonment pursuant to subdivision (h) of Section 1170 of the Penal Code.

(e) The court also shall impose upon a person convicted of violating subdivision (b), (c), or (d), a fine of not less than five thousand dollars ($5,000) nor more than one hundred thousand dollars ($100,000) for each day of violation, except as further provided in this subdivision. If the act which violated subdivision (b), (c), or (d) caused great bodily injury, or caused a substantial probability that death could result, the person convicted of violating subdivision (b), (c), or (d) may be punished by imprisonment pursuant to subdivision (h) of Section 1170 of the Penal Code for one, two, or three years, in addition and consecutive to the term specified in subdivision (b), (c), or (d), and may be fined up to two hundred fifty thousand dollars ($250,000) for each day of violation.

(f) For purposes of this section, except as otherwise provided in this subdivision, "each day of violation" means each day on which a violation continues. In any case where a person has disposed or caused the disposal of any hazardous waste in violation of this section, each day that the waste remains disposed of in violation of this section and the person has knowledge thereof is a separate additional violation, unless the person has filed a report of the disposal with the department and is complying with any order concerning the disposal issued by the department, a hearing officer, or court of competent jurisdiction.

Health & Safety Code § 25189.6

(Amended by Stats. 2011, Ch. 15, Sec. 189. (AB 109) Effective April 4, 2011. Operative October 1, 2011, by Sec. 636 of Ch. 15, as amended by Stats. 2011, Ch. 39, Sec. 68.)

(a) Any person who knowingly, or with reckless disregard for the risk, treats, handles, transports, disposes, or stores any hazardous waste in a manner which causes any unreasonable risk of fire, explosion, serious injury, or death is guilty of a public offense and shall, upon conviction, be punished by a fine of not less than five thousand dollars ($5,000) nor more than two hundred fifty thousand dollars ($250,000) for each day of violation, or by imprisonment in a county jail for not more than one year, or by imprisonment pursuant to subdivision (h) of Section 1170 of the Penal Code, or by both that fine and imprisonment.

(b) Any person who knowingly, at the time the person takes the actions specified in subdivision (a), places another person in imminent danger of death or serious bodily injury, is guilty of a public offense and shall, upon conviction, be punished by a fine of not less than five thousand dollars ($5,000) nor more than two hundred fifty thousand dollars ($250,000) for each day of violation, and by imprisonment pursuant to subdivision (h) of Section 1170 of the Penal Code for three, six, or nine years.

Health & Safety Code § 25189.7

(Amended by Stats. 2011, Ch. 15, Sec. 190. (AB 109) Effective April 4, 2011. Operative October 1, 2011, by Sec. 636 of Ch. 15, as amended by Stats. 2011, Ch. 39, Sec. 68.)

(a) The burning or incineration of any hazardous waste, or the causing thereof, is prohibited when the burning or incineration is at a facility which does not have a permit from the department issued pursuant to this chapter, or at any point which is not authorized according to this chapter.

(b) Any person who is convicted of knowingly burning or incinerating, or causing the burning or incineration of, any hazardous waste, or who reasonably should have known that he or she was burning or incinerating, or causing the burning or incineration of, any hazardous waste, at a facility which does not have a permit from the department issued pursuant to this chapter, or at any point which is not authorized according to this chapter, shall, upon conviction, be punished by imprisonment in a county jail for not more than one year or by imprisonment pursuant to subdivision (h) of Section 1170 of the Penal Code.

(c) The court also shall impose upon a person convicted of violating subdivision (b) a fine of not less than five thousand dollars ($5,000) nor more than one hundred thousand dollars ($100,000) for each day of violation, except as otherwise provided in this subdivision. If the act which violated subdivision (b) caused great bodily injury or caused a substantial probability that death could result, the person convicted of violating subdivision (b) may be punished by imprisonment pursuant to subdivision (h) of Section 1170 of the Penal Code for one, two, or three years, in addition and consecutive to the term specified in subdivision (b), and may be fined up to two hundred fifty thousand dollars ($250,000) for each day of violation.

Health and Safety Code § 100425

(Amended by Stats. 2021, Ch. 576, Sec. 3. (AB 45) Effective October 6, 2021.)

(a) The fees or charges for the issuance or renewal of any permit, license, registration, or document pursuant to Sections 1639.5, 1676, 1677, 2805, 11839.25, 103625, 106700, 106890, 106925, 107080, 107090, 107095, 107160, 110210, 110470, 110471, 111130, 111140, 111630, 111923.5, 111923.6, 112405, 112510, 112750, 112755, 113060, 113065, 114065, 115035, 115065, 115080, 117923, 117995, 118045, 118210, and 118245 shall be adjusted annually by the percentage change printed in the Budget Act for those items appropriating funds to the state department. After the first annual adjustment of fees or charges pursuant to this section, the fees or charges subject to subsequent adjustment shall be the fees or charges for the prior calendar year. The percentage change shall be determined by the Department of Finance, and shall include at least the total percentage change in salaries and operating expenses of the state department. However, the total increase in amounts collected under this section shall not exceed the total increased cost of the program or service provided.

(b) The state department shall publish annually a list of the actual numerical fee charges for each permit, license, certification, or registration governed by this section.

(c) This adjustment of fees and publication of the fee list shall not be subject to the requirements of Chapter 3.5 (commencing with Section 11340) of Part 1 of Division 3 of Title 2 of the Government Code.

(d) With respect to the fees or charges pursuant to Section 103625, the actual dollar fee or charge shall be rounded to the nearest whole dollar.

Health and Safety Code § 109925

(Amended by Stats. 2017, Ch. 27, Sec. 160. (SB 94) Effective June 27, 2017.)

(a) "Drug" means any of the following:

(1) An article recognized in an official compendium.

(2) An article used or intended for use in the diagnosis, cure, mitigation, treatment, or prevention of disease in human beings or any other animal.

(3) An article other than food, that is used or intended to affect the structure or any function of the body of human beings or any other animal.

(4) An article used or intended for use as a component of an article designated in paragraphs (1) to (3), inclusive.

(b) The term "drug" does not include any device.

(c) Any food for which a claim (as described in Sections 403(r)(1)(B) (21 U.S.C. Sec. 343(r)(1)(B)) and 403(r)(3) (21 U.S.C. Sec. 343(r)(3)) or Sections 403(r)(1)(B) (21 U.S.C. Sec. 343(r)(1)(B)) and 403(r)(5)(D) (21 U.S.C. Sec. 343(r)(5)(D)) of the federal act), is made in accordance with the requirements set forth in Section 403(r) (21 U.S.C. Sec. 343(r)) of the federal act, is not a drug under subdivision (b) solely because the label or labeling contains such a claim.

(d) Cannabis product, including any cannabis product intended for external use, is not a drug.

Health and Safety Code § 110036

(Added by Stats. 2021, Ch. 576, Sec. 4. (AB 45) Effective October 6, 2021.)

All laws and regulations pertaining to industrial hemp products shall remain in effect until the adoption of regulations pursuant to the federal law that authorizes industrial hemp products. At that time, the department shall adopt new regulations either as necessary pursuant to the federal law or deemed necessary to protect consumers.

Health and Safety Code § 110065

(Amended by Stats. 2021, Ch. 576, Sec. 5. (AB 45) Effective October 6, 2021.)

(a) The department may adopt any regulations that it determines are necessary for the enforcement of this part. The regulations shall be adopted by the department in the manner prescribed by Chapter 3.5 (commencing with Section 11340) of Part 1 of Division 3 of Title 2 of the Government Code. The department shall, insofar as practicable, make these regulations conform with those adopted under the federal act or by the United States Department of Agriculture or by the Internal Revenue Service of the United States Treasury Department.

(b) (1) The department may adopt emergency regulations to implement this division.

(2) The department may readopt any emergency regulation authorized by this section that is the same as, or substantially equivalent to, an emergency regulation previously adopted as authorized by this section. That readoption shall be limited to one time for each regulation.

(3) Notwithstanding any other law, the initial adoption of emergency regulations and the readoption of emergency regulations authorized by this section shall be deemed an emergency and necessary for the immediate preservation of the public peace, health, safety, or general welfare. The initial emergency regulations and the readopted emergency regulations authorized by this section shall be each submitted to the Office of Administrative Law for filing with the Secretary of State and shall remain in effect for no more than 180 days, by which time final regulations shall be adopted.

(c) Initial regulations regarding industrial hemp shall be exempt from the Administrative Procedure Act (Chapter 3.5 (commencing with Section 11340) of Part 1 of Division 3 of Title 2 of the Government Code), except that the department shall post the proposed regulations on its internet website for public comment for 30 days. The comments received shall be considered by the department and the final adopted regulations shall be filed with the Office of Administrative Law for publication in the California Code of Regulations. This exemption does not apply to regulations adopted pursuant to Section 111921.3 or 111922.

Health and Safety Code § 110407

(Added by Stats. 2021, Ch. 576, Sec. 6. (AB 45) Effective October 6, 2021.)

(a) A manufacturer, distributor, or seller of an industrial hemp product shall not include on the label of the product, or publish or disseminate in advertising or marketing, any health-related statement that is untrue in any particular manner as to the health effects of consuming products containing industrial hemp or cannabinoids, extracts, or derivatives from industrial hemp in violation of this part.

(b) For purposes of this section, "health-related statement" means a statement related to health, and includes a statement of a curative or therapeutic nature that, expressly or impliedly, suggests a relationship between the consumption of industrial hemp or industrial hemp products and health benefits or effects on health. However, "health-related statement" does not include statements required to be made pursuant to federal Food and Drug Administration regulations for active ingredients in prescription drugs, nonprescription over-the-counter drugs containing inactive ingredients, or structure-function claims allowed for dietary supplements made in accordance with the Federal Food, Drug, and Cosmetic Act (21 U.S.C. Sec. 343(r)(6)).

Health and Safety Code § 110469

(Added by Stats. 2021, Ch. 576, Sec. 7. (AB 45) Effective October 6, 2021.)

(a) A wholesale food manufacturing facility that manufactures products that contain industrial hemp shall be registered in accordance with Section 110460 and shall comply with good manufacturing practices as defined in Section 110105 and as determined by the department in regulation.

(b) Industrial hemp shall not be used in dietary supplements or food products unless the manufacturer demonstrates both of the following:

(1) All parts of the hemp plant used in dietary supplements or food products come from a state or country that has an established and approved industrial hemp program that inspects or regulates hemp under a food safety program or equivalent criteria to ensure safety for human or animal consumption.

(2) The industrial hemp cultivator or grower is in good standing and in compliance with the governing laws of the state or country of origin.

Health and Safety Code § 110611

(Added by Stats. 2021, Ch. 576, Sec. 8. (AB 45) Effective October 6, 2021.)

Except as provided in Section 25621.5 of the Business and Professions Code, a dietary supplement, food, or beverage is not adulterated by the inclusion of industrial hemp, as defined in Section 11018.5, as long as the cannabinoids, extracts, or derivatives from industrial hemp meet the requirements established in Chapter 9 (commencing with Section 111920). The sale of a dietary supplement, food, or beverage that includes industrial hemp or cannabinoids, extracts, or derivatives from industrial hemp shall not be restricted or prohibited based solely on the inclusion of industrial hemp provided that the cannabinoids, extracts, or derivatives from industrial hemp meet the requirements of Chapter 9 (commencing with Section 111920).

Health and Safety Code § 111691

(Added by Stats. 2021, Ch. 576, Sec. 9. (AB 45) Effective October 6, 2021.)

A cosmetic is not adulterated because it includes industrial hemp, as defined in Section 11018.5, as long as the cannabinoids, extracts, or derivatives from industrial hemp meet the requirements established in Chapter 9 (commencing with Section 111920). The sale of a cosmetic that includes industrial hemp or cannabinoids, extracts, or derivatives from industrial hemp shall not be restricted or prohibited based solely on the inclusion of industrial hemp provided that the cannabinoids, extracts, or derivatives from industrial hemp meet the requirements established in Chapter 9 (commencing with Section 111920).

Chapter 9. Industrial Hemp

ARTICLE 1. DEFINITIONS

Health and Safety Code § 111920

(Added by Stats. 2021, Ch. 576, Sec. 10. (AB 45) Effective October 6, 2021.)

For purposes of this chapter, the following definitions apply:

(a) "Department" means the State Department of Public Health.

(b) "Established and approved industrial hemp program" means a program that meets any applicable requirements set forth in federal law regarding the lawful and safe cultivation of industrial hemp.

(c) "Final form product" is a product intended for consumer use to be sold at a retail premise.

(d) "Hemp manufacturer" means either of the following:

(1) A processor extracting cannabinoids from hemp biomass.

(2) A processor purchasing industrial hemp raw extract for the purpose of manufacturing a final form product.

(e) "Independent testing laboratory" means a laboratory that meets all of the following requirements:

(1) Does not have a direct or indirect interest in the entity for which testing is being done.

(2) Does not have a direct or indirect interest in a facility that cultivates, processes, distributes, dispenses, or sells raw hemp products in this state or in another jurisdiction.

(3) Does not have a license issued pursuant to Division 10 (commencing with Section 26000) of the Business and Professions Code, other than as a licensed testing laboratory.

(4) Is either of the following:

(A) A testing laboratory licensed pursuant to Division 10 (commencing with Section 26000) of the Business and Professions Code, if the licensed testing lab has notified the Department of Cannabis Control.

(B) Accredited by a third-party accrediting body as a competent testing laboratory pursuant to ISO/IEC 17025 of the International Organization for Standardization.

(f) "Industrial hemp" has the same meaning as in Section 11018.5. "Industrial hemp" does not include cannabinoids produced through chemical synthesis.

(g) (1) "Industrial hemp product" or "hemp product" means a finished product containing industrial hemp that meets all of the following conditions:

(A) Is a cosmetic, food, food additive, dietary supplement, or herb.

(B) (i) Is for human or animal consumption.

(ii) "Animal" does not include livestock or a food animal as defined in Section 4825.1 of the Business and Professions Code.

(iii) Does not include THC isolate as an ingredient.

(2) "Industrial hemp product" does not include industrial hemp or a hemp product that has been approved by the United States Food and Drug Administration or a hemp product that includes industrial hemp or hemp that has

received Generally Recognized As Safe (GRAS) designation. For purposes of nonfood applications, "industrial hemp product" does not include a hemp product that contains derivatives, substances, or compounds derived from the seed of industrial hemp.

(h) (1) "Manufacture" or "manufacturing" means to compound, blend, extract, infuse, or otherwise make or prepare an industrial hemp product.

(2) "Manufacturing" includes all aspects of the extraction process, infusion process, and packaging and labeling processes, including processing, preparing, holding, and storing of industrial hemp products.

(3) "Manufacturing" also includes processing, preparing, holding, or storing hemp components and ingredients.

(4) "Manufacturing" does not include planting, growing, harvesting, drying, curing, grading, or trimming a plant or part of a plant.

(i) "Raw extract" or "industrial hemp raw extract" means extract not intended for consumer use and that contains a THC concentration of not more than an amount determined by the department in regulation.

(j) "Raw hemp product" means a product that is derived from industrial hemp that is intended to be included in a food, beverage, dietary supplement, or cosmetic.

(k) "Retail" has the same meaning as in Section 113895.

(l) "THC" or "THC or comparable cannabinoid" means any of the following:

(1) Tetrahydrocannabinolic acid.

(2) Any tetrahydrocannabinol, including, but not limited to, Delta-8-tetrahydrocannabinol, Delta-9-tetrahydrocannabinol, and Delta-10-tetrahydrocannabinol, however derived, except that the department may exclude one or more isomers of tetrahydrocannabinol from this definition under subdivision (a) of Section 111921.7.

(3) Any other cannabinoid, except cannabidiol, that the department determines, under subdivision (b) of Section 111921.7, to cause intoxication.

(m) "THCA" means tetrahydrocannabinolic acid, CAS number 23978-85-0.

(n) "Total THC" means the sum of THC and THCA. Total THC shall be calculated using the following equation: total THC concentration (mg/g) +/- the measurement of uncertainty, as defined by the United States Department of Agriculture.

ARTICLE 2. GENERAL PROVISIONS

Health and Safety Code § 111921

(Added by Stats. 2021, Ch. 576, Sec. 10. (AB 45) Effective October 6, 2021.)

An industrial hemp product shall not be distributed or sold in the state except in conformity with all applicable state laws and regulations, including this chapter and any regulations promulgated thereunder, and with documentation that includes both of the following:

(a) A certificate of analysis from an independent testing laboratory that confirms both of the following:

(1) The industrial hemp raw extract, in its final form, does not exceed THC concentration of an amount determined allowable by the department in regulation, or the mass of the industrial hemp extract used in the

final form product does not exceed a THC concentration of 0.3 percent.

(2) The industrial hemp product was tested for any hemp derivatives identified on the product label or in associated advertising in accordance with Section 111926.2.

(b) The industrial hemp product was produced from industrial hemp grown in compliance with Division 24 (commencing with Section 81000) of the Food and Agricultural Code if sourced from within California, or licensed in accordance with United States Department of Agriculture (USDA) requirements if sourced from outside the state.

Health and Safety Code § 111921.3

(Added by Stats. 2021, Ch. 576, Sec. 10. (AB 45) Effective October 6, 2021.)

The department may adopt regulations imposing an age requirement for the sale of certain industrial hemp products upon a finding of a threat to public health.

Health and Safety Code § 111921.5

(Added by Stats. 2021, Ch. 576, Sec. 10. (AB 45) Effective October 6, 2021.)

(a) Unless explicitly approved by the federal Food and Drug Administration, industrial hemp shall not be included in products in any of the following categories:

(1) Medical devices.

(2) Prescription drugs.

(3) A product containing nicotine or tobacco.

(4) An alcoholic beverage.

(b) The department may prohibit the inclusion of industrial hemp in other products when it poses a risk to human or animal health through regulation.

(c) Cannabis and cannabis products are not subject to this section.

Health and Safety Code § 111921.6

(Added by Stats. 2021, Ch. 576, Sec. 10. (AB 45) Effective October 6, 2021. Conditionally repealed as prescribed by its own provisions.)

(a) Manufacture or sale of inhalable products is prohibited. Manufacture of inhalable products for the sole purpose of sale in other states is not prohibited.

(b) This section shall become inoperative and is repealed on the effective date of a measure passed by the Legislature that establishes a tax on inhalable products and states the intent of the Legislature to fulfill the requirements of this section.

Health and Safety Code § 111921.7

(Added by Stats. 2021, Ch. 576, Sec. 10. (AB 45) Effective October 6, 2021.)

(a) The department may exclude from the definition of "THC or Comparable Cannabinoid" one or more isomers of tetrahydrocannabinol if the department determines, consistent with subdivisions (c) and (d), that the tetrahydrocannabinol isomer does not cause intoxication.

(b) The department may include any other cannabinoid, in addition to those expressly listed in subdivision (l) of Section 111920, in the definition of "THC" if the department determines, consistent with subdivisions (c) and (d), that the cannabinoid causes intoxication.

(c) In making a determination under subdivision (a) or (b), the department shall consider scientific evidence concerning the pharmacological effects of the tetrahydrocannabinol or other cannabinoid in humans or other animals, if that evidence is available.

(d) Any initial determination under subdivision (a) or (b) shall not be subject to the administrative rulemaking requirements of Chapter 3.5 (commencing with Section 11340) of Part 1 of Division 3 of Title 2 of the Government Code, but the department, without being subject to those administrative rulemaking requirements, shall establish a process to receive public comment regarding those determinations, and shall publicly post all determinations on its internet website. However, any initial determination shall be confirmed subject to the administrative rulemaking requirements no later than 18 months following the date of the initial determination.

ARTICLE 3. MANUFACTURE

Health and Safety Code § 111922

(Added by Stats. 2021, Ch. 576, Sec. 10. (AB 45) Effective October 6, 2021.)

(a) The department, through regulation, may determine maximum serving sizes for hemp-derived cannabinoids, hemp extract, and products derived therefrom, active cannabinoid concentration per serving size, the number of servings per container, and any other requirements for foods and beverages.

(b) Food and beverages shall be prepackaged and shelf stable.

Health and Safety Code § 111922.3

(Added by Stats. 2021, Ch. 576, Sec. 10. (AB 45) Effective October 6, 2021.)

(a) A hemp manufacturer who produces raw extract that will only be used for dietary supplements, foods, beverages, and cosmetics, or a hemp manufacturer who produces industrial hemp products shall comply with this chapter and, to the extent applicable, this part.

(b) A hemp manufacturer who produces processed pet food products shall comply with this chapter and Chapter 10 (commencing with Section 113025) of Part 6 and shall follow good manufacturing practices pursuant to those provisions.

ARTICLE 4. REGISTRATION AND FEES

Health and Safety Code § 111923

(Added by Stats. 2021, Ch. 576, Sec. 10. (AB 45) Effective October 6, 2021.)

The Industrial Hemp Enrollment and Oversight Fund is hereby established in the State Treasury. All money received by the department pursuant to Section 111923.5 shall be deposited into this fund and shall be expended by the department, upon appropriation by the Legislature, to carry out and implement this chapter. Moneys in this fund shall not be redirected for any other purpose.

Health and Safety Code § 111923.3

(Added by Stats. 2021, Ch. 576, Sec. 10. (AB 45) Effective October 6, 2021.)

(a) (1) A hemp manufacturer who produces an industrial hemp product that is a food or beverage shall register with the department pursuant to Article 2 (commencing with Section 110460) of Chapter 5.

(2) Sections 110473 and 110474 shall not apply to dietary supplements and food products that include industrial hemp.

(b) Notwithstanding the voluntary nature of registration provided in Section 111795, a hemp manufacturer who produces an industrial hemp product that is a cosmetic shall register pursuant to Article 4 (commencing with Section 111795) of Chapter 7.

(c) A hemp manufacturer who produces an industrial hemp product that is a processed pet food shall obtain a license pursuant to Article 2 (commencing with Section 113060) of Chapter 10 of Part 6.

(d) (1) An in-state hemp manufacturer who produces raw hemp extract and who does not produce an industrial hemp product, or an out-of-state hemp manufacturer who produces raw hemp extract with the intent to import that raw hemp extract into this state, shall register with the department pursuant to Article 2 (commencing with Section 110460) of Chapter 5.

(2) Sections 110473 and 110474 shall not apply to hemp manufacturers who register pursuant to this subdivision.

(e) All hemp manufacturers shall notify the department immediately of any change of information in their application for a license of registration.

Health and Safety Code § 111923.5

(Added by Stats. 2021, Ch. 576, Sec. 10. (AB 45) Effective October 6, 2021.)

(a) In addition to licensing and registration requirements and fees required pursuant to other applicable laws, as specified in Section 111923.3, a hemp manufacturer shall obtain an industrial hemp enrollment and oversight authorization from the department. Authorization shall be renewed annually.

(b) The department shall assess an authorization fee and renewal fee to cover the actual reasonable costs of implementing the regulatory program in this chapter. Fees may be set at different amounts for different hemp manufacturer types, including food products, cosmetic products, and pet food products, based on the differing costs associated with regulatory requirements, including, but not limited to, the nature and scope of the authorization activities and oversight, inspection, and enforcement activities.

(c) The fee shall be adjusted pursuant to Section 100425.

(d) Fees may be prorated based upon the date of the renewal or issuance of the authorization.

Health and Safety Code § 111923.7

(Added by Stats. 2021, Ch. 576, Sec. 10. (AB 45) Effective October 6, 2021.)

A hemp manufacturer located outside the state shall reimburse the department for travel and per diem required to perform necessary onsite inspections at the facility to ensure compliance with this chapter and related activities pursuant to this part.

Health and Safety Code § 111923.9

(Added by Stats. 2021, Ch. 576, Sec. 10. (AB 45) Effective October 6, 2021.)

A hemp manufacturer or retailer who is operating in conformance with this part and in good faith compliance with their responsibilities under this chapter may manufacture or sell industrial hemp products or raw hemp extract without authorization for three months after the effective date of the act that added this chapter.

ARTICLE 5. RECORDKEEPING

Health and Safety Code § 111924

(Added by Stats. 2021, Ch. 576, Sec. 10. (AB 45) Effective October 6, 2021.)

The department may adopt regulations for recordkeeping standards that shall apply to transporters, manufacturers, and retailers of industrial hemp product and raw extract.

ARTICLE 6. TESTING REQUIREMENTS

Health and Safety Code § 111925

(Added by Stats. 2021, Ch. 576, Sec. 10. (AB 45) Effective October 6, 2021.)

(a) A hemp manufacturer shall meet all of the following testing requirements:

(1) Industrial hemp shall be tested in raw extract final form, to allow its use as an ingredient, prior to being incorporated into a product.

(2) Testing shall be completed by an independent testing laboratory.

(3) The manufacturer of the hemp extract in its final form or the final form industrial hemp product shall be able to prove total THC concentration does not exceed 0.3 percent. A manufacturer of raw extract shall be able to prove that the THC concentration meets department requirements set forth pursuant to subdivision (a) of Section 111921.

(b) The department may regulate and restrict the cap on extract and may cap the amount of total THC concentration at the product level based on the product form, volume, number of servings, ratio of cannabinoids to THC in the product, or other factors, as needed.

Health and Safety Code § 111925.2

(Added by Stats. 2021, Ch. 576, Sec. 10. (AB 45) Effective October 6, 2021.)

A raw hemp product shall not be distributed or sold in this state without a certificate of analysis from an independent testing laboratory that confirms all of the following:

(a) The raw hemp product is the product of a batch of industrial hemp that was tested by the independent testing laboratory.

(b) A tested representative sample of the batch of industrial hemp contained a total THC concentration that did not exceed 0.3 percent on a dry-weight basis.

(c) The tested sample of the batch did not contain contaminants that are unsafe for human or animal consumption.

Health and Safety Code § 111925.4

(Added by Stats. 2021, Ch. 576, Sec. 10. (AB 45) Effective October 6, 2021.)

(a) As of the effective date of the act adding this chapter, testing requirements for contaminant levels shall be the same as those for cannabis, as established in paragraph (2) of subdivision (d) of Section 26100 of the Business and Professions Code and regulations adopted pursuant thereto.

(b) The department may adjust the specific contaminant levels for industrial hemp by regulation to protect consumers.

Health and Safety Code § 111925.6

(Added by Stats. 2021, Ch. 576, Sec. 10. (AB 45) Effective October 6, 2021.)

(a) A product batch may be reprocessed or remediated after failed testing, but the batch shall not be distributed or sold unless the reprocessed or remediated batch has been retested and successfully passed all the analyses required pursuant to this article.

(b) If the batch cannot be reprocessed or remediated, the product batch shall be destroyed.

(c) If a failed product batch is not reprocessed or remediated in any way, it shall not be retested. Subsequent certificates of analysis produced without reprocessing or remediation of the failed product batch shall not supersede the initial regulatory compliance testing certificate of analysis.

(d) This section shall not prevent a product batch from being retested when the certificate of analysis was obtained 12 months prior or more.

(e) (1) Reprocessing or remediation shall be an available remedy for failed product batches in all industrial hemp product categories and raw extract.

(2) Remediation is not allowed once a product enters the retail market.

(f) A failed product batch that cannot be reprocessed or remediated shall be destroyed, at the expense of the owner, on video surveillance, as authorized by the department, or under the supervision of an authorized agent of the department.

ARTICLE 7. LABELING AND ADVERTISEMENT

Health and Safety Code § 111926

(Added by Stats. 2021, Ch. 576, Sec. 10. (AB 45) Effective October 6, 2021.)

(a) A manufacturer, distributor, or seller of an industrial hemp product shall follow packaging, labeling, and advertising laws, including, but not limited to, Chapter 4 (commencing with Section 110290), and federal laws incorporated or applicable in this state, including, but not limited to, Sections 110100, 110340, 110371, 110380, 110382, and 110407 and shall not violate this part.

(b) A hemp manufacturer shall not directly target advertising or marketing to children or to persons who are pregnant or breastfeeding.

(c) Advertising or marketing placed in broadcast, cable, radio, print, or digital communications shall only be displayed where at least 70 percent of the audience is reasonably expected to be 18 years of age or older, as determined by reliable, up-to-date audience composition data.

Health and Safety Code § 111926.2

(Added by Stats. 2021, Ch. 576, Sec. 10. (AB 45) Effective October 6, 2021.)

(a) An industrial hemp product that is a dietary supplement, food, or beverage shall not be distributed or sold in the state without packaging and labeling on the product that includes all of the following information:

(1) A label, scannable barcode, internet website, or quick response (QR) code linked to the certificate of analysis of the final form product batch by an independent testing laboratory that provides all of the following information:

(A) The product name.

(B) The name of the product's manufacturer, packer, or distributor, and their address and telephone number.

(C) The batch number, which matches the batch number on the product.

(D) The concentration of cannabinoids present in the product batch, including, at minimum, total THC and any marketed cannabinoids or ingredient, as required by the department in regulation.

(E) The levels within the product batch of contaminants, as required in subdivision (c) of Section 111925.2.

(2) The product expiration or best by date, if applicable.

(3) A statement indicating that children or those who are pregnant or breastfeeding should avoid using the product prior to consulting with a health care professional about its safety.

(4) A statement that products containing cannabinoids should be kept out of reach of children.

(5) The following statement, "THE FDA HAS NOT EVALUATED THIS PRODUCT FOR SAFETY OR EFFICACY."

(b) The requirements of this section shall apply to products manufactured 90 days or more after the enactment of this section.

Health and Safety Code § 111926.3

(Added by Stats. 2021, Ch. 576, Sec. 10. (AB 45) Effective October 6, 2021.)

(a) An industrial hemp product that is a cosmetic shall not be distributed or sold in the state without packaging and labeling on the product that includes all of the following information:

(1) A label, scannable barcode, internet website, or quick response (QR) code linked to the certificate of analysis

of the final form extract or the final form product batch by an independent testing laboratory that provides all of the following information:

(A) The product name.

(B) The name of the product's manufacturer, packer, or distributor, and their address and telephone number.

(C) The batch number, which matches the batch number on the product.

(D) The concentration of cannabinoids present in the product batch, including, at minimum, total THC and any marketed cannabinoids.

(E) The levels within the product batch of contaminants, as required in subdivision (c) of Section 111925.2.

(2) The product expiration or best by date, if applicable.

(3) The following statement, "THE FDA HAS NOT EVALUATED THIS PRODUCT FOR SAFETY OR EFFICACY."

(b) The requirements of this section shall apply to products manufactured 90 days or more after the enactment of this section.

ARTICLE 8. ENFORCEMENT

Health and Safety Code § 111927

(Added by Stats. 2021, Ch. 576, Sec. 10. (AB 45) Effective October 6, 2021.)

(a) The department shall have the seizure and embargo powers provided for in Article 3 (commencing with Section 111860) of Chapter 7 with respect to industrial hemp products and raw extract.

(b) The department shall have the ability to recall industrial hemp products or raw extract that it determines to be dangerous to the public in the manner prescribed in Section 110806.

Health and Safety Code § 111927.2

(Added by Stats. 2021, Ch. 576, Sec. 10. (AB 45) Effective October 6, 2021.)

(a) In addition to the inspection authority provided elsewhere in this part, the department may inspect financial data, sales data, and personnel data, as needed to enforce this chapter.

(b) State, local, or law enforcement officials may review paperwork from those handling or transporting industrial hemp plant material, raw extract, intermediary industrial hemp product, or final finished product and take samples at any point along the supply chain to test that sample for verification.

(c) Upon inspection, if the industrial hemp plant material, raw extract, intermediary industrial hemp product, or final finished product does not meet the definition of industrial hemp, the state, local, or law enforcement official shall notify the department.

(d) (1) State, local, and law enforcement officials shall immediately notify the department of an arrest made for a violation over which the department has jurisdiction that involves a person authorized pursuant to this chapter.

(2) The department shall promptly investigate whether grounds exist for suspension or revocation of the

authorization or if other actions are warranted under this part.

Health and Safety Code § 111927.4

(Added by Stats. 2021, Ch. 576, Sec. 10. (AB 45) Effective October 6, 2021.)

Violations of this chapter are subject to the fines and penalties established in Article 1 (commencing with Section 111825) of Chapter 8.

ARTICLE 9. AGENCY COORDINATION

Health and Safety Code § 111928

(Amended by Stats. 2022, Ch. 28, Sec. 103. (SB 1380) Effective January 1, 2023.)

(a) The Department of Food and Agriculture and the State Department of Public Health, in consultation with the Department of Cannabis Control, if necessary, shall develop a process to share license, registration, cultivar, and enforcement information to facilitate compliance and enforcement against unlicensed manufacturers or the sale of industrial hemp that does not meet the requirements of this part.

(b) Communications shared between state agencies and local and law enforcement officials regarding license, registration, cultivar, and enforcement information of manufacturers and retailers of industrial hemp products and raw extract shall not be subject to the California Public Records Act (Division 10 (commencing with Section 7920.000) of Title 1 of the Government Code) and shall be considered "official information" pursuant to Section 1040 of the Evidence Code.

ARTICLE 10. INHALABLE PRODUCTS

Health and Safety Code § 111929

(Added by Stats. 2021, Ch. 576, Sec. 10. (AB 45) Effective October 6, 2021. Conditionally operative as prescribed by Section 111929.4.)

Inhalable products shall not be sold to consumers under 21 years of age.

Health and Safety Code § 111929.1

(Added by Stats. 2021, Ch. 576, Sec. 10. (AB 45) Effective October 6, 2021. Conditionally operative as prescribed by Section 111929.4.)

A hemp manufacturer who produces inhalable products shall comply with this chapter and, to the extent applicable, with the provisions of this part.

Health and Safety Code § 111929.2

(Added by Stats. 2021, Ch. 576, Sec. 10. (AB 45) Effective October 6, 2021. Conditionally operative as prescribed by Section 111929.4.)

An inhalable product shall not contain any of the following:

(a) Flavorings other than natural terpenes.

(b) Polyethylene glycol (PEG).

(c) Vitamin E acetate.

(d) Medium chain triglycerides (MCT oil).

(e) Squalene or squalane.

(f) Any other substance that the department finds to be a danger to public health.

Health and Safety Code § 111929.3

(Added by Stats. 2021, Ch. 576, Sec. 10. (AB 45) Effective October 6, 2021. Conditionally operative as prescribed by Section 111929.4.)

The department may enter into a memorandum of understanding or other interagency agreement with another state agency to administer and enforce provisions of this chapter as they relate to inhalable products, including, but not limited to, testing provisions, advertising and labeling provisions, and the provisions relating to the manufacture and sale of inhalable products.

Health and Safety Code § 111929.4

(Added by Stats. 2021, Ch. 576, Sec. 10. (AB 45) Effective October 6, 2021. Note: Operative provisions affect Article 10, commencing with Section 111929.)

This article shall become operative upon the effective date of a measure passed by the Legislature that establishes a tax on inhalable products and states the intent of the Legislature to fulfill the requirements of this section.

Health and Safety Code § 113091

(Added by Stats. 2021, Ch. 576, Sec. 11. (AB 45) Effective October 6, 2021.)

A processed pet food is not adulterated because it includes industrial hemp, as defined in Section 11018.5, or cannabinoids, extracts, or derivatives from industrial hemp, if the cannabinoids, extracts, or derivatives from industrial hemp meet the requirements established in Chapter 9 (commencing with Section 111920) of Part 5. The sale of processed pet food that includes industrial hemp or cannabinoids, extracts, or derivatives from industrial hemp shall not be restricted or prohibited based solely on the inclusion of industrial hemp or cannabinoids, extracts, or derivatives from industrial hemp, if the cannabinoids, extracts, or derivatives from industrial hemp meet the requirements established in Chapter 9 (commencing with Section 111920) of Part 5.

IX. Labor Code Sections

Labor Code § 147.5

(Added by Stats. 2015, Ch. 689, Sec. 7. (AB 266) Effective January 1, 2016.)

(a) By January 1, 2017, the Division of Occupational Safety and Health shall convene an advisory committee to evaluate whether there is a need to develop industry-specific regulations related to the activities of facilities issued a license pursuant to Chapter 3.5 (commencing with Section 19300) of Division 8 of the Business and Professions Code.

(b) By July 1, 2017, the advisory committee shall present to the board its findings and recommendations for consideration by the board. By July 1, 2017, the board shall render a decision regarding the adoption of industry-specific regulations pursuant to this section.

Labor Code § 147.6

(Added November 8, 2016, by initiative Proposition 64, Sec. 6.2.)

(a) By March 1, 2018, the Division of Occupational Safety and Health shall convene an advisory committee to evaluate whether there is a need to develop industry-specific regulations related to the activities of licensees under Division 10 of the Business and Professions Code, including but not limited to, whether specific requirements are needed to address exposure to second-hand marijuana smoke by employees at facilities where on-site consumption of marijuana is permitted under subdivision (d) of Section 26200 of the Business and Professions Code, and whether specific requirements are needed to address the potential risks of combustion, inhalation, armed robberies or repetitive strain injuries.

(b) By October 1, 2018, the advisory committee shall present to the board its findings and recommendations for consideration by the board. By October 1, 2018, the board shall render a decision regarding the adoption of industry-specific regulations pursuant to this section.

Labor Code § 432.8

(Added by Stats. 1976, Ch. 952.)

The limitations on employers and the penalties provided for in Section 432.7 shall apply to a conviction for violation of subdivision (b) or (c) of Section 11357 of the Health and Safety Code or a statutory predecessor thereof, or subdivision (c) of Section 11360 of the Health and Safety Code, or Section 11364, 11365, or 11550 of the Health and Safety Code as they related to marijuana prior to January 1, 1976, or a statutory predecessor thereof, two years from the date of such a conviction.

Labor Code § 1140

(Added by Stats. 1975, 3rd Ex. Sess., Ch. 1.)

This part shall be known and may be referred to as the Alatorre-Zenovich-Dunlap-Berman Agricultural Labor Relations Act of 1975.

Labor Code § 1140.2

(Added by Stats. 1975, 3rd Ex. Sess., Ch. 1.)

It is hereby stated to be the policy of the State of California to encourage and protect the right of agricultural employees to full freedom of association, self-organization, and designation of representatives of their own choosing, to negotiate the terms and conditions of their employment, and to be free from the interference, restraint, or coercion of employers of labor, or their agents, in the designation of such representatives or in self-organization or in other concerted activities for the purpose of collective bargaining or other mutual aid or protection. For this purpose this part is adopted to provide for collective-bargaining rights for agricultural employees.

Labor Code § 1140.4

(Amended by Stats. 1994, Ch. 1010, Sec. 181. Effective January 1, 1995.)

As used in this part:

(a) The term "agriculture" includes farming in all its branches, and, among other things, includes the cultivation and tillage of the soil, dairying, the production, cultivation, growing, and harvesting of any agricultural or horticultural commodities (including commodities defined as agricultural commodities in Section 1141j(g) of Title 12 of the United States Code), the raising of livestock, bees, furbearing animals, or poultry, and any practices (including any forestry or lumbering operations) performed by a farmer or on a farm as an incident to or in conjunction with such farming operations, including preparation for market and delivery to storage or to market or to carriers for transportation to market.

(b) The term "agricultural employee" or "employee" shall mean one engaged in agriculture, as such term is defined in subdivision (a). However, nothing in this subdivision shall be construed to include any person other than those employees excluded from the coverage of the National Labor Relations Act, as amended, as agricultural employees, pursuant to Section 2(3) of the Labor Management Relations Act (Section 152(3), Title 29, United States Code), and Section 3(f) of the Fair Labor Standards Act (Section 203(f), Title 29, United States Code).

Further, nothing in this part shall apply, or be construed to apply, to any employee who performs work to be done at the site of the construction, alteration, painting, or repair of a building, structure, or other work (as these terms have been construed under Section 8(e) of the Labor Management Relations Act, 29 U.S.C. Sec. 158(e)) or logging or timber-clearing operations in initial preparation of land for farming, or who does land leveling or only land surveying for any of the above.

As used in this subdivision, "land leveling" shall include only major land moving operations changing the contour of the land, but shall not include annual or seasonal tillage or preparation of land for cultivation.

(c) The term "agricultural employer" shall be liberally construed to include any person acting directly or indirectly in the interest of an employer in relation to an agricultural employee, any individual grower, corporate grower, cooperative grower, harvesting association, hiring association, land management group, any association of persons or cooperatives engaged in agriculture, and shall include any person who owns or leases or manages land used for agricultural purposes, but shall exclude any person supplying agricultural workers to an employer, any farm labor contractor as defined by Section 1682, and any person functioning in the capacity of a labor contractor. The employer engaging such labor contractor or person shall be deemed the employer for all purposes under this part.

(d) The term "person" shall mean one or more individuals, corporations, partnerships, limited liability companies, associations, legal representatives, trustees in bankruptcy, receivers, or any other legal entity, employer, or labor organization having an interest in the outcome of a proceeding under this part.

(e) The term "representatives" includes any individual or labor organization.

(f) The term "labor organization" means any organization of any kind, or any agency or employee representation committee or plan, in which employees participate and which exists, in whole or in part, for the purpose of dealing with employers concerning grievances, labor disputes, wages, rates of pay, hours of employment, or conditions of work for agricultural employees.

(g) The term "unfair labor practice" means any unfair labor practice specified in Chapter 4 (commencing with Section 1153) of this part.

(h) The term "labor dispute" includes any controversy concerning terms, tenure, or conditions of employment, or concerning the association or representation of persons in negotiating, fixing, maintaining, changing, or seeking to arrange terms or conditions of employment, regardless of whether the disputants stand in the proximate relation of employer and employee.

(i) The term "board" means Agricultural Labor Relations Board.

(j) The term "supervisor" means any individual having the authority, in the interest of the employer, to hire, transfer, suspend, lay off, recall, promote, discharge, assign, reward, or discipline other employees, or the responsibility to direct them, or to adjust their grievances, or effectively to recommend such action, if, in connection with the foregoing, the exercise of such authority is not of a merely routine or clerical nature, but requires the use of independent judgment.

X. Penal Code Sections

Penal Code § 182

(Amended by Stats. 2011, Ch. 15, Sec. 272. (AB 109) Effective April 4, 2011. Operative October 1, 2011, by Sec. 636 of Ch. 15, as amended by Stats. 2011, Ch. 39, Sec. 68.)

(a) If two or more persons conspire:

(1) To commit any crime.

(2) Falsely and maliciously to indict another for any crime, or to procure another to be charged or arrested for any crime.

(3) Falsely to move or maintain any suit, action, or proceeding.

(4) To cheat and defraud any person of any property, by any means which are in themselves criminal, or to obtain money or property by false pretenses or by false promises with fraudulent intent not to perform those promises.

(5) To commit any act injurious to the public health, to public morals, or to pervert or obstruct justice, or the due administration of the laws.

(6) To commit any crime against the person of the President or Vice President of the United States, the Governor of any state or territory, any United States justice or judge, or the secretary of any of the executive departments of the United States. They are punishable as follows: When they conspire to commit any crime against the person of any official specified in paragraph (6), they are guilty of a felony and are punishable by imprisonment pursuant to subdivision (h) of Section 1170 for five, seven, or nine years. When they conspire to commit any other felony, they shall be punishable in the same manner and to the same extent as is provided for the punishment of that felony. If the felony is one for which different punishments are prescribed for different degrees, the jury or court which finds the defendant guilty thereof shall determine the degree of the felony the defendant conspired to commit. If the degree is not so determined, the punishment for conspiracy to commit the felony shall be that prescribed for the lesser degree, except in the case of conspiracy to commit murder, in which case the punishment shall be that prescribed for murder in the first degree. If the felony is conspiracy to commit two or more felonies which have different punishments and the commission of those felonies constitute but one offense of conspiracy, the penalty shall be that prescribed for the felony which has the greater maximum term.

When they conspire to do an act described in paragraph (4), they shall be punishable by imprisonment in a county jail for not more than one year, or by imprisonment pursuant to subdivision (h) of Section 1170, or by a fine not exceeding ten thousand dollars ($10,000), or by both that imprisonment and fine. When they conspire to do any of the other acts described in this section, they shall be punishable by imprisonment in a county jail for not more than one year, or pursuant to subdivision (h) of Section 1170, or by a fine not exceeding ten thousand dollars ($10,000), or by both that imprisonment and fine. When they receive a felony conviction for conspiring to commit identity theft, as defined in Section 530.5, the court may impose a fine of up to twenty-five thousand dollars ($25,000). All cases of conspiracy may be prosecuted and tried in the superior court of any county in which any overt act tending to effect the conspiracy shall be done.

(b) Upon a trial for conspiracy, in a case where an overt act is necessary to constitute the offense, the defendant cannot be convicted unless one or more overt acts are expressly alleged in the indictment or information, nor unless one of the acts alleged is proved; but other overt acts not alleged may be given in evidence.

Penal Code § 290

(Amended (as amended by Stats. 2020, Ch. 79, Sec. 2) by Stats. 2021, Ch. 626, Sec. 25. (AB 1171) Effective January 1, 2022.)

(a) Sections 290 to 290.024, inclusive, shall be known, and may be cited, as the Sex Offender Registration Act. All references to "the Act" in those sections are to the Sex Offender Registration Act.

(b) Every person described in subdivision (c), for the period specified in subdivision (d) while residing in California, or while attending school or working in California, as described in Sections 290.002 and 290.01, shall register with the chief of police of the city in which the person is residing, or the sheriff of the county if the person is residing in an unincorporated area or city that has no police department, and, additionally, with the chief of police of a campus of the University of California, the California State University, or community college if the person is residing upon the campus or in any of its facilities, within five working days of coming into, or changing the person's residence within, any city, county, or city and county, or campus in which the person temporarily resides, and shall register thereafter in accordance with the Act, unless the duty to register is terminated pursuant to Section 290.5 or as otherwise provided by law.

(c) (1) The following persons shall register:

Every person who, since July 1, 1944, has been or is hereafter convicted in any court in this state or in any federal or military court of a violation of Section 187 committed in the perpetration, or an attempt to perpetrate, rape, or any act punishable under Section 286, 287, 288, or 289 or former Section 288a, Section 207 or 209 committed with intent to violate Section 261, 286, 287, 288, or 289 or former Section 288a, Section 220, except assault to commit mayhem, subdivision (b) or (c) of Section 236.1, Section 243.4, Section 261, paragraph (1) of subdivision (a) of former Section 262 involving the use of force or violence for which the person is sentenced to the state prison, Section 264.1, 266, or 266c, subdivision (b) of Section 266h, subdivision (b) of Section 266i, Section 266j, 267, 269, 285, 286, 287, 288, 288.3, 288.4, 288.5, 288.7, 289, or 311.1, or former Section 288a, subdivision (b), (c), or (d) of Section 311.2, Section 311.3, 311.4, 311.10, 311.11, or 647.6, former Section 647a, subdivision (c) of Section 653f, subdivision 1 or 2 of Section 314, any offense involving lewd or lascivious conduct under Section 272, or any felony violation of Section 288.2; any statutory predecessor that includes all elements of one of the offenses described in this subdivision; or any person who since that date has been or is hereafter convicted of the attempt or conspiracy to commit any of the offenses described in this subdivision.

(2) Notwithstanding paragraph (1), a person convicted of a violation of subdivision (b) of Section 286, subdivision (b) of Section 287, or subdivision (h) or (i) of Section 289 shall not be required to register if, at the time of the offense, the person is not more than 10 years older than the minor, as measured from the minor's date of birth to the person's date of birth, and the conviction is the only one requiring the person to register. This paragraph does not preclude the court from requiring a person to register pursuant to Section 290.006.

(d) A person described in subdivision (c), or who is otherwise required to register pursuant to the Act shall register for 10 years, 20 years, or life, following a conviction and release from incarceration, placement, commitment, or release on probation or other supervision, as follows:

(1) (A) A tier one offender is subject to registration for a minimum of 10 years. A person is a tier one offender if the person is required to register for conviction of a misdemeanor described in subdivision (c), or for conviction of a felony described in subdivision (c) that was not a serious or violent felony as described in subdivision (c) of Section 667.5 or subdivision (c) of Section 1192.7.

(B) This paragraph does not apply to a person who is subject to registration pursuant to paragraph (2) or (3).

(2) (A) A tier two offender is subject to registration for a minimum of 20 years. A person is a tier two offender if the person was convicted of an offense described in subdivision (c) that is also described in subdivision (c) of Section 667.5 or subdivision (c) of Section 1192.7, Section 285, subdivision (g) or (h) of Section 286, subdivision (g) or (h) of Section 287 or former Section 288a, subdivision (b) of Section 289, or Section 647.6 if it is a second or subsequent conviction for that offense that was brought and tried separately.

(B) This paragraph does not apply if the person is subject to lifetime registration as required in paragraph (3).

(3) A tier three offender is subject to registration for life. A person is a tier three offender if any one of the following applies:

(A) Following conviction of a registerable offense, the person was subsequently convicted in a separate proceeding of committing an offense described in subdivision (c) and the conviction is for commission of a violent felony described in subdivision (c) of Section 667.5, or the person was subsequently convicted of committing an offense for which the person was ordered to register pursuant to Section 290.006, and the conviction is for the commission of a violent felony described in subdivision (c) of Section 667.5.

(B) The person was committed to a state mental hospital as a sexually violent predator pursuant to Article 4 (commencing with Section 6600) of Chapter 2 of Part 2 of Division 6 of the Welfare and Institutions Code.

(C) The person was convicted of violating any of the following:

(i) Section 187 while attempting to commit or committing an act punishable under Section 261, 286, 287, 288, or 289 or former Section 288a.

(ii) Section 207 or 209 with intent to violate Section 261, 286, 287, 288, or 289 or former Section 288a.

(iii) Section 220.

(iv) Subdivision (b) of Section 266h.

(v) Subdivision (b) of Section 266i.

(vi) Section 266j.

(vii) Section 267.

(viii) Section 269.

(ix) Subdivision (b) or (c) of Section 288.

(x) Section 288.2.

(xi) Section 288.3, unless committed with the intent to commit a violation of subdivision (b) of Section 286, subdivision (b) of Section 287 or former Section 288a, or subdivision (h) or (i) of Section 289.

(xii) Section 288.4.

(xiii) Section 288.5.

(xiv) Section 288.7.

(xv) Subdivision (c) of Section 653f.

(xvi) Any offense for which the person is sentenced to a life term pursuant to Section 667.61.

(D) The person's risk level on the static risk assessment instrument for sex offenders (SARATSO), pursuant to Section 290.04, is well above average risk at the time of release on the index sex offense into the community, as defined in the Coding Rules for that instrument.

(E) The person is a habitual sex offender pursuant to Section 667.71.

(F) The person was convicted of violating subdivision (a) of Section 288 in two proceedings brought and tried separately.

(G) The person was sentenced to 15 to 25 years to life for an offense listed in Section 667.61.

(H) The person is required to register pursuant to Section 290.004.

(I) The person was convicted of a felony offense described in subdivision (b) or (c) of Section 236.1.

(J) The person was convicted of a felony offense described in subdivision (a), (c), or (d) of Section 243.4.

(K) The person was convicted of violating paragraph (2), (3), or (4) of subdivision (a) of Section 261 or was convicted of violating Section 261 and punished pursuant to paragraph (1) or (2) of subdivision (c) of Section 264.

(L) The person was convicted of violating paragraph (1) of subdivision (a) of former Section 262.

(M) The person was convicted of violating Section 264.1.

(N) The person was convicted of any offense involving lewd or lascivious conduct under Section 272.

(O) The person was convicted of violating paragraph (2) of subdivision (c) or subdivision (d), (f), or (i) of Section 286.

(P) The person was convicted of violating paragraph (2) of subdivision (c) or subdivision (d), (f), or (i) of Section 287 or former Section 288a.

(Q) The person was convicted of violating paragraph (1) of subdivision (a) or subdivision (d), (e), or (j) of Section 289.

(R) The person was convicted of a felony violation of Section 311.1 or 311.11 or of violating subdivision (b), (c), or (d) of Section 311.2, Section 311.3, 311.4, or 311.10.

(4) (A) A person who is required to register pursuant to Section 290.005 shall be placed in the appropriate tier if the offense is assessed as equivalent to a California registerable offense described in subdivision (c).

(B) If the person's duty to register pursuant to Section 290.005 is based solely on the requirement of registration in another jurisdiction, and there is no equivalent California registerable offense, the person shall be subject to registration as a tier two offender, except that the person is subject to registration as a tier three offender if one of the following applies:

(i) The person's risk level on the static risk assessment instrument (SARATSO), pursuant to Section 290.06, is well above average risk at the time of release on the index sex offense into the community, as defined in the Coding Rules for that instrument.

(ii) The person was subsequently convicted in a separate proceeding of an offense substantially similar to an offense listed in subdivision (c) which is also substantially similar to an offense described in subdivision (c) of Section 667.5, or is substantially similar to Section 269 or 288.7.

(iii) The person has ever been committed to a state mental hospital or mental health facility in a proceeding substantially similar to civil commitment as a sexually violent predator pursuant to Article 4 (commencing with Section 6600) of Chapter 2 of Part 2 of Division 6 of the Welfare and Institutions Code.

(5) (A) The Department of Justice may place a person described in subdivision (c), or who is otherwise required to register pursuant to the Act, in a tier-to-be-determined category if the appropriate tier designation described in this subdivision cannot be immediately ascertained. An individual placed in this tier-to-be-determined category shall continue to register in accordance with the Act. The individual shall be given credit toward the mandated minimum registration period for any period for which the individual registers.

(B) The Department of Justice shall ascertain an individual's appropriate tier designation as described in this subdivision within 24 months of the individual's placement in the tier-to-be-determined category.

(e) The minimum time period for the completion of the required registration period in tier one or two commences on the date of release from incarceration, placement, or commitment, including any related civil commitment on the registerable offense. The minimum time for the completion of the required registration period for a designated tier is tolled during any period of subsequent incarceration, placement, or commitment, including any subsequent civil commitment, except that arrests not resulting in conviction, adjudication, or revocation of probation or parole shall not toll the required registration period. The minimum time period shall be extended by one year for each misdemeanor conviction of failing to register under this act, and by three years for each felony conviction of failing to register under this act, without regard to the actual time served in custody for the conviction. If a registrant is subsequently convicted of another offense requiring registration pursuant to the Act, a new minimum time period for the completion of the registration requirement for the applicable tier shall commence upon that person's release from incarceration, placement, or commitment, including any related civil commitment. If the subsequent conviction requiring registration pursuant to the Act occurs prior to an order to terminate the registrant from the registry after completion of a tier associated with the first conviction for a registerable offense, the applicable tier shall be the highest tier associated with the convictions.

(f) This section does not require a ward of the juvenile court to register under the Act, except as provided in Section 290.008.

Penal Code § 374.8

(Amended by Stats. 2011, Ch. 15, Sec. 338. (AB 109) Effective April 4, 2011. Operative October 1, 2011, by Sec. 636 of Ch. 15, as amended by Stats. 2011, Ch. 39, Sec. 68.)

(a) In any prosecution under this section, proof of the elements of the offense shall not be dependent upon the requirements of Title 22 of the California Code of Regulations.

(b) Any person who knowingly causes any hazardous substance to be deposited into or upon any road, street, highway, alley, or railroad right-of-way, or upon the land of another, without the permission of the owner, or into the waters of this state is punishable by imprisonment in the county jail for not more than one year or by imprisonment pursuant to subdivision (h) of Section 1170 for a term of 16 months, two years, or three years, or by a fine of not less than fifty dollars ($50) nor more than ten thousand dollars ($10,000), or by both the fine and imprisonment, unless the deposit occurred as a result of an emergency that the person promptly reported to the appropriate regulatory authority.

(c) For purposes of this section, "hazardous substance" means either of the following:

(1) Any material that, because of its quantity, concentration, or physical or chemical characteristics, poses a significant present or potential hazard to human health and safety or to the environment if released into the environment, including, but not limited to, hazardous waste and any material that the administering agency or

a handler, as defined in Chapter 6.91 (commencing with Section 25410) of Division 20 of the Health and Safety Code, has a reasonable basis for believing would be injurious to the health and safety of persons or harmful to the environment if released into the environment.

(2) Any substance or chemical product for which one of the following applies:

(A) The manufacturer or producer is required to prepare a MSDS, as defined in Section 6374 of the Labor Code, for the substance or product pursuant to the Hazardous Substances Information Training Act (Chapter 2.5 (commencing with Section 6360) of Part 1 of Division 5 of the Labor Code) or pursuant to any applicable federal law or regulation.

(B) The substance is described as a radioactive material in Chapter 1 of Title 10 of the Code of Federal Regulations maintained and updated by the Nuclear Regulatory Commission.

(C) The substance is designated by the Secretary of Transportation in Chapter 27 (commencing with Section 1801) of the appendix to Title 49 of the United States Code and taxed as a radioactive substance or material.

(D) The materials listed in subdivision (b) of Section 6382 of the Labor Code.

Penal Code § 667

(Amended by Stats. 2021, Ch. 626, Sec. 27. (AB 1171) Effective January 1, 2022.)

(a) (1) A person convicted of a serious felony who previously has been convicted of a serious felony in this state or of any offense committed in another jurisdiction that includes all of the elements of any serious felony, shall receive, in addition to the sentence imposed by the court for the present offense, a five-year enhancement for each such prior conviction on charges brought and tried separately. The terms of the present offense and each enhancement shall run consecutively.

(2) This subdivision shall not be applied when the punishment imposed under other provisions of law would result in a longer term of imprisonment. There is no requirement of prior incarceration or commitment for this subdivision to apply.

(3) The Legislature may increase the length of the enhancement of sentence provided in this subdivision by a statute passed by majority vote of each house thereof.

(4) As used in this subdivision, "serious felony" means a serious felony listed in subdivision (c) of Section 1192.7.

(5) This subdivision does not apply to a person convicted of selling, furnishing, administering, or giving, or offering to sell, furnish, administer, or give to a minor any methamphetamine-related drug or any precursors of methamphetamine unless the prior conviction was for a serious felony described in subparagraph (24) of subdivision (c) of Section 1192.7.

(b) It is the intent of the Legislature in enacting subdivisions (b) to (i), inclusive, to ensure longer prison sentences and greater punishment for those who commit a felony and have been previously convicted of one or more serious or violent felony offenses.

(c) Notwithstanding any other law, if a defendant has been convicted of a felony and it has been pled and proved that the defendant has one or more prior serious or violent felony convictions as defined in subdivision (d), the court shall adhere to each of the following:

(1) There shall not be an aggregate term limitation for purposes of consecutive sentencing for any subsequent felony conviction.

(2) Probation for the current offense shall not be granted, nor shall execution or imposition of the sentence be

suspended for any prior offense.

(3) The length of time between the prior serious or violent felony conviction and the current felony conviction shall not affect the imposition of sentence.

(4) There shall not be a commitment to any other facility other than the state prison. Diversion shall not be granted, nor shall the defendant be eligible for commitment to the California Rehabilitation Center as provided in Article 2 (commencing with Section 3050) of Chapter 1 of Division 3 of the Welfare and Institutions Code.

(5) The total amount of credits awarded pursuant to Article 2.5 (commencing with Section 2930) of Chapter 7 of Title 1 of Part 3 shall not exceed one-fifth of the total term of imprisonment imposed and shall not accrue until the defendant is physically placed in the state prison.

(6) If there is a current conviction for more than one felony count not committed on the same occasion, and not arising from the same set of operative facts, the court shall sentence the defendant consecutively on each count pursuant to subdivision (e).

(7) If there is a current conviction for more than one serious or violent felony as described in paragraph (6), the court shall impose the sentence for each conviction consecutive to the sentence for any other conviction for which the defendant may be consecutively sentenced in the manner prescribed by law.

(8) A sentence imposed pursuant to subdivision (e) shall be imposed consecutive to any other sentence that the defendant is already serving, unless otherwise provided by law.

(d) Notwithstanding any other law and for the purposes of subdivisions (b) to (i), inclusive, a prior conviction of a serious or violent felony shall be defined as:

(1) An offense defined in subdivision (c) of Section 667.5 as a violent felony or an offense defined in subdivision (c) of Section 1192.7 as a serious felony in this state. The determination of whether a prior conviction is a prior felony conviction for purposes of subdivisions (b) to (i), inclusive, shall be made upon the date of that prior conviction and is not affected by the sentence imposed unless the sentence automatically, upon the initial sentencing, converts the felony to a misdemeanor. The following dispositions shall not affect the determination that a prior conviction is a prior felony for purposes of subdivisions (b) to (i), inclusive:

(A) The suspension of imposition of judgment or sentence.

(B) The stay of execution of sentence.

(C) The commitment to the State Department of State Hospitals as a mentally disordered sex offender following a conviction of a felony.

(D) The commitment to the California Rehabilitation Center or any other facility whose function is rehabilitative diversion from the state prison.

(2) A prior conviction in another jurisdiction for an offense that, if committed in California, is punishable by imprisonment in the state prison constitutes a prior conviction of a particular serious or violent felony if the prior conviction in the other jurisdiction is for an offense that includes all of the elements of a particular violent felony as defined in subdivision (c) of Section 667.5 or serious felony as defined in subdivision (c) of Section 1192.7.

(3) A prior juvenile adjudication constitutes a prior serious or violent felony conviction for purposes of sentence enhancement if it meets all of the following:

(A) The juvenile was 16 years of age or older at the time the juvenile committed the prior offense.

(B) The prior offense is listed in subdivision (b) of Section 707 of the Welfare and Institutions Code or described in paragraph (1) or (2) as a serious or violent felony.

(C) The juvenile was found to be a fit and proper subject to be dealt with under the juvenile court law.

(D) The juvenile was adjudged a ward of the juvenile court within the meaning of Section 602 of the Welfare and Institutions Code because the person committed an offense listed in subdivision (b) of Section 707 of the Welfare and Institutions Code.

(e) For purposes of subdivisions (b) to (i), inclusive, and in addition to any other enhancement or punishment provisions that apply, the following apply if a defendant has one or more prior serious or violent felony convictions:

(1) If a defendant has one prior serious or violent felony conviction as defined in subdivision (d) that has been pled and proved, the determinate term or minimum term for an indeterminate term shall be twice the term otherwise provided as punishment for the current felony conviction.

(2) (A) Except as provided in subparagraph (C), if a defendant has two or more prior serious or violent felony convictions as defined in subdivision (d) that have been pled and proved, the term for the current felony conviction shall be an indeterminate term of life imprisonment with a minimum term of the indeterminate sentence calculated as the greatest of:

(i) Three times the term otherwise provided as punishment for each current felony conviction subsequent to the two or more prior serious or violent felony convictions.

(ii) Imprisonment in the state prison for 25 years.

(iii) The term determined by the court pursuant to Section 1170 for the underlying conviction, including any enhancement applicable under Chapter 4.5 (commencing with Section 1170) of Title 7 of Part 2, or any period prescribed by Section 190 or 3046.

(B) The indeterminate term described in subparagraph (A) shall be served consecutive to any other term of imprisonment for which a consecutive term may be imposed by law. Any other term imposed subsequent to an indeterminate term described in subparagraph (A) shall not be merged therein but shall commence at the time the person would otherwise have been released from prison.

(C) If a defendant has two or more prior serious or violent felony convictions as defined in subdivision (c) of Section 667.5 or subdivision (c) of Section 1192.7 that have been pled and proved, and the current offense is not a serious or violent felony as defined in subdivision (d), the defendant shall be sentenced pursuant to paragraph (1) of subdivision (e) unless the prosecution pleads and proves any of the following:

(i) The current offense is a controlled substance charge, in which an allegation under Section 11370.4 or 11379.8 of the Health and Safety Code was admitted or found true.

(ii) The current offense is a felony sex offense, defined in subdivision (d) of Section 261.5 or former Section 262, or a felony offense that results in mandatory registration as a sex offender pursuant to subdivision (c) of Section 290 except for violations of Sections 266 and 285, paragraph (1) of subdivision (b) and subdivision (e) of Section 286, paragraph (1) of subdivision (b) and subdivision (e) of Section 288a, Section 311.11, and Section 314.

(iii) During the commission of the current offense, the defendant used a firearm, was armed with a firearm or deadly weapon, or intended to cause great bodily injury to another person.

(iv) The defendant suffered a prior serious or violent felony conviction, as defined in subdivision (d) of this section, for any of the following felonies:

(I) A "sexually violent offense" as defined in subdivision (b) of Section 6600 of the Welfare and Institutions Code.

(II) Oral copulation with a child who is under 14 years of age and more than 10 years younger than the defendant as defined by Section 288a, sodomy with another person who is under 14 years of age and more than 10 years younger than the defendant as defined by Section 286, or sexual penetration with another person who is under 14 years of age and more than 10 years younger than the defendant, as defined by Section 289.

(III) A lewd or lascivious act involving a child under 14 years of age, in violation of Section 288.

(IV) Any homicide offense, including any attempted homicide offense, defined in Sections 187 to 191.5, inclusive.

(V) Solicitation to commit murder as defined in Section 653f.

(VI) Assault with a machinegun on a peace officer or firefighter, as defined in paragraph (3) of subdivision (d) of Section 245.

(VII) Possession of a weapon of mass destruction, as defined in paragraph (1) of subdivision (a) of Section 11418.

(VIII) Any serious or violent felony offense punishable in California by life imprisonment or death.

(f) (1) Notwithstanding any other law, subdivisions (b) to (i), inclusive, shall be applied in every case in which a defendant has one or more prior serious or violent felony convictions as defined in subdivision (d). The prosecuting attorney shall plead and prove each prior serious or violent felony conviction except as provided in paragraph (2).

(2) The prosecuting attorney may move to dismiss or strike a prior serious or violent felony conviction allegation in the furtherance of justice pursuant to Section 1385, or if there is insufficient evidence to prove the prior serious or violent felony conviction. If upon the satisfaction of the court that there is insufficient evidence to prove the prior serious or violent felony conviction, the court may dismiss or strike the allegation. This section shall not be read to alter a court's authority under Section 1385.

(g) Prior serious or violent felony convictions shall not be used in plea bargaining as defined in subdivision (b) of Section 1192.7. The prosecution shall plead and prove all known prior serious or violent felony convictions and shall not enter into any agreement to strike or seek the dismissal of any prior serious or violent felony conviction allegation except as provided in paragraph (2) of subdivision (f).

(h) All references to existing statutes in subdivisions (c) to (g), inclusive, are to statutes as they existed on November 7, 2012.

(i) If any provision of subdivisions (b) to (h), inclusive, or the application thereof to any person or circumstance is held invalid, that invalidity shall not affect other provisions or applications of those subdivisions that can be given effect without the invalid provision or application, and to this end the provisions of those subdivisions are severable.

(j) The provisions of this section shall not be amended by the Legislature except by statute passed in each house by rollcall vote entered in the journal, two-thirds of the membership concurring, or by a statute that becomes effective only when approved by the electors.

Penal Code § 830.2

(Amended by Stats. 2021, Ch. 70, Sec. 106. (AB 141) Effective July 12, 2021.)

The following persons are peace officers whose authority extends to any place in the state:

(a) Any member of the Department of the California Highway Patrol including those members designated under subdivision (a) of Section 2250.1 of the Vehicle Code, provided that the primary duty of the peace officer is the enforcement of any law relating to the use or operation of vehicles upon the highways, or laws pertaining to the provision of police services for the protection of state officers, state properties, and the occupants of state properties, or both, as set forth in the Vehicle Code and Government Code.

(b) A member of the University of California Police Department appointed pursuant to Section 92600 of the Education Code, provided that the primary duty of the peace officer shall be the enforcement of the law within the area specified in Section 92600 of the Education Code.

(c) A member of the California State University Police Departments appointed pursuant to Section 89560 of the Education Code, provided that the primary duty of the peace officer shall be the enforcement of the law within the area specified in Section 89560 of the Education Code.

(d) (1) Any member of the Office of Correctional Safety of the Department of Corrections and Rehabilitation, provided that the primary duties of the peace officer shall be the investigation or apprehension of inmates, wards, parolees, parole violators, or escapees from state institutions, the transportation of those persons, the investigation of any violation of criminal law discovered while performing the usual and authorized duties of employment, and the coordination of those activities with other criminal justice agencies.

(2) Any member of the Office of Internal Affairs of the Department of Corrections and Rehabilitation, provided that the primary duties shall be criminal investigations of Department of Corrections and Rehabilitation personnel and the coordination of those activities with other criminal justice agencies. For purposes of this subdivision, the member of the Office of Internal Affairs shall possess certification from the Commission on Peace Officer Standards and Training for investigators, or have completed training pursuant to Section 6126.1.

(e) Employees of the Department of Fish and Game designated by the director, provided that the primary duty of those peace officers shall be the enforcement of the law as set forth in Section 856 of the Fish and Game Code.

(f) Employees of the Department of Parks and Recreation designated by the director pursuant to Section 5008 of the Public Resources Code, provided that the primary duty of the peace officer shall be the enforcement of the law as set forth in Section 5008 of the Public Resources Code.

(g) The Director of Forestry and Fire Protection and employees or classes of employees of the Department of Forestry and Fire Protection designated by the director pursuant to Section 4156 of the Public Resources Code, provided that the primary duty of the peace officer shall be the enforcement of the law as that duty is set forth in Section 4156 of the Public Resources Code.

(h) Persons employed by the Department of Alcoholic Beverage Control for the enforcement of Division 9 (commencing with Section 23000) of the Business and Professions Code and designated by the Director of Alcoholic Beverage Control, provided that the primary duty of any of these peace officers shall be the enforcement of the laws relating to alcoholic beverages, as that duty is set forth in Section 25755 of the Business and Professions Code.

(i) Marshals and police appointed by the Board of Directors of the California Exposition and State Fair pursuant to Section 3332 of the Food and Agricultural Code, provided that the primary duty of the peace officers shall be the enforcement of the law as prescribed in that section.

(j) Persons employed by the Department of Cannabis Control for the enforcement of Division 10 (commencing with Section 26000) of the Business and Professions Code and designated by the Director of the Department of Cannabis Control, provided that the primary duty of any of these peace officers shall be the enforcement of the laws as that duty is set forth in Section 26015 of the Business and Professions Code.

Penal Code § 830.11

(Amended by Stats. 2022, Ch. 474, Sec. 1.5. (SB 1496) Effective January 1, 2023.)

(a) The following persons are not peace officers but may exercise the powers of arrest of a peace officer as specified in Section 836 and the power to serve warrants as specified in Sections 1523 and 1530 during the course and within the scope of their employment, if they receive a course in the exercise of those powers pursuant to Section 832. The authority and powers of the persons designated under this section extend to any place in the state:

(1) A person employed by the Department of Financial Protection and Innovation designated by the Commissioner of Financial Protection and Innovation, provided that the person's primary duty is the enforcement of, and investigations relating to, the provisions of law administered by the Commissioner of Financial Protection and Innovation.

(2) A person employed by the Bureau of Real Estate designated by the Real Estate Commissioner, provided that the person's primary duty is the enforcement of the laws set forth in Part 1 (commencing with Section 10000) and Part 2 (commencing with Section 11000) of Division 4 of the Business and Professions Code. The Real Estate Commissioner may designate a person under this section who, at the time of their designation, is assigned to the Special Investigations Unit, internally known as the Crisis Response Team.

(3) A person employed by the State Lands Commission designated by the executive officer, provided that the person's primary duty is the enforcement of the law relating to the duties of the State Lands Commission.

(4) A person employed as an investigator of the Investigations Bureau of the Department of Insurance, who is designated by the Chief of the Investigations Bureau, provided that the person's primary duty is the enforcement of the Insurance Code and other laws relating to persons and businesses, licensed and unlicensed by the Department of Insurance, who are engaged in the business of insurance.

(5) A person employed as an investigator or investigator supervisor by the Public Utilities Commission, who is designated by the commission's executive director and approved by the commission, provided that the person's primary duty is the enforcement of the law as that duty is set forth in Section 308.5 of the Public Utilities Code.

(6) (A) A person employed by the California Department of Tax and Fee Administration, who is designated by the department's director, provided that the person's primary duty is the enforcement of laws administered by the California Department of Tax and Fee Administration.

(B) A person designated pursuant to this paragraph is not entitled to peace officer retirement benefits.

(7) A person employed by the Department of Food and Agriculture and designated by the Secretary of Food and Agriculture as an investigator, investigator supervisor, or investigator manager, provided that the person's primary duty is enforcement of, and investigations relating to, the Food and Agricultural Code or Division 5 (commencing with Section 12001) of the Business and Professions Code.

(8) The Inspector General and those employees of the Office of the Inspector General designated by the Inspector General, provided that the person's primary duty is the enforcement of the law relating to the duties of the Office of the Inspector General.

(9) A person employed by the Department of Cannabis Control and designated by the director of the department as an investigator, investigator supervisor, or investigator manager, provided that the person's primary duty is enforcement of, and investigations relating to, Division 10 (commencing with Section 26000) of the Business and Professions Code. This section shall apply to only those investigator positions occupied by persons previously designated by the Secretary of the Department of Food and Agriculture as an investigator, investigator supervisor, or investigative manager whose primary duty was to enforce Division 10 (commencing with Section 26000) of the Business and Professions Code.

(b) Notwithstanding any other law, a person designated pursuant to this section may not carry a firearm.

(c) A person designated pursuant to this section shall be included as a "peace officer of the state" under paragraph (2) of subdivision (c) of Section 11105 for the purpose of receiving state summary criminal history information and shall be furnished that information on the same basis as other peace officers designated in paragraph (2) of subdivision (c) of Section 11105.

Penal Code § 1000

(Amended by Stats. 2017, Ch. 778, Sec. 1. (AB 208) Effective January 1, 2018.)

(a) This chapter shall apply whenever a case is before any court upon an accusatory pleading for a violation of Section 11350, 11357, 11364, or 11365, paragraph (2) of subdivision (b) of Section 11375, Section 11377, or Section 11550 of the Health and Safety Code, or subdivision (b) of Section 23222 of the Vehicle Code, or Section 11358 of the Health and Safety Code if the marijuana planted, cultivated, harvested, dried, or processed is for personal use, or Section 11368 of the Health and Safety Code if the narcotic drug was secured by a fictitious prescription and is for the personal use of the defendant and was not sold or furnished to another, or subdivision (d) of Section 653f if the solicitation was for acts directed to personal use only, or Section 381 or subdivision (f) of Section 647 of the Penal Code, if for being under the influence of a controlled substance, or Section 4060 of the Business and Professions Code, and it appears to the prosecuting attorney that, except as provided in subdivision (b) of Section 11357 of the Health and Safety Code, all of the following apply to the defendant:

(1) Within five years prior to the alleged commission of the charged offense, the defendant has not suffered a conviction for any offense involving controlled substances other than the offenses listed in this subdivision.

(2) The offense charged did not involve a crime of violence or threatened violence.

(3) There is no evidence of a contemporaneous violation relating to narcotics or restricted dangerous drugs other than a violation of the offenses listed in this subdivision.

(4) The defendant has no prior felony conviction within five years prior to the alleged commission of the charged offense.

(b) The prosecuting attorney shall review his or her file to determine whether or not paragraphs (1) to (4), inclusive, of subdivision (a) apply to the defendant. If the defendant is found eligible, the prosecuting attorney shall file with the court a declaration in writing or state for the record the grounds upon which the determination is based, and shall make this information available to the defendant and his or her attorney. This procedure is intended to allow the court to set the hearing for pretrial diversion at the arraignment. If the defendant is found ineligible for pretrial diversion, the prosecuting attorney shall file with the court a declaration in writing or state for the record the grounds upon which the determination is based, and shall make this information available to the defendant and his or her attorney. The sole remedy of a defendant who is found ineligible for pretrial diversion is a postconviction appeal.

(c) All referrals for pretrial diversion granted by the court pursuant to this chapter shall be made only to programs that have been certified by the county drug program administrator pursuant to Chapter 1.5 (commencing with Section 1211) of Title 8, or to programs that provide services at no cost to the participant and have been deemed by the court and the county drug program administrator to be credible and effective. The defendant may request to be referred to a program in any county, as long as that program meets the criteria set forth in this subdivision.

(d) Pretrial diversion for an alleged violation of Section 11368 of the Health and Safety Code shall not prohibit any administrative agency from taking disciplinary action against a licensee or from denying a license. This subdivision does not expand or restrict the provisions of Section 1000.4.

(e) Any defendant who is participating in a program authorized in this section may be required to undergo analysis of his or her urine for the purpose of testing for the presence of any drug as part of the program. However, urinalysis results shall not be admissible as a basis for any new criminal prosecution or proceeding.

Penal Code § 1170

(Amended by Stats. 2022, Ch. 744, Sec. 1. (AB 960) Effective January 1, 2023.)

(a) (1) The Legislature finds and declares that the purpose of sentencing is public safety achieved through punishment, rehabilitation, and restorative justice. When a sentence includes incarceration, this purpose is best served by terms that are proportionate to the seriousness of the offense with provision for uniformity in the sentences of offenders committing the same offense under similar circumstances.

(2) The Legislature further finds and declares that programs should be available for incarcerated persons, including, but not limited to, educational, rehabilitative, and restorative justice programs that are designed to promote behavior change and to prepare all eligible offenders for successful reentry into the community. The Legislature encourages the development of policies and programs designed to educate and rehabilitate all eligible offenders. In implementing this section, the Department of Corrections and Rehabilitation is encouraged to allow all eligible incarcerated persons the opportunity to enroll in programs that promote successful return to the community. The Department of Corrections and Rehabilitation is directed to establish a mission statement consistent with these principles.

(3) In any case in which the sentence prescribed by statute for a person convicted of a public offense is a term of imprisonment in the state prison, or a term pursuant to subdivision (h), of any specification of three time periods, the court shall sentence the defendant to one of the terms of imprisonment specified unless the convicted person is given any other disposition provided by law, including a fine, jail, probation, or the suspension of imposition or execution of sentence or is sentenced pursuant to subdivision (b) of Section 1168 because they had committed their crime prior to July 1, 1977. In sentencing the convicted person, the court shall apply the sentencing rules of the Judicial Council. The court, unless it determines that there are circumstances in mitigation of the sentence prescribed, shall also impose any other term that it is required by law to impose as an additional term. Nothing in this article shall affect any provision of law that imposes the death penalty, that authorizes or restricts the granting of probation or suspending the execution or imposition of sentence, or expressly provides for imprisonment in the state prison for life, except as provided in subdivision (d). In any case in which the amount of preimprisonment credit under Section 2900.5 or any other provision of law is equal to or exceeds any sentence imposed pursuant to this chapter, except for a remaining portion of mandatory supervision imposed pursuant to subparagraph (B) of paragraph (5) of subdivision (h), the entire sentence shall be deemed to have been served, except for the remaining period of mandatory supervision, and the defendant shall not be actually delivered to the custody of the secretary or the county correctional administrator. The court shall advise the defendant that they shall serve an applicable period of parole, postrelease community supervision, or mandatory supervision and order the defendant to report to the parole or probation office closest to the defendant's last legal residence, unless the in-custody credits equal the total sentence, including both confinement time and the period of parole, postrelease community supervision, or mandatory supervision. The sentence shall be deemed a separate prior prison term or a sentence of imprisonment in a county jail under subdivision (h) for purposes of Section 667.5, and a copy of the judgment and other necessary documentation shall be forwarded to the secretary.

(b) (1) When a judgment of imprisonment is to be imposed and the statute specifies three possible terms, the court shall, in its sound discretion, order imposition of a sentence not to exceed the middle term, except as otherwise provided in paragraph (2).

(2) The court may impose a sentence exceeding the middle term only when there are circumstances in aggravation of the crime that justify the imposition of a term of imprisonment exceeding the middle term, and the facts underlying those circumstances have been stipulated to by the defendant, or have been found true beyond a reasonable doubt at trial by the jury or by the judge in a court trial. Except where evidence supporting an aggravating circumstance is admissible to prove or defend against the charged offense or enhancement at trial, or it is otherwise authorized by law, upon request of a defendant, trial on the circumstances in aggravation alleged in the indictment or information shall be bifurcated from the trial of charges and enhancements. The jury shall not be informed of the bifurcated allegations until there has been a conviction of a felony offense.

(3) Notwithstanding paragraphs (1) and (2), the court may consider the defendant's prior convictions in determining sentencing based on a certified record of conviction without submitting the prior convictions to a jury. This paragraph does not apply to enhancements imposed on prior convictions.

(4) At least four days prior to the time set for imposition of judgment, either party or the victim, or the family of the victim if the victim is deceased, may submit a statement in aggravation or mitigation to dispute facts in the record

or the probation officer's report, or to present additional facts. The court may consider the record in the case, the probation officer's report, other reports, including reports received pursuant to Section 1203.03, and statements in aggravation or mitigation submitted by the prosecution, the defendant, or the victim, or the family of the victim if the victim is deceased, and any further evidence introduced at the sentencing hearing.

(5) The court shall set forth on the record the facts and reasons for choosing the sentence imposed. The court may not impose an upper term by using the fact of any enhancement upon which sentence is imposed under any provision of law. A term of imprisonment shall not be specified if imposition of sentence is suspended.

(6) Notwithstanding paragraph (1), and unless the court finds that the aggravating circumstances outweigh the mitigating circumstances that imposition of the lower term would be contrary to the interests of justice, the court shall order imposition of the lower term if any of the following was a contributing factor in the commission of the offense:

(A) The person has experienced psychological, physical, or childhood trauma, including, but not limited to, abuse, neglect, exploitation, or sexual violence.

(B) The person is a youth, or was a youth as defined under subdivision (b) of Section 1016.7 at the time of the commission of the offense.

(C) Prior to the instant offense, or at the time of the commission of the offense, the person is or was a victim of intimate partner violence or human trafficking.

(7) Paragraph (6) does not preclude the court from imposing the lower term even if there is no evidence of those circumstances listed in paragraph (6) present.

(c) The court shall state the reasons for its sentence choice on the record at the time of sentencing. The court shall also inform the defendant that as part of the sentence after expiration of the term they may be on parole for a period as provided in Section 3000 or 3000.08 or postrelease community supervision for a period as provided in Section 3451.

(d) (1) (A) When a defendant who was under 18 years of age at the time of the commission of the offense for which the defendant was sentenced to imprisonment for life without the possibility of parole has been incarcerated for at least 15 years, the defendant may submit to the sentencing court a petition for recall and resentencing.

(B) Notwithstanding subparagraph (A), this paragraph shall not apply to defendants sentenced to life without parole for an offense where it was pled and proved that the defendant tortured, as described in Section 206, their victim or the victim was a public safety official, including any law enforcement personnel mentioned in Chapter 4.5 (commencing with Section 830) of Title 3, or any firefighter as described in Section 245.1, as well as any other officer in any segment of law enforcement who is employed by the federal government, the state, or any of its political subdivisions.

(2) The defendant shall file the original petition with the sentencing court. A copy of the petition shall be served on the agency that prosecuted the case. The petition shall include the defendant's statement that the defendant was under 18 years of age at the time of the crime and was sentenced to life in prison without the possibility of parole, the defendant's statement describing their remorse and work towards rehabilitation, and the defendant's statement that one of the following is true:

(A) The defendant was convicted pursuant to felony murder or aiding and abetting murder provisions of law.

(B) The defendant does not have juvenile felony adjudications for assault or other felony crimes with a significant potential for personal harm to victims prior to the offense for which the sentence is being considered for recall.

(C) The defendant committed the offense with at least one adult codefendant.

(D) The defendant has performed acts that tend to indicate rehabilitation or the potential for rehabilitation, including, but not limited to, availing themselves of rehabilitative, educational, or vocational programs, if those programs have been available at their classification level and facility, using self-study for self-improvement, or showing evidence of remorse.

(3) If any of the information required in paragraph (2) is missing from the petition, or if proof of service on the prosecuting agency is not provided, the court shall return the petition to the defendant and advise the defendant that the matter cannot be considered without the missing information.

(4) A reply to the petition, if any, shall be filed with the court within 60 days of the date on which the prosecuting agency was served with the petition, unless a continuance is granted for good cause.

(5) If the court finds by a preponderance of the evidence that one or more of the statements specified in subparagraphs (A) to (D), inclusive, of paragraph (2) is true, the court shall recall the sentence and commitment previously ordered and hold a hearing to resentence the defendant in the same manner as if the defendant had not previously been sentenced, provided that the new sentence, if any, is not greater than the initial sentence. Victims, or victim family members if the victim is deceased, shall retain the rights to participate in the hearing.

(6) The factors that the court may consider when determining whether to resentence the defendant to a term of imprisonment with the possibility of parole include, but are not limited to, the following:

(A) The defendant was convicted pursuant to felony murder or aiding and abetting murder provisions of law.

(B) The defendant does not have juvenile felony adjudications for assault or other felony crimes with a significant potential for personal harm to victims prior to the offense for which the defendant was sentenced to life without the possibility of parole.

(C) The defendant committed the offense with at least one adult codefendant.

(D) Prior to the offense for which the defendant was sentenced to life without the possibility of parole, the defendant had insufficient adult support or supervision and had suffered from psychological or physical trauma, or significant stress.

(E) The defendant suffers from cognitive limitations due to mental illness, developmental disabilities, or other factors that did not constitute a defense, but influenced the defendant's involvement in the offense.

(F) The defendant has performed acts that tend to indicate rehabilitation or the potential for rehabilitation, including, but not limited to, availing themselves of rehabilitative, educational, or vocational programs, if those programs have been available at their classification level and facility, using self-study for self-improvement, or showing evidence of remorse.

(G) The defendant has maintained family ties or connections with others through letter writing, calls, or visits, or has eliminated contact with individuals outside of prison who are currently involved with crime.

(H) The defendant has had no disciplinary actions for violent activities in the last five years in which the defendant was determined to be the aggressor.

(7) The court shall have the discretion to resentence the defendant in the same manner as if the defendant had not previously been sentenced, provided that the new sentence, if any, is not greater than the initial sentence. The discretion of the court shall be exercised in consideration of the criteria in paragraph (6). Victims, or victim family members if the victim is deceased, shall be notified of the resentencing hearing and shall retain their rights to participate in the hearing.

(8) Notwithstanding paragraph (7), the court may also resentence the defendant to a term that is less than the initial sentence if any of the following were a contributing factor in the commission of the alleged offense:

(A) The person has experienced psychological, physical, or childhood trauma, including, but not limited to, abuse, neglect, exploitation, or sexual violence.

(B) The person is a youth, or was a youth as defined under subdivision (b) of Section 1016.7 at the time of the commission of the offense.

(C) Prior to the instant offense, or at the time of the commission of the offense, the person is or was a victim of intimate partner violence or human trafficking.

(9) Paragraph (8) does not prohibit the court from resentencing the defendant to a term that is less than the initial sentence even if none of the circumstances listed in paragraph (8) are present.

(10) If the sentence is not recalled or the defendant is resentenced to imprisonment for life without the possibility of parole, the defendant may submit another petition for recall and resentencing to the sentencing court when the defendant has been committed to the custody of the department for at least 20 years. If the sentence is not recalled or the defendant is resentenced to imprisonment for life without the possibility of parole under that petition, the defendant may file another petition after having served 24 years. The final petition may be submitted, and the response to that petition shall be determined, during the 25th year of the defendant's sentence.

(11) In addition to the criteria in paragraph (6) the court may consider any other criteria that the court deems relevant to its decision, so long as the court identifies them on the record, provides a statement of reasons for adopting them, and states why the defendant does or does not satisfy the criteria.

(12) This subdivision shall have retroactive application.

(13) Nothing in this paragraph is intended to diminish or abrogate any rights or remedies otherwise available to the defendant.

(e) Notwithstanding subdivision (a), the court may recall and resentence an incarcerated person pursuant to the compassionate release program set forth in Section 1172.2.

(f) Notwithstanding any other provision of this section, for purposes of paragraph (3) of subdivision (h), any allegation that a defendant is eligible for state prison due to a prior or current conviction, sentence enhancement, or because the defendant is required to register as a sex offender shall not be subject to dismissal pursuant to Section 1385.

(g) A sentence to the state prison for a determinate term for which only one term is specified, is a sentence to state prison under this section.

(h) (1) Except as provided in paragraph (3), a felony punishable pursuant to this subdivision where the term is not specified in the underlying offense shall be punishable by a term of imprisonment in a county jail for 16 months, or two or three years.

(2) Except as provided in paragraph (3), a felony punishable pursuant to this subdivision shall be punishable by imprisonment in a county jail for the term described in the underlying offense.

(3) Notwithstanding paragraphs (1) and (2), where the defendant (A) has a prior or current felony conviction for a serious felony described in subdivision (c) of Section 1192.7 or a prior or current conviction for a violent felony described in subdivision (c) of Section 667.5, (B) has a prior felony conviction in another jurisdiction for an offense that has all the elements of a serious felony described in subdivision (c) of Section 1192.7 or a violent felony described in subdivision (c) of Section 667.5, (C) is required to register as a sex offender pursuant to Chapter 5.5 (commencing with Section 290) of Title 9 of Part 1, or (D) is convicted of a crime and as part of the sentence an enhancement pursuant to Section 186.11 is imposed, an executed sentence for a felony punishable pursuant to this subdivision shall be served in the state prison.

(4) Nothing in this subdivision shall be construed to prevent other dispositions authorized by law, including pretrial diversion, deferred entry of judgment, or an order granting probation pursuant to Section 1203.1.

(5) (A) Unless the court finds, in the interest of justice, that it is not appropriate in a particular case, the court, when imposing a sentence pursuant to paragraph (1) or (2), shall suspend execution of a concluding portion of the term for

a period selected at the court's discretion.

(B) The portion of a defendant's sentenced term that is suspended pursuant to this paragraph shall be known as mandatory supervision, and, unless otherwise ordered by the court, shall commence upon release from physical custody or an alternative custody program, whichever is later. During the period of mandatory supervision, the defendant shall be supervised by the county probation officer in accordance with the terms, conditions, and procedures generally applicable to persons placed on probation, for the remaining unserved portion of the sentence imposed by the court. The period of supervision shall be mandatory, and may not be earlier terminated except by court order. Any proceeding to revoke or modify mandatory supervision under this subparagraph shall be conducted pursuant to either subdivisions (a) and (b) of Section 1203.2 or Section 1203.3. During the period when the defendant is under that supervision, unless in actual custody related to the sentence imposed by the court, the defendant shall be entitled to only actual time credit against the term of imprisonment imposed by the court. Any time period which is suspended because a person has absconded shall not be credited toward the period of supervision.

(6) When the court is imposing a judgment pursuant to this subdivision concurrent or consecutive to a judgment or judgments previously imposed pursuant to this subdivision in another county or counties, the court rendering the second or other subsequent judgment shall determine the county or counties of incarceration and supervision of the defendant.

(7) The sentencing changes made by the act that added this subdivision shall be applied prospectively to any person sentenced on or after October 1, 2011.

(8) The sentencing changes made to paragraph (5) by the act that added this paragraph shall become effective and operative on January 1, 2015, and shall be applied prospectively to any person sentenced on or after January 1, 2015.

(9) Notwithstanding the separate punishment for any enhancement, any enhancement shall be punishable in county jail or state prison as required by the underlying offense and not as would be required by the enhancement. The intent of the Legislature in enacting this paragraph is to abrogate the holding in People v. Vega (2014) 222 Cal. App.4th 1374, that if an enhancement specifies service of sentence in state prison, the entire sentence is served in state prison, even if the punishment for the underlying offense is a term of imprisonment in the county jail.

Penal Code § 12022

(Amended by Stats. 2013, Ch. 76, Sec. 166. (AB 383) Effective January 1, 2014.)

(a) (1) Except as provided in subdivisions (c) and (d), a person who is armed with a firearm in the commission of a felony or attempted felony shall be punished by an additional and consecutive term of imprisonment pursuant to subdivision (h) of Section 1170 for one year, unless the arming is an element of that offense. This additional term shall apply to a person who is a principal in the commission of a felony or attempted felony if one or more of the principals is armed with a firearm, whether or not the person is personally armed with a firearm.

(2) Except as provided in subdivision (c), and notwithstanding subdivision (d), if the firearm is an assault weapon, as defined in Section 30510 or 30515, or a machinegun, as defined in Section 16880, or a .50 BMG rifle, as defined in Section 30530, the additional and consecutive term described in this subdivision shall be three years imprisonment pursuant to subdivision (h) of Section 1170 whether or not the arming is an element of the offense of which the person was convicted. The additional term provided in this paragraph shall apply to any person who is a principal in the commission of a felony or attempted felony if one or more of the principals is armed with an assault weapon, machinegun, or a .50 BMG rifle, whether or not the person is personally armed with an assault weapon, machinegun, or a .50 BMG rifle.

(b) (1) A person who personally uses a deadly or dangerous weapon in the commission of a felony or attempted felony shall be punished by an additional and consecutive term of imprisonment in the state prison for one year, unless use of a deadly or dangerous weapon is an element of that offense.

(2) If the person described in paragraph (1) has been convicted of carjacking or attempted carjacking, the

additional term shall be in the state prison for one, two, or three years.

(3) When a person is found to have personally used a deadly or dangerous weapon in the commission of a felony or attempted felony as provided in this subdivision and the weapon is owned by that person, the court shall order that the weapon be deemed a nuisance and disposed of in the manner provided in Sections 18000 and 18005.

(c) Notwithstanding the enhancement set forth in subdivision (a), a person who is personally armed with a firearm in the commission of a violation or attempted violation of Section 11351, 11351.5, 11352, 11366.5, 11366.6, 11378, 11378.5, 11379, 11379.5, or 11379.6 of the Health and Safety Code shall be punished by an additional and consecutive term of imprisonment pursuant to subdivision (h) of Section 1170 for three, four, or five years.

(d) Notwithstanding the enhancement set forth in subdivision (a), a person who is not personally armed with a firearm who, knowing that another principal is personally armed with a firearm, is a principal in the commission of an offense or attempted offense specified in subdivision (c), shall be punished by an additional and consecutive term of imprisonment pursuant to subdivision (h) of Section 1170 for one, two, or three years.

(e) For purposes of imposing an enhancement under Section 1170.1, the enhancements under this section shall count as a single enhancement.

(f) Notwithstanding any other provision of law, the court may strike the additional punishment for the enhancements provided in subdivision (c) or (d) in an unusual case where the interests of justice would best be served, if the court specifies on the record and enters into the minutes the circumstances indicating that the interests of justice would best be served by that disposition.

XI. Revenue and Taxation Code Sections

Revenue and Taxation Code § 6369.6

(Added by Stats. 2022, Ch. 56, Sec. 12. (AB 195) Effective June 30, 2022.)

(a) There are exempted from the taxes imposed by this part the gross receipts from the sale in this state of, and the storage, use, or other consumption in this state of, medicinal cannabis or medicinal cannabis products as those terms are defined in Division 10 (commencing with Section 26000) of the Business and Professions Code when a person with an identification card or primary caregiver furnishes the seller with both their card issued under Section 11362.71 of the Health and Safety Code and a valid government-issued identification card.

(b) For purposes of this section, "person with an identification card" and "primary caregiver" have the same meanings as those terms are defined in Section 11362.7 of the Health and Safety Code.

Revenue and Taxation Code § 6414

(Amended by Stats. 2021, Ch. 70, Sec. 110. (AB 141) Effective July 12, 2021. Repealed on the date prescribed by its own conditions.)

(a) The storage, use, or other consumption in this state of medicinal cannabis or medicinal cannabis product shall be exempt from the use tax in either of the following circumstances:

(1) The medicinal cannabis or medicinal cannabis product is donated by a cannabis retailer licensed under Division 10 (commencing with Section 26000) of the Business and Professions Code to a medicinal cannabis patient.

(2) The medicinal cannabis or medicinal cannabis product is donated by a person licensed under Division 10 (commencing with Section 26000) of the Business and Professions Code to a cannabis retailer for subsequent donation to a medicinal cannabis patient.

(b) (1) The exemption specified in subdivision (a) shall apply only if the cannabis retailer certifies in writing to the licensee that donates the medicinal cannabis or medicinal cannabis product, in such a form as the department may prescribe, that the medicinal cannabis and medicinal cannabis product will be used in a manner and for a purpose specified in subdivision (a). The licensee that donates the medicinal cannabis or medicinal cannabis product shall keep a copy of the certification for no less than seven years. The certification in writing shall relieve the licensee that donates the medicinal cannabis or medicinal cannabis product of liability for use tax only if it is taken in good faith.

(2) If a licensee uses the donated medicinal cannabis or medicinal cannabis product in some manner or for some purpose other than those specified in subdivision (a), the licensee shall be liable for the payment of use tax, the measure of tax to the licensee shall be deemed that licensee's purchase price for similar product, and the licensee shall be subject to having their license suspended by the Department of Cannabis Control pursuant to Section 26031 of the Business and Professions Code.

(c) "Medicinal cannabis" and "medicinal cannabis product" shall have the same meaning as those terms are defined in Section 26001 of the Business and Professions Code.

(d) "Cannabis retailer" shall have the same meaning as that term is defined in Section 34010.

(e) "Medicinal cannabis patient" shall mean a qualified patient, as defined in Section 11362.7 of the Health and Safety Code, who possesses a physician's recommendation that complies with Article 25 (commencing with Section 2525) of Chapter 5 of Division 2 of the Business and Professions Code, or a qualified patient or primary caregiver for a qualified patient issued a valid identification card pursuant to Section 11362.71 of the Health and Safety Code.

(f) (1) This section shall become operative upon completion of the necessary changes to the track and trace program in order to implement the act adding this section, as determined by the Department of Food and Agriculture, or on March 1, 2020, whichever occurs first.

(2) This section shall remain in effect only until five years after it becomes operative, and as of that date is repealed.

Revenue and Taxation Code § 6479.3

(Amended by Stats. 2022, Ch. 56, Sec. 13. (AB 195) Effective June 30, 2022.)

(a) Except as provided in subdivision (k), any person whose estimated tax liability under this part averages ten thousand dollars ($10,000) or more per month, as determined by the department pursuant to methods of calculation prescribed by the department, shall remit amounts due by an electronic funds transfer under procedures prescribed by the department. Any person who collects use tax on a voluntary basis is not required to remit amounts due by electronic funds transfer.

(b) Any person whose estimated tax liability under this part averages less than ten thousand dollars ($10,000) per month or any person who voluntarily collects use tax may elect to remit amounts due by electronic funds transfer with the approval of the department.

(c) Any person remitting amounts due pursuant to subdivision (a) or (b) shall perform electronic funds transfer in compliance with the due dates set forth in Article 1 (commencing with Section 6451) and Article 1.1 (commencing with Section 6470). Payment is deemed complete on the date the electronic funds transfer is initiated, if settlement to the state's demand account occurs on or before the banking day following the date the transfer is initiated. If settlement to the state's demand account does not occur on or before the banking day following the date the transfer is initiated, payment is deemed to occur on the date settlement occurs.

(d) Any person remitting taxes by electronic funds transfer shall, on or before the due date of the remittance, file a return for the preceding reporting period in the form and manner prescribed by the department. Any person who fails to timely file the required return shall pay a penalty of 10 percent of the amount of taxes, exclusive of prepayments, with respect to the period for which the return is required.

(e) (1) Except as provided in paragraph (2), any person required to remit taxes pursuant to this article who remits those taxes by means other than appropriate electronic funds transfer shall pay a penalty of 10 percent of the taxes incorrectly remitted.

(2) A person required to remit prepayments pursuant to this article who remits a prepayment by means other than an appropriate electronic funds transfer shall pay a penalty of 6 percent of the prepayment amount incorrectly remitted.

(f) Except as provided in Sections 6476 and 6477, any person who fails to pay any tax to the state or any amount of tax required to be collected and paid to the state, except amounts of determinations made by the department under Article 2 (commencing with Section 6481) or Article 3 (commencing with Section 6511), within the time required shall pay a penalty of 10 percent of the tax or amount of tax, in addition to the tax or amount of tax, plus interest at the modified adjusted rate per month, or fraction thereof, established pursuant to Section 6591.5, from the date on which the tax or the amount of tax required to be collected became due and payable to the state until the date of payment.

(g) In determining whether a person's estimated tax liability averages ten thousand dollars ($10,000) or more per month, the department may consider tax returns filed pursuant to this part and any other information in the department's possession.

(h) Except as provided in subdivision (i), the penalties imposed by subdivisions (d), (e), and (f) shall be limited to a maximum of 10 percent of the taxes due, exclusive of prepayments, for any one return. Any person remitting taxes by electronic funds transfer shall be subject to the penalties under this section and not Section 6591.

(i) The penalties imposed with respect to paragraph (2) of subdivision (e) and Sections 6476 and 6477 shall be limited to a maximum of 6 percent of the prepayment amount.

(j) The department shall promulgate regulations pursuant to Chapter 3.5 (commencing with Section 11340) of Part 1 of Division 3 of Title 2 of the Government Code for purposes of implementing this section.

(k) (1) On and after January 1, 2022, a person licensed to engage in commercial cannabis activity under Division 10 (commencing with Section 26000) of the Business and Professions Code, may remit amounts due by a means other than electronic funds transfer, if the department deems it necessary to facilitate collection of amounts due.

(2) A person licensed to engage in commercial cannabis activity under Division 10 (commencing with Section 26000) of the Business and Professions Code that failed to remit amounts due by means of electronic funds transfer on and after January 1, 2022, and before January 1, 2023, is not subject to or is relieved of any of the penalties imposed by this section for that failure.

Revenue and Taxation Code § 17053.64

(Added by Stats. 2022, Ch. 56, Sec. 14. (AB 195) Effective June 30, 2022. Repealed as of December 1, 2028, by its own provisions.)

(a) (1) For each taxable year beginning on or after January 1, 2023, and before January 1, 2028, there shall be allowed a credit against the "net tax," as defined in Section 17039, to a qualified taxpayer equal to 25 percent of the total amount of the qualified taxpayer's qualified expenditures in the taxable year, subject to paragraph (2).

(2) (A) The credit allowable under this section in any taxable year to any qualified taxpayer shall be limited to a maximum of two hundred fifty thousand dollars ($250,000).

(B) For qualified taxpayers that are required to be included in a combined report under Section 25101 or authorized to be included in a combined report under Section 25101.15, the limit specified in subparagraph (A) shall be the aggregate amount of the credit claimed by all taxpayers that are required to be or authorized to be included in a combined report and in no instance shall the aggregate amount of credit claimed by a combined group exceed the limit specified in subparagraph (A).

(b) For purposes of this section:

(1) "Full-time employee" means an individual who is either of the following:

(A) Paid wages subject to withholding under Division 6 (commencing with Section 13000) of the Unemployment Insurance Code by the qualified taxpayer for services not less than an average of 35 hours per week.

(B) A salaried employee who was paid compensation during the taxable year for full-time employment, as described in Section 515 of the Labor Code, by the qualified taxpayer that is paid wages subject to withholding under Division 6 (commencing with Section 13000) of the Unemployment Insurance Code.

(2) "Minimum wage" means the wage established pursuant to Chapter 1 (commencing with Section 1171) of Part 4 of Division 2 of the Labor Code.

(3) "Qualified expenditures" means amounts paid or incurred by a qualified taxpayer for any of the following:

(A) Employment compensation for the full-time employees of the qualified taxpayer. For purposes of this subparagraph, "employment compensation" means wages paid to full-time employees who are paid no less than 150 percent but no more than 350 percent of the applicable minimum wage. The calculation of wages pursuant to this subparagraph may include the monetary value to the full-time employee of employer-provided group health insurance benefits, childcare benefits, employer contributions to employer-provided retirement benefits, or employer contributions to pension benefits.

(B) Safety-related equipment, training, and services. For purposes of this subparagraph, "safety-related equipment, training, and services" means equipment primarily used by employees of cannabis licensees to ensure their personal and occupational safety or the safety of customers of the cannabis licensees; training for nonmanagement employees on workplace hazards, including, but not limited to, training required pursuant to subparagraph (A) of paragraph (11) of subdivision (a) of Section 26051.5 of the Business and Professions Code; and services, including, but not limited to, safety audits, security guards, security cameras, and fire risk mitigation.

(C) Workforce development and safety training for employees of the qualified taxpayer. For purposes of this subparagraph, "workforce development" includes, but is not limited to, joint labor management training programs, membership in a joint apprenticeship training committee registered by the Division of Apprenticeship Standards, and a state-recognized high road training partnership as defined in Section 14005 of the Unemployment Insurance Code.

(4) "Qualified taxpayer" means a commercial cannabis business, licensed pursuant to Division 10 (commencing with Section 26000) of the Business and Professions Code, and that provides full-time employees with all of the following:

(A) Employment compensation, as described in subparagraph (A) of paragraph (3).

(B) Employer-provided group health insurance.

(C) Employer-provided retirement benefits or pension benefits, including stock in the duly licensed commercial cannabis employer to employees under employee stock ownership plans where the employer pays for the full value of the stock.

(D) Possesses a Type-10 or a Type-12 license pursuant to Section 26050 of the Business and Professions

Code.

(c) The total aggregate amount of the credit that may be allocated by credit reservations to all qualified taxpayers pursuant to this section and Section 23664 shall not exceed twenty million dollars ($20,000,000) for all taxable years, cumulatively.

(d) To be eligible for the credit allowed by this section, a qualified taxpayer shall request a credit reservation from the Franchise Tax Board during the month of July for each taxable year or within 30 days of the start of their taxable year if the qualified taxpayer's taxable year begins after July, in the form and manner prescribed by the Franchise Tax Board.

(e) To obtain a credit reservation with respect to a qualified expenditure, the qualified taxpayer shall provide all necessary information, as determined by the Franchise Tax Board.

(f) The Franchise Tax Board shall approve tentative credit reservations with respect to qualified expenditures incurred during a taxable year for qualified taxpayers, subject to the cap established under this section and Section 23664.

(g) In the case where the credit allowed by this section exceeds the "net tax," the excess may be carried over to reduce the "net tax" in the following taxable year, and the seven succeeding years if necessary, until the credit is exhausted.

(h) If the credit allowed by this section is claimed by the qualified taxpayer, any deduction or credit otherwise allowed under this part for any qualified expenditure made by the qualified taxpayer as a trade or business expense shall be reduced by the amount of the credit allowed by this section.

(i) The Franchise Tax Board may prescribe rules, guidelines, or procedures necessary or appropriate to carry out the purposes of this section, including any guidelines regarding the allocation of the credit allowed under this section. Chapter 3.5 (commencing with Section 11340) of Part 1 of Division 3 of Title 2 of the Government Code shall not apply to any rule, guideline, or procedure prescribed by the Franchise Tax Board pursuant to this section.

(j) This section shall remain in effect only until December 1, 2028, and as of that date is repealed.

Revenue and Taxation Code § 17053.82

(Added by Stats. 2022, Ch. 56, Sec. 15. (AB 195) Effective June 30, 2022. Repealed as of December 1, 2028, by its own provisions.)

(a) For each taxable year beginning on or after January 1, 2023, and before January 1, 2028, there shall be allowed a credit against the "net tax," as defined in Section 17039, to a qualified taxpayer in an amount equal to ten thousand dollars ($10,000).

(b) For purposes of this section, "qualified taxpayer" means an equity licensee that has received approval, including approval contingent upon the availability of funds, for the fee waiver and deferral program established pursuant to Section 26249 of the Business and Professions Code, as administered by the Department of Cannabis Control.

(c) On January 1, 2024, and every 6 months thereafter, the Department of Cannabis Control shall provide the Franchise Tax Board with a list of qualified taxpayers for the purposes of administering this section. The Department of Cannabis Control may satisfy this requirement by maintaining a database that makes this information available to the Franchise Tax Board.

(d) In the case where the credit allowed by this section exceeds the "net tax," the excess may be carried over to reduce the "net tax" in the following taxable year, and succeeding seven years if necessary, until the credit is exhausted.

(e) The Franchise Tax Board may prescribe rules, guidelines, or procedures necessary or appropriate to carry out the purposes of this section, including any guidelines regarding the allocation of the credit allowed under this section.

Chapter 3.5 (commencing with Section 11340) of Part 1 of Division 3 of Title 2 of the Government Code shall not apply to any rule, guideline, or procedure prescribed by the Franchise Tax Board pursuant to this section.

(f) This section and Section 23682 shall be known and may be cited as the Cannabis Equity Tax Credit.

(g) This section shall remain in effect only until December 1, 2028, and as of that date is repealed.

Revenue and Taxation Code § 17209

(Added by Stats. 2019, Ch. 792, Sec. 1. (AB 37) Effective October 12, 2019. Repealed as of December 1, 2025, by its own provisions.)

(a) For each taxable year beginning on or after January 1, 2020, and before January 1, 2025, Section 280E of the Internal Revenue Code, relating to expenditures in connection with the illegal sale of drugs, shall not apply to the carrying on of any trade or business that is commercial cannabis activity by a licensee.

(b) For purposes of this section, "commercial cannabis activity" and "licensee" shall have the same meanings as set forth in Division 10 (commencing with Section 26000) of the Business and Professions Code.

(c) This section shall remain in effect only until December 1, 2025, and as of that date is repealed.

Revenue and Taxation Code § 23664

(Added by Stats. 2022, Ch. 56, Sec. 16. (AB 195) Effective June 30, 2022. Repealed as of December 1, 2028, by its own provisions.)

(a) (1) For each taxable year beginning on or after January 1, 2023, and before January 1, 2028, there shall be allowed a credit against the "tax," as defined in Section 23036, to a qualified taxpayer equal to 25 percent of the total amount of the qualified taxpayer's qualified expenditures in the taxable year, subject to paragraph (2).

(2) (A) The credit allowable under this section in any taxable year to any qualified taxpayer shall be limited to a maximum of two hundred fifty thousand dollars ($250,000).

(B) For qualified taxpayers that are required to be included in a combined report under Section 25101 or authorized to be included in a combined report under Section 25101.15, the limit specified in subparagraph (A) shall be the aggregate amount of the credit claimed by all taxpayers that are required to be or authorized to be included in a combined report and in no instance shall the aggregate amount of credit claimed by a combined group exceed the limit specified in subparagraph (A).

(b) For purposes of this section:

(1) "Full-time employee" means an individual who is either of the following:

(A) Paid wages subject to withholding under Division 6 (commencing with Section 13000) of the Unemployment Insurance Code by the qualified taxpayer for services not less than an average of 35 hours per week.

(B) A salaried employee who was paid compensation during the taxable year for full-time employment, as described in Section 515 of the Labor Code, by the qualified taxpayer that is paid wages subject to withholding under Division 6 (commencing with Section 13000) of the Unemployment Insurance Code.

(2) "Minimum wage" means the wage established pursuant to Chapter 1 (commencing with Section 1171) of Part 4 of Division 2 of the Labor Code.

(3) "Qualified expenditures" means amounts paid or incurred by a qualified taxpayer for any of the following:

(A) Employment compensation for the full-time employees of the qualified taxpayer. For purposes of this subparagraph, "employment compensation" means wages paid to full-time employees who are paid no less than 150 percent but no more than 350 percent of the applicable minimum wage. The calculation of wages pursuant to this subparagraph may include the monetary value to the full-time employee of employer-provided group health insurance benefits, childcare benefits, employer contributions to employer-provided retirement benefits, or employer contributions to pension benefits.

(B) Safety-related equipment, training, and services. For purposes of this subparagraph, "safety-related equipment, training, and services" means equipment primarily used by employees of cannabis licensees to ensure their personal and occupational safety or the safety of customers of the cannabis licensees; training for nonmanagement employees on workplace hazards, including, but not limited to, training required pursuant to subparagraph (A) of paragraph (11) of subdivision (a) of Section 26051.5 of the Business and Professions Code; and services, including, but not limited to, safety audits, security guards, security cameras, and fire risk mitigation.

(C) Workforce development and safety training for employees of the qualified taxpayer. For purposes of this subparagraph, "workforce development" includes, but is not limited to, joint labor management training programs, membership in a joint apprenticeship training committee registered by the Division of Apprenticeship Standards, and a state-recognized high road training partnership as defined in Section 14005 of the Unemployment Insurance Code.

(4) "Qualified taxpayer" means a commercial cannabis business, licensed pursuant to Division 10 (commencing with Section 26000) of the Business and Professions Code, and that provides full-time employees with all of the following:

(A) Employment compensation, as described in subparagraph (A) of paragraph (3).

(B) Employer-provided group health insurance.

(C) Employer-provided retirement benefits or pension benefits, including stock in the duly licensed commercial cannabis employer to employees under employee stock ownership plans where the employer pays for the full value of the stock.

(D) Possesses a Type-10 or a Type-12 license pursuant to Section 26050 of the Business and Professions Code.

(c) The total aggregate amount of the credit that may be allocated by credit reservations to all qualified taxpayers pursuant to this section and Section 17053.64 shall not exceed twenty million dollars ($20,000,000) for all taxable years, cumulatively.

(d) To be eligible for the credit allowed by this section, a qualified taxpayer shall request a credit reservation from the Franchise Tax Board during the month of July for each taxable year or within 30 days of the start of their taxable year if the qualified taxpayer's taxable year begins after July, in the form and manner prescribed by the Franchise Tax Board.

(e) To obtain a credit reservation with respect to a qualified expenditure, the qualified taxpayer shall provide all necessary information, as determined by the Franchise Tax Board.

(f) The Franchise Tax Board shall approve tentative credit reservations with respect to qualified expenditures incurred during a taxable year for qualified taxpayers, subject to the cap established under this section and Section 17053.64.

(g) In the case where the credit allowed by this section exceeds the "tax," the excess may be carried over to reduce the "tax" in the following taxable year, and the seven succeeding years if necessary, until the credit is exhausted.

(h) If the credit allowed by this section is claimed by the qualified taxpayer, any deduction or credit otherwise allowed under this part for any qualified expenditure made by the qualified taxpayer as a trade or business expense shall be reduced by the amount of the credit allowed by this section.

(i) The Franchise Tax Board may prescribe rules, guidelines, or procedures necessary or appropriate to carry out the purposes of this section, including any guidelines regarding the allocation of the credit allowed under this section. Chapter 3.5 (commencing with Section 11340) of Part 1 of Division 3 of Title 2 of the Government Code shall not apply to any rule, guideline, or procedure prescribed by the Franchise Tax Board pursuant to this section.

(j) This section shall remain in effect only until December 1, 2028, and as of that date is repealed.

Revenue and Taxation Code § 23682

(Added by Stats. 2022, Ch. 56, Sec. 17. (AB 195) Effective June 30, 2022. Repealed as of December 1, 2028, by its own provisions.)

(a) For each taxable year beginning on or after January 1, 2023, and before January 1, 2028, there shall be allowed a credit against the "tax," as defined in Section 23036, to a qualified taxpayer in an amount equal to ten thousand dollars ($10,000).

(b) For purposes of this section, "qualified taxpayer" means an equity licensee that has received approval, including approval contingent upon the availability of funds, for the fee waiver and deferral program established pursuant to Section 26249 of the Business and Professions Code, as administered by the Department of Cannabis Control.

(c) On January 1, 2024, and every six months thereafter, the Department of Cannabis Control shall provide the Franchise Tax Board with a list of qualified taxpayers for the purposes of administering this section. The Department of Cannabis Control may satisfy this requirement by maintaining a database that makes this information available to the Franchise Tax Board.

(d) In the case where the credit allowed by this section exceeds the "tax," the excess may be carried over to reduce the "tax" in the following taxable year, and succeeding seven years if necessary, until the credit is exhausted.

(e) This section and Section 17053.82 shall be known and may be cited as the Cannabis Equity Tax Credit.

(f) The Franchise Tax Board may prescribe rules, guidelines, or procedures necessary or appropriate to carry out the purposes of this section, including any guidelines regarding the allocation of the credit allowed under this section. Chapter 3.5 (commencing with Section 11340) of Part 1 of Division 3 of Title 2 of the Government Code shall not apply to any rule, guideline, or procedure prescribed by the Franchise Tax Board pursuant to this section.

(g) This section shall remain in effect only until December 1, 2028, and as of that date is repealed.

Revenue and Taxation Code § 34010

(Amended by Stats. 2022, Ch. 56, Sec. 18. (AB 195) Effective June 30, 2022. Note: This section was added on Nov. 8, 2016, by initiative Prop. 64.)

This part shall be known, and may be cited, as the "Cannabis Tax Law." For purposes of this part:

(a) "2020–21 fiscal year baseline" means the total amount of funds disbursed in the sub-trust accounts in fiscal year 2021–22 for the third allocation of the fiscal year 2020–21 revenue, pursuant to subdivision (f) of Section 34019, as determined by the Department of Finance.

(b) "Arm's length transaction" shall mean a sale entered into in good faith and for valuable consideration that reflects the fair market value in the open market between two informed and willing parties, neither under any compulsion to participate in the transaction.

(c) "Average market price" shall mean both of the following:

(1) (A) In an arm's length transaction, the average retail price determined by the wholesale cost of the cannabis or cannabis products sold or transferred to a cannabis retailer, plus a mark-up, as determined by the department on a biannual basis in six-month intervals.

(B) Notwithstanding subparagraph (A), the department shall not increase the mark-up amount during the period beginning on and after the operative date of the act amending this section by adding this subparagraph and before July 1, 2021.

(2) In a nonarm's length transaction, the cannabis retailer's gross receipts from the retail sale of the cannabis or cannabis products.

(d) "Cannabis" has the same meaning as set forth in Section 11018 of the Health and Safety Code and shall also mean medicinal cannabis.

(e) "Cannabis products" has the same meaning as set forth in Section 11018.1 of the Health and Safety Code and shall also mean medicinal concentrates and medicinal cannabis products.

(f) "Cannabis flowers" means the dried flowers of the cannabis plant as defined by the department.

(g) "Cannabis leaves" means all parts of the cannabis plant other than cannabis flowers that are sold or consumed.

(h) "Cannabis retailer" means a person required to be licensed pursuant to Division 10 (commencing with Section 26000) of the Business and Professions Code as a retailer, non-storefront retailer, microbusiness, or nonprofit, or any other person otherwise authorized under Division 10 (commencing with Section 26000) of the Business and Professions Code to engage in retail sales.

(i) "Cultivator" means all persons required to be licensed to cultivate cannabis pursuant to Division 10 (commencing with Section 26000) of the Business and Professions Code.

(j) "Department" means the California Department of Tax and Fee Administration or its successor agency.

(k) "Designated for donation" means medicinal cannabis donated by a cultivator to a cannabis retailer for subsequent donation to a medicinal cannabis patient pursuant to Section 26071 of the Business and Professions Code.

(l) "Distributor" means a person required to be licensed as a distributor pursuant to Division 10 (commencing with Section 26000) of the Business and Professions Code.

(m) "Enters the commercial market" means cannabis or cannabis products, except for immature cannabis plants and seeds, that complete and comply with a quality assurance review and testing, as described in Section 26110 of the Business and Professions Code.

(n) "Gross receipts" has the same meaning as set forth in Section 6012.

(o) "Manufacturer" means a person required to be licensed as a manufacturer pursuant to Division 10 (commencing with Section 26000) of the Business and Professions Code.

(p) "Medicinal cannabis patient" means a qualified patient, as defined in Section 11362.7 of the Health and Safety Code, who possesses a physician's recommendation that complies with Article 25 (commencing with Section 2525) of Chapter 5 of Division 2 of the Business and Professions Code, or a qualified patient or primary caregiver for a qualified patient issued a valid identification card pursuant to Section 11362.71 of the Health and Safety Code.

(q) "Microbusiness" has the same meaning as set forth in Section 26001 of the Business and Professions Code.

(r) "Nonprofit" has the same meaning as set forth in Section 26070.5 of the Business and Professions Code.

(s) "Person" has the same meaning as set forth in Section 6005.

(t) "Retail sale" has the same meaning as set forth in Section 6007.

(u) "Sale" and "purchase" mean any change of title or possession, exchange, or barter, conditional or otherwise, in any manner or by any means whatsoever, for consideration.

(v) "Sub-trust accounts" means the sub-trust accounts created under subdivision (f) of Section 34019.

(w) "Tax fund" means the California Cannabis Tax Fund created by Section 34018.

(x) "Transfer" means to grant, convey, hand over, assign, sell, exchange, or barter, in any manner or by any means, with or without consideration.

(y) "Unprocessed cannabis" includes cannabis flowers, cannabis leaves, or other categories of harvested cannabis, categories for unprocessed or frozen cannabis or immature plants, or cannabis that is shipped directly to manufacturers.

Revenue and Taxation Code § 34011

(Amended by Stats. 2022, Ch. 56, Sec. 19. (AB 195) Effective June 30, 2022. Inoperative April 1, 2023, by its own provisions. Conditionally inoperative as prescribed by Stats. 2022, Ch. 56, Sec. 41. Repealed conditionally as prescribed by Stats. 2022, Ch. 56, Sec. 41. See later operative version as amended by Stats. 2021, Ch. 70. Note: This section was added on Nov. 8, 2016, by initiative Prop. 64.)

(a) (1) Effective on and after January 1, 2018, and before January 1, 2023, a cannabis excise tax shall be imposed upon purchasers of cannabis or cannabis products sold in this state at the rate of 15 percent of the average market price of any retail sale by a cannabis retailer. A purchaser's liability for the cannabis excise tax is not extinguished until the cannabis excise tax has been paid to this state except that an invoice, receipt, or other document from a cannabis retailer given to the purchaser pursuant to this subdivision is sufficient to relieve the purchaser from further liability for the tax to which the invoice, receipt, or other document refers.

(2) Each cannabis retailer shall provide a purchaser with an invoice, receipt, or other document that includes a statement that reads: "The cannabis excise taxes are included in the total amount of this invoice."

(3) The department may prescribe other means to display the cannabis excise tax on an invoice, receipt, or other document from a cannabis retailer given to the purchaser.

(b) (1) A distributor in an arm's length transaction shall collect the cannabis excise tax imposed by this section from the cannabis retailer on or before 90 days after the sale or transfer of cannabis or cannabis product to the cannabis retailer. A distributor in a nonarm's length transaction shall collect the cannabis excise tax from the cannabis retailer on or before 90 days after the sale or transfer of cannabis or cannabis product to the cannabis retailer, or at the time of retail sale by the cannabis retailer, whichever is earlier. A distributor shall report and remit the cannabis excise tax to the department pursuant to Section 34015. A cannabis retailer shall be responsible for collecting the cannabis excise tax from the purchaser and remitting the cannabis excise tax to the distributor in accordance with rules and procedures established under law and any regulations adopted by the department.

(2) A distributor shall provide an invoice, receipt, or other similar document to the cannabis retailer that identifies the licensee receiving the product, the distributor from which the product originates, including the associated unique identifier, the amount of cannabis excise tax, and any other information deemed necessary by the department. The department may authorize other forms of documentation under this paragraph.

(c) The cannabis excise tax imposed by this section shall be in addition to the sales and use tax imposed by the state and local governments.

(d) Gross receipts from the sale of cannabis or cannabis products for purposes of assessing the sales and use taxes under Part 1 (commencing with Section 6001) shall include the tax levied pursuant to this section.

(e) Cannabis or cannabis products shall not be sold to a purchaser unless the cannabis excise tax imposed by this section has been paid by the purchaser at the time of sale.

(f) This section shall not be construed to impose a cannabis excise tax upon medicinal cannabis, or medicinal cannabis product, donated for no consideration to a medicinal cannabis patient pursuant to Section 26071 of the Business and Professions Code.

(g) (1) This section shall not be construed to impose a cannabis excise tax upon cannabis or cannabis products designated as a trade sample pursuant to Section 26153.1 of the Business and Professions Code.

(2) A person licensed under Division 10 (commencing with Section 26000) of the Business and Professions Code that sells cannabis or cannabis products designated as a trade sample pursuant to Section 26153.1 of the Business and Professions Code shall be liable for the cannabis excise tax imposed by this section as if the person were a cannabis retailer at the time of sale.

(h) This section shall be inoperative on April 1, 2023.

Revenue and Taxation Code § 34011.01

(Added by Stats. 2022, Ch. 56, Sec. 20. (AB 195) Effective June 30, 2022.)

(a) Any amount owed by a cannabis retailer to a distributor in connection with the collection of cannabis excise tax owed prior to January 1, 2023, shall be paid by the retailer to the distributor on or before April 1, 2023. This section shall not be construed to require the department to enforce this obligation.

(b) A cannabis retailer may claim a credit on the cannabis excise tax return for cannabis excise tax amounts paid to a distributor, pursuant to Section 34011, before January 1, 2023, on cannabis or cannabis products sold to a purchaser on or after January 1, 2023, for which the cannabis retailer is responsible for remitting to the department.

Revenue and Taxation Code § 34011.1

(Added by Stats. 2022, Ch. 56, Sec. 21. (AB 195) Effective June 30, 2022. Conditionally inoperative as prescribed by Stats. 2022, Ch. 56, Sec. 41. Repealed conditionally as prescribed by Stats. 2022, Ch. 56, Sec. 41.)

(a) (1) Until December 31, 2025, a licensed cannabis retailer that has received approval from the Department of Cannabis Control for a fee waiver under Section 26249 of the Business and Professions Code may retain vender compensation in an amount equal to 20 percent of the cannabis excise tax. For purposes of this paragraph, approval for a fee waiver under Section 26249 includes approval for a fee waiver that is contingent upon the availability of funds.

(2) To apply to retain vendor compensation pursuant to this section, a cannabis retailer shall complete a one-page application in a form and manner prescribed by the department that sets forth the name under which they transact or intend to transact business, the location of their place or places of business, and any other information the department may require. The cannabis retailer shall also include with the application their seller's permit number and cannabis tax permit number and a copy of their cannabis license and Department of Cannabis Control approved fee waiver. An application for a permit shall be authenticated in a form or pursuant to methods as may be prescribed by the department.

(3) Upon verification that a licensed cannabis retailer meets the requirements of this subdivision, the department shall issue the cannabis retailer a notice approving vendor compensation under this section.

(4) To maintain eligibility for vendor compensation under this section, a licensed cannabis retailer shall maintain eligibility for a fee waiver under Section 26249 of the Business and Professions Code and any relevant implementing

regulations. An approval for vendor compensation under this section shall expire on the last day of the calendar quarter following notification to the department pursuant to paragraph (5) that a cannabis retailer is no longer eligible for a fee waiver. If a cannabis retailer maintains eligibility for a fee waiver, an approval for vendor compensation under this subdivision shall remain valid for one year commencing on the first day of the calendar quarter following the date the department issues the notice, and may be renewed pursuant to paragraph (2) or other procedures as may be prescribed by the department.

(5) To notify the department of a cannabis retailer's eligibility for vendor compensation under this section, the Department of Cannabis Control shall do either of the following:

(A) Maintain a database accessible to the department reflecting whether a cannabis retailer is eligible or has become ineligible for a fee waiver under Section 26249 of the Business and Professions Code and implementing regulations.

(B) Otherwise provide information upon request of the department for purposes of verifying a cannabis retailer's eligibility under this section.

(b) This section shall become operative on January 1, 2023.

Revenue and Taxation Code § 34011.2

(Added by Stats. 2022, Ch. 56, Sec. 22. (AB 195) Effective June 30, 2022. Conditionally inoperative as prescribed by Stats. 2022, Ch. 56, Sec. 41. Repealed conditionally as prescribed by Stats. 2022, Ch. 56, Sec. 41.)

(a) (1) Effective on and after January 1, 2023, a cannabis excise tax shall be imposed upon purchasers of cannabis or cannabis products sold in this state at 15 percent of the gross receipts of any retail sale by a cannabis retailer.

(2) For the 2025–26 fiscal year and every two years thereafter, the department, in consultation with the Department of Finance, shall on or before May 1 of the fiscal year immediately preceding the applicable fiscal year, adjust the cannabis excise tax rate upon purchasers of cannabis or cannabis products imposed in paragraph (1) by the additional percentage of the gross receipts of any retail sale by a cannabis retailer that the department estimates will generate an amount of revenue equivalent to the amount that would have been collected in the previous fiscal year pursuant to the weight-based cultivation tax imposed under Section 34012 as it read on the date before the effective date of the act adding this section. In no case shall the cannabis excise tax exceed 19 percent of the gross receipts of retail sale. The department shall round the rate calculated under this subdivision to the nearest one-quarter of 1 percent. The adjusted rate shall become operative the following July 1.

(3) On or before May 1, 2025, and each May 1 every two years thereafter, the department, in consultation with the Department of Finance, shall estimate the amount of revenue that would have been collected in the previous fiscal year pursuant to the weight-based cultivation tax imposed under Section 34012 as it read on the date before the effective date of the act adding this section. The department shall estimate this amount by projecting the revenue from weight-based cultivation taxes that would have been collected in the previous calendar year based on information available to the department, including, but not limited to, information in the track and trace system required pursuant to Chapter 6.5 (commencing with Section 26067) of Division 10 of the Business and Professions Code, or any implementing regulations, as a percentage of gross receipts from the retail sale of cannabis and cannabis products by cannabis retailers in the previous calendar year.

(b) A purchaser's liability for the cannabis excise tax is not extinguished until the cannabis excise tax has been paid to this state, except that an invoice, receipt, or other document from a cannabis retailer given to the purchaser pursuant to this section is sufficient to relieve the purchaser from further liability for the tax to which the invoice, receipt, or other document refers.

(c) A cannabis retailer shall be responsible for collecting the cannabis excise tax from the purchaser and remitting that tax to the department in accordance with this division.

(d) The cannabis retailer shall provide each purchaser with an invoice, receipt, or other document that separately states the cannabis excise tax.

(e) The cannabis excise tax imposed by this section shall be in addition to the sales and use tax imposed by the state and local governments.

(f) Gross receipts from the sale of cannabis or cannabis products for purposes of assessing the sales and use taxes under Part 1 (commencing with Section 6001) shall include the tax levied pursuant to this section.

(g) Cannabis or cannabis products shall not be sold to a purchaser unless the cannabis excise tax imposed by this section has been paid by the purchaser at the time of sale.

(h) This section shall not be construed to impose a cannabis excise tax upon medicinal cannabis, or medicinal cannabis product, donated for no consideration to a medicinal cannabis patient pursuant to Section 26071 of the Business and Professions Code.

(i) (1) This section shall not be construed to impose a cannabis excise tax upon cannabis or cannabis products designated as a trade sample pursuant to Section 26153.1 of the Business and Professions Code.

(2) A person licensed under Division 10 (commencing with Section 26000) of the Business and Professions Code that sells cannabis or cannabis products designated as a trade sample pursuant to Section 26153.1 of the Business and Professions Code shall be liable for the cannabis excise tax imposed by this section as if the person were a cannabis retailer at the time of sale.

(j) This section shall become operative on January 1, 2023.

Revenue and Taxation Code § 34012

(Amended by Stats. 2022, Ch. 56, Sec. 23. (AB 195) Effective June 30, 2022. Conditionally inoperative as prescribed by Stats. 2022, Ch. 56, Sec. 41. Repealed conditionally as prescribed by Stats. 2022, Ch. 56, Sec. 41. See later operative version as amended by Stats. 2021, Ch. 70. Note: This section was added on Nov. 8, 2016, by initiative Prop. 64.)

(a) (1) Effective January 1, 2018, and before July 1, 2022, there is hereby imposed a cultivation tax on all harvested cannabis that enters the commercial market upon all cultivators. The tax shall be due after the cannabis is harvested and enters the commercial market.

> (A) The tax for cannabis flowers shall be nine dollars and twenty-five cents ($9.25) per dry-weight ounce.
>
> (B) The tax for cannabis leaves shall be set at two dollars and seventy-five cents ($2.75) per dry-weight ounce.

(2) Notwithstanding paragraph (1), the cultivation tax imposed by this subdivision shall not apply to harvested cannabis that enters the commercial market and no tax collection is required pursuant to subdivision (h) if any of the following apply:

> (A) The harvested cannabis was first sold or transferred by a cultivator to a manufacturer on or after July 1, 2022.
>
> (B) The harvested cannabis was first sold or transferred by a cultivator to a distributor on or after July 1, 2022.
>
> (C) The harvested cannabis, or cannabis products containing that harvested cannabis, was first sold or transferred by a microbusiness to a distributor or manufacturer that arranges for laboratory testing pursuant to subdivision (a) of Section 26110 of the Business and Professions Code on or after July 1, 2022.

(3) It is the intent of the Legislature that the suspension of the cultivation tax imposed by paragraph (2) apply only to cannabis that is ultimately subject, at retail sale as either cannabis or as cannabis products containing the harvested cannabis, to the cannabis excise tax imposed pursuant to Section 34011.2.

(b) The department may adjust the tax rate for cannabis leaves annually to reflect fluctuations in the relative price of cannabis flowers to cannabis leaves.

(c) The department may from time to time establish other categories of harvested cannabis, categories for unprocessed or frozen cannabis or immature plants, or cannabis that is shipped directly to manufacturers. These categories shall be taxed at their relative value compared with cannabis flowers.

(d) The department may prescribe by regulation a method and manner for payment of the cultivation tax that utilizes tax stamps or state-issued product bags that indicate that all required tax has been paid on the product to which the tax stamp is affixed or in which the cannabis is packaged.

(e) The tax stamps and product bags shall be of the designs, specifications, and denominations as may be prescribed by the department and may be purchased by any licensee under Division 10 (commencing with Section 26000) of the Business and Professions Code.

(f) Subsequent to the establishment of a tax stamp program, the department may by regulation provide that cannabis shall not be removed from a licensed cultivation facility or transported on a public highway unless in a state-issued product bag bearing a tax stamp in the proper denomination.

(g) The tax stamps and product bags shall be capable of being read by a scanning or similar device and must be traceable utilizing the track and trace system pursuant to Section 26068 of the Business and Professions Code.

(h) Cultivators shall be responsible for payment of the tax pursuant to regulations adopted by the department. A cultivator's liability for the tax is not extinguished until the tax has been paid to this state except that an invoice, receipt, or other document from a distributor or manufacturer given to the cultivator pursuant to paragraph (3) is sufficient to relieve the cultivator from further liability for the tax to which the invoice, receipt, or other document refers. Cannabis shall not be sold unless the tax has been paid as provided in this part.

(1) A distributor shall collect the cultivation tax from a cultivator on all harvested cannabis that enters the commercial market. This paragraph shall not apply where a cultivator is not required to send, and does not send, the harvested cannabis to a distributor.

(2) (A) A manufacturer shall collect the cultivation tax from a cultivator on the first sale or transfer of unprocessed cannabis by a cultivator to a manufacturer. The manufacturer shall remit the cultivation tax collected on the cannabis product sold or transferred to a distributor for quality assurance, inspection, and testing, as described in Section 26110 of the Business and Professions Code. This paragraph shall not apply where a distributor collects the cultivation tax from a cultivator pursuant to paragraph (1).

(B) Notwithstanding subparagraph (A), the department may prescribe a substitute method and manner for collection and remittance of the cultivation tax under this paragraph, including a method and manner for collection of the cultivation tax by a distributor.

(3) A distributor or manufacturer shall provide to the cultivator, and a distributor that collects the cultivation tax from a manufacturer pursuant to paragraph (2) shall provide to the manufacturer, an invoice, receipt, or other similar document that identifies the licensee receiving the product, the cultivator from which the product originates, including the associated unique identifier, the amount of cultivation tax, and any other information deemed necessary by the department. The department may authorize other forms of documentation under this paragraph.

(4) The department may adopt regulations prescribing procedures for the refund of cultivation tax collected on cannabis or cannabis product that fails quality assurance, inspection, and testing as described in Section 26110 of the Business and Professions Code.

(i) All cannabis removed from a cultivator's premises, except for plant waste or medicinal cannabis or medicinal cannabis products designated for donation, shall be presumed to be sold and thereby taxable under this section, except as otherwise exempt pursuant to Section 34012.2.

(j) The tax imposed by this section shall be imposed on all cannabis cultivated in the state pursuant to rules and regulations promulgated by the department, but shall not apply to cannabis cultivated for personal use under Section 11362.1 of the Health and Safety Code or cultivated by a qualified patient or primary caregiver in accordance with the Compassionate Use Act of 1996 (Proposition 215), found in Section 11362.5 of the Health and Safety Code.

(k) (1) For the 2020 calendar year, the rates set forth in subdivisions (a), (b), and (c) shall be adjusted by the department for inflation.

(2) For the 2021 calendar year, the rates shall be those imposed for the 2020 calendar year in paragraph (1) and shall not be adjusted for inflation unless the adjustment is for an inflation rate that is less than zero.

(3) For the 2022 calendar year, until July 1, 2022, the rates shall be those imposed for the 2021 calendar year in paragraph (2) and shall be adjusted by the department for inflation.

(l) The Department of Cannabis Control is not responsible for enforcing any provisions of the cultivation tax.

Revenue and Taxation Code § 34012.1

(Added by Stats. 2019, Ch. 837, Sec. 12. (SB 34) Effective January 1, 2020. Operative on or before March 1, 2020, as prescribed by its own conditions. Repealed on the date prescribed by its own conditions.)

(a) Notwithstanding Section 34012, on and after the operative date of the act adding this section, the cultivation tax shall not be imposed on medicinal cannabis designated for donation by a cultivator in the track and trace system.

(b) A person licensed under Division 10 (commencing with Section 26000) of the Business and Professions Code that certifies in writing that medicinal cannabis or a medicinal cannabis product will be donated to a medicinal cannabis patient and sells or uses the medicinal cannabis or medicinal cannabis product in some manner or for some purpose other than donation, shall be liable for the taxes under this part. The certification in writing shall relieve the cultivator that donates the medicinal cannabis from liability for the taxes imposed and shall relieve the distributor from liability for the taxes required to be collected under this part, only if the certification is taken in good faith.

(c) A distributor or manufacturer shall not collect or remit the cultivation tax for medicinal cannabis or medicinal cannabis products designated for donation by a cultivator.

(d) A cultivator shall keep records of any medicinal cannabis or medicinal cannabis products designated for donation.

(e) Nothing in this part shall be construed to impose a cultivation tax upon medicinal cannabis or medicinal cannabis products designated for donation.

(f) For purposes of this section, "medicinal cannabis" and "medicinal cannabis product" shall mean cannabis and cannabis product, as defined in Section 26001 of the Business and Professions Code, intended for use pursuant to the Compassionate Use Act of 1996 (Proposition 215), found in Section 11362.5 of the Health and Safety Code, by a medicinal cannabis patient.

(g) (1) This section shall become operative upon completion of the necessary changes to the track and trace program in order to implement the act adding this section, as determined by the Department of Food and Agriculture, or on March 1, 2020, whichever occurs first.

(2) This section shall remain in effect only until five years after it becomes operative, and as of that date is repealed.

Revenue and Taxation Code § 34012.2

(Added by Stats. 2021, Ch. 70, Sec. 114. (AB 141) Effective July 12, 2021.)

(a) On and after January 1, 2022, there is exempt from the cultivation tax imposed pursuant to Section 34012 the cultivation of all harvested cannabis that will be, or has been, designated a trade sample pursuant to Section 26153.1 of the Business and Professions Code and all harvested cannabis that is used to manufacture a cannabis product that is designated a trade sample pursuant to Section 26153.1 of the Business and Professions Code.

(b) The department shall adopt regulations prescribing the procedures for how the exemption provided in subdivision (a) shall be implemented.

(c) A person licensed under Division 10 (commencing with Section 26000) of the Business and Professions Code that sells cannabis exempt from the cultivation tax pursuant to subdivision (a) or sells any cannabis product that is manufactured with cannabis exempt from the cultivation tax pursuant to subdivision (a) shall be liable for the cultivation tax imposed by Section 34012 as if the person were a cultivator of the cannabis at the time of sale.

(d) Notwithstanding any other law, the department may adopt and readopt emergency regulations to implement this section. The provisions of this section shall be applicable to emergency regulations adopted or readopted pursuant to this section. The emergency regulations authorized by this section shall be deemed an emergency and necessary for the immediate preservation of public peace, health, safety or general welfare.

Revenue and Taxation Code § 34012.3

(Added by Stats. 2022, Ch. 56, Sec. 24. (AB 195) Effective June 30, 2022. Operative January 1, 2023, by its own provisions.)

(a) The cannabis excise tax required to be collected by a cannabis retailer, and any amount not returned to the purchaser that is not tax but was collected from the purchaser under the representation by the cannabis retailer that it was tax, constitutes debt owed by the cannabis retailer to this state.

(b) This section shall become operative on January 1, 2023.

Revenue and Taxation Code § 34012.5

(Amended by Stats. 2022, Ch. 56, Sec. 25. (AB 195) Effective June 30, 2022.)

(a) The cultivation tax and cannabis excise tax imposed pursuant to Section 34011 required to be collected by the distributor, or required to be collected by the manufacturer pursuant to paragraph (2) of subdivision (h) of Section 34012, and any amount unreturned to the cultivator or cannabis retailer that is not tax but was collected from the cultivator or cannabis retailer under the representation by the distributor or the manufacturer that it was tax constitute debts owed by the distributor or the manufacturer to this state.

(b) A distributor or manufacturer that has collected any amount of tax in excess of the amount of tax imposed by this part and actually due from a cultivator or cannabis retailer, may refund such amount to the cultivator or cannabis retailer, even though such tax amount has already been paid over to the department and no corresponding credit or refund has yet been secured. The distributor or manufacturer may claim credit for that overpayment against the amount of tax imposed by this part that is due upon any other quarterly return, providing that credit is claimed in a return dated no later than three years from the date of overpayment.

(c) Any tax collected from a cultivator, cannabis retailer, or purchaser that has not been remitted to the department shall be deemed a debt owed to the State of California by the person required to collect and remit the tax.

Revenue and Taxation Code § 34013

(Amended by Stats. 2022, Ch. 474, Sec. 40. (SB 1496) Effective January 1, 2023. Note: This section was added on Nov.

8, 2016, by initiative Prop. 64.)

(a) The department shall administer and collect the taxes imposed by this part pursuant to the Fee Collection Procedures Law (Part 30 (commencing with Section 55001)). For purposes of this part, the references in the Fee Collection Procedures Law to "fee" shall include the taxes imposed by this part, and references to "feepayer" shall include a person required to pay or collect the taxes imposed by this part.

(b) (1) A person licensed to engage in commercial cannabis activity under Division 10 (commencing with Section 26000) of the Business and Professions Code that failed to remit amounts due by means of electronic funds transfer on and after January 1, 2022, and before January 1, 2023, is not subject to or is relieved of any of the penalties imposed by Section 55050 for that failure.

(2) On or after January 1, 2022, subdivision (a) of Section 55050 shall not apply to a person required to pay or collect the taxes imposed by this part on a person licensed to engage in commercial cannabis activity under Division 10 (commencing with Section 26000) of the Business and Professions Code if the department deems it necessary to facilitate the collection of amounts due.

(c) The department may prescribe, adopt, and enforce regulations relating to the administration and enforcement of this part, including, but not limited to, collections, reporting, refunds, and appeals.

(d) The department shall adopt necessary rules and regulations to administer the taxes in this part. Such rules and regulations may include methods or procedures to tag cannabis or cannabis products, or the packages thereof, to designate prior tax payment.

(e) Until January 1, 2024, the department may prescribe, adopt, and enforce any emergency regulations as necessary to implement, administer, and enforce its duties under this division. Any emergency regulation prescribed, adopted, or enforced pursuant to this section shall be adopted in accordance with Chapter 3.5 (commencing with Section 11340) of Part 1 of Division 3 of Title 2 of the Government Code, and, for purposes of that chapter, including Section 11349.6 of the Government Code, the adoption of the regulation is an emergency and shall be considered by the Office of Administrative Law as necessary for the immediate preservation of the public peace, health and safety, and general welfare. Notwithstanding any other law, the emergency regulations adopted by the department may remain in effect for two years from adoption, and may be readopted in accordance with subdivision (h) of Section 11346.1 of the Government Code.

(f) Any person required to be licensed pursuant to Division 10 (commencing with Section 26000) of the Business and Professions Code who fails to pay the taxes imposed under this part shall, in addition to owing the taxes not paid, be subject to a penalty of at least one-half the amount of the taxes not paid, and shall be subject to having its license revoked pursuant to Section 26031 of the Business and Professions Code.

(g) The department may bring such legal actions as are necessary to collect any deficiency in the tax required to be paid, and, upon the department's request, the Attorney General shall bring the actions.

Revenue and Taxation Code § 34014

(Amended by Stats. 2022, Ch. 56, Sec. 27. (AB 195) Effective June 30, 2022. Note: This section was added on Nov. 8, 2016, by initiative Prop. 64.)

(a) (1) Until January 1, 2023, all distributors must obtain a separate permit from the department pursuant to regulations adopted by the department. No fee shall be charged to any person for issuance of the permit. Any person required to obtain a permit who engages in business as a distributor without a permit or after a permit has been canceled, suspended, or revoked, and each officer of any corporation that so engages in business, is guilty of a misdemeanor.

(2) On and after January 1, 2023, all cannabis retailers shall obtain a separate cannabis tax permit from the

department pursuant to regulations adopted by the department. A fee shall not be charged to any person for issuance of the permit. Any person required to obtain a permit who engages in business as a cannabis retailer without a permit or after a permit has been canceled, suspended, or revoked, and each officer of any corporation that so engages in business, is guilty of a misdemeanor.

(b) The department may require every licensed distributor, retailer, cultivator, microbusiness, nonprofit, or other person required to be licensed, to provide security to cover the liability for taxes imposed by state law on cannabis produced or received by the retailer, cultivator, microbusiness, nonprofit, or other person required to be licensed in accordance with procedures to be established by the department. Notwithstanding anything herein to the contrary, the department may waive any security requirement it imposes for good cause, as determined by the department. "Good cause" includes, but is not limited to, the inability of a distributor, retailer, cultivator, microbusiness, nonprofit, or other person required to be licensed to obtain security due to a lack of service providers or the policies of service providers that prohibit service to a cannabis business.

(c) In fixing the amount of any security required by the department, the department shall give consideration to the financial hardship that may be imposed on licensees as a result of any shortage of available surety providers.

Revenue and Taxation Code § 34014.1

(Added by Stats. 2022, Ch. 56, Sec. 28. (AB 195) Effective June 30, 2022.)

(a) Whenever any person fails to comply with any provision of this part relating to the cannabis excise tax or any rule or regulation of the department relating to the cannabis excise tax prescribed and adopted under this part, or when a person's seller's permit has been suspended or revoked under Part 1 (commencing with Section 6001), or when a person's license has been suspended or revoked under Division 10 (commencing with Section 26000) of the Business and Professions Code, the department upon conducting a hearing, after giving the person 10 days' notice in writing specifying the time and place of hearing and requiring the person to show cause why the person's permit or permits should not be revoked, may revoke or suspend any one or more of the permits held by the person. The department shall give to the person written notice of the suspension or revocation of any of the person's permits. The notices herein required may be served personally or by mail in the manner prescribed for service of notice of a deficiency determination under subdivision (d) of Section 55061 of the Revenue and Taxation Code. The department shall not issue a new permit after the revocation of a permit unless it is satisfied that the former holder of the permit will comply with the provisions of this part relating to the cannabis excise tax and the regulations of the department.

(b) A person whose permit has been previously suspended or revoked shall pay the department a new issuance fee of one hundred dollars ($100) for the reissuance of a permit.

Revenue and Taxation Code § 34015

(Amended by Stats. 2022, Ch. 56, Sec. 29. (AB 195) Effective June 30, 2022. Repealed as of April 30, 2023, by its own provisions. See later operative date added by Sec. 30 of Stats. 2022, Ch. 56. Note: This section was added on Nov. 8, 2016, by initiative Prop. 64.)

(a) Unless otherwise prescribed by the department pursuant to subdivision (c), the cannabis excise tax imposed by Section 34011 and cultivation tax imposed by this part is due and payable to the department quarterly on or before the last day of the month following each quarterly period of three months. On or before the last day of the month following each quarterly period, a return for the preceding quarterly period shall be filed with the department by each distributor using electronic media. Returns shall be authenticated in a form or pursuant to methods as may be prescribed by the department. If the cultivation tax is paid by stamp pursuant to subdivision (d) of Section 34012, the department may by regulation determine when and how the tax shall be paid.

(b) The department may require every person engaged in the cultivation, distribution, manufacturing, retail sale of cannabis or cannabis products, or any other person required to be licensed pursuant to Division 10 (commencing with Section 26000) of the Business and Professions Code to file, on or before the 25th day of each month, a report using electronic media respecting the person's inventory, purchases, and sales during the preceding month and any other information as the department may require to carry out the purposes of this part. Reports shall be authenticated in a form or pursuant to methods as may be prescribed by the department.

(c) The department may adopt regulations prescribing the due date for returns and remittances of cannabis excise tax collected by a distributor in an arm's length transaction pursuant to subdivision (b) of Section 34011.

(d) The department may make examinations of the books and records of any person licensed, or required to be licensed, pursuant to Division 10 (commencing with Section 26000) of the Business and Professions Code, as it may deem necessary in carrying out this part.

(e) This section shall remain in effect only until April 30, 2023, and as of that date is repealed.

Revenue and Taxation Code § 34015

(Repealed (in Sec. 29) and added by Stats. 2022, Ch. 56, Sec. 30. (AB 195) Effective June 30, 2022. Operative January 1, 2023, by its own provisions.)

(a) Unless otherwise prescribed by the department, the cannabis excise tax imposed by Section 34011.2 is due and payable to the department quarterly on or before the last day of the month following each quarterly period of three months. On or before the last day of the month following each quarterly period, each cannabis retailer shall file a return for the preceding quarterly period with the department using electronic media prescribed by the department. Returns shall be authenticated in a form or pursuant to methods as may be prescribed by the department.

(b) The department may require every person engaged in the cultivation, distribution, manufacturing, or retail sale of cannabis or cannabis products, or any other person required to be licensed pursuant to Division 10 (commencing with Section 26000) of the Business and Professions Code to file, on or before the 25th day of each month, a report using electronic media prescribed by the department with respect to the person's inventory, purchases, and sales during the preceding month and any other information as the department may require to carry out the purposes of this part. Reports shall be authenticated in a form or pursuant to methods as may be prescribed by the department.

(c) The department may examine the books and records of any person licensed, or required to be licensed, pursuant to Division 10 (commencing with Section 26000) of the Business and Professions Code, as it may deem necessary in carrying out this part.

(d) This section shall become operative on January 1, 2023.

Revenue and Taxation Code § 34015.1

(Added by Stats. 2022, Ch. 56, Sec. 31. (AB 195) Effective June 30, 2022.)

(a) (1) Any unlicensed person who is required to be licensed pursuant to Division 10 (commencing with Section 26000) of the Business and Professions Code and who possesses, keeps, stores, or retains for the purpose of sale, or sells or offers to sell any cannabis or cannabis products, shall be liable for the cultivation tax imposed pursuant to Section 34012 as if the person were the cultivator of the harvested cannabis and that cannabis entered the commercial market, the cannabis excise tax imposed pursuant to Section 34011 or 34011.2 as if the person were the purchaser of the cannabis or cannabis product in a retail sale from a cannabis retailer, and for applicable penalties and interest, if any, which shall become immediately due and payable.

(2) (A) The department shall ascertain as best it may the category and amount of the harvested cannabis deemed as having entered the commercial market, and the average market price or gross receipts, based on any information

within the department's possession or that may come into its possession, of the retail sale of the cannabis or cannabis product deemed as purchased from a cannabis retailer, and shall determine immediately the tax on that amount, adding to the tax a penalty of 25 percent of the amount of tax or five hundred dollars ($500), whichever is greater, and shall give the unlicensed person notice of that determination in the same manner as prescribed for service of notice by Section 55061. However, if the department determines that the failure to secure a license was due to reasonable cause, the department may waive the penalty. Sections 55101 and 55102 shall be applicable with respect to the finality of the determination and the right of the person to petition for a redetermination.

(B) Any person seeking to be relieved of the penalty imposed pursuant to subparagraph (A) shall file with the department a signed statement setting forth the facts upon which they base the claim for relief. Any person who signs a statement pursuant to this section that asserts the truth of any material matter that they know to be false is guilty of a misdemeanor punishable by imprisonment of up to one year in the county jail, or a fine of not more than one thousand dollars ($1,000), or both the imprisonment and the fine.

(3) If the department believes that the collection of any amount of tax required to be paid by any person under this part will be jeopardized by delay, it may make a jeopardy determination pursuant to Article 4 (commencing with Section 55101) of Chapter 3 of Part 30.

(4) The department may collect the tax, penalty, and interest due from the person by seizure and sale of property in the manner prescribed for the collection pursuant to Section 55181.

(5) In the suit, a copy of the jeopardy determination certified by the department shall be prima facie evidence that the person is indebted to the state in the amount of the tax, penalties, and interest at the modified adjusted rate per month, or fraction thereof, established pursuant to Section 6591.5, from the date the amount, or any portion thereof, should have been reported until the date of payment.

(6) The foregoing remedies of the state are cumulative.

(7) No action taken pursuant to this section relieves the person in any way from the penal provisions of this part or the Fee Collection Procedures Law (Part 30 (commencing with Section 55001)).

(b) Any licensed person, on or after January 1, 2023, who sells or transfers to any person cannabis or cannabis products and who knowingly does not report or falsely reports that sale or transfer in the track and trace system required pursuant to Chapter 6.5 (commencing with Section 26067) of Division 10 of the Business and Professions Code or any regulations promulgated for purposes of that chapter, shall be, with respect to the cannabis or cannabis products knowingly not reported or falsely reported in the track and trace system, liable for the cannabis excise tax imposed pursuant to Section 34011 or 34011.2 as if the person were the purchaser of the cannabis or cannabis product in a retail sale from a cannabis retailer, and for applicable penalties and interest, if any, which shall become immediately due and payable.

Revenue and Taxation Code § 34015.2

(Added by Stats. 2022, Ch. 56, Sec. 32. (AB 195) Effective June 30, 2022.)

(a) Upon the termination, dissolution, or abandonment of the business of a corporation, partnership, limited partnership, limited liability partnership, or limited liability company, any officer, member, manager, partner, or other person having control or supervision of, or who is charged with the responsibility for the filing of returns or the payment of tax for, or who is under a duty to act for the corporation, partnership, limited partnership, limited liability partnership, or limited liability company in complying with any requirement of this part, shall, notwithstanding any provision in the Corporations Code to the contrary, be personally liable for any unpaid taxes and interest and penalties on those taxes, if the officer, member, manager, partner, or other person willfully fails to pay or to cause to be paid any taxes due from the corporation, partnership, limited partnership, limited liability partnership, or limited liability company pursuant to this part.

(b) The officer, member, manager, partner, or other person shall be liable only for taxes that became due during the period they had the control, supervision, responsibility, or duty to act for the corporation, partnership, limited partnership, limited liability partnership, or limited liability company described in subdivision (a), plus interest and penalties on those taxes.

(c) Personal liability may be imposed pursuant to this section only if the department can establish that the corporation, partnership, limited partnership, limited liability partnership, or limited liability company is required to collect the cannabis excise tax imposed pursuant to Section 34011 or 34011.2 or cultivation tax imposed pursuant to Section 34012 and that it failed to report and pay the tax.

(d) Except as provided in subdivision (e), the sum due for the liability under this section may be collected by determination and collection in the manner provided in Chapter 3 (commencing with Section 55040) and Chapter 4 (commencing with Section 55121) of Part 30.

(e) A notice of deficiency determination under this section shall be mailed within three years after the last day of the calendar month following the quarterly period in which the department obtains actual knowledge, through its audit or compliance activities, or by written communication by the business or its representative, of the termination, dissolution, or abandonment of the business of the corporation, partnership, limited partnership, limited liability partnership, or limited liability company, or, within eight years after the last day of the calendar month following the quarterly period in which the corporation, partnership, limited partnership, limited liability partnership, or limited liability company business was terminated, dissolved, or abandoned, whichever period expires earlier. If a business or its representative files a notice of termination, dissolution, or abandonment of its business with a state or local agency other than the department, this filing shall not constitute actual knowledge by the department under this section.

(f) For purposes of this section, "willfully fails to pay or to cause to be paid" means that the failure was the result of an intentional, conscious, and voluntary course of action.

Revenue and Taxation Code § 34016

(Amended by Stats. 2022, Ch. 474, Sec. 42. (SB 1496) Effective January 1, 2023. Note: This section was added on Nov. 8, 2016, by initiative Prop. 64.)

(a) Any peace officer or department employee granted limited peace officer status pursuant to paragraph (6) of subdivision (a) of Section 830.11 of the Penal Code, upon presenting appropriate credentials, is authorized to enter any place as described in paragraph (2) and to conduct inspections in accordance with the following paragraphs, inclusive.

(1) Inspections shall be performed in a reasonable manner and at times that are reasonable under the circumstances, taking into consideration the normal business hours of the place to be entered.

(2) Inspections may be at any place at which cannabis or cannabis products are sold to purchasers, cultivated, or stored, or at any site where evidence of activities involving evasion of tax may be discovered.

(3) Inspections shall be conducted no more than once in a 24-hour period.

(b) Any person who fails or refuses to allow an inspection shall be guilty of a misdemeanor. Each offense shall be punished by a fine not to exceed five thousand dollars ($5,000), or imprisonment not exceeding one year in a county jail, or both the fine and imprisonment. The court shall order any fines assessed be deposited in the California Cannabis Tax Fund.

(c) (1) (A) The department or a law enforcement agency may seize cannabis or cannabis products from a person who possesses, stores, owns, or has made a retail sale of those cannabis or cannabis products if any of the following apply:

(i) Until January 1, 2023, the cannabis or cannabis products are without evidence of tax payment.

(ii) The cannabis or cannabis products are not contained in secure packaging.

(iii) The person is an unlicensed person specified in paragraph (1) of subdivision (a) of Section 34015.1.

(iv) The cannabis or cannabis products were not reported in the track and trace system, as specified in subdivision (b) of Section 34015.1.

(B) Any cannabis or cannabis products seized by a law enforcement agency or the department shall be deemed forfeited and the department shall comply with the procedures set forth in Sections 30436 through 30449, inclusive.

(2) Any seizures authorized pursuant to paragraph (1) of this subdivision are in addition to any criminal or civil penalties that may be imposed by law, including subdivision (e) of this section.

(d) Any person who renders a false or fraudulent report is guilty of a misdemeanor and subject to a fine not to exceed one thousand dollars ($1,000) for each offense.

(e) Any violation of any provisions of this part, except as otherwise provided, is a misdemeanor and is punishable as such.

(f) All moneys remitted to the department under this part shall be credited to the California Cannabis Tax Fund.

Revenue and Taxation Code § 34017

(Added November 8, 2016, by initiative Proposition 64, Sec. 7.1.)

The Legislative Analyst's Office shall submit a report to the Legislature by January 1, 2020, with recommendations to the Legislature for adjustments to the tax rate to achieve the goals of undercutting illicit market prices and discouraging use by persons younger than 21 years of age while ensuring sufficient revenues are generated for the programs identified in Section 34019.

Revenue and Taxation Code § 34018

(Amended by Stats. 2022, Ch. 474, Sec. 43. (SB 1496) Effective January 1, 2023. Note: This section was added on Nov. 8, 2016, by initiative Prop. 64.)

(a) The California Cannabis Tax Fund is hereby created in the State Treasury. The Tax Fund shall consist of all taxes, interest, penalties, and other amounts collected and paid to the department pursuant to this part, less payment of refunds.

(b) Notwithstanding any other law, the California Cannabis Tax Fund is a special trust fund established solely to carry out the purposes of the Control, Regulate and Tax Adult Use of Marijuana Act and all revenues deposited into the Tax Fund, together with interest or dividends earned by the fund, are hereby continuously appropriated for the purposes of the Control, Regulate and Tax Adult Use of Marijuana Act without regard to fiscal year and shall be expended only in accordance with the provisions of this part and its purposes.

(c) Notwithstanding any other law, the taxes imposed by this part and the revenue derived therefrom, including investment interest, shall not be considered to be part of the General Fund, as that term is used in Chapter 1 (commencing with Section 16300) of Part 2 of Division 4 of Title 2 of the Government Code, shall not be considered General Fund revenue for purposes of Section 8 of Article XVI of the California Constitution and its implementing statutes, and shall not be considered "moneys" for purposes of subdivisions (a) and (b) of Section 8 of Article XVI of the California Constitution and its implementing statutes.

Revenue and Taxation Code § 34019

(Amended by Stats. 2022, Ch. 394, Sec. 1. (AB 2925) Effective January 1, 2023. Note: This section was added on Nov. 8, 2016, by initiative Prop. 64.)

(a) (1) For each fiscal year, the Department of Finance shall estimate revenues to be received pursuant to Sections 34011, 34011.2, and 34012 and provide those estimates to the Controller no later than June 15 of each year. The Controller shall use these estimates when disbursing funds pursuant to this section. Except as provided in paragraph (2), before any funds are disbursed pursuant to subdivisions (b), (c), (d), and (e) of this section, the Controller shall disburse from the tax fund to the appropriate account, without regard to fiscal year, the following:

(A) Reasonable costs incurred by the board for administering and collecting the taxes imposed by this part; provided, however, such costs shall not exceed 4 percent of tax revenues received.

(B) Reasonable costs incurred by the Department of Cannabis Control for implementing, administering, and enforcing Division 10 (commencing with Section 26000) of the Business and Professions Code to the extent those costs are not reimbursed pursuant to Section 26180 of the Business and Professions Code. This paragraph shall remain operative through the 2022–23 fiscal year.

(C) Reasonable costs incurred by the Department of Fish and Wildlife, the State Water Resources Control Board, and the Department of Pesticide Regulation for carrying out their respective duties under Division 10 (commencing with Section 26000) of the Business and Professions Code to the extent those costs are not otherwise reimbursed.

(D) Reasonable costs incurred by the Governor's Office of Business and Economic Development for implementing, administering, and enforcing Chapter 23 (commencing with Section 26240) of Division 10 of the Business and Professions Code.

(E) Reasonable costs incurred by the Controller for performing duties imposed by the Control, Regulate and Tax Adult Use of Marijuana Act, including the audit required by Section 34020.

(F) Reasonable costs incurred by the Department of Finance for conducting the performance audit pursuant to Section 26191 of the Business and Professions Code.

(G) Reasonable costs incurred by the Legislative Analyst's Office for performing duties imposed by Section 34017.

(H) Sufficient funds to reimburse the Division of Labor Standards Enforcement and the Division of Occupational Safety and Health within the Department of Industrial Relations and the Employment Development Department for the costs of applying and enforcing state labor laws to licensees under Division 10 (commencing with Section 26000) of the Business and Professions Code.

(2) Notwithstanding paragraph (1), the Controller shall not make disbursements pursuant to subparagraph (A), (B), (C), (E) or (H) for the 2022–23 and 2023–24 fiscal years.

(b) The Controller shall next disburse the sum of ten million dollars ($10,000,000) to a public university or universities in California annually beginning with the 2018–19 fiscal year until the 2028–29 fiscal year to research and evaluate the implementation and effect of the Control, Regulate and Tax Adult Use of Marijuana Act, and shall, if appropriate, make recommendations to the Legislature and Governor regarding possible amendments to the Control, Regulate and Tax Adult Use of Marijuana Act. The recipients of these funds shall publish reports on their findings at a minimum of every two years and shall make the reports available to the public. The Department of Cannabis Control shall select the universities to be funded. The research funded pursuant to this subdivision shall include but not necessarily be limited to:

(1) Impacts on public health, including health costs associated with cannabis use, as well as whether cannabis use is associated with an increase or decrease in use of alcohol or other drugs.

(2) The impact of treatment for maladaptive cannabis use and the effectiveness of different treatment

programs.

(3) Public safety issues related to cannabis use, including studying the effectiveness of the packaging and labeling requirements and advertising and marketing restrictions contained in the act at preventing underage access to and use of cannabis and cannabis products, and studying the health-related effects among users of varying potency levels of cannabis and cannabis products.

(4) Cannabis use rates, maladaptive use rates for adults and youth, and diagnosis rates of cannabis-related substance use disorders.

(5) Cannabis market prices, illicit market prices, tax structures and rates, including an evaluation of how to best tax cannabis based on potency, and the structure and function of licensed cannabis businesses.

(6) Whether additional protections are needed to prevent unlawful monopolies or anticompetitive behavior from occurring in the adult-use cannabis industry and, if so, recommendations as to the most effective measures for preventing such behavior.

(7) The economic impacts in the private and public sectors, including, but not necessarily limited to, job creation, workplace safety, revenues, taxes generated for state and local budgets, and criminal justice impacts, including, but not necessarily limited to, impacts on law enforcement and public resources, short- and long-term consequences of involvement in the criminal justice system, and state and local government agency administrative costs and revenue.

(8) Whether the regulatory agencies tasked with implementing and enforcing the Control, Regulate and Tax Adult Use of Marijuana Act are doing so consistent with the purposes of the act, and whether different agencies might do so more effectively.

(9) Environmental issues related to cannabis production and the criminal prohibition of cannabis production.

(10) The geographic location, structure, and function of licensed cannabis businesses, and demographic data, including race, ethnicity, and gender, of licenseholders.

(11) The outcomes achieved by the changes in criminal penalties made under the Control, Regulate and Tax Adult Use of Marijuana Act for cannabis-related offenses, and the outcomes of the juvenile justice system, in particular, probation-based treatments and the frequency of up-charging illegal possession of cannabis or cannabis products to a more serious offense.

(c) The Controller shall next disburse the sum of three million dollars ($3,000,000) annually to the Department of the California Highway Patrol beginning with the 2018–19 fiscal year until the 2022–23 fiscal year to establish and adopt protocols to determine whether a driver is operating a vehicle while impaired, including impairment by the use of cannabis or cannabis products, and to establish and adopt protocols setting forth best practices to assist law enforcement agencies. The department may hire personnel to establish the protocols specified in this subdivision. In addition, the department may make grants to public and private research institutions for the purpose of developing technology for determining when a driver is operating a vehicle while impaired, including impairment by the use of cannabis or cannabis products.

(d) The Controller shall next disburse the sum of ten million dollars ($10,000,000) beginning with the 2018–19 fiscal year and increasing ten million dollars ($10,000,000) each fiscal year thereafter until the 2022–23 fiscal year, at which time the disbursement shall be fifty million dollars ($50,000,000) each year thereafter, to the Governor's Office of Business and Economic Development, in consultation with the Labor and Workforce Development Agency and the State Department of Social Services, to administer a community reinvestments grants program to local health departments and at least 50 percent to qualified community-based nonprofit organizations to support job placement, mental health treatment, substance use disorder treatment, system navigation services, legal services to address barriers to reentry, and linkages to medical care for communities disproportionately affected by past federal and state drug policies. The office shall solicit input from community-based job skills, job placement, and legal service providers with relevant expertise as to the administration of the grants program. In addition, the office shall periodically evaluate the programs it is funding to determine the effectiveness of the programs, shall not spend more than 4 percent for administrative costs related to implementation, evaluation, and oversight of the programs, and shall award grants annually, beginning no later than January 1, 2020.

(e) The Controller shall next disburse the sum of two million dollars ($2,000,000) annually to the University of California San Diego Center for Medicinal Cannabis Research to further the objectives of the center, including the enhanced understanding of the efficacy and adverse effects of cannabis as a pharmacological agent.

(f) By July 15 of each fiscal year beginning in the 2018–19 fiscal year, the Controller shall, after disbursing funds pursuant to subdivisions (a), (b), (c), (d), and (e), disburse funds deposited in the tax fund during the prior fiscal year into sub-trust accounts, which are hereby created, as follows:

(1) Sixty percent shall be deposited in the Youth Education, Prevention, Early Intervention and Treatment Account, and disbursed by the Controller to the State Department of Health Care Services for programs for youth that are designed to educate about and to prevent substance use disorders and to prevent harm from substance use. The State Department of Health Care Services shall enter into interagency agreements with the State Department of Public Health and the State Department of Education to implement and administer these programs. The programs shall emphasize accurate education, effective prevention, early intervention, school retention, and timely treatment services for youth, their families, and caregivers. The programs may include, but are not limited to, the following components:

(A) Prevention and early intervention services including outreach, risk survey and education to youth, families, caregivers, schools, primary care health providers, behavioral health and substance use disorder service providers, community and faith-based organizations, fostercare providers, juvenile and family courts, and others to recognize and reduce risks related to substance use, and the early signs of problematic use and of substance use disorders.

(B) Grants to schools to develop and support student assistance programs, or other similar programs, designed to prevent and reduce substance use, and improve school retention and performance, by supporting students who are at risk of dropping out of school and promoting alternatives to suspension or expulsion that focus on school retention, remediation, and professional care. Schools with higher than average dropout rates should be prioritized for grants.

(C) Grants to programs for outreach, education, and treatment for homeless youth and out-of-school youth with substance use disorders.

(D) Access and linkage to care provided by county behavioral health programs for youth, and their families and caregivers, who have a substance use disorder or who are at risk for developing a substance use disorder.

(E) Youth-focused substance use disorder treatment programs that are culturally and gender competent, trauma informed, evidence based, and that provide a continuum of care that includes screening and assessment (substance use disorder as well as mental health), early intervention, active treatment, family involvement, case management, overdose prevention, prevention of communicable diseases related to substance use, relapse management for substance use and other cooccurring behavioral health disorders, vocational services, literacy services, parenting classes, family therapy and counseling services, medication-assisted treatments, psychiatric medication, and psychotherapy. When indicated, referrals must be made to other providers.

(F) To the extent permitted by law and where indicated, interventions shall utilize a two-generation approach to addressing substance use disorders with the capacity to treat youth and adults together. This would include supporting the development of family-based interventions that address substance use disorders and related problems within the context of families, including parents, foster parents, caregivers, and all their children.

(G) Programs to assist individuals, as well as families and friends of drug using young people, to reduce the stigma associated with substance use including being diagnosed with a substance use disorder or seeking substance use disorder services. This includes peer-run outreach and education to reduce stigma, anti-stigma campaigns, and community recovery networks.

(H) Workforce training and wage structures that increase the hiring pool of behavioral health staff with substance use disorder prevention and treatment expertise. Provide ongoing education and coaching that increases substance use treatment providers' core competencies and trains providers on promising and evidenced-based practices.

(I) Construction of community-based youth treatment facilities.

(J) The departments may contract with each county behavioral health program for the provision of services.

(K) Funds shall be allocated to counties based on demonstrated need, including the number of youth in the county, the prevalence of substance use disorders among adults, and confirmed through statistical data, validated assessments, or submitted reports prepared by the applicable county to demonstrate and validate need.

(L) The departments shall periodically evaluate the programs they are funding to determine the effectiveness of the programs.

(M) The departments may use up to 4 percent of the moneys allocated to the Youth Education, Prevention, Early Intervention and Treatment Account for administrative costs related to implementation, evaluation, and oversight of the programs.

(N) If the Department of Finance ever determines that funding pursuant to cannabis taxation exceeds demand for youth prevention and treatment services in the state, the departments shall provide a plan to the Department of Finance to provide treatment services to adults as well as youth using these funds.

(O) The departments shall solicit input from volunteer health organizations, physicians who treat addiction, treatment researchers, family therapy and counseling providers, and professional education associations with relevant expertise as to the administration of any grants made pursuant to this paragraph.

(P) On or before July 10, 2023, the State Department of Health Care Services shall provide to the Legislature, pursuant to Section 9795 of the Government Code, a spending report of funds from the Youth Education, Prevention, Early Intervention and Treatment Account for the 2021–22 and 2022–23 fiscal years. On or before July 10, 2024, and annually thereafter, the State Department of Health Care Services shall provide to the Legislature, pursuant to Section 9795 of the Government Code, a spending report of funds from the Youth Education, Prevention, Early Intervention and Treatment Account for the prior fiscal year.

(2) Twenty percent shall be deposited in the Environmental Restoration and Protection Account, and disbursed by the Controller as follows:

(A) To the Department of Fish and Wildlife and the Department of Parks and Recreation for the cleanup, remediation, and restoration of environmental damage in watersheds affected by cannabis cultivation and related activities including, but not limited to, damage that occurred prior to enactment of this part, and to support local partnerships for this purpose. The Department of Fish and Wildlife and the Department of Parks and Recreation may distribute a portion of the funds they receive from the Environmental Restoration and Protection Account through grants for purposes specified in this paragraph.

(B) To the Department of Fish and Wildlife and the Department of Parks and Recreation for the stewardship and operation of state-owned wildlife habitat areas and state park units in a manner that discourages and prevents the illegal cultivation, production, sale, and use of cannabis and cannabis products on public lands, and to facilitate the investigation, enforcement, and prosecution of illegal cultivation, production, sale, and use of cannabis or cannabis products on public lands.

(C) To the Department of Fish and Wildlife to assist in funding the watershed enforcement program and multiagency taskforce established pursuant to subdivisions (b) and (c) of Section 12029 of the Fish and Game Code to facilitate the investigation, enforcement, and prosecution of these offenses and to ensure the reduction of adverse impacts of cannabis cultivation, production, sale, and use on fish and wildlife habitats throughout the state.

(D) For purposes of this paragraph, the Secretary of the Natural Resources Agency shall determine the allocation of revenues between the departments. During the first five years of implementation, first consideration should be given to funding purposes specified in subparagraph (A).

(E) Funds allocated pursuant to this paragraph shall be used to increase and enhance activities described in subparagraphs (A), (B), and (C), and not replace allocation of other funding for these purposes. Accordingly, annual General Fund appropriations to the Department of Fish and Wildlife and the Department of Parks and Recreation shall not be reduced below the levels provided in the Budget Act of 2014 (Chapter 25 of the Statutes of 2014).

(3) Twenty percent shall be deposited into the State and Local Government Law Enforcement Account and disbursed by the Controller as follows:

(A) To the Department of the California Highway Patrol for conducting training programs for detecting, testing, and enforcing laws against driving under the influence of alcohol and other drugs, including driving under the influence of cannabis. The department may hire personnel to conduct the training programs specified in this subparagraph.

(B) To the Department of the California Highway Patrol to fund internal California Highway Patrol programs and grants to qualified nonprofit organizations and local governments for education, prevention, and enforcement of laws related to driving under the influence of alcohol and other drugs, including cannabis; programs that help enforce traffic laws, educate the public in traffic safety, provide varied and effective means of reducing fatalities, injuries, and economic losses from collisions; and for the purchase of equipment related to enforcement of laws related to driving under the influence of alcohol and other drugs, including cannabis.

(C) To the Board of State and Community Corrections for making grants to local governments to assist with law enforcement, fire protection, or other local programs addressing public health and safety associated with the implementation of the Control, Regulate and Tax Adult Use of Marijuana Act. The board shall not make any grants to local governments that ban both indoor and outdoor commercial cannabis cultivation, or ban retail sale of cannabis or cannabis products pursuant to Section 26200 of the Business and Professions Code or as otherwise provided by law.

(D) For purposes of this paragraph, the Department of Finance shall determine the allocation of revenues between the agencies; provided, however, beginning in the 2022–23 fiscal year the amount allocated pursuant to subparagraph (A) shall not be less than ten million dollars ($10,000,000) annually and the amount allocated pursuant to subparagraph (B) shall not be less than forty million dollars ($40,000,000) annually. In determining the amount to be allocated before the 2022–23 fiscal year pursuant to this paragraph, the Department of Finance shall give initial priority to subparagraph (A).

(g) Funds allocated pursuant to subdivision (f) shall be used to increase the funding of programs and purposes identified and shall not be used to replace allocation of other funding for these purposes.

(h) Effective July 1, 2028, the Legislature may amend this section by majority vote to further the purposes of the

Control, Regulate and Tax Adult Use of Marijuana Act, including allocating funds to programs other than those specified in subdivisions (d) and (f). Any revisions pursuant to this subdivision shall not result in a reduction of funds to accounts established pursuant to subdivisions (d) and (f) in any subsequent year from the amount allocated to each account in the 2027–28 fiscal year. Prior to July 1, 2028, the Legislature may not change the allocations to programs specified in subdivisions (d) and (f).

Revenue and Taxation Code § 34019.01

(Added by Stats. 2022, Ch. 56, Sec. 34. (AB 195) Effective June 30, 2022.)

Notwithstanding subdivision (f) of Section 34019, for the 2021–22 fiscal year, the 2022–23 fiscal year, and the 2023–24 fiscal year, after disbursing funds pursuant to subdivisions (a), (b), (c), (d), and (e) of Section 34019, by November 1 following the fiscal year, the Controller shall disburse funds deposited in the tax fund during the prior fiscal year into sub-trust accounts in an amount not to exceed the 2020–21 fiscal year baseline. Any amount of funds that exceeds the 2020–21 fiscal year baseline shall remain in the tax fund for that fiscal year and shall be disbursed, as follows:

(a) (1) For the 2021–22 fiscal year, by November 1, 2022, the Controller shall disburse from the tax fund, to the extent available, an amount necessary to enable funds disbursed to the sub-trust accounts for the 2021–22 fiscal year pursuant to subdivision (f) of Section 34019 and Section 34019.1 to be equal to the 2020–21 fiscal year baseline.

(2) For the 2022–23 fiscal year, by November 1, 2023, the Controller shall disburse, to the extent available, an amount necessary to enable funds disbursed to the sub-trust accounts for the 2022–23 fiscal year pursuant to subdivision (f) of Section 34019 and Section 34019.1 to be equal to the 2020–21 fiscal year baseline.

(3) For the 2023–24 fiscal year, by November 1, 2024, the Controller shall disburse, to the extent available, an amount necessary to enable funds disbursed to the sub-trust accounts for the 2023–24 fiscal year pursuant to subdivision (f) of Section 34019 and Section 34019.1 to be equal to the 2020–21 fiscal year baseline.

(b) On or before January 1, 2026, any remaining moneys in the tax fund retained pursuant to this section and any interest derived shall be disbursed to the sub-trust accounts pursuant to subdivision (f) of Section 34019.

Revenue and Taxation Code § 34019.1

(Added by Stats. 2022, Ch. 56, Sec. 35. (AB 195) Effective June 30, 2022. Repealed as of December 31, 2026, by its own provisions.)

(a) In the 2022–23 fiscal year, the sum of ten thousand dollars ($10,000) is hereby appropriated from the General Fund for the purposes of this section. In the 2023–24 fiscal year, the sum of one hundred fifty million dollars ($150,000,000) is hereby appropriated from the General Fund, as specified in subdivision (b), for the purposes of this section. In no event shall any funds in excess of those amounts be transferred pursuant to this section. These funds shall be available for encumbrance or expenditure until June 30, 2025.

(b) Upon the order of the Department of Finance, the Controller shall make the following transfers from the General Fund, in an amount not to exceed one hundred fifty million dollars ($150,000,000) in fiscal years 2023–24 and 2024–25, cumulatively:

> (1) By November 1, 2023, the Controller shall, subject to the limitation in subdivision (a), transfer from the General Fund an amount that would enable funds disbursed to the sub-trust accounts for the 2022–23 fiscal year, pursuant to subdivision (f) of Section 34019, Section 34019.01, and this paragraph, to be equal to the 2020–21 fiscal year baseline.
>
> (2) By November 1, 2024, the Controller shall, subject to the limitation in subdivision (a), transfer from the General Fund an amount that would enable funds disbursed to the sub-trust accounts for the 2023–24 fiscal

year, pursuant to subdivision (f) of Section 34019, Section 34019.01, and this paragraph, to be equal to the 2020–21 fiscal year baseline.

(c) This section shall remain in effect only until December 31, 2026, and as of that date is repealed.

Revenue and Taxation Code § 34019.5

(Added by Stats. 2019, Ch. 40, Sec. 16. (AB 97) Effective July 1, 2019.)

Contracts entered into or amended by the State Department of Health Care Services to implement and administer the programs identified in paragraph (1) of subdivision (f) of Section 34019 shall be exempt from Chapter 6 (commencing with Section 14825) of Part 5.5 of Division 3 of Title 2 of the Government Code, Section 19130 of the Government Code, Part 2 (commencing with Section 10100) of Division 2 of the Public Contract Code, shall be exempt from the State Administrative Manual, and shall not be subject to the review or approval of any division of the Department of General Services.

Revenue and Taxation Code § 34020

(Added November 8, 2016, by initiative Proposition 64, Sec. 7.1.)

The Controller shall periodically audit the Tax Fund to ensure that those funds are used and accounted for in a manner consistent with this part and as otherwise required by law.

Revenue and Taxation Code § 34020.1

(Added by Stats. 2022, Ch. 56, Sec. 36. (AB 195) Effective June 30, 2022.)

(a) On or before March 1, 2025, the Department of Cannabis Control, in consultation with the Department of Finance and the California Department of Tax and Fee Administration, shall submit a report to the Legislature on the condition and health of the cannabis industry in the state. The report shall include, but is not limited to, the following information:

(1) How many local jurisdictions have permitted commercial cannabis activity.

(2) How many local jurisdictions have not permitted commercial cannabis activity.

(3) Information or analysis concerning the potential expansion or contraction of the cannabis market in the state, which may include information concerning any increase in retail cannabis sales and activity in the illicit market.

(4) How many equity licensees have been approved by the Department of Cannabis Control.

(5) In what counties the state equity licensees located.

(6) The health of the Cannabis Tax Fund, and any future projections of Cannabis Tax Fund revenues.

(7) Information on the viability of cannabis businesses in the state, and the ability to continue to operate cannabis businesses in the state, from a general and equity licensee standpoint.

(8) The impacts of the suspension of the cultivation tax imposed by paragraph (2) of subdivision (a) of Section 34012, including whether that suspension resulted in a decrease in retail cannabis prices or increased participation in the legal cannabis market.

(b) The report may include recommendations to strengthen the state's legal cannabis market.

(c) The Department of Cannabis Control may contract with a public university or universities in California to prepare the report. Subject to approval by the Department of Cannabis Control, the university or universities may contract with other organizations in connection with the report.

(d) The Department of Cannabis Control may consolidate this report with any other reports required under Division 10 (commencing with Section 26000) of the Business and Professions Code.

Revenue and Taxation Code § 34021

(Added November 8, 2016, by initiative Proposition 64, Sec. 7.1.)

(a) The taxes imposed by this Part shall be in addition to any other tax imposed by a city, county, or city and county.

Revenue and Taxation Code § 34021.5

(Amended by Stats. 2017, Ch. 27, Sec. 172. (SB 94) Effective June 27, 2017. Note: This section was added on Nov. 8, 2016, by initiative Prop. 64.)

(a) (1) A county may impose a tax on the privilege of cultivating, manufacturing, producing, processing, preparing, storing, providing, donating, selling, or distributing cannabis or cannabis products by a licensee operating under Division 10 (commencing with Section 26000) of the Business and Professions Code.

(2) The board of supervisors shall specify in the ordinance proposing the tax the activities subject to the tax, the applicable rate or rates, the method of apportionment, if necessary, and the manner of collection of the tax. The tax may be imposed for general governmental purposes or for purposes specified in the ordinance by the board of supervisors.

(3) In addition to any other method of collection authorized by law, the board of supervisors may provide for the collection of the tax imposed pursuant to this section in the same manner, and subject to the same penalties and priority of lien, as other charges and taxes fixed and collected by the county. A tax imposed pursuant to this section is a tax and not a fee or special assessment. The board of supervisors shall specify whether the tax applies throughout the entire county or within the unincorporated area of the county.

(4) The tax authorized by this section may be imposed upon any or all of the activities set forth in paragraph (1), as specified in the ordinance, regardless of whether the activity is undertaken individually, collectively, or cooperatively, and regardless of whether the activity is for compensation or gratuitous, as determined by the board of supervisors.

(b) A tax imposed pursuant to this section shall be subject to applicable voter approval requirements imposed by law.

(c) This section is declaratory of existing law and does not limit or prohibit the levy or collection of any other fee, charge, or tax, or a license or service fee or charge upon, or related to, the activities set forth in subdivision (a) as otherwise provided by law. This section shall not be construed as a limitation upon the taxing authority of a county as provided by law.

(d) This section shall not be construed to authorize a county to impose a sales or use tax in addition to the sales and use taxes imposed under an ordinance conforming to the provisions of Sections 7202 and 7203 of this code.

Revenue and Taxation Code § 55044

(Amended by Stats. 2022, Ch. 474, Sec. 100. (SB 1496) Effective January 1, 2023.)

(a) If the department finds that a person's failure to make a timely return or payment is due to reasonable cause and circumstances beyond the person's control, and occurred notwithstanding the exercise of ordinary care and the absence of willful neglect, the person may be relieved of the penalty provided by Sections 34013, 55042, 55050, and 55086.

(b) Except as provided in subdivisions (c) and (d), any person seeking to be relieved of the penalty shall file with the department a statement, under penalty of perjury, setting forth the facts upon which the person bases the claim for relief.

(c) (1) Subject to paragraph (2), the department may grant relief of the penalty for any person in an area identified in a state of emergency proclamation made by the Governor for the period the state of emergency proclamation is effective, regardless of whether the person has filed a statement with the department pursuant to subdivision (b).

(2) The department may grant the relief in paragraph (1) only during the first 12 months following the issuance of the state of emergency proclamation or the duration of the state of emergency, whichever is less.

(d) The department shall establish criteria that provide for efficient resolution of requests for relief pursuant to this section.

XII. Vehicle Code Sections

Vehicle Code § 2429.7

(Added by Stats. 2017, Ch. 27, Sec. 173. (SB 94) Effective June 27, 2017.)

(a) The commissioner shall appoint an impaired driving task force to develop recommendations for best practices, protocols, proposed legislation, and other policies that will address the issue of impaired driving, including driving under the influence of cannabis and controlled substances. The task force shall also examine the use of technology, including field testing technologies and validated field sobriety tests, to identify drivers under the influence of prescription drugs, cannabis, and controlled substances. The task force shall include, but is not limited to, the commissioner, who shall serve as chairperson, and at least one member from each of the following:

(1) The Office of Traffic Safety.

(2) The National Highway Traffic Safety Administration.

(3) Local law enforcement.

(4) District attorneys.

(5) Public defenders.

(6) California Association of Crime Laboratory Directors.

(7) California Attorneys for Criminal Justice.

(8) The California Cannabis Research Program, known as the Center for Medicinal Cannabis Research, authorized pursuant to Section 11362.9 of the Health and Safety Code.

(9) An organization that represents medicinal cannabis patients.

(10) Licensed physicians with expertise in substance abuse disorder treatment.

(11) Researchers with expertise in identifying impairment caused by prescription medications and controlled substances.

(12) Nongovernmental organizations committed to social justice issues.

(13) A nongovernmental organization that focuses on improving roadway safety.

(b) The members of the task force shall serve at the pleasure of the commissioner and without compensation.

(c) The task force members shall be free of economic relationships with any company that profits from the sale of technologies or equipment that is intended to identify impairment. Members and their organizations shall not receive pay from, grants from, or any form of financial support from companies or entities that sell such technologies or equipment.

(d) The task force shall make recommendations regarding prevention of impaired driving, means of identifying impaired driving, and responses to impaired driving that reduce reoccurrence, including, but not limited to, evidence-based approaches that do not rely on incarceration.

(e) The task force shall make recommendations regarding how to best capture data to evaluate the impact that cannabis legalization is having on roadway safety.

(f) By January 1, 2021, the task force shall report to the Legislature its policy recommendations and the steps state agencies are taking regarding impaired driving. The report shall be submitted in compliance with Section 9795 of the Government Code.

Vehicle Code § 23152

(Amended by Stats. 2016, Ch. 765, Sec. 1. (AB 2687) Effective January 1, 2017.)

(a) It is unlawful for a person who is under the influence of any alcoholic beverage to drive a vehicle.

(b) It is unlawful for a person who has 0.08 percent or more, by weight, of alcohol in his or her blood to drive a vehicle.

For purposes of this article and Section 34501.16, percent, by weight, of alcohol in a person's blood is based upon grams of alcohol per 100 milliliters of blood or grams of alcohol per 210 liters of breath.

In any prosecution under this subdivision, it is a rebuttable presumption that the person had 0.08 percent or more, by weight, of alcohol in his or her blood at the time of driving the vehicle if the person had 0.08 percent or more, by weight, of alcohol in his or her blood at the time of the performance of a chemical test within three hours after the driving.

(c) It is unlawful for a person who is addicted to the use of any drug to drive a vehicle. This subdivision shall not apply to a person who is participating in a narcotic treatment program approved pursuant to Article 3 (commencing with Section 11875) of Chapter 1 of Part 3 of Division 10.5 of the Health and Safety Code.

(d) It is unlawful for a person who has 0.04 percent or more, by weight, of alcohol in his or her blood to drive a commercial motor vehicle, as defined in Section 15210. In a prosecution under this subdivision, it is a rebuttable presumption that the person had 0.04 percent or more, by weight, of alcohol in his or her blood at the time of driving the vehicle if the person had 0.04 percent or more, by weight, of alcohol in his or her blood at the time of the performance of a chemical test within three hours after the driving.

(e) Commencing July 1, 2018, it shall be unlawful for a person who has 0.04 percent or more, by weight, of alcohol in his or her blood to drive a motor vehicle when a passenger for hire is a passenger in the vehicle at the time of the offense. For purposes of this subdivision, "passenger for hire" means a passenger for whom consideration is contributed or expected as a condition of carriage in the vehicle, whether directly or indirectly flowing to the owner, operator, agent, or any other person having an interest in the vehicle. In a prosecution under this subdivision, it is a rebuttable presumption that the person had 0.04 percent or more, by weight, of alcohol in his or her blood at the time of driving the vehicle if the person had 0.04 percent or more, by weight, of alcohol in his or her blood at the time of the performance of a chemical test within three hours after the driving.

(f) It is unlawful for a person who is under the influence of any drug to drive a vehicle.

(g) It is unlawful for a person who is under the combined influence of any alcoholic beverage and drug to drive a vehicle.

Vehicle Code § 23152.5

(Added by Stats. 2019, Ch. 68, Sec. 1. (AB 127) Effective July 10, 2019.)

Notwithstanding Section 23152, a person who is under the influence of a drug or the combined influence of an alcoholic beverage and drug who is under the supervision of, and on the property of, the Department of the California Highway Patrol may drive a vehicle for purposes of conducting research on impaired driving.

Vehicle Code § 23155

(Added by Stats. 2019, Ch. 610, Sec. 1. (AB 397) Effective January 1, 2020.)

Beginning January 1, 2022, when a disposition described in Section 13151 of the Penal Code is a conviction for a violation of subdivision (f) of Section 23152 or subdivision (f) of Section 23153 for which cannabis was the sole drug, the disposition report shall state that the convicted offense was due to cannabis.

Vehicle Code § 23220

(Amended by Stats. 2017, Ch. 232, Sec. 1. (SB 65) Effective January 1, 2018.)

(a) A person shall not drink any alcoholic beverage or smoke or ingest marijuana or any marijuana product while driving a motor vehicle on any lands described in subdivision (c).

(b) A person shall not drink any alcoholic beverage or smoke or ingest marijuana or any marijuana product while riding as a passenger in any motor vehicle being driven on any lands described in subdivision (c).

(c) As used in this section, "lands" means those lands to which the Chappie-Z'berg Off-Highway Motor Vehicle Law of 1971 (Division 16.5 (commencing with Section 38000)) applies as to off-highway motor vehicles, as described in Section 38001.

(d) A violation of subdivision (a) or (b) shall be punished as an infraction.

Vehicle Code § 23221

(Amended by Stats. 2017, Ch. 232, Sec. 2. (SB 65) Effective January 1, 2018.)

(a) A driver shall not drink any alcoholic beverage or smoke or ingest marijuana or any marijuana product while driving a motor vehicle upon a highway.

(b) A passenger shall not drink any alcoholic beverage or smoke or ingest marijuana or any marijuana product while in a motor vehicle being driven upon a highway.

(c) A violation of this section shall be punished as an infraction.

Vehicle Code § 23222

(Amended by Stats. 2019, Ch. 610, Sec. 2. (AB 397) Effective January 1, 2020.)

(a) A person shall not have in their possession on their person, while driving a motor vehicle upon a highway or on lands, as described in subdivision (c) of Section 23220, a bottle, can, or other receptacle, containing an alcoholic beverage which has been opened, or a seal broken, or the contents of which have been partially removed.

(b) (1) Except as authorized by law, a person who has in their possession on their person, while driving a motor vehicle upon a highway or on lands, as described in subdivision (c) of Section 23220, a receptacle containing cannabis or cannabis products, as defined by Section 11018.1 of the Health and Safety Code, which has been opened or has a seal broken, or loose cannabis flower not in a container, is guilty of an infraction punishable by a fine of not more than one hundred dollars ($100).

(2) Paragraph (1) does not apply to a person who has a receptacle containing cannabis or cannabis products that has been opened, has a seal broken, or the contents of which have been partially removed, or to a person who has a loose cannabis flower not in a container, if the receptacle or loose cannabis flower not in a container is in the trunk of the vehicle.

(c) Subdivision (b) does not apply to a qualified patient or person with an identification card, as defined in Section 11362.7 of the Health and Safety Code, if both of the following apply:

(1) The person is carrying a current identification card or a physician's recommendation.

(2) The cannabis or cannabis product is contained in a container or receptacle that is either sealed, resealed, or closed.

Vehicle Code § 40000.15

(Amended by Stats. 2006, Ch. 609, Sec. 6. Effective January 1, 2007.)

A violation of any of the following provisions shall constitute a misdemeanor, and not an infraction:

Subdivision (g), (j), (k), (l), or (m) of Section 22658, relating to unlawfully towed or stored vehicles.

Sections 23103 and 23104, relating to reckless driving.

Section 23109, relating to speed contests or exhibitions.

Subdivision (a) of Section 23110, relating to throwing at vehicles.

Section 23152, relating to driving under the influence.

Subdivision (b) of Section 23222, relating to possession of marijuana.

Subdivision (a) or (b) of Section 23224, relating to persons under 21 years of age knowingly driving, or being a passenger in, a motor vehicle carrying any alcoholic beverage.

Section 23253, relating to directions on toll highways or vehicular crossings.

Section 23332, relating to trespassing.

Section 24002.5, relating to unlawful operation of a farm vehicle.

Section 24011.3, relating to vehicle bumper strength notices.

Section 27150.1, relating to sale of exhaust systems.

Section 27362, relating to child passenger seat restraints.

Section 28050, relating to true mileage driven.

Section 28050.5, relating to nonfunctional odometers.

Section 28051, relating to resetting odometers.

Section 28051.5, relating to devices to reset odometers.

Subdivision (d) of Section 28150, relating to possessing four or more jamming devices.

XIII. Water Code Sections

Water Code § 25

(Added by Stats. 1967, Ch. 284.)

"Board," unless otherwise specified, means the State Water Resources Control Board.

Water Code § 1052

(Amended by Stats. 2022, Ch. 56, Sec. 37. (AB 195) Effective June 30, 2022.)

(a) The diversion or use of water subject to this division other than as authorized in this division is a trespass.

(b) (1) An action for the issuance of injunctive relief as may be warranted by way of temporary restraining order, preliminary injunction, or permanent injunction, may be brought by the Attorney General on behalf of the board, or in the Attorney General's independent capacity in the name of the people of the State of California, where the diversion or use of water is threatened, is occurring, or has occurred.

(2) (A) A civil action for a violation under this section resulting from unlicensed cannabis cultivation may also be brought by a city attorney or county counsel, upon approval of the board, in the name of the people of the State of California.

(B) A city attorney or county counsel shall inform and coordinate with the board as to the investigation of potential violations of this section related to unlicensed cannabis cultivation. Unless the board withholds its approval within 21 days after the local jurisdiction provides notice of its intent to file, the local jurisdiction may deem the board's silence as approval.

(c) A person or entity committing a trespass as defined in this section may be liable in an amount not to exceed the following:

> (1) If the unauthorized diversion or use occurs in a critically dry year immediately preceded by two or more consecutive below normal, dry, or critically dry years, or during a period for which the Governor has issued a proclamation of a state of emergency under the California Emergency Services Act (Chapter 7 (commencing with Section 8550) of Division 1 of Title 2 of the Government Code) based on drought conditions, the sum of the following:

(A) One thousand dollars ($1,000) for each day in which the trespass occurs.

(B) Two thousand five hundred dollars ($2,500) for each acre-foot of water diverted or used in excess of that diverter's water rights.

(2) If the unauthorized diversion or use is not described by paragraph (1), five hundred dollars ($500) for each day in which the unauthorized diversion or use occurs.

(3) Notwithstanding paragraphs (1) and (2), up to three thousand five hundred dollars ($3,500) for each day in which the unauthorized diversion or use for unlicensed cannabis cultivation occurs.

(d) Civil liability for a violation of this section may be imposed by the superior court or the board as follows:

(1) The superior court may impose civil liability in an action brought by the Attorney General, upon request of the board, to impose, assess, and recover any sums pursuant to subdivision (c). In determining the appropriate amount, the court shall take into consideration all relevant circumstances, including, but not limited to, the extent of harm caused by the violation, the nature and persistence of the violation, the length of time over which the violation occurs, and the corrective action, if any, taken by the violator.

(2) The superior court may impose civil liability in an action for a violation under this section resulting from unlicensed cannabis cultivation brought by a city attorney or county counsel to impose, assess, and recover any sums pursuant to subdivision (c). In determining the appropriate amount, the court shall take into consideration all relevant circumstances, including, but not limited to, the extent of harm caused by the violation, whether the violation was intentional or committed knowingly, the nature and persistence of the violation, the length of time over which the violation has occurred, and the corrective action, if any, taken by the violator. The court shall make its findings on the record.

(3) The board may impose civil liability in accordance with Section 1055.

(e) (1) Upon appropriation by the Legislature, funds recovered in an action pursuant to this section shall be used to proportionally reimburse the Attorney General, city attorney, county counsel, and the board for costs of bringing the action, including reasonable attorney's fees, and of investigating the violation and supporting the prosecution of the action.

(2) Except for reimbursements to the Attorney General, city attorney, or county counsel, as specified in paragraph (1), all funds recovered pursuant to this section shall be deposited in the Water Rights Fund established pursuant to Section 1550.

(f) The remedies prescribed in this section are cumulative and not alternative.

Water Code § 1525

(Amended by Stats. 2020, Ch. 18, Sec. 6. (AB 92) Effective June 29, 2020.)

(a) Each person or entity who holds a permit or license to appropriate water, and each lessor of water leased under Chapter 1.5 (commencing with Section 1020) of Part 1, shall pay an annual fee according to a fee schedule established by the board.

(b) Each person or entity who files any of the following shall pay a fee according to a fee schedule established by the board:

(1) An application for a permit to appropriate water.

(2) A registration of appropriation for a small domestic use, small irrigation use, or livestock stockpond use.

(3) A petition for an extension of time within which to begin construction, to complete construction, or to

apply the water to full beneficial use under a permit.

(4) A petition to change the point of diversion, place of use, or purpose of use, under a permit, license, or registration.

(5) A petition to change the conditions of a permit or license, requested by the permittee or licensee, that is not otherwise subject to paragraph (3) or (4).

(6) A petition to change the point of discharge, place of use, or purpose of use, of treated wastewater, requested pursuant to Section 1211.

(7) An application for approval of a water lease agreement.

(8) A request for release from priority pursuant to Section 10504.

(9) An application for an assignment of a state-filed application pursuant to Section 10504.

(10) A statement of water diversion and use pursuant to Part 5.1 (commencing with Section 5100) that reports that water was used for cannabis cultivation.

(c) (1) The board shall set the fee schedule authorized by this section so that the total amount of fees collected pursuant to this section equals that amount necessary to recover costs incurred in connection with the issuance, administration, review, monitoring, and enforcement of permits, licenses, certificates, and registrations to appropriate water, water leases, statements of water diversion and use for cannabis cultivation, and orders approving changes in point of discharge, place of use, or purpose of use of treated wastewater. The board may include, as recoverable costs, but is not limited to including, the costs incurred in reviewing applications, registrations, statements of water diversion and use for cannabis cultivation, petitions and requests, prescribing terms of permits, licenses, registrations, and change orders, enforcing and evaluating compliance with permits, licenses, certificates, registrations, change orders, and water leases, inspection, monitoring, planning, modeling, reviewing documents prepared for the purpose of regulating the diversion and use of water, applying and enforcing the prohibition set forth in Section 1052 against the unauthorized diversion or use of water subject to this division and the water diversion related provisions of Chapter 6 (commencing with Section 26060) of Division 10 of the Business and Professions Code, and the administrative costs incurred in connection with carrying out these actions.

(2) In setting the fee schedule for fees subject to subdivision (b) of Section 1433.2 and subdivision (b) of Section 1443.2, the board shall also include an amount estimated by the board, in consultation with the Department of Fish and Wildlife, necessary to recover costs incurred by the Department of Fish and Wildlife under Article 2 (commencing with Section 1433) of Chapter 6.5 and Article 2 (commencing with Section 1443) of Chapter 6.6.

(d) (1) The board shall adopt the schedule of fees authorized under this section as emergency regulations in accordance with Section 1530.

(2) For filings subject to subdivision (b), the schedule may provide for a single filing fee or for an initial filing fee followed by an annual fee, as appropriate to the type of filing involved, and may include supplemental fees for filings that have already been made but have not yet been acted upon by the board at the time the schedule of fees takes effect.

(3) The board shall set the amount of total revenue collected each year through the fees authorized by this section at an amount equal to the amounts appropriated by the Legislature for expenditure for support of water rights program activities from the Water Rights Fund established under Section 1550, taking into account the reserves in the Water Rights Fund. The board shall review and revise the fees each fiscal year as necessary to conform to the amounts appropriated. If the board determines that the revenue collected during the preceding year was greater than, or less than, the amounts appropriated, the board may further adjust the annual fees to compensate for the over or under collection of revenue.

(e) Annual fees imposed pursuant to this section for the 2003–04 fiscal year shall be assessed for the entire 2003–04 fiscal year.

Water Code § 1535

(Amended by Stats. 2016, Ch. 32, Sec. 95. (SB 837) Effective June 27, 2016.)

(a) Any fee subject to this chapter that is required in connection with the filing of an application, registration, request, statement, or proof of claim, other than an annual fee required after the period covered by the initial filing fee, shall be paid to the board.

(b) If a fee established under subdivision (b) of Section 1525, Section 1528, or Section 13160.1 is not paid when due, the board may cancel the application, registration, petition, request, statement, or claim, or may refer the matter to the State Board of Equalization for collection of the unpaid fee.

Water Code § 1831

(Amended by Stats. 2017, Ch. 27, Sec. 175. (SB 94) Effective June 27, 2017.)

(a) When the board determines that any person is violating, or threatening to violate, any requirement described in subdivision (d), the board may issue an order to that person to cease and desist from that violation.

(b) The cease and desist order shall require that person to comply forthwith or in accordance with a time schedule set by the board.

(c) The board may issue a cease and desist order only after notice and an opportunity for hearing pursuant to Section 1834.

(d) The board may issue a cease and desist order in response to a violation or threatened violation of any of the following:

(1) The prohibition set forth in Section 1052 against the unauthorized diversion or use of water subject to this division.

(2) Any term or condition of a permit, license, certification, or registration issued under this division.

(3) Any decision or order of the board issued under this part, Section 275, Chapter 11 (commencing with Section 10735) of Part 2.74 of Division 6, or Article 7 (commencing with Section 13550) of Chapter 7 of Division 7, in which decision or order the person to whom the cease and desist order will be issued, or a predecessor in interest to that person, was named as a party directly affected by the decision or order.

(4) A regulation adopted under Section 1058.5.

(5) Any extraction restriction, limitation, order, or regulation adopted or issued under Chapter 11 (commencing with Section 10735) of Part 2.74 of Division 6.

(6) Any diversion or use of water for cannabis cultivation if any of paragraphs (1) to (5), inclusive, or any of the following applies:

(A) A license is required, but has not been obtained, under Chapter 6 (commencing with Section 26060) or Chapter 7 (commencing with Section 26070) of Division 10 of the Business and Professions Code.

(B) The diversion is not in compliance with an applicable limitation or requirement established by the board or the Department of Fish and Wildlife under Section 13149.

(C) The diversion or use is not in compliance with a requirement imposed under paragraphs (1) and (2) of subdivision (b) of Section 26060.1 of, and paragraph (3) of subdivision (a) of Section 26070 of, the Business and Professions Code.

(e) This article does not alter the regulatory authority of the board under other provisions of law.

Water Code § 1840

(Amended by Stats. 2016, Ch. 32, Sec. 98. (SB 837) Effective June 27, 2016.)

(a) (1) Except as provided in subdivision (b), a person who, on or after January 1, 2016, diverts 10 acre-feet of water per year or more under a permit or license shall install and maintain a device or employ a method capable of measuring the rate of direct diversion, rate of collection to storage, and rate of withdrawal or release from storage. The measurements shall be made using the best available technologies and best professional practices, as defined in Section 5100, using a device or methods satisfactory to the board, as follows:

(A) A device shall be capable of continuous monitoring of the rate and quantity of water diverted and shall be properly maintained. The permittee or licensee shall provide the board with evidence that the device has been installed with the first report submitted after installation of the device. The permittee or licensee shall provide the board with evidence demonstrating that the device is functioning properly as part of the reports submitted at five-year intervals after the report documenting installation of the device, or upon request of the board.

(B) In developing regulations pursuant to Section 1841, the board shall consider devices and methods that provide accurate measurement of the total amount diverted and the rate of diversion. The board shall consider devices and methods that provide accurate measurements within an acceptable range of error, including the following:

(i) Electricity records dedicated to a pump and recent pump test.

(ii) Staff gage calibrated with an acceptable streamflow rating curve.

(iii) Staff gage calibrated for a flume or weir.

(iv) Staff gage calibrated with an acceptable storage capacity curve.

(v) Pressure transducer and acceptable storage capacity curve.

(2) The permittee or licensee shall maintain a record of all diversion monitoring that includes the date, time, and diversion rate at time intervals of one hour or less, and the total amount of water diverted. These records shall be included with reports submitted under the permit or license, as required under subdivision (c), or upon request of the board.

(b) (1) The board may modify the requirements of subdivision (a) upon finding either of the following:

(A) That strict compliance is infeasible, is unreasonably expensive, would unreasonably affect public trust uses, or would result in the waste or unreasonable use of water.

(B) That the need for monitoring and reporting is adequately addressed by other conditions of the permit or license.

(2) The board may increase the 10-acre-foot reporting threshold of subdivision (a) in a watershed or subwatershed, after considering the diversion reporting threshold in relation to quantity of water within the watershed or subwatershed. The board may increase the 10-acre-foot reporting threshold to 25 acre-feet or above if it finds that the benefits of the additional information within the watershed or subwatershed are substantially outweighed by the cost of installing measuring devices or employing methods for measurement for diversions at the 10-acre-foot threshold.

(c) At least annually, a person who diverts water under a registration, permit, or license shall report to the board the following information:

(1) The quantity of water diverted by month.

(2) The maximum rate of diversion by months in the preceding calendar year.

(3) The information required by subdivision (a), if applicable.

(4) The amount of water used, if any, for cannabis cultivation.

(d) Compliance with the applicable requirements of this section is a condition of every registration, permit, or license.

Water Code § 1845

(Amended by Stats. 2016, Ch. 32, Sec. 99. (SB 837) Effective June 27, 2016.)

(a) Upon the failure of any person to comply with a cease and desist order issued by the board pursuant to this chapter, the Attorney General, upon the request of the board, shall petition the superior court for the issuance of prohibitory or mandatory injunctive relief as appropriate, including a temporary restraining order, preliminary injunction, or permanent injunction.

(b) (1) A person or entity who violates a cease and desist order issued pursuant to this chapter may be liable in an amount not to exceed the following:

(A) If the violation occurs in a critically dry year immediately preceded by two or more consecutive below normal, dry, or critically dry years or during a period for which the Governor has issued a proclamation of a state of emergency under the California Emergency Services Act (Chapter 7 (commencing with Section 8550) of Division 1 of Title 2 of the Government Code) based on drought conditions, ten thousand dollars ($10,000) for each day in which the violation occurs.

(B) If the violation is not described by subparagraph (A), one thousand dollars ($1,000) for each day in which the violation occurs.

(2) Civil liability may be imposed by the superior court. The Attorney General, upon the request of the board, shall petition the superior court to impose, assess, and recover those sums.

(3) Civil liability may be imposed administratively by the board pursuant to Section 1055.

Water Code § 1846

(Amended by Stats. 2016, Ch. 32, Sec. 100. (SB 837) Effective June 27, 2016.)

(a) A person or entity may be liable for a violation of any of the following in an amount not to exceed five hundred dollars ($500) for each day in which the violation occurs:

(1) A term or condition of a permit, license, certificate, or registration issued under this division.

(2) A regulation or order adopted by the board.

(b) Civil liability may be imposed by the superior court. The Attorney General, upon the request of the board, shall petition the superior court to impose, assess, and recover those sums.

(c) Civil liability may be imposed administratively by the board pursuant to Section 1055.

Water Code § 1847

(Amended by Stats. 2017, Ch. 27, Sec. 176. (SB 94) Effective June 27, 2017.)

(a) A person or entity may be liable for a violation of any of the requirements of subdivision (b) in an amount not to exceed the sum of the following:

(1) Five hundred dollars ($500), plus two hundred fifty dollars ($250) for each additional day on which the violation continues if the person fails to correct the violation within 30 days after the board has called the violation to the attention of that person.

(2) Two thousand five hundred dollars ($2,500) for each acre-foot of water diverted or used in violation of the applicable requirement.

(b) Liability may be imposed for any of the following violations:

(1) Violation of a principle, guideline, or requirement established by the board or the Department of Fish and Wildlife under Section 13149.

(2) Failure to submit information, or making a material misstatement in information submitted, under Section 26060.1 of the Business and Professions Code.

(3) Violation of any requirement imposed under subdivision (b) of Section 26060.1 of the Business and Professions Code.

(4) Diversion or use of water for cannabis cultivation for which a license is required, but has not been obtained, under Chapter 6 (commencing with Section 26060) or Chapter 7 (commencing with Section 26070) of Division 10 of the Business and Professions Code.

(c) Civil liability may be imposed by the superior court. The Attorney General, upon the request of the board, shall petition the superior court to impose, assess, and recover those sums.

(d) Civil liability may be imposed administratively by the board pursuant to Section 1055.

Water Code § 5100

(Amended by Stats. 2009, 7th Ex. Sess., Ch. 2, Sec. 3. (SB 8 7x) Effective February 3, 2010.)

As used in this part:

(a) "Best available technologies" means technologies at the highest technically practical level, using flow totaling devices, and if necessary, data loggers and telemetry.

(b) "Best professional practices" means practices attaining and maintaining the accuracy of measurement and reporting devices and methods.

(c) "Diversion" means taking water by gravity or pumping from a surface stream or subterranean stream flowing through a known and definite channel, or other body of surface water, into a canal, pipeline, or other conduit, and includes impoundment of water in a reservoir.

(d) "Person" means all persons whether natural or artificial, including the United States of America, State of California, and all political subdivisions, districts, municipalities, and public agencies.

Water Code § 5101

(Amended by Stats. 2021, Ch. 258, Sec. 44. (SB 155) Effective September 23, 2021.)

(a) Each person who, after December 31, 1965, diverts water shall file with the board a statement of their diversion and use, as provided in subdivision (b), except that a statement is not required to be filed if the diversion is any of the following:

(1) From a spring that does not flow off the property on which it is located and from which the person's aggregate diversions do not exceed 25 acre-feet in any year.

(2) Covered by a registration for small domestic use, small irrigation use, or livestock stockpond use, or permit or license to appropriate water on file with the board.

(3) Included in a notice filed pursuant to Part 5 (commencing with Section 4999).

(4) Regulated by a watermaster appointed by the department and included in annual reports filed with a court or the board by the watermaster, which reports identify the persons who have diverted water and describe the general purposes and the place, the use, and the quantity of water that has been diverted from each source.

(5) Included in annual reports filed with a court or the board by a watermaster appointed by a court or pursuant to statute to administer a final judgment determining rights to water, which reports identify the persons who have diverted water and give the general place of use and the quantity of water that has been diverted from each source.

(6) For use in compliance with Article 2.5 (commencing with Section 1226) or Article 2.7 (commencing with Section 1228) of Chapter 1 of Part 2.

(7) A diversion that occurs before January 1, 2009, if any of the following applies:

(A) The diversion is from a spring that does not flow off the property on which it is located, and the person's aggregate diversions do not exceed 25 acre-feet in any year.

(B) The diversion is covered by an application to appropriate water on file with the board.

(C) The diversion is reported by the department in its hydrologic data bulletins.

(D) The diversion is included in the consumptive use data for the Delta lowlands published by the department in its hydrologic data bulletins.

(b) (1) For diversions after December 31, 1965, and before January 1, 2021, the statement shall be filed before July 1 of the year after the diversion.

(2) For diversions after December 31, 2020, and before October 1, 2021, the statement shall be filed before April 1, 2022.

(3) For diversions after September 30, 2021, the statement shall include diversions during the one-year period from October 1 of each year through September 30, inclusive, of the following year, and shall be filed before February 1 of the year after that one-year period.

Water Code § 5102

(Amended by Stats. 1967, Ch. 62.)

The statement may be filed either by the person who is diverting water or, on his behalf, by an agency which he designates and which maintains a record of the water diverted. A separate statement shall be filed for each point of diversion.

Water Code § 5103

(Amended by Stats. 2016, Ch. 32, Sec. 103. (SB 837) Effective June 27, 2016.)

Each statement shall be prepared on a form provided by the board. The statement shall include all of the following information:

(a) The name and address of the person who diverted water and of the person filing the statement.

(b) The name of the stream or other source from which water was diverted, and the name of the next major stream or other body of water to which the source is tributary.

(c) The place of diversion. The location of the diversion works shall be depicted on a specific United States Geological Survey topographic map, or shall be identified using the California Coordinate System, or latitude and longitude measurements. If assigned, the public land description to the nearest 40-acre subdivision and the assessor's parcel number shall also be provided.

(d) The capacity of the diversion works and of the storage reservoir, if any, and the months in which water was used during the preceding calendar year.

(e) (1) (A) At least monthly records of water diversions. The measurements of the diversion shall be made in accordance with Section 1840.

(B) (i) On and after July 1, 2016, the measurement of a diversion of 10 acre-feet or more per year shall comply with regulations adopted by the board pursuant to Article 3 (commencing with Section 1840) of Chapter 12 of Part 2.

(ii) The requirement of clause (i) is extended to January 1, 2017, for any statement filer that enters into a voluntary agreement that is acceptable to the board to reduce the statement filer's diversions during the 2015 irrigation season.

(2) (A) The terms of, and eligibility for, any grant or loan awarded or administered by the department, the board, or the California Bay-Delta Authority on behalf of a person that is subject to paragraph (1) shall be conditioned on compliance with that paragraph.

(B) Notwithstanding subparagraph (A), the board may determine that a person is eligible for a grant or loan even though the person is not complying with paragraph (1), if both of the following apply:

(i) The board determines that the grant or loan will assist the grantee or loan recipient in complying with paragraph (1).

(ii) The person has submitted to the board a one-year schedule for complying with paragraph (1).

(C) It is the intent of the Legislature that the requirements of this subdivision shall complement and not affect the scope of authority granted to the board by provisions of law other than this article.

(f) (1) The purpose of use.

(2) The amount of water used, if any, for cannabis cultivation.

(g) A general description of the area in which the water was used. The location of the place of use shall be depicted on a specific United States Geological Survey topographic map and on any other maps with identifiable landmarks. If assigned, the public land description to the nearest 40-acre subdivision and the assessor's parcel number shall also be provided.

(h) The year in which the diversion was commenced as near as is known.

Water Code § 13149

(Amended by Stats. 2021, Ch. 70, Sec. 116. (AB 141) Effective July 12, 2021.)

(a) (1) (A) The board, in consultation with the Department of Fish and Wildlife, shall adopt principles and guidelines for diversion and use of water for cannabis cultivation in areas where cannabis cultivation may have the potential to substantially affect instream flows. The principles and guidelines adopted under this section may include, but are not limited to, instream flow objectives, limits on diversions, and requirements for screening of diversions and elimination of barriers to fish passage. The principles and guidelines may include requirements that apply to groundwater extractions where the board determines those requirements are reasonably necessary for purposes of this section.

(B) Prior to adopting principles and guidelines under this section, the board shall allow for public comment and hearing, pursuant to Section 13147. The board shall provide an opportunity for the public to review and comment on the proposal for at least 60 days and shall consider the public comments before adopting the principles and guidelines.

(2) The board, in consultation with the Department of Fish and Wildlife, shall adopt principles and guidelines pending the development of long-term principles and guidelines under paragraph (1). The principles and guidelines, including the interim principles and guidelines, shall include measures to protect springs, wetlands, and aquatic habitats from negative impacts of cannabis cultivation. The board may update the interim principles and guidelines as it determines to be reasonably necessary for purposes of this section.

(3) The Department of Fish and Wildlife, in consultation with the board, may establish interim requirements to protect fish and wildlife from the impacts of diversions for cannabis cultivation pending the adoption of long-term principles and guidelines by the board under paragraph (1). The requirements may also include measures to protect springs, wetlands, and aquatic habitats from negative impacts of cannabis cultivation.

(b) (1) Notwithstanding Section 15300.2 of Title 14 of the California Code of Regulations, actions of the board and the Department of Fish and Wildlife under this section shall be deemed to be within Section 15308 of Title 14 of the California Code of regulations, provided that those actions do not involve relaxation of existing streamflow standards.

(2) The board shall adopt principles and guidelines under this section as part of state policy for water quality control adopted pursuant to Article 3 (commencing with Section 13140) of Chapter 3 of Division 7.

(3) If the Department of Fish and Wildlife establishes interim requirements under this section, it shall do so as emergency regulations in accordance with Chapter 3.5 (commencing with Section 11340) of Part 1 of Division 3 of Title 2 of the Government Code. The adoption of those interim requirements is an emergency and shall be considered by the Office of Administrative Law as necessary for the immediate preservation of the public peace, health, safety, and general welfare. Notwithstanding Chapter 3.5 (commencing with Section 11340) of Part 1 of Division 3 of Title 2 of the Government Code, the emergency regulations shall remain in effect until revised by the Department of Fish and Wildlife, provided that the emergency regulations shall not apply after long-term principles and guidelines adopted by the board under this section take effect for the stream or other body of water where the diversion is located.

(4) A diversion for cannabis cultivation is subject to both the interim principles and guidelines and the interim requirements in the period before final principles and guidelines are adopted by the board.

(5) The board shall have primary enforcement responsibility for principles and guidelines adopted under this section, and shall notify the Department of Cannabis Control of any enforcement action taken.

Water Code § 13260

(Amended by Stats. 2022, Ch. 678, Sec. 3. (SB 891) Effective January 1, 2023.)

(a) Each of the following persons shall file with the appropriate regional board a report of the discharge, containing the information that may be required by the regional board:

(1) A person discharging waste, or proposing to discharge waste, within any region that could affect the quality of the waters of the state, other than into a community sewer system.

(2) A person who is a citizen, domiciliary, or political agency or entity of this state discharging waste, or proposing to discharge waste, outside the boundaries of the state in a manner that could affect the quality of the waters of the state within any region.

(3) A person operating, or proposing to construct, an injection well.

(b) No report of waste discharge need be filed pursuant to subdivision (a) if the requirement is waived pursuant to Section 13269.

(c) Each person subject to subdivision (a) shall file with the appropriate regional board a report of waste discharge relative to any material change or proposed change in the character, location, or volume of the discharge.

(d) (1) (A) Each person who is subject to subdivision (a) or (c) shall submit an annual fee according to a fee schedule established by the state board.

(B) The total amount of annual fees collected pursuant to this section shall equal that amount necessary to recover costs incurred in connection with the issuance, administration, reviewing, monitoring, and enforcement of waste discharge requirements and waivers of waste discharge requirements.

(C) Recoverable costs may include, but are not limited to, costs incurred in reviewing waste discharge reports, prescribing terms of waste discharge requirements and monitoring requirements, enforcing and evaluating compliance with waste discharge requirements and waiver requirements, conducting surface water and groundwater monitoring and modeling, analyzing laboratory samples, adopting, reviewing, and revising water quality control plans and state policies for water quality control, and reviewing documents prepared for the purpose of regulating the discharge of waste, and administrative costs incurred in connection with carrying out these actions.

(D) In establishing the amount of a fee that may be imposed on a confined animal feeding and holding operation pursuant to this section, including, but not limited to, a dairy farm, the state board shall consider all of the following factors:

(i) The size of the operation.

(ii) Whether the operation has been issued a permit to operate pursuant to Section 1342 of Title 33 of the United States Code.

(iii) Any applicable waste discharge requirement or conditional waiver of a waste discharge requirement.

(iv) The type and amount of discharge from the operation.

(v) The pricing mechanism of the commodity produced.

(vi) Any compliance costs borne by the operation pursuant to state and federal water quality regulations.

(vii) Whether the operation participates in a quality assurance program certified by a regional water quality control board, the state board, or a federal water quality control agency.

(2) (A) Subject to subparagraph (B), the fees collected pursuant to this section shall be deposited in the Waste Discharge Permit Fund, which is hereby created. The money in the fund is available for expenditure by the state board, upon appropriation by the Legislature, solely for the purposes of carrying out this division.

(B) (i) Notwithstanding subparagraph (A), the fees collected pursuant to this section from stormwater dischargers that are subject to a general industrial or construction stormwater permit under the national pollutant discharge elimination system (NPDES) shall be separately accounted for in the Waste Discharge Permit Fund.

(ii) Not less than 50 percent of the money in the Waste Discharge Permit Fund that is separately accounted for pursuant to clause (i) is available, upon appropriation by the Legislature, for expenditure by the regional board with jurisdiction over the permitted industry or construction site that generated the fee to carry out stormwater programs in the region.

(iii) Each regional board that receives money pursuant to clause (ii) shall spend not less than 50 percent of that money solely on stormwater inspection and regulatory compliance issues associated with industrial and construction stormwater programs.

(3) A person who would be required to pay the annual fee prescribed by paragraph (1) for waste discharge requirements applicable to discharges of solid waste, as defined in Section 40191 of the Public Resources Code, at a waste management unit that is also regulated under Division 30 (commencing with Section 40000) of the Public Resources Code, shall be entitled to a waiver of the annual fee for the discharge of solid waste at the waste management unit imposed by paragraph (1) upon verification by the state board of payment of the fee imposed by Section 48000 of the Public Resources Code, and provided that the fee established pursuant to Section 48000 of the Public Resources Code generates revenues sufficient to fund the programs specified in Section 48004 of the Public Resources Code and the amount appropriated by the Legislature for those purposes is not reduced.

(e) Each person that discharges waste in a manner regulated by this section shall pay an annual fee to the state board. The state board shall establish, by regulation, a timetable for the payment of the annual fee. If the state board or a regional board determines that the discharge will not affect, or have the potential to affect, the quality of the waters of the state, all or part of the annual fee shall be refunded.

(f) (1) The state board shall adopt, by emergency regulations, a schedule of fees authorized under subdivision (d). The total revenue collected each year through annual fees shall be set at an amount equal to the revenue levels set forth in the Budget Act for this activity. The state board shall automatically adjust the annual fees each fiscal year to conform with the revenue levels set forth in the Budget Act for this activity. If the state board determines that the revenue collected during the preceding year was greater than, or less than, the revenue levels set forth in the Budget Act, the state board may further adjust the annual fees to compensate for the over and under collection of revenue.

(2) The emergency regulations adopted pursuant to this subdivision, any amendment thereto, or subsequent adjustments to the annual fees, shall be adopted by the state board in accordance with Chapter 3.5 (commencing with Section 11340) of Part 1 of Division 3 of Title 2 of the Government Code. The adoption of these regulations is an emergency and shall be considered by the Office of Administrative Law as necessary for the immediate preservation of the public peace, health, safety, and general welfare. Notwithstanding Chapter 3.5 (commencing with Section 11340) of Part 1 of Division 3 of Title 2 of the Government Code, any emergency regulations adopted by the state board, or adjustments to the annual fees made by the state board pursuant to this section, shall not be subject to review by the Office of Administrative Law and shall remain in effect until revised by the state board.

(g) The state board shall adopt regulations setting forth reasonable time limits within which the regional board shall determine the adequacy of a report of waste discharge submitted under this section.

(h) Each report submitted under this section shall be sworn to, or submitted under penalty of perjury.

(i) The regulations adopted by the state board pursuant to subdivision (f) shall include a provision that annual fees shall not be imposed on those who pay fees under the national pollutant discharge elimination system until the time when those fees are again due, at which time the fees shall become due on an annual basis.

(j) A person operating or proposing to construct an oil, gas, or geothermal injection well subject to paragraph (3) of subdivision (a) shall not be required to pay a fee pursuant to subdivision (d) if the injection well is regulated by the Geologic Energy Management Division of the Department of Conservation, in lieu of the appropriate California regional water quality control board, pursuant to the memorandum of understanding, entered into between the state board and the Department of Conservation on May 19, 1988. This subdivision shall remain operative until the memorandum of understanding is revoked by the state board or the Department of Conservation.

(k) In addition to the report required by subdivision (a), before a person discharges mining waste, the person shall first submit both of the following to the regional board:

(1) A report on the physical and chemical characteristics of the waste that could affect its potential to cause pollution or contamination. The report shall include the results of all tests required by regulations adopted by the board, any test adopted by the Department of Toxic Substances Control pursuant to Section 25141 of the Health and Safety Code for extractable, persistent, and bioaccumulative toxic substances in a waste or other material, and any other tests that the state board or regional board may require, including, but not limited to, tests needed to determine the acid-generating potential of the mining waste or the extent to which hazardous substances may persist in the waste after disposal.

(2) A report that evaluates the potential of the discharge of the mining waste to produce, over the long term, acid mine drainage, the discharge or leaching of heavy metals, or the release of other hazardous substances.

(l) Except upon the written request of the regional board, a report of waste discharge need not be filed pursuant to subdivision (a) or (c) by a user of recycled water that is being supplied by a supplier or distributor of recycled water for whom a master recycling permit has been issued pursuant to Section 13523.1.

Water Code § 13264

(Amended by Stats. 2003, Ch. 683, Sec. 1. Effective January 1, 2004.)

(a) No person shall initiate any new discharge of waste or make any material changes in any discharge, or initiate a discharge to, make any material changes in a discharge to, or construct, an injection well, prior to the filing of the report required by Section 13260 and no person shall take any of these actions after filing the report but before whichever of the following occurs first:

(1) The issuance of waste discharge requirements pursuant to Section 13263.

(2) The expiration of 140 days after compliance with Section 13260 if the waste to be discharged does not create or threaten to create a condition of pollution or nuisance and any of the following applies:

(A) The project is not subject to the California Environmental Quality Act (Division 13 (commencing with Section 21000) of the Public Resources Code).

(B) The regional board is the lead agency for purposes of the California Environmental Quality Act, a negative declaration is required, and at least 105 days have expired since the regional board assumed lead agency responsibility.

(C) The regional board is the lead agency for the purposes of the California Environmental Quality Act, and environmental impact report or written documentation prepared to meet the requirements of Section 21080.5 of the Public Resources Code is required, and at least one year has expired since the regional board assumed lead agency responsibility.

(D) The regional board is a responsible agency for purposes of the California Environmental Quality Act, and at least 90 days have expired since certification or approval of environmental documentation by the lead agency.

(3) The issuance of a waiver pursuant to Section 13269.

(b) The Attorney General, at the request of a regional board, shall petition the superior court for the issuance of a temporary restraining order, preliminary injunction, or permanent injunction, or combination thereof, as may be appropriate, prohibiting any person who is violating or threatening to violate this section from doing any of the following, whichever is applicable:

(1) Discharging the waste or fluid.

(2) Making any material change in the discharge.

(3) Constructing the injection well.

(c) (1) Notwithstanding any other provision of law, moneys collected under this division for a violation pursuant to paragraph (2) of subdivision (a) shall be deposited in the Waste Discharge Permit Fund and separately accounted for in that fund.

(2) The funds described in paragraph (1) shall be expended by the state board, upon appropriation by the Legislature, to assist regional boards, and other public agencies with authority to clean up waste or abate the effects of the waste, in cleaning up or abating the effects of the waste on waters of the state or for the purposes authorized in Section 13443.

Water Code § 13272

(Amended by Stats. 2014, Ch. 35, Sec. 184. (SB 861) Effective June 20, 2014.)

(a) Except as provided by subdivision (b), any person who, without regard to intent or negligence, causes or permits any oil or petroleum product to be discharged in or on any waters of the state, or discharged or deposited where it is, or probably will be, discharged in or on any waters of the state, shall, as soon as (1) that person has knowledge of the discharge, (2) notification is possible, and (3) notification can be provided without substantially impeding cleanup or other emergency measures, immediately notify the Office of Emergency Services of the discharge in accordance with the spill reporting provision of the California oil spill contingency plan adopted pursuant to Article 3.5 (commencing with Section 8574.1) of Chapter 7 of Division 1 of Title 2 of the Government Code.

(b) The notification required by this section shall not apply to a discharge in compliance with waste discharge requirements or other provisions of this division.

(c) Any person who fails to provide the notice required by this section is guilty of a misdemeanor and shall be punished by a fine of not less than five hundred dollars ($500) or more than five thousand dollars ($5,000) per day for each day of failure to notify, or imprisonment of not more than one year, or both. Except where a discharge to the waters of this state would have occurred but for cleanup or emergency response by a public agency, this subdivision shall not apply to any discharge to land that does not result in a discharge to the waters of this state. This subdivision shall not apply to any person who is fined by the federal government for a failure to report a discharge of oil.

(d) Notification received pursuant to this section or information obtained by use of that notification shall not be used against any person providing the notification in any criminal case, except in a prosecution for perjury or giving a false statement.

(e) Immediate notification to the appropriate regional board of the discharge, in accordance with reporting requirements set under Section 13267 or 13383, shall constitute compliance with the requirements of subdivision (a).

(f) The reportable quantity for oil or petroleum products shall be one barrel (42 gallons) or more, by direct discharge to the receiving waters, unless a more restrictive reporting standard for a particular body of water is adopted.

Water Code § 13276

(Amended by Stats. 2018, Ch. 92, Sec. 217. (SB 1289) Effective January 1, 2019. Note: This section was amended on

Nov. 8, 2016, by initiative Prop. 64.)

(a) The multiagency task force, the Department of Fish and Wildlife and state board pilot project to address the Environmental Impacts of Cannabis Cultivation, assigned to respond to the damages caused by cannabis cultivation on public and private lands in California, shall continue its enforcement efforts on a permanent basis and expand them to a statewide level to ensure the reduction of adverse impacts of cannabis cultivation on water quality and on fish and wildlife throughout the state.

(b) The state board or the appropriate regional board shall address discharges of waste resulting from cannabis cultivation under Division 10 (commencing with Section 26000) of the Business and Professions Code and associated activities, including by adopting a general permit, establishing waste discharge requirements, or taking action pursuant to Section 13269. In addressing these discharges, the state board or the regional board shall include conditions to address items that include, but are not limited to, all of the following:

(1) Site development and maintenance, erosion control, and drainage features.

(2) Stream crossing installation and maintenance.

(3) Riparian and wetland protection and management.

(4) Soil disposal.

(5) Water storage and use.

(6) Irrigation runoff.

(7) Fertilizers and soil.

(8) Pesticides and herbicides.

(9) Petroleum products and other chemicals.

(10) Cultivation-related waste.

(11) Refuse and human waste.

(12) Cleanup, restoration, and mitigation.

Water Code § 13387

(Amended by Stats. 2011, Ch. 15, Sec. 616. (AB 109) Effective April 4, 2011. Operative October 1, 2011, by Sec. 636 of Ch. 15, as amended by Stats. 2011, Ch. 39, Sec. 68.)

(a) Any person who knowingly or negligently does any of the following is subject to criminal penalties as provided in subdivisions (b), (c), and (d):

(1) Violates Section 13375 or 13376.

(2) Violates any waste discharge requirements or dredged or fill material permit issued pursuant to this chapter or any water quality certification issued pursuant to Section 13160.

(3) Violates any order or prohibition issued pursuant to Section 13243 or 13301, if the activity subject to the order or prohibition is subject to regulation under this chapter.

(4) Violates any requirement of Section 301, 302, 306, 307, 308, 318, 401, or 405 of the Clean Water Act (33 U.S.C. Sec. 1311, 1312, 1316, 1317, 1318, 1328, 1341, or 1345), as amended.

(5) Introduces into a sewer system or into a publicly owned treatment works any pollutant or hazardous

substances that the person knew or reasonably should have known could cause personal injury or property damage.

(6) Introduces any pollutant or hazardous substance into a sewer system or into a publicly owned treatment works, except in accordance with any applicable pretreatment requirements, which causes the treatment works to violate waste discharge requirements.

(b) Any person who negligently commits any of the violations set forth in subdivision (a) shall, upon conviction, be punished by a fine of not less than five thousand dollars ($5,000), nor more than twenty-five thousand dollars ($25,000), for each day in which the violation occurs, by imprisonment for not more than one year in a county jail, or by both that fine and imprisonment. If a conviction of a person is for a violation committed after a first conviction of the person under this subdivision, subdivision (c), or subdivision (d), punishment shall be by a fine of not more than fifty thousand dollars ($50,000) for each day in which the violation occurs, by imprisonment pursuant to subdivision (h) of Section 1170 of the Penal Code for 16, 20, or 24 months, or by both that fine and imprisonment.

(c) Any person who knowingly commits any of the violations set forth in subdivision (a) shall, upon conviction, be punished by a fine of not less than five thousand dollars ($5,000), nor more than fifty thousand dollars ($50,000), for each day in which the violation occurs, by imprisonment pursuant to subdivision (h) of Section 1170 of the Penal Code, or by both that fine and imprisonment. If a conviction of a person is for a violation committed after a first conviction of the person under this subdivision or subdivision (d), punishment shall be by a fine of not more than one hundred thousand dollars ($100,000) for each day in which the violation occurs, by imprisonment pursuant to subdivision (h) of Section 1170 of the Penal Code for two, four, or six years, or by both that fine and imprisonment.

(d) (1) Any person who knowingly commits any of the violations set forth in subdivision (a), and who knows at the time that the person thereby places another person in imminent danger of death or serious bodily injury, shall, upon conviction, be punished by a fine of not more than two hundred fifty thousand dollars ($250,000), imprisonment pursuant to subdivision (h) of Section 1170 of the Penal Code for 5, 10, or 15 years, or by both that fine and imprisonment. A person that is an organization shall, upon conviction under this subdivision, be subject to a fine of not more than one million dollars ($1,000,000). If a conviction of a person is for a violation committed after a first conviction of the person under this subdivision, the punishment shall be by a fine of not more than five hundred thousand dollars ($500,000), by imprisonment pursuant to subdivision (h) of Section 1170 of the Penal Code for 10, 20, or 30 years, or by both that fine and imprisonment. A person that is an organization shall, upon conviction for a violation committed after a first conviction of the person under this subdivision, be subject to a fine of not more than two million dollars ($2,000,000). Any fines imposed pursuant to this subdivision shall be in addition to any fines imposed pursuant to subdivision (c).

(2) In determining whether a defendant who is an individual knew that the defendant's conduct placed another person in imminent danger of death or serious bodily injury, the defendant is responsible only for actual awareness or actual belief that the defendant possessed, and knowledge possessed by a person other than the defendant, but not by the defendant personally, cannot be attributed to the defendant.

(e) Any person who knowingly makes any false statement, representation, or certification in any record, report, plan, notice to comply, or other document filed with a regional board or the state board, or who knowingly falsifies, tampers with, or renders inaccurate any monitoring device or method required under this division shall be punished by a fine of not more than twenty-five thousand dollars ($25,000), by imprisonment pursuant to subdivision (h) of Section 1170 of the Penal Code for 16, 20, or 24 months, or by both that fine and imprisonment. If a conviction of a person is for a violation committed after a first conviction of the person under this subdivision, punishment shall be by a fine of not more than twenty-five thousand dollars ($25,000) per day of violation, by imprisonment pursuant to subdivision (h) of Section 1170 of the Penal Code for two, three, or four years, or by both that fine and imprisonment.

(f) For purposes of this section, a single operational upset which leads to simultaneous violations of more than one pollutant parameter shall be treated as a single violation.

(g) For purposes of this section, "organization," "serious bodily injury," "person," and "hazardous substance" shall have the same meaning as in Section 309(c) of the Clean Water Act (33 U.S.C. Sec. 1319(c)), as amended.

(h) (1) Subject to paragraph (2), funds collected pursuant to this section shall be deposited in the State Water Pollution Cleanup and Abatement Account.

(2) (A) Notwithstanding any other provision of law, fines collected for a violation of a water quality certification in accordance with paragraph (2) of subdivision (a) or for a violation of Section 401 of the Clean Water Act (33 U.S.C. Sec. 1341) in accordance with paragraph (4) of subdivision (a) shall be deposited in the Water Discharge Permit Fund and separately accounted for in that fund.

(B) The funds described in subparagraph (A) shall be expended by the state board, upon appropriation by the Legislature, to assist regional boards, and other public agencies with authority to clean up waste or abate the effects of the waste, in cleaning up or abating the effects of the waste on waters of the state, or for the purposes authorized in Section 13443.

Water Code § 13575

(Amended by Stats. 1998, Ch. 753, Sec. 1. Effective January 1, 1999.)

(a) This chapter shall be known and may be cited as the Water Recycling Act of 1991.

(b) As used in this chapter, the following terms have the following meanings:

(1) "Customer" means a person or entity that purchases water from a retail water supplier.

(2) "Entity responsible for groundwater replenishment" means any person or entity authorized by statute or court order to manage a groundwater basin and acquire water for groundwater replenishment.

(3) "Recycled water" has the same meaning as defined in subdivision (n) of Section 13050.

(4) "Recycled water producer" means any local public entity that produces recycled water.

(5) "Recycled water wholesaler" means any local public entity that distributes recycled water to retail water suppliers and which has constructed, or is constructing, a recycled water distribution system.

(6) "Retail water supplier" means any local entity, including a public agency, city, county, or private water company, that provides retail water service.

(7) "Retailer" means the retail water supplier in whose service area is located the property to which a customer requests the delivery of reycled water service.

XIV. Welfare and Institutions Code

Welfare and Institutions Code § 328.2

(Added by Stats. 2022, Ch. 260, Sec. 1. (AB 2595) Effective January 1, 2023.)

The State Department of Social Services shall update all regulations, all-county letters, and other instructions relating to the investigation of a minor who may be described by Section 300 to ensure that, when a social worker is investigating an alleged case of child abuse or neglect, a parent's or guardian's use or possession of cannabis is treated in the same manner as a parent's or guardian's use or possession of alcohol and legally prescribed medication.

Part 2: Regulations

I. Title 3. Food and Agriculture

DIVISION 4. PLANT INDUSTRY

Chapter 8. Industrial Hemp Cultivation

ARTICLE 1. REGISTRATION OF INDUSTRIAL HEMP GROWERS

§ 4890. Definitions.

(a) For purposes of this chapter, the following definitions apply:

(1) "Acceptable hemp THC level" means a THC concentration that falls within the distribution or range that includes three-tenths of one percent or less that is produced when the measurement of uncertainty is applied to the reported THC concentration. For example, if the reported THC concentration of a sample is 0.35% and the measurement of uncertainty is ± 0.06%, the measured THC concentration would range from 0.29% to 0.41%. Because 0.3% is within the distribution or range, the sample is within the acceptable hemp THC level.

(2) "Cannabis" has the same meaning as defined in subdivision (e) of Section 26001 of the Business and Professions Code.

(3) "Central cola" means a cut stem that could develop into a bud of the flowering top of the plant.

(4) "Criminal history report" means the Federal Bureau of Investigation's Identity History Summary.

(5) "Cultivar" means a cultivated variety of industrial hemp.

(6) "Cultivation" means the planting, growing, irrigation, or harvesting of an industrial hemp plant or crop.

(7) "Cultivation site" means contiguous land area on which the applicant plans to engage in industrial hemp cultivation, storage, or both.

(8) "Cultivator" means a person planting, cultivating, growing, irrigating, or harvesting industrial hemp plants or crop.

(9) "Destroy" or "dispose" means an activity that transitions the non-compliant product into a non-retrievable or non-ingestible form. Such activities include plowing, tilling, or disking plant material into the soil; mulching, composting, chopping, or bush mowing plant material into green manure; burning plant material; burying plant material into the earth and covering with soil.

(10) "Disqualifying conviction" means any plea of guilty or nolo contendere, or any finding of guilt for a State or Federal felony related to a controlled substance, except:

(A) when the finding of guilt is subsequently overturned on appeal, pardoned, or expunged, or

(B) where an individual is allowed to withdraw an original plea of guilty or nolo contendere and enter a plea of not guilty and the case is subsequently dismissed.

(11) "Established agricultural research institution" means an institution of higher education, as defined in Section 101 of the federal Higher Education Act of 1965 (20 U.S.C. Sec. 1001), that grows, cultivates, or manufactures industrial hemp for purposes of agricultural or academic research.

(12) "Grower" means a person that is registered with the commissioner to cultivate hemp for sale.

(13) "Harvest" means the collection of any portion of industrial hemp plant.

(14) "Hemp breeder" means a person that is registered with the commissioner to develop cultivars intended for sale or research.

(15) "Industrial hemp" or "hemp" means an agricultural product, whether growing or not, that is limited to types of the plant Cannabis sativa L. and any part of that plant, including the seeds of the plant and all derivatives, extracts, the resin extracted from any part of the plant, cannabinoids, isomers, acids, salts, and salts of isomers, with a total delta-9 tetrahydrocannabinol concentration of no more than 0.3 percent on a dry weight basis.

(16) "Industrial hemp nursery stock" means any industrial hemp plant or any part of an industrial hemp plant for planting or propagation.

(17) "Key participants" includes the registrant and means any person in the entity producing industrial hemp who is:

(A) a sole proprietor, a partner in partnership, or a person with executive managerial control in a corporation producing industrial hemp, or

(B) a person with executive managerial control over the entity producing industrial hemp, including persons such as a chief executive officer, chief operating officer and chief financial officer.

(C) This definition does not include a person in a management position with no executive managerial control over the entity producing industrial hemp, such as farm, field, or shift managers.

(D) For established agricultural research institutions, this definition does not include a person that is a member of the leadership of the established agricultural research institution unless the member of the leadership exercises executive managerial control over the hemp production.

(18) "Measurement of uncertainty" means the parameter associated with the result of a measurement that characterizes the dispersion of the values that could reasonably be attributed to the particular quantity subject to measurement.

(19) "Person" means any individual, partnership, association, corporation, limited liability company, or any organized group of persons whether incorporated or not.

(20) "Premises" has the same meaning as defined in subdivision (aq) of Section 26001 of the Business and Professions Code.

(21) "Research plan" means a strategy devised by an established agricultural research institution, or applicant established agricultural research institution, detailing its approach to growing or cultivating hemp for academic or agricultural research.

(22) "THC concentration" or "percentage concentration of THC" means the post-decarboxylated value of the percentage of delta-9 THC content derived from the sum of THC and THCA content and reported on a dry weight basis to the nearest thousandth, or three decimal places. The percentage concentration of THC may be measured by using either:

(A) a suitable analytical instrumentation described in Section 4942(b) that results in the decarboxylation of THC-acid to delta-9 THC, or

(B) a calculated value using a conversion formula of the percentage concentration of delta-9 THC plus eighty-seven and seven tenths (87.7) percent of the percentage concentration of THC-acid when a suitable analytical instrumentation described in Section 4942(b) does not result in the decarboxylation of

THC-acid to delta-9 THC.

(23) "Tissue culture" means in vitro material introduced into culture from nodal cuttings at a particular time and from a single plant and grown in aseptic conditions to be used as a source of propagative plant material.

(24) "Valid registration" means the registration is unexpired, unsuspended, and unrevoked.

(25) "Variety development plan" means a strategy devised by a hemp breeder, or applicant hemp breeder, detailing their approach to growing and developing a new cultivar for industrial hemp.

NOTE: Authority cited: Sections 407, 81003, 81004, 81004.5, 81006 and 81013, Food and Agricultural Code. Reference: Sections 81000, 81003, 81004, 81004.5, 81006 and 81013, Food and Agricultural Code.

§ 4900. Registration Fees.

(a) The Secretary establishes the following fees for registration of growers of industrial hemp and hemp breeders to be submitted along with the registration application as authorized in sections 81003 and 81004 of the Food and Agricultural Code:

(1) Prior to cultivation, a fee of nine-hundred dollars ($900) per applicant shall be submitted with the application to the commissioner.

(2) A separate registration is required for each county in which the applicant intends to grow industrial hemp.

(3) This registration is valid for one year from date of issuance by the commissioner.

(b) The Secretary establishes the following fee for registration renewal of growers of industrial hemp and hemp breeders:

(1) Upon expiration of registration, a fee of nine-hundred dollars ($900) per registrant shall be due to the commissioner in each county in which the applicant intends to continue to grow industrial hemp.

(2) Renewed registration is valid for one year from date of issuance of renewal by the commissioner.

NOTE: Authority cited: Sections 407, 483 and 81005, Food and Agricultural Code. Reference: Sections 81003, 81004 and 81005, Food and Agricultural Code.

§ 4901. Registration Application for Industrial Hemp.

(a) Registration.

(1) Any person cultivating industrial hemp must have a valid registration prior to cultivation.

(2) Except for an established agricultural research institution subject to Food and Agricultural Code Section 81004.5 or a hemp breeder subject to Food and Agricultural Code Section 81004, a grower of industrial hemp, before cultivation, shall register with the commissioner of the county in which the grower intends to engage in industrial hemp cultivation. The registration application for growers of industrial hemp shall include:

(A) the name, physical address, and contact information of the applicant, including mailing address, telephone number, and email (if available),

(B) the business type (sole proprietor, partnership, corporation, limited liability company, or specified other type), business name(s) including all DBAs ("doing business as"), principal business address, and the employer identification number (EIN) of the business entity as provided by the Internal Revenue Service,

(C) the name(s), title(s), and email(s) (if available) of all key participants,

(D) the legal description, Global Positioning System coordinates, size, and map of the cultivation site(s),

(E) the approved cultivar to be grown, including the state or country of origin, and supporting documentation to demonstrate compliance with Section 4920, and

(F) the applicant's signature certifying the following:

1. the information provided on the application is true and correct,

2. the cultivation site(s) to be registered for industrial hemp cultivation is not on premises licensed by the Department of Cannabis Control to cultivate or process cannabis,

3. the applicant shall comply with all the requirements outlined in Division 24 of the Food and Agricultural Code and this chapter, and

4. any changes to the registration shall be provided to the commissioner in accordance with Section 4901(b).

(3) Except for an established agricultural research institution subject to Food and Agricultural Code Section 81004.5 or a grower of industrial hemp subject to Food and Agricultural Code Section 81003, a hemp breeder, before cultivation, shall register with the commissioner of the county in which the hemp breeder intends to engage in industrial hemp cultivation. The registration application for hemp breeders shall include:

(A) the name, physical address, and contact information of the applicant, including mailing address, telephone number, and email (if available),

(B) the business type (sole proprietor, partnership, corporation, limited liability company, or specified other type), business name(s) including all DBAs ("doing business as"), principal business address, and the employer identification number (EIN) of the business entity as provided by the Internal Revenue Service,

(C) the name(s), title(s), and email(s) (if available) of all key participants,

(D) the legal description, Global Positioning System coordinates, size, and map of the cultivation site(s),

(E) a variety development plan, which shall include:

1. the name of the seed-certifying agency that will be conducting the certification if a new cultivar is to be certified by a seed-certifying agency,

2. the hemp varieties that will be used and, if applicable, how those varieties will be used in the development of a new cultivar,

3. a plan for testing the THC concentration of a representative sample of the plants grown,

a. Industrial hemp produced by registered hemp breeders that does not enter the stream of commerce shall not be subject to the sampling requirements outlined in Section 4941(b) if the sampling method to test THC concentration has the potential to ensure, at a confidence level of 95 percent, that the plants grown will not test above the acceptable hemp THC level pursuant to Part 990.3 in Title 7 of the Code of Federal Regulations (October 31, 2019) which is hereby incorporated by reference, and

b. Industrial hemp produced by registered hemp breeders that enters the stream of commerce shall be sampled in accordance with the sampling procedures outlined in Sections 4940 through 4941 and tested in accordance with the testing procedures outlined in Sections 4942 through 4944.

4. the measures that will be taken to destroy any plants with THC concentrations that test above the acceptable hemp THC level, given that

a. Any hemp destruction shall be conducted in accordance with Section 297B of the federal Agricultural Marketing Act of 1946 (added by Section 10113 of the federal Agriculture Improvement Act of 2018 (December 20, 2018) (Public Law 115-334)), implementing regulations, and guidance which is hereby incorporated by reference.

5. the measures that will be taken to prevent the unlawful use of hemp under Division 24 of the Food and Agricultural Code and this chapter,

6. a procedure for the maintenance of records documenting the development of the new cultivar, and

(F) the applicant's signature certifying the following:

1. the information provided on the application is true and correct,

2. the cultivation site(s) to be registered for industrial hemp cultivation is not on premises licensed by the Department of Cannabis Control to cultivate or process cannabis,

3. the applicant shall comply with all the requirements outlined in Division 24 of the Food and Agricultural Code and this chapter, and

4. any changes to the registration shall be provided to the commissioner in accordance with Section 4901(b).

(4) Except for a grower of industrial hemp subject to Food and Agricultural Code Section 81003 or a hemp breeder subject to Food and Agricultural Code Section 81004, an established agricultural research institution, before cultivation, shall register with the commissioner of the county in which the established agricultural research institution intends to engage in industrial hemp cultivation. Subsection (b)(4) shall become operative as of the date on which a state plan for California is approved in accordance with Food and Agricultural Code Section 81004.5(h). The registration application for established agricultural research institutions shall include:

(A) the name, physical address, and contact information of the applicant, including mailing address, telephone number, and email (if available),

(B) the business type (sole proprietor, partnership, corporation, limited liability company, or specified other type), business name(s) including all DBAs ("doing business as" designations), and principal business address,

(C) the name(s), title(s), and email(s) (if available) of all key participants,

(D) the legal description, Global Positioning System coordinates, size, and map of the cultivation site(s),

(E) a research plan, which shall include:

1. the hemp varieties that will be used and, if applicable, how those varieties will be used for the purposes of agricultural or academic research,

2. a plan for testing a representative sample of the plants cultivated,

a. Industrial hemp produced by registered established agricultural research institutions that does not enter the stream of commerce shall not be subject to the sampling requirements outlined in Section 4941(b) if the sampling method to test THC concentration has the potential to ensure, at a confidence level of 95 percent, that the plants grown will not test above the acceptable hemp THC level, and is adopted by the department and approved by the United States Department of Agriculture pursuant to Part 990.3 in Title 7 of the Code of

Federal Regulations (October 31, 2019) which is hereby incorporated by reference, and

b. Industrial hemp produced by registered established agricultural research institutions that enters the stream of commerce shall be sampled in accordance with the sampling procedures outlined in Sections 4940 through 4941 and tested in accordance with the testing procedures outlined in Sections 4942 through 4944.

3. the measures that will be taken to destroy any plants with THC concentrations that test above the acceptable hemp THC level, given that,

a. Any hemp destruction shall be conducted in accordance with Section 297B of the federal Agricultural Marketing Act of 1946 (added by Section 10113 of the federal Agriculture Improvement Act of 2018 (December 20, 2018) (Public Law 115-334)), implementing regulations, and guidance which is hereby incorporated by reference,

b. Registered established agricultural research institutions registered with the United States Drug Enforcement Administration to handle marijuana may possess industrial hemp with a laboratory test report that indicates a percentage concentration of THC that is greater than the acceptable hemp THC level if the possession contributes to the development of types of industrial hemp that will fall within the acceptable hemp THC level, until the end of the study, at which point the industrial hemp testing greater than the acceptable hemp THC level must be disposed of according to Section 4901(a)(4)(E)3.a.

4. a procedure for the maintenance of records documenting the agricultural or academic research, and

(F) the applicant's signature certifying the following:

1. the information provided on the application is true and correct,

2. the cultivation site(s) to be registered for industrial hemp cultivation is(are) not on premises licensed by the Department of Cannabis Control to cultivate or process cannabis,

3. the applicant shall comply with all the requirements outlined in Division 24 of the Food and Agricultural Code and this chapter, and

4. any changes to the registration shall be provided to the commissioner in accordance with Section 4901(b).

(5) Each registration application, except for established agricultural research institutions, shall be accompanied with the registration or renewal fee in accordance with Section 4900.

(6) Each registration application shall be accompanied by criminal history reports for all key participants in accordance with Section 4902.

(b) Alterations or changes to registration.

(1) Registration is non-transferrable to another person. A new registration application shall be submitted in accordance with Section 4901(a) for any change in ownership of the business or registered plants.

(2) Registrants shall submit an updated registration application to the commissioner for any of the following alterations or changes:

(A) Any alterations or changes to business name, contact information, or key participants must be submitted within 15 calendar days of the change.

(B) Any alterations or changes to cultivation sites, approved cultivars, variety development plans, or research plans, must be approved by the commissioner prior to planting.

(3) Any alterations or changes not submitted to the commissioner in accordance with the specified timeframes outlined in Section 4901(b) shall result in the existing crop being considered non-compliant and subject to destruction in accordance with Section 4950.

(c) Registration renewal.

(1) A registrant shall submit a registration application in accordance with the registration procedures outlined in Section 4901(a) to the commissioner in each county in which the applicant intends to renew the registration at least 30 calendar days prior to the expiration of registration. Renewal applications received less than 30 calendar days from registration expiration may result in noncompliance with Section 4901(a).

(2) If the registration application for renewal is received less than 30 calendar days from registration expiration and registration is not renewed prior to registration expiration, any existing plantings shall be considered noncompliant with Section 4901(a) upon registration expiration.

(d) Commissioner approval, refusal, or revocation.

(1) Once the commissioner receives the application in accordance with the registration procedures outlined in Section 4901(a) and Section 4901(b) for registration, registration amendment, or renewal and determines that the registration requirements pursuant to Division 24 of the Food and Agricultural Code and this chapter are met, the commissioner shall issue a registration to the applicant and notify the registrant that the key participants as defined in Section 4890(a)(17) with no disqualifying convictions may cultivate hemp using the registered cultivar(s), cultivation site(s), research plan(s), and variety development plan(s). For new registrations and registration amendments, the commissioner shall issue such registration and notice within 30 calendar days from the application submission date. For registration renewals, the commissioner shall issue such registration and notice prior to registration expiration, unless the application is received less than 30 calendar days prior to registration expiration, in which case the commissioner shall issue the registration and notice as soon as reasonably possible but not necessarily before expiration.

(2) The commissioner may verify the registration application by conducting field inspections. The commissioner shall be provided with complete and unrestricted access during business hours to all hemp and other cannabis plants, whether growing or harvested, and all land, buildings, and other structures used for the cultivation, handling, and storage of all hemp and other cannabis plants, and all locations registered as a cultivation site.

(3) If the commissioner determines that the application for registration or renewal does not meet the registration requirements outlined in Division 24 of the Food and Agricultural Code and this chapter, the commissioner shall provide written notification to the applicant of the deficiencies in the application. If the deficiency is a lack of requested information, the applicant shall have 30 calendar days from the receipt of the notification to provide the requested information to the commissioner. If the requested information is not provided within the timeframe, the commissioner shall deny registration.

(A) If registration is denied due to deficiencies in the application for registration or renewal, the applicant must submit a new application and registration or renewal fee (if applicable) to the commissioner in order to register to cultivate hemp.

(e) The following information shall be transmitted by the commissioner to the department no more than 10 business days, and submitted by the department to the United States Department of Agriculture no more than 30 business days, after the date on which it is collected, or, in the case of subparagraph (b), the date of a change in registration status:

(1) the name and contact information for each registrant,

(2) the employer identification number (EIN) of the business entity as provided by the Internal Revenue Service,

(3) a legal description of the land on which the registrant engages in hemp cultivation,

(4) the registration status of the registrant,

(5) the registration number for each registrant associated with each location in the state where hemp will be produced, and

(6) the name, business title, and email address (if available) of all key participants for each registration.

(f) The department and the commissioner shall retain information collected under this section for at least three years after collecting or receiving it.

NOTE: Authority cited: Sections 407, 81003, 81004, 81004.5, 81005, 81006 and 81013, Food and Agricultural Code. Reference: Sections 81003, 81004, 81004.5, 81005, 81006 and 81013, Food and Agricultural Code.

§ 4902. Criminal History Report for Industrial Hemp Registration.

(a) Registration requirements.

(1) A criminal history report for each key participant listed pursuant to Section 4901 shall be submitted along with the application in accordance with the registration procedures outlined in Section 4901(a) for registration, registration amendment, or renewal to the commissioner. A registration application will not be considered complete without all required criminal history reports.

(2) Any changes to key participants must be reported along with criminal history reports for any additional key participants to the commissioner as an amendment to the registration within 15 calendar days of the change.

(3) All criminal history reports must be dated within 60 calendar days of submission of the application for registration, registration amendment, or renewal.

(4) Registrants shall notify the commissioner in writing within 48 hours of the registrant or a key participant receiving a disqualifying conviction.

(5) If an applicant, registrant, or key participant is found to have a disqualifying conviction, the applicant or key participant shall be ineligible to participate in the hemp program for ten (10) years from the date of the conviction.

(6) Any falsification of criminal history reports shall be considered as materially falsifying information in an application or registration and shall result in revocation or refusal of registration and ineligibility to participate in the industrial hemp program.

(7) The commissioner may require additional criminal history reports during the registration period as deemed necessary to ensure all registered key participants do not have a disqualifying conviction.

NOTE: Authority cited: Sections 407, 81003, 81004, 81004.5 and 81013, Food and Agricultural Code. Reference: Sections 81003, 81004, 81004.5, 81013 and 81014, Food and Agricultural Code.

ARTICLE 2. REGULATIONS FOR INDUSTRIAL HEMP CULTIVATION

§ 4920. List of Approved Seed Cultivars.

(a) The Secretary, as provided in Section 81002 of the Food and Agricultural Code, adopts the following list of approved cultivars.

(1) Industrial hemp seed or propagative materials certified as breeder, foundation, registered, or certified seed or stock by one of the following agencies:

(A) Member organizations of the Association of Official Seed Certifying Agencies,

(B) Organization of Economic Cooperation and Development, or

(C) An officially approved and recognized seed-certifying agency listed in Title 3, California Code of Regulations, Section 3875, as provided in Section 52401 of the Food and Agricultural Code.

(2) Industrial hemp seed or propagative materials produced in a quality assurance program approved by one of the following agencies:

(A) Member organizations of the Association of Official Seed Certifying Agencies,

(B) Organization of Economic Cooperation and Development, or

(C) An officially approved and recognized seed-certifying agency listed in Title 3, California Code of Regulations, Section 3875, as provided in Section 52401 of the Food and Agricultural Code.

(3) Industrial hemp seed or propagative materials produced by an authorized participant in a state industrial hemp agricultural pilot program, pursuant to Section 7606 of the federal Agricultural Act of 2014 (7 U.S.C. Sec. 5940) or an authorized participant under an approved state, tribal, or federal regulatory plan for hemp production pursuant to Section 297B of the federal Agriculture Improvement Act of 2018 (December 20, 2018) (Public Law 115-334).

(A) The crop from which the seed or propagative materials were harvested from shall have been tested in accordance with a testing method approved by the regulatory authority in the state of origin and found to have no more than three-tenths of one percent tetrahydrocannabinol (THC) on a dry weight basis.

(B) The commissioner shall be notified of the importation of all propagative materials into the county. The shipment is subject to inspection by the commissioner and shall not be used for cultivation until released by the commissioner (California Food and Agricultural Code Division 4, Part 2, Chapter 2 Sections 6401 and 6501).

(4) Industrial hemp seeds or tissue culture plants imported from outside the United States that meets federal importation requirements.

(A) The crop from which the seeds or tissue culture plants were harvested from shall have been tested in accordance with a testing method approved by the department of agriculture in the country of origin and found to have no more than three-tenths of one percent THC on a dry weight basis.

(B) The commissioner shall be notified of the importation of all propagative materials into the county. The shipment is subject to inspection by the commissioner and shall not be used for cultivation until released by the commissioner (California Food and Agricultural Code Division 4, Part 2, Chapter 2 Sections 6401 and 6501).

(C) For the purposes of this section, the term “tissue culture” means in vitro material introduced into culture from nodal cuttings at a particular time and from a single plant and grown in aseptic conditions to be used as a source of propagative material.

(5) Industrial hemp seed or propagative materials produced in California in accordance with the provisions of Division 24 of the Food and Agricultural Code and this chapter.

(A) The crop from which the seed or propagative materials were harvested from shall have been tested by a department-approved laboratory and found to have no more than three-tenths of one percent THC on a dry weight basis.

(B) The commissioner shall be notified of the importation of all propagative materials into the county. The shipment is subject to inspection by the commissioner and shall not be used for cultivation until released by the commissioner (California Food and Agricultural Code Division 4, Part 2, Chapter 2 Sections 6401 and 6501).

NOTE: Authority cited: Sections 407 and 81002, Food and Agricultural Code. Reference: Sections 81001 and 81002, Food and Agricultural Code.

§ 4921. Methodology and Procedure to Update the List of Approved Seed Cultivars.

(a) The Secretary adopts the following methodology and procedure to add, amend or remove a cultivar from the list of approved cultivars.

(1) Upon request from the chair of the Board, or of any four members of the Board, the Department shall schedule a public hearing to consider a proposal to update the list of approved cultivars by adding, amending, or removing cultivars. A notice and text of the proposal shall be made available to the public no less than 30 days prior to the hearing.

(2) The public hearing to consider a proposal to update the list of approved cultivars shall be part of a regularly scheduled meeting of the Industrial Hemp Advisory board.

(3) The public hearing shall include:

(A) Presentation of the proposal to update the list of approved cultivars;

(B) Presentation of the purpose for the update; and

(C) Opportunity for public comment, pursuant to Section 11125.7 of the Government Code.

(4) After receiving comments from the public, the Board shall vote to accept, amend and accept, or deny a proposal for recommendation to the Secretary.

(5) Upon recommendation by the Board to adopt a proposal and approval by the Secretary, the Department shall amend the list of approved cultivars and shall submit the amended list to the Office of Administrative Law to be filed promptly with the Secretary of State. Pursuant to Section 81002 of the Food and Agricultural Code, the proposal shall not be subject to further review.

(6) The Department shall post the list of approved cultivars to its website and shall provide electronic and/or mail notification of amendments to list of approved cultivars to parties that have requested notification. An interested party may go to the Department's website and elect to receive automatic notifications of any changes to the list of approved cultivars via an electronic mail listserv.

(b) Amendment of the methodology and procedure.

(1) By motion, the Board may recommend amending the methodology and procedure in subsection (a). In consultation with the chair of the Board, the Department shall schedule a public hearing to consider the recommendation, and a notice and text of the proposed amendment shall be made available to the public no less than 30 days prior to the hearing.

(2) The public hearing to consider a proposal to amend the methodology and procedure shall be part of a regularly scheduled meeting of the Industrial Hemp Advisory Board.

(3) The public hearing shall include:

(A) Presentation of the proposal to amend the methodology and procedure;

(B) Presentation of the purpose for the amendment; and

(C) Opportunity for public comment, pursuant to Section 11125.7 of the Government Code.

(4) After receiving comments from the public, the Board shall vote to accept, amend and accept, or deny the proposal for recommendation to the Secretary.

(5) Upon recommendation by the Board to adopt the amendment and approval by the Secretary, the Department shall amend the methodology and procedure, and shall submit the amended methodology and procedure to the Office of Administrative Law to be filed promptly with the Secretary of State. Pursuant to Section 81002 of the Food and Agricultural Code, the proposal shall not be subject to further review.

(6) The Department shall provide electronic and/or mail notification of the amendment to the methodology and procedure to parties that have requested notification. An interested party may go to the Department's website and elect to receive automatic notifications of any changes to the methodology and procedure via an electronic mail listserv.

NOTE: Authority cited: Sections 407 and 81002, Food and Agricultural Code. Reference: Sections 81001 and 81002, Food and Agricultural Code.

§ 4930. Inspections of Industrial Hemp.

(a) The commissioner shall conduct annual inspections of a random group of registrants to verify that industrial hemp is not produced in violation of Division 24 of the Food and Agricultural Code and this chapter.

(b) The commissioner shall be provided with complete and unrestricted access during business hours to all hemp and other cannabis plants, whether growing or harvested, and all land, buildings, and other structures used for the cultivation, handling, and storage of all hemp and other cannabis plants, and all locations registered as a cultivation site.

(c) Registered hemp breeders and registered established agricultural research institutions shall provide records that document the varietal development or research activities conducted under the approved plan upon the request of the commissioner.

NOTE: Authority cited: Sections 407, 81003, 81004, 81004.5 and 81006, Food and Agricultural Code. Reference: Sections 81006, Food and Agricultural Code.

§ 4934. Planting Location Requirements.

(a) Except when grown by a registered established agricultural research institution or a registered hemp breeder, the industrial hemp shall be grown in acreages of not less than one-tenth of an acre at the same time.

(b) All plantings shall have signage indicating they are industrial hemp.

NOTE: Authority cited: Sections 407, 81003, 81004, 81004.5 and 81006, Food and Agricultural Code. Reference: Sections 81006, Food and Agricultural Code.

§ 4935. Planting Report for Industrial Hemp.

(a) In order to confirm that industrial hemp was planted at a registered cultivation site, registrants shall submit a signed planting report to the commissioner within 72 hours following the completion of the planting. A separate planting report shall be completed for each planting. The planting report shall include the:

(1) registrant's registration number,

(2) name and contact information of the registrant,

(3) planting date(s),

(4) name(s) of the cultivar(s) and the quantity planted,

(5) physical address, Global Positioning System coordinates, general description of the planting location, and total acreage or square footage of the planting, and

(6) planned growing period for each cultivar planted.

(b) The Department shall make a template of a planting report form available on the Department's website.

(c) The commissioner may confirm the planting of the crop by conducting field inspections. The commissioner shall be provided with complete and unrestricted access during business hours to all hemp and other cannabis plants, whether growing or harvested, and all land, buildings, and other structures used for the cultivation, handling, and storage of all hemp and other cannabis plants, and all locations registered as a cultivation site.

(d) All registrants shall report on all hemp production in the state and any changes to where hemp will be produced to the United States Department of Agriculture Farm Service Agency within 30 calendar days of completion of a planting and shall provide, at minimum, all of the following information and changes:

(1) registrant's registration number,

(2) physical address, Global Positioning System coordinates, general description of the planting location, and

(3) acreage dedicated to the production of hemp, or greenhouse or indoor square footage.

NOTE: Authority cited: Sections 407, 81003, 81004, 81004.5, 81004.6 and 81006, Food and Agricultural Code. Reference: Section 81006, Food and Agricultural Code.

§ 4936. Movement of Industrial Hemp Nursery Stock.

(a) No less than 72 hours prior to the movement of industrial hemp nursery stock from its registered cultivation site or a change in ownership of the industrial hemp nursery stock, the registrant shall sign and complete a transfer form, provided by the commissioner of the county where the industrial hemp nursery stock is registered, and:

(1) for movement or change of ownership within California, submit the completed form to the commissioner of the destination county, if different than the county of origin, or

(2) for interstate movement or change in ownership, submit the completed form to the destination state's department of agriculture.

(b) The transfer form shall include:

(1) originating registrant's name, registration number, contact information, and physical address of the origin site,

(2) receiving registrant's name, registration number, contact information, physical address of the destination site,

(3) anticipated start and end date of the movement or date of change in ownership, and

(4) name and number of each cultivar of plants moved or transferred to new ownership.

(c) The bill of lading shall be provided to the Department, the commissioner, or local law enforcement upon request.

NOTE: Authority cited: Sections 407, 81003, 81004, 81004.5 and 81006, Food and Agricultural Code. Reference: Sections 81006, Food and Agricultural Code.

§ 4940. Sampling Timeframe and Pre-Harvest Notification for Industrial Hemp.

(a) Sampling Timeframe.

(1) Samples shall be collected no more than 11 calendar days prior to the anticipated harvest start date listed on the pre-harvest report.

(2) Any changes to the harvest date that result in harvest activities to occur more than 30 calendar days after the sample collection date shall require additional sampling for THC concentration prior to harvest.

(b) Sampling Request and Pre-Harvest Report.

(1) In order to request sampling, registrants shall submit a signed pre-harvest report to the commissioner at least 30 calendar days before the anticipated harvest start date to initiate the sampling process.

(2) A separate pre-harvest report shall be completed for each planting to be harvested. The pre-harvest report shall include the:

(A) registrant's registration number,

(B) name and contact information of the registrant,

(C) anticipated harvest start date,

(D) name(s) of the cultivar(s) to be harvested,

(E) physical address, Global Positioning System coordinates, general description of the planting location, and total acreage or square footage of the planting to be harvested, and

(F) name and contact information of the laboratory to conduct the testing for THC concentration.

(3) The pre-harvest report shall be accompanied by a sample analysis request form for each composite sample to be taken. The sample analysis request form shall be used to record the following information during the sampling and testing process:

(A) name, contact information, and signature of the sample analysis requester,

(B) registrant's registration number,

(C) name and contact information of the commissioner,

(D) physical address, general description of the planting location, and total acreage or square footage of the planting sampled,

(E) lot identification number as provided by United States Department of Agriculture Farm Service Agency,

(F) name of the cultivar sampled,

(G) description of the planting to be sampled including estimated average height, appearance, approximate density, homogeneity, condition of the plants, and degree of maturity of flowering material,

(H) unique sample identification number for the composite sample,

(I) number of the samples taken,

(J) date and time of the sample collection,

(K) name and signature of the sampler,

(L) name and contact information of the approved laboratory conducting the THC testing,

(M) name and signature of the person testing the sample,

(N) date and time of the sample testing,

(O) testing instrumentation used to analyze the sample for THC concentration,

(P) laboratory determination of THC concentration in accordance with Section 4890(a)(22) and limit of detection (LOD), and

(Q) chain of custody information including the name and signature of the person who received and delivered the sample, and the date, time, and location of each possession or transfer of the sample.

(4) The Department shall make a template of a pre-harvest report and sample analysis request form available on the Department's website.

(5) The sampler, as described in Section 4941(a)(1), shall schedule a sampling date.

(6) Registrants shall notify the commissioner of any changes to the above information no less than two calendar days prior to the scheduled sampling date.

NOTE: Authority cited: Sections 407 and 81006, Food and Agricultural Code. Reference: Section 81006, Food and Agricultural Code.

§ 4941. Sampling Procedures for Testing Industrial Hemp for THC Concentration.

(a) Collection of Samples.

(1) Samples for THC testing shall be collected by USDA-certified samplers. Samples shall not be collected by a hemp registrant or key participant.

(A) All samplers shall complete training using USDA training procedures and submit the certificate of completion electronically to the Department to the email industrialhemp@cdfa.ca.gov.

(B) The Department shall maintain a publicly available list of USDA-certified samplers on the Department's website.

(2) Prior to the collection of the samples, the sampler as described in Section 4941(a)(1) shall verify that the planting to be sampled corresponds to the registered cultivation site using the physical address, Global Positioning System coordinates, general description, and total acreage or square footage provided on the pre-harvest report and registration application.

(3) The registrant or an authorized representative of the registrant shall be present to observe the collection of samples and shall allow the sampler as described in Section 4941(a)(1), complete and unrestricted access during business hours to all hemp and other cannabis plants, whether growing or harvested, and all land, buildings, and other structures used for the cultivation, handling, and storage of all hemp and other cannabis

plants, and all locations registered as a cultivation site.

(b) Sample Volume and Composition.

(1) Each sample shall be collected from different plants. Each sample shall consist of the terminal eight inches from the main stem that includes leaves and flowers, terminal bud that occurs at the end of a stem, or central cola. If the plant is less than eight inches tall, the whole plant above ground shall be taken.

(2) A composite sample shall consist of the following:

(A) one sample from each plant for plantings that have fewer than six plants.

(B) six samples for plantings that are less than or equal to six acres.

(C) one sample from each acre for plantings that are greater than six acres but less than ten acres.

(D) For plantings equal to or greater than ten acres, the number of samples shall be calculated at a confidence level of 95 percent that the plants grown will not test above the acceptable hemp THC level, using the following formula where n is the number of plants to be selected and N is the planting acreage:

$n = 299 / (1 + (298 / N))$

(3) A separate composite sample shall be taken for:

(A) each cultivar within each contiguous planting, and

(B) indoor and outdoor growing areas shall be treated as separate plantings.

(c) Handling of Samples.

(1) All plant material collected for a composite sample shall be placed together in a permeable bag, and kept in a manner not conducive to mold growth. Each composite sample shall be stored in separate bags.

(2) The bag containing the composite sample shall be sealed and labeled in a manner to detect tampering and ensure chain of custody. Sample labels shall be signed by both the registrant and the sampler as described in Section 4941(a)(1).

(3) Samples shall be labeled with a unique sample identification number as assigned on the sample analysis request form and accompanied by the following documentation:

(A) registrant's proof of registration,

(B) pre-harvest report,

(C) sample analysis request form containing information outlined in Sections 4940(b)(3)(B) through 4940(b)(3)(L) provided by the commissioner and Section 4940(b)(3)(A) provided by the registrant.

(4) Samples shall be delivered to the testing laboratory within 24 hours of collection.

NOTE: Authority cited: Sections 407 and 81006, Food and Agricultural Code. Reference: Section 81006, Food and Agricultural Code.

§ 4942. Approved Testing Method for Testing Industrial Hemp for THC Concentration.

(a) Sample Preparation.

(1) The laboratory shall maintain chain of custody upon receiving the samples by documenting the chain of custody information on the sample analysis request form. The laboratory shall provide the information outlined in Sections 4940(b)(3)(M) through 4940(b)(3)(Q) on the sample analysis request form.

(2) The laboratory shall check the sample for any signs of tampering. The laboratory shall immediately notify the commissioner and not test the sample if there is evidence of tampering. New samples shall be collected and submitted to the laboratory for testing in accordance with the procedures outlined in Section 4941.

(3) Each composite sample shall be maintained and tested separately for THC concentration.

(4) All plant material included in the composite sample shall be processed and tested as a single sample.

(5) Each composite sample shall be tested for THC concentration on dry weight basis. The laboratory can either:

(A) Dry all plant material included in the composite sample until the weight of the composite sample remains constant after drying intervals (typically five to 12 percent moisture content). Drying temperature shall not exceed 90 degrees Celsius. The moisture content shall be expressed as the ratio of the amount of moisture in the sample to the amount of dry solid in the sample; or

(B) Analyze the moisture content of the sample and factor the measured moisture content into the THC concentration for a dry weight basis by using the following formula:

THC concentration on dry weight basis = THC concentration of the wet sample/(1.0 - (percentage weight of the wet sample/100)).

(6) All of the dried plant material included in the composite sample shall be ground using a centrifugal rotor mill or a similar method to mill and combine the sample into a homogenous powder-like consistency before analysis.

(b) Suitable analytical instrumentation used to determine THC concentration in industrial hemp includes the following:

(1) gas chromatography with flame ionization detector,

(2) gas chromatography coupled with mass spectrometry,

(3) liquid chromatography coupled with mass spectrometry, or

(4) liquid chromatography coupled with diode-array or variable wavelength detector.

(c) Sample Retention and Disposal.

(1) If the laboratory test report indicates a percentage concentration of THC that is equal to or less than the acceptable hemp THC level, the laboratory shall retain the sample for a minimum of 30 calendar days from the testing date.

(2) If the laboratory test report indicates a percentage concentration of THC that exceeds the acceptable hemp THC level, the laboratory shall retain the sample for a minimum of 60 calendar days from the testing date. Between 60 and 120 calendar days from testing date, the laboratory shall destroy the samples in a manner compliant with Section 297B of the federal Agricultural Marketing Act of 1946 (added by Section 10113 of the federal Agriculture Improvement Act of 2018 (December 20, 2018) (Public Law 115-334)) which is hereby incorporated by reference.

NOTE: Authority cited: Sections 407 and 81006, Food and Agricultural Code. Reference: Section 81006, Food and Agricultural Code.

§ 4943. Approved Laboratory for Testing Industrial Hemp for THC Concentration.

(a) Testing of industrial hemp for THC concentration shall be conducted by a laboratory with International Organization for Standardization (ISO) / International Electrotechnical Commission (IEC) 17025 accreditation using a validated method in accordance with Sections 4942, 4944, and 4945 for THC analysis on plant material from an accreditation body that is a signatory to the International Laboratory Accreditation Cooperation (ILAC) Mutual Recognition Arrangement.

(1) Laboratories testing industrial hemp for THC concentration shall register with the United States Drug Enforcement Administration no later than December 31, 2022.

(2) Laboratories shall meet the AOAC International Standard Method Performance Requirements (SMPR) for Quantitation of Cannabinoids in Plant Materials of Hemp (Low THC Varieties Cannabis sp.) (SMPR 2019.003, October 9, 2019), which is hereby incorporated by reference, for each testing method used.

(b) A laboratory shall obtain written approval from the Department before testing industrial hemp for THC concentration. A laboratory shall submit a signed laboratory approval application with the following information to the Department for review and approval:

(1) name and contact information of the applicant,

(2) name and physical address of the testing laboratory,

(3) starting December 31, 2022, a copy of the testing laboratory's DEA registration certificate, if applicable,

(4) a copy of the testing laboratory's ISO/IEC 17025 certificate of accreditation,

(5) a copy of the testing laboratory's ISO/IEC 17025 scope of accreditation,

(6) a copy of the testing laboratory's standard operating procedures for THC testing, and

(7) a copy of the laboratory sample test report in accordance with Section 4944(b).

(c) Once the Department receives the application in accordance with the application procedures outlined in Section 4943(b) for approval or renewal and determines that the requirements outlined in this section are met and the laboratory's standard operating procedures for THC testing and sample test report comply with the requirements outlined in Sections 4942, 4944, and 4945, the Department shall approve the laboratory to conduct THC testing on industrial hemp using the approved standard operating procedures in 4943(b)(6) for THC testing and laboratory test report by issuing a proof of approval, and adding the testing laboratory to the list of approved testing laboratories.

(d) If the Department determines that the application for approval or renewal does not meet the testing laboratory requirements outlined Division 24 of the Food and Agricultural Code and this chapter, the Department shall provide written notification to the laboratory applicant of the deficiencies in the application. If the deficiency is a lack of requested information required in 4943(b), the applicant shall have 30 calendar days from the receipt of the notification to provide the requested information to the Department. If the requested information is not provided within the timeframe, the Department will deny approval.

(1) If laboratory approval is denied due to deficiencies in the application for approval or renewal, the applicant must submit a new application to the Department in order to obtain approval to test industrial hemp for THC concentration.

(e) If the Department determines that the approved testing laboratory no longer meets the testing laboratory requirements outlined in Division 24 of the Food and Agricultural Code and this chapter, the Department shall revoke the approval and provide written notification to the laboratory applicant regarding the revocation. The revocation is effective as of the date on the notification.

(f) Laboratory approval shall be valid for one year from date of approval by the Department, after which the laboratory shall renew the approval.

(g) Laboratories shall request renewal of Department approval in accordance with the procedures outlined in Section 4943(b). Renewed approval shall be valid for one year from date of renewal by the Department.

(h) Any changes to the approved laboratory's standard operating procedures shall be submitted to the Department for review and approval prior to implementation. Once the Department has determined that the requirements outlined in this section are met and the laboratory's standard operating procedures comply with testing requirements outlined in Sections 4942, 4944, and 4945, the Department shall notify the laboratory that testing may be completed under the revised standard operating procedures.

(i) The Department shall make a template of a laboratory application and the list of approved testing laboratories available on the Department's website.

NOTE: Authority cited: Sections 407 and 81006, Food and Agricultural Code. Reference: Section 81006, Food and Agricultural Code.

§ 4944. Notification of Laboratory Test Report.

(a) Laboratories shall issue a separate laboratory test report for each composite sample.

(b) The laboratory test report shall include the:

(1) registration number,

(2) unique sample identification number as assigned on the sample analysis request form,

(3) name and contact information of the registrant,

(4) name of the sampler,

(5) dates and times of the sample collection, testing, and test report,

(6) name of the cultivar tested,

(7) physical address, Global Positioning System coordinates, general description of the planting location, and total acreage or square footage of the planting sampled,

(8) lot identification number as provided by United States Department of Agriculture Farm Service Agency,

(9) name and contact information of the laboratory,

(10) name of approved analytical instrumentation used and the limit of detection (LOD),

(11) name of the person who received the sample,

(12) name of the person who tested the sample

(13) DEA registration number of the laboratory, if applicable,

(14) identification of a retest, if applicable,

(15) percentage concentration of THC in accordance with Section 4890(a)(22),

(16) measurement of uncertainty as a ± percentage value to the nearest thousandth, or three decimal places, at 95% confidence level,

(17) the words "OFFICIAL CALIFORNIA REGULATORY SAMPLE",

(18) and words "PASSED AS CALIFORNIA INDUSTRIAL HEMP" or "FAILED AS CALIFORNIA INDUSTRIAL HEMP" at or near the top of page.

(A) If the laboratory test report indicates a percentage concentration of THC that is within the acceptable hemp THC level, the words "PASSED AS CALIFORNIA INDUSTRIAL HEMP" shall appear.

(B) If the laboratory test report indicates a percentage concentration of THC that is greater than the acceptable hemp THC level, the words "FAILED AS CALIFORNIA INDUSTRIAL HEMP" shall appear.

(c) Laboratories shall provide an electronic copy of the laboratory test report to the registrant and commissioner concurrently within 10 calendar days of the collection of samples.

(d) Following the electronic notification of the laboratory test report, the laboratory shall:

(1) report the results for all samples required to be tested to the United States Department of Agriculture,

(2) provide the registrant no fewer than ten original paper copies with wet signatures of a passing laboratory test report, signed by an employee authorized to sign by the laboratory,

(3) provide the registrant one or more paper copies of a failed laboratory test report, signed by an employee authorized to sign by the laboratory,

(e) Upon request from the commissioner, the laboratory shall provide a copy of the completed sample analysis request form.

(f) The laboratory shall retain one or more original copies of each laboratory test report and the completed sample analysis request form for a minimum of three years from the date of sampling.

NOTE: Authority cited: Sections 407 and 81006, Food and Agricultural Code. Reference: Section 81006, Food and Agricultural Code.

§ 4945. Approved Testing Method for Retesting of Industrial Hemp for THC Concentration.

(a) Additional samples for retesting shall be collected in accordance with the sampling procedures outlined in Section 4941 and tested in accordance with the testing procedures outlined in Sections 4942 through 4944.

NOTE: Authority cited: Sections 407 and 81006, Food and Agricultural Code. Reference: Section 81006, Food and Agricultural Code.

§ 4946. Final Disposition for Registered Industrial Hemp Crops.

(a) Registrants shall harvest the sampled crop only upon receipt of an electronic copy of a passing laboratory test report.

(1) Registrants shall submit a harvest report to the commissioner within 72 hours following the completion of the harvest. The harvest report shall include the:

(A) registration number,

(B) name and contact information of the registrant,

(C) harvest timeframe including start and end dates,

(D) name(s) of the cultivar(s),

(E) unique sample identification number(s) as assigned on the sample analysis request form and the percentage concentration of THC for each cultivar as reported on the laboratory test report,

(F) physical address, Global Positioning System coordinates, general description of the planting location, and total acreage or square footage of the harvested planting, and

(G) description and quantity of the material harvested.

(2) The Department shall make a template of a harvest report form available on the Department's website.

(3) Harvest shall be completed within 30 calendar days from the sampling date.

(A) Registrants may request additional sampling and testing in accordance with the procedures outlined in Section 4940 to extend the harvest timeframe.

1. The most recent laboratory test report electronically received by the commissioner in compliance with Sections 4940 through 4945 shall be considered the effective THC concentration for determining whether the planting may be harvested and determining compliance with Division 24 of the Food and Agricultural Code.

2. All previous laboratory test reports received for the same planting shall be invalid upon the commissioner's receipt of an electronic copy of the most recent laboratory test report. If the most recent laboratory test report indicates a percentage concentration of THC that is greater than the acceptable hemp THC level but does not exceed one percent, the registrant may request one additional retest in accordance with Section 4945.

(4) The commissioner may confirm the completion of the harvest by conducting field inspections. The commissioner shall be provided with complete and unrestricted access during business hours to all hemp and other cannabis plants, whether growing or harvested, and all land, buildings, and other structures used for the cultivation, handling, and storage of all hemp and other cannabis plants, and all locations registered as a cultivation site.

(5) Registrant shall provide an original copy of the passing test report to any person transporting, purchasing, or obtaining the industrial hemp.

(b) Registrants shall not harvest the sampled crop that received a failed laboratory test report. Hemp crops that received a failed laboratory test report cannot be further handled or processed, except in accordance with Section 4950, and may not enter the stream of commerce.

(1) If the initial laboratory test report indicates a percentage concentration of THC that is greater than the acceptable hemp THC level but does not exceed one percent, the registrant may request one additional retest in accordance with Section 4945.

(c) Registrants shall destroy a crop that receives a failed laboratory test report within the following timeframes:

(1) If a laboratory test report indicates the percentage concentration of THC exceeds one percent, the destruction shall begin within 48 hours, and be completed within seven calendar days, after the registrant's receipt of an electronic copy of the laboratory test report. The commissioner shall issue a notice of abatement to the registrant within 48 hours of the receipt of the electronic copy of the laboratory test report.

(2) If a second laboratory test report from retesting indicates the percentage concentration of THC exceeds the acceptable hemp THC level but is less than one percent, the destruction shall take place as soon as practicable, but no later than 45 calendar days after the registrant's receipt of an electronic copy of the second laboratory test report. The commissioner shall issue a notice of abatement to the registrant within 48 hours of the receipt of the electronic copy of the laboratory test report.

(d) Registrant shall retain an original signed copy of the laboratory test report for two years from the date of sampling and make the original signed copy of the laboratory test report available to the Department, the commissioner, or law enforcement officials or their designees upon request.

NOTE: Authority cited: Sections 407 and 81006, Food and Agricultural Code. Reference: Section 81006, Food and Agricultural Code.

ARTICLE 3. ABATEMENT AND ENFORCEMENT

§ 4950. Destruction of Non-Compliant Industrial Hemp Crops.

(a) Any industrial hemp crop that does not meet the requirements of Division 24 of the Food and Agricultural Code and this chapter shall be destroyed in a manner compliant with Section 297B of the federal Agricultural Marketing Act of 1946 (added by Section 10113 of the federal Agriculture Improvement Act of 2018 (December 20, 2018) (Public Law 115-334), implementing regulations, and guidance which is hereby incorporated by reference.

(1) Unless otherwise specified in Section 4946 (c), any non-compliant industrial hemp crop shall be destroyed as soon as practical, but destruction must be completed no later than 45 calendar days after the cultivator's receipt of notification of abatement from the commissioner.

(b) The cultivator of the industrial hemp crop shall submit a signed destruction plan to the commissioner at least 24 hours prior to the start of the destruction, unless a shorter timeframe is allowed by the commissioner. The destruction plan shall include the:

(1) registration number, if applicable,

(2) name and contact information of the cultivator,

(3) anticipated destruction date(s) of the crop to be destroyed,

(4) name(s) of the cultivar(s) to be destroyed,

(5) unique sample identification number(s) as assigned on the sample analysis request form and percentage concentration of THC for each cultivar as reported on the laboratory test report, if applicable,

(6) physical address, Global Positioning System coordinates, general description and location type of the planting location, and total square footage or acreage of the destroyed planting,

(7) lot identification number as provided by United States Department of Agriculture Farm Service Agency, if available, and

(8) destruction method compliant with Section 297B of the federal Agricultural Marketing Act of 1946 (added by Section 10113 of the federal Agriculture Improvement Act of 2018 (December 20, 2018) (Public Law 115-334), implementing regulations, and guidance which is hereby incorporated by reference.

(c) The destruction plan shall be approved by the commissioner prior to the start of the destruction.

(d) Unless destroyed by a reverse distributor registered with the United States Drug Enforcement Administration or by law enforcement, the destruction shall be conducted at the planting site.

(e) The cultivator shall submit a signed destruction report to the commissioner within 72 hours following the completion of the destruction. The destruction report shall include the:

(1) registration number, if applicable,

(2) name and contact information of the cultivator,

(3) date(s) and time(s) of destruction,

(4) name(s) of the cultivar(s) destroyed,

(5) unique sample identification number(s) and percentage concentration of THC for each cultivar as reported on the laboratory test report, if applicable,

(6) physical address, Global Positioning System coordinates, general description and location type of the planting location, and total square footage or acreage of the destroyed planting,

(7) lot identification number as provided by United States Department of Agriculture Farm Service Agency, if available, and

(8) description and quantity of the material destroyed.

(f) The commissioner shall confirm the destruction of the crop by either conducting field inspections or directing cultivators to provide pictures or videos that disposal occurred successfully. The commissioner shall be provided with complete and unrestricted access during business hours to all hemp and other cannabis plants, whether growing or harvested, and all land, buildings, and other structures used for the cultivation, handling, and storage of all hemp and other cannabis plants, and all locations registered as a cultivation site.

(g) The Department shall make a template of a destruction plan and destruction report available on the Department's website.

(h) The Department shall notify the United States Department of Agriculture by certified mail or electronically by the first of each month of any occurrence of non-compliant plants or plant material and provide a disposal record for those plants and materials in accordance with the procedure outlined in Part 990.70(b) in Title 7 of the Code of Federal Regulations.

NOTE: Authority cited: Sections 407, 81003, 81004, 81004.5 and 81006, Food and Agricultural Code. Reference: Section 81006, Food and Agricultural Code.

§ 4950.1. Voluntary Destruction of Industrial Hemp Crops.

(a) Any cultivator that wishes to voluntarily destroy a crop shall destroy the crop in a manner compliant with Section 297B of the federal Agricultural Marketing Act of 1946 (added by Section 10113 of the federal Agriculture Improvement Act of 2018 (December 20, 2018) (Public Law 115-334), implementing regulations, and guidance which is hereby incorporated by reference.

(b) The cultivator shall report destruction of the crop to the commissioner in accordance with procedures outlined in Section 4950(b) through (e).

NOTE: Authority cited: Sections 407, 81003, 81004, 81004.5 and 81006, Food and Agricultural Code. Reference: Section 81006, Food and Agricultural Code.

§ 4951. Corrective Action Plan.

(a) If the commissioner finds a cultivator has negligently violated Food and Agricultural Code Division 24 or this chapter, the commissioner shall issue a notice of violation and require a corrective action plan be provided by the cultivator. Negligent violations, defined as the failure to exercise the standard of care that a reasonably prudent person would have exercised in a similar situation shall include:

(1) failing to provide a legal description of the land on which the cultivator cultivates hemp,

(2) failing to obtain registration prior to cultivation, or

(3) producing hemp with a THC concentration greater than the acceptable hemp THC level except that cultivators do not commit a negligent violation for producing hemp with a THC concentration greater than the acceptable hemp THC level if the crop does not have a total delta-9 tetrahydrocannabinol concentration of more than 1.0 percent on a dry weight basis.

(c) A notice of violation shall describe:

(1) the violations charged to the recipient,

(2) the right to request a hearing before the commissioner via a written appeal, as specified in Section 4952 (a), including the email, mailing address, physical address, and/or website that may be used to submit an appeal

(3) a corrective action plan, and

(4) an administrative hold, if applicable.

(c) A notice of violation that is sent by certified mail to the last known address of the person charged shall be considered received even if delivery is refused or the notice is not accepted at that address.

(d) If the commissioner determines that hemp grown not in compliance with Food and Agricultural Code Division 24 or this chapter will negatively affect the welfare or well-being of the general public, it is in the public interest to issue an order for the administrative hold of hemp:

(1) The order shall provide a description of the hemp to be subject to the administrative hold.

(2) Within twenty-four (24) hours of receipt of the order for administrative hold, the person in possession of the hemp subject to the hold shall physically segregate, safeguard and preserve all industrial hemp subject to the hold in the area designated on the licensee's premises diagram.

(3) While the administrative hold is in effect, the person in possession of the industrial hemp is restricted from selling, donating, transferring, transporting, gifting, giving away, or destroying the industrial hemp that is subject to the hold.

(4) Nothing herein shall prevent a registrant from continued possession, cultivation, or harvesting of the industrial hemp subject to the administrative hold. While the administrative hold is in effect, all industrial hemp subject to the hold shall be segregated from industrial hemp that is not subject to hold.

(5) Nothing herein shall prevent a person in possession of the hemp from voluntarily surrendering industrial hemp subject to an administrative hold to the commissioner. The registrant shall identify the hemp being voluntarily surrendered. Voluntary surrender does not waive the right to a hearing and any associated rights.

(6) Nothing herein shall prevent the person who is in possession of the hemp from inspecting it or from taking a sample according to Section 4941 and testing according to Section 4942 for evidence while in the presence of a person designated by the commissioner.

(7) The hold order shall be nullified upon issuance of a decision under Section 4952(a), (b), or (q) that finds the person charged in the notice of violation was not and is not in violation as so charged.

(8) If the notice of violation places a hold on hemp, or requires a person to cease operations, the notice of violation shall remain in effect pending the outcome of the hearings in Section 4952(a), (b), or (q).

(9) Nothing herein shall be construed to extend required destruction timeframes and waive prohibitions on cultivation or harvest in Division 24 of the Food and Agricultural Code or this chapter.

(10) The Commissioner shall remove a hold order upon finding that the violation that caused the hold order has been corrected.

(e) The commissioners or the Department shall not apply more than one negligent violation towards the eligibility requirement outlined in Section 4951(k) per calendar year.

(f) The cultivator will be required to provide a corrective action plan to the commissioner within 15 calendar days from the receipt of the notice of violation. The corrective action plan shall include:

(1) a reasonable date, not to exceed 45 calendar days, by which the cultivator shall correct the violation,

(2) measures to correct the violation, and

(3) periodic reporting to the commissioner on its compliance with the requirements of Division 24 of the Food and Agricultural Code, this chapter, and the corrective action plan for a minimum of two years from the date of the violation.

(g) The corrective action plan shall be approved by the commissioner prior to implementation of the corrective action plan.

(h) The commissioner shall confirm compliance with the corrective action plan by conducting field inspections. The commissioner shall be provided with complete and unrestricted access during business hours to all hemp and other cannabis, whether growing or harvested, and all land, buildings, and other structures used for the cultivation, handling, and storage of all hemp and other cannabis plants, and all locations registered as a cultivation site.

(i) Failure to comply with this section shall result in revocation of registration and the existing crop may be considered non-compliant and subject to destruction in accordance with Section 4950.

(j) Revocation shall be effective within 30 calendar days from the notice of violation unless appealed pursuant to Section 4952.

(k) A grower of industrial hemp, established agricultural research institution, or hemp breeder that commits a negligent violation three times in a five-year period shall be ineligible to participate in the industrial hemp program for a period of five years beginning on the date of the finding of the third violation.

(l) A cultivator shall not, as a result of a negligent violation, be subject to any criminal enforcement action by the state or local government.

(m) The Secretary shall immediately report any violations that are determined by the department or commissioner to have been conducted with a mental state greater than negligence which is defined as acting intentionally, knowingly, willfully, recklessly, or with criminal negligence including, but not limited to, intentionally, with recklessness, or with gross negligence, to the Attorney General of the United States and the Attorney General of California. Subsections (a) through (g) of this section shall not apply to such violations.

NOTE: Authority cited: Sections 407, 81003, 81004, 81004.5 and 81012, Food and Agricultural Code. Reference: Section 81012, Food and Agricultural Code.

§ 4952. Appeals.

(a) Appeals to the commissioner. A respondent may contest a notice of violation or a lab report issued pursuant to Food and Agricultural Code Section 81006(e) within 30 calendar days from the date of the notice of violation by submitting a written request, via email, mailing address, physical address, or website, as specified in the notice of violation, for a hearing before the commissioner.

(1) Failure to present a timely request for a hearing constitutes a waiver of the respondent's right to contest the notice of violation or lab report.

(2) At the hearing, the person shall be given an opportunity to review the commissioner's evidence and to present evidence on his or her own behalf.

(3) Within 60 calendar days of the receipt of a written request for a hearing, the commissioner shall hold a hearing, a hearing officer assigned by the commissioner shall issue a proposed decision and order, and the commissioner shall mail notice of the order to the respondent. The order is effective as of the date on the notice.

(b) Appeals to the Secretary. If the person upon whom the commissioner issued a notice of violation requested and appeared at the hearing, the person may appeal the commissioner's decision to the Secretary within 30 calendar days of the date of receiving a copy of the commissioner's decision.

(1) To appeal the commissioner's decision, the appellant shall send a written request to the Legal Office of Hearings and Appeals of the Department of Food and Agriculture, 1220 N Street, Room 315, Sacramento, California 95814 or via email to CDFA.LegalOffice@cdfa.ca.gov.

(A) The written request shall include:

1. a copy of the commissioner's decision,

2. the notice of violation,

3. a clear and concise statement of the basis for the appeal, and

4. the signature of the appellant or his or her authorized agent.

(2) The appellant shall submit a copy of the appeal with the commissioner at the same time it is filed with the Secretary.

(3) Both the appellant and the commissioner, at the time appellant files the appeal or within 10 calendar days thereafter, may submit the record of the hearing and a written argument to the Secretary stating the ground for affirming, modifying, or reversing the commissioner's decision. All documents must be submitted to the Legal Office of Hearings and Appeals of the California Department of Food and Agriculture, 1220 N Street, Suite 315, Sacramento, California 95814 or via email at CDFA.LegalOffice@cdfa.ca.gov.

(4) The department shall schedule an informal hearing within 45 calendar days from receipt of the request for an informal hearing. The department shall provide a notice of informal hearing to the appellant containing the following information:

(A) date, location, and time of the informal hearing, and

(B) a statement to the appellant that the appellant may, but need not, be represented by counsel at any or all stages of the proceedings.

(5) Any objection to the department's selection of the informal hearing procedure instead of a formal hearing procedure shall be made in writing to the Legal Office of Hearings and Appeals and shall be resolved by the hearing officer prior to the hearing.

(6) Hearings shall be presided over and conducted by a hearing officer designated by the Secretary. In no instance shall any employee of the Industrial Hemp Program serve as the hearing officer in any hearing conducted pursuant to this section.

(7) If the hearing officer finds substantial evidence in the record to support the commissioner's decision, the Secretary shall affirm the commissioner's decision.

(8) Hearings may be conducted by teleconference, at the discretion of the hearing officer.

(9) The decision of the hearing officer shall be in writing and include a statement of the factual legal basis of

the decision.

(10) The decision shall be issued within 30 calendar days after the conclusion of the hearing and may be issued orally at the conclusion of the hearing subject to written confirmation.

(11) The written decision shall be served on the respondent either by personal service, facsimile transmission, or email.

(12) The hearing officer's decision shall be effective immediately upon first articulation under subsection (10) and shall be final and not appealable to the Secretary or any other officer of the department.

(13) The person charged may challenge the hearing officer's decision by filing a writ of administrative mandamus in the appropriate court pursuant to Code of Civil Procedure Section 1094.5.

(c) The commissioner may deny, suspend, or revoke a registration for any violation of the Division 24 of the Food and Agricultural Code or this chapter.

(1) The commissioner shall notify the person charged with a violation pursuant to the notice requirements of Section 4951 (a).

(2) Any person who is noticed of denial, suspension, or revocation of registration may request a hearing before the Secretary within 30 calendar days of the date of receiving a copy of the commissioner's notice.

(3) The hearing shall be scheduled by the Department consistent with the provisions of Chapter 5 (commencing with Section 11500), Part 1, Division 3, Title 2 of the Government Code, and any applicable regulations enacted pursuant to these provisions.

(4) Hearings concerning the denial, suspension, or revocation of a registration shall be conducted pursuant to Chapter 5 (commencing with Section 11500) Part 1, Division 3, Title 2 of the Government Code.

(5) The standard of proof to be applied by the Department is preponderance of the evidence. The commissioner shall have the burden of proof and the burden of producing evidence.

NOTE: Authority cited: Sections 407, 81003, 81004, 81004.5 and 81012, Food and Agricultural Code. Reference: Section 81012, Food and Agricultural Code.

DIVISION 8. CANNABIS CULTIVATION

Chapter 1. Cannabis Cultivation Program [Renumbered]

Change without regulatory effect renumbering and amending title 3, division 8, chapter 1 (articles 1-7, sections 8000-8609) to new title 4, division 19, chapter 9, (articles 1-7, sections 16000-16609), including repealer of sections 8111 and 8407.

Chapter 2. Cannabis Appellations Program

ARTICLE 1. DEFINITIONS

§ 9000. Definitions.

The following definitions apply to this chapter:

(a) "Cultivar" means a cultivated variety, trade designation, or strain of cannabis.

(b) "Petitioning organization" means a group of licensed cultivators representing three or more unique businesses within the geographical area of the proposed appellation of origin.

(c) "Petitioner" means the licensee designated by the petitioning organization to be the primary contact for the petition.

(d) "Practice" means an allowed or prohibited method of cultivation or method of conducting commercial cannabis activity.

(e) "Standard" means a measurable, scorable, or certified requirement applicable to the cannabis or cultivation.

Note: Authority cited: Section 26063, Business and Professions Code. Reference: Section 26063, Business and Professions Code.

ARTICLE 2. PETITIONS

§ 9100. Submission of Petitions.

(a) A petitioning organization may submit a petition to the department to:

(1) Establish a new appellation of origin; or

(2) Amend an existing appellation of origin.

(b) Petitions shall be submitted to the mailing address or email address listed on the Cannabis Appellations Program webpage on the department's website.

(c) Petition submission fees, pursuant to section 9101 of this chapter, shall be paid at the time the petition is submitted to the department.

(d) Petition proposal fees, pursuant to section 9101 of this chapter, shall be paid at the request of the department according to section 9200, subdivision (b) of this chapter.

Note: Authority cited: Section 26063, Business and Professions Code. Reference: Section 26063, Business and Professions Code.

§ 9101. Petition Fees.

(a) The following are the non-refundable petition fees for the specified petitions:

(1) Petition to Establish an Appellation of Origin:

(A) A petition submission fee of $2,850; and

(B) A petition proposal fee of $14,250.

(2) Petition to Amend an Appellation of Origin:

(A) A petition submission fee of $1,425; and

(B) A petition proposal fee of $7,125.

Note: Authority cited: Sections 26012, 26013, 26063, and 26180, Business and Professions Code. Reference: Sections

26012, 26013 and 26180, Business and Professions Code.

§ 9102. Petition to Establish an Appellation of Origin.

A petition to establish a new appellation of origin shall include:

(a) Petitioner name, license numbers issued by the department, primary contact phone number, email address, and preferred method of contact;

(b) Names, license numbers issued by the department, and signatures of individuals in the petitioning organization;

(c) A general description and location of the proposed geographical area which may include information such as total acreage of the area, total canopy acreage within the area that is currently occupied under licensed commercial cannabis cultivation, and estimated cannabis canopy acreage eligible to use the proposed appellation of origin;

(d) Evidence of name use pursuant to section 9104 of this chapter;

(e) A description and documentation of the boundary of the proposed appellation of origin pursuant to section 9105 of this chapter;

(f) A description and evidence of distinctive geographical features affecting cannabis produced in the boundary of the proposed appellation of origin pursuant to section 9106 of this chapter;

(g) Identification and definition of all standard, practice, and cultivar requirements of the proposed appellation of origin pursuant to section 9107 of this chapter;

(h) A description and evidence of the legacy, history, reputation, and economic importance of cannabis production in the area;

(i) If the proposed appellation of origin is located either partially or fully within the geographical area of another appellation of origin, an explanation of how the proposed appellation of origin is distinct from the existing appellation of origin; and

(j) Practice requirements described according to section 9107 of this chapter ensuring that the appellation of origin be applicable only to cannabis that is planted in the ground in the canopy area; cultivated without the use of structures including a greenhouse, hoop house, glasshouse, conservatory, hothouse, or any similar structure covering the plant or modifying the natural light received by the plant in the canopy area; and cultivated without any artificial light in the canopy area pursuant to Business and Professions Code section 26063, subdivision (c).

Note: Authority cited: Section 26063, Business and Professions Code. Reference: Sections 26061 and 26063, Business and Professions Code.

§ 9103. Petition to Amend an Appellation of Origin.

A petition to amend any parts of an established appellation of origin shall include:

(a) All requirements of section 9102;

(b) A summary description of the amendments to the appellation of origin and the reason for each amendment;

(c) An explanation of how the amended appellation of origin preserves the causal links between the geographical features and the cannabis, consistent with section 9106; and

(d) Evidence supporting the amendments.

Note: Authority cited: Section 26063, Business and Professions Code. Reference: Section 26063, Business and Professions Code.

§ 9104. Evidence of Name Use.

The petition shall describe the name and history of the proposed appellation of origin, including:

(a) In narrative form, an explanation of how the name has been used in the geographical area covered by the proposed appellation of origin, supported by evidence of name usage. The relationship of the name and boundary of the proposed appellation of origin should be thoroughly explained; and

(b) Evidence of name usage shall conform to the following requirements:

(1) Evidence shall be appropriately cross-referenced in the petition;

(2) Evidence shall demonstrate the proposed name is directly associated with an area in which licensed cannabis cultivation exists;

(3) Evidence to support the proposed name shall come from sources independent of the petitioner; and

(4) Appropriate name evidence sources include but are not limited to historical and modern government or commercial maps, books, newspapers, magazines, tourist and other promotional materials, local business or school names, and road names.

Note: Authority cited: Section 26063, Business and Professions Code. Reference: Section 26063, Business and Professions Code.

§ 9105. Maps and Boundary Description.

The petition shall describe the area and boundary of the proposed appellation of origin, including:

(a) The proposed boundary shall be depicted on United States Geological Survey topographical maps and shall conform to the following:

(1) The scale shall be large enough to show adequate geographical detail of the proposed boundary line.

(2) The exact boundary of the appellation of origin shall be prominently and clearly drawn on the maps without obscuring the underlying features that define the boundary line.

(b) A detailed narrative description of the proposed boundary. The description shall have a specific beginning point, shall proceed unbroken from that point in a clockwise direction, and shall return to that beginning point to complete the boundary description. The proposed boundary description may rely on any of the following map features:

(1) State, county, township, forest, and other political entity lines; except the boundary cannot be based solely on the political entity lines of a single county, city, or city and county;

(2) Highways, roads (including unimproved roads), and trails;

(3) Contour or elevation lines;

(4) Natural geographical features, including rivers, streams, creeks, ridges, and marked elevation points (such as summits or benchmarks);

(5) Human-made features (such as bridges, buildings, windmills, or water tanks); and

(6) Straight lines between marked intersections, human-made features, or other map points.

Note: Authority cited: Section 26063, Business and Professions Code. Reference: Section 26063, Business and Professions Code.

§ 9106. Geographical Features.

The petition shall include:

(a) A narrative description of the distinctive geographical features affecting cannabis production. Examples include, but are not limited to:

(1) Climate information which may include temperature, precipitation, wind, fog, solar orientation and radiation;

(2) Geological information which may include underlying formations, landforms, and such geophysical events as earthquakes, eruptions, and major floods;

(3) Soil features which may include microbiology and soil series or phases of a soil series;

(4) Physical features which may include flat, hilly, or mountainous topography, geographical formations, bodies of water, watersheds, and irrigation resources; and

(5) Minimum and maximum elevations.

(b) Substantial evidence that the geographical area is distinctive when compared to areas outside the proposed boundary and to other relevant areas which produce cannabis for sale into the marketplace;

(c) A description of the quality or characteristics of the cannabis which are essentially or exclusively caused by one or more distinctive geographical feature(s), including an explanation of how the distinctive geographical feature(s) cause(s) the cannabis to have that quality or characteristic; and

(d) Identification of at least one specific standard, practice, or cultivar requirement which acts to preserve the causal link(s) between one or more distinctive geographical feature(s) and the cannabis, including:

(1) Description of the mechanism by which the requirement preserves or maintains the causal link; and

(2) A clear distinction between cultivation methods which are allowed and prohibited under each requirement.

Note: Authority cited: Section 26063, Business and Professions Code. Reference: Section 26063, Business and Professions Code.

§ 9107. Standard, Practice, and Cultivar Requirements.

The petition shall identify and define at least one of each of the following production requirements for the proposed appellation of origin: standard, practice, and cultivar.

(a) Standard, practice, and cultivar requirements shall be reviewed for clarity. To satisfy this review the following conditions shall be met:

(1) The standard, practice, and cultivar requirements must be reasonable and logical and cannot have more than one meaning;

(2) The standard, practice, and cultivar requirements cannot conflict with one another or any other information provided in the petition;

(3) The meaning of terms used in the standard, practice, and cultivar requirements are generally familiar to

other licensed cultivators;

(4) The language used for the standard, practice, and cultivar requirements is correct including grammar, punctuation, and spelling;

(5) The standard, practice, and cultivar requirements are presented in a format that is readily understandable by the public; and

(6) Licensees understand the requirements necessary to qualify for use of the appellation of origin.

(b) Standard requirements in a petition shall be either:

(1) Composed of upper limits, lower limits, or accepted ranges of measurable or scorable characteristics, including measurement and variance tolerances; or

(2) Program-level certifications granted by a certifier in good standing according to the certification owner; including but not limited to those associated with the department's comparable-to-organics certification program or certification marks registered with the United States Patent and Trademark Office and applicable to cannabis.

(c) Practice requirements in a petition shall:

(1) Include a description of the practice requirement to allow any licensed cultivator within the appellation of origin to comply without substantial additional research, and in plain language to provide clear understanding to the public; and

(2) Not use any term likely to mislead consumers as to the practice or its implementation.

(d) Cultivar requirements in a petition may take the form of:

(1) Allowed or prohibited lists of cultivar names, which may contain any number of entries including zero; or

(2) Requirements including genetic testing, seed or plant specimen preservation, or cultivar identity certification with identified limits on acceptable methods, vendors, and practices.

(e) Each standard, practice, and cultivar requirement shall include description of a mandatory mechanism by which compliance with the requirement shall be documented and supported by record retention pursuant to cannabis licensing record retention regulations. Appellation compliance documentation shall be thorough and appropriate to the requirement to allow determination of compliance based solely upon review of the records.

Note: Authority cited: Section 26063, Business and Professions Code. Reference: Section 26063, Business and Professions Code.

ARTICLE 3. PETITION REVIEW PROCESS

§ 9200. Petition Review.

(a) The department shall notify the petitioner by e-mail when the petition is received. A petition shall not be deemed received unless the petition submission fee is submitted in full along with the petition.

(b) If the department finds that the petition is complete and accepts it for further review, the department shall send a notice to the petitioner requesting payment of the petition proposal fee. The petitioner shall pay the petition proposal fee before the notice of proposed action is issued pursuant to section 9201. The petitioner shall have 120 days from the date of the request to submit the payment to the department. If the petition proposal fee is not submitted in full, the department shall notify the petitioner by e-mail that the petition is abandoned and shall no longer be considered by the department.

(c) If the department receives the petition proposal fee in full, the department shall issue notice of proposed action on the petition pursuant to Section 9201.

(d) If the department finds that the petition is incomplete or additional information is required to make a decision on the petition, the department shall notify the petitioner in writing of what information the petitioner needs to provide.

(e) If the department has not received a response acknowledging receipt of an appellation petition deficiency notice from the petitioner within 60 days from the date on the appellation petition deficiency notice, or if the petitioner fails to provide the requested information within 180 days from the date on the appellation petition deficiency notice, the department shall notify the petitioner by e-mail that the petition is abandoned and shall no longer be considered by the department.

Note: Authority cited: Section 26063, Business and Professions Code. Reference: Section 26063, Business and Professions Code.

§ 9201. Notice of Proposed Action on Appellation of Origin.

(a) Following determination that a petition is complete and payment of the petition proposal fee pursuant to section 9200 of this chapter, the department shall provide public notice of proposed action to establish or amend the appellation of origin. The public will have 90 days from the initial date identified in the notice to provide comments on the petition. Comments shall be submitted to the contact person identified in the notice and received by the final day identified in the notice. The department may extend the comment period in response to a request showing a reasonable basis for extension.

(b) A notice of proposed action on an appellation of origin shall include weblinks to:

(1) The completed petition;

(2) A map of the area described by the petition; and

(3) The standard, practice, and cultivar requirements identified in the petition.

Note: Authority cited: Section 26063, Business and Professions Code. Reference: Section 26063, Business and Professions Code.

§ 9202. Notice of Final Decision on Appellation of Origin.

(a) The department shall provide notice of final decision on a petition for an appellation of origin (i.e. established, amended, or denied on its website and by e-mail to:

(1) The petitioner;

(2) Designated responsible parties of licenses issued by the department and located within the areas directly impacted by the decision; and

(3) Stakeholders enrolled on the department's Cannabis Appellations Program Mailing List. Enrollment on to the department's Cannabis Appellations Program Mailing List can be requested by any stakeholder using an electronic request form on the Department of Food and Agriculture's Cannabis Appellations Program webpage or by submitting a written request to the mailing address or email address listed on the Cannabis Appellations Program webpage.

(b) If the petition is denied, the notice of final decision shall include all of the reasons why the petition was denied.

Note: Authority cited: Section 26063, Business and Professions Code. Reference: Section 26063, Business and Professions Code.

§ 9203. Denial of Petition for Appellation of Origin.

The Department may deny the petition for the following reasons:

(a) Evidence is not sufficient to demonstrate the legacy, history, reputation, and economic importance of cannabis production in the proposed geographical area pursuant to section 9102, subdivision (h);

(b) Evidence is not sufficient to demonstrate that the proposed appellation name has been used in direct association with a cannabis production area pursuant to section 9104, subdivisions (b)(2) through (b)(4) of this chapter;

(c) Evidence is not sufficient to demonstrate that the proposed geographical area is distinctive with respect to the geographical features affecting cannabis pursuant to section 9106, subdivision (b) of this chapter;

(d) Proposed geographical features as described are not causally-linked to the cannabis or the causal links are not maintained according to the standards set forth in section 9106, subdivisions (c) and (d) of this chapter;

(e) Proposed standard, practice, and cultivar requirements do not meet the clarity, form, or recordkeeping standards set forth in section 9107, subdivisions (a) through (e) of this chapter;

(f) Amendments to the appellation of origin are not consistent with the proposed geographical features according to section 9103, subdivisions (b) through (d) of this chapter; and

(g) Any other reasonable cause submitted through the public comment process that the department determines would preclude the appellation from being established or amended.

Note: Authority cited: Section 26063, Business and Professions Code. Reference: Section 26063, Business and Professions Code.

Chapter 3. Ocal Program

ARTICLE 1. DEFINITIONS

§ 10000. Definitions.

The following definitions, including definitions in section 26001 of the Business and Professions Code, and definitions included in title 4, section 16000 of the California Code of Regulations apply to this chapter.

(a) "Accreditation" means a determination made by the California Department of Food and Agriculture that authorizes a private entity or local jurisdiction to conduct certification activities when registered as a certifying agent pursuant to this chapter.

(b) "Action level" means the limit at or above which the U. S. Food and Drug Administration will take legal action against a product to remove it from the market. Action levels are based on unavoidability of poisonous or deleterious substances and do not represent permissible levels of contamination where it is avoidable.

(c) "Agricultural inputs" means all substances or materials used in the production of OCal cannabis or nonmanufactured cannabis products.

(d) "Allowed synthetic" means a substance that is included on the National List of synthetic substances allowed for use in organic production, as provided in The National List of Allowed and Prohibited Substances, 7 Code of Federal Regulations (7 CFR) section 205.601.

(e) "Applicant" means an owner of the applicant entity or sole proprietor applying for accreditation, registration, or certification pursuant to this chapter.

(f) "Area of operation" means the types of operations a certifying agent may be accredited to certify pursuant to this chapter.

(g) "Audit trail" means documentation that is sufficient to determine the source, transfer of ownership, and transportation of any cannabis or nonmanufactured cannabis product labeled "OCal."

(h) "Biodegradable" means subject to biological decomposition into simpler biochemical or chemical components.

(i) "Buffer zone" means an area located between land maintained under OCal or NOP certified Organic management and an adjacent land area not maintained under OCal or NOP certified Organic management.

(j) "Certification" or "certified" means a determination made by the registered certifying agent, and documented by a certificate, that a cultivation or distribution operation is in compliance with this chapter.

(k) "Certified operation" means a cannabis cultivator or distributor that has received OCal certification.

(l) "Certifying agent" means any entity that currently certifies operations.

(m) "Certifying agent's operation" means all sites, facilities, personnel, and records used by a certifying agent.

(n) "Claims" means oral, written, implied, or symbolic representations, statements, advertising or other forms of communication presented to the public or consumers that relate to the OCal certification process or the term "OCal".

(o) "Clone" means an asexually produced plant grown by taking a cutting from a mother plant or a tissue culture from a source plant that is genetically identical to the mother plant or source plant.

(p) "Commercially available" means the ability to obtain a production input in an appropriate form, quality, or quantity to fulfill an essential function in a system of production as determined by the registered certifying agent in the course of reviewing the OCal system plan.

(q) "Commingling" means physical contact between OCal produced and non-OCal produced cannabis and nonmanufactured cannabis products.

(r) "Compost" means the product of a managed process through which microorganisms break down plant and animal materials into more available forms suitable for application to the soil.

(s) "Control" means any method that reduces or limits damage by populations of pests, weeds, or diseases to levels that do not significantly reduce productivity.

(t) "Crop" means pastures, cover crops, green manure crops, catch crops, or any plant or part of a plant intended to be marketed as an agricultural product, or used in the field to manage nutrients and soil fertility.

(u) "Crop residues" means the plant parts remaining in a field after the harvest of a crop, which include stalks, stems, leaves, roots, and weeds.

(v) "Crop rotation" means a method of reducing soil erosion and increasing soil fertility, biodiversity, and crop yield through the practice of alternating the annual crops grown on a specific field in a planned pattern or sequence in successive crop years so that crops of the same species or family are not grown repeatedly, without interruption, on the same field.

(w) "Cultivation" means any activity involving the planting, growing, harvesting, drying, curing, grading, or trimming of cannabis.

(x) “Cultural methods” means methods used to enhance crop health and prevent weed, pest, or disease problems without the use of substances, such as the selection of appropriate varieties and planting sites, proper timing and density of plantings, irrigation, and extending or compressing a growing season by manipulating the microclimate with green houses, cold frames, or wind breaks.

(y) “Detectable residue” means the amount or presence of chemical residue or sample component that can be reliably observed or found in the sample matrix by current approved analytical methodology.

(z) “Disease vectors” means plants or animals that harbor or transmit disease organisms or pathogens which may attack crops.

(aa) “Drift” means the physical movement of prohibited substances from the intended target site onto an OCal operation or portion thereof.

(ab) “Emergency pest or disease treatment program” means a mandatory program authorized by a federal, state, or local agency for the purpose of controlling or eradicating a pest or disease.

(ac) “Employee” means any person providing paid or volunteer services for the registered certifying agent.

(ad) “Excluded methods” means a variety of methods used to genetically modify organisms or influence their growth and development by means that are not possible under natural conditions or processes and are not considered compatible with organic and OCal production. Such methods include cell fusion (except when the donor cells/protoplasts fall within the same taxonomic plant family), microencapsulation and macroencapsulation, and recombinant DNA technology (including gene deletion, gene doubling, introducing a foreign gene, and changing the positions of genes when achieved by recombinant DNA technology). Such methods do not include the use of traditional breeding, conjugation, fermentation, hybridization, in vitro fertilization , or tissue culture.

(ae) “Fertilizer” means a single or blended substance containing one or more recognized plant nutrient(s) which is used primarily for its plant nutrient content and which is designed for use or claimed to have value in promoting plant growth.

(af) “Field” means an area of land identified as a discrete unit within a production operation.

(ag) “Handling” means the touching or manipulating of post-harvest OCal cannabis and nonmanufactured cannabis products, processing of OCal cannabis and nonmanufactured cannabis products, or accessing OCal cannabis and nonmanufactured cannabis products via an open container or an unsealed package at any point in the supply chain.

(ah) “Immediate family” means the spouse, minor children, or blood relatives who reside in the immediate household of the registered certifying agent or an employee, inspector, contractor, or other personnel of the registered certifying agent.

(ai) “Inert ingredient” means any substance (or group of substances with similar chemical structures if designated by the United States Environmental Protection Agency) other than an active ingredient which is intentionally included in any pesticide product.

(aj) “Information panel” means any part of the cannabis or nonmanufactured cannabis product label that is not the primary panel and that contains required labeling information.

(ak) “Ingredient” means any substance that is used in the manufacture of a cannabis product and that is intended to be present in the product’s final form.

(al) “Inspection” means the act of examining and evaluating an operation to determine compliance with this chapter.

(am) “Inspector” means any person retained or used by the registered certifying agent to conduct inspections of certification applicants or certified operations.

(an) “Label” means a display of written, printed, or graphic matter upon a cannabis product, upon its container or wrapper, or that accompanies any cannabis product.

(ao) “Labeling” means any label or other written, printed, or graphic matter upon a cannabis product, upon its container or wrapper, or that accompanies any cannabis product.

(ap) “Laboratory or Testing laboratory” means a laboratory, facility, or entity in the state that offers or performs tests of cannabis and cannabis products is licensed by the Bureau of Cannabis Control and is accredited by an accrediting body that is independent from all other persons involved in commercial cannabis activity in the state.

(aq) “Licensee” means any person holding a cannabis cultivation or distribution license in the State of California.

(ar) “Limited-access area” means an area that is only accessible to the operator and authorized personnel of an operation.

(as) “Local jurisdiction” means a city, county, or city and county.

(at) “Manufacture” means to compound, blend, extract, infuse, or otherwise make or prepare a cannabis product.

(au) “Manure” means feces, urine, other excrement, and bedding produced by livestock that has not been composted.

(av) “Mother plant” means a plant used for the sole purpose of taking cuttings or offsets in order to grow more of the same plant.

(aw) “Mulch” means any nonsynthetic material, such as wood chips, leaves, or straw, or any synthetic material included on the National List for such use, such as newspaper or plastic that serves to suppress weed growth, moderate soil temperature, or conserve soil moisture.

(ax) “National List” means the list of allowed and prohibited substances included in National Organic Program regulations, 7 CFR sections 205.600 through 205.607.

(ay) “National Organic Program” or “NOP” means the federal regulatory program that develops and enforces uniform national standards for organically-produced agricultural products sold in the United States.

(az) “Natural resources of the operation” means the physical, hydrological, and biological features of a production operation, including but not limited to soil, water, wetlands, woodlands, and wildlife.

(ba) “Nonmanufactured cannabis product” means flower, shake, leaf, pre-rolls, and kief that is obtained from accumulation in containers or sifted from loose, dry cannabis flower or leaf with a mesh screen or sieve.

(bb) “Nonsynthetic (natural)” means a substance that is derived from mineral, plant, or animal matter and does not undergo a synthetic process, as defined in (cd) of this section.

(bc) “Nonretail container” means any container used for shipping or storage of nonmanufactured OCal cannabis products that is not used in the retail display or sale of the product.

(bd) “Nursery” means all activities associated with producing clones, immature plants, seeds, and other agricultural products used specifically for the propagation and cultivation of cannabis.

(be) “OCal” means a labeling term that refers to cannabis and nonmanufactured cannabis products produced pursuant to this chapter or a certification program for manufactured cannabis products authorized under Business and Professions Code section 26062.

(bf) “OCal production” means a production system that is managed pursuant to this chapter to respond to site-specific conditions by integrating cultural, biological, and mechanical practices that foster cycling of resources, promote ecological balance, and conserve biodiversity.

(bg) “OCal Program” means the program authorized by Business and Professions Code section 26062(a)(1) to assure consumers that cannabis and nonmanufactured cannabis products certified under the OCal designation are produced pursuant to this chapter and comparable to the National Organic Program regulations, 7 CFR part 205.

(bh) "OCal system plan" means a plan of management of an OCal operation that has been agreed to by an operator and the registered certifying agent and that includes written plans concerning all aspects of cannabis production described in this chapter.

(bi) "Operation" means a person that holds a valid and active California commercial cannabis cultivator or distributor license.

(bj) "Organic" means a labeling term that refers to an agricultural product produced in accordance with the Organic Foods Production Act and the National Organic Program regulations, 7 CFR part 205.

(bk) "Organic matter" means the remains, residues, or waste products of any organism.

(bl) "Pest" means any of the following that is, or is liable to become, dangerous or detrimental to the agricultural or nonagricultural environment of the state: (1) Any insect, predatory animal, rodent, nematode, or weed; and (2) Any form of terrestrial, aquatic, or aerial plant or animal virus, fungus, bacteria, or other microorganism (except viruses, fungi, bacteria, or other microorganisms on or in living man or other living animals).

(bm) "Pesticide" means: (1) Any spray adjuvant. (2) Any substance, or mixture of substances which is intended to be used for defoliating plants, regulating plant growth, or for preventing, destroying, repelling, or mitigating any pest, as defined in section 12754.5 of the Food and Agricultural Code, which may infest or be detrimental to vegetation, man, animals, or households, or be present in any agricultural or nonagricultural environment whatsoever.

(bn) "Planting stock" means any plant or plant tissue, including shoots and stem cuttings, used in plant cultivation or propagation.

(bo) "Practice standard" means the guidelines and requirements through which a production operation implements a required component of its OCal system plan.

(bp) "Premises" means the designated structure or structures and land specified in the application that is owned, leased, or otherwise held under the control of the applicant or licensee where the commercial cannabis activity will be or is conducted. The premises shall be a contiguous area and shall only be occupied by one licensee.

(bq) "Principal display panel" means that part of a label that is most likely to be displayed, presented, shown, or examined under customary conditions of display for sale.

(br) "Private entity" means any domestic nongovernmental for-profit or not-for-profit organization providing certification services.

(bs) "Process," "Processing," and "Processes" mean all activities associated with the drying, curing, grading, trimming, rolling, storing, packaging, and labeling of cannabis or nonmanufactured cannabis products.

(bt) "Production" means the cultivation or distribution of cannabis or nonmanufactured cannabis products.

(bu) "Prohibited substance" means a substance that shall not be used in any aspect of United States Department of Agriculture Organic or OCal production and is prohibited by the National Organic Program.

(bv) "Records" means any information in written, visual, or electronic form that documents the activities undertaken by an operation or registered certifying agent to comply with this chapter.

(bw) "Registered certifying agent" means any entity accredited by the department or the National Organic Program and registered by the department to certify an operation under the OCal Program pursuant to sections 10500 through 10506 of this chapter.

(bx) "Registered certifying agent's operation" means all sites, facilities, personnel, and records used by the certifying agent registered by the department to conduct certification activities pursuant to this chapter.

(by) "Residue testing" means an official or validated analytical procedure that detects, identifies, and measures the presence of chemical substances, their metabolites, or degradation products in or on raw or processed agricultural products.

(bz) "Responsibly connected" means any person who is a partner, officer, director, holder, manager, or owner of 10 percent or more of the voting stock of an applicant or a recipient of certification, accreditation, or registration.

(ca) "Sewage sludge" means a solid, semisolid, or liquid residue generated during the treatment of domestic sewage in a treatment works. Sewage sludge includes but is not limited to: domestic septage; scum or solids removed in primary, secondary, or advanced wastewater treatment processes; and a material derived from sewage sludge. Sewage sludge does not include ash generated during the firing of sewage sludge in a sewage sludge incinerator or grit and screenings generated during preliminary treatment of domestic sewage in a treatment works.

(cb) "Soil and water quality" means observable indicators of the physical, chemical, or biological condition of soil and water, including the presence of environmental contaminants.

(cc) "Split operation" means an operation that produces both certified and noncertified products. The department does not consider an operation certified to produce both organic and OCal products a "split operation."

(cd) "Synthetic" means a substance that is formulated or manufactured by a chemical process or by a process that chemically changes a substance extracted from naturally occurring plant, animal, or mineral sources, except that such term shall not apply to substances created by naturally occurring biological processes.

(ce) "Temporary" and "Temporarily" mean occurring for a limited time only (e.g., overnight, throughout a storm, the period of time specified by the department when granting a temporary variance), not permanent or lasting.

(cf) "Tolerance" means the maximum legal level of a pesticide chemical residue in or on a raw or processed agricultural commodity or processed food.

(cg) "Track-and-trace system" means the state-approved system used to track commercial cannabis activity and movement.

(ch) "Transplant" means a seedling which has been removed from its original place of production, transported, and replanted.

(ci) "Type of operation" means the type of operation that may be certified under this chapter.

(cj) "Unavoidable residual environmental contamination (UREC)" means background levels of naturally occurring or synthetic chemicals that are present in the soil or present in organically produced agricultural products that are below established tolerances.

(ck) "Willful" means intentional or deliberate.

Note: Authority cited: Sections 26012 and 26013, Business and Professions Code. Reference: Sections 26001, 26013 and 26062, Business and Professions Code.

§ 10001. Incorporation by Reference.

(a) The following OCal guidance and instructions for registered certifying agents and certified operations are incorporated by reference into this chapter:

(1) OCal 1000 Methods and Materials in OCal Production, April 23, 2021

(2) OCal 2006 Separation of Duties in Certification Decisions, April 23, 2021

(3) OCal 2602 Recordkeeping for Certified Operations, April 23, 2021

(4) OCal 2608 Responding to Noncompliances, April 23, 2021

(5) OCal 2609 Unannounced Inspections, April 23, 2021

(6) OCal 2610 Sampling Procedures for OCal Cannabis Residue Testing, April 23, 2021

(7) OCal 2611 Laboratory Selection Criteria for Prohibited Substance Testing, April 23, 2021

(8) OCal 2611-1 Prohibited Pesticides for OCal Residue Testing, April 23, 2021

(9) OCal 2613 Responding to Results of Pesticide Residue Testing, April 23, 2021

(10) OCal 2614 Technical Assistance Instruction, April 23, 2021

(11) OCal 2615 OCal System Plans, OCal System Plan Updates, and Notification of Changes, April 23, 2021

(12) OCal 3012 Material Review, April 23, 2021

(13) OCal 5006 Processed Animal Manures in OCal Production, April 23, 2021

(14) OCal 5008 Reassessed Inert Ingredients, April 23, 2021

(15) OCal 5020 Natural Resources and Biodiversity Conservation, April 23, 2021

(16) OCal 5021 Compost and Vermicompost in OCal Production, April 23, 2021

(17) OCal 5023 Substances Used in Post-Harvest Handling of OCal Products, April 23, 2021

(18) OCal 5025 Commingling and Contamination Prevention in OCal Production, April 23, 2021

(19) OCal 5026 The Use of Chlorine Materials in OCal Production, April 23, 2021

(20) OCal 5029 Seeds and Planting Stock in OCal Cultivation, April 23, 2021

(21) OCal 5033 Classification of Unique Materials, April 23, 2021

(22) OCal 5033-1 Decision Tree for Classification of Materials, April 23, 2021

(23) OCal 5034 Materials for OCal Cannabis Production, April 23, 2021

(24) OCal 5034-1 List of Materials for Use in OCal Cannabis Production, April 23, 2021

(25) OCal 5034-2 List of Materials Prohibited for Use in OCal Cannabis Production, April 23, 2021

(26) OCal 5036 Treated Lumber, April 23, 2021

(b) Food and Drug Administration regulation, 21 CFR section 179.26 (April 23, 2021) is incorporated by reference into this chapter.

Note: Authority cited: Sections 26012 and 26013, Business and Professions Code. Reference: Sections 26013, 26062 and 26062.5, Business and Professions Code.

ARTICLE 2. APPLICABILITY

§ 10100. Who May Certify.

(a) A private entity or local jurisdiction shall satisfy the following criteria to certify cannabis operations under the department:

(1) Be accredited by either the department pursuant to sections 10400 through 10407 of this chapter or the National Organic Program 7 CFR sections 205.500 through 205.510; and

(2) Be registered by the department to certify under the OCal Program.

Note: Authority cited: Sections 26012 and 26013, Business and Professions Code. Reference: Sections 26013, 26062 and 26062.5, Business and Professions Code.

§ 10101. What Must be Certified.

(a) Except for operations excluded in section 10102 of this chapter, each operation or specified portion of an operation that holds a commercial cannabis license from the department or other cannabis licensing authority and produces cannabis and nonmanufactured cannabis products that are intended to be sold, labeled, or represented as OCal shall be certified pursuant to the provisions of Article 6 of this chapter and shall meet all other applicable requirements of this chapter.

(b) A cultivation or distribution operation or specified portion of a cultivation or distribution operation shall be deemed to be certified under this chapter on the date its certifying agent receives registration under this chapter until the operation's next certification anniversary date if the certifier can demonstrate the operation's compliance with this chapter.

(c) Such recognition under subdivision (b) shall only be available to those operations certified by a certifying agent that is registered before January 1, 2022.

Note: Authority cited: Sections 26012 and 26013, Business and Professions Code. Reference: Sections 26013, 26062 and 26062.5, Business and Professions Code.

§ 10102. Exclusions from Certification.

(a) A licensed commercial cannabis operation that does not handle cannabis and nonmanufactured cannabis products to be labeled, sold or represented as OCal is excluded from the requirements of this chapter. These operations include:

(1) Distribution operations if nonmanufactured OCal cannabis products:

(A) Are received enclosed in a package or container;

(B) Remain enclosed in the same package or container while under the control of the distributor, except for Bureau sampling; and

(C) Are in a container labeled pursuant to section 10301(a) of this chapter.

(2) Laboratory operations.

(3) Retail operations.

Note: Authority cited: Sections 26012 and 26013, Business and Professions Code. Reference: Sections 26013, 26062, and 26062.5, Business and Professions Code.

§ 10103. Use of the Terms OCal and Organic.

(a) Any cannabis or nonmanufactured cannabis product that is sold, labeled, or represented as OCal shall be produced pursuant to the requirements of this chapter.

(b) No cannabis or nonmanufactured cannabis product shall be advertised or labeled OCal or similar terminology that leaves in doubt whether the product is being sold, labeled, or represented as certified pursuant to the requirements of this chapter.

(c) Cannabis operations are prohibited from selling, labeling, or referring to their products as organic, pursuant to section 26062.5 of the California Business and Professions Code.

Note: Authority cited: Sections 26012 and 26013, Business and Professions Code. Reference: Sections 26013, 26062 and 26062.5, Business and Professions Code; Section 46027, Food and Agriculture Code.

§ 10104. Recordkeeping by Certified Operations.

(a) A certified operation shall maintain records concerning the production of cannabis and nonmanufactured cannabis products that are intended to be sold, labeled, or represented as OCal.

(b) Such records shall:

(1) Fully disclose all activities and transactions of the certified operation in enough detail as to be readily understood and audited;

(2) Be maintained for not less than five years beyond their creation; and

(3) Demonstrate compliance with the regulations in this chapter.

(c) The certified operation shall make such records available to authorized representatives of the department or the registered certifying agent for inspection and copying during standard business hours. For the purposes of this section, standard business hours are 8:00am - 5:00pm (Pacific Time), Monday through Friday, excluding holidays.

(d) A certified cultivation or distribution operation shall identify within the Track-and-Trace system, in a manner specified by the Department of Cannabis Control regulations, 4 CCR sections 15048, 15049, 15051, 16109, 16402, 16403, 16404, 16405, and 16406, cannabis or nonmanufactured cannabis products that are intended to be sold, labeled, or represented as OCal.

Note: Authority cited: Sections 26012 and 26013, Business and Professions Code. Reference: Sections 26013, 26062, 26062.5 and 26067, Business and Professions Code.

§ 10105. Allowed and Prohibited Substances and Methods in OCal Production.

(a) To be sold or labeled OCal, cannabis and nonmanufactured cannabis products shall be produced without the use of:

(1) Synthetic substances and ingredients, except as provided in The National List of Allowed and Prohibited Substances 7 CFR section 205.601;

(2) Nonsynthetic substances prohibited in The National List of Allowed and Prohibited Substances 7 CFR section 205.602;

(3) Substances prohibited for use on cannabis as described in the Department of Cannabis Control regulations, 4 CCR section 15719;

(4) Excluded methods;

(5) Ionizing radiation, as described in Food and Drug Administration regulation, 21 CFR section 179.26; and

(6) Sewage sludge.

(b) Certified operations shall only use fertilizing materials pursuant to Fertilizing Materials Registration requirements for Organic Input Materials, 3 CCR section 2320.3.

(c) Agricultural inputs shall not be used in OCal production if the input utilizes or includes:

(1) Synthetic substances and ingredients, except as provided in The National List of Allowed and Prohibited Substances 7 CFR section 205.601;

(2) Nonsynthetic substances prohibited in The National List of Allowed and Prohibited Substances 7 CFR section 205.602;

(3) Excluded methods;

(4) Ionizing radiation, as described in Food and Drug Administration regulation, 21 CFR section 179.26; and

(5) Sewage sludge.

(d) If a production practice is not prohibited or otherwise restricted under this chapter, such practice shall be permitted if it complies with the requirements of this chapter.

Note: Authority cited: Sections 26012 and 26013, Business and Professions Code. Reference: Sections 26013, 26062 and 26062.5, Business and Professions Code.

ARTICLE 3. OCAL CULTIVATION AND DISTRIBUTION REQUIREMENTS

§ 10200. General.

(a) An operation intending to sell, label, or represent cannabis or nonmanufactured cannabis products as "OCal," shall comply with the applicable provisions of this chapter.

(b) Production practices implemented in accordance with this chapter shall maintain or improve the natural resources of the operation, including soil, water, wetlands, woodlands, and wildlife, and respond to site-specific conditions by integrating cultural, biological, and mechanical practices that foster cycling of resources, promote ecological balance, and conserve biodiversity.

(c) A certified operation shall meet or exceed all practice standards set forth in sections 10202 through 10209 of this chapter.

Note: Authority cited: Sections 26012 and 26013, Business and Professions Code. Reference: Sections 26013, 26062, and 26062.5, Business and Professions Code.

§ 10201. OCal System Plans.

(a) A cultivator or distributor intending to sell, label, or represent cannabis or nonmanufactured cannabis products as OCal shall develop an OCal system plan that is agreed to by the cultivator or distributor and the registered certifying agent.

(b) An OCal system plan shall meet the requirements set forth in this chapter for OCal production.

(c) A certified operation shall use the practice standards set forth in sections 10202 through 10209 of this article to define and implement required components of its OCal system plan. The OCal system plan shall include:

(1) A description of practices and procedures to be performed and maintained, including the frequency with which they will be performed;

(2) A list of each substance to be used as an OCal production input and material, indicating its composition, source, location(s) where it will be used, and documenting commercial availability, as applicable;

(A) Documentation of commercial availability of OCal seeds and planting stock is not required for the first 12 months of the program.

(3) A description of the monitoring practices and procedures to be performed and maintained, including the frequency with which they will be performed, to verify that the plan is effectively implemented;

(4) A description of the recordkeeping system implemented to comply with the requirements established in section 10104 of this chapter;

(5) A description of the management practices and physical barriers established to prevent commingling of OCal and non-OCal or non-organic products on a split operation and to prevent contact of OCal operations and products with prohibited substances;

(6) A description of practices implemented to maintain or improve the natural resources of the operation, including soil, water, wetlands, woodlands, and wildlife, and respond to site-specific conditions by integrating cultural, biological, and mechanical practices that foster cycling of resources, promote ecological balance, and conserve biodiversity. These practices may also be integrated into subdivisions (1) through (5) above; and

(7) Additional information deemed necessary by the registered certifying agent to evaluate compliance with this chapter.

Note: Authority cited: Sections 26012 and 26013, Business and Professions Code. Reference: Sections 26013, 26062 and 26062.5, Business and Professions Code.

§ 10202. Land Requirements.

(a) Any field or farm parcel from which harvested cannabis is intended to be sold, labeled, or represented as "OCal" shall:

(1) Have been managed pursuant to sections 10203 through 10206 of this chapter;

(2) Have had no prohibited substances, pursuant to section 10105 of this chapter, applied to it for a period of three years immediately preceding harvest of cannabis; and

(3) Have on the operator's field or farm parcel distinct, defined boundaries and buffer zones sufficient in size or other features (e.g. windbreaks or a diversion ditch) to prevent the unintended application of a prohibited substance to the cannabis or contact with a prohibited substance applied to adjoining land that is not under organic management. Split operations shall use obviously visible onsite signage to identify OCal and non-OCal production areas.

Note: Authority cited: Sections 26012 and 26013, Business and Professions Code. Reference: Sections 26013, 26062 and 26062.5, Business and Professions Code.

§ 10203. Soil Fertility and Crop Nutrient Management Practice Standard.

(a) A cultivator shall select and implement tillage and cultivation practices that maintain or improve the physical, chemical, and biological condition of soil and minimize soil erosion.

(b) A cultivator shall manage crop nutrients and soil fertility through rotations, cover crops, intercropping, alley cropping, hedgerows or the application of plant and animal materials.

(c) A cultivator shall manage plant and animal materials to maintain or improve soil organic matter content, biological diversity, nutrient cycling, and microbial activity in a manner that does not contribute to contamination of crops, soil, or water by plant nutrients, pathogenic organisms, heavy metals, or residues of prohibited substances. Animal and plant materials include:

(1) Raw animal manure, which shall be composted unless it is:

(A) Incorporated into the soil not less than 120 days prior to the harvest of cannabis whose consumable portion has direct contact with the soil surface or soil particles; or

(B) Incorporated into the soil not less than 90 days prior to the harvest of cannabis whose consumable portion does not have direct contact with the soil surface or soil particles.

(2) Composted plant and animal materials produced through a process that:

(A) Established an initial C:N ratio of between 25:1 and 40:1; and

(B) Maintained a temperature of between 131oF and 170oF for three days using an in-vessel or static aerated pile system; or

(C) Maintained a temperature of between 131oF and 170oF for 15 days using a windrow composting system, during which period, the materials shall be turned a minimum of five times.

(3) Uncomposted plant materials.

(4) Vermicompost.

(d) Pursuant to the following requirements, a cultivator may manage plant nutrients and soil fertility to maintain or improve soil organic matter content, biological diversity, nutrient cycling, and microbial activity in a manner that does not contribute to contamination of crops, soil, or water by plant nutrients, pathogenic organisms, heavy metals, or residues of prohibited substances by applying:

(1) A plant nutrient or soil amendment included on the National List of synthetic substances allowed for use in organic crop production, pursuant to The National List of Allowed and Prohibited Substances 7 CFR section 205.601;

(2) A mined substance of low solubility;

(3) A mined substance of high solubility provided that the substance is used in compliance with the conditions established on the National List of nonsynthetic substances prohibited for use in organic crop production pursuant The National List of Allowed and Prohibited Substances 7 CFR section 205.602;

(4) Ash obtained from the burning of a plant or animal material, except as prohibited in paragraph (e) of this section, provided that the material burned has not been treated or combined with a prohibited substance or the ash is not included on the National List of nonsynthetic substances prohibited for use in organic crop production, pursuant to The National List of Allowed and Prohibited Substances 7 CFR section 205.602; and

(5) A plant or animal material that has been chemically altered by a manufacturing process provided that the material is included on The National List of Allowed and Prohibited Substances 7 CFR section 205.601.

(e) The cultivator shall not use:

(1) Any fertilizer or composted plant and animal material that contains a synthetic substance not included on

The National List of Allowed and Prohibited Substances 7 CFR section 205.601;

(2) Sewage sludge in accordance with section 10105(a)(6) of this chapter; and

(3) Burning as a means of disposal for crop residues produced on the operation except that burning may be used to suppress the spread of disease or to stimulate seed germination consistent with local and state laws and regulations.

Note: Authority cited: Sections 26012 and 26013, Business and Professions Code. Reference: Sections 26013, 26062 and 26062.5, Business and Professions Code.

§ 10204. Seeds and Planting Stock Practice Standard.

(a) A cultivator shall use its own OCal grown cannabis seeds and planting stock or OCal seeds and planting stock from a nursery licensed by the department and certified pursuant to the requirements of this chapter except under the following conditions:

(1) Non-OCal grown untreated seeds and planting stock may be used to produce OCal cannabis when equivalent OCal grown seeds and planting stock are not commercially available;

(2) Non-OCal grown seeds and planting stock that have been treated with a substance allowed for use in organic crop production pursuant to the National List of Allowed and Prohibited Substances may be used to produce OCal cannabis when an equivalent OCal grown or untreated variety is not commercially available;

(3) Non-OCal grown seeds and planting stock may be used to produce an OCal crop when a temporary variance has been granted in accordance with section 10210(d) of this chapter; and

(4) Seeds and planting stock treated with prohibited substances may be used to produce OCal cannabis when the application of the materials is a requirement of federal or state phytosanitary regulations.

Note: Authority cited: Sections 26012 and 26013, Business and Professions Code. Reference: Sections 26013, 26062 and 26062.5, Business and Professions Code.

§ 10205. Crop Rotation Practice Standard.

(a) A cultivator shall implement a crop rotation which may include but is not limited to sod, cover crops, green manure crops, and catch crops. As applicable to the operation, crops shall:

(1) Maintain or improve soil organic matter content;

(2) Provide for pest management;

(3) Manage deficient or excess plant nutrients; and

(4) Provide erosion control.

Note: Authority cited: Sections 26012 and 26013, Business and Professions Code. Reference: Sections 26013, 26062 and 26062.5, Business and Professions Code.

§ 10206. Crop Pest, Weed, and Disease Management Practice Standard.

(a) A cultivator shall use management practices to prevent crop pests, weeds, and diseases, including but not limited to:

(1) Crop rotation and soil and crop nutrient management practices, as provided for in section 10203 and section 10205 of this chapter;

(2) Sanitation measures to remove disease vectors, weed seeds, and habitat for pest organisms; and

(3) Cultural practices that enhance crop health, including selection of plant species and varieties with regard to suitability to site-specific conditions and resistance to prevalent pests, weeds, and diseases.

(b) Pest problems may be controlled through mechanical or physical methods, including but not limited to:

(1) Augmentation or introduction of predators or parasites of the pest species;

(2) Development of habitat for natural enemies of pests; and

(3) Nonsynthetic controls such as lures, traps, and repellents.

(c) Weed problems may be controlled through:

(1) Mowing;

(2) Livestock grazing;

(3) Hand weeding and mechanical cultivation;

(4) Flame, heat, or electrical means; and

(5) Plastic or other synthetic mulches, provided they are removed from the field at the end of the growing or harvest season.

(d) Disease problems may be controlled through:

(1) Management practices which suppress the spread of disease organisms; or

(2) Application of nonsynthetic biological, botanical, or mineral inputs.

(e) A biological or botanical substance or a substance included on the National List of synthetic substances allowed for use in organic crop production, pursuant to The National List of Allowed and Prohibited Substances 7 CFR section 205.601, may be applied to prevent, suppress, or control pests, weeds, or diseases when the practices provided for in paragraphs (a) through (d) of this section are insufficient to prevent or control crop pests, weeds, and diseases. Conditions for using the substance must be documented in the OCal system plan.

(f) A cultivator shall not use lumber treated with arsenate or other prohibited materials for new installations or replacement purposes if the treated lumber comes into contact with soil or cannabis intended to be sold, labeled or represented as OCal.

Note: Authority cited: Sections 26012 and 26013, Business and Professions Code. Reference: Sections 26013, 26062 and 26062.5, Business and Professions Code.

§ 10207. OCal Handling Requirements.

(a) A cultivator or processor may process by drying, curing, grading, trimming, rolling, packaging, re-packaging, labeling, or re-labeling cannabis or nonmanufactured cannabis products intended to be sold, labeled, or represented as OCal.

(b) A distributor may process by packaging, re-packaging, labeling, re-labeling, or rolling cannabis or nonmanufactured cannabis products intended to be sold, labeled, or represented as OCal.

(c) A cultivator or distributor shall not use substances or methods prohibited in paragraph (a) of section 10105 of this chapter in or on cannabis or nonmanufactured cannabis products intended to be sold, labeled, or represented as OCal.

Note: Authority cited: Sections 26012 and 26013, Business and Professions Code. Reference: Sections 26013, 26062 and 26062.5, Business and Professions Code.

§ 10208. Facility Pest Management Practice Standard.

(a) Pest prevention practices at a facility that produces OCal products may include but are not limited to:

(1) Removal of pest habitat, food sources, and breeding areas;

(2) Prevention of access to facilities in which cannabis products are handled; and

(3) Management of environmental factors, such as temperature, light, humidity, atmosphere, and air circulation, to prevent pest reproduction.

(b) Pests may be controlled through:

(1) Mechanical or physical controls including but not limited to traps, light, or sound; and

(2) Lures and repellents using nonsynthetic or synthetic substances consistent with The National List of Allowed and Prohibited Substances 7 CFR section 205.601 through 205.602.

(c) If the practices provided for in paragraphs (a) and (b) of this section are not effective to prevent or control pests, a nonsynthetic or synthetic substance consistent with The National List of Allowed and Prohibited Substances 7 CFR sections 205.601 through 205.602 may be applied.

(d) If the practices provided for in paragraphs (a), (b), and (c) of this section are not effective to prevent or control facility pests, a synthetic substance not included on The National List of Allowed and Prohibited Substances 7 CFR section 205.601, may be applied, provided that the operation and registered certifying agent agree on the substance, method of application, and measures to be taken to prevent contact of nonmanufactured OCal cannabis products with the substance used.

(e) The cultivator or distributor of an OCal operation who applies a nonsynthetic or synthetic substance to prevent or control pests shall update the operation's OCal system plan to reflect the use of such substances and methods of application. The updated OCal system plan shall include a list of all measures taken to prevent contact of nonmanufactured OCal cannabis products with the substance used.

(f) Notwithstanding the practices provided for in paragraphs (a), (b), (c), and (d) of this section, an operation may use substances to prevent or control pests as required by federal, state, or local laws and regulations provided that measures are taken to prevent contact of nonmanufactured OCal cannabis products with the substance used.

Note: Authority cited: Sections 26012 and 26013, Business and Professions Code. Reference: Sections 26013.,26062 and 26062.5, Business and Professions Code.

§ 10209. Commingling and Contact with Prohibited Substance Prevention Practice Standard.

(a) A cultivator or distributor shall implement measures necessary to prevent the commingling of OCal and non-OCal cannabis and nonmanufactured cannabis products and protect OCal cannabis and nonmanufactured OCal cannabis products from contact with prohibited substances.

(b) The following are prohibited for use in the handling of any cannabis or nonmanufactured cannabis product to be sold, labeled, or represented as OCal:

(1) Packaging materials, storage containers, or bins that contain a synthetic fungicide, preservative, or fumigant;

(2) Use or reuse of any bag or container that has been in contact with any substance in such a manner as to compromise the integrity of OCal cannabis and nonmanufactured cannabis products placed in those containers, unless such reusable bag or container has been thoroughly cleaned and poses no risk of contact of OCal cannabis and nonmanufactured cannabis products with the substance used.

Note: Authority cited: Sections 26012 and 26013, Business and Professions Code. Reference: Sections 26013, 26062 and 26062.5, Business and Professions Code.

§ 10210. Temporary Variances.

(a) The department may establish temporary variances from the requirements in sections 10203 through 10208 for:

(1) A disaster for which the Governor has proclaimed a state of emergency in accordance with Government Code sections 8558 and 8625, or for which a local jurisdiction has proclaimed an emergency or disaster in accordance with Government Code sections 8558 and 8630. For the purposes of this chapter, "disaster" means the condition of extreme peril to the safety of persons and property within the state or a county, city and county, or city caused by conditions such as, fire, flood, storm, epidemic, drought, sudden and severe energy shortage, plant or animal infestation or disease, an earthquake, or similar public calamity; and

(2) Conduct of research or trials of techniques, varieties, or ingredients used in OCal cultivation.

(b) The registered certifying agent shall submit a written request for temporary variance to the department accompanied by a copy of the emergency proclamation.

(c) The department will provide written notification to registered certifying agents upon establishing a temporary variance that is applicable to the registered certifying agent's certified operations. The temporary variance shall specify the period of time it shall remain in effect, subject to extension as the department deems necessary.

(d) The registered certifying agent, when notified that the department has established a temporary variance, shall notify each cultivation or distribution operation it certifies to which the temporary variance applies.

(e) Temporary variances will not be granted for any practice, material, or procedure prohibited under section 10105 of this chapter.

Note: Authority cited: Sections 26012 and 26013, Business and Professions Code. Reference: Sections 26013, 26062 and 26062.5, Business and Professions Code.

ARTICLE 4. LABELS, LABELING, AND MARKET INFORMATION

§ 10300. Cannabis and Nonmanufactured Cannabis Products Labeled OCal.

(a) Cannabis or a nonmanufactured cannabis product to be sold, labeled, or represented as OCal must contain 100 percent OCal produced cannabis. The OCal cannabis or nonmanufactured cannabis product shall be labeled pursuant to section 10302 of this chapter.

(b) The ingredient statement of nonmanufactured OCal cannabis products shall not include ingredients:

(1) produced using excluded methods, pursuant to section 10105(a) of this chapter;

(2) produced using ionizing radiation, pursuant to section 10105(a)(5) of this chapter; and

(3) processed using sewage sludge, pursuant to section 10105(a)(6) of this chapter.

(c) OCal cannabis or cannabis product packages may display, on the principal display panel, information panel, any other panel of the package and on any labeling or marketing information concerning the product, one or more of the following:

(1) The term OCal to modify the name of the product;

(2) The OCal seal; or

(3) The seal, logo, or other identifying mark of the registered certifying agent that certified the operation that produced the finished product, provided that such seals or marks are not individually displayed more prominently than the OCal seal.

d) The registered certifying agent of the cultivator or distributer that handled the finished product must be identified on the information panel, above the statement, "Certified OCal by * * *," or similar phrase. The label may also display the business address, business website address, or telephone number of the identified registered certifying agent.

(e) Nonmanufactured OCal cannabis must be identified in the ingredient statement with the word, "OCal," or with an asterisk or other reference mark which is defined below the ingredient statement to indicate that the cannabis has been OCal produced.

Note: Authority cited: Sections 26012 and 26013, Business and Professions Code. Reference: Sections 26013, 26062 and 26062.5, Business and Professions Code.

§ 10301. Storage and Transport of Nonretail Containers Used for Nonmanufactured OCal Cannabis Products.

Nonretail containers used to store or transport nonmanufactured OCal cannabis products shall display on the outside of the container obviously visible OCal identifiers.

Note: Authority cited: Sections 26012 and 26013, Business and Professions Code. Reference: Sections 26013, 26062 and 26062.5, Business and Professions Code.

§ 10302. OCal Seal.

(a) The OCal seal described in paragraph (b) of this section may be used only for cannabis products described in section 10300 of this chapter.

(b) The OCal seal must replicate the form and design of the example in figure 1 and must be printed legibly and conspicuously:

(1) On a white background and with the term "OCal" ("O" in green with white cannabis flower inside "O" and "Cal" in orange overlapping the "O").

(2) On a white or transparent background with the term "OCal" ("O" in dark gray with white cannabis flower inside "O" and "Cal" in black overlapping the "O").

Note: Image not shown.

See https://www.omarfigueroa.com/book/

Figure 1

Note: Authority cited: Sections 26012 and 26013, Business and Professions Code. Reference: Sections 26013, 26062 and 26062.5, Business and Professions Code.

§ 10303. Registered Certifying Agent Seal, Logo, or Other Identifying Mark.

(a) A private entity or local jurisdiction registered as a certifying agent under this chapter may establish a seal, logo, or other identifying mark to be used by cultivation operations certified by the registered certifying agent to indicate affiliation with the registered certifying agent provided that the registered certifying agent:

(1) Does not require as a condition of certification use of its seal, logo, or other identifying mark on any product sold, labeled, or represented as OCal; and

(2) Does not require as a condition of use of its identifying mark compliance with any cultivation or distribution practices other than those provided for in this chapter.

Note: Authority cited: Sections 26012 and 26013, Business and Professions Code. Reference: Sections 26013, 26062 and 26062.5, Business and Professions Code.

ARTICLE 5. ACCREDITATION AND REGISTRATION OF CERTIFYING AGENTS

§ 10400. Areas and Duration of Accreditation and Registration.

(a) The department shall accredit or register a qualified applicant to certify cannabis operations under the OCal Program.

(b) Accreditation shall be for a period of five years from the date of approval of accreditation pursuant to section 10405 of this chapter.

(c) Registration shall be until January 1 of the following year pursuant to section 10409 of this chapter.

Note: Authority cited: Sections 26012 and 26013, Business and Professions Code. Reference: Sections 26013, 26062 and 26062.5, Business and Professions Code.

§ 10401. Requirements for Accreditation.

(a) A private entity or local jurisdiction accredited as a certifying agent under this section shall comply with each of the items listed below.

(1) Have expertise in organic production techniques to fully comply with and implement the terms and conditions of the certification program established under the regulations in this chapter.

(2) Demonstrate the ability to fully comply with the requirements for accreditation set forth in this chapter.

(3) Carry out all applicable provisions of the regulations in this chapter, including the provisions of sections 10500 through 10506 and 10710 of this chapter.

(4) Have enough trained and knowledgeable personnel, including inspectors and certification review personnel, to competently and efficiently comply with and implement the regulations of this chapter.

(5) Ensure that its responsibly connected persons, employees, and contractors with inspection, analysis, and decision-making responsibilities have ample expertise in organic production techniques to successfully perform the duties assigned.

(6) Conduct an annual performance evaluation of all persons who review applications for certification, perform on-site inspections, review certification documents, evaluate qualifications for certification, make recommendations concerning certification, or make certification decisions and implement measures to correct any deficiencies in certification services.

(7) Conduct an annual internal program review of the certification activities executed by certifying agent staff. The internal program review shall be performed by the certifying agent's staff, an outside auditor, or a consultant who has the expertise to conduct such reviews and implement measures to correct any non-compliances with the regulations in this chapter.

(8) Provide enough information to persons seeking certification to enable them to comply with the regulations in this chapter.

(9) Maintain records according to the following schedule:

(A) Records obtained from applicants for certification and certified operations shall be maintained for not less than five years beyond their receipt;

(B) Records created by the certifying agent regarding applicants for certification and certified operations shall be maintained for not less than 10 years beyond their creation; and

(C) Records created or received by a certifying agent pursuant to the accreditation requirements of this chapter, excluding any records covered by section 10401(a)(9)(B), shall be maintained for not less than five years beyond their creation or receipt.

(10) Make all records in paragraph (9), above, available for inspection and copying during standard business hours or mail to the physical or email address listed on the OCal Program website within 10 business days of a request by the department. For the purposes of this section, standard business hours are 8:00am - 5:00pm (Pacific Time), Monday through Friday, excluding holidays.

(11) Maintain strict confidentiality with respect to its clients under the OCal Program and not disclose to third parties, except for the department, business-related information concerning any client obtained while implementing the regulations of this chapter, except as provided for in section 10402(c)(5) of this chapter.

(12) Prevent conflicts of interest by:

(A) Not certifying an operation if a certifying agent or a responsibly connected party of such certifying agent has or previously held a commercial interest in the operation, including an immediate family interest or the delivery of consulting services, within the 12-month period prior to the application for certification;

(B) Excluding any person, including contractors, with conflicts of interest from work, discussions, and decisions in all stages of the certification process and the monitoring of certified operations for all entities in which such person has or previously held a commercial interest, including an immediate family interest or the delivery of consulting services, within the 12-month period prior to the application for certification;

(C) Not permitting any employee, inspector, contractor, or other personnel to accept payment, gifts, or favors of any kind, other than prescribed fees, from any business inspected, except that a certifying agent that is a not-for-profit organization with an Internal Revenue Code tax exemption, may accept voluntary labor from certified operations;

(D) Not giving advice or providing consultancy services, to certification applicants or certified operations, for overcoming identified barriers to certification;

(E) Requiring all persons who review applications for certification, perform on-site inspections, review certification documents, evaluate qualifications for certification, make recommendations concerning certification, or make certification decisions, and all parties responsibly connected to the certifying agent, to complete an annual conflict-of-interest disclosure report;

(F) Ensuring that the decision to certify an operation is made by a person different from those who conducted the review of documents and on-site inspection;

(G) Reconsidering a certified operation's application for certification and, if necessary, perform a new on-site inspection when it is determined, within 12 months of certifying the operation, that any person participating in the certification process and covered under section 10401(a)(12)(B) of this chapter has or had a conflict of interest involving the applicant. All costs associated with a reconsideration of application, including onsite inspection costs, shall be borne by the certifying agent; and

(H) Referring a certified operation to a different registered certifying agent for recertification and reimburse the operation for the cost of the recertification when it is determined that any person covered under section 10401(a)(12)(A) of this chapter at the time of certification of the applicant had a conflict of interest involving the applicant.

(13) Accept the certification decisions made by another certifying agent registered by the department to certify under the OCal Program pursuant to section 10409 of this chapter.

(14) Refrain from making false or misleading claims about its accreditation or registration status, the department's accreditation or registration program for certifying agents, or the nature or qualities of nonmanufactured OCal cannabis products.

(15) Charge applicants for certification and certified operations only those certification fees and charges that are on file with the department pursuant to section 10402(a)(8) of this chapter.

(16) Pay and submit accreditation fee, payment, or fine to the department pursuant to sections 10600, 10603, and 10701(e) of this chapter.

(17) Provide the inspector, prior to each annual on-site certification or re-certification inspection, with previous on-site inspection reports and notify the inspector of its decision regarding certification of an operation site inspected by the inspector and of any requirements for the correction of minor non-compliances.

(18) Accept all applications within its accredited certification type(s) and certify all qualified applicants, to the extent of its administrative capacity to do so, without regard to size or membership in any association or group.

(19) Comply with, implement, and carry out all terms and conditions pursuant to this chapter.

(b) The department may initiate suspension or revocation of an accreditation if the registered certifying agent fails to meet, conduct, or maintain accreditation requirements pursuant to this chapter.

(c) The accredited certifying agent may request amendment to its accredited certification types at any time. The application for amendment shall be sent to the department and shall contain information applicable to the requested change in accreditation, a complete and accurate update of the most recent information submitted pursuant to sections 10402 and 10407 of this chapter, and the applicable fee, payment, or fine pursuant to sections 10600, 10601, and 10701(e) of this chapter.

Note: Authority cited: Sections 26012 and 26013, Business and Professions Code. Reference: Sections 26013, 26062 and 26062.5, Business and Professions Code.

§ 10402. Application for Accreditation.

An application for certifying agent accreditation shall be submitted by mail to the physical or email address listed on the OCal Program website, or such other address as required by the department. Each application shall include the following, if applicable:

(a) Business information:

(1) Legal name;

(2) Employer Identification or Taxpayer Identification Number;

(3) Primary office physical address, mailing address, web address, and name of the person(s) responsible for the applicant's day-to-day operations and their contact number(s) and email address;

(4) Subsidiary office(s) physical address(es), mailing address(es), phone number(s), and a contact name(s) and number(s) for each subsidiary office;

(5) Business entity structure, including, but not limited to, a corporation, general partnership, joint venture, limited liability company, limited liability partnership, sovereign entity, sole proprietorship, not for profit corporation, and/or trust;

(6) For a local jurisdiction, a copy of the official's authority to conduct certification activities under this chapter;

(7) For a private entity, copies of all formation documents, which may include, but are not limited to, articles of incorporation, operating agreements, partnership agreements, and/or fictitious business name statements. The applicant shall also provide all documents filed with the California Secretary of State, which may include, but are not limited to, articles of incorporation, certificates of stock, articles of organization, certificates of limited partnership, and/or statements of partnership authority. If the applicant is a foreign corporation, the applicant shall provide a certificate of qualification issued by the California Secretary of State; and

(8) Each area of operation for which accreditation is requested and the estimated number of each type of operation anticipated to be certified annually by the applicant along with a copy of the applicant's schedule of fees for all services to be provided under these regulations by the applicant.

(b) Personnel information:

(1) Copy of the applicant's policies and procedures for training, evaluating, and supervising personnel;

(2) Name and position description of all personnel to be employed within the cannabis certification operation, including administrative staff, certification inspectors, members of any certification review and evaluation committees, contractors, and all parties responsibly connected to the applicant;

(3) Description of qualifications, including experience, training, and education in agriculture, organic production, and organic handling for each inspector to be used by the applicant and each person to be designated by the applicant to review or evaluate applications for certification; and

(4) Description of training the applicant has provided or intends to provide to personnel to ensure that they comply with and implement the requirements of this chapter.

(c) Administrative policies and procedures:

(1) Copy of the procedures to be used to evaluate certification applicants, make certification decisions, and issue certificates.

(2) Copy of the procedures to be used to review and investigate certified operation compliance with this chapter and to report any violations of this chapter to the department.

(3) Copy of the procedures to be used for complying with the recordkeeping requirements set forth in section 10401(a)(9) of this chapter.

(4) Copy of the procedures to be used for maintaining the confidentiality of any business-related information as set forth in section 10401(a)(11) of this chapter.

(5) Copy of the procedures to be used, including any fees to be assessed, for making the following information available to any member of the public upon request:

(A) Copies of certification certificates issued during the current and three preceding calendar years;

(B) A list of operations certified during the current and three preceding calendar years as well as certification status (certified, surrendered, suspended, revoked), city or cities in which the operation is located, products certified by the operation, and commercial cannabis license number(s).

(C) The results of laboratory analyses for residues of pesticides and other prohibited substances conducted to assist with verifying certified operation compliance during the current year and three preceding calendar years; and

(D) Other business information as permitted in writing by the certified operation.

(6) Copy of the procedures to be used for sampling and residue testing pursuant to section 10711 of this chapter.

(d) Conflicts of interest:

(1) Copy of the procedures intended to be implemented to prevent the occurrence of conflicts of interest, as described in section 10401(a)(12) of this chapter; and

(2) A conflict-of-interest disclosure report for all persons who review applications for certification, perform on-site inspections, review certification documents, evaluate qualifications for certification, make certification recommendations, make certification decisions, and all parties responsibly connected to the applicant. The conflict-of-interest disclosure report shall identify, for each of these persons, any cannabis-related business interests, including business interests of immediate family members, that may cause a conflict of interest.

(e) Current private entity or local jurisdiction certification activities:

(1) Number of operations certified (cannabis or other crop) during the current and previous three years;

(2) For each accreditation type requested, an OCal system plan (or equivalent), inspection report, and any other relevant documentation for three or more operations (cannabis or other crop) certified by the certifying agent during the current or previous year; and

(3) If the applicant underwent an accreditation process during the current or previous year, the name of the accrediting body and a copy of the written evaluation.

(f) Attestation to the following statement: "Under penalty of perjury, I hereby declare that the information contained within and submitted with the application is complete, true, and accurate. I understand that a misrepresentation of fact is cause for denial of the application, or revocation or suspension of the accreditation issued."

(g) Any other information the department requires to assist in the evaluation of the application for accreditation, which may include, but be not limited to, additional inspection reports, an external program review, and evidence that an applicant without certification experience can comply with the regulations.

Note: Authority cited: Sections 26012 and 26013, Business and Professions Code. Reference: Sections 26013, 26062 and 26062.5, Business and Professions Code.

§ 10403. Review of Accreditation Application.

(a) The department shall notify the applicant in writing:

(1) That the application is complete and accepted for further review.

(2) That the application is incomplete, the reasons for incompleteness, and the date by which any missing information, fee, payment or fine (10601, 10603 or 10701(e)) is due.

(A) The department shall receive the missing information, fee, payment, or fine from the applicant no later than 30 calendar days from the date of notification from the department. The application will be deemed abandoned if the missing information, fee, payment, or fines is not provided within the specified timeframe.

(B) If the application is deemed abandoned, the applicant may reapply and pay a new application fee.

Note: Authority cited: Sections 26012 and 26013, Business and Professions Code. Reference: Sections 26013, 26062 and 26062.5, Business and Professions Code.

§ 10404. Withdrawal of Accreditation Application.

(a) The applicant may withdraw an application at any time prior to the department's issuance of accreditation or denial of accreditation.

(b) Requests to withdraw an application shall be submitted to the department in writing, dated, and signed by the applicant.

(c) The department will not refund application fees for a withdrawn application.

(d) The applicant may reapply and pay a new application fee at any time following the withdrawal of an application.

Note: Authority cited: Sections 26012 and 26013, Business and Professions Code. Reference: Sections 26013, 26062 and 26062.5, Business and Professions Code.

§ 10405. Granting Accreditation and Registration.

(a) If the department determines the accreditation applicant meets the requirements for accreditation, pursuant to section 10401 of this chapter, the department shall notify the accreditation applicant in writing of the determination and bill the amount due. Payment shall be due 10 calendar days past the date the notice was issued.

(b) Accreditation shall be granted and the accredited certifying agent shall be registered when the required payment has been submitted pursuant to section 10600 of this chapter.

(c) The department shall notify the accredited certifying agent of the granting of accreditation and registration in writing. The notice shall state the effective and expiration dates of accreditation, the type(s) of certification for which the accreditation is granted, and the registration effective and expiration dates.

(d) The accredited certifying agent shall be registered pursuant to section 10409(e) of this chapter.

(e) The accreditation shall be valid for a period of five years from the effective date of accreditation. The department shall grant the accredited certifying agent a grace period between the accreditation date and January 1 of the following year so that accreditation and registration renewals may be applied for and completed concurrently. Accreditation may be renewed pursuant to section 10407 of this chapter unless the accredited certifying agent voluntarily ceases its certification activities or the accreditation is suspended or revoked pursuant to the requirements of section 10703 of this chapter.

Note: Authority cited: Sections 26012 and 26013, Business and Professions Code. Reference: Sections 26013, 26062 and 26062.5, Business and Professions Code.

§ 10406. Denial of Accreditation.

(a) If the department determines the accreditation applicant does not meet the requirements for accreditation pursuant to section 10401 of this chapter, the department shall provide written notification of accreditation denial to the applicant. Such notification shall include the reasons for the department's assessment and appeal procedures.

(b) The applicant who receives notification of accreditation denial may appeal the denial of accreditation pursuant to section 10706 of this chapter within 30 days after the date of the notice of accreditation denial.

(c) The applicant who receives notification of accreditation denial may apply for accreditation again at any time and pay a new application fee.

Note: Authority cited: Sections 26012 and 26013, Business and Professions Code. Reference: Sections 26013, 26062 and 26062.5, Business and Professions Code.

§ 10407. Accreditation Renewal.

An accreditation renewal application shall be submitted by mail to the physical or email address listed on the OCal Program website, or such other address as required by the department.

(a) The accredited certifying agent shall renew its accreditation every five years concurrently with its annual registration renewal pursuant to sections 10405(e) and 10410 of this chapter, except for the following:

> (1) The accredited certifying agent renewing both accreditation and registration shall receive a notice of expiration of registration and accreditation approximately six months prior to the registration expiration date;
>
> (2) The dual accreditation and registration renewal package shall be submitted no more than four months and no less than three months prior to the registration expiration date; and
>
> (3) The department shall conduct a site evaluation within three months of the registration expiration date.

(b) If the department determines the accredited certifying agent meets the requirements for accreditation, the accredited certifying agent's accreditation and registration shall be renewed pursuant to section 10405 of this chapter except that the notice will state any terms and conditions for continued accreditation, including minor non-compliances and the date by which such non-compliances shall be satisfied by the accredited certifying agent.

(c) The department shall issue a notice of proposed suspension or revocation of accreditation to the accredited certifying agent that does not satisfy all terms and conditions, including non-compliances, by the date specified on the notice of accreditation renewal.

(d) The department shall issue a written notice of denial of accreditation renewal pursuant to section 10406 of this chapter and the certifying agent shall be disqualified from registration pursuant to section 10410 of this chapter if it finds the accredited certifying agent unable to comply with the regulations of this chapter. The notice will specify the date the accreditation and registration shall expire and provide accreditation denial appeal instructions pursuant to section 10707 of this chapter.

(e) The accredited certifying agent who receives a notice of denial of accreditation renewal shall transfer to the department or make available all records or copies of records concerning the accredited certifying agent's certification activities, pursuant to section 10408(a)(4).

(f) The accredited certifying agent who no longer wishes to maintain its department accreditation must surrender its accreditation by submitting written notification to the department and shall transfer to the department or make available all records or copies of records concerning the accredited certifying agent's certification activities.

Note: Authority cited: Sections 26012 and 26013, Business and Professions Code. Reference: Sections 26013, 26062 and 26062.5, Business and Professions Code.

§ 10408. Requirements for Registration.

(a) A private entity or local jurisdiction registered as an accredited certifying agent under this chapter shall:

(1) Be accredited by the department as set forth in section 10401 of this chapter or possess current and valid accreditation by the National Organic Program, pursuant to 7 CFR part 205. The scope of accreditation shall be comparable to the scope of registration.

(2) Comply with, implement, and carry out all terms and conditions pursuant to this chapter;

(3) Annually renew registration and report activities as set forth in section 10410 of this chapter unless the accredited certifying agent voluntarily ceases its certification activities, its accreditation is suspended or revoked pursuant to 7 CFR part 205 or section 10705 of this chapter, as applicable, or its registration is suspended or revoked pursuant to section 10705 of this chapter;

(4) Transfer to the department or make available all records or copies of records concerning the registered certifying agent's certification activities if the registered certifying agent no longer wishes to maintain its registration, dissolves, or loses its registration;

(5) Pay and submit the registration fee and any payments or fines owed to the department in accordance with sections 10601, 10603 and 10701(e) of this chapter; and

(6) Demonstrate the ability to fully comply with the requirements for registration set forth in this section.

(b) The registered certifying agent shall notify the department in writing of receipt of payment and amount paid for certification or recertification of the operation. The notification shall also contain the operation's business name, commercial cannabis license number(s), license type(s), mailing address, physical address, telephone number, number of square feet certified, and products produced.

(1) Upon receipt of notification, the department will issue a certification number.

(2) The certification number shall be valid from the date the notification was received by the department.

(c) The department may initiate suspension or revocation of a registration if the certifying agent fails to meet, conduct, or maintain registration requirements pursuant to this chapter.

(d) The accredited certifying agent's registration shall expire unless renewed prior to the scheduled expiration date. Accredited certifying agents with an expired registration shall not perform certification activities under the regulations of this chapter.

§ 10409. Registration.

Registration information for an accredited certifying agent shall be submitted by mail to the physical or email address listed on the OCal Program website, or such other address as required by the department.

(a) Each application shall include the following, if applicable:

(1) Legal business name;

(2) Registration application fee pursuant to section 10601 of this chapter;

(3) A copy of the accredited certifying agent's current and valid accreditation certificate issued by the National Organic Program, if applicable;

(4) Employer Identification or Taxpayer Identification Number;

(5) Primary office physical address, mailing address, web address, and name of the person(s) responsible for the applicant's day-to-day operations and their contact number(s) and email address.

(6) Subsidiary office(s) physical address(es), mailing address(es), phone number(s), and a contact name(s) and number(s) for each subsidiary office;

(7) Business entity structure, including, but not limited to, a corporation, general partnership, joint venture, limited liability company, limited liability partnership, sovereign entity, sole proprietorship, not for profit corporation, and/or trust);

(8) The accredited areas of operation for which registration is requested and the estimated number of each type of operation anticipated to be certified annually by the accredited certifying agent;

(9) A schedule of fees for all services to be provided by the accredited certifying agent under these regulations;

(10) A conflict-of-interest disclosure report pursuant to section 10402(d)(2) of this chapter or 7 CFR section 205.504(c)(2), as applicable;

(11) The most recent annual internal program review of the accredited certifying agent's certification activities conducted by accredited certifying agent staff, an outside auditor, or a consultant, accompanied by a summary of findings which documents the results of the report, pursuant to section 10401(a)(7) of this chapter or 7 CFR section 205.501(a)(7), as applicable, and a description of adjustments to the accredited certifying agent's operation and procedures implemented or to be implemented in response to the program review; and

(12) Attestation to the following statement: "Under penalty of perjury, I hereby declare that the information contained within and submitted with the application is complete, true, and accurate. I understand that a misrepresentation of fact is cause for denial of the application, or revocation or suspension of the accreditation issued."

(b) The accredited certifying agent shall receive written notification of disqualification if the registration is disqualified due to missing information or ineligibility.

(c) The accredited certifying agent shall receive written notification of registration that includes the effective and expiration dates of the registration when:

(1) The accredited certifying agent has submitted the information pursuant to this section; and

(2) The accredited certifying agent has paid the required fee or fines pursuant to sections 10601, 10603 and

10701(e) of this chapter.

(d) Registration is valid through January 1 of the following year and may be renewed pursuant to section 10410 of this chapter unless the certifying agent voluntarily ceases its certification activities or registration is suspended or revoked pursuant to section 10705 of this chapter.

Note: Authority cited: Sections 26012 and 26013, Business and Professions Code. Reference: Sections 26013, 26062 and 26062.5, Business and Professions Code.

§ 10410. Registration Renewal and Reporting.

(a) The registered certifying agent's registration renewal shall be due by January 1 of each year and submitted by mail to the physical or email address listed on the OCal Program website, or such other address as required by the department.

(b) The department will send the registered certifying agent a notice of pending expiration of registration approximately ninety 90 calendar days prior to the scheduled date of expiration. The notice will include the registration number, the date of expiration, and any outstanding fines. Fines shall be paid prior to consideration for renewal, pursuant to section 10701(e)(4) of this chapter.

(c) Failure to receive a notice of pending registration expiration does not relieve the registered certifying agent of the obligation to renew registration as required.

(d) Registration renewal shall be submitted prior to registration expiration and include the following:

(1) The legal name of the registered certifying agent.

(2) The registration number and expiration date.

(3) A complete and accurate update of information submitted pursuant to section 10409 of this chapter, or, if applying for concurrent accreditation and registration renewal, a complete and accurate update of information submitted pursuant to section 10402 (a) through (d) of this chapter.

(4) A renewal application fee pursuant to section 10601 of this chapter.

(5) Full payment of any outstanding fees, payments, or fines pursuant to sections 10601, 10603 and 10701(e) of this chapter.

(6) A list of each cannabis operation granted certification during the previous year, which includes the business name, commercial cannabis license number(s), license type(s), mailing address, physical address, county, telephone number, number of square feet certified, and products.

(7) A copy of the inspection report for each cannabis operation granted certification during the previous year.

(8) Certificates of Analysis (COA) for no less than 5 percent of the registered certifying agent's certified operations tested in the previous year pursuant to section 10711 of this chapter.

(9) Any other information the department requires to assist in evaluating the application, including, but not limited to, OCal system plans, a notice of violation issued to an operation, and results of an NOP audit that took place during the previous year, when applicable.

(e) Registration renewals submitted before the expiration date printed on the notification of pending expiration will not expire prior to a renewal decision by the department.

(f) If a renewal is not submitted prior to the expiration date printed on the notification of pending expiration, the registered certifying agent may submit a registration renewal up to 30 calendar days after the expiration date printed on the notification of pending expiration. Registered certifying agents with an expired registration shall not perform certification activities under this chapter.

(1) A late renewal will be subject to a fee of 50 percent of the flat renewal fee to be paid in addition to the required renewal fee.

(g) The registered certifying agent that does not submit a complete registration renewal to the department within 30 calendar days after the expiration date printed on the notification of pending expiration shall forfeit its eligibility for renewal and may register pursuant to section 10409 of this chapter.

(h) The department shall notify the registered certifying agent in writing if the renewal is incomplete and the reason(s) for the incompleteness.

(1) The department shall receive any missing information, fee, payment, or fine, pursuant to sections 10403, 10601, 10603 and 10701(e) of this chapter, from the applicant no more than 15 calendar days after the date of the notification.

(2) The registered certifying agent that fails to provide the missing information, fees, payments, or fines, pursuant to sections 10403, 10601, 10603 and 10701(e) of this chapter, within the time allotted shall forfeit its eligibility for renewal and may re-register pursuant to section 10409 of this chapter.

Note: Authority cited: Sections 26012 and 26013, Business and Professions Code. Reference: Sections 26013, 26062 and 26062.5, Business and Professions Code.

§ 10411. Registration Renewal Acceptance.

(a) The registered certifying agent shall receive written notice of renewal acceptance, which includes the registration number and the effective and expiration dates of the renewal when:

(1) All required information has been submitted pursuant to section 10410 of this chapter; and

(2) Required fee(s) or fine(s) have been paid pursuant to sections 10601, 10603, and 10701(e) of this chapter.

(b) A registration renewal will be valid for a period of one year and may be renewed as provided in section 10410 of this chapter unless the registered certifying agent voluntarily ceases its certification activities or registration is suspended or revoked pursuant to section 10705 of this chapter.

Note: Authority cited: Sections 26012 and 26013, Business and Professions Code. Reference: Sections 26013, 26062 and 26062.5, Business and Professions Code.

§ 10412. Site Evaluations for Accredited and Registered Certifying Agents.

(a) Site evaluations shall be conducted for the purpose of examining the certifying agent's operations and evaluating its compliance with the regulations in this chapter. Site evaluations shall include an on-site review of the registered certifying agent's certification procedures, decisions, facilities, administrative and management systems, and operations certified by the registered certifying agent. Site evaluations shall be conducted by a representative of the department.

(b) One or more site evaluations may be conducted at any time during the accreditation or registration periods to determine registered certifying agent's compliance with this chapter.

Note: Authority cited: Sections 26012 and 26013, Business and Professions Code. Reference: Sections 26013, 26062 and 26062.5, Business and Professions Code.

ARTICLE 6. CERTIFICATION OF OPERATIONS

§ 10500. General Requirements for Certification.

A person seeking to receive or maintain OCal certification under the regulations in this chapter shall:

(a) Have an active and valid state commercial cannabis license;

(b) Comply with all applicable requirements of this chapter;

(c) Complete, implement, and update annually an OCal system plan that is submitted to the registered certifying agent pursuant to section 10201 of this chapter;

(d) Permit on-site inspections by authorized representatives of the department and the registered certifying agent with complete access to the production operation, including noncertified production areas, structures, and offices pursuant to section 10503 of this chapter;

(e) Maintain all records applicable to the certified operation for not less than five years beyond their creation and allow authorized representatives of the department and the registered certifying agent access to such records during standard business hours for review and copying to determine compliance with this chapter pursuant to section 10104 of this chapter. For the purposes of this section, standard business hours are 8:00am - 5:00pm (Pacific Time), Monday through Friday, excluding holidays.

(f) Submit the applicable fees charged by the registered certifying agent; and

(g) Immediately notify the registered certifying agent concerning any:

> (1) Application, including drift, of a prohibited substance to any product, field, production unit, site, or facility that is certified under the department;
>
> (2) Change in a certified operation or any portion of a certified operation that may affect certified operations compliance with this chapter; and
>
> (3) Change in commercial cannabis license status that would make an operation ineligible for certification.

Note: Authority cited: Sections 26012 and 26013, Business and Professions Code. Reference: Sections 26013, 26062 and 26062.5, Business and Professions Code.

§ 10501. Application for Certification.

(a) A person seeking certification of an operation under this chapter shall submit an application for certification to the registered certifying agent. The application shall include the following information:

> (1) An OCal system plan, as required in section 10201 of this chapter;
>
> (2) The name, business name, and business telephone number of the individual completing the application,
>
> (3) The name, business address, and business telephone number of the commercial cannabis licensee;
>
> (4) The name, address, email address, and telephone number of the commercial cannabis licensee;
>
> (5) A list of all valid commercial cannabis license types the commercial cannabis licensee holds and the

associated license numbers from the licensing authority;

(6) The name(s) of any OCal registered certifying agent(s) to which application has previously been made; the year(s) of application; the outcome of the application(s) submission, including, when available, a copy of any notification of non-compliance or denial of certification issued to the applicant for certification; and a description of the actions taken by the applicant to correct the non-compliances noted in the notification of non-compliance, including evidence of such correction;

(7) A statement of consent allowing the department to obtain all information regarding OCal certification from any certifying agent registered by the department to certify under the OCal program; and

(8) Other information deemed necessary by the registered certifying agent to determine compliance with this chapter, including, but not limited to, additional information regarding the origin of inputs, amendments to the OSP, and information regarding substances used on adjacent land.

Note: Authority cited: Sections 26012 and 26013, Business and Professions Code. Reference: Sections 26013, 26062 and 26062.5, Business and Professions Code.

§ 10502. Review of Certification Application.

(a) Upon acceptance of an application for certification, the registered certifying agent shall:

(1) Review the application to ensure completeness pursuant to section 10501 of this chapter;

(2) Determine by a review of the application materials whether the applicant can comply with the applicable requirements of this chapter;

(3) Verify the applicant who previously applied to another registered certifying agent and received a notification of non-compliance or denial of certification, pursuant to section 10505 of this chapter, has submitted documentation to support the correction of any non-compliances identified in the notification of non-compliance or denial of certification, as required in section 10505(e) of this chapter; and

(4) Schedule an on-site inspection of the operation to determine whether the applicant qualifies for certification if the review of application materials reveals the operation may be in compliance with the applicable requirements of this chapter.

(b) The registered certifying agent shall:

(1) Review the application materials received and communicate its findings to the applicant;

(2) Provide the applicant with a copy of the on-site inspection report for any on-site inspection performed; and

(3) Provide the applicant with a copy of the test results for any samples taken by an inspector.

(c) The applicant may withdraw its application at any time. The applicant that withdraws its application shall be liable for the costs of services provided up to the time of withdrawal of its application. An applicant that voluntarily withdraws its re-certification application prior to the issuance of a notice of non-compliance will not be issued a notice of non-compliance. Similarly, an applicant that voluntarily withdraws its application prior to the issuance of a notice of certification denial will not be issued a notice of certification denial.

Note: Authority cited: Sections 26012 and 26013, Business and Professions Code. Reference: Sections 26013, 26062 and 26062.5, Business and Professions Code.

§ 10503. On-site Inspections.

(a) On-site inspections.

(1) The registered certifying agent shall conduct an initial on-site inspection of each operation. An on-site inspection shall be conducted annually thereafter for the purpose of determining whether the certification of the operation should continue. Initial and annual on-site inspections shall include each of the operation's units, facilities, or sites intended for the production of OCal cannabis.

(2) (A) The registered certifying agent may conduct additional on-site inspections of applicants for certification and certified operations to determine compliance with this chapter.

(B) The department may require additional inspections be performed by the registered certifying agent for the purpose of determining compliance with this chapter.

(C) Additional inspections may be announced or unannounced at the discretion of the registered certifying agent or as required by the department.

(D) The registered certifying agent shall follow-up on any deficiencies found, which may include a subsequent inspection, to ensure compliance with this chapter.

(b) Scheduling.

(1) Following a review of the certification application pursuant to this section, the initial on-site inspection shall be conducted.

(2) All on-site inspections shall be conducted when an authorized representative of the operation who is knowledgeable about the operation is present and at a time when land, facilities, and activities that demonstrate the operation's compliance with or capability to comply with the applicable provisions of this chapter can be observed, except that this requirement does not apply to unannounced on-site inspections.

(c) Verification of information. The on-site inspection of an operation shall verify:

(1) The operation's compliance or capability to comply with this chapter;

(2) That the information, including the OCal system plan requirements provided pursuant to sections 10201, 10501(a)(1), and 10506(a)(1) of this chapter, accurately reflects the practices used or to be used by the applicant for certification or by the certified operation;

(3) That prohibited substances have not been and are not being applied to the operation through means which, at the discretion of the registered certifying agent, may include the collection and testing of soil, water, waste, seeds, plant tissue, plant, or cannabis product samples.

(d) Exit interview. The inspector shall conduct an exit interview with an authorized representative of the operation who is knowledgeable about the inspected operation to confirm the accuracy and completeness of inspection observations and information gathered during the on-site inspection. The inspector shall also address the need for any additional information as well as any issues of concern.

(e) Documents to the inspected operation.

(1) At the time of the inspection, the inspector shall provide the operation's authorized representative with a receipt for any samples taken by the inspector. There shall be no charge to the inspector for the samples taken.

(2) The registered certifying agency shall send a copy of the on-site inspection report and any test results to the inspected operation.

Note: Authority cited: Sections 26012 and 26013, Business and Professions Code. Reference: Sections 26013, 26062 and 26062.5, Business and Professions Code.

§ 10504. Granting Certification.

(a) Upon completion of the initial on-site inspection, the registered certifying agent shall review the on-site inspection report, the results of any analyses for substances conducted, and any additional information requested from or supplied by the applicant. If the registered certifying agent determines that the OCal system plan and all procedures and activities of the applicant's operation are in compliance with the requirements of this chapter and that the applicant is able to conduct operations in accordance with the plan, the registered certifying agent shall begin granting certification. The certification may include requirements for the correction of correctable non-compliances within a specified time period as a condition of continued certification. The operation is certified upon issuance of the certificate.

(b) The department shall issue each operation a certification number pursuant to section 10408(b) of this chapter.

(c) The registered certifying agent shall issue a certificate of OCal operation which specifies:

(1) Name and premises address of the certified operation;

(2) Department-issued certification number;

(3) Effective date of initial certification;

(4) Most recent inspection date;

(5) The operation's commercial cannabis license numbers and license types;

(6) Name, address, and telephone number of the registered certifying agent.

(d) Subject to section 10506 of this chapter once certified, a production operation's OCal certification continues in effect until surrendered, suspended or revoked by the registered certifying agent or the department, or if the operation no longer holds a valid commercial cannabis license.

(e) The OCal certificate shall be prominently displayed by the certified operation where it can be viewed by state or local government agencies.

Note: Authority cited: Sections 26012 and 26013, Business and Professions Code. Reference: Sections 26013, 26062 and 26062.5, Business and Professions Code.

§ 10505. Denial of Certification.

(a) When the registered certifying agent has reason to believe, based on a review of the information specified in section 10502 or 10504 of this chapter, that the applicant for certification is not able to comply or is not in compliance with the requirements of this chapter, the registered certifying agent shall provide a written notification of non-compliance to the applicant. When correction of a notice of non-compliance is not possible, a notification of non-compliance and a notification of denial of certification may be combined in one notification. The notification of non-compliance shall provide:

(1) A description of each non-compliance;

(2) The facts upon which the notification of non-compliance is based; and

(3) The date by which the applicant shall rebut or correct each non-compliance and submit supporting documentation of each such correction when correction is possible.

(b) Upon receipt of such notification of non-compliance, the applicant may:

(1) Correct non-compliances and submit a description of the corrective actions taken, with supporting

documentation, to the registered certifying agent;

(2) Correct non-compliances and submit a new application to another registered certifying agent and include, with the completed application, the notification of non-compliance received from the first registered certifying agent and a description of the corrective actions taken along with supporting documentation; or

(3) Submit written information to the issuing registered certifying agent to rebut the non-compliance described in the notification of non-compliance.

(c) After issuance of a notification of non-compliance, the registered certifying agent shall:

(1) Evaluate the applicant's corrective actions taken and supporting documentation submitted or the written rebuttal, conduct an on-site inspection if necessary, and

(A) When the corrective action or rebuttal is sufficient for the applicant to qualify for certification, issue the applicant an approval of certification pursuant to section 10504 of this chapter, or

(B) When the corrective action or rebuttal is not sufficient for the applicant to qualify for certification, issue the applicant a written notice of denial of certification.

(2) Issue a written notice of denial of certification to the applicant who fails to respond to the notification of non-compliance.

(3) Provide notice of approval or denial to the department.

(d) A notice of denial of certification shall state the reason(s) for denial and the applicant's right to:

(1) Reapply for certification pursuant to sections 10501 and 10505(e) of this chapter;

(2) Request mediation pursuant to section 10704 of this chapter;

(3) File an appeal of the denial of certification pursuant to section 10706 of this chapter.

(e) The applicant for certification who has received a written notification of non-compliance or a written notice of denial of certification may apply for certification again at any time with any registered certifying agent pursuant to section 10501 of this chapter. When such applicant submits a new application to the registered certifying agent other than the agent who issued the notification of non-compliance or notice of denial of certification, the applicant for certification shall include a copy of the notification of non-compliance or notice of denial of certification and a description of the actions taken, with supporting documentation, to correct the non-compliances noted in the notification of non-compliance.

(f) The registered certifying agent that receives a new application for certification, which includes a notification of non-compliance or a notice of denial of certification, shall treat the application as a new application and begin a new application process pursuant to section 10501 of this chapter.

(g) Notwithstanding paragraph (a) of this section, if the registered certifying agent has reason to believe that the applicant for certification has willfully made a false statement or otherwise purposefully misrepresented the applicant's operation or its compliance with the certification requirements pursuant to this chapter, the registered certifying agent may deny certification pursuant to paragraph (c)(1)(B) of this section without first issuing a notification of non-compliance.

Note: Authority cited: Sections 26012 and 26013, Business and Professions Code. Reference: Sections 26013, 26062 and 26062.5, Business and Professions Code.

§ 10506. Continuation of Certification.

(a) To continue certification, a certified operation shall annually pay the certification fees and submit the following information, as applicable, to the registered certifying agent:

(1) An updated OCal system plan that includes:

(A) A summary statement, supported by documentation, detailing any deviations from, changes to, modifications to, or other amendments made to the previous year's OCal system plan during the previous year; and

(B) Any additions or deletions to the previous year's OCal system plan, intended to be undertaken in the coming year, detailed pursuant to section 10201 of this chapter;

(2) Any additions to or deletions from the information required pursuant to section 10501 of this chapter;

(3) An update on the correction of minor non-compliances previously identified by the registered certifying agent as requiring correction for continued certification; and

(4) Other information as deemed necessary by the registered certifying agent to determine compliance with this chapter, including, but not limited to, additional information regarding the origin of inputs and evidence of correction of minor noncompliances.

(b) Following receipt of the information specified in paragraph (a) of this section, the registered certifying agent shall arrange and conduct an on-site inspection of the certified operation pursuant to section 10503 of this chapter, except when it is impossible for the registered certifying agent to conduct the annual on-site inspection following receipt of the certified operation's annual update of information. In such cases the registered certifying agent may allow continuation of certification and issue an updated certificate of OCal operation on the basis of the information submitted and the most recent on-site inspection conducted during the previous 12 months, provided that the annual on-site inspection, required pursuant to section 10503 of this chapter, is conducted within the first six months following the certified operation's scheduled date of annual update.

(c) If the registered certifying agent has reason to believe, based on the on-site inspection and a review of the information specified in section 10501 of this chapter, a certified operation is not complying with the requirements of this chapter, the registered certifying agent shall provide a written notification of non-compliance to the operation pursuant to section 10703(b) of this chapter.

(d) If the registered certifying agent determines the certified operation is in compliance with this chapter, the registered certifying agent shall issue an updated certificate of OCal operation pursuant to section 10504 of this chapter.

Note: Authority cited: Sections 26012 and 26013, Business and Professions Code. Reference: Sections 26013, 26062 and 26062.5, Business and Professions Code.

ARTICLE 7. FEES

§ 10600. Fees and Other Charges for Accreditation and Accreditation Renewal.

(a) A non-refundable application fee of $500.00 shall be due at the time of application. This fee will be applied to the total amount due for accreditation.

(b) The department shall charge an hourly fee for service of $55.00 for time spent on accreditation or accreditation renewal. Accreditation fees are based on the time required to render the service provided calculated to the nearest 15-minute period. Fees cover the review of applications and accompanying documents and information, evaluator travel time, the conduct of on-site evaluations, review of annual reports and updated documents and information, and the time required to prepare reports and any other documents in connection with the performance of service.

(c) Travel and per diem charges shall be administratively determined by the California Department of Human Resources, California Code of Regulations, title 2, division 1, chapter 3, subchapter 1, article 2, (commencing with section 599.615). Per diem charges to the applicant will cover the same period of time for which the evaluator(s) receives per diem reimbursement. The accreditation or accreditation renewal applicant will not be charged a new travel or per diem rate without notification before the service is rendered.

(d) When costs other than costs specified in paragraphs (a), (b), and (c) of this section are associated with providing the services, the accreditation or accreditation renewal applicant will be charged for these costs. Such costs include, but are not limited to, equipment rental, photocopying, delivery, facsimile, telephone, or translation charges incurred in association with accreditation services. The amount of the costs charged will be determined administratively by the department.

(e) The balance due upon completion of accreditation or accreditation renewal shall be billed to the applicant and due to the department 10 calendar days after the bill or notice date. Fees shall be collected from applicant prior to issuance of accreditation or accreditation renewal.

Note: Authority cited: Sections 26012 and 26013, Business and Professions Code. Reference: Sections 26013, 26062 and 26062.5, Business and Professions Code.

§ 10601. Fees for Registration and Registration Renewal.

(a) Fees for initial registration shall be due at the time of registration. Initial registration shall expire on January 1 of the year following initial registration.

(1) 12-month incentive fee. The initial registration fee shall be a flat fee of $1,000.00 if a certifying agent is registered during first nine months following the program's start date, or $750.00 if a certifying agent is registered during the final three months of the 12-month period following the program's start date.

(2) Regular, on-going fee. At the end of the 12-month period following the program's start date, the initial registration fee shall be a flat fee of $5,000.00 if a certifying agent is registered during the first three quarters of the year, and $3,000.00 if a certifying agent is registered during the final quarter of the year

(b) Fees for registration renewal shall be due by January 1 of each year. Registration shall expire on January 1 of the following year.

(1) The annual registration renewal fee of 26 percent of gross revenue earned from certification during the previous calendar year or a flat fee of $100.00, whichever is higher.

(c) Fees and other charges shall be collected from applicants prior to issuance of initial registration and registration renewal.

§ 10602. Fees and Other Charges for Certification.

(a) Fees charged by a registered certifying agent must be reasonable and a registered certifying agent shall charge applicants for certification and certified cultivation and distribution operations only those fees and charges that it has filed with the department.

(b) The registered certifying agent shall provide each applicant with an estimate of the total cost of certification and an estimate of the annual cost of updating the certification.

(c) The certifying agent may require applicants for certification to pay at the time of application a nonrefundable fee which shall be applied to the applicant's fees-for-service account.

(1) The certifying agent may set the nonrefundable portion of certification fees; however, the nonrefundable portion of certification fees must be explained in the fee schedule submitted to the department.

(2) The fee schedule must explain what fee amounts are nonrefundable and at what stage during the certification process fees become nonrefundable.

(d) The certifying agent shall provide all persons inquiring about the application process with a copy of its fee schedule.

Note: Authority cited: Sections 26012 and 26013, Business and Professions Code. Reference: Sections 26013, 26062 and 26062.5, Business and Professions Code.

§ 10603. Payment of Department Fees and Other Charges.

Fees shall be paid in accordance with sections 10600 or 10601 and pursuant to the directions on the bill or notice.

Note: Authority cited: Sections 26012 and 26013, Business and Professions Code. Reference: Sections 26013, 26062 and 26062.5, Business and Professions Code.

ARTICLE 8. COMPLIANCE

§ 10700. General.

The department may inspect, audit, review or investigate a certified operation's or a registered certifying agent's compliance with this chapter with or without prior notice.

Note: Authority cited: Sections 26012 and 26013, Business and Professions Code. Reference: Sections 26013, 26062 and 26062.5, Business and Professions Code.

§ 10701. Adverse Actions.

(a) The department may initiate one or a combination of the following actions on a registration, accreditation, or certification:

(1) Notice of Non-compliance;

(2) Notice of Proposed Suspension;

(3) Notice of Proposed Revocation; or

(4) Notice of Suspension or Revocation.

(b) The registered certifying agent may initiate one or a combination of the following actions on a certification:

(1) Notice of Non-compliance

(2) Notice of Proposed Suspension; or

(3) Notice of Proposed Revocation.

(c) The department may initiate suspension, for a term of no less than six months, or revocation of a certification:

(1) When the department has reason to believe a certified operation has violated or is not in compliance with this chapter; or

(2) When the department has reason to believe a certified operation has violated or is not in compliance with this chapter and the registered certifying agent fails to take appropriate action to enforce this chapter.

(d) The department may initiate suspension or revocation of an accreditation or registration if the registered certifying agent fails to meet, conduct, or maintain accreditation or registration requirements pursuant to this chapter. The suspension term will be no less than six months.

(e) The department may issue administrative fines to certifying agents and certified operations for violations of this chapter. The amount of the fine assessed for each violation shall be based upon the scope of the violation, the seriousness of the deception, and the impact of the fine on the violator, including the deterrent effect on future violations.

(1) Up to $17,952.00 per violation for knowingly labeling or selling a product as:

(A) "OCal," except in accordance with this chapter, or

(B) "Organic," except in accordance with the Organic Foods Production Act of 1990.

(2) Up to $20,000.00 per violation with a Proposed Suspension or Revocation, a Suspension or Revocation, or in response to a Willful violation

(3) The department shall receive payment of fines no more than 30 calendar days past the date of notification unless the fine is being appealed.

(4) All fines shall be paid prior to consideration for reinstatement or renewal of accreditation or registration, regardless of due date.

(f) All correspondence issued pursuant to sections 10702, 10703, 10704, and 10705 of this chapter and responses to correspondence shall be sent to the recipient's place of business via a delivery service which provides dated return receipts.

Note: Authority cited: Sections 26012, 26013, 26030 and 26031.5, Business and Professions Code. Reference: Sections 26013, 26031, 26062 and 26062.5, Business and Professions Code.

§ 10702. Investigation of Certified Operations.

(a) The registered certifying agent shall investigate suspected non-compliance and credible complaints of non-compliance with this chapter concerning operations certified as OCal by the registered certifying agent.

(b) The registered certifying agent must notify the department of all compliance proceedings and actions taken pursuant to this chapter.

(c) The department may assign a complaint against a certified operation to its registered certifying agent for investigation and specify a timeframe during which the investigation shall take place as agreed upon between the department and the registered certifying agent.

(d) The registered certifying agent shall investigate a complaint against a certified operation within the specified timeframe determined in subdivision (c).

(e) The registered certifying agent may refer an investigation back to the department, within the specified timeframe determined in subdivision (c), if the registered certifying agent lacks resources, expertise, or for some other reason beyond its control is unable to resolve the case. The registered certifying agent shall provide the department written explanation for its inability to reach a conclusion along with all findings.

(f) The registered certifying agent shall, in a timely manner, take appropriate action against a certified operation.

(g) If the registered certifying agent fails to comply with paragraphs (a) through (f) of this section, the department will resolve the complaint or take appropriate action against a certified operation and may begin non-compliance proceedings against the registered certifying agent pursuant to section 10705 of this chapter.

Note: Authority cited: Sections 26012 and 26013, Business and Professions Code. Reference: Sections 26013, 26062 and 26062.5, Business and Professions Code.

§ 10703. Non-compliance Procedures for Certified Operations.

(a) The registered certifying agent shall notify the certified operation and the department of any denial of certification or proposed fine, proposed suspension, or proposed revocation of a certification pursuant to this chapter.

(b) Notice of non-compliance. When an inspection, audit, or review of a certified operation by the registered certifying agent or the department reveals any non-compliance with this chapter, a written notification of non-compliance shall be sent to the certified operation. Such notification shall provide:

(1) A description of each non-compliance;

(2) The facts upon which the notification of non-compliance is based; and

(3) The date by which the certified operation shall rebut or correct each non-compliance and submit supporting documentation of each such correction when correction is possible.

(c) Resolution. When a certified operation demonstrates that each non-compliance has been resolved, the registered certifying agent or the department, as applicable, shall send the certified operation a written notification of non-compliance resolution.

(d) Proposed suspension or revocation. When rebuttal is unsuccessful or correction of the non-compliance is not completed within the prescribed time period, the registered certifying agent or department official shall send the certified operation a written notification of proposed suspension or revocation of certification of the entire operation or a portion of the operation, as applicable to the non-compliance. When correction of a non-compliance is not possible, the notification of non-compliance and the proposed suspension or revocation of certification may be combined in one notification. The notification of proposed suspension or revocation of certification shall state:

(1) The reasons for the proposed suspension or revocation;

(2) The proposed effective and expiration dates of such suspension;

(3) The proposed effective date and impact of a revocation on future eligibility for certification;

(4) The right to request mediation pursuant to section 10704 or request an appeal pursuant to section 10706 of this chapter.

(e) Willful violations. Notwithstanding paragraph (b) of this section, if the registered certifying agent or the department has reason to believe that a certified operation has willfully violated the regulations in this chapter, the registered certifying agent or the department shall send the certified operation a notification of proposed suspension or revocation of certification of the entire operation or a portion of the operation, as applicable to the non-compliance.

(f) Suspension or revocation. If the certified operation fails to correct the non-compliance, to resolve the issue through rebuttal or mediation, or to file an appeal of the proposed suspension or revocation of certification, the department shall send the certified operation a written notification of suspension or revocation that includes the amount of the administrative fine, pursuant to section 10701(e), if applicable.

(g) Eligibility for reinstatement.

(1) A certified operation whose certification has been suspended under this section may apply for reinstatement of certification, effective after the period of suspension has ended, by submitting to the registered certifying agent:

(A) A copy of the notice showing the suspension expiration date;

(B) A new application for certification in compliance with section 10501 of this chapter.

(C) Evidence demonstrating correction of each non-compliance and corrective actions taken to comply and remain in compliance with this chapter; and

(D) Evidence of payment of all fines in accordance with section 10701(e)(3) and (4).

(2) When the items in (g)(1) in this section have been satisfied, the registered certifying agent may issue a new OCal certificate to the operation pursuant to section 10504 of this chapter.

(3) A certified operation or a person responsibly connected with an operation whose certification has been revoked will be ineligible to receive certification for a period of five years following the effective date of such revocation.

Note: Authority cited: Sections 26012 and 26013, Business and Professions Code. Reference: Sections 26013, 26062 and 26062.5, Business and Professions Code.

§ 10704. Mediation for Certified Operations.

Any dispute with respect to denial of certification or proposed suspension or revocation of certification under this chapter may be mediated at the request of the applicant for certification or certified operation and with acceptance by the registered certifying agent. Mediation shall be requested in writing to the applicable registered certifying agent. If the registered certifying agent rejects the request for mediation, the registered certifying agent shall provide written notification to the applicant for certification or certified operation. The written notification shall advise the applicant for certification or certified operation of the right to request an appeal, pursuant to section 10706 of this chapter, within 30 calendar days of the date of the written notification of rejection of the request for mediation. If mediation is accepted by the registered certifying agent, such mediation shall be conducted by a qualified mediator mutually agreed upon by the parties to the mediation. The parties to the mediation shall have no more than 30 calendar days to reach an agreement following a mediation session. If mediation is unsuccessful, the applicant for certification or certified operation shall have 30 calendar days from termination of mediation to appeal the registered certifying agent's decision pursuant to section 10706 of this chapter. Any agreement reached during or as a result of the mediation process shall be in compliance with the regulations in this chapter. The department may review any mediated agreement for conformity to the regulations in this chapter and may reject any agreement or provision not in conformance with this chapter.

Note: Authority cited: Sections 26012 and 26013, Business and Professions Code. Reference: Sections 26013, 26062 and 26062.5, Business and Professions Code.

§ 10705. Non-compliance Procedure for Registered Certifying Agents.

(a) Notice of non-compliance. When an inspection, audit, or review of the registered certifying agent by the department reveals any non-compliance with this chapter, a written notification of non-compliance shall be sent to the registered certifying agent. Such notification shall provide:

(1) A description of each non-compliance;

(2) The facts upon which the notification of non-compliance is based;

(3) The date by which the registered certifying agent shall rebut or correct each non-compliance and submit supporting documentation of each correction when correction is possible.

(b) Resolution. When the registered certifying agent demonstrates that each non-compliance has been resolved, the department shall send the registered certifying agent a written notification of non-compliance resolution.

(c) Proposed suspension or revocation. When rebuttal is unsuccessful or correction of the non-compliance is not completed within the prescribed time period, the department shall send a written notification of proposed suspension or revocation of accreditation or registration to the registered certifying agent. The notification of proposed suspension or revocation will state whether the registered certifying agent's accreditation or specified areas of accreditation are to be suspended or revoked. When correction of a non-compliance is not possible, the notification of non-compliance and the proposed suspension or revocation may be combined in one notification. The notification of proposed suspension or revocation of accreditation or registration will state:

(1) The reasons for the proposed suspension or revocation;

(2) The proposed effective and expiration dates of the suspension or revocation;

(3) The proposed effective date of the revocation and its impact on future eligibility for accreditation;

(4) The right to file an appeal pursuant to section 10706 of this chapter.

(d) Willful violations. Notwithstanding paragraph (a) of this section, if the department has reason to believe that the registered certifying agent has willfully violated the regulations in this chapter, the department shall send a written notification of proposed suspension or revocation of accreditation or registration to the registered certifying agent.

(e) Suspension or revocation. When the accredited registered certifying agent fails to file an appeal of the proposed suspension or revocation of accreditation or registration, the department shall send a written notice of suspension or revocation of accreditation or registration to the certifying agent.

(f) Cessation of certification activities. The registered certifying agent whose accreditation or registration is suspended or revoked shall:

(1) Cease all certification activities.

(2) Transfer to the department and make available to department officials all records concerning its certification activities that were suspended or revoked.

(g) Eligibility for reinstatement.

(1) A certifying agent whose accreditation or registration has been suspended under this chapter may submit a request to the department for reinstatement of its accreditation or registration, to take effect after the expiration date of the suspension or revocation. The request shall be accompanied by evidence demonstrating correction of each non-compliance and corrective actions taken to comply and remain in compliance with this chapter. All fines shall be paid pursuant to section 10701(e)(3) and (4).

(2) A certifying agent whose accreditation or registration is revoked by the department will be ineligible to be accredited or registered as a certifying agent under this chapter for a period of not less than three years following the date of such revocation.

Note: Authority cited: Sections 26012 and 26013, Business and Professions Code. Reference: Sections 26013, 26062 and 26062.5, Business and Professions Code.

§ 10706. Appeals - General.

(a) The certified operation or certifying agent (respondent) may appeal a denial, the imposition of administrative fines pursuant to section 10701(e), or proposed notice of suspension or revocation to the department.

(b) All appeals shall be reviewed, heard, and decided by persons not involved with the decision being appealed.

Note: Authority cited: Sections 26012 and 26013, Business and Professions Code. Reference: Sections 26013, 26062 and 26062.5, Business and Professions Code.

§ 10707. Appeals - Submission.

(a) The registered certifying agent or certified operation may appeal a notice of denial, proposed suspension or revocation, suspension or revocation, or the imposition of administrative fines pursuant to section 10701(e), by submitting a written request for an informal hearing to the Department of Food and Agriculture, Legal Office of Hearings and Appeals, 1220 "N" Street, Suite 315, Sacramento, California 95814 or via email to CDFA.LegalOffice@cdfa.ca.gov. The request shall be received by the department within 30 calendar days after the date of the notice. The request shall include the following:

(1) Certifying agent or certified operation's (respondent's) name, mailing address, and daytime phone number;

(2) Respondent's certification number (if applicable);

(3) A copy of the notice; and

(4) A request for a telephonic hearing, if preferred.

(b) If the respondent fails to submit a request for hearing pursuant to subdivision (a) of this section, the proposed suspension or revocation may not be appealed and the department may proceed without a hearing.

Note: Authority cited: Sections 26012 and 26013, Business and Professions Code. Reference: Sections 26013, 26062 and 26062.5, Business and Professions Code.

§ 10708. Appeals - Evidence Provided by Certifying Agent.

(a) If the certified operation (respondent) appeals the proposed suspension or revocation action, notice of denial, or imposition of administrative fines by the certifying agent, the department shall request in writing evidence from the certifying agent to support the proposed suspension or revocation action.

(b) Within 30 days from the date of the request by the department, the certifying agent shall provide or send all information supporting the proposed suspension or revocation action to the department.

(c) If the certifying agent fails to send supporting information to the department within the specified time frame, the appeal shall be sustained with no impact on the respondent's certification.

(d) Within 45 days from the date of the request for supporting evidence, the department shall send the respondent either a notice of informal hearing pursuant to section 10709 of this chapter or notify the respondent that the appeal is sustained with no impact on the respondent's certification.

Note: Authority cited: Sections 26012 and 26013, Business and Professions Code. Reference: Sections 26013, 26062 and 26062.5, Business and Professions Code.

§ 10709. Appeals - Informal Hearing Schedule and Notification.

(a) The department shall schedule an informal hearing within 45 calendar days from receipt of the request for an informal hearing.

(b) The department shall provide notice of the informal hearing to the respondent. The notice shall contain the following information:

(1) Date, location, and time of the informal hearing;

(2) A statement to the respondent that the respondent may, but need not, be represented by counsel at any or all stages of the proceedings;

(3) Summary of the violations;

(4) Any other information or documentation necessary for the hearing; and

(5) A copy of California Code of Regulations, title 3, section 10710.

Note: Authority cited: Sections 26012, 26013, and 26031, Business and Professions Code. Reference: Sections 26013 and 26031, Business and Professions Code.

§ 10710. Appeals - Conduct of Informal Hearing.

Informal hearings shall be conducted as follows:

(a) The standard of proof to be applied by the hearing officer shall be a preponderance of the evidence.

(b) The respondent may request a hearing by phone by submitting the request with the appeal pursuant to section 10707.

(c) The hearing officer shall issue a written decision:

(1) Within 30 calendar days after the conclusion of the hearing;

(2) That includes a statement of the factual legal basis of the decision; and

(3) By personal service, mail, email, or via facsimile, depending upon the method by which the appeal was received.

(d) Review of the department's decision may be sought by the respondent within 30 calendar days from the date of the decision pursuant to section 1094.5 of the Code of Civil Procedure.

Note: Authority cited: Sections 26012, 26013, and 26031, Business and Professions Code. Reference: Sections 26013 and 26031, Business and Professions Code.

§ 10711. Inspection, Testing, and Reporting.

(a) A certified operation shall make all agricultural inputs, cannabis waste or cannabis that is to be sold, labeled, or represented as OCal accessible for examination and sampling by the department or the certified operation's registered certifying agent.

(b) The department or the registered certifying agent may require preharvest or postharvest testing of any agricultural input used, cannabis waste, or cannabis that is to be sold, labeled, or represented as OCal when there is reason to believe the agricultural input or cannabis has come into contact with a prohibited substance or has been produced using excluded methods. Samples collected and tested may include soil, water, cannabis waste, seeds, plant tissue, and whole plants. Such tests shall be conducted by the department or the registered certifying agent at the department's or the registered certifying agent's own expense.

(c) The registered certifying agent shall conduct periodic residue testing of cannabis waste and pre- and post-harvest cannabis that is to be sold, labeled, or represented as OCal. Samples collected and tested may include soil, water, cannabis waste, seeds, plant tissue, and whole plants. Such tests shall be conducted by the registered certifying agent at the registered certifying agent's own expense.

(d) The registered certifying agent shall, on an annual basis, sample and test from a minimum of 5 percent of the operations it certifies, rounded to the nearest whole number. The registered certifying agent that certifies fewer than 30 operations on an annual basis shall sample and test from at least one operation annually.

(e) Sample collection in accordance with this section shall be performed by a representative of the department or the registered certifying agent. Sample integrity shall be maintained throughout the chain of custody.

(f) Testing shall be performed by the Department of Food and Agriculture Center for Analytical Chemistry or a laboratory located in California that is a California commercial cannabis licensee or is accredited by an accrediting body that is independent from all other persons involved in commercial cannabis activity in the state and approved by the department.

(g) When testing detects prohibited substances, the registered certifying agent shall investigate to determine the cause of the prohibited substance.

(h) A certified operation must provide its registered certifying agent with a copy of the Certificate of Analysis (COA) for any batch tested, pursuant to section 26100 of the Business and Professions Code, that is destroyed within three business days after notification of destruction. If the batch was held or destroyed due to residue from prohibited substances, the registered certifying agent shall investigate pursuant to section 10702 of this chapter.

(i) Results of all analyses and tests performed under this chapter will be available for public access unless the testing is part of a compliance investigation or action. Results may be reviewed as part of a department audit pursuant to section 10412 of this chapter.

Note: Authority cited: Sections 26012 and 26013, Business and Professions Code. Reference: Sections 26013, 26062 and 26062.5, Business and Professions Code.

§ 10712. Exclusion from Sale as OCal and Reporting.

When residue testing detects unavoidable residual environmental contamination or prohibited substances at levels greater than 0.01 parts per million (ppm) or greater than the action level set by the Bureau of Cannabis Control if this action level is greater than 0.01 parts per million (ppm), the cannabis product shall not be sold, labeled, or represented as OCal. The registered certifying agent shall investigate pursuant to section 10702 of this chapter.

Note: Authority cited: Sections 26012 and 26013, Business and Professions Code. Reference: Sections 26013, 26062 and 26062.5, Business and Professions Code.

§ 10713. Emergency Pest or Disease Treatment.

When a prohibited substance is applied to a certified operation due to a federal or state emergency pest or disease treatment program and the certified operation otherwise meets the requirements of this chapter, the certification status of the operation shall not be affected as a result of the application of the prohibited substance, but , any harvested crop or plant part to be harvested that has contact with a prohibited substance applied as the result of a federal or state emergency pest or disease treatment program cannot be sold, labeled, or represented as OCal.

Note: Authority cited: Sections 26012 and 26013, Business and Professions Code. Reference: Sections 26013, 26062 and 26062.5, Business and Professions Code.

Title 4. Business Regulations

DIVISION 19. DEPARTMENT OF CANNABIS CONTROL

Chapter 1. All Licensees

ARTICLE 1. DIVISION DEFINITIONS AND GENERAL REQUIREMENTS

§ 15000. Definitions.

(a) "Act" means the Medicinal and Adult-Use Cannabis Regulation and Safety Act, codified in Business and Professions Code section 26000, et seq.

(b) "Adulterated" or "adulteration" has the meaning stated in section 26039.6(a) of the Act.

(c) "Allergen" means a major food allergen as defined in 21 U.S.C § 321(qq).

(d) "Appellation of Origin" means a designation to indicate that the cannabis meets the requirements developed by the program established pursuant to section 26063 of the Act.

(e) "Applicant" means an owner that is applying for a Department-issued license.

(f) "Batch" means a specific quantity of homogeneous cannabis or cannabis product that is one of the following types:

> (1) "Harvest batch" means a specifically identified quantity of dried flower or trim, leaves, and other cannabis plant matter that is harvested at the same time, and, if applicable, cultivated using the same pesticides and other agricultural chemicals.
>
> (2) "Manufactured cannabis batch" or "production batch" means either:
>
> > (A) An amount of cannabis concentrate or extract produced in one production cycle using the same extraction methods and standard operating procedures; or
> >
> > (B) An amount of a type of cannabis product produced in one production cycle using the same formulation and standard operating procedures.

(g) "Cannabis accessories" has the meaning stated in Health and Safety Code section 11018.2.

(h) "Cannabis concentrate" means cannabis that has undergone a process to concentrate one or more active cannabinoids, thereby increasing the product's potency. For purposes of this division, "cannabis concentrate" includes, but is not limited to, the kief, tinctures, capsules, suppositories, extracts, butter, vape cartridges, inhaled products (e.g., dab, shatter, and wax), and tablets as defined in subsection (nnn).

(i) "Cannabis goods" means cannabis and cannabis products in final form and packaged and labeled as they will be sold at retail. For the purposes of section 15311, "cannabis goods" includes all cannabis and cannabis products in any form.

(j) "Cannabis product" means cannabis that has undergone a process whereby the plant material has been transformed into a concentrate, including, but not limited to, concentrated cannabis, or an edible or topical product containing cannabis or concentrated cannabis and other ingredients.

(k) "Cannabis product quality," "quality cannabis product," or "quality" means that the cannabis product consistently meets the established specifications for identity, cannabinoid concentration, homogeneity, composition, and testing standards pursuant to sections 15718 through 15724, and has been manufactured, packaged, labeled, and held under conditions to prevent adulteration and misbranding.

(l) "Cannabis waste" means any material intended for disposal that contains cannabis but is not otherwise considered a hazardous waste. Cannabis waste consisting solely of plant material shall be considered an organic waste as defined in Public Resources Code section 42649.8(d).

(m) "Canopy" means the designated area(s) at a licensed premises that will contain mature plants at any point in time.

(n) "CBD" means the compound cannabidiol, CAS number 13956-29-1. "Total CBD" is defined in section 15700(qqq).

(o) "Commercial cannabis activity" includes the cultivation, possession, manufacture, distribution, processing, storing, laboratory testing, packaging, labeling, transportation, delivery, or sale of cannabis or cannabis products as provided for in this division, or acting as a cannabis event organizer for temporary cannabis events.

(p) "Commercial-grade, non-residential door lock" means a lock manufactured for commercial use.

(q) "Cultivation" means any activity involving the planting, growing, harvesting, drying, curing, grading, or trimming of cannabis.

(r) "Cultivation site" means a location where commercial cannabis is planted, grown, harvested, dried, cured, graded, or trimmed, or a location where any combination of those activities occurs.

(s) "Delivery employee" means an individual employed by a licensed retailer or licensed microbusiness authorized to engage in retail sales who delivers cannabis goods from the licensed retailer or licensed microbusiness premises to a customer at a physical address.

(t) "Designated responsible party" means the individual identified by the commercial cannabis business who has legal authority to bind the commercial cannabis business and who is the primary contact for the application and license-related issues.

(u) "Distribution" means the procurement, sale, and transport of cannabis and cannabis products between licensees.

(v) "Dried flower" means all dead cannabis that has been harvested, dried, cured, or otherwise processed, excluding leaves and stems.

(w) "Edible cannabis product" means a cannabis product intended to be used orally, in whole or in part, for human consumption. For purposes of this division, "edible cannabis product" includes cannabis products that dissolve or disintegrate in the mouth, but does not include any product otherwise defined as "cannabis concentrate."

(x) "Extraction" means a process by which cannabinoids are separated from cannabis plant material through chemical or physical means.

(y) "Final form" refers to cannabis and cannabis products that are in the form in which the cannabis or cannabis product will be consumed or used.

(z) "Flowering" means that a cannabis plant has formed a mass of pistils measuring greater than one-half inch wide at its widest point.

(aa) "Free cannabis goods" means any amount of cannabis goods provided to any person without cost or payment or exchange of any other thing of value.

(bb) “Immature plant” or “immature” means, for purposes of cultivation: a cannabis plant that has a first true leaf measuring greater than one-half inch long from base to tip if started from seed or a mass of roots measuring greater than one-half inch wide at its widest point if vegetatively propagated and outside of a tissue container, but that is not flowering; or a container with one or more cannabis protoplasts, cells, shoots, or plantlets in culture. For retail purposes, “immature plant” or “immature” means a cannabis plant that is nonflowering and shorter and narrower than 18 inches.

(cc) “Indoor cultivation” means the cultivation of cannabis within a permanent structure using exclusively artificial light or within any type of structure using artificial light at a rate above twenty-five watts per square foot.

(dd) “Informational panel” means any part of the cannabis product label that is not the primary panel and that contains required labeling information.

(ee) “Infusion” means a process by which cannabis, cannabinoids, or cannabis concentrates are directly incorporated into a product formulation to produce a cannabis product.

(ff) “Infused pre-roll” means a pre-roll into which cannabis concentrate (other than kief) or other ingredients have been incorporated.

(gg) “Ingredient” means any substance that is used in the manufacture of a cannabis product and that is intended to be present in the finished cannabis product.

(hh) “Kief” means the resinous trichomes of cannabis that have been separated from the cannabis plant.

(ii) “Labeling” means any label or other written, printed, or graphic matter upon cannabis or a cannabis product, upon its container or wrapper, or that accompanies any cannabis or cannabis product.

(jj) “Licensee” means any person holding a license issued under the Act.

(kk) “Light deprivation” means the use of any technique to eliminate natural light in order to induce flowering.

(ll) “Limited-access area” means an area in which cannabis or cannabis products are stored or held and is only accessible to a licensee and authorized persons.

(mm) “Lot” means a batch, or specifically identified portion of a batch.

(nn) “Lot number” or “batch number” means a distinctive group of numbers, letters, or symbols or any combination of these that is unique to a group of cannabis or cannabis products.

(oo) “Manufacture” means to compound, blend, extract, infuse, or otherwise make or prepare a cannabis product.

(1) The term “manufacture” includes the following processes:

(A) Extraction.

(B) Infusion.

(C) Packaging or repackaging of cannabis products.

(D) Labeling or relabeling the packages of cannabis products.

(E) “Post-extraction processing” or “post-processing,” which means a process by which one or more active cannabinoids in cannabis concentrate are further concentrated either by chemical or physical means.

(F) Remediation of failed harvest batches or cannabis product batches.

(2) The term “manufacture” does not include the following:

(A) The repacking of cannabis products from a bulk shipping container by a distributor or retailer where the product's original packaging and labeling is not otherwise altered.

(B) The preparation of pre-rolls by a licensed distributor in accordance with the requirements of section 15303.

(C) The collection of the resinous trichomes that are dislodged or sifted from the cannabis plant incidental to cultivation activities by a licensed cultivator.

(D) The processing of nonmanufactured cannabis products, as defined in subsection (eee).

(E) The labeling or relabeling of a package containing cannabis goods with the amount of cannabinoids and terpenoids based on regulatory compliance testing results by a distributor in accordance with sections 15303 and 17407.

(pp) "Manufacturing" or "manufacturing operation" means all aspects of the extraction process, infusion process, post-processing, remediation, and packaging and labeling processes, including processing, preparing, holding, and storing of cannabis products. Manufacturing also includes any processing, preparing, holding, or storing of components and ingredients.

(qq) "Mature plant" or "mature" means a cannabis plant that is flowering.

(rr) "Medicinal cannabis patient" includes both a qualified patient as defined in Health and Safety Code section 11362.7 and a person in possession of a valid identification card issued under Health and Safety Code section 11362.71.

(ss) "Mixed-light cultivation" means the cultivation of mature cannabis in a greenhouse, hoop-house, glasshouse, conservatory, hothouse, or other similar structure using a combination of:

(1) Natural light and either of the models listed below:

(A) "Mixed-light Tier 1," without the use of artificial light or the use of artificial light at a rate above zero, but no more than six watts per square foot; or

(B) "Mixed-light Tier 2," the use of artificial light at a rate above six and below or equal to twenty-five watts per square foot.

(tt) "Nonmanufactured cannabis products" means final form items that contain only cannabis, leaf, pre-roll filter tips, or paper.

(uu) "Nonvolatile solvent" means any solvent used in the extraction process that is not a volatile solvent. "Nonvolatile solvent" includes carbon dioxide, ethanol, and nonhydrocarbon-based or other solvents such as water, vegetable glycerin, vegetable oil, animal fat, and glycerin.

(vv) "Nursery" means all activities associated with producing clones, immature plants, seeds, and other agricultural products used specifically for the propagation and cultivation of cannabis.

(ww) "Orally consumed concentrate" means a cannabis concentrate that is intended to be consumed by mouth and is not otherwise an edible cannabis product. "Orally consumed concentrate" includes tinctures, capsules, and tablets as defined in subsection (nnn).

(xx) "Outdoor cultivation" means the cultivation of mature cannabis without the use of artificial lighting in the canopy area at any point in time.

(yy) "Package" or "packaging" means any container or wrapper that may be used for enclosing or containing any cannabis or cannabis product. "Package" does not include a shipping container or outer wrapping used solely for the transport of cannabis or cannabis products in bulk quantity to a licensed premises.

(zz) "Person" includes any individual, firm, partnership, joint venture, association, corporation, limited liability company, estate, trust, business trust, receiver, syndicate, or any other group or combination acting as a unit, and the plural as well as the singular.

(aaa) "Pest" means an undesired insect, rodent, nematode, fungus, bird, vertebrate, invertebrate, weed, virus, bacteria, or other microorganism (except microorganisms on or in living humans or other living animals) that is, or is liable to become, injurious, dangerous, or detrimental to health, the environment, or the agricultural environment of the state.

(bbb) "Pre-roll" means any combination of the following rolled in paper: flower, shake, leaf, or kief that is obtained from accumulation in containers or sifted from loose, dry cannabis flower or leaf with a mesh screen or sieve.

(ccc) "Premises" means the designated structure(s) and land specified in the application that is owned, leased, or otherwise held under the control of the applicant or licensee where the commercial cannabis activity will be or is conducted. The premises shall be a contiguous area and shall only be occupied by one licensee.

(ddd) "Primary panel" means the part of a cannabis goods label that is most likely to be displayed, presented, shown, or examined under customary conditions of display for retail sale.

(eee) "Processing" means all activities associated with the drying, curing, sifting, grading, trimming, rolling, storing, packaging, and labeling of cannabis or nonmanufactured cannabis products.

(fff) "Product Identity" or "identity of the product" means the generic, common, or usual name of a product by which it is most commonly known.

(ggg) "Promotional materials" means any form, letter, circular, pamphlet, publication, or other written material directed to a customer or prospective customer to induce retail sales. Promotional material does not include permitted signs, displays, decorations, cannabis accessories, or cannabis or cannabis products furnished by a licensed cultivator, licensed manufacturer, licensed distributor, licensed microbusiness, or licensed cannabis event organizer to a retail licensee for advertising purposes. Promotional materials shall have no intrinsic or secondary value.

(hhh) "Publicly owned land" means any building or real property that is owned, leased, or occupied by a city, county, state, federal, or other government entity.

(iii) "Quarantine" means the storage or identification of cannabis or cannabis product to prevent use, movement or transfer of the cannabis or cannabis product.

(jjj) "Residential area" is an area that is within 600 feet of any single-family or multifamily residence, other than commercial hotels, motels, and similar establishments for temporary lodging.

(kkk) "Retail area" means a building, room, or other area that is open to the public, upon the licensed retailer or licensed microbusiness premises authorized to engage in retail sales in which cannabis goods are sold or displayed.

(lll) "Serving" means the designated amount of cannabis product established by the manufacturer to constitute a single unit.

(mmm) "Sublet" means to lease or rent all or part of a leased or rented property.

(nnn) "Tablet" means a solid preparation containing a single serving of THC or other cannabinoid that is intended to be swallowed whole, not formulated to be chewable, dispersible, effervescent, orally disintegrating, used as a suspension, or consumed in a manner other than swallowed whole, and does not contain any added natural or artificial flavor or sweetener.

(ooo) "Tamper-evident" means that the cannabis goods packaging is sealed in a manner that prevents the packaging from being opened without obvious destruction of the seal.

(ppp) "Terpenes" means terpenes, terpenoids, flavonoids, polyphenols, and other naturally occurring phytochemicals and secondary metabolites contributing to the aroma or flavor of cannabis.

(qqq) "THC" or "delta-9 THC" means the compound tetrahydrocannabinol, CAS number 1972-08-3. "Total THC" is defined in section 15700(rrr).

(rrr) "Tincture" means a solution of cannabis extract, derived either directly from the cannabis plant or from a manufactured cannabis extract, dissolved in alcohol, glycerin, or vegetable oils. For purposes of this definition, "vegetable" includes botanically classified fruits and vegetables and their seeds.

(sss) "Topical cannabis product" means a cannabis product intended to be applied to the skin rather than ingested or inhaled.

(ttt) "Track and trace system" means the program for reporting the movement of cannabis and cannabis products through the distribution chain established by the Department in accordance with section 26067 of the Act.

(uuu) "Transport" means the physical movement of cannabis or cannabis products from one licensed premises to another licensed premises.

(vvv) "Unique identifier" or "UID" means an alphanumeric code or designation used for reference to a specific plant and any cannabis or cannabis product derived or manufactured from that plant.

(www) "Universal symbol" means the symbol developed by the Department pursuant to section 26130(c)(7) of the Act to indicate that a product contains cannabinoids.

(xxx) "Vehicle alarm system" is a device or series of devices installed to discourage theft of the vehicle or its contents and is intended to summon general attention or to summon law enforcement as a result of an indication of an attempted breach of the vehicle.

(yyy) "Volatile solvent" means any solvent that is or produces a flammable gas or vapor that, when present in the air in sufficient quantities, will create explosive or ignitable mixtures. Examples of volatile solvents include, but are not limited to, butane, hexane, and propane.

(zzz) "Watts per square foot" means the sum of the maximum wattage of all lights identified in the designated canopy area(s) in the premises diagram divided by the sum of the dimensions in square feet of the same designated canopy area(s).

(aaaa) "Wholesale cost" has the meaning stated in title 18, California Code of Regulations, section 3700.

NOTE: Authority cited: Section 26013, Business and Professions Code. Reference: Section 26013, Business and Professions Code.

§ 15000.1. General Requirements.

(a) Every person who conducts commercial cannabis activity shall obtain and maintain a valid license from the Department for each separate premises at which commercial cannabis activity is conducted.

(b) Commercial cannabis activity shall only be conducted between licensees. Licensed retailers and licensed microbusinesses authorized to engage in retail sales may conduct commercial cannabis activity with customers or nonprofits in accordance with this division.

(c) The licensee shall only conduct commercial cannabis activities authorized by the license and on the premises licensed for the activity.

(d) All transfers of cannabis and cannabis product shall be conducted by a licensed distributor.

(e) Licenses shall not be transferrable or assignable to another person or premises, except as provided in section

26050.2 of the Business and Professions Code. In the event of the sale or other transfer of the commercial cannabis business, changes in ownership shall be made in accordance with section 15023.

(f) Applicants and licensees shall use their legal business name on all documents related to commercial cannabis activity.

NOTE: Authority cited: Section 26013, Business and Professions Code. Reference: Sections 26012, 26053, 26057 and 26070, Business and Professions Code.

§ 15000.2. A- and M-Designations.

(a) Licensees may conduct business with other licensees irrespective of the A-designation or M-designation on their licenses.

(b) Licensees authorized to engage in distribution shall only transport and sell cannabis goods designated as "For Medical Use Only" to M-designated retailers or M-designated microbusinesses authorized to engage in retail sales.

(c) Licensees authorized to engage in retail sales shall only sell cannabis goods designated as "For Medical Use Only" to medicinal customers.

NOTE: Authority cited: Section 26013, Business and Professions Code. Reference: Sections 26001, 26013, 26050 and 26053, Business and Professions Code.

§ 15000.3. Premises Requirements.

(a) A licensed premises shall not be in a location that requires persons to pass through a business that sells alcohol or tobacco or a private residence to access the licensed premises.

(b) A licensed premises shall not be in a location that requires persons to pass through the licensed premises to access a business that sells alcohol or tobacco or a private residence.

(c) A licensed premises shall not include the living areas of a private residence, such as bathrooms, bedrooms, kitchens, and living rooms, unless living areas are required to be included in the licensed premises. If the local jurisdiction requires living areas of a private residence to be included in the licensed premises, licensees shall designate living areas on their premises diagram as required by section 15006(k) but shall not conduct any commercial cannabis activity within the designated living areas. Nothing in this section shall prohibit a licensee from utilizing the living areas of a private residence for non-commercial cannabis activity, such as staff breaks. Areas of a private residence that are not considered to be living areas may include garages, offices, sheds, barns, and other areas regularly used for commercial cannabis activity

(d) Licensees shall ensure that the Department has immediate access to their licensed premises. If the Department is denied access to a licensee's premises for any reason, the licensee shall be held responsible and subject to discipline. If the Department is denied access to one licensee's premises because of another licensee's refusal to grant access when the only access to one licensed premises is through another licensed premises, all licensees shall be held responsible and subject to discipline.

(e) Nothing in this section shall be interpreted to prohibit two or more licensed premises from occupying separate portions of the same parcel of land or sharing common use areas, such as a bathroom, breakroom, hallway, or building entrance.

(f) All structures included as part of the licensed premises shall be permanent structures. Structures that are considered permanent structures include, but are not limited to, buildings, barns, sheds, shipping containers, and modular buildings. Structures that are not considered to be permanent structures include, but are not limited to, structures that rest on wheels or any structure that can be readily moved.

(g) Personal cultivation of cannabis as permitted by Health and Safety Code section 11362.1 shall not occur on the licensed premises unless the local jurisdiction requires that all areas of the land parcel be included in the premises. If the local jurisdiction requires all areas of the land parcel be included, then the licensee may conduct personal cultivation in a separate and distinct area on the premises, which shall be identified on the premises diagram pursuant to section 15006. "Separate and distinct," for purposes of this section, shall mean that the personally cultivated cannabis is cultivated, processed, and stored in a manner that clearly identifies it as personally cultivated cannabis and prevents it from coming into contact with commercially cultivated cannabis.

(h) Notwithstanding any other provision of law, a licensed premises that is not in compliance with subsections (c) and (f) at the time this subsection becomes effective shall come into compliance within six months of the effective date of this subsection by submitting a premises modification in accordance with section 15027. Premises that must be modified to comply with this subsection shall not be subject to the premises modification fee specified in section 15014.

NOTE: Authority cited: Section 26013, Business and Professions Code. Reference: Sections 26012, 26050, 26051.5, 26054, 26055 and 26160, Business and Professions Code.

§ 15000.4. Subletting of Premises.

Except as allowed pursuant to article 2 of chapter 8, a licensee shall not sublet or allow another person to conduct operations in any area designated as the licensed premises for the licensee's commercial cannabis activity.

NOTE: Authority cited: Section 26013, Business and Professions Code. Reference: Sections 26012 and 26070, Business and Professions Code.

§ 15000.5. Licensee's Responsibility for Acts of Employees and Agents.

In construing and enforcing the provisions of the Act and the regulations in this division, the act, omission, or failure of an agent, officer, representative, or other person acting for or employed by a licensee, within the scope of their employment or office, shall in every case be deemed the act, omission, or failure of the licensee.

NOTE: Authority cited: Section 26013, Business and Professions Code. Reference: Sections 26031 and 26110, Business and Professions Code.

§ 15000.6. Age Restriction.

Employees or persons retained by a licensee to work within or on a licensed premises or to handle cannabis or cannabis products shall be at least 21 years of age.

NOTE: Authority cited: Section 26013, Business and Professions Code. Reference: Section 26140, Business and Professions Code.

§ 15000.7. Storage of Inventory.

(a) All cannabis and cannabis products must be stored within the licensed premises.

(b) A licensee shall not store cannabis goods outdoors.

(c) Bathrooms and changing facilities shall be separated from all storage areas by solid walls that extend from the floor to the ceiling. Employee break areas, if any, shall be separate and distinct from areas where cannabis and cannabis products are stored.

(d) Licensees may use additional shipping containers as temporary storage space on their licensed premises when their storage needs exceed the capacity of their storage space. Licensees using storage containers pursuant to this subsection shall notify the Department of the premises modification in accordance with subsection (h) of section 15027.

NOTE: Authority cited: Section 26013, Business and Professions Code. Reference: Sections 26012, 26053 and 26070, Business and Professions Code.

ARTICLE 2. APPLICATIONS

§ 15001. Provisional Licenses.

(a) A provisional licensee shall comply with all laws applicable to a licensee holding an annual license of the same type.

(b) A provisional license does not create a vested right in the holder to renewal of the provisional license or issuance of an annual license.

(c) A provisional license shall no longer be valid upon issuance of an annual license, denial of an annual license, abandonment of an application for licensure, withdrawal of an application for licensure, or surrender of the provisional license.

(d) A provisional licensee must actively and diligently pursue requirements for an annual license to continue to hold a provisional license, which includes meeting all the following requirements:

> (1) Paying the license fee within 60 calendar days of the date the Department sends a notification that the license fee is due.
>
> (2) Providing all information requested by the Department or otherwise elaborating upon information previously provided to the Department, or providing a statement demonstrating that the information cannot be provided due to circumstances beyond the provisional licensee's control. The information or statement shall be provided by the response date specified by the Department, or within 30 calendar days of the date the Department sends the information request to the provisional licensee if the Department does not specify a response date.

(e) Refusal by the Department to issue or renew a provisional license pursuant to section 15001.1 or section 15001.2 shall not entitle the applicant to a hearing or an appeal of the decision. Chapter 2 (commencing with section 480) of division 1.5, chapter 4 (commencing with section 26040), and sections 26031 and 26058 of the Business and Professions Code shall not apply to licenses issued pursuant to this section.

(f) No provisional license issued by the Department shall be effective after January 1, 2026.

NOTE: Authority cited: Section 26013, Business and Professions Code. Reference: Section 26050.2, Business and Professions Code.

§ 15001.1. Issuance of Provisional License.

(a) Until June 30, 2022, the Department may, in its sole discretion, issue a provisional license to a commercial cannabis business if:

(1) The applicant submits a complete application, in accordance with section 15002, and the required application fee to the Department on or before March 31, 2022.

(2) For an application for a license that includes cultivation activities, the applicant provides any of the following documents:

(A) A final streambed alteration agreement;

(B) A draft streambed alteration agreement provided by the Department of Fish and Wildlife and signed and returned to the Department of Fish and Wildlife;

(C) Written verification by the Department of Fish and Wildlife that a streambed alteration agreement is not needed; or

(D) Written verification by the Department of Fish and Wildlife that the applicant submitted a notification described in section 1602 of the Fish and Game Code, submitted payment of applicable fees pursuant to section 1609 of the Fish and Game Code, and is responsive to the Department of Fish and Wildlife as prescribed in section 26050.2 of the Business and Professions Code.

(3) Issuance of the license would not cause the commercial cannabis business to hold multiple cultivation licenses on contiguous premises to exceed one acre of total canopy for outdoor cultivation, or 22,000 square feet for mixed-light or indoor cultivation, if the application is received on or after January 1, 2022. For purposes of this subsection, premises will be considered contiguous if they are connected, touching, or adjoining.

(b) After June 30, 2022, and until September 30, 2022, the Department may, in its sole discretion, issue a provisional license for cultivation to a commercial cannabis business if:

(1) The applicant submits a complete application, in accordance with section 15002, and the required application fee to the Department on or before June 30, 2022.

(2) The commercial cannabis business is not applying for a cultivation license for a premises that exceeds 20,000 square feet of total canopy for outdoor cultivation.

(3) The commercial cannabis business provides any of the following documents:

(A) A final streambed alteration agreement;

(B) A draft streambed alteration agreement provided by the Department of Fish and Wildlife and signed and returned to the Department of Fish and Wildlife;

(C) Written verification by the Department of Fish and Wildlife that a streambed alteration agreement is not needed; or

(D) Written verification by the Department of Fish and Wildlife that the applicant has submitted a notification described in section 1602 of the Fish and Game Code, submitted payment of applicable fees pursuant to section 1609 of the Fish and Game Code, and is responsive to the Department of Fish and Wildlife as prescribed in section 26050.2 of the Business and Professions Code.

(4) Issuance of the license would not cause the commercial cannabis business to hold multiple cultivation licenses on contiguous premises to exceed one acre of total canopy for outdoor cultivation, or 22,000 square feet for mixed-light or indoor cultivation, if the application is received on or after January 1, 2022. For the purposes of this subsection, premises will be considered contiguous if they are connected, touching, or adjoining.

(c) After June 30, 2022, and until June 30, 2023, the Department may, in its sole discretion, issue a provisional license to a local equity license applicant, as defined in section 26240(c) of the Business and Professions Code, if:

(1) The applicant submits a complete application, in accordance with section 15002, and the required application fee to the Department on or before March 31, 2023.

(2) For an application for a license that includes cultivation activities, the following conditions are met:

(A) The local equity license applicant provides any of the following documents:

(i) A final streambed alteration agreement;

(ii) A draft streambed alteration agreement provided by the Department of Fish and Wildlife and signed and returned to the Department of Fish and Wildlife;

(iii) Written verification by the Department of Fish and Wildlife that a streambed alteration agreement is not needed; or

(iv) Written verification by the Department of Fish and Wildlife that the applicant has submitted a notification described in section 1602 of the Fish and Game Code, submitted payment of applicable fees pursuant to section 1609 of the Fish and Game Code, and is responsive to the Department of Fish and Wildlife as prescribed in section 26050.2 of the Business and Professions Code.

(B) The local equity applicant is not applying for a cultivation license for a premises that exceeds one acre of total canopy for outdoor cultivation, or 22,000 square feet for mixed-light or indoor cultivation.

(C) Issuance of the license would not cause the local equity applicant to hold multiple cultivation licenses on contiguous premises to exceed one acre of total canopy for outdoor cultivation, or 22,000 square feet for mixed-light or indoor cultivation. For the purposes of this subsection, premises will be considered contiguous if they are connected, touching, or adjoining.

NOTE: Authority cited: Section 26013, Business and Professions Code. Reference: Section 26050.2, Business and Professions Code.

§ 15001.2. Renewal of Provisional License.

(a) To timely renew a provisional license, the provisional licensee shall comply with the requirements of section 15020.

(b) For provisional license renewals from July 1, 2022, through June 30, 2023, in addition to the requirements of section 15020, a provisional licensee must also provide to the Department:

(1) Evidence that one of the following California Environmental Quality Act (CEQA) (Division 13 (commencing with section 21000) of the Public Resources Code) requirements has been met:

(A) Documentation, such as a letter, report, notice or other type of written communication from the local jurisdiction, demonstrating that the local jurisdiction is in the process of preparing a site-specific initial study, addendum, or checklist pursuant to title 14, California Code of Regulations, section 15063, 15164, 15168, or 15183 to demonstrate whether it is consistent with a previously circulated and adopted negative declaration, mitigated negative declaration, or environmental impact report;

(B) Documentation, such as a letter, report, notice or other type of written communication from the local jurisdiction, demonstrating that the local jurisdiction has made substantial progress during the previous 12-month licensure term toward completing project specific environmental review by drafting, preparing, or circulating for public review an environmental document pursuant to CEQA;

(C) Documentation requested by the Department of the provisional licensee that demonstrates the furtherance of environmental review during the previous 12-month licensure term;

(D) Other information requested by the Department from the provisional licensee that demonstrates evidence of substantial progress toward compliance with CEQA during the previous 12-month licensure term; or

(E) Documentation that demonstrates compliance with CEQA is complete.

(2) For cultivation licenses, a provisional licensee must also provide one of the following forms of documentation demonstrating progress with compliance with chapter 6 (commencing with section 1600) of division 2 of the Fish and Game Code:

(A) A final streambed alteration agreement issued by the Department of Fish and Wildlife;

(B) A draft streambed alteration agreement provided by the Department of Fish and Wildlife and signed and returned to the Department of Fish and Wildlife by the provisional licensee;

(C) Written verification by the Department of Fish and Wildlife that the provisional licensee has submitted a complete notification described in section 1602 of the Fish and Game Code; or

(D) Written verification by the Department of Fish and Wildlife that a streambed alteration agreement is not needed.

(c) For provisional license renewals on or after July 1, 2023, in addition to the information required in section 15020, a provisional licensee must also provide to the Department:

(1) Documentation, such as a full or partial copy of the administrative record, demonstrating that one of the following CEQA requirements has been met:

(A) The local jurisdiction has prepared and circulated for public review a negative declaration or a mitigated negative declaration;

(B) The local jurisdiction has determined that an environmental impact report is required pursuant to section 21157 of the Public Resources Code and has either made substantial progress in preparing that environmental impact report or has a contract or contracts with consultants in place for the preparation of that environmental impact report;

(C) The local jurisdiction has certified that it has conducted a reasonably comprehensive site-specific review and has reviewed, prepared, and deemed complete an initial study, addendum, or checklist pursuant to title 14, California Code of Regulations, section 15063, 15164, 15168, or 15183 demonstrating consistency with a previously circulated and adopted negative declaration, mitigated negative declaration, or environmental impact report, in preparation for approval of an annual license; or

(D) The local jurisdiction has reviewed, prepared, and deemed complete a notice of exemption pursuant to section 21108 or 21152 of the Public Resources Code, except for ministerial projects not subject to the California Environmental Quality Act pursuant to section 21080(b)(1) of the Public Resources Code.

(E) Documentation submitted pursuant to subsection (c)(1) may include, but is not limited to:

(i) Any environmental documentation, including, but not limited to, an exemption, initial study, negative declaration, mitigated negative declaration, and/or environmental impact report;

(ii) Any staff reports and related documents prepared by the local jurisdiction;

(iii) Any written transcript or minutes of the proceedings of the local jurisdiction;

(iv) Any notice(s) issued by the local jurisdiction to comply with CEQA and the CEQA Guidelines;

(v) Any proposed decisions or findings considered by the local jurisdiction by its staff or the applicant; and

(vi) Any documentation of the local jurisdiction's final decision.

(2) For cultivation licensees, one of the following forms of documentation demonstrating progress with compliance with chapter 6 (commencing with section 1600) of division 2 of the Fish and Game Code:

(A) A final streambed alteration agreement issued by the Department of Fish and Wildlife;

(B) A draft streambed alteration agreement provided by the Department of Fish and Wildlife and signed and returned to the Department of Fish and Wildlife by the provisional licensee; or

(C) Written verification from the Department of Fish and Wildlife that a streambed alteration agreement is not needed.

(d) The Department will not renew a provisional license authorizing cultivation if:

(1) The State Water Resources Control Board has notified the Department that the provisional licensee is not in compliance with section 26060.1(a) or (b) of the Business and Professions Code or the principles, guidelines, and requirements established pursuant to section 13149 of the Water Code.

(2) The Department of Fish and Wildlife has notified the Department that the provisional licensee is not in compliance with any final streambed alteration agreement, any conditions set forth in a signed draft streambed alteration agreement, or a condition established pursuant to section 26060.1(a) or (b)(1) and (2) of the Business and Professions Code.

(3) After January 1, 2023, if renewing the license would cause a licensee to hold multiple cultivation licenses on contiguous premises to exceed one acre of total canopy for outdoor cultivation or 22,000 square feet for mixed-light or indoor cultivation. For the purposes of this section, premises will be considered contiguous if they are connected, touching, or adjoining.

NOTE: Authority cited: Section 26013, Business and Professions Code. Reference: Section 26050.2, Business and Professions Code.

§ 15001.3. Notice of Provisional License Review.

(a) When the Department is considering the suspension, revocation, or denial of renewal of a provisional license pursuant to Business and Professions Code section 26050.2, the Department shall issue a Notice of Provisional License Review to a provisional licensee for failure to comply with the Act or its implementing regulations.

(b) The Notice of Provisional License Review shall be in writing and state the following:

(1) The nature and facts of each violation, including a reference to the statutory and/or regulatory section(s) violated;

(2) The manner in which the provisional licensee must correct the violation(s) to achieve compliance;

(3) That the Department is considering suspending, revoking, or denying the renewal of the provisional license.

(4) That the provisional licensee may provide the Department with information related to the observed violation(s) and potential license action for the Department's consideration during its provisional license review. The information may include statements, including a statement that the Department should not take the action under consideration, and any relevant documentation, including evidence that the violation(s) did not occur, of correction of the violation(s), or of mitigation. The provisional licensee may also request an informal meeting with the Department to discuss the matter and may be accompanied by an attorney or other

representative.

(c) The Department shall serve the Notice of Provisional License Review by mail or electronic mail to the provisional licensee's designated responsible party, or in person to the licensee or an employee or agent of the provisional licensee.

NOTE: Authority cited: Section 26013, Business and Professions Code. Reference: Section 26050.2, Business and Professions Code.

§ 15001.4. Immediate Suspension of Provisional License.

(a) The Department may immediately suspend any provisional license, or immediately impose licensing restrictions or other conditions upon any provisional licensee, if necessary to protect public health, safety, or welfare.

(b) An order issued pursuant to subsection (a) shall be in writing and describe the following:

> (1) The nature and facts of each violation, including a reference to the statutory and/or regulatory section(s) violated; and
>
> (2) Whether the provisional license is suspended or the provisional licensee may continue to operate subject to restrictions or other conditions.

(c) Following the issuance of an order pursuant to subsection (a), the Department shall serve the provisional licensee with a Notice of Provisional License Review pursuant to section 15001.3.

NOTE: Authority cited: Section 26013, Business and Professions Code. Reference: Section 26050.2, Business and Professions Code.

§ 15002. Annual License Application Requirements.

(a) Applications may be completed and submitted online at www.cannabis.ca.gov.

(b) Applicants who submit their applications online shall first register for a user account if required by the licensing system. To register for a user account, the applicant shall do all of the following as requested by the licensing system:

> (1) Create a username, password, and security question and answer;
>
> (2) Provide an email address; and
>
> (3) Provide the owner's first and last name, primary phone number, Social Security number or individual taxpayer identification number, date of birth, and mailing address.

(c) An application must be completed by an owner as defined by section 15003. An application for an annual cannabis license includes the following:

> (1) The legal first and last name of the applicant and the legal business name of the commercial cannabis business.
>
> (2) Every business trade name, fictitious business name, and doing business as ("DBA") under which the commercial cannabis business will operate.
>
> (3) The commercial cannabis license for which the applicant is applying, and whether the applicant is requesting that the license be designated as medicinal, adult-use, or both, if applicable.
>
> (4) Payment of an application fee pursuant to section 15014.

(5) The physical address of the premises or the assessor parcel number. If the Department is unable to confirm that the address provided is valid, then the applicant shall provide a document that confirms the physical address or location of the premises. Such a document may include a utility bill, printed information from the county assessor, deed, or title.

(6) The mailing address for the commercial cannabis business, if different from the premises address.

(7) The telephone number for the commercial cannabis business.

(8) The website address of the commercial cannabis business, if any.

(9) The number under which the commercial cannabis business files federal taxes, such as a federal employer identification number, federal taxpayer identification number, individual taxpayer identification number, Social Security number, or national identification number.

(10) Contact information for the owner of the commercial cannabis business who will serve as the designated primary contact person or designated responsible party for the business, including the name, title, phone number, and email address of the individual.

(11) The full legal name, mailing address, primary contact phone number, email address, and preferred method of written communication (e.g., standard mail or email) of each individual or entity serving as agent for service of process for the commercial cannabis business, if any.

(12) A description of the business organizational structure of the commercial cannabis business, such as partnership, joint venture, limited liability company, sole proprietorship, trust, or corporation.

(13) Upon request, business formation documents that are not available online through the California Secretary of State, which may include, but are not limited to operating agreements, bylaws, and other documents that establish ownership or control over the commercial cannabis business. If the commercial cannabis business is held in trust, the applicant shall provide a copy of the certificate of trust establishing trustee authority.

(14) A commercial cannabis business that is a foreign corporation or foreign limited liability company shall include in its application a certificate of qualification, certificate of registration, or certificate of status issued by the California Secretary of State.

(15) A complete list of every financial interest holder of the commercial cannabis business as defined in section 15004, who is not an owner as defined in section 15003. The list of financial interest holders shall include:

> (A) For financial interest holders that are individuals, the first and last name of the individual, a contact phone number and email address, and the type and number of the individual's government-issued identification, such as a driver's license.
>
> (B) For financial interest holders that are entities, the legal business name, the name and phone number and email address of the entity's primary contact, and federal taxpayer identification number of the entity.

(16) A complete list of every owner of the commercial cannabis business, as defined in section 15003. Each individual named on this list shall submit the following information:

> (A) The full name of the owner.
>
> (B) The owner's title within the commercial cannabis business.
>
> (C) The owner's date of birth and place of birth.
>
> (D) The owner's Social Security number or individual taxpayer identification number.
>
> (E) The owner's mailing address.

(F) The owner's telephone number. This may include a number for the owner's home, business, or mobile telephone.

(G) The owner's email address.

(H) The owner's current employer.

(I) The percentage of the ownership interest held in the commercial cannabis business by the owner.

(J) The number of the owner's government-issued identification. Acceptable forms of identification are a document issued by a federal, state, county, or municipal government that includes the name, date of birth, gender, and photo of the person, such as a driver's license or passport.

(K) A copy of the owner's completed application for electronic fingerprint images submitted to the Department of Justice.

(L) A statement of rehabilitation may be submitted by the owner for any conviction, but is not required. The statement of rehabilitation is to be written by the owner and may contain evidence that the owner would like the Department to consider that demonstrates the owner's fitness for licensure. Supporting evidence may be attached to the statement of rehabilitation and may include, but is not limited to, a certificate of rehabilitation under Penal Code section 4852.01, and dated letters of reference from employers, instructors, or professional counselors that contain valid contact information for the individual providing the reference.

(M) If applicable, a detailed description of any administrative orders or civil judgments for violations of labor standards, any suspension of a commercial cannabis license, revocation of a commercial cannabis license, or sanctions for unlicensed commercial cannabis activity by a licensing authority, local agency, or state agency against the owner in their individual capacity or a business entity in which the owner was an owner or officer within the three years immediately preceding the date of the application. The owner may provide mitigating information including, but not limited to, a statement of rehabilitation to the Department for consideration if any prior discipline disclosed pursuant to this section may result in denial of the application.

(N) Attestation to the following statement: Under penalty of perjury, I hereby declare that the information contained within and submitted with this application is complete, true, and accurate. I understand that a misrepresentation of fact is cause for rejection of this application, denial of the license, or revocation of a license issued.

(17) Evidence that the commercial cannabis business has the legal right to occupy and use the proposed location that complies with section 15007.

(18) An attestation that the proposed premises is in compliance with Business and Professions Code section 26054(b) and, if requested, evidence of compliance. For purposes of this section, evidence of compliance with Business and Professions Code section 26054(b) may be a copy of a valid license, permit, or other authorization issued by the applicable local jurisdiction or a notification from the applicable local jurisdiction stating that the commercial cannabis business is in compliance with local ordinances and regulations.

(19) For a commercial cannabis business with 20 or more employees, the applicant shall either provide a notarized statement that the commercial cannabis business will enter into and abide by the terms of a labor peace agreement or demonstrate that the commercial cannabis business has entered into a labor peace agreement by providing a copy of the signature page of the agreement. For a commercial cannabis business with fewer than 20 employees that has not yet entered into a labor peace agreement, provide a notarized statement indicating that the applicant will enter into and abide by the terms of a labor peace agreement within 60 days of employing its 20th employee.

(20) The applicant shall provide a valid seller's permit number issued by the California Department of Tax and

Fee Administration, if applicable. If the commercial cannabis business has not yet received a seller's permit, the commercial cannabis business shall attest that the commercial cannabis business is currently applying for a seller's permit.

(21) A diagram of the premises as required by section 15006.

(22) Proof of a surety bond of at least $5,000 payable to the State of California for each licensed premises. All bonds required under this section shall be issued by a corporate surety licensed to transact surety business in the State of California. An aggregated bond may be used when multiple licenses are held by the same commercial cannabis business.

(23) Additional information as required by section 15011.

(24) When an applicant provides a license, permit, or other authorization from the local jurisdiction where the licensed premises will be or is located, the Department will notify the applicable local jurisdiction to confirm the validity of the authorization. If the local jurisdiction does not respond within 10 calendar days, the Department shall consider the authorization valid.

(25) The limited waiver of sovereign immunity required by section 15009, if applicable.

(26) Evidence of exemption from, or compliance with, the California Environmental Quality Act as required by section 15010.

(27) The commercial cannabis business' State Employer Identification Number (SEIN) issued by the California Employment Development Department, if applicable.

(28) For a commercial cannabis business with more than one employee, the applicant shall attest that the commercial cannabis business employs, or will employ within one year of receiving a license, one supervisor and one employee who have successfully completed a Cal-OSHA 30-hour general industry outreach course offered by a training provider that is authorized by an OSHA Training Institute Education Center to provide the course.

(29) An applicant shall disclose whether they have been denied a license or had a license suspended or revoked by the Department or any other state cannabis licensing authority. The applicant shall provide the type of license denied, suspended, or revoked, the name of the licensing authority, and the date of the denial, suspension, or revocation.

(d) An applicant for a cannabis event organizer license shall not be required to comply with subsections (c)(5), (c)(17), (c)(20), (c)(21), (c)(22), (c)(24), (c)(25), and (c)(26).

NOTE: Authority cited: Section 26013, Business and Professions Code. Reference: Sections 26012, 26050, 26051.5 and 26055, Business and Professions Code.

§ 15002.1. Temporary Cannabis Event Application.

(a) A temporary cannabis event license shall only be issued to a person who holds a cannabis event organizer license issued by the Department.

(b) An application for a temporary cannabis event license shall include the following:

(1) The name of the applicant. For applicants who are individuals, the applicant shall provide both the first and last name of the individual. For applicants who are business entities, the applicant shall provide the legal business name of the entity.

(2) The license number for each state cannabis license held by the applicant.

(3) The address of the location where the temporary cannabis event will be held, or if no address exists, the assessor parcel number, or street description.

(4) The name of the temporary cannabis event.

(5) A diagram of the physical layout of the temporary cannabis event. The diagram shall clearly indicate where the temporary cannabis event will be taking place on the location grounds, all entrances and exits that will be used by participants during the event, all cannabis goods consumption areas, and all areas where cannabis and cannabis products will be sold or displayed. The hours during which cannabis goods will be sold shall be noted on the diagram. The diagram shall also clearly indicate the area where cannabis waste will be stored, all areas where cannabis goods will be stored, and the specific location of each cannabis licensee and non-cannabis vendor who will be participating in the event. Each cannabis licensee and non-cannabis vendor participating in the event shall be identified with an assigned temporary cannabis event location number. The diagram shall also designate a limited-access area that can only be accessed by the cannabis event organizer and Department representatives.

(6) The dates and hours of operation for which the temporary cannabis event license is being sought. A temporary event license is required for any date in which the applicant engages in onsite cannabis goods sales or allows onsite cannabis goods consumption.

(7) Contact information for the applicant's designated primary contact person regarding the temporary event license, including the name, title, address, phone number, and email address of the individual.

(8) Contact information for a designated contact person(s) who shall be onsite at the event and reachable by telephone at all times during the event.

(9) Written approval from the local jurisdiction authorizing the applicant to engage in onsite cannabis goods sales to, and onsite consumption by, persons 21 years of age or older at the temporary cannabis event at the proposed location.

(10) A list of all licensees who will be participating in the event that provides a designated contact for each licensee who will be responsible for that licensee's activities during the event and will be available to the Department in person or by phone throughout the event, whether the licensee will be selling cannabis goods at the event, whether the licensee will be selling any non-cannabis products at the event, and a description of the type of non-cannabis products that will be sold, if applicable.

(11) A list of all non-cannabis vendors who will be participating in the event, a description of the type of product they will be selling or displaying, and contact information for a designated contact person.

(12) Attestation to the following statement: Under penalty of perjury, I hereby declare that the information contained within and submitted with this application is complete, true, and accurate. I understand that a misrepresentation of fact is cause for rejection of this application, denial of the license, or revocation of a license issued.

NOTE: Authority cited: Section 26013, Business and Professions Code. Reference: Sections 26012 and 26200, Business and Professions Code.

§ 15003. Owners of Commercial Cannabis Businesses.

(a) An applicant for a commercial cannabis license or a licensee shall disclose all owners of the commercial cannabis business. An owner of the commercial cannabis business includes all of the following:

(1) A person with an aggregate ownership interest of 20 percent or more in the commercial cannabis business, unless the interest is solely a security, lien, or encumbrance. For purposes of this section, "aggregate" means the total ownership interest held by a single person through any combination of individually held ownership

interests in a commercial cannabis business and ownership interests in an entity that has an ownership interest in the same commercial cannabis business. For example, a person who owns 10 percent of the stock in a commercial cannabis business as an individual shareholder and 100 percent of the stock in an entity that owns 10 percent of the stock in the same commercial cannabis business has a 20 percent aggregate ownership interest in the commercial cannabis business.

(2) An individual who manages, directs, or controls the operations of the commercial cannabis business, including but not limited to:

(A) A member of the board of directors of a nonprofit.

(B) A general partner of a commercial cannabis business that is organized as a partnership.

(C) A non-member manager or managing member of a commercial cannabis business that is organized as a limited liability company.

(D) The trustee(s) and all persons who have control of the trust and/or the commercial cannabis business that is held in trust.

(E) The chief executive officer, president or their equivalent, or an officer, director, vice president, general manager or their equivalent.

(b) If the commercial cannabis business is owned in whole or in part by an entity and the entity includes individuals who manage, direct, or control the operations of the commercial cannabis business, as described in subsection (a)(2)(E), those individuals shall also be disclosed as owners.

(c) If available evidence indicates that an individual qualifies as an owner, the Department may notify the applicant or licensee that they must either disclose the individual as an owner and submit the information required by section 15002 or demonstrate that the individual does not qualify as an owner.

NOTE: Authority cited: Section 26013, Business and Professions Code. Reference: Sections 26001 and 26012, Business and Professions Code.

§ 15004. Financial Interest in a Commercial Cannabis Business.

(a) An applicant for a commercial cannabis license or a licensee shall disclose all financial interest holders. A financial interest holder of the commercial cannabis business includes all of the following, except as provided in subsection (b):

(1) A person with an aggregate ownership interest of less than 20 percent.

(2) A person providing a loan to the commercial cannabis business.

(3) A person entitled to receive 10 percent or more of the profits of the commercial cannabis business, including:

(A) An employee who has entered into a profit share plan with the commercial cannabis business.

(B) A landlord who has entered into a lease agreement with the commercial cannabis business for a share of the profits.

(C) A consultant who is providing services to the commercial cannabis business for a share of the profits.

(D) A person acting as an agent, such as an accountant or attorney, for the commercial cannabis business for a share of the profits.

(E) A broker who is engaging in activities for the commercial cannabis business for a share of the profits.

(F) A salesperson who earns a commission.

(G) A person who has entered into an intellectual property licensing agreement for a share of the profits.

(b) Financial interest holders do not include any of the following:

(1) A bank or financial institution whose interest constitutes a loan;

(2) Persons whose only financial interest in the commercial cannabis business is through an interest in a diversified mutual fund, blind trust, or similar instrument;

(3) Persons whose only financial interest is a security interest, lien, or encumbrance on property that will be used by the commercial cannabis business; and

(4) Persons who hold a share of stock that is less than 10 percent of the total shares in a publicly traded or privately held company.

NOTE: Authority cited: Section 26013, Business and Professions Code. Reference: Sections 26012 and 26051.5, Business and Professions Code.

§ 15004.1. Independence of Testing Laboratories.

(a) A licensed testing laboratory shall maintain independence from persons who hold a license or an interest in a commercial cannabis business licensed for any activity other than testing.

(b) A person who is an owner or financial interest holder of a licensed testing laboratory shall not be an owner or financial interest holder of a commercial cannabis business licensed for any activity other than testing.

(c) A licensed testing laboratory shall not lease real or personal property from or to a commercial cannabis business licensed for any activity other than testing.

(d) A licensed testing laboratory shall not employ any person who is employed by, or is an owner or financial interest holder of, a commercial cannabis business licensed for any activity other than testing.

(e) A licensed testing laboratory shall not offer or agree to provide preferential treatment, including discounted testing services, to any other licensee unless the offer or agreement is available to all licensees.

NOTE: Authority cited: Section 26013, Business and Professions Code. Reference: Section 26053, Business and Professions Code.

§ 15005. Personnel Prohibited from Holding Licenses.

(a) A license authorized by the Act and issued by the Department may not be held by, or issued to, any person holding office in, or employed by, any agency of the State of California or any of its political subdivisions when the duties of such person have to do with the enforcement of the Act or any other penal provisions of law of this State prohibiting or regulating the sale, use, possession, transportation, distribution, testing, manufacturing, or cultivation of cannabis or cannabis products.

(b) This section applies to, but is not limited to, any person employed in the State of California Department of Justice as a peace officer, in any district attorney's office, in any city attorney's office, in any sheriff's office, or in any local police department.

(c) No person listed in subsection (a) or (b) may have any ownership interest, directly or indirectly, in any business to be operated or conducted under a cannabis license.

(d) This section does not apply to any person who holds a license in the capacity of executor, administrator, or guardian.

NOTE: Authority cited: Section 26013, Business and Professions Code. Reference: Section 26012, Business and Professions Code.

§ 15006. Premises Diagram.

(a) An applicant shall submit to the Department, with the application, a complete and detailed diagram of the proposed premises. The diagram shall be used by the Department to determine whether the premises meets the requirements under this division and the Act. The Department shall deny an application if the premises does not qualify for licensure pursuant to Business and Professions Code section 26057.

(b) The diagram shall show the boundaries of the property and the proposed premises to be licensed, showing all boundaries, entrances and exits, interior partitions, walls, rooms, windows, and doorways, and shall include a brief statement or description of the principal activity to be conducted therein. The diagram shall also include the dimensions of the boundaries of the premises and structures, including interior and exterior dimensions, to clearly identify the bounds of the premises.

(c) The diagram shall show and identify commercial cannabis activities that will take place in each area of the premises, and identify limited-access areas. Commercial cannabis activities that shall be identified on the diagram include the following, if applicable to the business operations: storage, batch sampling, loading or unloading of shipments, packaging and labeling, customer sales, loading for deliveries, extraction, infusion, cultivation, and processing.

(d) The diagram shall show where all cameras are located and assign a number to each camera for identification purposes unless the premises is exempt from the video surveillance requirement pursuant to section 15315 or section 15044.

(e) The diagram shall be to scale to clearly determine the bounds of the premises.

(f) If the proposed premises consists of only a portion of a property, the diagram must be labeled indicating which part of the property is the proposed premises and for what purpose(s) the remaining property is used.

(g) If the proposed premises consists of only a portion of a property that will contain two or more licensed premises, the diagram shall clearly show the designated entrances and walls under the exclusive control of the commercial cannabis business for the premises, as well as the designated entrances and walls for each additional premises. The diagram shall also show all proposed common or shared areas of the property. Such areas may include lobbies, bathrooms, hallways, and breakrooms.

(h) If the commercial cannabis business is seeking a license to conduct cultivation activities on the proposed premises, the following must be clearly identified on the premises diagram:

> (1) All roads and water crossings on the property.
>
> (2) All water sources identified and labeled for beneficial use type, including but not limited to, irrigation, domestic, fire protection, power, fish and wildlife preservation and enhancement, and recreation.
>
> (3) If the commercial cannabis business is proposing to use a diversion from a waterbody or an underground stream flowing in a known and definite channel, groundwater well, or rain catchment system as a water source for cultivation, include the following locations on the premises diagram with locations also provided as geographic coordinates in either latitude and longitude or the California Coordinate System:
>
> > (A) Sources of water used, including the location of waterbody diversions(s), pump locations(s), and distribution system; and

(B) Location, type, and capacity of each water storage unit to be used for cultivation.

(4) The assessor's parcel number(s).

(5) For applicants for a Specialty Cottage, Specialty, Small, Medium, and Large license:

(A) Canopy area(s), including dimensions in feet and aggregate square footage if the canopy areas are noncontiguous. All unique areas separated by identifiable boundaries pursuant to section 15000(m) shall be clearly described and labeled in the premises diagram. If mature plants are being cultivated using a shelving system, the surface area of each level shall be included in the total canopy calculation;

(B) Area(s) outside of the canopy where only immature plants shall be maintained, including their dimensions in feet, if applicable. This area may not be shared among multiple licenses held by one licensee;

(C) Designated pesticide and other agricultural chemical storage area(s);

(D) Designated processing area(s) if the licensee will process onsite. This area may not be shared among multiple licenses held by one licensee;

(E) Designated packaging area(s) if the licensee will package products onsite. This area may not be shared among multiple licenses held by one licensee;

(F) Designated composting area(s) if the licensee will compost cannabis waste onsite;

(G) Designated secured area(s) for cannabis waste if different from subsection (F) above;

(H) Designated area(s) for harvested cannabis storage. This area may not be shared among multiple licenses held by one licensee;

(I) Designated area(s) that are shared between licenses held by one licensee. The shared area(s) must be contiguous, be indicated on the premises diagram for each application, and be one or more of the following designated area(s) shared between licenses held by one licensee: pesticide and other agricultural chemical storage area(s), composting area(s), and secured area(s) for cannabis waste; and

(J) Common use area(s), such as hallways, bathrooms, and breakrooms. This area may be shared by multiple licensees.

(6) For indoor and Mixed-light license type applications, a lighting diagram with the following information must be included:

(A) Location of all lights in the canopy area(s); and

(B) Maximum wattage, or wattage equivalent, of each light.

(7) For applicants for a nursery license:

(A) Designated pesticide and other agricultural chemical storage area(s);

(B) Designated composting area(s) if the licensee will compost cannabis waste onsite;

(C) Designated secured area(s) for cannabis waste if different from subsection (B) above;

(D) At least one of the following areas:

(i) Area(s) that shall contain only immature plants; or

(ii) Designated seed production area(s) that may contain mature plants; and

(E) Designated research and development area(s) that may contain mature plants, if the licensee will be conducting research and development activities that require a plant to flower.

(8) For applicants for a processor license:

(A) Designated processing area(s);

(B) Designated packaging area(s), if the licensee will package and label products onsite;

(C) Designated composting area(s) if the licensee will compost cannabis waste onsite;

(D) Designated secured area(s) for cannabis waste if different from subsection (C) above; and

(E) Designated area(s) for harvested cannabis storage.

(i) If the commercial cannabis business is seeking a Type S license to manufacture cannabis products or registering as a manufacturing Shared-Use Facility, the premises diagram must also comply with all applicable requirements in sections 15011(b)(13)(D) and 17124-17128.

(j) If a proposed premises is located on only a portion of a property that also includes a residence, the diagram shall clearly show the designated buildings for the premises and the residence.

(k) If the commercial cannabis business is seeking a license to conduct manufacturing activities using a closed-loop extraction system, the diagram shall include the location of the closed-loop extraction system and clearly display the systems serial number.

NOTE: Authority cited: Section 26013, Business and Professions Code. Reference: Sections 26012 and 26051.5, Business and Professions Code.

§ 15007. Landowner Approval.

(a) If the commercial cannabis business is not the landowner of the real property upon which the premises is located, the commercial cannabis business shall provide to the Department a document from the landowner or the landowner's agent that states that the commercial cannabis business has the right to occupy the property and acknowledges that the commercial cannabis business may use the property for the commercial cannabis activity for which the commercial cannabis business is applying for licensure. An applicant shall also provide a copy of the rental agreement, as applicable.

(b) If the commercial cannabis business is the landowner of the real property upon which the premises is located, the commercial cannabis business shall provide to the Department a copy of the title or deed to the property.

(c) If the landowner is a trust, the landowner approval shall come from the person who holds equitable title in the real property.

NOTE: Authority cited: Section 26013, Business and Professions Code. Reference: Section 26051.5, Business and Professions Code.

§ 15007.1. Electronic Signature.

The Department will accept an electronic signature that complies with Civil Code section 1633.2(h) on any documents required to be submitted to the Department and that are submitted electronically, except documents that are required to be notarized.

NOTE: Authority cited: Section 26013, Business and Professions Code. Reference: Section 26013, Business and Professions Code.

§ 15007.2. Use of Legal Business Name. [Repealed]

Note: Authority cited: Section 26013, Business and Professions Code. Reference: Section 26013, Business and Professions Code.

§ 15008. Bond. [Repealed]

Note: Authority cited: Section 26013, Business and Professions Code. Reference: Section 26051.5, Business and Professions Code.

§ 15009. Limited Waiver of Sovereign Immunity.

a) Any applicant or licensee that may fall within the scope of sovereign immunity that may be asserted by a federally recognized tribe or other sovereign entity must waive any sovereign immunity defense that the applicant or licensee may have, may be asserted on its behalf, or may otherwise be asserted in any state administrative or judicial enforcement actions against the applicant or licensee, regardless of the form of relief sought, whether monetary or otherwise, under the state laws and regulations governing commercial cannabis activity. The applicant or licensee must submit a written waiver of sovereign immunity to the Department with any license application or renewal, which is valid for the period of the license. The written waiver shall include that the applicant or licensee has the lawful authority to enter into the waiver required by this section, the applicant or licensee hereby waives sovereign immunity, and the applicant or licensee agrees to do all of the following:

(1) Provide documentation to the Department that establishes that the applicant or licensee has the lawful authority to enter into the waiver required by this section;

(2) Conduct all commercial cannabis activity in full compliance with the state laws and regulations governing commercial cannabis activity, including submission to all enforcement provisions thereof;

(3) Allow access as required by state statute or regulation by persons or entities charged with duties under the state laws and regulations governing commercial cannabis activity to any licensed premises or property at which the applicant conducts any commercial cannabis activity, including licensed premises or property where records of commercial cannabis activity are maintained by or for the applicant or licensee;

(4) Provide any and all records, reports, and other documents as may be required under the state laws and regulations governing commercial cannabis activity;

(5) Conduct commercial cannabis activity with other state commercial cannabis licensees only, unless otherwise specified by state law;

(6) Meet all of the requirements for licensure under the state laws and regulations governing the conduct of commercial cannabis activity, and provide truthful and accurate documentation and other information of the applicant's qualifications and suitability for licensure as may be requested; and

(7) Submit to the personal and subject matter jurisdiction of the California courts to address any matter related to the waiver or the commercial cannabis application, license, or activity, and that all such matters and proceedings shall be governed, construed and enforced in accordance with California substantive and procedural law, including but not limited to the Medicinal and Adult- Use Regulation and Safety Act and the Administrative Procedure Act.

(b) The Department shall not approve an application for a state license if approval of the license would violate the provisions of any local ordinance or regulation adopted in accordance with Business and Professions Code section 26200 that is issued by the county or, if within a city, the city, within which the licensed premises is to be located.

(c) Any applicant or licensee must immediately notify the Department of any changes that may materially affect the applicant or licensee's compliance with subsection (a) of this section.

(d) Any failure by an applicant or licensee to comply with the requirements of subsections (b) or (c) of this section shall be a basis for denial of an application or renewal or discipline of a licensee.

NOTE: Authority cited: Section 26013, Business and Professions Code. Reference: Sections 26012, 26050 and 26051.5, Business and Professions Code.

§ 15010. Compliance with the California Environmental Quality Act (CEQA).

(a) "CEQA Guidelines" means the Guidelines for Implementation of the California Environmental Quality Act codified at title 14, California Code of Regulations, section 15000 et seq.

(b) An applicant shall provide evidence of compliance with, or exemption from, CEQA (division 13 (commencing with section 21000) of the Public Resources Code). The evidence provided may be any one of the following:

(1) A signed copy of a project-specific Notice of Determination or Notice of Exemption and a copy of the associated CEQA document, or reference to where it may be located electronically, a project description, and any accompanying permitting documentation from the local jurisdiction used for review in determining site-specific environmental compliance. Documentation may include a copy of the administrative record previously certified or adopted by the local jurisdiction that has already reviewed the commercial cannabis business' proposed commercial cannabis activities. For purposes of this section, the administrative record may include, but is not limited to:

(A) Environmental documentation, including, but not limited to, exemptions, initial studies, negative declarations, mitigated negative declarations, and environmental impact reports;

(B) Staff reports and related documents prepared by the local jurisdiction;

(C) Transcripts or minutes of the proceedings of the local jurisdiction;

(D) Notice(s) issued by the local jurisdiction to comply with CEQA and the CEQA Guidelines;

(E) Proposed decisions or findings considered by the local jurisdiction by its staff or the commercial cannabis business; and

(F) Documentation of the local jurisdiction's final decision.

(2) If the applicant does not have the evidence specified in subsection (b)(1), or if the Department determines that the evidence submitted is not sufficient to determine compliance or exemption from CEQA, then the applicant shall submit the information on a form to be prescribed by the Department. Such information shall include at least the following:

(A) The project location and surrounding land use, which shall:

(i) Describe the project location, including street address, city, county, Assessor's Parcel Number, major cross streets, general plan designation, zoning designation, and any other physical description that clearly indicates the project site location.

(ii) Describe the surrounding land uses and zoning designations within a one-half mile radius of the project and list all abutting land uses.

(iii) Include a vicinity map and aerial image to show the project location.

(iv) Include photographs, not larger than 8.5 by 11 inches, of existing visual conditions as observed from publicly accessible vantage point(s).

(B) A project description, which shall:

(i) Describe the activities included in the project application and identify any other commercial cannabis activity or activities occurring at the proposed premises.

(ii) Quantify the project size (total floor area of the project), and the lot size on which the project is located, in square feet.

(iii) List and describe any other related public agency permits and approvals, including any entitlements, required for this project, including those required by a planning commission, local air district, or regional water board.

(iv) Identify whether the commercial cannabis business is licensed by, or has applied for licensure from, the Department or one of the prior state cannabis licensing authorities (the Bureau of Cannabis Control, the California Department of Food and Agriculture, and the California Department of Public Health) to engage in commercial cannabis activity at the proposed premises.

(v) Estimate the number of anticipated employees onsite, occupancy during operating hours, and frequency of deliveries or shipments originating from and/or arriving to the project site.

(C) The environmental setting, which shall:

(i) Describe natural characteristics (e.g., topography, vegetation, drainage, soil stability, habitat, etc.) on the project site.

(ii) Identify whether there are any watercourses or riparian habitats (e.g., drainage swales, stream courses, springs, ponds, lakes, creeks, tributary of creeks, wetlands) within 150 feet of the proposed premises.

(iii) Identify the approximate number of vehicle trips per day to be generated by the project and information regarding the days and times most trips are expected to occur.

(iv) Identify whether the property contains natural features of scenic value or rare or unique characteristics (e.g., rock outcroppings, mature trees).

(v) Identify whether the property has any historic designations or archeological remains onsite.

(vi) Identify whether the property contains habitat(s) for special status species.

(vii) Identify the location, type, and quantity of hazardous materials, as defined by Health and Safety Code section 25260, that are stored, used, or disposed of at the project site and a copy of the Hazardous Material Business Plan (HMBP) prepared for the proposed premises, if any.

(viii) Discuss whether the project will increase the quantity and type of solid waste, as defined by Public Resources Code section 40191, or hazardous waste, as defined by Health and Safety Code section 25117, that is generated or stored onsite.

(ix) Describe the project's anticipated operational energy needs, identify the source of energy supplied for the project and the anticipated amount of energy per day, and explain whether the project will require an increase in energy demand and the need for additional energy resources.

(c) If the Department determines that a project does not qualify for an exemption and further environmental review is required pursuant to the CEQA Guidelines, the Department may charge the applicant for the costs of preparation of any supplemental environmental document as well as the Department's costs for procedures to comply with CEQA.

NOTE: Authority cited: Section 26013, Business and Professions Code. Reference: Section 26055, Business and Professions Code.

§ 15010.1. Review of Previously Prepared Environmental Documents Pursuant to CEQA. [Repealed]

Note: Authority cited: Section 26013, Business and Professions Code. Reference: Section 26055, Business and Professions Code; and Section 21166, Public Resources Code.

§ 15010.2. CEQA Exempt Projects. [Repealed]

Note: Authority cited: Section 26013, Business and Professions Code. Reference: Section 26055, Business and Professions Code.

§ 15010.3. Preparation of CEQA Environmental Documents for Applicant. [Repealed]

Note: Authority cited: Section 26013, Business and Professions Code. Reference: Section 26055, Business and Professions Code.

§ 15011. Additional Information.

(a) A commercial cannabis business applying for a license to cultivate cannabis shall provide the following information:

(1) The hours of operation for each day of the week the commercial cannabis business will have staff on the licensed premises. Applicants may include annual scheduled closure periods for their site.

(2) For commercial cannabis businesses that are a cannabis cooperative as defined by division 10, chapter 22 (commencing with section 26220) of the Business and Professions Code, identification of all members, identifying information shall include each member's license number for commercial cannabis activity, and the name of the licensed business.

(3) For all cultivator license types except processor, evidence of enrollment in an order or waiver of waste discharge requirements with the State Water Resources Control Board or the appropriate Regional Water Quality Control Board. Acceptable documentation for evidence of enrollment may be a Notice of Applicability letter. Acceptable documentation that enrollment is not necessary may be a Notice of Non-Applicability.

(4) Evidence that the commercial cannabis business has conducted a hazardous materials record search of the EnviroStor database for the proposed premises. If hazardous sites were encountered, the applicant shall provide documentation of protocols implemented to protect employee health and safety.

(5) For indoor and mixed-light license types, identification of all power sources for cultivation activities, including, but not limited to, illumination, heating, cooling, and ventilation.

(6) A proposed cultivation plan that complies with the requirements in section 16309.

(7) Identification of all water sources used for cultivation activities as required in section 16311.

(8) A copy of any final lake or streambed alteration agreement issued by the California Department of Fish and Wildlife, pursuant to sections 1602 or 1617 of the Fish and Game Code, or written verification from the California Department of Fish and Wildlife that a lake and streambed alteration agreement is not required.

(9) An attestation that the applicant entity is an "agricultural employer" as defined by the Alatorre-Zenovich-Dunlap-Berman Agricultural Labor Relations Act of 1975; division 2, part 3.5 (commencing with section 1140) of the Labor Code.

(10) An attestation that the local fire department has been notified of the cultivation site if the application is for an indoor license type.

(11) If applicable, the applicant shall provide evidence that the proposed premises is not located in whole or in part in a watershed or other geographic area that the State Water Resources Control Board or the Department of Fish and Wildlife has determined to be significantly adversely impacted by cannabis cultivation pursuant to section 26060(a)(2) of the Business and Professions Code.

(12) For all cultivator license types except processor, a signed attestation that states the commercial cannabis business shall contact the appropriate County Agricultural Commissioner regarding requirements for legal use of pesticides on cannabis prior to using any of the active ingredients or products included in the pest management plan and shall comply with all pesticide laws.

(b) A commercial cannabis business applying for a license to manufacture cannabis products shall provide the following information:

(1) The type(s) of activity that will be conducted at the proposed licensed premises (extraction, infusion, packaging, or labeling).

(2) The types of products that will be manufactured, packaged, or labeled at the premises, including a product list.

(3) The name, title, email address, and phone number of the onsite individual who manages the operation of the premises.

(4) The name, title, email address, and phone number of an alternate contact person for the premises, if applicable.

(5) The number of employees at the premises.

(6) Upon request by the Department, a description of inventory control procedures sufficient to demonstrate how the commercial cannabis business will comply with the requirements of section 17218, or a copy of the standard operating procedure addressing inventory control.

(7) Upon request by the Department, a description of quality control procedures sufficient to demonstrate how the commercial cannabis business will comply with all of the applicable requirements specified in sections 17208 through 17216, or a copy of the standard operating procedure addressing quality control.

(8) Upon request by the Department, a description of the transportation process describing how cannabis or cannabis products will be transported into and out of the premises, or a copy of the standard operating procedure addressing transportation.

(9) Upon request by the Department, a description of security procedures sufficient to demonstrate how the commercial cannabis business will comply with the applicable security requirements of sections 15042 through 15047, or a copy of the standard operating procedure addressing security procedures.

(10) Upon request by the Department, a description of the cannabis waste management procedures sufficient to demonstrate how the commercial cannabis business will comply with the requirements of section 17223, or a copy of the standard operating procedure addressing cannabis waste management.

(11) A copy of the signed closed-loop system certification required pursuant to section 17206.1, if applicable.

(12) Any manufacturer submitting operating procedures and protocols to the Department pursuant to the Act and this division may claim such information as a trade secret or confidential by clearly identifying such information as "confidential" on the document at the time of submission. Any claim of confidentiality by a manufacturer must be based on the manufacturer's good faith belief that the information marked as confidential constitutes a trade secret as defined in Civil Code section 3426.1(d), or is otherwise exempt from public disclosure under the California Public Records Act, Government Code section 6250 et seq.

(13) Applications for a Type S manufacturing license shall:

(A) Be submitted in accordance with section 15002;

(B) Include the license number and address of the registered shared-use facility at which the commercial cannabis business will conduct manufacturing operations;

(C) Include a copy of the use agreement signed by both the Type S applicant and the primary licensee; and

(D) On the premises diagram submitted pursuant to section 15002(c)(21), indicate the designated area to be used by the Type S commercial cannabis business and detail where the commercial cannabis business will store its cannabis and cannabis products.

(E) A Type S license shall only be available to commercial cannabis businesses with a gross annual revenue of less than $1,000,000 as calculated pursuant to section 15014.

(F) A Type S licensee may conduct the following operational activities:

(i) Infusions, as defined in section 15000(ee);

(ii) Packaging and labeling of cannabis products; and

(iii) Extractions with water, glycerin, vegetable oil, animal fat, or using mechanical methods, provided that the resulting extract or concentrate shall be used solely in the manufacture of the Type S licensee's infused product and shall not be sold to any other licensee.

(c) A commercial cannabis business applying for a license to distribute cannabis and cannabis products shall provide the following information, upon the request of the Department:

(1) Standard Operating Procedures, Form DCC-LIC-019 (New 2/22), incorporated herein by reference.

(2) Proof of compliance with the insurance requirements in section 15308.

(3) Transport vehicle information required by section 15312.

(d) A commercial cannabis business applying for a license to sell cannabis and cannabis products at retail shall provide the following information, upon request by the Department:

(1) Standard Operating Procedures, Form DCC-LIC-019 (New 2/22).

(2) Delivery employee information required by section 15415.

(3) Delivery vehicle information required by section 15417.

(e) A commercial cannabis business applying for a license to operate as a microbusiness shall provide the information required in subsections (a) through (d) as applicable for the activities they will be conducting under the license.

(f) Applicants for a cannabis event organizer license shall indicate whether the cannabis event organizer plans to hold 0-5 events, 6-10 events, 11-20 events, or more than 20 events during the license period.

(g) Applicants for a testing laboratory license shall provide the following information:

(1) The certificate(s) of accreditation required by sections 15701 and 15702, or the information required for an interim license required by section 15703.

(2) Upon the request by the Department, Standard Operating Procedures, Form DCC-LIC-019 (New 2/22).

(3) The operating procedures required by chapter 6.

(h) The Department may request additional information and documents from the applicant. The Department will provide the applicant with a deadline for submittal of additional information. The Department will consider the complexity of the information requested and the ease with which the information can be obtained and transmitted to the Department by the applicant in determining the deadline.

(i) Items required by this section may also be requested by the Department at any time following the issuance of a license. Licensees shall maintain the information required by this section and provide it to the Department upon request.

NOTE: Authority cited: Sections 26013 and 26130, Business and Professions Code. Reference: Sections 26031, 26050, 26051.5 and 26130, Business and Professions Code.

§ 15012. Incomplete and Abandoned Applications.

(a) Incomplete applications will not be processed. Applications will only be considered complete if all of the information required under sections 15002 and 15011 is included. The Department shall issue a written notice to the applicant, by mail, email, or through the Department's licensing system, informing them that the application is incomplete and identifying the information missing from the application.

(b) If the applicant fails to submit all required information within 180 days from the date of the initial written notice, the application shall be deemed abandoned.

(c) If the applicant fails to submit payment of the license fee within 60 calendar days from the date of the request for payment of the license fee, the application shall be deemed abandoned.

(d) The Department will not refund application fees for an incomplete or abandoned application.

(e) An applicant may reapply at any time following an abandoned application and will be required to submit a new application and application fee.

NOTE: Authority cited: Sections 26013 and 26130, Business and Professions Code. Reference: Sections 26012, 26050 and 26051.5, Business and Professions Code.

§ 15013. Withdrawal of Application.

(a) An applicant may withdraw an application at any time prior to the Department issuance of a license or denial of a license.

(b) Requests to withdraw an application must be submitted to the Department by mail in writing, dated, and signed by the applicant, or in writing by electronic mail to licensing@cannabis.ca.gov.

(c) In accordance with Business and Professions Code section 26057, withdrawal of an application shall not, unless the Department has consented in writing to such withdrawal, deprive the Department of its authority to institute or continue a proceeding against the commercial cannabis business for the denial of the license upon any ground provided by law or to enter an order denying the license upon any such ground.

(d) The Department will not refund application fees for a withdrawn application.

(e) An applicant may reapply at any time following the withdrawal of an application and will be required to submit a new application and application fee.

NOTE: Authority cited: Section 26013, Business and Professions Code. Reference: Sections 26050 and 26057, Business and Professions Code.

ARTICLE 3. LICENSING

§ 15014. Fees.

(a) The application fee for an annual license under section 15002, a cannabis event organizer license under section 15600, a temporary cannabis event license under section 15601 for each event, and physical modification of the premises under section 15027 shall be paid by an applicant or licensee as provided by this division. Applicants and licensees shall pay the appropriate fee as outlined in this section.

Application Fee Schedule

License Type	Fee Per Application
Testing Laboratory, Distributor, Retailer, Microbusiness Annual Licenses	$ 1,000
Cannabis Event Organizer License	$ 1,000
Temporary Cannabis Event License	$ 1,000
Physical Modification of Premises for Testing Laboratory, Distributor, Retailer, Microbusiness, and Manufacturing Licenses	$ 500
Type 6, 7, N, or P Annual Manufacturing Licenses	$ 1,000
Type S Annual Manufacturing License	$ 500
Cultivation Annual Licenses	See (f)

(b) The annual licensing fee for each license shall be paid by an applicant after the Department has approved the application. The renewal license fee shall be paid by the licensee as required by section 15020. The Department shall not issue the license until the annual licensing fee has been paid.

(c) To determine the appropriate annual license fee due for testing laboratory, distributor, retailer, and microbusiness license types, the applicant or licensee shall first estimate the gross revenue for the 12-month license period. Based on the license type sought, the applicant or licensee shall identify the appropriate tier category in which their expected gross revenue belongs, as identified in the Annual License Fee Schedule charts found in this section. The license fee associated with the licensing tier category the applicant or licensee has identified using their expected gross revenue shall be the license fee due for the original license or renewal. The following are the annual license fees due for these license types to be paid prior to issuance of a license or renewed license:

Annual License Fee Schedule for Testing Laboratory (Type 8)

Gross Revenue ($ Max. Per License)	Fee Per License
Less than or equal to $160,000	$3,000
More than $160,000 and less or equal to $320,000	$6,000
More than $320,000 and less or equal to $480,000	$8,000
More than $480,000 and less or equal to $800,000	$13,000
More than $800,000 and less or equal to $1.2 million	$20,000
More than $1.2 million and less or equal to $2.0 million	$32,000
More than $2.0 million and less or equal to $2.8 million	$48,000
More than $2.8 million and less or equal to $4.4 million	$72,000
More than $4.4 million	$112,000

Annual License Fee Schedule for Distributor (Type 11 or 13), unless only engaging in transport only self-distribution

Gross Revenue ($ Max. Per License)	Fee Per License
Less than or equal to $1.0 million	$1,500
More than $1.0 million and less or equal to $2.5 million	$6,000
More than $2.5 million and less or equal to $5.0 million	$11,250
More than $5.0 million and less or equal to $10.0 million	$22,500
More than $10.0 million and less or equal to $20.0 million	$45,000
More than $20.0 million and less or equal to $30.0 million	$75,000

Gross Revenue ($ Max. Per License)	Fee Per License
More than $30.0 million and less or equal to $50.0 million	$120,000
More than $50.0 million and less or equal to $70.0 million	$180,000
More than $70.0 million	$240,000

Annual License Fee Schedule for Distributor Transport Only Self-Distribution (Type 13)

Gross Revenue ($ Max. Per License)	Fee Per License
Less than or equal to $1,000	$200
More than $1,000 and less or equal to $3,000	$500
More than $3,000	$1,000

Annual License Fee Schedule for Retailer (Type 9 or 10)

Gross Revenue ($ Max. Per License)	Fee Per License
Less than or equal to $500,000	$2,500
More than $500,000 and less or equal to $750,000	$5,500
More than $750,000 and less or equal to $1.0 million	$7,500
More than $1.0 million and less or equal to $1.5 million	$11,000
More than $1.5 million and less or equal to $2.0 million	$14,500
More than $2.0 million and less or equal to $3.0 million	$22,500
More than $3.0 million and less or equal to $4.0 million	$30,500
More than $4.0 million and less or equal to $5.0 million	$38,500
More than $5.0 million and less or equal to $6.0 million	$46,500

Gross Revenue ($ Max. Per License)	Fee Per License
More than $6.0 million and less or equal to $7.5 million	$57,000
More than $7.5 million	$96,000

Annual License Fee Schedule for Microbusiness (Type 12)

Gross Revenue ($ Max. Per License)	Fee Per License
Less than or equal to $1.0 million	$5,000
More than $1.0 and less or equal to $2.0 million	$12,000
More than $2.0 and less or equal to $3.0 million	$20,000
More than $3.0 and less or equal to $4.0 million	$32,000
More than $4.0 and less or equal to $6.0 million	$45,000
More than $6.0 and less or equal to $7.0 million	$60,000
More than $7.0 and less or equal to $10.0 million	$80,000
More than $10.0 and less or equal to $20.0 million	$100,000
More than $20.0 and less or equal to $30.0 million	$120,000
More than $30.0 and less or equal to $40.0 million	$140,000
More than $40.0 and less or equal to $50.0 million	$160,000
More than $50.0 and less or equal to $60.0 million	$180,000
More than $60.0 and less than or equal to $80.0 million	$220,000
More than $80 million	$300,000

(d) The annual license fee for a cannabis event organizer license shall be based on the number of planned operations during the license period as indicated in the chart below.

Annual License Fee Schedule for Cannabis Event Organizers

Planned Operations (Number of Operations)	Fee Per License
0-5 events annually	$3,000
6-10 events annually	$5,000
11-20 events annually	$9,000
Greater than 20 events annually	$20,000

(e) The annual license fee for a manufacturer license shall be based on gross revenue as indicated in the chart below.

(1) The applicant shall calculate the gross annual revenue for the licensed premises based on the annual gross sales of cannabis products and, if applicable, the annual revenue received from manufacturing, packaging, labeling or otherwise handling cannabis or cannabis products for other licensees, in the 12 months preceding the date of application.

(2) For a new license applicant, the gross annual revenue shall be based on the gross sales and revenue expected during the first 12 months following licensure.

(3) For a manufacturer licensee that is also licensed as a distributor or retailer, and that sells or transfers cannabis products manufactured on the licensed premises in a non-arm's length transaction, the annual gross sales or revenue for such transactions shall be based on the product's fair market value if it were to be sold in an arm's length transaction at wholesale.

(4) For purposes of this section, an "arm's length transaction" means a sale entered into in good faith and for valuable consideration that reflects the fair market value in the open market between two informed and willing parties, neither under any compulsion to participate in the transaction.

Annual License Fee Schedule for Manufacturing (Type 6, 7, N, P, or S)

Gross Revenue ($ Max. Per License)	Fee Per License
Less than or equal to $100,000	$2,000
More than $100,000 and less or equal to $500,000	$7,500
More than $500,000 and less or equal to $1.5 million	$15,000
More than $1.5 million and less or equal to $3.0 million	$25,000
More than $3.0 million and less or equal to $5.0 million	$35,000

Gross Revenue ($ Max. Per License)	Fee Per License
More than $5.0 million and less or equal to $10 million	$50,000
More than $10 million	$75,000

(f) The following are the application fees due for the specified annual cultivation license types to be paid at the time the complete application is submitted to the Department:

Application Fee Schedule for Cultivation

License Type	Fee Per License
Specialty Cottage Outdoor	$135
Specialty Cottage Indoor	$205
Specialty Cottage Mixed-Light Tier 1	$340
Specialty Cottage Mixed-Light Tier 2	$580
Specialty Outdoor	$270
Specialty Indoor	$2,170
Specialty Mixed Light-Tier 1	$655
Specialty Mixed Light-Tier 2	$1,125
Small Outdoor	$535
Small Indoor	$3,935
Small Mixed-Light Tier 1	$1,310
Small Mixed-Light Tier 2	$2,250
Medium Outdoor	$1,555
Medium Indoor	$8,655

License Type	Fee Per License
Medium Mixed-Light Tier 1	$2,885
Medium Mixed-Light Tier 2	$4,945
Nursery	$520
Processor	$1,040

(g) The following are the annual license fees due for the specified annual cultivation license types to be paid prior to issuance of a license or renewal of a license:

Annual License Fee Schedule for Cultivation

License Type	Fee Per License
Specialty Cottage Outdoor	$1,205
Specialty Cottage Indoor	$1,830
Specialty Cottage Mixed-Light Tier 1	$3,035
Specialty Cottage Mixed-Light Tier 2	$5,200
Specialty Outdoor	$2,410
Specialty Indoor	$19,540
Specialty Mixed-Light Tier 1	$5,900
Specialty Mixed-Light Tier 2	$10,120
Small Outdoor	$4,820
Small Indoor	$35,410
Small Mixed-Light Tier 1	$11,800
Small Mixed-Light Tier 2	$20,235

License Type	Fee Per License
Medium Outdoor	$13,990
Medium Indoor	$77,905
Medium Mixed-Light Tier 1	$25,970
Medium Mixed-Light Tier 2	$44,517
Nursery	$4,685
Processor	$9,370

(i) All fees are nonrefundable.

Note: Authority cited: Section 26013, Business and Professions Code. Reference: Sections 26012, 26051.5 and 26180, Business and Professions Code.

§ 15014.1. Equity Fee Relief.

(a) For the purposes of this section, the following definitions apply:

(1) "Qualified equity applicant or licensee" means a person who is an owner in a commercial cannabis business pursuant to section 15003(a) and is either:

(A) A locally verified equity applicant or licensee in a jurisdiction with a local equity program as defined in subsection (a)(2); or

(B) An applicant or licensee who qualifies for the fee waiver program under the provisions of subsection (d).

(2) "Locally verified equity applicant or licensee" means an applicant or licensee that satisfies the following conditions:

(A) The applicant or licensee has submitted an application to a local jurisdiction to engage in commercial cannabis activity;

(B) The applicant or licensee's commercial cannabis operation is located within the boundaries of that jurisdiction;

(C) The applicant or licensee meets the requirements of that jurisdiction's local equity program; and

(D) The applicant or licensee has attested that they meet one of the criteria set in subsection (d).

(b) Commercial cannabis businesses with at least one qualified equity applicant or licensee shall be eligible for equity fee relief in the form of one fee waiver during each calendar year and one fee deferral for each additional license during each calendar year if they satisfy all of the following:

(1) The applicant or licensee has submitted a complete application for licensure, in accordance with section

15002, or has satisfied the licensure renewal requirements of section 15020.

(2) Only for fee waiver requests, the applicant or licensee expects a gross revenue less than or equal to $5,000,000, or a licensee with a gross revenue less than or equal to $5,000,000 and the applicant has submitted documentation demonstrating gross revenue. Documentation demonstrating gross revenue may include, but is not limited to, a copy of the licensee's state tax return filed with the California Department of Tax and Fee Administration.

(3) The qualified equity applicant or licensee, either individually or in combination with other qualified equity applicants or licensees, owns no less than 50 percent of the commercial cannabis business that is applying for licensure or is licensed.

(4) The applicant or licensee has timely submitted a request for equity fee relief with the information enumerated in subsections (c) and (d).

(A) To be eligible for a license fee waiver or deferral in the initial 12-month licensure period, the qualified equity applicant must indicate on the application for commercial cannabis license that they are also applying for equity fee relief from the Department.

(B) To be eligible for a license fee waiver or deferral at the time of renewal, the qualified equity licensee must submit a request for equity fee relief at least 60 calendar days before the expiration of the license. The Department will accept requests for equity fee relief from qualified equity licensees who on the effective date of this section are less than 60 days from the date of license expiration. The Department will provide a refund if the Department determines the qualified equity licensee is eligible for a fee waiver or deferral after the licensee has paid all annual licensing fees, subject to available funding.

(c) To submit a request for equity fee relief, the qualified equity applicant or licensee shall submit all of the following to the Department:

(1) A complete list of every qualified equity applicant or licensee which includes the percentage of the aggregate ownership interest held by the qualified equity applicant or licensee in the commercial cannabis business.

(2) Contact information for each qualified equity applicant or licensee of the commercial cannabis business, including the name, title, phone number, and email address.

(3) Only for equity fee relief requestors that are locally verified equity applicants or licensees in a jurisdiction with a local equity program, an attestation to the following statement: Under penalty of perjury, I hereby declare that I am a locally verified equity applicant or licensee. I further declare that I satisfy at least one of the criteria set forth in California Code of Regulations, title 4, section 15014.1(d). I understand that the Department may investigate the accuracy of these declarations, and that a misrepresentation of fact is cause for rejection of this request for equity fee relief.

(4) An attestation that the qualified equity applicant or licensee, either individually or in combination with other qualified equity applicants or licensees, own no less than 50 percent of the commercial cannabis business that is applying for licensure or is licensed.

(d) All applicants or licensees must satisfy at least one of the following criteria to be granted a fee waiver or deferral. Qualified equity applicants or licensees that are locally verified equity applicants may establish that they satisfy at least one of these criteria by attestation, as set forth in subsection (c)(3). Qualified equity applicants or licensees that are not locally verified in a jurisdiction with a local equity program must submit evidence of at least one of the following for each equity applicant or licensee:

(1) The qualified equity applicant or licensee was convicted of an offense related to the sale, possession, use, manufacture, or cultivation of cannabis, prior to November 8, 2016. Proof of conviction shall be demonstrated by copies of federal or state court records indicating the disposition of the criminal matter; records reflecting

the post-conviction dismissal or expungement of a conviction, including records reflecting the destruction of records under Health and Safety Code section 11361.5; or any other court or law enforcement record that shows proof of conviction.

(2) The qualified equity applicant or licensee was arrested for an offense related to the sale, possession, use, manufacture, or cultivation of cannabis, prior to November 8, 2016. Proof of arrest shall be demonstrated by copies of federal or state court records indicating the disposition of the criminal matter, records of expungement documentation, or any other law enforcement record that shows proof of arrest.

(3) The qualified equity applicant or licensee resides in a household with a household income less than or equal to 60 percent of the area median income for the local jurisdiction they reside, as reported in the most recent United States decennial or special census.

(A) Proof of income shall be demonstrated by the qualified equity applicant or licensee for each earner in their household using copies of at least one of the following records with a residential address in the local jurisdiction, which is not a post office box, dated within the last two years from the date of the request for equity fee relief :

(i.) Individual federal tax returns, state tax returns, and W-2s;

(ii.) At least two consecutive paystubs;

(iii.) Proof of eligibility for a general assistance program that provides financial aid to adults without sufficient income or resources, including but not limited to CalFresh, MediCal/CalWORKS, supplemental security income, or social security disability.

(B) For the purposes of this subsection, "income" means the money income received in the preceding calendar year using the income measurement defined by the U.S. Census Bureau in their most recent United States decennial or special census.

(4) Proof that the qualified equity applicant or licensee resided for at least five years between 1980 and 2016 in an area with a population that was disproportionately impacted by past criminal justice policies implementing cannabis prohibition during their period of residency and that they satisfy one of the following:

(A) The qualified equity applicant or licensee resided in a census tract that is among the top 25 percent for civilian unemployment and poverty in the state based on the United States Census Bureau's 2013-2017 American Community Survey; or

(B) The qualified equity applicant or licensee has an immediate family member who was convicted or arrested of an offense related to the sale, possession, use, manufacture, or cultivation of cannabis, prior to November 8, 2016.

(C) For the purposes of this subsection, the following definitions apply:

(i) "An area with a population that was disproportionately impacted by past criminal justice policies implementing cannabis prohibition for at least five years" means a county within California with a per capita drug related arrest rate higher than the state's per capita drug related arrest rate between 1980 and 2016; these counties are: Alameda, Alpine, Contra Costa, Del Norte, Fresno, Glenn, Humboldt, Imperial, Inyo, Kern, Lake, Los Angeles, Mendocino, Merced, Riverside, Sacramento, San Bernardino, San Diego, San Francisco, San Joaquin, Santa Cruz, Sierra, Solano, Stanislaus, Tehama, Trinity, Tulare, Yolo, and Yuba.

(ii) "Immediate family member" means child, stepchild, parent, stepparent, brother, sister, half-brother, half-sister, stepsibling, legal guardian, grandparent, or great grandparent.

(D) Proof of residence shall be demonstrated by providing copies of at least two of the following records with a residential address in the local jurisdiction, which is not a post office box:

(i) California Driver's License or State Identification Card;

(ii) Property tax billing or payment, or evidence that the qualified equity applicant or licensee is otherwise exempt from property tax payment by law;

(iii) Signed residential lease agreement, or deed or title to residential real property;

(iv) Copies of state or federal tax returns;

(v) School records;

(vi) Banking or credit card records;

(vii) Voter registration;

(viii) Credit reports;

(ix) Utility, cable, or internet billing or payment; or

(x) Vehicle titles or proof of vehicle registration.

(E) Proof of an immediate family member's conviction or arrest shall be demonstrated by copies of federal or state court records indicating the disposition of the criminal matter; records reflecting the post-conviction dismissal or expungement of a conviction, including records reflecting the destruction of records under Health and Safety Code section 11361.5; or any other court or law enforcement record that shows proof of conviction or arrest.

(F) Proof of immediate family member shall be demonstrated by copies of documentation showing a familial relationship, including but not limited to, birth certificates or court records.

(e) Incomplete requests for equity fee relief will be denied. The Department will notify the applicant or licensee that the request for equity fee relief is denied and identify the deficiencies which caused the denial. An applicant or licensee may resubmit subsequent requests for equity fee relief after denial.

(f) The Department will process complete requests for equity fee relief in the order in which the application or renewal for commercial cannabis licensure has been approved by the Department. If a commercial cannabis business has submitted multiple requests for fee waivers, the Department will grant only one fee waiver to the applicant or licensee based on the first application or renewal for commercial cannabis licensure that has been approved by the Department.

(g) Issuance of fee waivers by the Department shall be subject to available funding; thus, all eligible applicants and licensees may not be granted a fee waiver. In the event that insufficient funding is available to issue a fee waiver, the Department will grant a fee deferral to qualified equity applicants and licensees.

(h) Fee deferrals granted by the Department shall be subject to the following conditions:

(1) All license fees must be paid in full no later than six months after the issuance or renewal of the license.

(2) The licensee's failure to pay the appropriate licensing fee as required by section 15014, will result in further action being taken by the Department, including, but not limited to, denial of licensure renewal, suspension, or revocation of a license.

(3) No fee deferrals will be granted by the Department prior to January 1, 2023.

NOTE: Authority cited: Section 26013, Business and Professions Code. Reference: Sections 26012, 26051.5, 26180 and 26249, Business and Professions Code.

§ 15014.2. Fees-Large Cultivation License.

(a) Notwithstanding section 15014, the following are the application fees due for the specified large cultivation license types to be paid at the time the complete application is submitted to the Department:

Application Fee Schedule for Large Cultivation Licenses

Large License Type	Fee Per Application
Outdoor	$1,555
Mixed-light Tier 1	$2,885
Mixed-light Tier 2	$4,945
Indoor	$8,655

(b) Notwithstanding section 15014, the following are the annual license fees due for the aggregate canopy size for the annual cultivation license to be paid prior to issuance of a license, renewal of a license, or a converted license:

License Fee Schedule for Large Outdoor Cultivation

Canopy Size	Fees
Base Annual Fee	$13,990
Per 2,000 sq. ft. of Canopy over 1 acre	$640

License Fee Schedule for Large Mixed-light Tier 1 Cultivation

Canopy Size	Fees
Base Annual Fee	$25,970
Fee Per 2,000 sq. ft over 22,000 sq. ft.	$2,360

License Fee Schedule for Large Mixed-light Tier 2 Cultivation

Canopy Size	Fees
Base Annual Fee	$44,517

Canopy Size	Fees
Fee Per 2,000 sq. ft over 22,000 sq. ft.	$4,040

License Fees Schedule for Large Indoor Cultivation

Canopy Size	Fees
Base Annual Fee	$77,905
Fee Per 2,000 sq. ft over 22,000 sq. ft.	$7,080

NOTE: Authority cited: Section 26013, Business and Professions Code. Reference: Sections 26012, 26051.5, 26060, 26120 and 26180, Business and Professions Code.

§ 15015. Payment of Fees.

(a) Any fee specified in this division shall be paid to the Department of Cannabis Control by cash, check, money order, debit card, or credit card. Check and money order payments may be made out to the Department of Cannabis Control.

(b) If the fee is paid by debit or credit card:

(1) The payment shall be made through the Department's online licensing system; and

(2) The applicant or licensee may be required to pay any associated processing or convenience fees to the third-party vendor processing the payment on behalf of the Department.

(c) Failure to pay the appropriate licensing fee is grounds for discipline. If the Department determines that the licensee paid an amount less than the appropriate licensing fee under section 15014, the licensee will be required to pay the balance of the appropriate fee and a penalty fee of 50 percent of the appropriate licensing fee. The Department in its discretion may waive the penalty fee.

NOTE: Authority cited: Section 26013, Business and Professions Code. Reference: Sections 26012, 26051.5 and 26180, Business and Professions Code.

§ 15017. Substantially Related Offenses and Criteria for Rehabilitation.

(a) When evaluating whether an applicant or licensee has been convicted of a criminal offense, act, or professional misconduct that is substantially related to the qualifications, functions, or duties of the business for which the application is made, the Department shall consider all of the following criteria:

(1) The nature and gravity of the offense;

(2) The number of years that have elapsed since the date of the offense; and

(3) The nature and duties of the particular license in which the applicant seeks licensure or in which the licensee is licensed.

(b) For the purpose of denial, suspension, or revocation of a license, convictions that are substantially related to the qualifications, functions, or duties of the business for which the application is made include, but are not limited to:

(1) A violent felony conviction, as specified in Penal Code section 667.5(c).

(2) A serious felony conviction, as specified in Penal Code section 1192.7(c).

(3) A felony conviction involving fraud, deceit, or embezzlement.

(4) A felony conviction for hiring, employing, or using a minor in transporting, carrying, selling, giving away, preparing for sale, or peddling, any controlled substance to a minor; or selling, offering to sell, furnishing, offering to furnish, administering, or giving any controlled substance to a minor.

(5) A felony conviction for drug trafficking with enhancements pursuant to Health and Safety Code section 11370.4 or 11379.8.

(c) For the purpose of denial of a license to engage in commercial cannabis manufacturing, a conviction or violation from any jurisdiction that is substantially related to the qualifications, functions, or duties of the business for which the application is made include:

(1) A violation of section 110620, 110625, 110630, 110760, 110765, 110770, 110775, 111295, 111300, 111305, 111440, 111445, 111450, or 111455 of the Health and Safety Code that resulted in suspension or revocation of a license, administrative penalty, civil proceeding, or criminal conviction;

(2) A violation of Chapter 4 (sections 111950 through 112130) of Part 6 of Division 104 of the Health and Safety Code that resulted in suspension or revocation of a license, administrative penalty, civil proceeding, or criminal conviction;

(3) A conviction under section 382 or 383 of the Penal Code; and

(4) A violation identified in subsections (c)(1) or (c)(2) committed by a business entity in which an owner was an officer or had an ownership interest.

(d) Except as provided in subsections (b)(4) and (b)(5) and notwithstanding Chapter 2 (commencing with Section 480) of Division 1.5 of the Business and Professions Code, a prior conviction, where the sentence, including any term of probation, incarceration, or supervised release, is completed, for possession of, possession for sale, sale, manufacture, transportation, or cultivation of a controlled substance is not considered substantially related, and shall not be the sole ground for denial of a license. Conviction for any controlled substance felony, subsequent to licensure, shall be grounds for revocation of a license or denial of the renewal of a license.

(e) When evaluating whether an applicant who has been convicted of a criminal offense, act, or professional misconduct that is substantially related to the qualifications, functions, or duties of the business for which the application is made should be issued a license, the Department shall consider the following criteria of rehabilitation:

(1) The nature and gravity of the act, professional misconduct, or offense;

(2) Whether the person has a felony conviction based on possession or use of cannabis or cannabis products that would not be a felony if the person was convicted of the offense on the date of the person's application;

(3) The applicant's criminal record as a whole;

(4) Evidence of any act, professional misconduct, or offense committed subsequent to the act, professional misconduct, or offense under consideration that could be considered grounds for denial, suspension, or revocation of a commercial cannabis activity license;

(5) The time that has elapsed since commission of the act, professional misconduct, or offense;

(6) The extent to which the applicant has complied with any terms of parole, probation, restitution, or any

other sanctions lawfully imposed against the applicant;

(7) If applicable, evidence of dismissal under Penal Code sections 1203.4, 1203.4a, 1203.41, 1203.42, or pursuant to another state's similar law;

(8) If applicable, evidence the applicant has been granted clemency or a pardon by a state or federal executive;

(9) If applicable, a certificate of rehabilitation obtained under Penal Code section 4852.01 or another state's similar law; and

(10) Other evidence of rehabilitation submitted by the applicant.

(f) If an applicant has been denied a license based on a conviction, the applicant may request a hearing pursuant to Business and Professions Code section 26058 to determine if the applicant should be issued a license.

(g) For the purpose of this section, "conviction" means a plea or verdict of guilty or a conviction following a plea of nolo contendere.

NOTE: Authority cited: Section 26013, Business and Professions Code. Reference: Sections 480, 481, 482, 26012 and 26057, Business and Professions Code.

§ 15018. Additional Grounds for Denial of a License.

In addition to the reasons for denial in Business and Professions Code section 26057, a license may be denied for the following reasons:

(a) The applicant's proposed premises does not fully comply with standards set in regulation.

(b) The applicant's proposed or licensed premises is substantially different from the diagram of the proposed premises submitted by the applicant, in that the size, layout, location of common entryways, doorways, or passage ways means of public entry or exit, or identification of limited- access areas within the licensed premises is not the same.

(c) The applicant denied the Department access to the licensed premises or the property identified in the application as the premises.

(d) The applicant made a material misrepresentation on the application.

(e) The applicant did not correct the deficiencies within the application in accordance with sections 15002 and 15012.

(f) The applicant has been denied a license, permit, or other authorization to engage in commercial cannabis activity by a state or local licensing authority.

(g) The applicant's proposed premises is not in compliance with Division 13 (commencing with Section 21000) of the Public Resources Code.

(h) The applicant has failed to remit taxes as required under the Revenue and Taxation Code.

(i) The applicant may be denied a license for any violations of law related to the operations of the commercial cannabis business or for any violations of law related to licensure.

(j) The applicant has engaged in conduct that is grounds for disciplinary action specified in section 26030 of the Act.

NOTE: Authority cited: Section 26013, Business and Professions Code. Reference: Sections 480, 490, 26012, 26030 and 26050, Business and Professions Code.

§ 15019. Excessive Concentration.

(a) In determining whether to grant, deny, or renew a license for a retail premises or microbusiness premises authorized to engage in retail sales, the Department shall consider if an excessive concentration exists in the area where the licensee will operate. For the purposes of this section "excessive concentration" applies when either of the following conditions exist:

(1) The ratio of licensees to population within the census tract or census division in which the applicant premises is located exceeds the ratio of licensees to population in the county in which the applicant premises is located, unless denial of the application would unduly limit the development of the legal market so as to perpetuate the illegal market for cannabis goods.

(2) The ratio of retail licenses or microbusiness licenses to the population within the census tract, census division, or jurisdiction exceeds that allowable by local ordinance adopted under Business and Professions Code section 26200.

(b) "Population Within the Census Tract or Census Division" as used in this section means the population as determined by the most recent United States decennial or special census. Such population determination shall not operate to prevent an applicant from establishing that an increase of resident population has occurred within the census tract or census division.

(c) "Population in the County" as used in this section shall be determined by the most recent annual population estimate for California counties published by the Demographic Research Unit, State Department of Finance.

(d) Beginning July 1, 2018, the Department shall calculate the ratios described in subsection (a) of this section once every six months using the most current available data. The Department's consideration of whether to grant, deny, or renew a license shall be based upon the most recent ratio calculated by the Department on the date of the Department's decision.

(e) The existence of an excessive concentration shall not be considered in determining whether to grant, deny, or extend a temporary license under Business and Professions Code section 26050.1.

(f) The applicant may provide reliable evidence establishing, to the satisfaction of the Department, that a denial of a license would unduly limit the development of the legal market so as to perpetuate the illegal market for cannabis goods.

NOTE: Authority cited: Section 26013, Business and Professions Code. Reference: Sections 26012 and 26051, Business and Professions Code.

§ 15020. Renewal of License.

(a) To timely renew a license, a completed license renewal form and annual license fee pursuant to section 15014 shall be received by the Department from the licensee no earlier than 60 calendar days before the expiration of the license and no later than 5:00 p.m. Pacific Time on the last business day before the expiration of the license if the renewal form is submitted to the Department at its office(s), or no later than 11:59 p.m. on the last business day before the expiration of the license if the renewal form is submitted to the Department through its electronic licensing system. Failure to receive a notice for license renewal does not relieve a licensee of the obligation to renew all licenses as required.

(b) In the event the license is not submitted for renewal prior to the expiration date, the licensee must not sell, transfer, transport, manufacture, test, or distribute any commercial cannabis or cannabis products until the license is renewed.

(c) A licensee may submit a license renewal form up to 30 calendar days after the license expires. Any late renewal form will be subject to a late fee equal to 50 percent of the applicable licensing fee required by subsection (a). A licensee who does not submit a complete license renewal application, including the late fee, to the Department within 30 calendar days after the expiration of the license shall forfeit their eligibility for a license renewal and be required to submit a new license application.

(d) The license renewal form shall contain the following:

(1) The name of the licensee. For licensees who are individuals, the applicant shall provide both the first and last name of the individual. For licensees who are business entities, the licensee shall provide the legal business name of the commercial cannabis business.

(2) The license number and expiration date.

(3) The licensee's mailing address and licensed premises address.

(4) Documentation demonstrating the licensee's gross revenue for the current licensed period, such as a copy of the licensee's state tax return filed with the California Department of Tax and Fee Administration. This subsection does not apply to the renewal of cultivation licenses.

(5) Documentation of any change to any item listed in the original application under section 15002 that has not been reported to the Department through another process pursuant to the Act or this division.

(6) An attestation that all information provided to the Department in the license renewal form and the original application under section 15002 or subsequent notification under sections 15023 and 15024 is accurate and current.

(7) If applicable, a limited waiver of sovereign immunity pursuant to section 15009.

(8) For a licensee with more than one employee, the licensee shall attest that it employs, or will employ within one year of renewing the license, one supervisor and one employee who has successfully completed a Cal-OSHA 30-hour general industry outreach course offered by a training provider that is authorized by an OSHA Training Institute Education Center to provide the course.

(e) Beginning January 1, 2022, an application for renewal of a license to engage in commercial cannabis cultivation shall include the following records, for each power source indicated on the application for licensure for the previous annual licensed period:

(1) Total electricity supplied by local utility provider, name of local utility provider, and greenhouse gas emission intensity per kilowatt hour reported by the utility provider under section 398.4(c) of the Public Utilities Code for the most recent calendar year available at time of submission;

(2) Total electricity supplied by a zero net energy renewable source, as set forth in section 398.4(h)(5) of the Public Utilities Code, that is not part of a net metering or other utility benefit;

(3) Total electricity supplied from other unspecified sources, as defined in section 398.2(e) of the Public Utilities Code, and other onsite sources of generation not reported to the local utility provider (e.g., generators, fuel cells) and the greenhouse gas emission intensity from these sources; and

(4) Average weighted greenhouse gas emission intensity considering all electricity use in subsections (e)(1)-(e)(3).

NOTE: Authority cited: Section 26013, Business and Professions Code. Reference: Sections 26012 and 26050, Business and Professions Code.

§ 15021. Denial of License.

(a) The Department may deny an application for a new license or a renewal of a license for any reason specified in Business and Professions Code section 26057, and on any additional grounds including grounds for denial under section 15018, and grounds for discipline under the Act or this division.

(b) Upon denial of an application for a license or renewal of a license, the Department shall notify the applicant in writing of the reasons for denial, and the right to a hearing to contest the denial.

(c) The applicant may request a hearing to contest the denial by submitting a written request to the Department at appeals@cannabis.ca.gov.

(1) The written request for a hearing must be received by the Department or postmarked within 30 calendar days of service of the notification of denial.

(2) If the written request for a hearing is not received within the required timeframe, the applicant's right to a hearing is waived.

(3) Upon timely receipt of the written request for hearing, the Department shall set a date for hearing to be conducted in accordance with chapter 5 (commencing with section 11500) of part 1 of division 3 of title 2 of the Government Code.

(d) If a license application is denied due to an owner's conviction history, the Department shall notify the applicant of the process for the owner to request a copy of their complete conviction history and question the accuracy or completeness of the record pursuant to Penal Code sections 11122 through 11127.

NOTE: Authority cited: Section 26013, Business and Professions Code; Reference: Sections 26012, 26057 and 26058, Business and Professions Code.

§ 15022. Cancellation of License. [Repealed]

Note: Authority cited: Section 26013, Business and Professions Code. Reference: Sections 26012 and 26050, Business and Professions Code.

§ 15023. Business Modifications.

Business modifications shall be made in accordance with the following:

(a) Changes to standard operating procedures may be made without providing notification to the Department, except as required by the Act or this division. Licensees shall maintain a copy of all current and prior operating procedures as required by section 15037.

(b) If at the time of licensure, a licensee employed fewer than 20 employees and later employs 20 or more employees, within 60 days of employing 20 or more employees, the licensee shall provide to the Department a notarized statement that the licensee will enter into a labor peace agreement and will abide by the terms of the agreement or demonstrate that the commercial cannabis business has entered into a labor peace agreement by providing a copy of the signature page of the agreement.

(c) Licenses are not transferrable or assignable to another person or owner. In the event of the sale or other transfer of the business or operations covered by the licensee, changes in ownership shall be made in accordance with the following:

(1) If one or more of the owners change, the new owners shall submit the information required under section 15002(c)(16) for each new owner to the Department within 14 calendar days of the effective date of the ownership change. The business may continue to operate under the active license while the Department reviews the qualifications of the new owner(s) in accordance with the Act and these regulations to determine

whether the change would constitute grounds for denial of the license, if at least one existing owner is not transferring their ownership interest and will remain as an owner under the new ownership structure. If all owners will be transferring their ownership interest, the business shall not operate under the new ownership structure until a new license application has been submitted to and approved by the Department, and all application and license fees for the new application have been paid. The former owner's inventory shall be transferred to the new owner's track and trace account upon issuance of the license.

(A) A change in ownership occurs when a new person meets the definition of owner in section 15003.

(B) A change in ownership does not occur when one or more owners leave the business by transferring their ownership interest to the other existing owner(s).

(2) In cases where one or more owners leave the business by transferring their ownership interest to the other existing owner(s), the owner or owners that are transferring their interest shall provide a signed statement to the Department confirming that they have transferred their interest within 14 calendar days of the change.

(d) When there is a change in financial interest holder(s) in the commercial cannabis business who do not meet the requirements for a new license application under this section, the licensee shall submit the information required by section 15002(c)(15) to the Department within 14 calendar days of the change.

(e) When any of the following changes occur, the licensee shall notify the Department within 14 calendar days of the change:

(1) Any change to contact information from the information provided to the Department in the original application.

(2) Any change in name if the licensee is an individual, or any change in legal business name if the licensee is a business entity.

(3) Any change in business trade names, fictitious business names, or doing business as ("DBA").

(4) Any change in the bond required under section 15002(c)(22).

(f) Licensees may request to add an A-designation or M-designation to their license by sending a notification to the Department signed by at least one owner as defined in section 15003. A licensee shall not operate under the requested designation until they have received approval from the Department.

(g) Microbusiness licensees may add a commercial cannabis activity to their license or remove a commercial cannabis activity from their license if doing so is consistent with the requirement set forth in section 15500(a) that licensees engage in at least three (3) commercial cannabis activities. Licensees shall request the modification by completing a request to modify the licensed premises pursuant to section 15027. A licensee shall not engage in a new commercial cannabis activity until they have paid for the modification and received approval from the Department.

(h) Except as permitted under Business and Professions Code section 26050.2(h), licensees may not be transferred from one premises to another. Licensees shall not operate out of a new premises until they have been issued a new license.

(i) For any business modification or notification under this section, licensees shall use and submit to the Department the Licensee Notification and Request Form, Notifications and Requests to Modify a License, DCC-LIC-027 (Amended 2/22), which is incorporated herein by reference, unless the change relates to contact information and can be made through the Department's online system.

NOTE: Authority cited: Section 26013, Business and Professions Code. Reference: Section 26012, Business and Professions Code.

§ 15024. Death, Incapacity, or Insolvency of a Licensee.

(a) In the event of the death, incapacity, receivership, assignment for the benefit of creditors or other event rendering one or more owners incapable of performing the duties associated with the license, the owner or owners' successor in interest (e.g., appointed guardian, executor, administrator, receiver, trustee, or assignee) shall notify the Department in writing, within 14 calendar days, by submitting the Licensee Notification and Request Form, Notifications and Requests to Modify a License, DCC-LIC-027 (Amended 2/22), which is incorporated herein by reference.

(b) To continue operations or surrender the existing license, the successor in interest shall submit to the Department the following:

(1) The name of the successor in interest;

(2) The name of the owner(s) for which the successor in interest is succeeding and the license number;

(3) The phone number, mailing address, and email address of the successor in interest; and

(4) Documentation demonstrating that the owner(s) is incapable of performing the duties associated with the license such as a death certificate or a court order, and documentation demonstrating that the person making the request is the owner or owners' successor in interest such as a court order appointing guardianship, receivership, or a will or trust agreement.

(c) The Department may give the successor in interest written approval to continue operations on the licensed business premises for a period of time specified by the Department:

(1) If the successor in interest or another person has applied for a license from the Department for the licensed premises and that application is under review;

(2) If the successor in interest needs additional time to destroy or sell cannabis or cannabis products; or

(3) At the discretion of the Department.

(d) The successor in interest is held subject to all terms and conditions under which a state cannabis license is held pursuant to the Act.

(e) The approval creates no vested right to the issuance of a state cannabis license.

NOTE: Authority cited: Section 26013, Business and Professions Code. Reference: Section 26012, Business and Professions Code.

§ 15024.1. Cannabis and Cannabis Products After Termination of License.

In the event a license is terminated for any reason while cannabis or cannabis products remain on the premises, the following actions may be taken:

(a) The cannabis or cannabis products may be destroyed by the former licensee; or

(b) A licensed distributor or licensed microbusiness authorized to engage in distribution may be authorized by the Department to procure and distribute the former licensee's entire inventory stock in accordance with the following;

(1) A licensed distributor or licensed microbusiness authorized to engage in distribution shall, within 14 calendar days of the termination of the former licensee's license, submit a written request to the Department, on the Licensee Notification and Request Form, Notifications and Requests Regarding Regulatory Compliance, DCC-LIC-028 (New 2/22), which is incorporated by reference, for authorization to procure the cannabis or cannabis products from the former licensee; and

(2) Upon approval from the Department, the licensed distributor or licensed microbusiness authorized to

engage in distribution shall transport the cannabis or cannabis products as follows:

(A) Cannabis goods shall be transported to a licensed distribution premises where the distributor shall arrange for laboratory testing and perform quality assurance in accordance with chapter 2. If the cannabis goods have already been tested in accordance with chapter 6 and have a valid certificate of analysis for regulatory compliance testing that is less than 12 months old, the cannabis goods are not required to undergo additional testing.

(B) Cannabis that requires further processing as defined in section 15000(e), or further manufacturing as defined in section 15000(pp), shall be transported to a licensee licensed to conduct the additional processing or manufacturing.

(C) Cannabis or cannabis products that require packaging and labeling shall be transported to a licensee licensed to conduct packaging and labeling of the cannabis or cannabis products.

(D) Cannabis products that require further manufacturing as defined in section 15000(pp) shall be transported to a licensed manufacturer.

NOTE: Authority cited: Section 26013, Business and Professions Code. Reference: Sections 26011.5 and 26013, Business and Professions Code.

§ 15025. Additional Premises Requirements for Retailers and Microbusinesses Authorized to Engage in Retail.

(a) Licensed retailers and licensed microbusinesses authorized to engage in retail sales shall only serve customers who are within the licensed premises, or at a delivery address that meets the requirements of this division.

(1) The sale and delivery of cannabis goods shall not occur through a pass-out window or a slide-out tray to the exterior of the licensed premises.

(2) Licensed retailers or licensed microbusinesses authorized to engage in retail sales shall not operate as or with a drive-in or drive-through at which cannabis goods are sold to persons within or about a motor vehicle, except for curbside delivery conducted pursuant to section 15404.

(b) Alcoholic beverages as defined in Business and Professions Code section 23004 shall not be stored or consumed on a licensed premises.

(c) Any licensed retailer or microbusiness authorized to conduct retail sales that is adjacent to another premises engaging in manufacturing, cultivation, or distribution shall be separated from those premises by solid walls that extend from floor to ceiling, and any doors leading to the cultivation, distribution, or manufacturing premises shall remain closed.

(d) Cannabis goods shall not be dispersed in the air throughout the premises or throughout a portion of the premises by an oil diffuser or any other vaporizing device that is intended to disperse the vapor throughout the premises or throughout a portion of the premises. This section shall not be interpreted to prohibit cannabis goods consumption on the premises of a licensed retailer or licensed microbusiness authorized to engage in retail sales that is conducted in accordance with Business and Professions Code section 26200(g).

(e) Notwithstanding subsection (a), a commercial cannabis business may have a drive-in or drive-through window only if, prior to June 1, 2018:

(1) The commercial cannabis business received a license or permit from the local jurisdiction for a premises including a drive-in or drive-through window which was disclosed on the local application; or

(2) The commercial cannabis business has submitted an application to the local jurisdiction for a license or

permit which, at the time of submission of the application, included information that a drive-in or drive-through window was already part of, or proposed to be part of, the premises, and after June 1, 2018, the local jurisdiction approves the premises with a drive-in or drive-through window.

NOTE: Authority cited: Section 26013, Business and Professions Code. Reference: Sections 26001, 26012 and 26053, Business and Professions Code.

§ 15026. Premises Location. [Repealed]

Note: Authority cited: Section 26013, Business and Professions Code. Reference: Sections 26012, 26051.5, 26054 and 26055, Business and Professions Code.

§ 15027. Modification of Premises or Operations.

(a) A licensee shall not, without the prior written approval of the Department, make a physical change, alteration, or modification of the licensed premises that materially or substantially alters the licensed premises or the use of the licensed premises from the premises diagram originally filed with the license application. A licensee whose licensed premises is to be materially or substantially changed, modified, or altered is responsible for filing a request for premises modification with the Department.

(b) Material or substantial changes, alterations, or modifications to a licensed cultivation premises requiring prior approval from the Department are:

(1) Modification to any area described in the licensee's cultivation plan including, but not limited to, the removal, creation, or relocation of canopy, processing, packaging, composting, harvest storage, and storage areas for pesticides and other chemicals.

(2) Change in water or power source(s).

(3) Any increase or decrease in the total physical size or capacity of the licensed premises.

(4) Any physical change that would require a building permit, zoning change, or other approval from the applicable local jurisdiction.

(c) Material or substantial changes, alterations, or modifications to a licensed manufacturing premises that require prior approval from the Department are:

(1) The addition of any ethanol, carbon dioxide, or volatile extraction method or extraction unit.

(2) Any increase or decrease in the total physical size or capacity of the licensed premises.

(3) Any physical change that would require the installation of additional video surveillance cameras or a change in the video surveillance system to meet the requirements of section 15044, or alarm system to meet the requirements of section 15047.

(4) Any physical change that would require a building permit, zoning change, or other approval from the applicable local jurisdiction.

(d) Material or substantial changes, alterations, or modifications to a licensed microbusiness premises that require prior approval from the Department are:

(1) The addition of a commercial cannabis activity pursuant to section 15500(h).

(2) Any material or substantial changes, alterations, or modifications listed in subsections (b), (c), or (e), as applicable to the licensed microbusiness' commercial cannabis activities.

(e) Material or substantial changes, alterations, or modifications to a licensed distribution, retail, or testing laboratory premises that require prior approval from the Department include, but are not limited to:

(1) Any increase or decrease in the total physical size or capacity of the licensed premises.

(2) Any physical change that would require the installation of additional video surveillance cameras or a change in the video surveillance system to meet the requirements of section 15044, or alarm system to meet the requirements of section 15047.

(3) Any physical change that would require a building permit, zoning change, or other approval from the applicable local jurisdiction.

(f) Licensees shall request approval of a physical change, alteration, or modification through the online licensing system or in writing, by submitting the Licensee Notification and Request Form, Notifications and Requests to Modify a License, DCC-LIC-027 (Amended 2/22), which is incorporated herein by reference, and the request shall include:

(1) A new premises diagram that conforms to requirements in section 15006; and

(2) A fee pursuant to section 15014 for all licensees except licensed cultivators.

(g) A licensee shall provide additional documentation requested by the Department to evaluate the licensee's request to modify the licensed premises.

(h) Licensees shall notify the Department of all changes, alterations, or modifications to a licensed premises or the licensee's operations that do not require prior approval pursuant to subsections (b), (c), (d), and (e) through the online licensing system or by submitting the Licensee Notification and Request Form, Notifications and Request to Modify a License, DCC-LIC-027 (Amended 2/22), which is incorporated herein by reference, and a new premises diagram that conforms to requirements in section 15006. Notifications pursuant to this subsection shall be submitted to the Department no later than three (3) business days after the changes, alterations, or modifications have been made to the licensed premises.

NOTE: Authority cited: Section 26013, Business and Professions Code. Reference: Sections 26012 and 26055, Business and Professions Code.

§ 15027.1. Conversion to Large and Medium Cultivation Licenses.

(a) A licensee may convert existing cultivation licenses into a Large or Medium Cultivation license if the following requirements are met:

(1) The location to be licensed consists of licensed or previously licensed cultivation sites, as listed in section 16201. The licensee must have at least one active license within the boundaries of the proposed premises at the time they request conversion.

(2) The licenses to be converted are held by the same person(s) as the requested converted Large or Medium Cultivation license.

(b) To obtain a conversion into a Large or Medium Cultivation license, an eligible licensee shall submit to the Department the following information:

(1) The name of the Designated Responsible Party requesting the conversion.

(2) The license numbers of the current or previous cultivation licenses to be converted.

(3) The physical address(es) for the current or previous cultivation licenses to be converted.

(4) A diagram of the proposed premises that meets the requirements of section 15006.

(5) A proposed cultivation plan that meets the requirements in section 16309.

(6) If the conversion necessitates additional review pursuant to CEQA (division 13 (commencing with section 21000) of the Public Resources Code); the licensee shall provide evidence of compliance with CEQA in accordance with section 15010.

(7) The identities of all owners and financial interest holders, as defined in sections 15003 and 15004, for the converted license. The information for all owners required in section 15002, subsection (c)(16) and all information required for financial interest holders in section 15002, subsection (c)(15) shall be submitted to the Department by entering the information into the appropriate fields within the Department's licensing system.

(c) The Department shall verify that all requirements for conversion have been met. If all requirements have been met, the Department shall notify the licensee in writing that the conversion requirements have been met and they may pay the applicable license fee provided for in section 15014.2 or 15014. The fee associated with the converted license shall be paid within 30 calendar days of the notification from the Department required by this subsection. The converted license will become active on the date the fee associated with the converted license is paid in full. If the licensee has been granted a fee deferral pursuant to Business and Professions Code section 26249, the converted license will become active on the date of the notification from the Department that all conversion requirements have been met and the fee associated with the converted license shall be paid in accordance with the provisions of the fee deferral.

(d) A conversion shall not be subject to an application fee.

(e) Notwithstanding sections 15014.2 and 15014, if time remains on any of the licenses to be converted, the prorated value for each day remaining on each license approved for conversion will be credited to the license fee amount for the converted license. The amount credited shall not exceed the license fee for the converted license.

(f) At the time a converted Large or Medium Cultivation license becomes active, the licenses that are converted or within the boundaries of the converted license shall be cancelled by the Department.

NOTE: Authority cited: Section 26013, Business and Professions Code. Reference: Sections 26012, 26013, 26050, 26055, 26060.1 and 26061, Business and Professions Code.

§ 15028. Subletting of Premises. [Repealed]

Note: Authority cited: Section 26013, Business and Professions Code. Reference: Sections 26012 and 26070, Business and Professions Code.

§ 15030. Licensee's Responsibility for Acts of Employees and Agents. [Repealed]

Note: Authority cited: Section 26013, Business and Professions Code. Reference: Sections 26031 and 26110, Business and Professions Code.

§ 15031. Age Restriction. [Repealed]

Note: Authority cited: Section 26013, Business and Professions Code. Reference: Section 26140, Business and Professions Code.

§ 15032. Commercial Cannabis Activity. [Repealed]

Note: Authority cited: Section 26013, Business and Professions Code. Reference: Sections 26001, 26013 and 26053, Business and Professions Code.

§ 15033. Storage of Inventory. [Repealed]

Note: Authority cited: Section 26013, Business and Professions Code. Reference: Sections 26012 and 26070, Business and Professions Code.

§ 15034. Significant Discrepancy in Inventory.

A significant discrepancy in inventory means a five percent difference between the licensee's physical inventory and the inventory recorded in the track and trace system.

NOTE: Authority cited: Section 26013, Business and Professions Code. Reference: Section 26070, Business and Professions Code.

§ 15035. Notification of Criminal Acts, Civil Judgments, Violations of Labor Standards, and Revocation of a Local License, Permit, or Other Authorization After Licensure.

(a) A licensee shall ensure that the Department is notified in writing of a criminal conviction of any owner, either by mail or electronic mail, within 48 hours of the conviction. The written notification to the Department shall include the date of conviction, the court docket number, the name of the court in which the licensee was convicted, and the specific offense(s) for which the licensee was convicted.

(b) A licensee shall ensure that the Department is notified in writing of a civil penalty or judgment rendered against the licensee or any owner in their individual capacity, either by mail or electronic mail, within 48 hours of delivery of the verdict or entry of judgment, whichever is sooner. The written notification shall include the date of verdict or entry of judgment, the court docket number, the name of the court in which the matter was adjudicated, and a description of the civil penalty or judgment rendered against the licensee.

(c) A licensee shall ensure that the Department is notified in writing of an administrative order or civil judgment for violations of labor standards against the licensee or any owner in their individual capacity, either by mail or electronic mail, within 48 hours of delivery of the order. The written notification shall include the date of the order, the name of the agency issuing the order, and a description of the administrative penalty or judgment rendered against the licensee.

(d) A licensee shall ensure that the Department is notified in writing of the revocation of a local license, permit, or other authorization held by the licensee or any owner in their individual capacity, either by mail or electronic mail, within 48 hours of receiving notice of the revocation. The written notification shall include the name of the local agency involved, a written explanation of the proceeding or enforcement action, and the specific violation(s) that led to revocation.

(e) For any notification required under this section, licensees shall use and submit to the Department the Licensee Notification and Request Form, Notifications and Requests to Modify a License, DCC-LIC-027 (Amended 2/22), which is incorporated herein by reference.

NOTE: Authority cited: Section 26013, Business and Professions Code. Reference: Sections 26030 and 26031, Business and Professions Code.

§ 15036. Notification of Theft, Loss, and Criminal Activity.

(a) A licensee shall notify the Department and local law enforcement within 24 hours of discovery of any of the following situations:

(1) The licensee discovers a significant discrepancy, as defined in section 15034, in its inventory.

(2) The licensee discovers diversion, theft, loss, or any other criminal activity pertaining to the operations of the licensee.

(3) The licensee discovers diversion, theft, loss, or any other criminal activity by an agent or employee of the licensee pertaining to the operations of the licensee.

(4) The licensee discovers loss or unauthorized alteration of records related to cannabis or cannabis products, customers, or the licensee's employees or agents.

(5) The licensee discovers any other breach of security.

(b) The notification to the Department pursuant to subsection (a) shall be submitted on the Licensee Notification and Request Form, Notifications and Requests Regarding Regulatory Compliance, DCC-LIC-028 (New 2/22), which is incorporated herein by reference, and shall include the date and time of occurrence of the theft, loss, or criminal activity, the name of the local law enforcement agency that was notified, and a description of the incident including, where applicable, the item(s) that were taken or lost.

NOTE: Authority cited: Section 26013, Business and Professions Code. Reference: Section 26070, Business and Professions Code.

§ 15037. General Record Retention Requirements.

(a) Licensees must keep and maintain records in connection with the licensed commercial cannabis business. Records must be kept for at least seven years from the date of creation, unless a shorter time is specified. Records include, but are not limited to:

(1) Financial records including, but not limited to, bank statements, sales invoices, receipts, tax records, and all records required by the California Department of Tax and Fee Administration (formerly Board of Equalization) under title 18, California Code of Regulations, sections 1698 and 4901.

(2) Personnel records, including each employee's full name, Social Security number or individual taxpayer identification number, date employment begins, and date of termination of employment, if applicable.

(3) Training records including, but not limited to, the content of the training provided and the names of the employees who received the training.

(4) Contracts regarding commercial cannabis activity.

(5) Permits, licenses, and other local authorizations to conduct the licensee's commercial cannabis activity.

(6) All other documents prepared or executed by an owner or their employees or assignees in connection with the licensed commercial cannabis business.

(7) Records required by the Act or this division.

(b) Records must be kept in a manner that allows the records to be produced for the Department in either hard-copy or electronic form.

(c) Records must be legible and accurate. No person may intentionally misrepresent or falsify records.

(d) Records must be stored in a secured area where the records are protected from debris, moisture, contamination, hazardous waste, and theft.

NOTE: Authority cited: Section 26013, Business and Professions Code. Reference: Sections 26160 and 26161, Business and Professions Code.

§ 15037.1. Licensee Authorization to Release Data to Financial Institutions.

(a) A licensee may authorize the Department to provide information to a financial institution for purposes of facilitating the provision of financial services. The authorization shall be made in writing, through a form prescribed by the Department, which shall include the following information:

(1) The name of the licensed business for which the licensee is authorizing the release of information;

(2) The business' license number(s);

(3) The financial institution authorized to receive information;

(4) The name, phone number, email address, and signature of the owner submitting the authorization;

(5) The categories of information specified in subsection (b) that are authorized for release; and

(6) An acknowledgement that the authorization to release information includes information that is otherwise protected from disclosure, that the licensee is waiving privilege and confidentiality, and that the scope of the release is strictly limited to the purposes of disclosure to the financial institution.

(b) After receipt of the authorization, the Department shall release the following information, as designated by the licensee, when requested by an authorized financial institution pursuant to section 15037.2 of this division:

(1) The license application(s), including renewal applications, excluding information required to be kept confidential pursuant to Penal Code section 11105 and confidential personal information of individual owners of the licensed business;

(2) Information captured in the track-and-trace system established pursuant to Business and Professions Code section 26067, including, but not limited to, aggregated sales or transfer information, as applicable; and

(3) Documents issued to the licensee pursuant to disciplinary or enforcement proceedings.

(c) A licensee may withdraw the authorization to provide information to a financial institution at any time. The withdrawal shall be made in writing, through a form prescribed by the Department, and shall include the following information:

(1) The name of the licensed business for which the licensee is withdrawing the authorization of the release of information;

(2) The business' license number(s);

(3) The financial institution from which authorization to receive information is withdrawn; and

(4) The name, phone number, email address, and signature of the owner submitting the withdrawal.

NOTE: Authority cited: Section 26013, Business and Professions Code. Reference: Section 26260, Business and Professions Code.

§ 15037.2. Financial Institution Request for Licensee Information.

A financial institution, as defined in Business and Professions Code section 26260(c)(3), may request information related to a licensee for purposes of facilitating the provision of financial services for that licensee. The request shall be made in writing, through a form prescribed by the Department, which shall include the following information:

(a) The name of the financial institution;

(b) The name, phone number, email, and signature of the representative of the financial institution requesting information;

(c) The business name and license number of the licensee for which the financial institution is requesting information;

(d) The type of financial services for which the information is requested (including, but not limited to, establishment or maintenance of bank accounts, extending loans, and providing insurance) and whether the request is for consideration of a new service or maintenance of an existing service;

(e) The specific information requested as described in section 15037.1(b), if authorized by the licensee; and

(f) An acknowledgment that use of the information is limited to that information which is necessary for the provision of financial services.

NOTE: Authority cited: Section 26013, Business and Professions Code. Reference: Section 26260, Business and Professions Code.

§ 15038. Disaster Relief.

(a) If a licensee is unable to comply with any licensing requirements due to a disaster, the licensee may notify the Department of this inability to comply and request relief from the specific licensing requirement.

(b) The Department may exercise its discretion to provide temporary relief from specific regulatory requirements in this division and from other licensing requirements when allowed by law.

(c) Temporary relief from specific licensing requirements shall be issued for a reasonable amount of time in order to allow the licensee to recover from the disaster.

(d) The Department may require that certain conditions be followed in order for a licensee to receive temporary relief from specific licensing requirements.

(e) A licensee shall not be subject to an enforcement action for a violation of a licensing requirement during the time in which the licensee has received temporary relief and is in compliance with any conditions of relief required by the Department.

(f) For the purposes of this section, "disaster" means condition of extreme peril to the safety of persons and property within the state or a county, city and county, or city caused by such conditions as air pollution, fire, flood, storm, tidal wave, epidemic, riot, drought, terrorism, sudden and severe energy shortage, plant or animal infestation or disease, Governor's warning of an earthquake or volcanic prediction, or an earthquake, or similar public calamity, other than conditions resulting from a labor controversy, for which the Governor has proclaimed a state of emergency in accordance with Government Code sections 8558 and 8625, or for which a local governing body has proclaimed a local emergency in accordance with Government Code sections 8558 and 8630.

(g) A licensed premises that has been vacated by a licensee due to a disaster shall not be deemed to have been abandoned.

(h) Notwithstanding subsection (a), if a licensee needs to move cannabis or cannabis products stored on the licensed premises to another location immediately to prevent loss, theft, or degradation of the cannabis or cannabis products from the disaster, the licensee may move the cannabis or cannabis products without obtaining prior approval from the Department if the following conditions are met:

(1) The cannabis or cannabis products are moved to a secure location where access to the cannabis or cannabis products can be restricted to the licensee, its employees, and contractors;

(2) The licensee notifies the Department in writing that the cannabis or cannabis products have been moved and that the licensee is requesting relief from complying with specific licensing requirements pursuant to subsection (a) within 24 hours of moving the cannabis or cannabis products;

(3) The licensee agrees to grant the Department access to the location where the cannabis or cannabis products have been moved for inspection; and

(4) The licensee submits a request for temporary relief as described in subsection (i) in writing to the Department within 14 calendar days of moving the cannabis or cannabis products.

(i) Requests for temporary disaster relief shall include the following:

(1) Name of the licensed commercial cannabis business requesting relief.

(2) License number issued by the Department.

(3) Premises address.

(4) Contact information for the owner submitting the request, including name, phone number, and email address.

(5) Date of request.

(6) Specific statutes and regulations from which relief is requested.

(7) Time period for which the relief is requested.

(8) Reason(s) for the request, including a clear explanation of how the relief requested is tied to the specific circumstances of the declared disaster.

NOTE: Authority cited: Section 26013, Business and Professions Code. Reference: Section 26012, Business and Professions Code.

ARTICLE 4. POSTING AND ADVERTISING

§ 15039. License Posting Requirement.

(a) Upon issuance of a license, the licensee shall prominently display the license on the licensed premises where it can be viewed by state and local agencies. If the licensed premises is open to the public, the license shall be displayed in an area that is within plain sight of the public.

(b) Upon issuance of any license, a retailer, whose licensed premises is open to the public, shall prominently display the Quick Response Code (QR Code) certificate issued by the Department so that it can be viewed and scanned from outside of the licensed premises.

(c) The QR Code certificate displayed by a licensee as required by subsection (b), shall be posted in the front window of the licensed premises within three (3) feet of any public entrance to the licensed premises, or in a locked display case mounted on the outside wall of the licensed premises within three (3) feet of any public entrance to the licensed premises. The QR Code certificate shall be posted in a manner that is clearly visible from outside of the licensed premises to the public and all persons entering the premises.

(d) The QR Code certificate displayed by the licensee as required by subsection (b) shall comply with the following requirements:

(1) The QR Code certificate shall be printed on paper, glass, metal, or other material not less than 8.5 inches by 11 inches.

(2) The QR Code on the certificate posted, as required by this section, shall not be less than 3.75 inches by 3.75 inches.

(3) The QR Code on the certificate shall be of sufficient clarity that the code can be read by a smartphone or device capable of reading QR Codes from a distance of at least three (3) feet.

NOTE: Authority cited: Section 26013, Business and Professions Code. Reference: Sections 26012 and 26053, Business and Professions Code.

§ 15040. Advertising Placement and Prohibitions.

(a) Any advertising or marketing, as defined in Business and Professions Code section 26150, that is placed in broadcast, cable, radio, print, and digital communications:

(1) Shall only be displayed after a licensee has obtained reliable up-to-date audience composition data demonstrating that at least 71.6 percent of the audience viewing the advertising or marketing is reasonably expected to be 21 years of age or older;

(2) Shall not use any depictions or images of minors or anyone under 21 years of age;

(3) Shall not use any images that are attractive to children, including, but not limited to:

(A) Cartoons;

(B) Any likeness to images, characters, or phrases that are popularly used to advertise to children;

(C) Any imitation of candy packaging or labeling; or

(D) The terms "candy" or "candies" or variants in spelling such as "kandy" or "kandeez."

(4) Shall not advertise free cannabis goods or cannabis accessories. This includes promotions such as:

(A) Buy one product, get one product free;

(B) Free product with any donation; and

(C) Contests, sweepstakes, or raffles.

(b) In addition to the requirements for advertising and marketing in subsection (a), all outdoor signs, including billboards, shall:

(1) Be affixed to a building or permanent structure; and

(2) Comply with the provisions of the Outdoor Advertising Act, commencing with section 5200 of the Business and Professions Code, if applicable.

(c) For the purposes of this section, "reliable up-to-date audience composition data" means data regarding the age and location demographics of the audience viewing a particular advertising or marketing medium. "Reliable up-to-date audience composition data" does not include data from the most recent United States decennial or special census, or the annual population estimate for California counties published by the Demographic Research Unit, State Department of Finance.

(d) Immediately upon request, a licensee shall provide to the Department audience composition data as required in subsection (a) for advertising or marketing placed by the licensee.

(e) If the Department determines that audience composition data for advertising or marketing provided by a licensee does not comply with the requirements of subsection (a), or the licensee fails to provide audience composition data to the Department upon request, the licensee shall remove the advertising or marketing placement in question.

(f) In construing and enforcing the advertising provisions of the Act and this division, any action, omission, or failure of an advertising agent, representative, or contractor retained by the licensee shall in every case be deemed the act, omission, or failure of the licensee.

NOTE: Authority cited: Section 26013, Business and Professions Code. Reference: Sections 26151 and 26152, Business and Professions Code.

§ 15040.1. Marketing Cannabis Goods as Alcoholic Products.

Licensees shall not market, advertise, sell or transport cannabis goods that are labeled as beer, wine, liquor, spirits, or any other term used to describe a type of alcohol or alcoholic beverage that may create a misleading impression that the product is an alcoholic beverage as defined in division 9 of the Business and Professions Code. Nothing in this section shall be interpreted as prohibiting a company or brand name associated with alcoholic beverages from appearing on cannabis goods or in marketing and advertisements for cannabis goods provided the cannabis goods do not create a misleading impression that the product is an alcoholic beverage.

NOTE: Authority cited: Section 26013, Business and Professions Code. Reference: Sections 26054, 26151 and 26152, Business and Professions Code.

§ 15040.2. Prohibited Business Promotions.

(a) A licensee shall not give away any amount of cannabis or cannabis products, or any cannabis accessory, as part of a business promotion.

(b) A licensee shall not hold a raffle or sweepstakes as part of a business promotion.

NOTE: Authority cited: Section 26013, Business and Professions Code. Reference: Section 26153, Business and Professions Code.

§ 15041. Age Confirmation in Advertising.

(a) Prior to any advertising or marketing from the licensee involving direct, individualized communication or dialogue, the licensee shall use age affirmation to verify that the recipient is 21 years of age or older.

(b) For the purposes of this section, direct, individualized communication or dialogue may occur through any form of communication, including in-person, telephone, physical mail, or electronic.

(c) A method of age verification is not necessary for a communication if the licensee can verify that the licensee has previously had the intended recipient undergo a method of age affirmation and the licensee is reasonably certain that the communication will only be received by the intended recipient.

(d) A licensee shall use a method of age affirmation before having a potential customer added to a mailing list, subscribe, or otherwise consent to receiving direct, individualized communication or dialogue controlled by a licensee.

NOTE: Authority cited: Section 26013, Business and Professions Code. Reference: Sections 26151 and 26152, Business and Professions Code.

§ 15041.1. Branded Merchandise.

(a) "Branded merchandise" means non-consumable consumer goods utilized by a licensee for advertising and marketing purposes. Examples of branded merchandise include clothing, bags, pens, keychains, mugs, water bottles, lanyards, stickers, pins, and posters. "Branded merchandise" does not include items containing cannabis or any items that are considered food as defined by Health and Safety Code section 109935.

(b) Branded merchandise shall identify the licensee responsible for its content by displaying the licensee's license number in a manner that is permanently affixed to the merchandise, legible, and clearly visible from the outside of the merchandise.

(c) Branded merchandise shall not be designed in any manner that is attractive to children as specified in section 15040(a)(3).

NOTE: Authority cited: Section 26013, Business and Professions Code. Reference: Sections 26013 and 26152, Business and Professions Code.

§ 15041.2. Trade Samples.

(a) For the purposes of this division, "trade sample" means a limited amount of cannabis or cannabis products that has been designated by a licensee to be provided to the licensee's employees or other licensees for the purposes of targeted advertising and product education.

(b) Cannabis or cannabis products that have been designated as trade samples may be provided from one licensee to another licensee for the purpose of providing the recipient licensee with product information to aid in making purchasing decisions about new or existing cannabis or cannabis products.

(c) Mature plants shall not be designated as trade samples. Immature plants, seeds and propagated material shall only be designated or provided to licensees as trade samples by licensed nurseries.

NOTE: Authority cited: Sections 26013 and 26153.1, Business and Professions Code. Reference: Section 26153.1, Business and Professions Code.

§ 15041.3. Designating Trade Samples.

(a) Licensees shall designate cannabis and cannabis products as trade samples through the track and trace system.

(b) At the time of designation as a trade sample, cannabis or cannabis products must be in the possession of the licensee making the designation.

(c) Once cannabis or cannabis products have been designated as a trade sample, the designation cannot be changed, unless the designation is changed to medicinal donation pursuant to section 15411 by the licensee originally designating the cannabis or cannabis products as a trade sample.

(d) After laboratory testing, cannabis and cannabis products that have been designated as trade samples may be transferred to a licensee's employees or other licensees in accordance with section 15041.4.

NOTE: Authority cited: Sections 26013 and 26153.1, Business and Professions Code. Reference: Section 26153.1, Business and Professions Code.

§ 15041.4. Providing Trade Samples.

(a) Cannabis or cannabis products that have been designated as trade samples may be provided to any licensee except licensed cannabis event organizers, distributor transport only licensees, and testing laboratory licensees.

(b) The following licensees may designate and provide trade samples to their own employees and other licensees:

(1) Cultivators;

(2) Manufacturers;

(3) Distributors; and

(4) Microbusinesses authorized to engage in cultivation, manufacturing, or distribution.

(c) Notwithstanding subsection (b), licensed nurseries may only provide trade samples to licensed cultivators and may not provide trade samples to their own employees.

(d) The following licenses shall not designate or provide trade samples to other licensees:

(1) Retailers;

(2) Cannabis event organizers;

(3) Distributor transport only licensees; and

(4) Testing laboratories.

(e) Licensed retailers may designate and provide trade samples to their own employees for product education but shall not provide them to another licensee as specified in subsection (d).

(f) Cannabis and cannabis products designated as trade samples may not be provided:

(1) For any payment or consideration;

(2) Without adhering to sales and excise tax requirements, if any;

(3) To employees as compensation;

(4) To an unlicensed person, including retail customers; or

(5) For a cost.

(g) The transfer from one licensee to another of cannabis and cannabis products designated as a trade sample must be recorded in the track and trace system.

(h) A licensee may provide cannabis and cannabis products that have been received from another licensee as a trade sample to an employee for that employee's inspection or consumption.

(i) Cannabis and cannabis products provided to employees as trade samples must be properly recorded in the track and trace system. The transaction shall be recorded as a package adjustment when provided to the employee. The adjustment note must include the name or licensee-assigned employee number of the employee and the date and time the cannabis and cannabis products were provided to the employee.

(j) Cannabis and cannabis products provided to employees as trade samples shall not be sold, given away, or otherwise transferred by the employee to any person.

NOTE: Authority cited: Sections 26013 and 26153.1, Business and Professions Code. Reference: Section 26153.1, Business and Professions Code.

§ 15041.5. Requirements for Trade Samples.

(a) In addition to the requirements of section 15041.3(d), cannabis and cannabis products provided to another licensee as a trade sample must be packaged and labeled in accordance with the packaging and labeling requirements found in the Act and this division for cannabis and cannabis products sold at retail.

(b) Cannabis and cannabis products provided to another licensee as a trade sample must comply with all laboratory testing requirements applicable to cannabis and cannabis products sold at retail, except for immature plants, seeds, and propagated material.

(c) All trade samples must be labeled with the following: "TRADE SAMPLE. NOT FOR RESALE OR DONATION."

(d) After laboratory testing, cannabis and cannabis products designated as trade samples must remain in the packaging until provided to a licensee's employee for inspection or consumption and must not be opened, resealed, or repackaged in any way.

(e) Transportation of cannabis and cannabis products designated as trade samples must be conducted in accordance with the transportation requirements in the Act and this division. Any licensee authorized to engage in distribution activities may transport trade samples.

(f) Notwithstanding subsection (e), an employee of a licensee authorized to engage in transportation may transport cannabis and cannabis products designated as trade samples in a vehicle that is not registered to the licensee and shall not be required to comply with the requirements of section 15311(g). Employees transporting cannabis and cannabis products under this subsection shall not transport an amount of cannabis or cannabis products that exceeds the possession limits established in section 11357 of the Health and Safety Code.

(g) Licensees who receive immature plants, seeds, and propagated material as trade samples shall not sell, give away, or distribute cannabis derived from the cultivated trade sample.

NOTE: Authority cited: Sections 26013 and 26153.1, Business and Professions Code. Reference: Section 26153.1, Business and Professions Code.

§ 15041.6. Consumption of Trade Samples.

(a) All consumption of cannabis and cannabis products provided as a trade sample must comply with all laws regarding the consumption of cannabis and cannabis products.

(b) Cannabis and cannabis products provided to employees as trade samples shall not be consumed by employees who are engaging in the transportation of cannabis and cannabis products, delivery of cannabis and cannabis products, any activity that requires the operation of a motor vehicle, or any activity that requires the use of heavy machinery, solvents, or asphyxiants.

(c) Cannabis trade samples provided to a licensee or their employees that are not consumed must be destroyed in accordance with the requirements of the Act and this division.

NOTE: Authority cited: Sections 26013 and 26153.1, Business and Professions Code. Reference: Section 26153.1, Business and Professions Code.

§ 15041.7. Trade Sample Limits.

(a) A licensee is limited to designating the following aggregate amounts of cannabis and cannabis products as trade samples in a calendar month period:

(1) For cannabis in the form of dried flower, a total of two pounds.

(2) For manufactured and nonmanufactured cannabis products, a total of 900 individual units.

(3) For seeds, immature plants, and other propagated material, 18 seeds, 12 seedlings, and 8 cuttings or tissue cultures, per strain.

(b) Licensees authorized to provide trade samples may provide trade samples to multiple employees or recipient licensees.

(c) A licensee is limited to providing the following aggregate amounts of cannabis and cannabis products as trade samples to each recipient licensee in a calendar month period:

(1) For cannabis in the form of dried flower, five (5) grams per strain and no more than six (6) strains to each recipient licensee.

(2) For manufactured and nonmanufactured cannabis products, five (5) individual units, as packaged for retail sale, per cannabis product line and no more than six (6) individual cannabis product lines to each recipient licensee.

(3) For seeds, immature plants, and other propagated material, no more than six (6) strains to each recipient licensee.

(d) A licensee is limited to providing no more than one (1) individual cannabis and cannabis product line to each recipient employee in a calendar month period.

(e) The limits provided in subsection (c) apply to the transfer of cannabis trade samples from one licensee to each recipient licensee and do not limit the total amount of cannabis trade samples that a licensed distributor may transport.

NOTE: Authority cited: Sections 26013 and 26153.1, Business and Professions Code. Reference: Section 26153.1, Business and Professions Code.

ARTICLE 5. SECURITY MEASURES

§ 15042. Premises Access Requirements.

(a) For a premises that is not open to the public, the licensee shall establish and implement an identification and sign-in/sign-out procedure for all persons accessing the premises, including authorized individuals, suppliers, and visitors.

(b) Licensees shall ensure that only employees of the licensee and other authorized individuals access the licensed premises.

(c) For the purpose of this section, "authorized individuals" include outside vendors, contractors, or other individuals conducting business that requires access to the licensed premises.

(d) An individual who enters the licensed premises and is not employed by the licensee shall be escorted by an employee of the licensee at all times while within the licensed premises.

(e) A licensee shall maintain a record of all authorized individuals who are not employees of the licensee who enter the licensed premises. The record shall include the name of the individual, the company the individual works for, the reason the individual entered the licensed premises, the date, and the times the individual entered and exited the licensed premises. These records shall be made available to the Department immediately upon request.

(f) A licensee shall not receive consideration or compensation for permitting an individual to enter the licensed premises.

NOTE: Authority cited: Section 26013, Business and Professions Code. Reference: Sections 26070 and 26160, Business and Professions Code.

§ 15042.1. Security Plan for Licensed Manufacturers.

A licensed manufacturer shall develop and implement a written security plan. At a minimum, the security plan shall include a description of the security measures to:

(a) Prevent access to the manufacturing premises by unauthorized persons and protect the physical safety of employees. This includes, but is not limited to:

(1) Establishing physical barriers to secure perimeter access and all points of entry into a manufacturing premises (such as locking primary entrances with commercial-grade, non-residential door locks, providing fencing around the grounds and driveway, and securing any secondary entrances including windows, roofs, and ventilation systems);

(2) Installing a security alarm system to notify and record incident(s) where physical barriers have been breached;

(3) Establishing an identification and sign-in/sign-out procedure for authorized personnel, individuals, suppliers, and visitors;

(4) Maintaining the premises such that visibility and security monitoring of the premises is possible; and

(5) Establishing procedures for the investigation of suspicious activities.

(b) Deterring theft or loss of cannabis and cannabis products. This includes, but is not limited to:

(1) Establishing an inventory system to track cannabis and cannabis products and the personnel responsible for processing it throughout the manufacturing process;

(2) Limiting access of personnel within the premises to those areas necessary to complete job duties, and to those timeframes specifically scheduled for completion of job duties, including access by outside vendors, suppliers, contractors or other individuals conducting business with the licensee that requires access to the premises;

(3) Supervising tasks or processes with high potential for diversion, including the loading and unloading of cannabis and cannabis products from transportation vehicles; and

(4) Providing areas in which personnel may store and access personal items that are separate from the manufacturing areas.

(c) Securing and backing up electronic records in a manner that prevents unauthorized access and ensures that the integrity of the records is maintained.

NOTE: Authority cited: Sections 26013 and 26130, Business and Professions Code. Reference: Sections 26011.5 and

26051.5, Business and Professions Code.

§ 15043. Licensee Employee Badge Requirement.

All agents, officers, or other persons acting for or employed by a licensee conducting retail sales or participating in a temporary cannabis event shall display a laminated or plastic-coated identification badge issued by the licensee at all times while engaging in commercial cannabis activity. The identification badge shall, at a minimum, include the licensee's "doing business as" name and license number, the employee's first name, an employee number exclusively assigned to that employee for identification purposes, and a color photograph of the employee that clearly shows the full front of the employee's face and that is at least 1 inch in width and 1.5 inches in height.

NOTE: Authority cited: Section 26013, Business and Professions Code. Reference: Section 26070, Business and Professions Code.

§ 15044. Video Surveillance System.

(a) Each licensed premises shall have a digital video surveillance system with a minimum camera resolution of 1280 x 720 pixels on the licensed premises. This requirement does not apply to a licensed premises authorized exclusively for cultivation activities or the cultivation area of a licensed microbusiness premises.

(b) The video surveillance system shall at all times be able to effectively and clearly record images of the area under surveillance.

(c) Each camera shall be permanently mounted and in a fixed location. Each camera shall be placed in a location that allows the camera to clearly record activity occurring within 20 feet of all points of entry and exit on the licensed premises, and allows for the clear and certain identification of any person and activities in all areas required to be filmed under subsection (d).

(d) Areas that shall be recorded on the video surveillance system include the following:

> (1) Areas where cannabis or cannabis products are weighed, packed, stored, loaded, and unloaded for transportation, prepared, or moved within the licensed premises;
>
> (2) Limited-access areas;
>
> (3) Security rooms;
>
> (4) Areas storing a surveillance-system storage device with at least one camera recording the access points to the secured surveillance recording area; and
>
> (5) Entrances and exits to the licensed premises, which shall be recorded from both indoor and outdoor vantage points.

(e) Licensed retailers and licensed microbusinesses authorized to engage in retail sales shall also record point-of-sale areas and areas where cannabis goods are displayed for sale on the video surveillance system. At each point-of-sale location, camera placement must allow for the recording of the facial features of any person purchasing or selling cannabis goods, or any person in the retail area, with sufficient clarity to determine identity.

(f) Cameras shall record continuously 24 hours per day and at a minimum of 15 frames per second (FPS).

(g) The physical media or storage device on which surveillance recordings are stored shall be secured in a manner to protect the recording from tampering or theft.

(h) Surveillance recordings shall be kept for a minimum of 90 calendar days.

(i) Surveillance recordings are subject to inspection by the Department and shall be kept in a manner that allows the Department to view and obtain copies of the recordings at the licensed premises immediately upon request. The licensee shall also send or otherwise provide copies of the recordings to the Department upon request within the time specified by the Department.

(j) Recorded images shall clearly and accurately display the time and date. Time is to be measured in accordance with the standards issued by the United States National Institute of Standards and Technology. The displayed date and time shall not cover the view of recorded images in a manner that prevents the ready identification of any person or activity in the captured image.

(k) The video surveillance system shall be equipped with a failure notification system that provides notification to the licensee of any interruption or failure of the video surveillance system or video surveillance-system storage device.

(l) If multiple licensed premises are contained within the same building or on the same parcel of land, a single video surveillance system covering the entire building or parcel of land may be used by all of the licensees if all licensees have immediate access to the surveillance recordings to produce them pursuant to subsection (i). All licensees sharing a video surveillance system shall be held responsible and subject to discipline for any violations of the video surveillance requirements.

(m) Notwithstanding subsection (a), a licensed distributor transport only licensee engaged in self-distribution whose premises is on the same parcel of land as their licensed cultivation premises shall not be required to comply with the provisions of this section.

NOTE: Authority cited: Section 26013, Business and Professions Code. Reference: Section 26070, Business and Professions Code.

§ 15045. Security Personnel.

(a) A licensed retailer or licensed microbusiness authorized to engage in retail sales shall hire or contract for security personnel who are at least 21 years of age to provide onsite security services for the licensed retail premises during the hours of operation. All security personnel hired or contracted for by the licensee shall be licensed by the Bureau of Security and Investigative Services and shall comply with chapters 11.4 and 11.5 of division 3 of the Business and Professions Code.

(b) Notwithstanding subsection (a), a licensed non-storefront retailer or licensed microbusiness who is not engaged in storefront retail sale is not required to hire or contract for security personnel.

(c) If multiple licensed premises are contained within the same building, security personnel may be shared by all of the licensees to cover the entire building. However, all licensees shall be held responsible and subject to discipline for any violations of the security personnel requirements.

NOTE: Authority cited: Section 26013, Business and Professions Code. Reference: Section 26070, Business and Professions Code.

§ 15046. Locks.

A licensee shall ensure that all limited-access areas can be securely locked using commercial-grade, nonresidential door locks. A licensee shall also use commercial-grade, nonresidential door locks on all points of entry and exit to the licensed premises. This requirement does not apply to a licensed premises authorized exclusively for cultivation activities or the cultivation area of a licensed microbusiness premises.

NOTE: Authority cited: Section 26013, Business and Professions Code. Reference: Section 26070, Business and Professions Code.

§ 15047. Alarm System.

(a) A licensee shall maintain an alarm system as defined in Business and Professions Code section 7590.1(c) at the licensed premises. This requirement does not apply to a licensed premises authorized exclusively for cultivation activities or the cultivation area of a licensed microbusiness premises.

(b) A licensee shall ensure a licensed alarm company operator or one or more of its registered alarm agents installs, maintains, monitors, and responds to the alarm system.

(c) Upon request, a licensee shall make available to the Department all information related to the alarm system, monitoring, and alarm activity.

(d) If multiple licensed premises are contained within the same building or parcel of land, a single alarm system covering the entire building or parcel of land may be used by all of the licensees if all licensees have access to and are able to provide the information under subsection (c). All licensees shall be held responsible and subject to discipline for any violations of the alarm system requirements.

NOTE: Authority cited: Section 26013, Business and Professions Code. Reference: Section 26070, Business and Professions Code.

§ 15047.1. Definitions.

(a) "Plant tag" means the tag that is labeled with a UID number and provided by the Department or the Department's designee for attaching to a cannabis plant.

(b) "Package tag" means the RFID-enabled tag that is labeled with a UID number and provided by the Department or the Department's designee for attaching to batches of cannabis or cannabis products.

NOTE: Authority cited: Section 26013, Business and Professions Code. Reference: Sections 26067, 26070, 26160 and 26161, Business and Professions Code.

§ 15047.2. General Requirements.

(a) A licensee shall create and maintain an account within the track and trace system prior to engaging in any commercial cannabis activity.

(b) All commercial cannabis activity shall be accurately recorded in the track and trace system.

(c) A licensee is responsible for the accuracy and completeness of all data and information entered into the track and trace system. The licensee is responsible for all actions taken by the designated account manager or other account users while performing track and trace activities.

(d) A person shall not intentionally misrepresent or falsify information entered into the track and trace system.

NOTE: Authority cited: Section 26013, Business and Professions Code. Reference: Sections 26067, 26070, 26160 and 26161, Business and Professions Code.

ARTICLE 6. TRACK AND TRACE REQUIREMENTS

§ 15048. Training and Credentialing.

(a) Each applicant or licensee shall identify an owner of the commercial cannabis business as the track and trace system account manager. A licensee may change the account manager by submitting a written request to the Department.

(b) No later than 10 calendar days after license issuance, the designated account manager shall:

(1) Complete new user system training provided by the Department.

(2) Email support@metrc.com from the designated account manager's email address to request access to the track and trace system.

(3) Complete the credentialing process to establish a login.

(c) The account manager and each user shall utilize a unique login, consisting of a username and password. The account manager and each user shall only access the track and trace system under their assigned login. No account manager or user shall share their login, username, or password, with any other individual for any reason.

NOTE: Authority cited: Section 26013, Business and Professions Code. Reference: Sections 26067, 26070, 26160 and 26161, Business and Professions Code.

§ 15048.1. Responsibilities of the Designated Account Manager.

(a) A licensee and their designated account manager(s) shall:

(1) Designate track and trace system users, as needed, and require the system users to be trained in the proper and lawful use of the track and trace system before the users are permitted to access the track and trace system;

(2) Maintain an accurate and complete list of all of the licensee's track and trace system users, including full names and usernames, and update the list immediately when changes occur;

(3) Remove a user from the licensee's track and trace system account when that individual is no longer authorized to represent the licensee;

(4) Correct any data entry errors within three (3) calendar days of discovery of the error;

(5) Tag and enter all inventory in the track and trace system as required by section 15049;

(6) Monitor all system notifications and resolve all issues identified. The notification shall not be dismissed by an account manager before resolution of the issue(s) identified in the notification;

(7) Notify the Department of any loss of access to the track and trace system that exceeds 72 hours; and

(8) Reconcile the inventory of cannabis and cannabis products on the licensed premises with the track and trace system database at least once every thirty (30) calendar days.

NOTE: Authority cited: Section 26013, Business and Professions Code. Reference: Sections 26067, 26070 and 26160, Business and Professions Code.

§ 15048.2. General Tag Requirements.

(a) A licensee shall only use plant and package tags provided and distributed by the Department or the Department's designee.

(b) A licensee shall only use plant and package tags assigned in the track and trace system to that licensee and shall not transfer unused tags to any other licensee.

(c) A licensee shall maintain a sufficient supply of tags to support tagging in accordance with this chapter.

(d) Plant and package tags shall be discarded after they are no longer required for use.

NOTE: Authority cited: Section 26013, Business and Professions Code. Reference: Sections 26050.1, 26067, 26070, 26160 and 26161, Business and Professions Code.

§ 15048.3. Ordering Tags.

(a) For licensees conducting cultivation, manufacturing, distribution, or testing:

(1) A licensee's account manager shall place the initial order of plant or package tags within ten (10) calendar days of initial credentialing into the track and trace system and shall reorder plant or package tags as needed.

(2) The receipt of plant or package tags shall be recorded in the track and trace system within three (3) calendar days of receipt. If ordered plant or package tags are not received by the licensee, the licensee shall notify the Department.

(3) For cultivation licensees, if the Department approves a request for a license designation change pursuant to section 15023(f), the licensee is required to order, apply, and report applicable plant and package tags in accordance with this article.

NOTE: Authority cited: Section 26013, Business and Professions Code. Reference: Sections 26013, 26067, 26069 and 26160, Business and Professions Code.

§ 15048.4. Tagging of Cannabis Plants.

(a) Immature cannabis plants shall be tagged as follows:

(1) Each established lot of immature plants shall be assigned a plant tag. Each lot of immature plants under a single plant tag shall be uniform in strain or cultivar and contain no more than 100 individual immature plants at any one time. The lot plant tag shall be visible and within clear view of an individual standing next to the immature lot and kept free from dirt and debris. Each lot shall either:

(A) Have each immature plant in the lot labeled with the UID number and placed contiguous to one another to facilitate identification by the Department; or

(B) Be fully separated from other lots of immature or mature plants by a physical barrier. In such cases, each individual plant does not need to be labeled with the corresponding UID number.

(2) Immature plants transferred from a licensed nursery for retail sale shall be transferred in a package with a package tag. The receiving licensee shall remove the licensed nursery's package tag and assign a plant or package tag, as applicable, belonging to the receiving licensee within three (3) calendar days of receiving the immature plants.

(3) A plant tag shall be applied to each individual plant in accordance with subsection (b) at the time the plant is moved to the designated canopy area or begins flowering.

(b) Mature cannabis plants shall be tagged as follows:

(1) Each mature plant shall be tagged with a plant tag. A plant tag shall be attached to the main stem at the base of each plant, placed in a position so it is visible and within clear view of an individual standing next to the mature plant, and kept free from dirt and debris.

(2) Licensees are prohibited from removing the plant tag from the mature plant to which it was attached and assigned until the plant is harvested, destroyed, or disposed of.

NOTE: Authority cited: Section 26013, Business and Professions Code. Reference: Sections 26013, 26067 and 26069, Business and Professions Code.

§ 15048.5. Use of Harvest Batch Name and Package Tags.

(a) Harvested plants that are hanging, drying, or curing shall be assigned a unique harvest batch name, which shall be recorded in the track and trace system and placed within clear view of an individual standing next to the batch. The assigned harvest batch name shall match what is in the track and trace system and the harvest batch name next to the batch shall be the same.

(b) Each harvest batch and manufactured cannabis batch shall be assigned a package tag and recorded in the track and trace system. For each harvest batch, the package tag shall be assigned and recorded in the track and trace system no later than the time at which any part of that harvest batch has finished undergoing any applicable drying, curing, grading, and trimming.

(c) For all cannabis and cannabis products held in a container, the package tag shall be affixed to the container holding the cannabis or cannabis products. If cannabis or cannabis products are held in multiple containers, the package tag shall be affixed to one of the containers and the other containers shall be labeled with the applicable UID number. Each unit within the container shall be labeled with the applicable UID number. All containers with the same UID number shall be placed contiguous to one another to facilitate identification by the Department.

NOTE: Authority cited: Section 26013, Business and Professions Code. Reference: Sections 26067, 26070, 26160 and 26161, Business and Professions Code.

§ 15049. Track and Trace Reporting.

(a) All cannabis and cannabis products on the licensed premises shall be assigned a plant or package tag, as applicable, except for harvested plants that are being dried, cured, graded, or trimmed, as specified in this division, and recorded in the track and trace system.

(b) Each of the following activities shall be recorded in the track and trace system within 24 hours of occurrence:

(1) Receipt of cannabis or cannabis products.

(2) Rejection of transferred cannabis or cannabis products.

(3) Manufacturing of cannabis or cannabis products.

(4) Use of cannabis or cannabis product for internal quality control testing or product research and development.

(5) Destruction or disposal of cannabis or cannabis products.

(6) Packaging or repackaging of cannabis or cannabis products, except that cultivation licensees shall comply with section 15049.1(b)(5).

(7) Laboratory testing, including testing results.

(8) Sale or donation of cannabis or cannabis products.

(c) The following information shall be recorded in the track and trace system for each activity entered pursuant to subsection (b):

(1) The type of cannabis or cannabis products.

(2) The weight, volume, or count of the cannabis or cannabis products.

(3) The date of activity.

(4) The UID assigned to the cannabis or cannabis products.

(5) The brand name of the cannabis goods.

(6) If cannabis or cannabis products are being destroyed or disposed of, the licensee shall record the following information in the notes section:

(A) The name of the employee performing the destruction or disposal;

(B) The reason for destruction or disposal; and

(C) The method of disposal.

(d) If a package adjustment is used to adjust the quantity of cannabis or cannabis products in the track and trace system, the licensee shall include a description explaining the reason for adjustment.

(e) If a licensee rejects a partial shipment of cannabis goods pursuant to section 15052.1(b), the licensee shall record the partial rejection in the track and trace system.

NOTE: Authority cited: Section 26013, Business and Professions Code. Reference: Sections 26013, 26067 and 26169, Business and Professions Code.

§ 15049.1. Additional Requirements for Recording Cultivation Activities.

(a) The licensee shall record the following cultivation activities in the track and trace system within three (3) calendar days of occurrence:

(1) Planting of an immature lot;

(2) Moving immature plants to a designated canopy area, flowering of an individual plant, or application of a plant tag to an immature plant, in accordance with section 15048.4;

(3) Destruction or disposal of an immature or mature plant; and

(4) Harvesting of a mature plant, or portion thereof.

(b) The following information shall be reported in the track and trace system for each harvest batch:

(1) The wet weight of each harvest batch, which shall be obtained by the licensee immediately after harvest;

(2) The weight of cannabis waste associated with each harvested plant;

(3) The unique name of the harvest batch; and

(4) The initiating date of the harvest. For purposes of this section, the "initiating date" of the harvest is the month, day, and year the first mature cannabis plants in the harvest batch were cut, picked, or removed from the soil or other growing media.

(c) After the entire harvest batch has been dried, trimmed, cured, and packaged, the licensee shall indicate in the track and trace system that the harvest is finished.

NOTE: Authority cited: Section 26013, Business and Professions Code. Reference: Sections 26013, 26067 and 26069, Business and Professions Code.

§ 15049.2. Recording Transfers of Cannabis and Cannabis Products.

(a) A licensee shall prepare a shipping manifest through the track and trace system prior to transferring cannabis and cannabis products off of a licensed premises. The following information shall be recorded on the shipping manifest by the licensee initiating the transfer:

(1) The name, license number, and premises address of the originating licensee;

(2) The name and license number of the distributor transporting the cannabis and cannabis products;

(3) The name, license number, and premises address of the licensee receiving the cannabis or cannabis products into inventory or storage;

(4) The UID numbers for all items being transferred;

(5) The item name, item category and weight or count of cannabis or cannabis products associated with each package tag;

(6) The estimated date and time of departure from the licensed premises;

(7) The estimated date and time of arrival at each licensed premises; and

(8) The driver's license number of the personnel transporting the cannabis and cannabis products, and the make, model, and license plate number of the vehicle used for transport.

(b) The distributor who transports the cannabis or cannabis product shall record the following additional information on the shipping manifest:

(1) The actual date and time of departure from the licensed premises; and

(2) The actual date and time of arrival at each licensed premises.

(c) Upon pick-up or receipt of cannabis and cannabis products for transport, storage, or inventory, a licensee shall ensure that the cannabis or cannabis products received are as described in the shipping manifest. The licensee shall record acceptance or receipt, and acknowledgment of the cannabis or cannabis products in the track and trace system.

(d) If there are any discrepancies between type or quantity of cannabis or cannabis products specified in the shipping manifest and the type or quantity received by the licensee, the licensee shall reject the shipment.

NOTE: Authority cited: Section 26013, Business and Professions Code. Reference: Sections 26067, 26070, 26160 and 26161, Business and Professions Code.

§ 15049.3. Track and Trace Requirements for Delivery.

(a) A licensed retailer conducting delivery of cannabis goods shall create a delivery inventory ledger in the track and trace system and record the information required under subsections (b)(1) through (7) prior to the delivery employee leaving the licensed retail premises for each delivery trip. A delivery trip begins when the delivery employee leaves the licensed retail premises to conduct delivery of cannabis goods.

(b) The delivery inventory ledger shall include the following information:

(1) The delivery inventory ledger number generated by the track and trace system and assigned to the specific delivery trip.

(2) The name and license number of the licensed retailer.

(3) The delivery employee's name, employee ID, and driver's license number.

(4) The delivery vehicle's make, model, and license plate number.

(5) The item name and category of each cannabis good to be carried on the delivery trip, the UID(s) assigned to those cannabis goods, and the number of units associated with each UID on the delivery inventory ledger.

(6) The UID(s) of any cannabis goods ordered by customers and processed by the licensed retailer prior to the delivery employee leaving the licensed retail premises.

(7) The date and time the delivery employee begins the delivery trip.

(c) For each delivery of cannabis goods, the following information shall be recorded within the track and trace system by the end of the calendar day on which the delivery was completed:

(1) The date and time the delivery was completed. A delivery is completed at the time the cannabis goods are physically provided to the customer.

(2) Whether the customer is an adult-use customer, medicinal cannabis patient, or patient's primary caregiver.

(3) The UID and quantity of each cannabis good delivered.

(4) The purchase price of each cannabis good delivered.

(5) The county in which the delivery was completed.

(d) If a delivery employee returns to the licensed retail premises to obtain additional inventory of cannabis goods for delivery to be conducted on the same day and by the same delivery employee, the licensed retailer may continue the existing delivery trip in the track and trace system. If the licensed retailer chooses to continue the existing delivery trip, the additional inventory is considered part of the existing delivery trip and a new delivery inventory ledger is not required. The licensed retailer shall record the following information within the track and trace system under the existing delivery inventory ledger number for any additional cannabis goods to be carried on the same delivery trip:

(1) The item name and category of each additional cannabis good to be carried on the delivery trip, the UID(s) assigned to those cannabis goods, and the number of units associated with each UID on the delivery inventory ledger.

(2) The date and time the delivery employee leaves the licensed retail premises to continue the delivery trip.

(e)(1) The end date and time of the delivery trip shall be:

(A) Except as provided in subsection (e)(1)(B), the date and time the delivery employee returned to the licensed retail premises after conducting all deliveries that are part of the same delivery trip.

(B) If the delivery employee does not carry any unsold cannabis goods and does not return to the licensed retail premises on the same day after delivering all cannabis goods carried in the vehicle on the delivery trip, the date and time at which the delivery employee completed the last delivery of cannabis goods on the delivery trip.

(2) No later than the end of the calendar day on which the delivery trip occurred:

(A) If a delivery employee still carries unsold cannabis goods at the end of a delivery trip, the delivery employee must return to the licensed premises, remove the unsold cannabis goods from the delivery inventory ledger, and return the unsold cannabis goods to the licensed retailer's inventory within the track and trace system.

(B) The licensed retailer shall record the end date and time of the delivery trip in the track and trace system.

(f) Notwithstanding subsections (a) through (e), prior to April 1, 2023, licensed retailers may comply with this section by maintaining delivery inventory ledgers in accordance with this subsection.

(1) Delivery inventory ledgers may be maintained by licensed retailers in hard copy or electronically and shall include the item name, category, UID, and unit quantity of each cannabis good carried on a delivery trip.

(2) All cannabis goods prepared for an order that was received and processed by the licensed retailer prior to the delivery employee's departure from the licensed retail premises must be clearly identified on the delivery inventory ledger.

(3) During a delivery trip, the delivery inventory ledger must be updated after each completed delivery to reflect the remaining inventory carried by the delivery employee.

(4) All sales of cannabis goods conducted by delivery must be entered into the track and trace system within 24 hours of the date and time the delivery trip was completed, as defined in subsection (e)(1).

NOTE: Authority cited: Section 26013, Business and Professions Code. Reference: Sections 26067, 26068 and 26090, Business and Professions Code.

§ 15050. Loss of Access.

(a) If at any point a licensee loses access to the track and trace system for any reason, the licensee shall prepare and maintain comprehensive records detailing all commercial cannabis activities that were conducted during the loss of access.

(b) The licensee shall not initiate transport for, receive, or deliver any cannabis or cannabis products until such time as access is restored.

(c) Once access has been restored, the licensee shall:

(1) Within three calendar days, enter all commercial cannabis activity that occurred during the loss of access into the track and trace system.

(2) Document the cause for loss of access, and the dates and times for when access to the track and trace system was lost and when it was restored.

NOTE: Authority cited: Section 26013, Business and Professions Code. Reference: Sections 26067, 26070 and 26160, Business and Professions Code.

§ 15051. Track and Trace System Reconciliation.

(a) The license shall review the information recorded in the track and trace system at least once every 30 calendar days to ensure its accuracy, including, at a minimum:

(1) Reconciling on-hand inventory of cannabis and cannabis product with the records in the track and trace system; and

(2) Reviewing the licensee's authorized users and removing any users who are no longer authorized to enter information into the track and trace system.

(b) If a licensee finds a discrepancy between the on-hand inventory and the track and trace system, the licensee shall conduct an audit and notify the Department in writing if the discrepancy is significant as defined in section 15034.

NOTE: Authority cited: Section 26013, Business and Professions Code. Reference: Sections 26067, 26070 and 26160, Business and Professions Code.

ARTICLE 7. ACCEPTANCE OR REJECTION OF SHIPMENTS

§ 15052. Returns.

(a) Cannabis and cannabis products may be returned from the licensee currently in possession to the originating licensee for any lawful business purpose in accordance with the following:

(1) Cannabis and cannabis products shall not be reprocessed, rebranded, relabeled, physically repackaged, have their expiration dates amended, or be modified in any way without prior approval from the Department. To receive approval to modify the cannabis or cannabis products, licensees shall submit a corrective action plan that meets the requirements specified in section 17305.

(2) After being returned, cannabis and cannabis products shall be transported to a licensed distributor to undergo laboratory testing in accordance with chapters 2 and 6 and quality assurance review pursuant to sections 15307 and 15307.1 prior to being transported to a licensed retailer.

(b) Returns of cannabis and cannabis products shall be recorded in the track and trace system on a return manifest that shall contain the reason for the return.

(c) Cannabis and cannabis products shall not be transported pursuant to a return unless the licensee returning the cannabis and cannabis products and the licensee receiving the cannabis and cannabis products have both consented to the return. The licensee who receives the return shall physically accept the return and enter it into the track and trace system.

NOTE: Authority cited: Section 26013, Business and Professions Code. Reference: Sections 26067, 26070 and 26160, Business and Professions Code.

§ 15052.1. Acceptance or Rejection of Shipments.

(a) Licensees shall accept or reject, in whole, shipments of cannabis or cannabis products.

(b) Notwithstanding subsection (a), partial shipments of cannabis or cannabis products shall be rejected in the following circumstances:

(1) If a licensee receives a shipment containing cannabis or cannabis products that differ from those listed on the sales invoice or receipt, the licensee shall reject the portion of the shipment that is not accurately reflected on the sales invoice or receipt.

(2) If a licensee receives a shipment containing any cannabis or cannabis products that were damaged during transportation, the licensee shall reject that portion of the shipment that was damaged.

(3) If a licensee receives a shipment containing cannabis or cannabis products that is non-compliant with labeling requirements or exceeds its provided expiration date, the licensee shall reject the portion of the shipment that is non-compliant with labeling requirements or expired.

(c) The licensee rejecting a shipment of cannabis or cannabis products, whether in whole or in part, shall record in the track and trace system and indicate on any relevant manifest, invoice, or sales receipt the specific reason for rejection.

(d) The licensee who originated a rejected shipment shall physically accept the rejected shipment and record it in the track and trace system.

NOTE: Authority cited: Section 26013, Business and Professions Code. Reference: Sections 26013, 26067, 26070 and 26161, Business and Professions Code.

§ 15053. Returns Between Licensees. [Repealed]

Note: Authority cited: Section 26013, Business and Professions Code. Reference: Sections 26013 and 26070, Business and Professions Code.

§ 15054. Destruction of Cannabis Goods Prior to Disposal. [Repealed]

Note: Authority cited: Section 26013, Business and Professions Code. Reference: Sections 26013 and 26070, Business and Professions Code.

Chapter 2. Distributors

§ 15300. Distribution Activities.

A licensed distributor shall distribute only cannabis and cannabis products, cannabis accessories, and licensees' branded merchandise or promotional materials.

NOTE: Authority cited: Section 26013, Business and Professions Code. Reference: Section 26070, Business and Professions Code.

§ 15301. Storage Services.

(a) A licensed distributor may provide storage services, including storage-only services that are unrelated to the quality assurance and laboratory testing processes, to a licensed cultivator, licensed manufacturer, licensed microbusiness, licensed retailer, or another licensed distributor.

(b) A licensed distributor may provide storage services to other licensees for cannabis goods packaged as they will be sold at retail, cannabis accessories, and licensees' branded merchandise or promotional materials only.

(c) A licensed distributor shall ensure that each batch of cannabis goods that are stored for another licensee are stored in accordance with section 15302.

(d) Notwithstanding subsection (b), a licensed distributor shall not store live plants, except for seeds, on the licensed premises.

(e) Items held for storage-only services by a licensed distributor pursuant to subsection (b) may be distributed from the premises of the licensed distributor providing the storage-only services.

NOTE: Authority cited: Section 26013, Business and Professions Code. Reference: Sections 26070 and 26110, Business and Professions Code.

§ 15302. Storage of Batches for Testing.

(a) A licensed distributor shall ensure that all batches of cannabis or cannabis products are stored separately and distinctly from other batches of cannabis or cannabis products on the licensed distributor's premises.

(b) In addition to any tag or label required by section 15048.5, a licensed distributor shall ensure a label with the following information is physically attached to each container of each batch:

(1) The name, license number, and licensed premises address of the licensee who provided the batch;

(2) The date of entry into the licensed distributor's storage area;

(3) The unique identifiers and batch number, if any, associated with the batch;

(4) A description of the cannabis or cannabis products with enough detail to easily identify the batch;

(5) The weight of or quantity of units in the batch; and

(6) The best-by, sell-by, or expiration date of the batch, if any.

NOTE: Authority cited: Section 26013, Business and Professions Code. Reference: Sections 26110 and 26120, Business and Professions Code.

§ 15303. Packaging, Labeling, and Rolling.

(a) A licensed distributor may package, repackage, label, and relabel cannabis in the form of dried flower, including pre-rolls, for retail sale. All packages of cannabis in the form of dried flower, including pre-rolls, shall comply with the requirements in chapter 11.

(b) A licensed distributor shall not process cannabis, but may roll pre-rolls that consist exclusively of any combination of flower, shake, leaf, or kief. Pre-rolls shall be rolled, packaged, and labeled prior to regulatory compliance testing.

(c) Licensed distributors may label and relabel a package containing manufactured cannabis or cannabis products with the amount of cannabinoids and terpenoids based on regulatory compliance testing results.

NOTE: Authority cited: Section 26013, Business and Professions Code. Reference: Sections 26013 and 26120, Business and Professions Code.

§ 15303.1. Net Weight of Dried Flower.

For purposes of this division, the net weight on any packaged cannabis good containing dried flower only shall not be considered inaccurate if the actual weight is within plus or minus 3% of the labeled weight.

NOTE: Authority cited: Section 26013, Business and Professions Code. Reference: Sections 26013, 26120 and 26152, Business and Professions Code.

§ 15304. Testing Arrangements.

After taking physical possession of a batch of cannabis or cannabis products, the licensed distributor shall contact a licensed testing laboratory and arrange for a laboratory employee to come to the licensed distributor's licensed premises to select a representative sample for laboratory testing.

NOTE: Authority cited: Section 26013, Business and Professions Code. Reference: Sections 26104 and 26110, Business and Professions Code.

§ 15305. Testing Sample.

(a) The licensed distributor shall ensure that the batch size from which the sample is taken meets the requirements of this division.

(b) A licensed distributor or an employee of the licensed distributor shall be physically present to observe the laboratory employee obtain the sample of cannabis or cannabis products for testing and shall ensure that the increments are taken from throughout the batch.

(c) The sampling shall be video-recorded with the batch number stated verbally or in writing on the video at the beginning of the video and a visible time and date indication on the video recording footage. The video recordings shall be maintained for 90 calendar days by the licensed distributor.

(d) After the sample has been selected, both the licensed distributor and the laboratory employee shall sign and date the chain of custody form pursuant to section 15706, attesting to the sample selection having occurred.

(e) A licensed distributor shall not assist the laboratory employee nor touch the cannabis or cannabis products or the sampling equipment while the laboratory employee is obtaining the sample.

NOTE: Authority cited: Section 26013, Business and Professions Code. Reference: Sections 26104 and 26110, Business and Professions Code.

§ 15305.1. Re-sampling.

Once a sample has been obtained from a batch for regulatory compliance testing, a licensed distributor may not arrange for or allow another licensed testing laboratory to sample or re- sample the same batch for regulatory compliance testing, unless all of the requirements of section 15705 subsection (g) of this division are met.

NOTE: Authority cited: Section 26013, Business and Professions Code. Reference: Sections 26100, 26104 and 26110, Business and Professions Code.

§ 15306. Regulatory Compliance Testing Results.

(a) A licensed distributor shall store a batch on its licensed premises until it either:

(1) Passes regulatory compliance testing as described in subsection (b); or

(2) If it fails regulatory compliance testing as described in subsection (d), a corrective action plan for remediation has been approved by the Department pursuant to section 17305.

(b) A batch passes regulatory compliance testing when the sample meets specifications in chapter 6. Once a batch has passed regulatory compliance testing, the batch shall not be repackaged into a new production batch in the track and trace system nor shall it be assigned a new batch number.

(c) When a batch passes regulatory compliance testing, the cannabis or cannabis products may be transported to one or more licensed retailers, licensed distributors, or licensed microbusinesses authorized to conduct distribution or retail. A copy of the certificate of analysis for regulatory compliance testing shall be provided to all licensed distributors receiving the batch for purposes of quality assurance review under section 15307. A copy of the certificate of analysis shall also be provided to the licensee who produced the batch. The copies of the certificate of analysis required by this subsection may be provided electronically.

(d) A batch fails regulatory compliance testing when the sample does not meet specifications in chapter 6.

(e) If a failed batch has been approved for remediation by the Department pursuant to section 17305, a licensed distributor may transport or arrange for the transportation of the batch to the licensed manufacturer or microbusiness authorized to engage in manufacturing that has received approval from the Department to conduct the remediation. Once a batch has been approved for remediation by the Department, the licensed distributor shall transport the batch to the approved manufacturer or microbusiness within 30 calendar days of the approval.

(f) A licensed distributor shall destroy a batch that failed regulatory compliance testing and cannot be remediated pursuant to section 17305 within 60 days of failure of the batch or 30 days of receiving notification from the Department that the batch may not be remediated. The distributor shall notify the licensed manufacturer or cultivator who produced the batch of the destruction and the reasons for it. Evidence of destruction including, but not limited to, video or photos of the destruction shall be provided to the Department upon request.

NOTE: Authority cited: Section 26013, Business and Professions Code. Reference: Sections 26070, 26100, 26104 and 26110, Business and Professions Code.

§ 15307. Quality-Assurance Review.

When a licensed distributor receives a certificate of analysis for regulatory compliance testing from the licensed testing laboratory or upon transfer from another licensed distributor stating that the batch meets specifications required by law, the licensed distributor shall ensure the following before transporting the cannabis goods to one or more licensed retailers or licensed microbusinesses authorized to engage in retail sales:

(a) The certificate of analysis for regulatory compliance testing that the licensed distributor received from the licensed testing laboratory or another licensed distributor is the certificate of analysis that corresponds to the batch;

(b) The date on the certificate of analysis for the regulatory compliance testing is less than 12 months old;

(c) The label on the cannabis goods is consistent with the certificate of analysis for regulatory compliance testing regarding cannabinoid content required to be listed by law as follows:

(1) If the cannabis goods are labeled with the content for cannabinoids, terpenoids, Total THC, and/or Total CBD prior to receiving the certificate of analysis for regulatory compliance testing, the licensed distributor shall ensure that the labeled amounts are accurate in accordance with section 15307.1, and

(2) If the cannabis goods are not labeled with the content for cannabinoids, terpenoids, Total THC, and/or Total CBD prior to receiving the certificate of analysis for regulatory compliance testing, the licensed distributor shall label the cannabis goods with the amounts listed on the certificate of analysis pursuant to section 15303;

(d) The packaging and labeling of the cannabis goods complies with Business and Professions Code section 26120 and this division, except cannabis goods are not required to be labeled or otherwise identified as medicinal products prior to retail sale unless the cannabis goods must be labeled as such pursuant to this division;

(e) The cannabis goods have not exceeded their expiration or sell-by date if one is provided;

(f) The weight or count of the batch comports with that in the track and trace system. A licensed distributor shall use scales as required by this division; and

(g) All events prior to receipt of the certificate of analysis for regulatory compliance testing have been entered into the track and trace system.

(h) If the licensed distributor determines that the cannabis goods are not fit for sale because they do not meet the requirements of this section, then the distributor may arrange for a corrective action plan to be submitted pursuant to section 17305 in accordance with the following:

(1) If the cannabis goods may be relabeled by the licensed distributor, another distributor, or microbusiness authorized to engage in distribution, then the distributor who will conduct the remediation shall submit a corrective action plan pursuant to section 17305. Transport to another licensed distributor or microbusiness authorized to engage in distribution shall not occur until the corrective action plan has been approved by the Department.

(2) If the cannabis goods may only be remediated by a licensed manufacturer or microbusiness authorized to engage in manufacturing because they must be repackaged or reprocessed, then the licensed distributor shall comply with the provisions of subsections (e) and (f) of section 15306.

NOTE: Authority cited: Section 26013, Business and Professions Code. Reference: Sections 26070, 26110 and 26120, Business and Professions Code.

§ 15307.1. Quality-Assurance Review for Labeling Cannabinoids and Terpenoids.

(a) For purposes of this division, any one cannabinoid, THC, Total THC, CBD and/or Total CBD claimed to be present on a label shall not be considered inaccurate if the difference in percentage on the certificate of analysis is plus or minus 10.0%.

(b) For purposes of this division, the terpenoid testing results on the label of any one terpenoid claimed to be present shall not be considered inaccurate if the difference in percentage on the certificate of analysis is plus or minus 10.0%.

(c) For purposes of this section, the difference in percent shall be calculated using the following equation:

Difference in percent = | (laboratory measurement--label claim) | / (label claim) x 100%

(d) For purposes of this section, Total THC and Total CBD shall have the same meaning as defined in chapter 6.

(e) Cannabis goods shall be labeled with accurate concentration limits in accordance with sections 17304 and 17407.

NOTE: Authority cited: Section 26013, Business and Professions Code. Reference: Sections 26100 and 26110, Business and Professions Code.

§ 15307.2. Licensed Distributor to Licensed Distributor Transfers.

(a) Cannabis goods that have undergone and passed regulatory compliance testing and have an accompanying certificate of analysis may be transferred to one or more licensed distributors.

(b) Cannabis goods that have not been transported to retail within 12 months of the date on the certificate of analysis must be destroyed or retested by the licensed distributor in possession of the cannabis goods. Retesting pursuant to this subsection shall only be conducted if the cannabis goods have not been modified in any way.

(c) If the licensed distributor, manufacturer, or microbusiness authorized to engage in manufacturing will be repackaging, relabeling, reformulating, or modifying the cannabis goods in any way, they shall submit a corrective action plan pursuant to section 17305 and receive approval from the Department before beginning modifications to the cannabis goods.

NOTE: Authority cited: Section 26013, Business and Professions Code. Reference: Sections 26070 and 26110, Business and Professions Code.

§ 15308. Insurance Requirements.

(a) A distributor licensee shall at all times carry and maintain commercial general liability insurance in the aggregate in an amount no less than $2,000,000 and in an amount no less than $1,000,000 for each loss.

(b) A distributor licensee shall maintain the insurance required in subsection (a) from an insurance company that is:

> (1) A non-admitted insurer that meets the requirements of Insurance Code section 1765.1 or 1765.2, and the insurance is placed pursuant to Insurance Code section 1763 and through a surplus line broker licensed under Insurance Code section 1765;
>
> (2) An insurer qualified to do business in California by the Secretary of State and authorized by the Insurance Commissioner to write the liability and property classes of insurance as defined by Insurance Code sections 102, 103, 107, 108, 114, and 120; or
>
> (3) A registered risk retention group compliant with the California Risk Retention Act of 1991. (See Insurance Code sections 125-140.)

(c) Admitted insurers and risk retention groups must show proof of capitalization in the amount of at least $10,000,000.

NOTE: Authority cited: Section 26013, Business and Professions Code. Reference: Sections 26051.5 and 26070, Business and Professions Code.

§ 15309. Inventory Accounting.

(a) A licensed distributor shall be able to account for all inventory and provide that information to the Department upon request.

(b) To account for inventory, a licensed distributor shall ensure all batches of cannabis or cannabis products are stored in accordance with section 15302 and shall be able to provide the Department with the status of the batch as follows:

> (1) The batch is being held in storage for another licensee;
>
> (2) The batch is awaiting sampling for regulatory compliance testing;
>
> (3) The batch has been sampled and is awaiting regulatory compliance testing results;
>
> (4) The batch has passed regulatory compliance testing;
>
> (5) The batch has failed regulatory compliance testing and is awaiting approval for remediation;
>
> (6) The batch has failed regulatory compliance testing and is awaiting destruction; and
>
> (7) The batch is being stored or held for any other lawful purpose under the Act or this division.

NOTE: Authority cited: Section 26013, Business and Professions Code. Reference: Sections 26070 and 26160, Business and Professions Code.

§ 15310. Records. [Repealed]

Note: Authority cited: Section 26013, Business and Professions Code. Reference: Section 26160, Business and Professions Code.

§ 15311. Requirements for the Transportation of Cannabis Products.

The following requirements apply when transporting cannabis and cannabis products between licensees or licensed premises:

(a) Transportation shall only be conducted by persons holding a distributor license under the Act, or employees of those persons. All vehicles and trailers used for transportation shall be owned or leased, in accordance with the Vehicle Code, by the licensee. The licensee is not required to be the sole owner or lessor of the vehicle or trailer and all owners and lessors may use the vehicle for non-commercial cannabis activity.

(b) Prior to transporting any cannabis and cannabis products, the licensed distributor shall have a completed sales invoice or receipt that meets the requirements of Business and Professions Code section 26161. The licensed distributor shall only transport cannabis and cannabis products listed on the sales invoice or receipt. The sales invoice or receipt may not be altered or changed once transport begins.

(c) A licensed distributor employee shall always carry a copy of the distributor's license and a copy of the QR Code certificate issued by the Department while engaging in the transportation of cannabis goods. The QR Code certificate shall comply with the requirements of section 15039, subsection (d).

(d) All vehicles transporting cannabis goods for hire shall be required to have a motor carrier permit issued to the licensed distributor pursuant to Chapter 2 (commencing with Section 34620) of Division 14.85 of the Vehicle Code.

(e) Transportation by means of aircraft, watercraft, drone, rail, human-powered vehicle, or unstaffed vehicle is prohibited.

(f) Cannabis and cannabis products shall only be transported inside of a vehicle or trailer and shall not be visible or identifiable from outside of the vehicle or trailer.

(g) Cannabis and cannabis products shall be transported in a fully enclosed, windowless, locked trailer or trunk that cannot be accessed from inside the vehicle, or in a secured area or compartment within the interior of the vehicle. A "secured area" is defined as an area where solid or locking metal partitions, cages, or high-strength shatterproof acrylic can be used to create a secure compartment in the fully enclosed vehicle. The secured area may be comprised on three sides of any part of the body of the vehicle, provided the parts of the vehicle used for the purposes of this section are shatterproof and are not made of glass.

(h) While left unattended, vehicles and trailers shall be locked and secured.

(i) A licensed distributor shall not leave a vehicle or trailer containing cannabis and cannabis products unattended in a residential area or parked overnight in a residential area.

(j) At a minimum, a licensed distributor shall have a vehicle alarm system on all transport vehicles and trailers. Motion detectors, pressure switches, duress, panic, and hold-up alarms may also be used.

(k) Packages or containers holding cannabis and cannabis products shall not be tampered with, or opened, during transport.

(l) A licensed distributor transporting cannabis and cannabis products shall only travel between licensees shipping or receiving cannabis and cannabis products and its own licensed premises when engaged in the transportation of cannabis and cannabis products. The licensed distributor may transport multiple shipments of cannabis and cannabis products at once in accordance with applicable laws. A licensed distributor shall not deviate from the travel requirements described in this section, except for necessary rest, fuel, or vehicle repair stops.

(m) Under no circumstances may non-cannabis goods, except for cannabis accessories and licensees' branded merchandise or promotional materials, be transported with cannabis and cannabis products.

(n) Vehicles and trailers transporting cannabis and cannabis products are subject to inspection by the Department at any licensed premises or during transport at any time.

(o) Notwithstanding subsections (e) through (g), if it is not operationally feasible to transport cannabis or cannabis products inside of a vehicle or trailer because the licensed premises that the cannabis or cannabis products will be transported from and the licensed premises that will be receiving the cannabis or cannabis products are located within the same building or on the same parcel of land, the cannabis or cannabis products may be transported by foot, hand truck, fork lift, or other similar means. A shipping manifest that complies with this division is required when transporting cannabis or cannabis products pursuant to this subsection.

(p) Notwithstanding subsection (e), transportation of cannabis and cannabis products may be conducted via waterway to licensees located on Catalina Island. The provisions of this section and other sections regarding vehicle requirements also apply to vessels used to transport cannabis and cannabis products via waterway pursuant to this section.

NOTE: Authority cited: Section 26013, Business and Professions Code. Reference: Section 26070, Business and Professions Code.

§ 15312. Required Transport Vehicle Information.

(a) Upon request, the licensed distributor shall provide the Department with a copy of the certificate of ownership or registration card issued by the California Department of Motor Vehicles, the year, make, model, license plate number, and Vehicle Identification Number in writing, and proof of insurance for any vehicle or trailer used to transport cannabis or cannabis products.

NOTE: Authority cited: Section 26013, Business and Professions Code. Reference: Section 26070, Business and Professions Code.

§ 15313. Transport Personnel Requirements.

(a) No person under the age of 21 years old shall be in a commercial vehicle or trailer transporting cannabis or cannabis products; and

(b) Only a licensee, an employee of the licensed distributor, or security personnel who meets the requirements of section 15045 shall be in a vehicle while transporting cannabis or cannabis products.

NOTE: Authority cited: Section 26013, Business and Professions Code. Reference: Section 26070, Business and Professions Code.

§ 15314. Shipping Manifest.

(a) Prior to transporting cannabis or cannabis products, a licensed distributor shall generate a shipping manifest through the track and trace system for the following activities:

(1) Regulatory compliance testing and sampling;

(2) Sale of cannabis or cannabis products to a licensee;

(3) Destruction or disposal of cannabis or cannabis products; and

(4) Any other activity, as required pursuant to this division, or by the Department.

(b) The licensed distributor shall transmit the shipping manifest to the Department and the licensee that will receive the cannabis or cannabis products prior to transporting the cannabis or cannabis products.

(c) The licensed distributor shall ensure and verify that the cannabis or cannabis products being taken into possession for transport at the originating licensed premises are as described and accurately reflected in the shipping manifest. For purposes of this section, the licensed distributor may verify that the cannabis or cannabis products are accurately reflected in the shipping manifest by confirming that the number of boxes of cannabis or cannabis products, type of cannabis or cannabis products, weight and/or units of cannabis or cannabis products matches the label on the boxes containing the cannabis or cannabis products.

(1) The licensed distributor shall not take into possession or transport:

(A) Any cannabis or cannabis products that are not on the shipping manifest; or

(B) Any cannabis or cannabis products that are less than or greater than the amount reflected on the shipping manifest.

(2) The licensed distributor is responsible for any discrepancies between the shipping manifest and the cannabis or cannabis products in its possession during transport, and subject to any enforcement or disciplinary action related to such discrepancy.

(3) A licensed distributor shall not void or change a shipping manifest after departing from the originating licensed premises.

(d) A shipping manifest shall accompany every transport of cannabis or cannabis products.

NOTE: Authority cited: Section 26013, Business and Professions Code. Reference: Sections 26067 and 26070, Business and Professions Code.

§ 15315. Distributor Transport Only License.

(a) A licensed distributor transport only licensee may transport cannabis or cannabis products between licensees; however, they shall not transport any cannabis or cannabis products except for immature cannabis plants, seeds, and trade samples to a licensed retailer or licensed microbusiness authorized to engage in retail sales.

(b) A complete application for a distributor transport only license shall include all the information required in an application for a distributor license.

(c) The licensing fee for a distributor transport only license will be based in part upon whether the licensee intends to transport only cannabis or cannabis products that the licensee has cultivated or manufactured (self-distribution), or whether the licensee intends to transport cannabis or cannabis products cultivated or manufactured by other licensees.

(d) A distributor transport only licensee shall comply with all of the requirements for a holder of a distributor license, except for those related to quality assurance and regulatory compliance testing.

(e) A distributor transport only licensee shall not hold title to any cannabis or cannabis products unless the licensee also holds a Department-issued cultivation, manufacturing, retailer, or microbusiness license.

(f) Holding a distributor transport only license shall not authorize a licensee to:

(1) Engage in the delivery of cannabis or cannabis products as defined in Business and Professions Code section 26001(o);

(2) Engage in the wholesale, destruction, packaging, labeling, or storing of cannabis or cannabis products; or

(3) Arrange for the regulatory compliance testing of cannabis or cannabis products by a testing laboratory.

(g) A distributor transport only licensee who is licensed to engage in self-distribution and whose licensed premises will be on the same property as their licensed cultivation or licensed manufacturing premises shall comply with the security provisions contained in chapter 1, article 5 that are applicable to their licensed cultivation or licensed manufacturing premises.

NOTE: Authority cited: Section 26013, Business and Professions Code. Reference: Sections 26012 and 26070, Business and Professions Code.

Chapter 3. Retailers

§ 15400. Access to Retailer Premises.

(a) Access to the licensed premises of a retailer with only an A-designation shall be limited to individuals who are at least 21 years of age.

(b) Access to the licensed premises of a retailer with only an M-designation shall be limited to individuals who are at least 18 years of age and have a valid physician's recommendation for medicinal cannabis, and individuals who are at least 21 years of age.

(c) Access to the licensed premises of a retailer with both an A- designation and an M- designation may include persons identified in subsections (a) and (b) of this section.

NOTE: Authority cited: Section 26013, Business and Professions Code. Reference: Sections 26070 and 26140, Business and Professions Code.

§ 15402. Customer Access to the Retail Area.

(a) Individuals shall be granted access to the retail area to purchase cannabis goods only after the retailer or an employee of the retailer has confirmed the individual's age and identity pursuant to section 15404.

(b) The licensed retailer or at least one employee shall be physically present in the retail area at all times when individuals who are not employees of the licensed retailer are in the retail area.

(c) All sales of cannabis goods must take place within the retail area of the retailer's licensed premises, except for cannabis goods sold through delivery, a drive-in or drive-through window as authorized by section 15025(e), or curbside delivery as provided in subsection (d).

(d) A licensed retailer or licensed microbusiness authorized to engage in storefront sales at their licensed premises may conduct sales through curbside delivery. Cannabis goods that have been purchased by a customer may be delivered to the customer in a vehicle parked immediately outside the licensed retail premises. Curbside delivery of cannabis goods must occur under video surveillance and meet the requirements of section 15044, subsection (e) for recording point-of-sale areas. Retail employees engaging in curbside delivery must verify each customer's age pursuant to subsection (a). Licensed retailers who are only authorized to engage in retail sales through delivery shall not conduct sales through curbside delivery.

NOTE: Authority cited: Section 26013, Business and Professions Code. Reference: Sections 26070 and 26140, Business and Professions Code.

§ 15403. Hours of Operation.

A licensed retailer shall sell and deliver cannabis goods only between the hours of 6:00 a.m. Pacific Time and 10:00 p.m. Pacific Time.

NOTE: Authority cited: Section 26013, Business and Professions Code. Reference: Section 26070, Business and Professions Code.

§ 15403.1. Requirements While Not Open for Business.

At any time the licensed premises is not open for retail sales, a licensed retailer shall ensure that:

(a) The licensed premises is securely locked with commercial-grade, nonresidential door locks as required in section 15046 of this division;

(b) The licensed premises is equipped with an active alarm system pursuant to section 15047 of this division, which shall be activated when the licensed retailer or its employees are not on the licensed premises; and

(c) Only employees of the licensee and other authorized individuals are allowed access to the licensed premises. For the purposes of this section, authorized individuals include individuals employed by the licensee as well as any outside vendors, contractors, or other individuals conducting business that requires access to the licensed premises.

NOTE: Authority cited: Section 26013, Business and Professions Code. Reference: Section 26070, Business and Professions Code.

§ 15404. Retail Customers.

(a) A licensed retailer shall only sell adult-use cannabis goods to individuals who are at least 21 years of age after confirming the customer's age and identity by inspecting a valid form of identification provided by the customer as required by subsection (c) of this section.

(b) A licensed retailer shall only sell medicinal cannabis goods to individuals who are at least 18 years of age and possesses a valid physician's recommendation after confirming the customer's age, identity, and physician's recommendation as required by subsection (c) of this section.

(c) Acceptable forms of identification include the following:

> (1) A document issued by a federal, state, county, or municipal government, or a political subdivision or agency thereof, including, but not limited to, a valid motor vehicle operator's license, that contains the name, date of birth, height, gender, and photo of the person;
>
> (2) A valid identification card issued to a member of the Armed Forces that includes the person's name, date of birth, and photo; or
>
> (3) A valid passport issued by the United States or by a foreign government.

NOTE: Authority cited: Section 26013, Business and Professions Code. Reference: Section 26140, Business and Professions Code.

§ 15405. Cannabis Goods Display.

(a) Cannabis goods for inspection and sale shall only be displayed in the retail area.

(b) Cannabis and cannabis products may be removed from their packaging and placed in containers to allow for customer inspection. The containers shall not be readily accessible to customers without assistance of retailer personnel. A container must be provided to the customer by the licensed retailer or its employees, who shall remain with the customer at all times that the container is being inspected by the customer.

(c) Cannabis and cannabis products removed from their packaging for display shall not be sold or consumed when the cannabis goods are no longer used for display.

NOTE: Authority cited: Section 26013, Business and Professions Code. Reference: Section 26070, Business and Professions Code.

§ 15406. Cannabis Goods for Sale.

A licensed retailer shall not make any cannabis goods available for sale or delivery to a customer unless:

(a) The cannabis goods were received by the licensed retailer from a licensed distributor or licensed microbusiness authorized to engage in distribution;

(b) The licensed retailer has verified that the cannabis goods have not exceeded their best-by, sell-by, or expiration date if one is provided;

(c) In the case of manufactured cannabis products, the product complies with all requirements of Business and Professions Code section 26130 and this division;

(d) The cannabis goods have undergone regulatory compliance testing as required by the Act and chapter 6;

(e) The batch number, if any, is labeled on the package of cannabis goods and matches the batch number on the corresponding certificate of analysis for regulatory compliance testing;

(f) The packaging and labeling of the cannabis goods complies with Business and Professions Code section 26120 and this division; and

(g) The cannabis goods comply with all applicable requirements found in the Act and the division.

NOTE: Authority cited: Section 26013, Business and Professions Code. Reference: Sections 26070 and 26120, Business and Professions Code.

§ 15407. Sale of Non-Cannabis Goods.

(a) In addition to cannabis goods, a licensed retailer may sell only cannabis accessories and the branded merchandise of any licensee. Licensed retailers may provide customers with promotional materials.

(b) Notwithstanding subsection (a), a licensed retailer or licensed microbusiness authorized for retail sales who operates a consumption area on the licensed premises in accordance with Business and Professions Code section 26200(g) may also sell prepackaged, non-cannabis-infused, non-alcoholic food and beverages if the applicable local jurisdiction allows such sales.

(c) Nothing in this section shall be interpreted to prevent consumers from bringing or receiving non-cannabis-infused, non-alcoholic food and beverages from a restaurant or food delivery service for consumption in the designated consumption area on the licensed premises, if the applicable local jurisdiction allows such activities.

NOTE: Authority cited: Section 26013, Business and Professions Code. Reference: Sections 26070, 26151 and 26152, Business and Professions Code.

§ 15408. Sale of Live Plants and Seeds.

(a) A licensed retailer shall only sell live, immature cannabis plants and cannabis seeds if all of the following requirements are met:

(1) The plant is not flowering and is shorter and narrower than 18 inches; and

(2) The plant or seed originated from a licensed nursery that holds a valid license from the Department or a licensed microbusiness authorized to engage in cultivation.

(b) A licensed retailer shall not apply or use any pesticide, on live plants. A licensed retailer shall not cause any pesticide to be applied or used on live plants.

NOTE: Authority cited: Section 26013, Business and Professions Code. Reference: Sections 26070 and 26100, Business and Professions Code.

§ 15409. Daily Limits.

(a) A licensed retailer shall not sell more than the following amounts to a single adult-use cannabis customer in a single day:

(1) 28.5 grams of non-concentrated cannabis.

(2) 8 grams of cannabis concentrate as defined in Business and Professions Code section 26001, including cannabis concentrate contained in cannabis products.

(3) 6 immature cannabis plants.

(b) A licensed retailer shall not sell more than the following amounts to a single medicinal cannabis patient, or to a patient's primary caregiver purchasing medicinal cannabis on behalf of the patient, in a single day:

(1) 8 ounces of medicinal cannabis in the form of dried mature flowers or the plant conversion as provided in Health and Safety Code section 11362.77.

(2) 12 immature cannabis plants.

(c) Notwithstanding subsection (b) of this section, if a medicinal cannabis patient's valid physician's recommendation contains a different amount than the limits listed in this section, the medicinal cannabis patient may purchase an amount of medicinal cannabis consistent with the patient's needs as recommended by a physician and documented in the physician's recommendation.

(d) The limits provided in subsection (a) and subsection (b) of this section shall not be combined to allow a customer to purchase cannabis goods in excess of any of the limits provided in this section.

(e) For the purposes of this section, a licensed retailer shall be responsible for determining that the amount of cannabis concentrates found in manufactured cannabis products sold to customers comply with the requirements of this section.

NOTE: Authority cited: Section 26013, Business and Professions Code. Reference: Section 26012, Business and Professions Code; and Sections 11362.1 and 11362.77, Health and Safety Code.

§ 15410. Customer Return of Cannabis Goods.

(a) For the purposes of this section, "customer return" means a customer's return of cannabis goods that were purchased from a licensed retailer, back to the licensed retailer from whom the cannabis goods were purchased.

(b) A licensed retailer may accept customer returns of cannabis goods that were previously sold to a customer.

(c) A licensed retailer shall not resell cannabis goods that have been returned.

(d) A licensed retailer shall treat any cannabis goods abandoned on the licensed retailer premises as a customer return.

(e) Defective manufactured cannabis products returned by customers to a licensed retailer may be destroyed or returned to the licensed distributor from whom the cannabis goods were obtained.

NOTE: Authority cited: Section 26013, Business and Professions Code. Reference: Sections 26011.5, 26012 and 26070, Business and Professions Code.

§ 15411. Requirements for Providing Free Cannabis Goods to Medicinal Consumers.

(a) A licensed retailer shall not provide free cannabis goods to any person. A licensed retailer shall not allow individuals who are not employed by the licensed retailer to provide free cannabis goods to any person on the licensed premises.

(b) Notwithstanding subsection (a), in order to provide access to medicinal cannabis patients who have difficulty accessing medicinal cannabis goods, a licensee who holds an M-Retailer license, an M-Retailer Non-storefront license, or an M-Microbusiness license that is authorized for retail sales may provide free medicinal cannabis goods if the following criteria are met:

(1) Free cannabis goods are provided only to a medicinal cannabis patient or primary caregiver who possesses a valid physician's recommendation for medicinal cannabis or cannabis products or a valid identification card issued under Health and Safety Code section 11362.71.

(A) Before providing free cannabis goods to a medicinal cannabis patient who does not possess a valid identification card issued under Health and Safety code section 11362.7, the licensed retailer shall do the following:

(i) Verify with the Medical Board of California, the Osteopathic Medical Board of California, or the California Board of Podiatric Medicine that the attending physician providing the patient's medicinal cannabis recommendation has a license in good standing to practice medicine or osteopathy in the State of California;

(ii) Keep a copy of the patient's or primary caregiver's driver's license or other government-issued identification; and

(iii) Prepare and retain written certification that the licensed retailer verified the physician's recommendation as required by this section that includes the date and time of the verification, the name of the employee who conducted the verification, the name of the licensing board(s) contacted, the method by which the licensing board was contacted, and the name of the person at the licensing board who provided the verification if it was conducted orally, or a copy of the verification if it was provided in writing.

(B) After initially verifying a physician's recommendation for a specific medicinal cannabis patient as required by this section, a licensed retailer shall also verify the physician's recommendation at least annually, for the time period that the physician's recommendation is valid.

(C) A licensee shall not provide free cannabis goods to a medicinal cannabis patient or the patient's primary caregiver if the physician's recommendation has expired.

(2) Prior to being provided to the patient or the patient's primary caregiver, the cannabis goods have been

properly designated for donation and recorded in the track and trace system.

(3) Except as provided under Revenue and Taxation Code section 34012.1, the donated cannabis goods shall comply with all statutory and regulatory requirements that apply to cannabis goods for sale, including those for cultivating, manufacturing, distributing, processing, storing, regulatory compliance testing, packaging, labeling, transporting, and delivering.

(4) The cannabis goods provided to a medicinal cannabis patient or the patient's primary caregiver pursuant to this section shall be applied toward the daily purchase limit for a medicinal cannabis customer contained in section 15409 and the possession limits contained in Health and Safety Code section 11362.77.

(5) If cannabis goods are donated by a licensed retailer, then the sales invoice or receipt for the cannabis goods shall indicate that the cannabis goods were donated.

(6) The provision of free cannabis goods shall be recorded in the track and trace system and the licensed retailer's inventory records. The inventory records shall also include either the number of the medicinal cannabis patient's identification card issued under Health and Safety Code section 11362.7 or a copy of a valid physician's recommendation and the written certification that the recommendation was verified as required by this section.

(c) In addition to the provision of free cannabis goods in subsection (b), a licensed retailer may donate cannabis goods and the use of equipment in compliance with any compassionate use, equity, or other similar program administered by a local jurisdiction. The licensee shall ensure that all cannabis goods provided pursuant to this subsection comply with subsections (b)(4), (b)(5), and (b)(6).

(d) A licensed retailer may contract with an individual or organization to coordinate the provision of free cannabis goods on the licensee's retail premises. All cannabis goods provided through an individual or organization pursuant to this subsection shall comply with the requirements of this section. The licensed retailer may be disciplined for violations of the Act that are committed by an individual or organization with whom the licensee has contracted.

(e) A licensed retailer authorized to engage in retail sales only through delivery shall provide free cannabis goods only by delivery. Free cannabis goods provided through delivery shall comply with the requirements of this section.

NOTE: Authority cited: Section 26013, Business and Professions Code. Reference: Sections 26013, 26153 and 26160, Business and Professions Code.

§ 15412. Prohibition on Packaging and Labeling by a Retailer.

(a) A licensed retailer shall not accept, possess, or sell cannabis goods that are not packaged as they will be sold at final sale, in compliance with this division.

(b) A licensed retailer shall not package or label cannabis goods.

(c) Notwithstanding subsection (b) of this section, a licensed retailer may place a barcode or similar sticker on the packaging of cannabis goods to be used in inventory tracking. A barcode or similar sticker placed on the packaging of a cannabis goods shall not obscure any labels required by the Act or this division.

NOTE: Authority cited: Section 26013, Business and Professions Code. Reference: Section 26120, Business and Professions Code.

§ 15413. Cannabis Goods Packaging and Exit Packaging.

(a) All cannabis goods sold by a licensed retailer shall be in compliance with the packaging requirements in chapter 11.

(b) A package containing cannabis goods shall be tamper-evident and child-resistant. If the package contains multiple servings, the package must also be resealable.

(c) All cannabis goods purchased by a customer shall not leave the licensed retailer's premises unless the goods are placed in an opaque exit package.

(d) Immature plants and seeds sold by a licensed retailer are not required to be placed in resealable, tamper-evident, child-resistant packaging.

NOTE: Authority cited: Section 26013, Business and Professions Code. Reference: Sections 26070.1 and 26120, Business and Professions Code.

§ 15414. Non-Storefront Retailer.

(a) A non-storefront retailer licensee shall be authorized to conduct retail sales exclusively by delivery as defined in Business and Professions Code section 26001(o).

(b) A complete application for a non-storefront retailer license shall include all the information required in an application for a retailer license.

(c) A non-storefront retailer licensee shall comply with all the requirements applicable to retailer licensees, except for those provisions related to public access to the licensed premises and the retail area.

(d) The licensed premises of a non-storefront retailer licensee shall be closed to the public.

NOTE: Authority cited: Section 26013, Business and Professions Code. Reference: Sections 26012 and 26070, Business and Professions Code.

§ 15415. Delivery Employees.

(a) All deliveries of cannabis goods shall be performed by a delivery employee who is directly employed by a licensed retailer.

(b) Each delivery employee of a licensed retailer shall be at least 21 years of age.

(c) All deliveries of cannabis goods shall be made in person. A delivery of cannabis goods shall not be made through the use of an unstaffed vehicle.

(d) Deliveries of cannabis goods shall be received by customers only during the hours of operation established by section 15403. Delivery employees shall return to the licensed premises after making their last delivery of the day if they have any unsold cannabis goods to return to the premises.

(e) During the process of delivery, the licensed retailer's delivery employee may not engage in any activities except for cannabis goods delivery and necessary rest, fuel, or vehicle repair stops.

(f) A delivery employee of a licensed retailer shall, during deliveries, carry a copy of the retailer's current license, a copy of the QR Code certificate issued by the Department, which complies with section 15039, subsection (d), the employee's government-issued identification, and an identification badge provided by the employer pursuant to section 15043. A delivery employee shall provide a copy of the retail license, a copy of the QR Code certificate, and their employee identification badge to a delivery customer upon request.

(g) Prior to providing cannabis goods to a delivery customer, a delivery employee shall confirm the identity and age of the delivery customer as required by section 15404 and ensure that all cannabis goods sold comply with requirements of section 15413.

(h) A licensed retailer shall maintain an accurate list of the retailer's delivery employees and shall provide the list to the Department upon request.

NOTE: Authority cited: Section 26013, Business and Professions Code. Reference: Sections 26070 and 26090, Business and Professions Code.

§ 15415.1. Deliveries Facilitated by Technology Platforms.

(a) A licensed retailer or licensed microbusiness shall not sell or otherwise transfer any cannabis goods to a customer through the use of an unlicensed third party, intermediary business, broker, or any other business or entity.

(b) Notwithstanding subsection (a) of this section, a licensed retailer or licensed microbusiness may contract with a service that provides a technology platform to facilitate the sale and delivery of cannabis goods, in accordance with all of the following:

(1) The licensed retailer or licensed microbusiness does not allow for delivery of cannabis goods by the technology platform service provider.

(2) The licensed retailer or licensed microbusiness does not share in the profits of the sale of cannabis goods with the technology platform service provider, or otherwise provide for a percentage or portion of the cannabis goods sales to the technology platform service provider.

(3) The licensed retailer or licensed microbusiness shall not advertise or market cannabis goods in conjunction with the technology platform service provider, outside of the technology platform, and shall ensure that the technology platform service provider does not use the licensed retailer's or licensed microbusiness's license number or legal business name on any advertisement or marketing that primarily promotes the services of the technology platform.

(4) The licensed retailer or licensed microbusiness shall ensure the following information is provided to customers:

(A) Any cannabis goods advertised or offered for sale on or through the technology platform shall disclose, at a minimum, the licensed retailer's or licensed microbusiness's legal business name and license number.

(B) Customers placing an order for cannabis goods through the technology platform shall be able to easily identify the licensed retailer or licensed microbusiness that each cannabis good is being ordered or purchased from. This information shall be available to the customer prior to the customer placing an order or purchasing the cannabis goods.

(5) All required sales invoices and receipts, including any receipts provided to the customer, shall disclose, at a minimum, the licensed retailer's or licensed microbusiness's legal business name and license number.

(6) All other delivery, marketing, and advertising requirements under this division are complied with.

NOTE: Authority cited: Section 26013, Business and Professions Code. Reference: Sections 26001, 26070, 26090, 26151 and 26152, Business and Professions Code.

§ 15416. Delivery to a Physical Address.

(a) A delivery employee may only deliver cannabis goods to a physical address in California.

(b) A delivery employee shall not leave the State of California while possessing cannabis goods.

(c) A delivery employee shall not deliver cannabis goods to an address located on publicly owned land or any address on land or in a building leased by a public agency. This prohibition applies to land held in trust by the United States for a tribe or an individual tribal member unless the delivery is authorized by and consistent with applicable tribal law.

(d) A delivery employee may deliver to any jurisdiction within the State of California provided that such delivery is conducted in compliance with all delivery provisions of this division.

(e) A delivery employee shall not deliver cannabis goods to a school providing instruction in kindergarten or any grades 1 through 12, day care center, or youth center.

NOTE: Authority cited: Section 26013, Business and Professions Code. Reference: Sections 26070 and 26090, Business and Professions Code.

§ 15417. Delivery Vehicle Requirements.

(a) A licensed retailer's delivery employee, carrying cannabis goods for delivery, shall only travel in an enclosed motor vehicle. Any vehicle used in the delivery of cannabis goods shall be operated by a delivery employee of the licensee. A vehicle used in the delivery of cannabis goods shall not have any marking or other indications on the exterior of the vehicle that may indicate that the delivery employee is carrying cannabis goods for delivery. Only the licensee or an employee of the retailer licensee for whom delivery is being performed shall be in the delivery vehicle.

(b) While carrying cannabis goods for delivery, a licensed retailer's delivery employee shall ensure the cannabis goods are not visible to the public. Cannabis goods shall be stored in a secure, fully enclosed trunk that cannot be accessed from inside the vehicle, or in a secured area or compartment within the interior of the vehicle. A "secured area" is defined as an area where solid or locking metal partitions, cages, or high-strength shatterproof acrylic can be used to create a secure compartment in the fully enclosed vehicle. The secured area may be comprised on three sides by any part of the body of the vehicle, provided the parts of the vehicle used for the purposes of this section are shatterproof and are not made of glass.

(c) A licensed retailer's delivery employee shall not leave cannabis goods in an unattended motor vehicle unless the motor vehicle is locked and equipped with an active vehicle alarm system. Any cannabis goods left in an unattended vehicle must be stored in a container as required in subsection (b).

(d) A vehicle used for the delivery of cannabis goods shall be outfitted with a dedicated Global Positioning System (GPS) device for identifying the geographic location of the delivery vehicle and recording a history of all locations traveled to by the delivery employee while engaged in delivery. A dedicated GPS device must be owned by the licensee and used for delivery only. The device shall be either permanently or temporarily affixed to the delivery vehicle and shall remain active and inside of the delivery vehicle at all times during delivery. At all times, the licensed retailer shall be able to identify the geographic location of all delivery vehicles that are making deliveries for the licensed retailer and document the history of all locations traveled to by a delivery employee while engaged in delivery. A licensed retailer shall provide this information to the Department upon request. The history of all locations traveled to by a delivery employee while engaging in delivery shall be maintained by the licensee for a minimum of 90 days.

(e) Upon request, a licensed retailer shall provide the Department with information regarding any motor vehicle used for the delivery of cannabis goods, including the vehicle's make, model, color, Vehicle Identification Number, license plate number and Department of Motor Vehicles registration information.

(f) Any motor vehicle used by a licensed retailer to deliver cannabis goods is subject to inspection by the Department. Vehicles used to deliver cannabis goods may be stopped and inspected by the Department at any licensed premises or during delivery.

NOTE: Authority cited: Section 26013, Business and Professions Code. Reference: Sections 26070 and 26090,

Business and Professions Code.

§ 15418. Cannabis Goods Carried During Delivery.

(a) A licensed retailer's delivery employee shall not carry cannabis goods in the delivery vehicle with a value in excess of $10,000 at any time.

(b) For the purposes of this section, the value of cannabis goods shall be determined using the current retail price of all cannabis goods carried by, or within the delivery vehicle of, the licensed retailer's delivery employee.

(c) A delivery employee may only carry cannabis goods, cannabis accessories, branded merchandise of any licensee, or promotional materials in the delivery vehicle and may only perform deliveries for one licensed retailer at a time. A delivery employee must depart and return to the same licensed premises before taking possession of any cannabis goods from another licensee to perform deliveries.

(d) Before leaving the licensed premises, the licensed retailer's delivery employee must have a delivery inventory ledger of all cannabis goods provided to the licensed retailer's delivery employee. The contents of the delivery inventory ledger must comply with the requirements of section 15049.3. During the delivery trip, as defined in section 15049.3, the delivery employee shall maintain the delivery inventory ledger in hard copy or electronically, the latter of which may be an electronic copy maintained in the track and trace system. The delivery inventory ledger must be updated after each completed delivery to reflect the remaining inventory carried by the delivery employee. The delivery inventory ledger must otherwise be updated in accordance with the requirements of section 15049.3, and then entered into the track and trace system no later than the end of the calendar day on which the delivery trip occurred.

(e) The licensed retailer's delivery employee shall maintain a log that includes all stops from the time the licensed retailer's delivery employee leaves the licensed premises to the time that the licensed retailer's delivery employee returns to the licensed premises, and the reason for each stop. The log shall be turned in to the licensed retailer when the licensed retailer's delivery employee returns to the licensed premises. The licensed retailer must maintain the log as a commercial cannabis activity record as required by this division. The log may be maintained electronically.

(f) Prior to arrival at any delivery location, the licensed retailer must have received a delivery request from the customer and provided the delivery request receipt to the licensed retailer's delivery employee electronically or in hard copy. The delivery request receipt provided to the licensed retailer's delivery employee shall contain all of the information required in section 15420, except for the date and time the delivery was made, and the signature of the customer.

(g) Immediately upon request by the Department or any law enforcement officer, the licensed retailer's delivery employee shall provide:

> (1) The delivery inventory ledgers from the time the licensed retailer's delivery employee left the licensed premises up to the time of the request;
>
> (2) All delivery request receipts for cannabis goods carried by the delivery employee, in the delivery vehicle, or any deliveries that have already been made to customers; and
>
> (3) The log of all stops from the time the licensed retailer's delivery employee left the licensed premises up to the time of the request.

(h) If a licensed retailer's delivery employee does not have any delivery requests to be performed for a 30-minute period, the licensed retailer's delivery employee shall not make any additional deliveries and shall return to the licensed premises. Required meal breaks shall not count toward the 30-minute period.

(i) Upon returning to the licensed premises, all undelivered cannabis goods shall be returned to the licensed retailer's inventory and recorded within the track and trace system in accordance with section 15049.3.

NOTE: Authority cited: Section 26013, Business and Professions Code. Reference: Sections 26067, 26068, 26070, 26090 and 26160, Business and Professions Code.

§ 15419. Cannabis Consumption During Delivery.

A licensed retailer's delivery employees shall not consume cannabis or cannabis products while delivering cannabis goods to customers.

NOTE: Authority cited: Section 26013, Business and Professions Code. Reference: Sections 26070 and 26090, Business and Professions Code.

§ 15420. Delivery Request Receipt.

A licensed retailer shall prepare a hard copy or electronic delivery request receipt for each delivery of cannabis goods.

(a) The delivery request receipt shall contain the following:

(1) The legal business name and license number of the licensed retailer;

(2) The first name and employee number of the licensed retailer's delivery employee who delivered the order;

(3) The first name and employee number of the licensed retailer's employee who prepared the order for delivery;

(4) The first name of the customer and a licensed retailer-assigned customer number for the person who requested the delivery;

(5) The date and time the delivery request was made;

(6) The delivery address;

(7) A detailed description of all cannabis goods requested for delivery. The description shall include the weight, volume, or any other accurate measure of the amount of all cannabis goods requested;

(8) The total amount paid for the delivery, including any taxes or fees, the cost of the cannabis goods, and any other charges related to the delivery; and

(9) Upon delivery, the date and time the delivery was made, and the handwritten or electronic signature of the customer who received the delivery.

(b) At the time of the delivery, the delivery employee of the retailer shall provide the customer who placed the order with a hard or electronic copy of the delivery request receipt. The delivery employee shall retain a hard or electronic copy of the signed delivery request receipt for the licensed retailer's records.

(c) For the purposes of this section, an employee number is a distinct number assigned by a licensed retailer to an employee that would allow the licensed retailer to identify the employee in documents or records using the employee number rather than the employee's full name. A licensed retailer shall be able to identify the employee associated with each employee number upon request from the Department.

(d) For the purposes of this section, a customer number is a distinct number assigned by a licensed retailer to a customer that would allow the licensed retailer to identify the customer in documents or records using the customer number rather than the customer's full name. A licensed retailer shall be able to identify the customer associated with each customer number upon request from the Department.

NOTE: Authority cited: Section 26013, Business and Professions Code. Reference: Sections 26070, 26090 and 26160, Business and Professions Code.

§ 15421. Delivery Route.

While making deliveries of cannabis goods, a licensed retailer's delivery employee shall only travel from the retailer's licensed premises to the delivery address; from one delivery address to another delivery address; or from a delivery address back to the retailer's licensed premises. A delivery employee of a licensed retailer shall not deviate from the delivery path described in this section, except for necessary rest, fuel, or vehicle repair stops, or because road conditions make continued use of the route unsafe, impossible, or impracticable.

NOTE: Authority cited: Section 26013, Business and Professions Code. Reference: Sections 26070 and 26090, Business and Professions Code.

§ 15422. Receiving Shipments of Inventory.

(a) A licensed retailer shall receive a shipment of cannabis goods only from a licensed distributor or licensed microbusiness authorized to engage in distribution.

(b) A licensed retailer shall accept shipments of cannabis goods only between the hours of 6:00 a.m. Pacific Time and 10:00 p.m. Pacific Time.

(c) During business hours, shipments of cannabis goods shall not enter the licensed premises through an entrance or exit that is available for use by the public.

(d) A licensed retailer whose licensed premises only has one entryway may be exempt from the requirements of subsection (c) of this section if the licensed retailer obtains authorization from the local jurisdiction explicitly authorizing this activity. The licensed retailer shall be required to provide this authorization to the Department upon request. For this section to apply, the licensed premises must physically have only one entryway and cannot have any other entryways.

NOTE: Authority cited: Section 26013, Business and Professions Code. Reference: Sections 26012 and 26070, Business and Professions Code.

§ 15423. Inventory Documentation.

A licensed retailer shall maintain an accurate record of its inventory. A licensed retailer shall provide the Department with the record of inventory immediately upon request. A licensed retailer shall keep a record of the following information for all cannabis goods the licensed retailer has in its inventory:

(a) A description of each item such that the cannabis goods can easily be identified;

(b) An accurate measurement of the quantity of the item;

(c) The date and time the cannabis goods were received by the licensed retailer;

(d) The sell-by or expiration date provided on the package of cannabis goods, if any;

(e) The name and license number of the licensed distributor or licensed microbusiness that transported the cannabis goods to the licensed retailer; and

(f) The price the licensed retailer paid for the cannabis goods, including taxes, delivery costs, and any other costs.

NOTE: Authority cited: Section 26013, Business and Professions Code. Reference: Section 26160, Business and Professions Code.

§ 15424. Inventory Reconciliation.

(a) A licensed retailer shall be able to account for all of its inventory.

(b) In conducting an inventory reconciliation, a licensed retailer shall verify that the licensed retailer's physical inventory is consistent with the licensed retailer's records pertaining to inventory.

(c) The result of inventory reconciliation shall be retained in the licensed retailer's records and shall be made available to the Department upon request.

(d) If a licensed retailer identifies any evidence of theft, diversion, or loss, the licensed retailer shall notify the Department and law enforcement pursuant to section 15036 of this division.

(e) If a significant discrepancy as defined in section 15034 of this division is discovered between a licensed retailer's physical inventory and the licensed retailer's inventory records, the licensed retailer shall notify the Department and law enforcement pursuant to section 15036 of this division.

NOTE: Authority cited: Section 26013, Business and Professions Code. Reference: Section 26160, Business and Professions Code.

§ 15426. Records. [Repealed]

Note: Authority cited: Section 26013, Business and Professions Code. Reference: Section 26160, Business and Professions Code.

§ 15427. Retailer Premises-to-Retailer Premises Transfer.

(a) A licensee who holds multiple retail licenses may arrange for the transfer of cannabis goods from one licensed retail premises to another licensed retail premises if both retail licenses are held by the same sole proprietor or business entity.

(b) Cannabis goods transferred to a licensed retail premises under subsection (a) may be sold by the licensed retailer receiving the cannabis goods only if the cannabis goods comply with all requirements found in the Act and this division.

(c) The transportation of cannabis goods under this section must comply with all requirements found within the Act and this division.

(d) Any movement of cannabis goods under this section shall be properly entered into the track and trace system.

NOTE: Authority cited: Section 26013, Business and Professions Code. Reference: Section 26070, Business and Professions Code.

Chapter 4. Microbusiness

§ 15500. Microbusiness.

(a) In order to hold a microbusiness license, a licensee must engage in at least three (3) of the following commercial cannabis activities: cultivation, manufacturing, distribution, and retail sale. License types created by the Department in regulation shall not be considered qualifying commercial cannabis activities for purposes of obtaining a microbusiness license, except for the Type N manufacturing license and the distributor transport only license.

(b) An applicant for a microbusiness license shall indicate on the application for licensure all commercial cannabis activities in which the applicant intends to engage.

(c) All cultivation, manufacturing, distribution, and retail activities performed by a licensee under a microbusiness license shall occur on the same licensed premises.

(d) A holder of a microbusiness license engaged in cultivation shall comply with all the rules and requirements applicable to the cultivation license type suitable for the cultivation activities of the licensee.

(e) A holder of a microbusiness license engaged in manufacturing shall comply with all the rules and requirements applicable to a Manufacturer 1 license in this division.

(f) A holder of a microbusiness license engaged in distribution shall comply with all the rules and requirements applicable to a distributor license in this division.

(g) A holder of a microbusiness license engaged in retail sale shall comply with all the rules and requirements applicable to a retailer license, or a non-storefront retailer license if retail sales are conducted by delivery only, in this division.

(h) A holder of a microbusiness license may only engage in the commercial cannabis activity requested in the license application and approved by the Department at the time the license is issued. If the holder of a microbusiness license wants to engage in an additional commercial cannabis activity after the license is issued, the licensee shall submit a request for a modification of the licensed premises pursuant to section 15027.

(i) A holder of a microbusiness license shall comply with all the security rules and requirements applicable to the corresponding license type suitable for the activities of the licensee.

(j) Areas of the licensed premises for manufacturing, cultivation, and distribution shall be separated from the retail areas by a wall and all doors between the areas shall remain closed when not in use.

(k) A suspension or revocation of a microbusiness licensee shall affect all commercial cannabis activities allowed pursuant to that license.

NOTE: Authority cited: Section 26013, Business and Professions Code. Reference: Sections 26012, 26050, 26051.5 and 26070, Business and Professions Code.

§ 15501. Microbusiness Applications Including Cultivation Activities. [Repealed]

Note: Authority cited: Section 26013, Business and Professions Code. Reference: Sections 26012, 26050, 26051.5 and 26070, Business and Professions Code.

§ 15502. Cultivation Plan Requirements. [Repealed]

Note: Authority cited: Section 26013, Business and Professions Code. Reference: Sections 26050, 26051.5 and 26070, Business and Professions Code.

§ 15503. Supplemental Water Source Information. [Repealed]

Note: Authority cited: Section 26013, Business and Professions Code. Reference: Sections 26050, 26051.5 and 26070, Business and Professions Code; and Section 13149, Water Code.

§ 15504. License Issuance in an Impacted Watershed. [Repealed]

Note: Authority cited: Section 26013, Business and Professions Code. Reference: Sections 26011.5, 26055 and 26070, Business and Professions Code.

§ 15505. Cultivation Records for Licensees Engaging in Cultivation Activities. [Repealed]

Note: Authority cited: Section 26013, Business and Professions Code. Reference: Sections 26069, 26160 and 26161, Business and Professions Code.

§ 15506. Microbusiness Applications Including Manufacturing Activities. [Repealed]

Note: Authority cited: Section 26013, Business and Professions Code. Reference: Sections 26012, 26050, 26051.5, 26055 and 26070, Business and Professions Code.

§ 15506.1. Microbusiness Failed Manufactured Cannabis Product Batches. [Repealed]

Note: Authority cited: Section 26013, Business and Professions Code. Reference: Sections 26012, 26050 and 26070, Business and Professions Code.

§ 15507. Microbusiness Records for Licensees Engaging in Manufacturing Activities. [Repealed]

Note: Authority cited: Section 26013, Business and Professions Code. Reference: Section 26160, Business and Professions Code.

Chapter 5. Cannabis Events

§ 15600. Cannabis Event Organizer License.

(a) To obtain a temporary cannabis event license, the event organizer must first apply for and obtain a cannabis event organizer license.

(b) A cannabis event organizer licensed under this section shall comply with chapter 1 except for sections 15006, 15007, 15010, 15019, 15025, 15027, 15034, 15038, 15042, 15044, and 15046-15052.1.

(c) A cannabis event organizer licensee is not authorized or licensed to cultivate, distribute, manufacture, or retail cannabis or cannabis products without first obtaining the appropriate licenses or authorizations to engage in such commercial cannabis activities.

NOTE: Authority cited: Section 26013, Business and Professions Code. Reference: Sections 26012 and 26200, Business and Professions Code.

§ 15601. Temporary Cannabis Event Requirements.

(a) A temporary cannabis event license authorizes a licensed cannabis event organizer to hold a temporary cannabis event where the onsite sale and consumption of cannabis goods is authorized at the location indicated on the license during the dates indicated on the license.

(b) Violations of the requirements applicable to temporary cannabis events may result in disciplinary action against the cannabis event organizer license or any other licenses held by a licensee participating in the temporary cannabis event and responsible for a violation under this division or the Act.

(c) A temporary cannabis event license shall only be issued for a single day or up to 4 consecutive days. No temporary cannabis event license will be issued for more than 4 days.

(d) An application for a temporary cannabis event license shall be submitted to the Department no less than 60 calendar days before the first day of the temporary cannabis event.

(e) A temporary cannabis event may only be held at a county fair event, district agricultural association event, or at another venue expressly approved by a local jurisdiction for the purpose of holding a temporary cannabis event.

(f) A temporary cannabis event license shall not be issued for a premises that is licensed for the sale of alcohol or tobacco.

(g) If the list of licensees and vendors participating in the temporary cannabis event changes after the application is submitted or after the license is issued, the applicant shall submit with the Licensee Notification and Request Form, Notifications and Requests Regarding Regulatory Compliance, DCC-LIC-028 (New 2/22), incorporated herein by reference, an updated list and an updated diagram, as required in section 15002.1(b)(5), to the Department no less than 72 hours before the event. Licensees not on the list submitted to the Department shall not participate in the temporary cannabis event. All employees of licensees participating in the event shall comply with the employee badge requirements in section 15403 at all times while participating in the temporary cannabis event and provide their badge to Department representatives upon request.

(h) The licensed cannabis event organizer shall hire or contract for security personnel to provide security services at the licensed temporary cannabis event. All security personnel hired or contracted for by the licensee shall be at least 21 years of age, licensed by the Bureau of Security and Investigative Services, and comply with chapters 11.4 and 11.5 of division 3 of the Business and Professions Code. Security personnel shall be present on the licensed premises at all times cannabis goods are available for sale and/or cannabis goods consumption is allowed on the licensed premises.

(i) A licensed cannabis event organizer shall maintain a clearly legible sign not less than 7 inches by 11 inches in size, reading "No Persons Under 21 Allowed" at or near each public entrance to any area where the sale or consumption of cannabis goods is allowed. The lettering of the sign shall be no less than 1 inch in height.

(j) All cannabis waste generated at a temporary cannabis event shall be collected and disposed of in accordance with the requirements of section 17223. The licensed cannabis event organizer may contract or arrange for the collection and disposal of cannabis waste generated during the temporary cannabis event.

(k) A licensed cannabis event organizer and all other licensees participating in a temporary cannabis event are required to comply with section 15037 and all other applicable requirements in the Act and this division pertaining to record keeping.

(l) The Department may require the event organizer and all participants to cease operations without delay if, in the opinion of the Department or local law enforcement, it is necessary to protect the immediate public health and safety of the people of the state. Upon notification from the Department that the event is to cease operations, the event organizer shall immediately stop the event and all participants shall be removed from the premises within the time frame provided by the Department.

(m) Upon notification from the Department, the event organizer shall immediately expel from the event any person selling cannabis goods without a license from the Department that authorizes the participant to sell cannabis goods. The event organizer or their representative shall remain with the person being expelled from the premises at all times until he or she vacates the premises. If the person does not vacate the premises, the Department may inform the event organizer that the event must cease operations. Upon notification from the Department that the event is to cease operations, the event organizer shall immediately stop the event and all participants shall be removed from the premises within the time frame provided by the Department.

(n) The event organizer shall designate a limited-access area that can only be accessed by the licensee and the Department. Upon request, the event organizer shall make the area available to the Department.

NOTE: Authority cited: Section 26013, Business and Professions Code. Reference: Sections 26012 and 26200, Business and Professions Code.

§ 15602. Temporary Cannabis Event Sales.

(a) Only persons age 21 or older may purchase and consume cannabis goods at a temporary cannabis event. Prior to selling cannabis goods to a customer, the licensee making the sale shall confirm, using valid identification as specified in section 15404, the age and identity of the customer.

(b) All sales of cannabis goods at a temporary cannabis event must occur in a retail area as designated in the premises diagram pursuant to section 15002.1(b)(5).

(c) Each sale at a temporary cannabis event shall be performed by a licensed retailer, a licensed non-storefront retailer, or licensed microbusiness that is authorized to engage in retail sales. The cannabis event organizer may also sell cannabis goods at the temporary cannabis event if the organizer separately holds a license authorizing the retail sale of cannabis goods.

> (1) Licensed retailers or licensed microbusinesses shall only conduct sales activities within their specifically assigned area, identified in the diagram of the physical layout of the temporary cannabis event.
>
> (2) Mobile sales activities via wagon, cart, or similar means are prohibited at the temporary cannabis event site.

(d) Licensed retailers or licensed microbusinesses must prominently display their temporary cannabis event location number and state license within plain sight of the public.

(e) All sales at a temporary cannabis event shall occur on the dates stated on the license and shall occur at the location stated on the license. All onsite sales of cannabis goods must comply with the hours of operation requirements of section 15403.

(f) Sale of alcohol or tobacco shall not be allowed on the licensed temporary cannabis event premises.

(g) The cannabis goods sold onsite at a temporary cannabis event shall be transported by a licensed distributor or licensed microbusiness in compliance with the Act and this division. All shipments of cannabis goods and non-cannabis goods intended for sale at a temporary cannabis event must be checked by the temporary cannabis event organizer staff to prevent prohibited items, such as alcohol and tobacco, from entering the licensed premises.

(h) Except small amounts of cannabis goods used for display, all cannabis goods for sale at a temporary cannabis event shall be stored in a secure, locked container that is not accessible to the public. Cannabis goods being stored by a licensee at a temporary cannabis event shall not be left unattended. Licensees may share the secure, locked container; however, each licensee using the container shall be held responsible for any violations of this section and subject to disciplinary action.

(i) All cannabis goods made available for sale at a cannabis event shall comply with all requirements for the retail sale of cannabis goods within the Act and section 15406.

(j) All cannabis goods made available for sale at a temporary cannabis event shall comply with all track and trace requirements within the Act and this division.

(k) All cannabis goods used for display at a temporary cannabis event shall comply with the requirements of section 15405.

(l) All cannabis goods sold at a temporary cannabis event shall comply with section 15413.

(m) All customer returns of cannabis goods at a temporary cannabis event shall comply with section 15410.

(n) The daily sales limits under section 15409 apply to all sales made at a temporary cannabis event.

(o) A licensed retailer shall only provide free cannabis goods to a person at a temporary cannabis event if the licensed retailer complies with all requirements of section 15411.

(p) The licensed cannabis event organizer shall be responsible for ensuring that all rules and requirements for the onsite sale of cannabis goods are followed.

(q) Any compensation paid from a licensed retailer to a licensed cannabis event organizer for participation in a temporary cannabis event shall not be determined based on, or be contingent on, the sale of cannabis goods.

NOTE: Authority cited: Section 26013, Business and Professions Code. Reference: Sections 26070 and 26200, Business and Professions Code.

§ 15603. Temporary Cannabis Event Consumption.

(a) Access to the area where cannabis consumption is allowed shall be restricted to persons 21 years of age or older.

(b) The event organizer licensee shall ensure that cannabis consumption is not visible from any public place or non-age-restricted area.

(c) Consumption of alcohol or tobacco shall not be allowed on the licensed premises.

(d) All requirements for onsite cannabis consumption imposed by the relevant local jurisdiction shall be followed and smoking of cannabis goods shall be prohibited in any areas where smoking is prohibited by law.

(e) The licensed cannabis event organizer, who holds the temporary cannabis event license, shall be responsible for ensuring that all rules and requirements for the onsite consumption of cannabis goods are followed.

(f) A licensed cannabis event organizer and all other licensees participating in a temporary cannabis event are required to follow all applicable requirements in this division pertaining to record keeping and waste management.

NOTE: Authority cited: Section 26013, Business and Professions Code. Reference: Section 26200, Business and Professions Code.

§ 15603.1. Participation in Temporary Cannabis Events by Non-

Retail Licensees.

(a) Licensees who are not retailers may participate in licensed temporary cannabis events and may display cannabis or cannabis products in accordance with the following:

(1) Cannabis or cannabis products displayed shall not exceed the following amounts:

(A) 85.5 grams of non-concentrated cannabis.

(B) 24 grams of cannabis concentrate.

(C) 18 immature plants.

(D) 21 seeds.

(2) Cannabis or cannabis products may be provided to attendees of the event for inspection and educational purposes only. Cannabis and cannabis products used for display shall comply with the provisions in subsections (b) and (c) of section 15405.

(3) Cannabis and cannabis products for display purposes by non-retail licensees only may be brought to the licensed event by the licensee or their employees. However, no individual shall transport an amount of cannabis or cannabis products that exceeds the possession limits established in section 11362.1 of the Health and Safety Code unless such individual is a licensed distributor or their employee transporting in a distribution vehicle.

(b) Licensees may display non-cannabis containing items such as cannabis accessories, packaging materials, promotional materials, and branded merchandise.

(c) Licensees may sell branded merchandise and cannabis accessories in compliance with local and state laws governing the sale of goods.

NOTE: Authority cited: Section 26013, Business and Professions Code. Reference: Section 26013, Business and Professions Code.

§ 15604. Informational or Educational Cannabis Events.

(a) Informational or educational cannabis events where no sales of cannabis goods or consumption of cannabis goods is occurring are not required to be licensed by the Department.

(b) A person may display cannabis or cannabis products for informational or educational purposes consistent with Health and Safety Code sections 11362.1 and 11362.77.

NOTE: Authority cited: Section 26013, Business and Professions Code. Reference: Section 26013, Business and Professions Code; and Sections 11362.1 and 11362.77, Health and Safety Code.

Chapter 6. Testing Laboratories

ARTICLE 1. CHAPTER DEFINITIONS

§ 15700. Definitions.

In addition to the definitions in section 15000, the following definitions apply to this chapter.

(a) "Acceptance criteria" means the specified limits placed on the characteristics of an item or method that are used to determine data quality.

(b) "Accreditation body" means an impartial non-profit organization that operates in conformance with the International Organization for Standardization (ISO) / International Electrotechnical Commission (IEC) standard 17011 and is a signatory to the International Laboratory Accreditation Cooperation (ILAC) Mutual Recognition Arrangement (MRA) for Testing.

(c) "Accredited college or university" means a college or university accredited by a regional or national accrediting agency that is an accreditor recognized by the Secretary of the US Department of Education.

(d) "Action level" means the threshold value that provides the criterion for determining whether a sample passes or fails an analytical test.

(e) "Analyte" means a chemical, compound, element, bacteria, yeast, fungus, or toxin to be identified or measured.

(f) "Analytical batch" means a set of no more than 20 samples that is prepared together for the same analysis and are prepared with laboratory quality control (LQC) samples.

(g) "Analytical method" means a technique used qualitatively or quantitatively to determine the composition of a sample or a microbial contamination of a sample.

(h) "Analytical sequence" means a group of samples that are analyzed sequentially using the same instrument calibration curve.

(i) "Cannabinoid" means a class of diverse chemical compounds derived from a cannabis plant.

(j) "CAS number" means the unique numerical identifier assigned to every chemical substance by Chemical Abstracts Service, a division of the American Chemical Society.

(k) "CBDA" means cannabidiolic acid, CAS number 1244-58-2.

(l) "CBG" means cannabigerol, CAS number 25654-31-3.

(m) "CBN" means cannabinol, CAS number 521-35-7.

(n) "Certificate of accreditation" means a document issued by an accreditation body that attests to the laboratory's competence to carry out specific testing analysis.

(o) "Certified reference material" means a reference material in cannabis or similar non-cannabis matrix prepared at a known concentration by a certifying body or a party independent of the laboratory with ISO/IEC 17034 accreditation. The laboratory will calculate the percent recovery of the certified reference material based on measured concentration relative to the known concentration.

(p) "Chain of Custody" (COC) means the chronological documentation that records the sequence of custody, control, transfer, analysis, and disposal of a sample.

(q) "Coefficient of Determination" (commonly denoted as "r2") means a statistical measure that determines how well the regression approximates the actual data points in the calibration curve, with a regression of 1 being a perfect fit.

(r) "Continuing calibration verification" (CCV) means a type of quality control sample that includes each of the target method analytes that is a mid-range calibration standard which checks the continued validity of the initial calibration of the instrument.

(s) "Corrective action" means an action taken by the laboratory to resolve, and prevent from recurrence, a problem with the technical operations of the laboratory.

(t) "Exclusivity" means the specificity of the test method for validating microbial testing methods. It evaluates the ability of the method to distinguish the target organisms from similar but genetically distinct non-target organisms.

(u) "Foreign material" means any filthy, putrid, or decomposed substance including hair, insects, excreta, or related adulterant that may be hazardous or cause illness or injury to the consumer.

(v) "Frequency" means the number of items occurring in each category. Frequency may be determined by analytical method or laboratory specific requirements for accuracy, precision of the analysis, or statistical calculation.

(w) "Good laboratory practice" (GLP) means a system of management controls for laboratories to ensure the uniformity, consistency, reliability, reproducibility, quality, and integrity of analyses performed by the testing laboratory.

(x) "Inclusivity" means, related to microbiological method validation, the sensitivity of the test method. It evaluates the ability of the test method to detect a wide range of target organisms by a defined relatedness.

(y) "Inhalable" means consumable through the lungs.

(z) "Initial Calibration Verification" (ICV) means a solution of each of the target method analytes of known concentration that is obtained from a source external to the laboratory and different from the source of calibration standards.

(aa) "ISO/IEC" means the joint technical committee of the International Organization for Standardization (ISO) and the International Electrotechnical Commission (IEC).

(bb) "ISO/IEC 17025" means the general requirements specified by the ISO/IEC for the competence of testing and calibration laboratories.

(cc) "ISO/IEC 17034" means the general requirements established by the ISO/IEC for the competence of reference material producers.

(dd) "ISO/IEC 17043" means the general requirements established by the ISO/IEC for proficiency testing.

(ee) "Laboratory" means "testing laboratory" as defined at Business and Professions Code section 26001(av).

(ff) "Laboratory Control Sample" (LCS) means a blank matrix to which known concentrations of each of the target method analytes are added. The spiked concentration must be at a mid-range concentration of the calibration curve for the target analytes. The LCS is analyzed in the same manner as the representative sample.

(gg) "Laboratory replicate sample" means a sub-sample taken of the representative sample used for laboratory quality control purposes to demonstrate reproducibility. It is prepared and analyzed in the identical manner as the representative sample. The results from replicate analyses are used to evaluate analytical precision.

(hh) "Laboratory employee" means any person directly employed by the laboratory for wages, salary, barter, or trade by the laboratory and who is not employed by any other licensee under the Act except for another testing laboratory. "Laboratory employee" does not mean an independent contractor, third party entity, or any other entity acting on behalf of the laboratory.

(ii) "Laboratory quality assurance" means the set of operating principles that enable laboratories to produce defensible data of known accuracy and precision and includes employee training, equipment preventative maintenance procedures, calibration procedures, and quality control testing, among other things.

(jj) "Limit of detection" (LOD) means the lowest quantity of a substance or analyte that can be distinguished from the absence of that substance within a stated confidence limit.

(kk) "Limit of quantitation" (LOQ) means the minimum concentration of an analyte in a specific matrix that can be reliably quantified while also meeting predefined goals for bias and imprecision.

(ll) "Linear regression" means the determination, in analytical chemistry, of the best linear equation for calibration data to generate a calibration curve. The concentrate of an analyte in a sample can then be determined by comparing a measurement of the unknown to the calibration curve. A linear regression uses the following equation:

$y = mx + b$; where m = slope, b = intercept

(mm) "Matrix" means the substances that are present in a sample except for the analyte(s) of interest.

(nn) "Matrix spike sample" means a sample prepared by adding a known quantity of each of the target analyte to a sample matrix or to a matrix that is as closely representative of the matrix being analyzed as possible. The spiked concentration must be at a mid-range concentration of the calibration curve for the target analytes.

(oo) "Method Blank" means an analyte free matrix to which all reagents are added in the same volumes or proportions as used in the sample preparation and is processed in exactly the same manner as the samples.

(pp) "Moisture content" means the percentage of water in a sample, by weight.

(qq) "Non-target organism" means an organism that the test method or analytical procedure is not testing for and can be used in evaluating the specificity of a test method.

(rr) "Percent recovery" means the percentage of a measured concentration relative to the added (spiked) concentration in a reference material or matrix spike sample. A laboratory shall calculate the percent recovery by dividing the sample result by the expected result then multiplying the quotient by 100.

(ss) "Practical experience" means experience performing scientific analytical tests in a laboratory setting using equipment, instruments, kits, and materials routinely found in a laboratory. "Practical experience" includes experience in any type of laboratory setting and is not limited to cannabis-specific laboratories.

(tt) "Proficiency test" means an evaluation of a laboratory's performance against pre-established criteria by means of interlaboratory comparisons of test measurements.

(uu) "Proficiency test sample" means a sample that is prepared by a party independent of the testing laboratory with the ISO/IEC 17043 accreditation, where the concentration and identity of an analyte is known to the independent party, but is unknown to the testing laboratory and testing laboratory employees.

(vv) "Quadratic regression" means the determination, in analytical chemistry, of the best parabola equation for calibration data to generate a calibration curve. The concentrate of an analyte in a sample can then be determined by comparing a measurement of the unknown to the calibration curve. A quadratic regression uses the following equation:

$y = ax2 + bx + c$; where a, b, and c are numerical coefficients

(ww) "Quality control" means the set of measures implemented within an analytical procedure to ensure that the measurement system is operating in a state of statistical control for which errors have been reduced to acceptable levels.

(xx) "Quality control sample" means a sample that is produced and used by a laboratory for the purpose of assuring the quality of the data and results. Quality control samples include blank samples, matrix spike samples, laboratory control samples, replicate samples, and reference material samples.

(yy) "Reagent" means a compound or mixture added to a system to cause a chemical reaction or test if a reaction occurs. A reagent may be used to tell whether a specific chemical substance is present by causing a reaction to occur with the chemical substance.

(zz) "Reference material" means material containing a known concentration of an analyte of interest that is in solution or in a homogeneous matrix.

(aaa) "Reference method" means the method by which the performance of an alternate method is measured or evaluated.

(bbb) “Relative percent difference” (RPD) means the comparative statistic that is used to calculate precision or random error. RPD is calculated using the following equation:

RPD = | (representative sample measurement - replicate sample measurement) / ([representative sample measurement + replicate sample measurement] / 2) x 100%

(ccc) “Relative standard deviation” (RSD) means the standard deviation expressed as a percentage of the means recovery. RSD is calculated using the following equation:

RSD = (s / x) x 100%; where s = standard deviation and x = mean

(ddd) “Representative” means a small quantity of the batch whose characteristics represent, as accurately as possible, the entire batch, thus allowing the results to be generalized.

(eee) “Representative sample” means a sample that is comprised of several sample increments of cannabis or cannabis products that are collected from a batch for testing.

(fff) “Requester” means the person who submits a request to the laboratory for testing of cannabis or cannabis products from an entity licensed under the Act.

(ggg) “Reserve sample” means any portion of a representative sample that was not used in the testing process.

(hhh) “Sample” means a representative part of, or a single item from, a batch which is comprised of several sample increments.

(jjj) “Sample increment” means a portion of a batch that, together with other increments, makes up the sample.

(kkk) “Sampler” means the laboratory employee responsible for obtaining samples of cannabis or cannabis products from a licensed distributor or licensed microbusiness authorized to engage in distribution.

(lll) “Sanitize” means to sterilize, disinfect, or make hygienic.

(mmm) “Scope of accreditation” means the tests or types of tests performed, materials or products tested, and the methods used for testing cannabis or cannabis products for which the accreditation has been granted.

(nnn) “Standard operating procedure” (SOP) means a written document that provides detailed instructions for the performance of all aspects of an analysis, operation, or action.

(ooo) “Target organism” means an organism that is being tested for in an analytical procedure or test method.

(ppp) “THCA” means tetrahydrocannabinolic acid, CAS number 23978-85-0.

(qqq) “Total CBD” means the sum of CBD and CBDA. Total CBD is calculated using the following equation:

Total CBD concentration (mg/g) = (CBDA concentration (mg/g) x 0.877) + CBD concentration (mg/g)

(rrr) “Total THC” means the sum of THC, delta 8 THC, and THCA. Total THC is calculated using the following equation:

Total THC (mg/g) = [(delta 8-THCA concentration (mg/g) + delta 9-THCA concentration (mg/g)) x 0.877] + [delta 8-THC concentration (mg/g) + delta 9-THC concentration (mg/g)]

(sss) “Validation” means the confirmation by examination and objective evidence that the requirements for a specific intended use or analytical method are fulfilled.

(ttt) “Water activity” means the measure of the quantity of water in a product that is available and therefore capable of supporting bacteria, yeasts, and fungi and which is reported in units Aw.

NOTE: Authority cited: Section 26013, Business and Professions Code. Reference: Sections 26013 and 26100,

Business and Professions Code.

ARTICLE 2. LABORATORY LICENSE

§ 15701. General Laboratory License Requirements.

(a) A licensed laboratory shall maintain ISO/IEC 17025 accreditation for the testing of the following:

(1) Cannabinoids;

(2) Heavy metals;

(3) Microbial impurities;

(4) Mycotoxins;

(5) Residual pesticides;

(6) Residual solvents and processing chemicals; and

(7) If tested, terpenoids.

(b) Each testing laboratory licensed premises shall have ISO/IEC 17025 accreditation.

(c) A licensed laboratory shall retain, and make available to the Department upon request, all records associated with the licensee's ISO/IEC 17025 certificate of accreditation.

(d) A licensed testing laboratory may test items not regulated by this division if they comply with the laws governing the testing of such items. A licensed testing laboratory shall maintain separate and distinct records of their activities regulated by this division and their activities that are subject to other laws.

NOTE: Authority cited: Section 26013, Business and Professions Code. Reference: Sections 26012 and 26100, Business and Professions Code.

§ 15702. Laboratory License Application.

In addition to the information required in section 15002, an application for a testing laboratory license includes the following:

(a) A valid certificate of accreditation, issued by an accreditation body, that attests to the laboratory's competence to perform testing, including all the required analytes for the following test methods:

(1) Cannabinoids;

(2) Heavy metals;

(3) Microbial impurities;

(4) Mycotoxins;

(5) Residual pesticides;

(6) Residual solvents and processing chemicals; and

(7) If tested, terpenoids.

(b) Standard operating procedures for the following testing methods:

(1) Cannabinoids;

(2) Foreign material;

(3) Heavy metals;

(4) Microbial impurities;

(5) Moisture content and water activity;

(6) Mycotoxins;

(7) Residual pesticides;

(8) Residual solvents and processing chemicals; and

(9) If tested, terpenoids.

(c) Method validation reports for the following testing methods:

(1) Cannabinoids;

(2) Heavy metals;

(3) Microbial impurities;

(4) Mycotoxins;

(5) Residual pesticides;

(6) Residual solvents; and processing chemicals; and

(7) If tested, terpenoids.

(d) Standard operating procedures for the sampling of cannabis or cannabis products.

NOTE: Authority cited: Section 26013, Business and Professions Code. Reference: Sections 26012, 26050, 26055, 26102 and 26104, Business and Professions Code.

§ 15703. Interim Testing Laboratory License.

(a) An applicant may apply for an interim license prior to receiving ISO/IEC 17025 accreditation provided that the commercial cannabis business meets all other licensure requirements for a testing laboratory and submits to the Department an application in compliance with section 15002 and an attestation that the commercial cannabis business has or intends to seek ISO/IEC 17025 accreditation for all testing methods required by this division.

(b) An interim testing laboratory license shall be valid for 12 months. The annual license fee for an interim license shall be determined pursuant to the requirements in section 15014 for determining the annual license fee for a testing laboratory license.

(c) To timely renew an interim license, a completed license renewal form and the annual renewal license fee pursuant to section 15014 shall be received by the Department from the licensee no earlier than 60 calendar days before the expiration of the license and no later than 5:00 p.m. Pacific Time on the last business day before the expiration of the license if the renewal form is submitted to the Department at its office(s), or no later than 11:59 p.m. on the last business day before the expiration of the license if the renewal form is submitted to the Department through its electronic licensing system. Failure to receive a notice for license renewal does not relieve a licensee of the obligation to renew an interim license as required.

(d) In the event the license is not renewed prior to the expiration date, the licensee must not test any commercial cannabis or cannabis products until the license is renewed.

(e) A licensee may submit a license renewal form up to 30 calendar days after the license expires. Any late renewal form will be subject to a late fee equal to 50 percent of the applicable licensing fees required by subsection (c).

(f) The license renewal application shall contain the following:

(1) The name of the licensee. For licensees who are individuals, the applicant shall provide both the first and last name of the individual. For licensees who are business entities, the licensee shall provide the legal business name of the commercial cannabis business;

(2) The license number and expiration date;

(3) The licensee's mailing address and licensed premises address; and

(4) An attestation that all information provided to the Department in the original application under section 15002 or subsequent notification under sections 15023 and 15024 is accurate and current.

(g) The Department may renew an interim license for an initial renewal period of 12 months.

(h) After one renewal, the Department may renew the interim license for additional 12-month periods if the licensee has submitted an application for the ISO/IEC 17025 accreditation. In addition to the information required for a renewal form pursuant to subsection (f), any renewal request pursuant to this section shall also include an attestation that the licensee's application for each ISO/IEC 17025 is pending with the accrediting body, the name of the accrediting body, and the date the application was submitted to the accrediting body.

(i) The licensee shall notify the Department if the application for each ISO/IEC 17025 accreditation is granted or denied within 1 business day of receiving the decision from the accrediting body. The licensee shall submit to the Department the information required, on the Licensee Notification and Request Form, Notifications and Requests Regarding Testing Laboratories, DCC-LIC-029 (New 2/22), which is incorporated herein by reference. If the accrediting body grants or denies the licensee's application for any ISO/IEC 17025 accreditation before the expiration of the interim license, the Department may terminate the interim license at that time.

(j) The Department may revoke an interim license at any time.

NOTE: Authority cited: Section 26013, Business and Professions Code. Reference: Sections 26012, 26031, 26050 and 26102, Business and Professions Code.

ARTICLE 3. SAMPLING CANNABIS AND CANNABIS PRODUCTS

§ 15704. Sampling Standard Operating Procedures.

(a) The licensed laboratory shall develop and implement a sampling standard operating procedure (SOP) that describes the laboratory's method for obtaining representative samples of cannabis or cannabis products. The licensed laboratory shall use and submit to the Department Sampling--Standard Operating Procedures, Form DCC-LIC-021 (Amended 2/22), which is incorporated herein by reference.

(b) The licensed laboratory shall retain a copy of the sampling SOP on the licensed laboratory premises and ensure that the sampling SOP is accessible to the sampler during sampling.

NOTE: Authority cited: Section 26013, Business and Professions Code. Reference: Sections 26100, 26102, 26104 and 26110, Business and Professions Code.

§ 15705. General Sampling Requirements.

(a) The licensed laboratory that obtains a representative sample from a licensed distributor or licensed microbusiness shall perform all the required testing at one licensed laboratory premises.

(b) The licensed laboratory may obtain and analyze samples only from cannabis products batches in final form as required by Business and Professions Code section 26100.

(c) The licensed laboratory sampler shall collect a representative sample from each batch following the procedures specified in the laboratory's sampling standard operating procedure(s).

(d) The licensed laboratory shall ensure that the sample is transported and subsequently stored at the licensed laboratory premises in a manner that prevents degradation, contamination, commingling, and tampering. If the cannabis or cannabis products specify on the label how the cannabis or cannabis products shall be stored, the laboratory shall store the sample as indicated on the label.

(e) The licensed laboratory shall complete a chain of custody form for each sample that the laboratory collects and analyzes.

(f) Once a representative sample has been obtained for regulatory compliance testing, the licensed laboratory that obtained the sample must complete the regulatory compliance testing.

(g) If a licensed laboratory is unable to competently complete the regulatory compliance testing after sampling and before a COA is issued, the licensed distributor or microbusiness authorized to engage in distribution who arranged for the testing of the batch may request approval from the Department to have the impacted batch re-sampled and tested by another licensed laboratory.

(1) The request shall be made in writing via email to testinglabs@cannabis.ca.gov and shall include all of the following:

(A) The name and license number of the distributor;

(B) The batch numbers;

(C) The type and quantity of cannabis or cannabis products;

(D) The name and license number of the laboratory that took the initial sample and is not able to competently complete the regulatory compliance testing;

(E) The name and license number of the laboratory proposed to re-sample and complete the regulatory compliance testing for the batch; and

(F) The reason why the laboratory that initially took the sample cannot competently complete the regulatory compliance testing.

(2) The Department will review the request and determine if the licensed laboratory that initially took the sample is unable to competently complete the regulatory compliance testing. If the Department determines that the licensed laboratory is unable to competently complete the regulatory compliance testing, the Department, in its discretion, may approve the request in whole or part and set conditions for the re-sampling and testing.

(3) No re-sampling of any batch shall occur prior to the licensed distributor or licensed microbusiness authorized to engaged in distribution receiving written approval from the Department.

NOTE: Authority cited: Section 26013, Business and Professions Code. Reference: Sections 26100, 26104 and 26110, Business and Professions Code.

§ 15706. Chain of Custody (COC).

(a) The licensed laboratory shall develop and implement a COC protocol to ensure accurate documentation is recorded for the transport, handling, storage, and destruction of samples.

(b) The COC protocol shall require the use of a COC form. The sampler shall use a COC to record the following information for each sampled batch:

(1) Laboratory's name, licensed premises address, and license number;

(2) Date and time sampling started and ended;

(3) Licensed distributor or licensed microbusiness' name, licensed premises address, and license number;

(4) Licensed cultivator's, licensed manufacturer's, licensed distributor's, or licensed microbusiness' name, licensed premises address, and license number;

(5) Batch number of the batch from which the representative sample was obtained and assigned unique sample identifier;

(6) Sample matrix;

(7) Total batch size, by weight, or unit count;

(8) Total weight, or unit count of the representative sample;

(9) Sampling conditions or problems encountered during the sampling process, if any;

(10) Printed name and signature of the licensed distributor or licensed microbusiness' authorized to engage in distribution employee; and

(11) Printed name and signature of the sampler.

(c) Each time a sample changes custody between licensees, is transported, or is destroyed, the date, time, and the names and signatures of persons involved in these activities shall be recorded on the COC form.

(d) Once the custody of the sample changes between licensees, the COC form for that change of custody may not be altered.

NOTE: Authority cited: Section 26013, Business and Professions Code. Reference: Sections 26100, 26102, 26104 and 26110, Business and Professions Code.

§ 15707. Harvest Batch Sampling.

(a) The sampler shall obtain a representative sample from each prepacked or unpacked harvest batch. The representative sample must weigh 0.35% of the total harvest batch weight.

(b) A sampler may collect a representative sample greater than 0.35% of the total harvest batch weight of a prepacked or unpacked harvest batch if necessary to perform the required testing or to ensure that the samples obtained are representative.

(c) The prepacked or unpacked harvest batch from which a sample is obtained shall weigh no more than 50.0 pounds. Laboratory analyses of a sample collected from a harvest batch weighing more than 50.0 pounds shall be deemed invalid and the harvest batch from which the sample was obtained shall not be released for retail sale.

(d) When the sampler obtains a representative sample from an unpacked harvest batch, the sampler shall do all the following:

(1) Collect the number of sample increments relative to the unpacked harvest batch size as listed in the following table;

(2) Obtain sample increments from random and varying locations of the unpacked harvest batch, both vertically and horizontally. To the extent practicable, the sample increments obtained from an unpacked harvest batch shall be of equal weight; and

(3) To the extent practicable, collect an equal number of sample increments from each container if the unpacked harvest batch is stored in multiple containers.

Unpacked Harvest Batch Size (pounds)	Number of Increments (per sample)
< or = 10.0	8
10.1 - 20.0	16
20.1 - 30.0	23
30.1 - 40.0	29
40.1 - 50.0	34

Note: Authority cited: Section 26013, Business and Professions Code. Reference: Sections 26100, 26104 and 26110, Business and Professions Code.

§ 15708. Cannabis Product Batch and Pre-Roll Sampling.

(a) The sampler shall obtain a representative sample from each cannabis product batch or pre-roll batch.

(b) The sampler may collect a greater number of sample increments if necessary to perform the required testing or to ensure that the samples obtained are representative.

(c) The cannabis product batch or pre-roll batch from which a representative sample is obtained shall contain no more than 150,000 units. Laboratory analyses of a sample collected from a cannabis product batch containing more than 150,000 units shall be deemed invalid and the cannabis product batch or pre-roll batch from which the representative sample was obtained shall not be released for retail sale.

(d) The sampler shall obtain a representative sample of a cannabis product or pre-roll batch by collecting, at minimum, the number of sample increments relative to the batch size as listed in the following table. Each sample increment consists of 1 packaged unit.

Cannabis Product or Pre-roll Batch Size (units)	Number of Sample Increments (per sample)
< or = 50	2
51 - 150	3

Cannabis Product or Pre-roll Batch Size (units)	Number of Sample Increments (per sample)
151 - 500	5
501 - 1,200	8
1,201 - 3,200	13
3,201 - 10,000	20
10,001 - 35,000	32
35,001 - 150,000	50

Note: Authority cited: Section 26013, Business and Professions Code. Reference: Sections 26100, 26104 and 26110, Business and Professions Code.

§ 15709. Laboratory Transportation of Cannabis and Cannabis Products Samples.

(a) The following requirements apply when a licensed testing laboratory transports cannabis or cannabis products samples:

(1) While transporting cannabis or cannabis products samples, a licensed testing laboratory employee shall ensure the cannabis or cannabis products are not visible to the public. Cannabis or cannabis products shall be stored in a secure, fully enclosed trunk that cannot be accessed from inside the vehicle, or in a secured area or compartment within the interior of the vehicle. A "secured area" is defined as an area where solid or locking metal partitions, cages, or high-strength shatterproof acrylic can be used to create a secure compartment in the fully enclosed vehicle. The secured area may be comprised on three sides by any part of the body of the vehicle, provided the parts of the vehicle used for the purposes of this section are shatterproof and are not made of glass.

(2) While left unattended, vehicles and trailers shall be locked and secured.

(3) The licensed laboratory shall not leave a vehicle or trailer containing cannabis or cannabis products samples unattended in a residential area or parked overnight in a residential area.

(4) The licensed laboratory shall ensure that any vehicle or trailer transporting cannabis or cannabis products samples has an alarm system.

(5) The licensed laboratory shall ensure that packages or containers holding cannabis or cannabis products samples are neither tampered with nor opened during transport.

(6) The licensed laboratory transporting cannabis or cannabis products samples shall only travel between licensees for whom the laboratory is conducting regulatory compliance testing or quality assurance testing. A laboratory shall not deviate from the travel requirements described in this section, except for necessary rest, fuel, or vehicle repair stops.

(7) The licensed laboratory may transport multiple cannabis or cannabis products samples obtained from multiple licensees at once.

(8) Vehicles or trailers transporting cannabis or cannabis products samples are subject to inspection by the Department at any licensed premises or during transport at any time.

(9) No person under the age of 21 years old shall be in a vehicle or trailer transporting cannabis or cannabis products samples.

(10) Only an employee of the licensed laboratory or security personnel who meets the requirement of section 15045 shall be in a vehicle while transporting cannabis or cannabis products samples.

(b) Upon request, the licensed laboratory shall provide the following required transport vehicle information to the Department:

(1) The certificate of ownership or registration card issued by the California Department of Motor Vehicles for each vehicle used to transport cannabis or cannabis products samples;

(2) The year, make, model, license plate number, and numerical Vehicle Identification Number (VIN) for each vehicle or trailer used to transport cannabis or cannabis products samples; and

(3) Proof of insurance for each vehicle used to transport cannabis or cannabis products samples.

(c) All vehicles and trailers used for transportation shall be owned or leased, in accordance with the Vehicle Code, by the licensee. The licensee is not required to be the sole owner or lessor of the vehicle or trailer and all owners and lessors may use the vehicle for non-commercial cannabis activity.

NOTE: Authority cited: Section 26013, Business and Professions Code. Reference: Sections 26100, 26102, 26104 and 26110, Business and Professions Code.

§ 15710. Laboratory Receipt of Samples Obtained from a Distributor or Microbusiness.

(a) The licensed laboratory may accept and analyze a sample from a licensed distributor or licensed microbusiness authorized to engage in distribution for the required testing under section 15714 only if there is an accompanying COC form for the sample.

(b) The licensed laboratory employee who receives the sample shall date, print, and sign their name on the accompanying sample COC.

(c) The licensed laboratory shall not analyze a sample obtained from a licensed distributor or licensed microbusiness authorized to engage in distribution, and the batch from which the sample was obtained may not be released for retail sale, if any of the following occur:

(1) The sample is received at the laboratory without the requisite COC form;

(2) The tamper-evident material is broken prior to the sample being received at the laboratory; or

(3) There is evidence of sample commingling, contamination, degradation, or a related occurrence rendering the sample unusable for analytical testing when the sample is received at the laboratory.

NOTE: Authority cited: Section 26013, Business and Professions Code. Reference: Sections 26100, 26104 and 26110, Business and Professions Code.

ARTICLE 4. STANDARD OPERATING PROCEDURES

§ 15711. Laboratory Analyses Standard Operating Procedures.

(a) The licensed laboratory shall develop, implement, and maintain written standard operating procedures (SOP) for sample preparation and each required test method. The licensed laboratory shall use and submit to the Department the following forms which are incorporated by reference:

(1) Sample Preparation--Standard Operating Procedures, Form DCC-LIC-022 (Amended 2/22), which is incorporated herein by reference; and

(2) Test Methods--Standard Operating Procedures, Form DCC-LIC-023 (Amended 2/22), which is incorporated herein by reference.

(b) The licensed laboratory shall keep each SOP at the licensed laboratory premises and ensure that each SOP is accessible to laboratory employees during operating hours.

(c) The licensed laboratory shall make each SOP available for inspection by the Department upon request, as well as any other SOPs associated with the licensee's ISO/IEC 17025 certificate of accreditation.

NOTE: Authority cited: Section 26013, Business and Professions Code. Reference: Sections 26012, 26100, 26102, 26104 and 26110, Business and Professions Code.

§ 15712. Test Methods.

(a) The laboratory shall develop, implement, and validate test methods for the analyses of samples as required under this division.

(b) To the extent practicable, the laboratory test methods shall comport with the following guidelines:

(1) US Food and Drug Administration's Bacterial Analytical Manual, 2016;

(2) AOAC International's Official Methods of Analysis for Contaminant Testing of AOAC International, 20th Edition, 2016; and

(3) United States Pharmacopeia and the National Formulary's Methods of Analysis for Contaminant Testing, 2016.

NOTE: Authority cited: Section 26013, Business and Professions Code. Reference: Sections 26100, 26102, 26104 and 26110, Business and Professions Code.

§ 15713. Validation of Test Methods.

(a) The licensed laboratory may use a nonstandard, amplified, or modified test method or a method that is designed or developed by the licensed laboratory to validate the methods for analyses of samples.

(b) The licensed laboratory shall follow the guidelines set forth in the US Food and Drug Administration's Guidelines for the Validation of Analytical Methods for the Detection of Microbial Pathogens in Foods and Feeds, 2nd Edition, April 2015, incorporated herein by reference, to validate test methods for the microbial analysis of samples. The licensed laboratory shall include and address the criteria listed in the following table when validating test methods for microbial analyses of samples.

Criteria	Requirement
Number of target organisms; inclusivity	5
Number of non-target organisms; exclusivity	5
Number of analyte levels per matrix: Qualitative methods	3 levels: high and low inoculum levels and 1 uninoculated level
Number of analyte levels per matrix: Quantitative methods	4 levels: low, medium and high inoculum levels and 1 uninoculated level
Replicates per food at each level tested	2 or more replicates per level

(c) The licensed laboratory shall follow the guidelines set forth in the US Food and Drug Administration's Guidelines for the Validation of Chemical Methods for the FDA FVM Program, 2nd Edition, April 2015, incorporated herein by reference, to validate test methods for chemical analysis of samples.

(1) The licensed laboratory shall include and address the following criteria to validate test methods for chemical analyses of samples:

(A) Accuracy;

(B) Precision;

(C) Linearity and range;

(i) The Coefficient of Determination (r2) for all calibration curves shall be greater than or equal to 0.99.

(ii) Linear regression or quadratic regression shall only be used for calibration curves. Curves shall not be weighted at all or only weighted at 1/x.

(iii) LOQ for analytes tested shall be within the range of the calibration curve.

(D) Calibration standard;

(i) For calibration curves, there shall be a minimum of five calibration standards, not including zero; and

(ii) Each calibration curve must include an Initial Calibration Verification (ICV). The percent recovery must be between 70% to 130%.

(E) Sensitivity and selectivity;

(F) Limit of detection and limit of quantitation;

(G) Recovery;

(H) Reproducibility; and

(I) Robustness.

(2) The licensed laboratory shall use certified reference materials to validate the following chemical analyses. The test method used for analysis is valid if the percent recovery of the certified reference material is between 80% to 120% for all required analytes.

(A) Cannabinoids, if available;

(B) Heavy metals;

(C) Microbial impurities;

(D) Mycotoxins;

(E) Residual pesticides;

(F) Residual solvents and processing chemicals; and

(G) Terpenoids, if available.

(d) The licensed laboratory shall generate a validation report for each test method. Each validation report shall include the following information:

(1) Instrument calibration data, if any;

(2) Raw data, including instrument raw data, for each test method, if any;

(3) Cannabis reference materials or certified reference material results;

(4) Data and calculations pertaining to LOD and LOQ determinations, if any;

(5) LQC report, as described in this chapter, for the validation of each method; and

(6) Worksheets, forms, pictures, or copies of laboratory notebook pages and any other documentation necessary to meet the requirements described in subsections (b) and (c).

(7) The supervisory or management laboratory employee shall review, approve, sign, and date the validation report for each test method.

(8) Upon new test methods or altered test methods being used in the laboratory, the new validation report shall be submitted to the Department within 5 business days, accompanied by the Licensee Notification and Request Form, Notifications and Requests Regarding Testing Laboratories, DCC-LIC-029 (New 2/22), which is incorporated herein by reference.

NOTE: Authority cited: Section 26013, Business and Professions Code. Reference: Sections 26012, 26100, 26104 and 26110, Business and Professions Code.

ARTICLE 5. LABORATORY TESTING AND REPORTING

§ 15714. Required Testing.

(a) All sample increments collected must be homogenized prior to sample analyses, notwithstanding foreign material testing.

(b) The licensed laboratory shall test each representative sample for the following:

(1) Cannabinoids;

(2) Foreign material;

(3) Heavy metals;

(4) Microbial impurities;

(5) Mycotoxins;

(6) Moisture content and water activity;

(7) Residual pesticides;

(8) Residual solvents and processing chemicals; and

(9) If applicable, terpenoids.

(c) The licensed laboratory shall report the results of each analysis performed by the laboratory on the certificate of analysis.

(d) The licensed laboratory that obtained the representative sample shall complete all required testing for each representative sample for regulatory compliance testing.

NOTE: Authority cited: Section 26013, Business and Professions Code. Reference: Sections 26100, 26104 and 26110, Business and Professions Code.

§ 15715. Phase-In of Required Laboratory Testing. [Repealed]

Note: Authority cited: Section 26013, Business and Professions Code. Reference: Sections 26100, 26104 and 26110, Business and Professions Code.

§ 15717. Moisture Content and Water Activity Testing.

(a) The licensed laboratory shall analyze at minimum 0.5 grams of the representative sample of dried flower to determine the level of water activity and the percentage of moisture content.

(1) The dried flower sample, including pre-rolls, shall be deemed to have passed water activity testing if the water activity does not exceed 0.65 Aw. The laboratory shall report the result of the water activity test on the certificate of analysis (COA) and indicate "pass" or "fail" on the COA.

(2) The licensed laboratory shall report the result of the moisture content test on the COA as a percentage.

(b) The licensed laboratory shall analyze at least 0.5 grams of the representative sample of solid edible cannabis products to determine the level of water activity. A solid edible cannabis product shall be deemed to have passed water activity testing if the water activity does not exceed 0.85 Aw. The laboratory shall report the result of the water activity test on the COA and indicate "pass" or "fail" on the COA.

(c) If the sample fails water activity testing, the batch from which the sample was collected fails water activity testing and shall not be released for retail sale.

NOTE: Authority cited: Section 26013, Business and Professions Code. Reference: Sections 26100, 26104 and 26110, Business and Professions Code.

§ 15718. Residual Solvents and Processing Chemicals Testing.

(a) The licensed laboratory shall analyze at minimum 0.25 grams of the representative sample of cannabis product or pre-rolls to determine whether residual solvents or processing chemicals are present.

(b) The licensed laboratory shall report the result of the residual solvents and processing chemicals testing in unit micrograms per gram (μg/g) on the COA and indicate "pass" or "fail" on the COA.

(c) The sample shall be deemed to have passed the residual solvents and processing chemicals testing if the presence of any residual solvent or processing chemical listed in the following tables in Category I and Category II does not exceed the indicated action levels.

(1) Notwithstanding subsection (c), the limit for ethanol does not apply to cannabis products that are tinctures.

(2) Notwithstanding subsection (c), the limit for ethanol or isopropyl alcohol does not apply to cannabis products that are topical cannabis products.

Category I Residual Solvent or Processing Chemical	**CAS No.**	**Cannabis Product or Pre-Roll Action Level (μg/g)**
1,2-Dichloroethane	107-06-2	1.0
Benzene	71-43-2	1.0
Chloroform	67-66-3	1.0
Ethylene oxide	75-21-8	1.0
Methylene chloride	75-09-2	1.0
Trichloroethylene	79-01-6	1.0

Category II Residual Solvent or Processing Chemical	**CAS No.**	**Cannabis Product or Pre-Roll Action Level (μg/g)**
Acetone	67-64-1	5000
Acetonitrile	75-05-8	410
Butane	106-97-8	5000
Ethanol	64-17-5	5000
Ethyl acetate	141-78-6	5000
Ethyl ether	60-29-7	5000

Category II Residual Solvent or Processing Chemical	CAS No.	Cannabis Product or Pre-Roll Action Level (µg/g)
Heptane	142-82-5	5000
Hexane	110-54-3	290
Isopropyl alcohol	67-63-0	5000
Methanol	67-56-1	3000
Pentane	109-66-0	5000
Propane	74-98-6	5000
Toluene	108-88-3	890
Total xylenes (ortho-, meta-, para-)	1330-20-7	2170

(d) If the sample fails residual solvents and processing chemicals testing, the batch from which the sample was collected fails residual solvents and processing chemicals testing and shall not be released for retail sale.

Note: Authority cited: Section 26013, Business and Professions Code. Reference: Sections 26100, 26104 and 26110, Business and Professions Code.

§ 15719. Residual Pesticides Testing.

(a) The licensed laboratory shall analyze at minimum 0.5 grams of the representative sample of cannabis and cannabis products to determine whether residual pesticides are present.

(b) The licensed laboratory shall report whether any Category I Residual Pesticides are detected above the limit of detection (LOD) and shall report the result of the Category II Residual Pesticides testing in unit micrograms per gram (µg/g) on the COA. The laboratory shall indicate "pass" or "fail" on the COA.

(c) The licensed laboratory shall establish a limit of quantitation (LOQ) of 0.10 µg/g or lower for all Category I Residual Pesticides.

(d) The sample shall be deemed to have passed the residual pesticides testing if both of the following conditions are met:

(1) The presence of any residual pesticide listed in the following tables in Category I are not detected, and

(2) The presence of any residual pesticide listed in the following tables in Category II does not exceed the indicated action levels.

Category I Residual Pesticide	CAS No.
Aldicarb	116-06-3
Carbofuran	1563-66-2
Chlordane	57-74-9
Chlorfenapyr	122453-73-0
Chlorpyrifos	2921-88-2
Coumaphos	56-72-4
Daminozide	1596-84-5
DDVP (Dichlorvos)	62-73-7
Dimethoate	60-51-5
Ethoprop(hos)	13194-48-4
Etofenprox	80844-07-1
Fenoxycarb	72490-01-8
Fipronil	120068-37-3
Imazalil	35554-44-0
Methiocarb	2032-65-7
Methyl parathion	298-00-0
Mevinphos	7786-34-7
Paclobutrazol	76738-62-0
Propoxur	114-26-1

Category I Residual Pesticide	CAS No.
Spiroxamine	118134-30-8
Thiacloprid	11988-49-9

Category II Residual Pesticide	CAS No.	Action Level (μg/g) for Inhalable Cannabis and Cannabis Products	Action Level (μg/g) for Non-Inhalable Cannabis and Cannabis Products
Abamectin	71751-41-2	0.1	0.3
Acephate	30560-19-1	0.1	5
Acequinocyl	57960-19-7	0.1	4
Acetamiprid	135410-20-7	0.1	5
Azoxystrobin	131860-33-8	0.1	40
Bifenazate	149877-41-8	0.1	5
Bifenthrin	82657-04-3	3	0.5
Boscalid	188425-85-6	0.1	10
Captan	133-06-2	0.7	5
Carbaryl	63-25-2	0.5	0.5
Chlorantraniliprole	500008-45-7	10	40
Clofentezine	74115-24-5	0.1	0.5
Cyfluthrin	68359-37-5	2	1
Cypermethrin	52315-07-8	1	1

Category II Residual Pesticide	CAS No.	Action Level (µg/g) for Inhalable Cannabis and Cannabis Products	Action Level (µg/g) for Non-Inhalable Cannabis and Cannabis Products
Diazinon	333-41-5	0.1	0.2
Dimethomorph	110488-70-5	2	20
Etoxazole	153233-91-1	0.1	1.5
Fenhexamid	126833-17-8	0.1	10
Fenpyroximate	111812-58-9	0.1	2
Flonicamid	158062-67-0	0.1	2
Fludioxonil	131341-86-1	0.1	30
Hexythiazox	78587-05-0	0.1	2
Imidacloprid	138261-41-3	5	3
Kresoxim-methyl	143390-89-0	0.1	1
Malathion	121-75-5	0.5	5
Metalaxyl	57837-19-1	2	15
Methomyl	16752-77-5	1	0.1
Myclobutanil	88671-89-0	0.1	9
Naled	300-76-5	0.1	0.5
Oxamyl	23135-22-0	0.5	0.2
Pentachloronitro- benzene	82-68-8	0.1	0.2
Permethrin	52645-53-1	0.5	20

Category II Residual Pesticide	CAS No.	Action Level (μg/g) for Inhalable Cannabis and Cannabis Products	Action Level (μg/g) for Non-Inhalable Cannabis and Cannabis Products
Phosmet	732-11-6	0.1	0.2
Piperonylbutoxide	51-03-6	3	8
Prallethrin	23031-36-9	0.1	0.4
Propiconazole	60207-90-1	0.1	20
Pyrethrins	8003-34-7	0.5	1
Pyridaben	96489-71-3	0.1	3
Spinetoram	187166-15-0, 187166-40-1	0.1	3
Spinosad	131929-60-7, 131929-63-0	0.1	3
Spiromesifen	283594-90-1	0.1	12
Spirotetramat	203313-25-1	0.1	13
Tebuconazole	107534-96-3	0.1	2
Thiamethoxam	153719-23-4	5	4.5
Trifloxystrobin	141517-21-7	0.1	30

(e) If the sample fails residual pesticides testing, the batch from which the sample was collected fails residual pesticides testing and shall not be released for retail sale.

Note: Authority cited: Section 26013, Business and Professions Code. Reference: Sections 26100, 26104 and 26110, Business and Professions Code.

§ 15720. Microbial Impurities Testing.

(a) The licensed laboratory shall analyze at minimum 1.0 grams of the representative sample of cannabis or cannabis products to determine whether microbial impurities are present.

(b) The licensed laboratory shall report the result of the microbial impurities testing by indicating "pass" or "fail" on the COA.

(c) The sample of inhalable cannabis and cannabis products shall be deemed to have passed the microbial impurities testing if all of the following conditions are met:

(1) Shiga toxin-producing Escherichia coli is not detected in 1 gram;

(2) Salmonella spp. is not detected in 1 gram; and

(3) Pathogenic Aspergillus species A. fumigatus, A. flavus, A. niger, and A. terreus are not detected in 1 gram.

(d) The sample of non-inhalable cannabis and cannabis products shall be deemed to have passed the microbial impurities testing if both the following conditions are met:

(1) Shiga toxin-producing Escherichia coli is not detected in 1 gram, and

(2) Salmonella spp. is not detected in 1 gram.

(e) If the sample fails microbial impurities testing, the batch from which the sample was collected fails microbial impurities testing and shall not be released for retail sale.

NOTE: Authority cited: Section 26013, Business and Professions Code. Reference: Sections 26100, 26104 and 26110, Business and Professions Code.

§ 15721. Mycotoxin Testing.

(a) The licensed laboratory shall analyze at minimum 0.5 grams of the representative sample of cannabis and cannabis products to determine whether mycotoxins are present.

(b) The licensed laboratory shall report the result of the mycotoxins testing in unit micrograms per kilograms (μg/kg) on the COA and indicate "pass" or "fail" on the COA.

(c) The sample shall be deemed to have passed mycotoxin testing if both the following conditions are met:

(1) Total of aflatoxin B1, B2, G1, and G2 does not exceed 20 μg/kg of substance, and

(2) Ochratoxin A does not exceed 20 μg/kg of substance.

(d) If the sample fails mycotoxin testing, the batch from which the sample was collected fails mycotoxin testing and shall not be released for retail sale.

NOTE: Authority cited: Section 26013, Business and Professions Code. Reference: Sections 26100, 26104 and 26110, Business and Professions Code.

§ 15722. Foreign Material Testing.

(a) The licensed laboratory shall analyze the representative sample of cannabis and cannabis products to determine whether foreign material is present.

(b) The licensed laboratory shall report the result of the foreign material test by indicating "pass" or "fail" on the COA.

(c) The licensed laboratory shall perform foreign material testing on the total representative sample prior to sample homogenization.

(d) When the licensed laboratory performs foreign material testing, at minimum, the laboratory shall do all of the following:

(1) Examine both the exterior and interior of the dried flower sample, and

(2) Examine the exterior of the cannabis product sample.

(e) The sample shall be deemed to have passed the foreign material testing if the presence of foreign material does not exceed:

(1) 1/4 of the total sample area covered by sand, soil, cinders, or dirt;

(2) 1/4 of the total sample area covered by mold;

(3) 1 insect fragment, 1 hair, or 1 count mammalian excreta per 3.0 grams; or

(4) 1/4 of the total sample area covered by an imbedded foreign material.

(f) If the sample fails foreign material testing, the batch from which the sample was collected fails foreign material testing and shall not be released for retail sale.

NOTE: Authority cited: Section 26013, Business and Professions Code. Reference: Sections 26100, 26104 and 26110, Business and Professions Code.

§ 15723. Heavy Metals Testing.

(a) The licensed laboratory shall analyze at minimum 0.5 grams of the representative sample of cannabis and cannabis products to determine whether heavy metals are present.

(b) The licensed laboratory shall report the result of the heavy metals test in unit micrograms per gram (μg/g) on the COA and indicate "pass" or "fail" on the COA.

(c) The sample shall be deemed to have passed the heavy metals testing if the presence of heavy metals does not exceed the action levels listed in the following table.

Heavy Metal	**Action Level (μg/g) for Inhalable Cannabis and Cannabis Products**	**Action Level (μg/g) for Non-Inhalable Cannabis and Cannabis Products**
Cadmium	0.2	0.5
Lead	0.5	0.5
Arsenic	0.2	1.5
Mercury	0.1	3.0

(d) If the sample fails heavy metals testing, the batch from which the sample was collected fails heavy metals testing and shall not be released for retail sale.

NOTE: Authority cited: Section 26013, Business and Professions Code. Reference: Sections 26100, 26104 and 26110,

Business and Professions Code.

§ 15724. Cannabinoid Testing.

(a) The licensed laboratory shall analyze at minimum 0.5 grams of the representative sample of cannabis and cannabis products to determine the cannabinoid profile such as THC; THCA; CBD; CBDA; CBG; and CBN.

(b) The licensed laboratory shall establish a limit of quantitation (LOQ) of 1.0 mg/g or lower for all cannabinoids analyzed and reported.

(c) The licensed laboratory shall report the result of the cannabinoid testing on the COA, including, at minimum:

(1) A percentage for THC, THCA, CBD, and CBDA;

(A) When the licensed laboratory reports the result of the cannabinoid testing for harvest batch representative samples on the COA in dry-weight percent, they shall use the following equation:

Dry-weight percent cannabinoid = wet-weight percent cannabinoid / (1- percent moisture / 100)

(2) A percentage for Total THC and Total CBD, if applicable;

(3) Milligrams per gram (mg/g) if by dry-weight or milligrams per milliliter (mg/mL) if by volume for THC, THCA, CBD, and CBDA.

(4) Milligrams per gram (mg/g) if by dry-weight or milligrams per milliliter (mg/mL) if by volume for Total THC and Total CBD, if applicable;

(A) The licensed laboratory shall calculate the total cannabinoid concentration as follows:

(i) For concentration expressed in weight:

Total cannabinoid concentration (mg/g) = (cannabinoid acid form concentration (mg/g) x 0.877) + cannabinoid concentration (mg/g)

(ii) For concentration expressed in volume:

Total cannabinoid concentration (mg/mL) = (cannabinoid acid form concentration (mg/mL) x 0.877) + cannabinoid concentration (mg/mL)

(5) Milligrams per package for THC and CBD;

(6) Milligrams per package for Total THC and Total CBD, if applicable;

(7) Milligrams per serving for THC and CBD, if any;

(8) Milligrams per serving for Total THC and Total CBD, if any and if applicable; and

(9) The licensed laboratory shall report the results of all other cannabinoids analyzed on the COA both as a percentage and in either milligrams per gram (mg/g) if by weight or milligrams per milliliter (mg/mL) if by volume.

(d) The sample shall be deemed to have passed the cannabinoid testing if the amount of THC does not exceed the limits established in section 17304.

(e) The licensed laboratory shall report the test results and indicate an overall "pass" or "fail" for the cannabinoid testing on the COA.

(f) Any cannabinoids found to be less than the LOQ shall be reported on the COA as "<1 mg/g" if by dry-weight or "<1 mg/mL" if by volume.

(g) If the sample fails cannabinoid testing, the batch from which the sample was collected fails cannabinoid testing and shall not be released for retail sale.

(h) For purposes of this division, any one cannabinoid, Total THC, and/or Total CBD claimed to be present on a label shall not be considered inaccurate if the difference in percentage on the certificate of analysis is plus or minus 10.0%.

NOTE: Authority cited: Section 26013, Business and Professions Code. Reference: Sections 26100, 26104 and 26110, Business and Professions Code.

§ 15725. Terpenoid Testing.

(a) If requested, the licensed laboratory shall analyze at minimum 0.5 grams of the representative sample of cannabis or cannabis products to determine the terpenoid profile of the sample.

(b) The licensed laboratory shall report the result of the terpenoid testing on the COA both as a percentage and in either milligrams per gram (mg/g) if by weight or milligrams per milliliter (mg/mL) if by volume.

NOTE: Authority cited: Section 26013, Business and Professions Code. Reference: Sections 26100, 26104 and 26110, Business and Professions Code.

§ 15726. Certificate of Analysis (COA).

(a) The licensed laboratory shall generate a COA for each representative sample that the laboratory analyzes.

(b) The licensed laboratory shall ensure that the COA contains the results of all required analyses performed for the representative sample.

(c) The licensed laboratory shall, within 1 business day of completing all analyses of a sample, both upload the COA into the track and trace system and simultaneously provide a copy of the COA to the Department via email at testinglabs@cannabis.ca.gov with a file name of "METRC UID Number and Test Sample ID" and "Passed" or "Failed" in the subject heading of the email.

(d) The licensed laboratory shall not release to any person any cumulative or individual test results prior to completing all analyses and providing the COA to the Department.

(e) The COA shall contain, at minimum, the following information:

> (1) The term "Regulatory Compliance Testing" in font no smaller than 14-point, which shall appear in the upper-right corner of each page of the COA. No text or images shall appear above the term "Regulatory Compliance Testing" on any page of the COA.
>
> (2) Laboratory's name, licensed premises address, and license number;
>
> (3) Licensed distributor's or licensed microbusiness authorized to engage in distribution's name, licensed premises address, and license number;
>
> (4) Licensed cultivator's, licensed manufacturer's, or licensed microbusiness' name, licensed premises address, and license number;
>
> (5) Batch number of the batch from which the sample was obtained. For cannabis and cannabis products that are already packaged at the time of sampling, the labeled batch number on the packaged cannabis and cannabis products shall match the batch number on the COA;

(6) Sample identifying information, including matrix type and unique sample identifiers;

(7) Sample history, including the date collected, the date received by the laboratory, and the date(s) of sample analyses and corresponding testing results;

(8) A picture of the sample of cannabis and cannabis products. If the sample is pre-packaged, the picture must include an unobstructed image of the packaging;

(9) For dried flower samples, the total weight of the batch, in grams or pounds, and the total weight, of the representative sample in grams;

(10) For cannabis product or pre-rolls samples, the total unit count of both the representative sample and the total batch size;

(11) Measured density of the cannabis and cannabis products;

(12) The analytical methods, analytical instrumentation used, and corresponding Limits of Detection (LOD) and Limits of Quantitation (LOQ);

(13) An attestation on the COA from the laboratory supervisory or management employee that all LQC samples required by section 15730 were performed and met the acceptance criteria; and

(14) Analytes detected during the analyses of the sample that are unknown, unidentified, or injurious to human health if consumed, if any.

(f) The licensed laboratory shall report test results for each representative sample on the COA as follows:

(1) Indicate an overall "pass" or "fail" for the entire batch;

(2) When reporting qualitative results for each analyte, the licensed laboratory shall indicate "pass" or "fail";

(3) When reporting quantitative results for each analyte, the licensed laboratory shall use the appropriate units of measurement as required under this chapter;

(4) When reporting results for each test method, the licensed laboratory shall indicate "pass" or "fail";

(5) When reporting results for any analytes that were detected below the analytical method LOQ, indicate "<LOQ", notwithstanding cannabinoid results;

(6) When reporting results for any analytes that were not detected or detected below the LOD, indicate "ND"; and

(7) Indicate "NT" for any test that the licensed laboratory did not perform.

(g) The licensed laboratory supervisory or management employee shall validate the accuracy of the information contained on the COA and sign and date the COA.

(h) The laboratory supervisory or management employee may request to amend a COA to correct minor errors. Requests must be emailed to the Department at testinglabs@cannabis.ca.gov for approval prior to making any corrections. Errors in results required to be reported pursuant to subsection (f) are not minor errors.

NOTE: Authority cited: Section 26013, Business and Professions Code. Reference: Sections 26100, 26104 and 26110, Business and Professions Code.

ARTICLE 6. POST TESTING PROCEDURES

§ 15727. Remediation and Retesting.

(a) A cannabis or cannabis product batch that has been additionally processed after failed regulatory compliance testing pursuant to section 17305 must be retested and successfully pass all the analyses required under this chapter.

(b) A cannabis or cannabis product batch may only be remediated twice. If the batch fails after the second remediation attempt and the second retesting, the entire batch shall be destroyed.

(c) Within one business day of completing the required analyses of a representative sample obtained from a remediated cannabis or cannabis product batch, the laboratory shall upload the COA information into the track and trace system, or if the licensee does not yet have access to the track and trace system, it shall be emailed to the Department.

NOTE: Authority cited: Section 26013, Business and Professions Code. Reference: Sections 26100, 26104 and 26110, Business and Professions Code.

§ 15728. Post Testing Sample Retention.

(a) The licensed laboratory shall retain the reserve sample, consisting of any portion of a sample that was not used in the testing process. The reserve sample shall be kept, at minimum, for 45 business days after the analyses, after which time it may be destroyed and denatured to the point the material is rendered unrecognizable and unusable.

(b) The licensed laboratory shall securely store the reserve sample in a manner that prohibits sample degradation, contamination, and tampering.

(c) The licensed laboratory shall provide the reserve sample to the Department upon request.

NOTE: Authority cited: Section 26013, Business and Professions Code. Reference: Sections 26100, 26104 and 26110, Business and Professions Code.

ARTICLE 7. LABORATORY QUALITY ASSURANCE AND QUALITY CONTROL

§ 15729. Laboratory Quality Assurance (LQA) Program.

(a) The licensed laboratory shall develop and implement a LQA program to assure the reliability and validity of the analytical data produced by the laboratory. The LQA program shall, at minimum, include a written LQA manual that addresses the following:

(1) Quality control procedures;

(2) Laboratory organization and employee training and responsibilities, including good laboratory practice (GLP);

(3) LQA objectives for measurement data;

(4) Traceability of data and analytical results;

(5) Instrument maintenance, calibration procedures, and frequency;

(6) Performance and system audits;

(7) Corrective action procedures;

(8) Steps to change processes when necessary;

(9) Record retention and document control;

(10) Test procedure standardization; and

(11) Method validation.

(b) The supervisory or management laboratory employee shall annually review, amend if necessary, and approve the LQA program and manual both when they are created and when there is a change in methods, laboratory equipment, or the supervisory or management laboratory employee.

NOTE: Authority cited: Section 26013, Business and Professions Code. Reference: Sections 26100, 26104 and 26110, Business and Professions Code.

§ 15730. Laboratory Quality Control (LQC) Samples.

The licensed laboratory shall use LQC samples and adhere to good laboratory practice (GLP) in the performance of each analysis according to the following specifications.

(a) The licensed laboratory shall analyze LQC samples in the same manner as the laboratory analyzes cannabis and cannabis products samples.

(b) The licensed laboratory shall use at least one negative control, one positive control, and one laboratory replicate sample in each analytical batch for each target organism during microbial testing. If one of the controls produces unexpected results, the samples shall be re-prepped and reanalyzed with a new set of controls.

(c) If the result of the microbial analyses is outside the specified acceptance criteria in the following table, the licensed laboratory shall determine the cause and take steps to remedy the problem until the result is within the specified acceptance criteria.

Laboratory Quality Control Sample	Acceptance Criteria	Corrective Action
Positive control	Produces expected result, positive result	Re-prep and reanalyze the entire analytical batch, once. If problem persists, locate and remedy the source of unexpected result, then re-prep samples and reanalyze with a new set of controls.
Negative control	Produces expected result, negative result	Re-prep and reanalyze the entire analytical batch, once. If problem persists, locate and remedy the source of unexpected result, then re-prep samples and reanalyze with a new set of controls.
Laboratory replicate sample	Sample results must concur	Reanalyze sample and associated replicate sample once. If problem persists, re-prep samples and reanalyze.

(d) The licensed laboratory shall prepare and analyze at least one of each of the following LQC samples for each analytical batch:

(1) Method blank;

(2) Laboratory control sample (LCS); and

(3) Laboratory replicate sample or matrix spike sample.

(e) The laboratory shall analyze, at minimum, a continuing calibration verification (CCV) sample at the beginning of each analytical sequence and every 10 samples thereafter.

(f) If the result of the chemical analyses is outside the specified acceptance criteria in the following table, the laboratory shall determine the cause and take steps to remedy the problem until the result is within the specified acceptance criteria.

Laboratory Quality Control Sample	Acceptance Criteria	Corrective Action
Method blank sample	Not to exceed LOQ	Reanalyze entire analytical batch once. If method blank is still greater than the LOQ for any analyte, locate the source of contamination then re-prep samples and reanalyze.
LCS	Percent recovery 70% to 130%	Reanalyze the entire analytical batch, once. If problem persists, re-prep samples and reanalyze or re-run the initial calibration curve.
Laboratory replicate sample	RPD < or = 30%	Reanalyze sample and associated replicate sample once. If problem persists, re-prep samples and reanalyze.
Matrix spike sample	Percent recovery between 70% to 130%	Reanalyze sample and associated matrix spike sample once. If problem persists, re-prep samples and reanalyze.
CCV	Percent recovery between 70% to 130%	Reanalyze all samples that followed the last CCV that met the acceptance criteria. If CCV still fails, re-run the initial calibration curve and all samples in the analytical sequence.

(g) If any analyte is detected above any action level, as described in this chapter, the sample shall be re-prepped and reanalyzed in replicate within another analytical batch.

(1) For quantitative analyses, the re-prepped sample and its associated replicate must meet the acceptance criteria of RPD ⩽30%.

(2) For qualitative analyses, the re-prepped sample and its associated replicate results must concur.

(h) If any LQC sample produces a result outside of the acceptance criteria, the laboratory cannot report the result and the entire batch cannot be released for retail sale. The laboratory shall determine the cause and take steps to remedy the problem until the result is within the specified acceptance criteria.

(i) If the licensed laboratory determines that the result is a false-positive or a false-negative, the Department may ask for the laboratory to re-sample or retest.

(j) The licensed laboratory shall compile and generate one LQC sample report for each analytical batch that includes LQC acceptance criteria, measurements, analysis date, and matrix.

NOTE: Authority cited: Section 26013, Business and Professions Code. Reference: Sections 26100, 26104 and 26110, Business and Professions Code.

§ 15731. Limits of Detection (LOD) and Limits of Quantitation (LOQ) for Quantitative Analyses.

(a) The licensed laboratory shall calculate the LOD for chemical method analyses according to any of the following methods:

(1) Signal-to-noise ratio of between 3:1 and 2:1;

(2) Standard deviation of the response and the slope of calibration curve using a minimum of 7 spiked blank samples calculated as follows; LOD = (3.3 x standard deviation of the response) / slope of the calibration curve; or

(3) A method published by the United States Food and Drug Administration (USFDA) or the United States Environmental Protection Agency (USEPA).

(b) The licensed laboratory shall calculate the LOQ for chemical method analyses according to any of the following methods:

(1) Signal-to-noise ratio of 10:1, at minimum;

(2) Standard deviation of the response and the slope using a minimum of 7 spiked blank samples calculated as follows:

LOQ = (10 x standard deviation of the response) / slope of the calibration curve; or

(3) A method published by the USFDA or the USEPA.

NOTE: Authority cited: Section 26013, Business and Professions Code. Reference: Sections 26100, 26104 and 26110, Business and Professions Code.

§ 15732. Data Package.

(a) The licensed laboratory shall compile and generate one data package for each representative sample that the laboratory analyzes.

(b) The licensed laboratory shall create a data package and use the Data Package Cover Page and Checklist Form, DCC-LIC-024 (Amended 2/22), which is incorporated herein by reference. The data package and form DCC-LIC-024 (Amended 2/22) shall be provided to the Department immediately upon request.

NOTE: Authority cited: Section 26013, Business and Professions Code. Reference: Sections 26100, 26104, 26110 and 26160, Business and Professions Code.

§ 15733. Required Proficiency Testing.

(a) The licensed laboratory shall participate in a proficiency testing program provided by an organization that operates in conformance with the requirements of ISO/IEC 17043, at least once every six months.

(b) The licensed laboratory shall annually, successfully participate in a proficiency testing program for each of the following test methods:

(1) Cannabinoids;

(2) Heavy metals;

(3) Microbial impurities;

(4) Mycotoxins;

(5) Residual pesticides;

(6) Residual solvents and processing chemicals; and

(7) If tested, terpenoids.

(c) The licensed laboratory shall report all analytes available by the proficiency testing program provider and for which the licensee is required to test as required under this chapter.

(d) The licensed laboratory shall participate in the proficiency testing program by following the laboratory's existing SOPs for testing cannabis and cannabis products.

(e) The licensed laboratory shall rotate the proficiency testing program among the laboratory employees who perform the test methods.

(f) Laboratory employees who participate in a proficiency testing program shall sign the corresponding analytical reports or attestation statements to certify that the proficiency testing program was conducted in the same manner as the laboratory tests of cannabis and cannabis products.

(g) A supervisory or management laboratory employee shall review and verify the accuracy of results reported for all proficiency testing program samples analyzed.

(h) The licensed laboratory shall request the proficiency testing program provider to send results concurrently to the Department, if available, or the laboratory shall provide the proficiency testing program results to the Department within 3 business days after the laboratory receives notification of their test results from the proficiency testing program provider. Any results shall be reported by submitting the Licensee Notification and Request Form, Notifications and Requests Regarding Testing Laboratories, DCC-LIC-029 (New 2/22), which is incorporated herein by reference.

NOTE: Authority cited: Section 26013, Business and Professions Code. Reference: Sections 26100 and 26110, Business and Professions Code.

§ 15734. Satisfactory and Unsatisfactory Proficiency Test Performance.

(a) The licensed laboratory shall be deemed to have successfully participated in a proficiency testing program for an analyte tested in a specific method if the test results demonstrate a "satisfactory" or otherwise proficient performance determination by the proficiency testing program provider.

(b) The licensed laboratory may not report test results for analytes that are deemed by the proficiency testing program provider as "unacceptable," "questionable," "unsatisfactory", or otherwise deficient.

(c) The licensed laboratory may resume reporting test results for analytes that were deemed "unacceptable," "questionable," "unsatisfactory", or otherwise deficient, only if both of the following conditions are met:

(1) The licensed laboratory satisfactorily remedies the cause of the failure for each analyte; and

(2) The licensed laboratory submits, to the Department, a written corrective action report demonstrating how the laboratory has fixed the cause of the failure.

NOTE: Authority cited: Section 26013, Business and Professions Code. Reference: Sections 26100 and 26110, Business and Professions Code.

§ 15735. Laboratory Audits.

(a) The licensed laboratory shall conduct an internal audit at least once per year or in accordance with the ISO/IEC 17025 accrediting body's requirement, whichever is more frequent.

(b) The internal audit must include all of the components required by the ISO/IEC 17025 internal-audit standards.

(c) Within 3 business days of completing the internal audit, the licensed laboratory shall submit the results of the internal audit to the Department.

(d) Within 3 business days of receiving the accrediting body onsite audit findings, the licensed laboratory shall submit the results to the Department.

(e) The licensed laboratory shall submit any audit results to the Department, accompanied by the Licensee Notification and Request Form, Notifications and Requests Regarding Testing Laboratories, DCC-LIC-029 (New 2/22), which is incorporated herein by reference.

NOTE: Authority cited: Section 26013, Business and Professions Code. Reference: Sections 26100 and 26104, Business and Professions Code.

ARTICLE 8. LABORATORY EMPLOYEE QUALIFICATIONS

§ 15736. General Laboratory Employee Qualifications.

(a) The licensed laboratory may only employ persons who are at least 21 years of age.

(b) The licensed laboratory shall develop and implement an employee training program to ensure competency of laboratory employees for their assigned functions.

(c) The licensed laboratory shall ensure and document that each laboratory employee meets the employee qualifications.

NOTE: Authority cited: Section 26013, Business and Professions Code. Reference: Sections 26102 and 26104, Business and Professions Code.

§ 15737. Supervisor or Management Responsibilities and Qualifications.

(a) The licensed laboratory shall employ a supervisor or management employee who must be responsible for:

(1) Overseeing and directing the scientific methods of the licensed laboratory;

(2) Ensuring that the licensed laboratory achieves and maintains a laboratory quality assurance program as required by section 15729; and

(3) Providing ongoing and appropriate training to laboratory employees.

(b) To be considered qualified, the supervisor or management employee must have at minimum:

(1) A doctoral degree in biological, chemical, agricultural, environmental, or related sciences from an accredited college or university;

(2) A master's degree in biological, chemical, agricultural, environmental, or related sciences from an accredited college or university, plus at least 2 years of full-time practical experience;

(3) A bachelor's degree in biological, chemical, agricultural, environmental, or related sciences from an accredited college or university, plus at least 4 years of full-time practical experience; or

(4) A bachelor's degree in any field from an accredited college or university, plus at least 8 years of full-time practical experience, 4 years of which must have been in a supervisory or management position.

NOTE: Authority cited: Section 26013, Business and Professions Code. Reference: Sections 26102 and 26104, Business and Professions Code.

§ 15738. Analyst and Sampler Qualifications.

(a) The licensed laboratory shall employ an analyst who, at minimum, must have either:

(1) Earned a master's degree or a bachelor's degree in biological, chemical, agricultural, environmental, or related sciences from an accredited college or university; or

(2) Completed 2 years of college or university education that included coursework in biological, chemical, agricultural, environmental, or related sciences from an accredited college or university, plus at least 3 years of full-time practical experience.

(b) The licensed laboratory shall employ a sampler who, at minimum, must have either:

(1) Completed 2 years college or university education; or

(2) Earned a High School Diploma or passed a General Educational Development or High School Equivalency exam, plus at least 1 year of full-time practical experience.

NOTE: Authority cited: Section 26013, Business and Professions Code. Reference: Sections 26102 and 26104, Business and Professions Code.

ARTICLE 9. RECORD RETENTION [REPEALED]

§ 15739. Records. [Repealed]

Note: Authority cited: Section 26013, Business and Professions Code. Reference: Section 26160, Business and Professions Code.

Chapter 7. Enforcement [Repealed]

§ 15800. Right of Access. [Repealed]

Note: Authority cited: Section 26013, Business and Professions Code. Reference: Sections 26012, 26015 and 26160, Business and Professions Code; and Section 11181, Government Code.

§ 15801. Notice to Comply. [Repealed]

Note: Authority cited: Section 26013, Business and Professions Code. Reference: Sections 26012 and 26018, Business and Professions Code.

§ 15802. Citations; Orders of Abatement; Administrative Fines. [Repealed]

Note: Authority cited: Sections 125.9 and 26013, Business and Professions Code. Reference: Sections 125.9, 148, 149 and 26012, Business and Professions Code.

§ 15803. Contesting Citations. [Repealed]

Note: Authority cited: Section 26013, Business and Professions Code. Reference: Sections 125.9, 26012 and 26016, Business and Professions Code.

§ 15804. Citation Compliance. [Repealed]

Note: Authority cited: Section 26013, Business and Professions Code. Reference: Sections 125.9 and 26012, Business and Professions Code.

§ 15805. Minor Decoys. [Repealed]

Note: Authority cited: Sections 26013 and 26140, Business and Professions Code. Reference: Section 26140, Business and Professions Code.

§ 15806. Attire and Conduct. [Repealed]

Note: Authority cited: Section 26013, Business and Professions Code. Reference: Section 26011.5, Business and Professions Code.

§ 15807. Entertainers and Conduct. [Repealed]

Note: Authority cited: Section 26013, Business and Professions Code. Reference: Section 26011.5, Business and Professions Code.

§ 15808. Additional Grounds for Discipline. [Repealed]

Note: Authority cited: Section 26013, Business and Professions Code. Reference: Sections 26011.5, 26012, 26030 and 26031, Business and Professions Code.

§ 15809. Disciplinary Actions. [Repealed]

Note: Authority cited: Section 26013, Business and Professions Code. Reference: Sections 26012, 26031 and 26034, Business and Professions Code.

§ 15810. Interim Suspension. [Repealed]

Note: Authority cited: Section 26013, Business and Professions Code. Reference: Sections 494, 26011.5, 26012 and 26031, Business and Professions Code.

§ 15811. Posting of Notice of Suspension. [Repealed]

Note: Authority cited: Section 26013, Business and Professions Code. Reference: Sections 26011.5 and 26012, Business and Professions Code.

§ 15812. Posting of Notice of Revocation. [Repealed]

Note: Authority cited: Section 26013, Business and Professions Code. Reference: Sections 26011.5 and 26012, Business and Professions Code.

§ 15813. Enforcement Costs. [Repealed]

Note: Authority cited: Section 26013, Business and Professions Code. Reference: Sections 125.3, 26012 and 26031, Business and Professions Code.

§ 15814. Disciplinary Guidelines. [Repealed]

Note: Authority cited: Section 26013, Business and Professions Code. Reference: Sections 26012 and 26031, Business and Professions Code.

§ 15815. Emergency Decision and Order. [Repealed]

Note: Authority cited: Section 26013, Business and Professions Code. Reference: Section 26012, Business and Professions Code; and Sections 11460.10, 11460.20, 11460.30, 11460.40, 11460.50, 11460.60, 11460.70 and 11460.80, Government Code.

§ 15900. Eligibility. [Repealed]

Note: Authority cited: Section 26013, Business and Professions Code. Reference: Section 34019, Revenue and Taxation Code.

§ 15901. Request for Proposals. [Repealed]

Note: Authority cited: Section 26013, Business and Professions Code. Reference: Section 34019, Revenue and Taxation Code.

§ 15902. Selection Process and Criteria. [Repealed]

Note: Authority cited: Section 26013, Business and Professions Code. Reference: Section 34019, Revenue and Taxation Code.

§ 15903. Release of Funds. [Repealed]

Note: Authority cited: Section 26013, Business and Professions Code. Reference: Section 34019, Revenue and Taxation Code.

§ 15904. Reports to the Department. [Repealed]

Note: Authority cited: Section 26013, Business and Professions Code. Reference: Section 34019, Revenue and Taxation Code.

§ 15905. Research Records. [Repealed]

Note: Authority cited: Section 26013, Business and Professions Code. Reference: Section 26160, Business and Professions Code; and Section 34019, Revenue and Taxation Code.

§ 16000. Definitions. [Repealed]

Note: Authority cited: Sections 26012 and 26013, Business and Professions Code. Reference: Sections 26001 and 26013, Business and Professions Code; and Section 12754.5, Food and Agricultural Code.

Chapter 7. Cultivators

ARTICLE 1. GENERAL CULTIVATION REQUIREMENTS

§ 16201. Cultivation License Types.

License types include:

(a) Specialty Cottage:

(1) "Specialty Cottage Outdoor" is an outdoor cultivation site with up to 25 mature plants or 2,500 square feet or less of total canopy.

(2) "Specialty Cottage Indoor" is an indoor cultivation site with 500 square feet or less of total canopy.

(3) "Specialty Cottage Mixed-Light Tier 1 and 2" is a mixed-light cultivation site with 2,500 square feet or less of total canopy.

(b) Specialty:

(1) "Specialty Outdoor" is an outdoor cultivation site with less than or equal to 5,000 square feet of total canopy, or up to 50 mature plants on noncontiguous plots.

(2) "Specialty Indoor" is an indoor cultivation site with between 501 and 5,000 square feet of total canopy.

(3) "Specialty Mixed-Light Tier 1 and 2" is a mixed-light cultivation site with between 2,501 and 5,000 square feet of total canopy.

(c) Small:

(1) "Small Outdoor" is an outdoor cultivation site with between 5,001 and 10,000 square feet of total canopy.

(2) "Small Indoor" is an indoor cultivation site with between 5,001 and 10,000 square feet of total canopy.

(3) "Small Mixed-Light Tier 1 and 2" is a mixed-light cultivation site with between 5,001 and 10,000 square feet of total canopy.

(d) Medium:

(1) "Medium Outdoor" is an outdoor cultivation site with between 10,001 square feet and one acre of total canopy.

(2) "Medium Indoor" is an indoor cultivation site with between 10,001 and 22,000 square feet of total canopy.

(3) "Medium Mixed-Light Tier 1 and 2" is a mixed-light cultivation site with between 10,001 and 22,000 square feet of total canopy.

(e) "Nursery" is a cultivation site that conducts only cultivation of clones, immature plants, seeds, and other agricultural products used specifically for the propagation of cultivation of cannabis.

(f) "Processor" is a cultivation site that conducts only trimming, drying, curing, grading, packaging, and labeling of cannabis and nonmanufactured cannabis products.

NOTE: Authority cited: Section 26013, Business and Professions Code. Reference: Sections 26012, 26013, 26050 and 26061, Business and Professions Code.

§ 16201.1. Large Cultivation Licenses.

(a) Beginning January 1, 2023, the Department may issue Large Cultivation licenses. Large license types include:

(1) "Large Outdoor" is an outdoor cultivation site with more than one acre of total canopy.

(2) "Large Indoor" is an indoor cultivation site with more than 22,000 square feet of total canopy.

(3) "Large Mixed-light" is a Mixed-light cultivation site with more than 22,000 square feet of total canopy.

NOTE: Authority cited: Section 26013, Business and Professions Code. Reference: Sections 26012, 26013, 26050 and 26061, Business and Professions Code.

§ 16202. General Cultivation Requirements.

(a) Licensees are prohibited from transferring any commercially cultivated cannabis or nonmanufactured cannabis products from their licensed premises. All transfers of cannabis and nonmanufactured cannabis product from a licensed cultivation premises must be conducted by a distributor licensed by the Department.

(b) Artificial lighting is permissible only to maintain immature plants outside the canopy area.

NOTE: Authority cited: Section 26013, Business and Professions Code. Reference: Sections 26010, 26012, 26013, 26050 and 26053, Business and Professions Code.

§ 16209. Medium Cultivation License Limits.

A person or owner shall be limited to one (1) Medium Outdoor, or one (1) Medium Indoor, or one (1) Medium Mixed-Light A-License or M-License. This section shall remain in effect until January 1, 2023.

NOTE: Authority cited: Section 26013, Business and Professions Code. Reference: Sections 26012, 26013, 26050 and 26061, Business and Professions Code.

ARTICLE 2. CULTIVATION SITE REQUIREMENTS

§ 16300. Cultivation Requirements for Specialty Cottage, Specialty, Small, and Medium Licenses.

(a) Cannabis plants maintained outside of the designated canopy area(s) for specialty cottage, specialty, small, and medium licenses are prohibited from flowering. Should a plant outside of the canopy area(s) begin flowering, a plant tag shall be applied, the plant shall be moved to a designated canopy area and reported in the track and trace system without delay.

(b) All plants or portions of a plant used for seed production shall be tagged with a plant tag pursuant to section 15048.4.

(c) A licensee propagating immature plants for distribution or seed for distribution to another licensee shall obtain a nursery license.

(d) Licensees shall process their harvested cannabis only in area(s) designated for processing in their cultivation plan, or transfer their harvested cannabis to a licensed processor, manufacturer, or distributor via a licensed distributor.

NOTE: Authority cited: Section 26013, Business and Professions Code. Reference: Sections 26013, 26060 and 26120, Business and Professions Code.

§ 16300.1. Additional Cultivation Requirements for Large Licenses.

(a) Commencing on January 1, 2023, a person that holds an ownership or financial interest in a Large Cultivation license shall not be eligible to apply for or hold an ownership or financial interest in a Type 8, Type 11, or Type 12 license.

(b) As part of the license application for a Large Cultivation license or a request for a conversion into a Large Cultivation license the applicant or licensee shall submit an attestation that:

(1) All persons who will hold an ownership or financial interest in the Large Cultivation license do not currently

hold any ownership or financial interest in a Type 8, Type 11, or Type 12 license; and

(2) No person who will hold an ownership or financial interest in the Large Cultivation license will apply for or hold an ownership or financial interest in a Type 8, Type 11, or Type 12 license while maintaining their ownership or financial interest in the Large Cultivation license.

NOTE: Authority cited: Section 26013, Business and Professions Code. Reference: Sections 26012, 26060, 26061 and 26180, Business and Professions Code.

§ 16301. Seed Production Requirements for Nursery Licensees.

Nursery licensees producing seed for distribution shall tag all mature plants with a plant tag pursuant to section 15048.4(b). All products, except seed, derived from these plants are prohibited from entering the commercial distribution chain.

NOTE: Authority cited: Section 26013, Business and Professions Code. Reference: Sections 26013, 26060 and 26067, Business and Professions Code.

§ 16302. Research and Development Requirements for Nursery Licensees.

Nursery licensees may maintain a research and development area, as identified in their cultivation plan, for the cultivation of mature plants. All mature plants shall be tagged with a plant tag pursuant to section 15048.4. All cannabis and cannabis products derived from these plants are prohibited from entering the commercial distribution chain or being transferred off the licensed premises.

NOTE: Authority cited: Section 26013, Business and Professions Code. Reference: Sections 26013, 26060 and 26067, Business and Professions Code.

§ 16303. Cultivation Requirements for Processor Licensees.

(a) Processor licensees shall comply with all of the following requirements:

(1) All aggregation of product shall adhere to track and trace requirements.

(2) Licensees may produce nonmanufactured cannabis products without a manufacturing license.

(3) Cultivation of cannabis plants is prohibited at a licensed processor premises.

NOTE: Authority cited: Section 26013, Business and Professions Code. Reference: Sections 26013, 26060, 26067, 26069 and 26120, Business and Professions Code.

§ 16304. General Environmental Protection Measures.

(a) All licensed cultivators shall comply with all of the following environmental protection measures:

(1) Principles, guidelines, and requirements adopted pursuant to section 13149 of the Water Code and implemented by the State Water Resources Control Board, Regional Water Quality Control Boards, or California Department of Fish and Wildlife;

(2) Any conditions of licensure included pursuant to section 26060.1(b)(1) of the Business and Professions

Code;

(3) Requirements of section 7050.5(b) of the Health and Safety Code if human remains are discovered during cultivation activities;

(4) Requirements for generators pursuant to section 16306;

(5) Requirements for pesticides pursuant to section 16307;

(6) Outdoor lights used for safety or security purposes are shielded and downward facing; and

(7) Lights used for indoor or mixed-light cultivation are shielded from sunset to sunrise to reduce nighttime glare.

NOTE: Authority cited: Section 26013, Business and Professions Code. Reference: Sections 26013, 26060, 26066 and 26201, Business and Professions Code.

§ 16305. Renewable Energy Requirements.

(a) Beginning January 1, 2023, all holders of indoor, tier 2 mixed-light license types of any size, and all holders of nursery licenses using indoor or tier 2 mixed-light techniques shall ensure that electrical power used for commercial cannabis activity meets the average electricity greenhouse gas emissions intensity required by their local utility provider pursuant to the California Renewables Portfolio Standard Program in division 1, part 1, chapter 2.3, article 16 (commencing with section 399.11) of the Public Utilities Code.

(b) If a licensed cultivator's average weighted greenhouse gas emission intensity, as calculated and reported upon license renewal pursuant to section 15020, is greater than the local utility provider's greenhouse gas emission intensity, the licensee shall obtain carbon offsets to cover the excess in carbon emissions from the previous annual licensed period. The carbon offsets shall be purchased from one or more of the following recognized voluntary carbon registries:

(1) American Carbon Registry;

(2) Climate Action Reserve; or

(3) Verified Carbon Standard.

NOTE: Authority cited: Section 26013, Business and Professions Code. Reference: Sections 26013, 26060, 26066 and 26201, Business and Professions Code.

§ 16306. Generator Requirements.

(a) For the purposes of this section, "generator" means a stationary or portable compression ignition engine, also known as a diesel engine, as defined in title 17, California Code of Regulations, section 93115.4.

(b) Licensed cultivators using generators rated at fifty (50) horsepower and greater shall demonstrate compliance with the Airborne Toxic Control Measure for stationary or portable engines, as applicable, established in title 17, California Code of Regulations, sections 93115-93116.5. Compliance shall be demonstrated by providing a copy of one of the following to the Department upon request:

(1) For portable engines, a Portable Equipment Registration Certificate provided by the California Air Resources Board; or

(2) For portable or stationary engines, a Permit to Operate or other proof of engine registration, obtained from the Local Air District with jurisdiction over the licensed premises.

(c) Licensed cultivators using generators rated below fifty (50) horsepower shall comply with the following by 2023:

(1) Either subsection (1)(A) or (1)(B):

(A) Meet the "emergency" definition for portable engines in title 17, California Code of Regulations, section 93116.2(a)(12), or the "emergency use" definition for stationary engines in title 17, California Code of Regulations, section 93115.4(a)(30); or

(B) Operate eighty (80) hours or less in a calendar year; and

(2) Either subsection (2)(A) or (2)(B):

(A) Meet Tier 3 with Level 3 diesel particulate filter requirements in title 13, California Code of Regulations, sections 2700-2711; or

(B) Meet Tier 4 requirements, or current engine requirements if more stringent, in title 40, Code of Federal Regulations, chapter I, subchapter U, part 1039, subpart B, section 1039.101.

(d) All generators used by licensed cultivators shall be equipped with non-resettable hour-meters. If a generator does not come equipped with a non-resettable hour-meter, an aftermarket non-resettable hour-meter shall be installed.

NOTE: Authority cited: Section 26013, Business and Professions Code. Reference: Sections 26013, 26060, 26066 and 26201, Business and Professions Code.

§ 16307. Pesticide Use Requirements.

(a) Licensed cultivators shall comply with all applicable pesticide statutes and regulations enforced by the Department of Pesticide Regulation.

(b) For all pesticides that are exempt from registration requirements, licensed cultivators shall comply with all applicable pesticide statutes and regulations enforced by the Department of Pesticide Regulation and the following pesticide application and storage protocols:

(1) Comply with all pesticide label directions;

(2) Store chemicals in a secure building or shed to prevent access by wildlife;

(3) Contain any chemical leaks and immediately clean up any spills;

(4) Apply the minimum amount of product necessary to control the target pest;

(5) Prevent offsite drift;

(6) Do not apply pesticides when pollinators are present;

(7) Do not allow drift to flowering plants attractive to pollinators;

(8) Do not spray directly to surface water or allow pesticide product to drift to surface water. Spray only when wind is blowing away from surface water bodies;

(9) Do not apply pesticides when they may reach surface water or groundwater; and

(10) Only use properly labeled pesticides. If no label is available, consult the Department of Pesticide Regulation.

NOTE: Authority cited: Section 26013, Business and Professions Code. Reference: Sections 26013, 26060, 26066 and 26201, Business and Professions Code.

§ 16308. Canopy Requirements.

(a) Licensed cultivators shall comply with the following requirements for canopy areas:

(1) Each canopy shall be marked with clearly identifiable physical boundaries around all areas that will contain mature plants. Physical boundaries include, but are not limited to, interior walls, shelves, greenhouse walls, hoop house walls, garden benches, hedgerows, fencing, garden beds, garden plots, or stakes delineating the perimeter.

(2) Each canopy shall be of sufficient size to contain the mature plants in their entirety at any point in time. No portion of the plant is permitted to hang over an established canopy boundary.

(b) Seeds, immature plants, or propagated material received from a licensed nursery as trade samples shall be cultivated in a canopy area dedicated to trade samples that meets the requirements of subsection (a). Canopy areas used to cultivate trade samples received from a licensed nursery shall be included in the licensed cultivator's cultivation plan and shall be included in the aggregate square footage of the canopy areas.

(c) Licensed cultivators may utilize canopy areas to produce seeds for their own use.

NOTE: Authority cited: Section 26013, Business and Professions Code. Reference: Sections 26013 and 26060, Business and Professions Code.

§ 16309. Cultivation Plan Requirements.

(a) Licensed cultivators shall establish and maintain a cultivation plan that includes all of the following:

(1) A premises diagram drafted in accordance with section 15006.

(2) A cannabis waste management plan developed in accordance with section 17223.

(3) A pest management plan developed in accordance with section 16310.

NOTE: Authority cited: Section 26013, Business and Professions Code. Reference: Sections 26013, 26051.5 and 26060, Business and Professions Code.

§ 16310. Pest Management Plan.

(a) The licensed cultivator shall develop a pest management plan that includes:

(1) The product name and active ingredient(s) of all pesticides to be applied to cannabis; and

(2) Any integrated pest management protocols, including chemical, biological, and cultural methods, that will be used to prevent and control pests on the cultivation site.

NOTE: Authority cited: Section 26013, Business and Professions Code. Reference: Sections 26013, 26051.5 and 26060, Business and Professions Code.

§ 16311. Supplemental Water Source Information.

The following information shall be provided for each water source identified by the applicant:

(a) Retail water supply sources:

(1) If the water source is a retail water supplier, as defined in section 13575 of the Water Code, such as a municipal provider, provide the following:

(A) Name of the retail water supplier; and

(B) A copy of the most recent water service bill or written documentation from the water supplier stating that service will be provided at the premises address.

(2) If the water source is a small retail water supplier, such as a delivery service, and is subject to section 26060.1(a)(1)(B) of the Business and Professions Code and the retail water supplier contract is for delivery or pickup of water from a surface water body or an underground stream flowing in a known and definite channel, provide all of the following:

(A) The name of the retail water supplier under the contract;

(B) The water source and geographic location coordinates, in either latitude and longitude or the California Coordinate System, of any point of diversion used by the retail water supplier to divert water delivered to the commercial cannabis business under the contract;

(C) The authorized place of use of any water right used by the retail water supplier to divert water delivered to the commercial cannabis business under the contract;

(D) The maximum amount of water delivered to the commercial cannabis business for cannabis cultivation in any year; and

(E) A copy of the most recent water service bill.

(3) If the water source is a small retail water supplier, such as a delivery service, and is subject to section 26060.1(a)(1)(B) of the Business and Professions Code and the retail water supplier contract is for delivery or pickup of water from a groundwater well, provide all of the following:

(A) The name of the retail water supplier under the contract;

(B) The geographic location coordinates for any groundwater well used to supply water delivered to the commercial cannabis business, in either latitude and longitude or the California Coordinate System;

(C) The maximum amount of water delivered to the commercial cannabis business for cannabis cultivation in any year;

(D) A copy of the well completion report filed with the Department of Water Resources pursuant to section 13751 of the Water Code for each percolating groundwater well used to divert water delivered to the commercial cannabis business. If no well completion report is available, the applicant shall provide evidence from the Department of Water Resources indicating that the Department of Water Resources does not have a record of the well completion report. When no well completion report is available, the State Water Resources Control Board may request additional information about the well; and

(E) A copy of the most recent water service bill.

(b) If the water source is a groundwater well, provide the following:

(1) The groundwater well's geographic location coordinates, in either latitude and longitude or the California Coordinate System; and

(2) A copy of the well completion report filed with the Department of Water Resources pursuant to section 13751 of the Water Code. If no well completion report is available, the applicant shall provide evidence from the Department of Water Resources indicating that the Department of Water Resources does not have a record of the well completion report. If no well completion report is available, the State Water Resources Control Board may request additional information about the well.

(c) If the water source is a rainwater catchment system, provide the following:

(1) The total square footage of the catchment footprint area(s).

(2) The total storage capacity, in gallons, of the catchment system(s).

(3) A detailed description and photographs of the rainwater catchment system infrastructure, including the location, size, and type of all surface areas that collect rainwater. Examples of rainwater collection surface areas include a rooftop and greenhouse.

(4) Geographic location coordinates of the rainwater catchment infrastructure in either latitude and longitude or the California Coordinate System.

(d) If the water source is a diversion from a waterbody (such as a river, stream, creek, pond, lake, etc.), provide any applicable water right statement, application, permit, license, or small irrigation use registration identification number(s), and a copy of any applicable statement, registration certificate, permit, license, or proof of a pending application issued under part 2 (commencing with section 1200) of division 2 of the California Water Code as evidence of approval of a water diversion by the State Water Resources Control Board.

NOTE: Authority cited: Section 26013, Business and Professions Code. Reference: Sections 26013 and 26060.1, Business and Professions Code.

ARTICLE 3. RELEASE OF INFORMATION TO FINANCIAL INSTITUTIONS

§ 16410. Cultivation Licensee Authorization to Release Data to Financial Institutions.

(a) A cultivation licensee may authorize the Department to provide information to a financial institution for purposes of facilitating the provision of financial services. The authorization shall be made in writing, through a form prescribed by the Department, which shall include the following information:

(1) The name of the licensed business for which the licensee is authorizing the release of information;

(2) The business's license number(s);

(3) The financial institution authorized to receive information;

(4) The name, phone number, email address, and signature of the owner submitting the authorization;

(5) The categories of information specified in subsection (b) that are authorized for release; and

(6) An acknowledgement that the authorization to release information includes information that is otherwise protected from disclosure, that the licensee is waiving privilege and confidentiality, and that the scope of the release is strictly limited for the purposes of disclosure to the financial institution.

(b) After receipt of the authorization from a cultivation licensee, the Department shall release the following information, when requested by an authorized financial institution pursuant to section 16411 of this division:

(1) The license application(s), including renewal applications, excluding information required to be kept confidential pursuant to Penal Code section 11105 and confidential personal information of individual owners of the licensed business;

(2) Information captured in the track and trace system established pursuant to Business and Professions Code section 26067, including, but not limited to, aggregated sales or transfer information, as applicable;

(3) Documents issued to the licensee pursuant to disciplinary or enforcement proceedings;

(c) A cultivation licensee may withdraw the authorization to provide information to a financial institution at any time. The withdrawal shall be made in writing, through a form prescribed by the Department, and shall include the following information:

(1) The name of the licensed business for which the licensee is withdrawing the authorization of the release of information;

(2) The business's license number(s);

(3) The financial institution from which authorization to receive information is withdrawn;

(4) The name, phone number, email address, and signature of the owner submitting the withdrawal.

NOTE: Authority cited: Section 26013, Business and Professions Code. Reference: Section 26260, Business and Professions Code.

§ 16411. Financial Institution Request for Cultivation Licensee Information.

A financial institution as defined in Business and Professions Code section 26260(c)(3) may request information related to a cultivation licensee for purposes of facilitating the provision of financial services for that licensee. The request shall be made in writing, through a form prescribed by the Department, which shall include the following information:

(a) The name of the financial institution;

(b) The name, phone number, email, and signature of the representative of the financial institution requesting information;

(c) The business name and license number of the licensee for which the financial institution is requesting information;

(d) The type of financial services for which the information is requested (including, but not limited to, establishment or maintenance of bank accounts, extending loans, and providing insurance) and whether the request is for consideration of a new service or maintenance of an existing service;

(e) The specific information requested as described in section 16410(b) if authorized by the licensee; and

(f) An acknowledgment that use of the information is limited to that which is necessary for the provision of financial services.

NOTE: Authority cited: Section 26013, Business and Professions Code. Reference: Section 26260, Business and Professions Code.

§ 17000. Definitions. [Repealed]

Note: Authority cited: Sections 26012, 26013 and 26130, Business and Professions Code. Reference: Sections 26001, 26120 and 26130, Business and Professions Code; and Section 11018.1, Health and Safety Code.

Chapter 8. Manufacturers

ARTICLE 1. MANUFACTURING LICENSE TYPES

§ 17006. Manufacturing License Types.

The following manufacturing license types are available from the Department:

(a) "Type 7," for extractions using volatile solvents as defined by section 15000(yyy). A Type 7 licensee may also:

(1) Conduct extractions using nonvolatile solvents or mechanical methods on the licensed premises, provided that the extraction process is noted on the application and the relevant information pursuant to section 15011(b) is provided to the Department;

(2) Conduct infusion operations on the licensed premises, provided the infusion operations and product types are noted on the application and the relevant information pursuant to section 15011(b) is provided to the Department;

(3) Conduct packaging and labeling of cannabis products on the licensed premises; and

(4) Register and operate the licensed premises as a shared-use facility in accordance with article 2 (commencing with section 17124) of chapter 8.

(b) "Type 6," for extractions using mechanical methods or nonvolatile solvents as defined by section 15000(uu). A Type 6 licensee may also:

(1) Conduct infusion operations on the licensed premises, provided the infusion operations and product types are noted on the application and the relevant information pursuant to section 15011(b) is provided to the Department;

(2) Conduct packaging and labeling of cannabis products on the licensed premises; and

(3) Register and operate the licensed premises as a shared-use facility in accordance with article 2 (commencing with section 17124) of chapter 8.

(c) "Type N," for manufacturers that produce cannabis products other than extracts or concentrates that are produced through extraction. A Type N licensee may also:

(1) Conduct packaging and labeling of cannabis products on the licensed premises; and

(2) Register and operate the licensed premises as a shared-use facility in accordance with article 2 (commencing with section 17124) of chapter 8.

(d) "Type P," for manufacturers that only package or repackage cannabis products or label or relabel cannabis product containers or wrappers.

(e) "Type S," for manufacturers that conduct commercial cannabis manufacturing activities in accordance with article 2 (commencing with section 17124) of chapter 8 at a registered shared-use facility.

NOTE: Authority cited: Sections 26013 and 26130, Business and Professions Code. Reference: Sections 26012, 26050 and 26130, Business and Professions Code.

§ 17009. Additional Activities.

In addition to the activities specified in section 17006, a licensed manufacturer may also roll and package pre-rolls and package dried cannabis flower.

NOTE: Authority cited: Sections 26013 and 26130, Business and Professions Code. Reference: Sections 26012 and 26130, Business and Professions Code.

§ 17117. License Constraints.

(a) A manufacturer licensee shall not manufacture, prepare, package or label any products other than cannabis products at the licensed premises.

(b) Notwithstanding subsection (a), a manufacturer licensee may manufacture, prepare, package, and label non-cannabis-infused product samples. For purposes of this section, a "non-cannabis-infused product sample" is a product that does not contain cannabis but contains all other components of a corresponding cannabis product and is used to provide information on flavor profiles, textures, smells, and other physical characteristics of the cannabis product. Non-cannabis-infused product samples shall not be sold and may be provided to other licensees except for licensed cultivators, transport only distributors, testing laboratories, and cannabis event organizers.

(c) A manufacturer licensee shall only use cannabinoid concentrates and extracts that are manufactured or processed from cannabis obtained from a licensed cannabis cultivator.

(d) A manufacturer licensee shall not manufacture, prepare, package, or label cannabis products in a location that is operating as a retail food establishment or as a processed food registrant.

(e) A manufacturer licensee shall not manufacture, prepare, package, or label cannabis products in a location that is licensed by the Department of Alcoholic Beverage Control pursuant to division 9 (commencing with section 23000) of the Business and Professions Code.

NOTE: Authority cited: Sections 26013 and 26130, Business and Professions Code. Reference: Sections 26050 and 26140, Business and Professions Code.

§ 17123.1. Manufacturing Licensee Authorization to Release Data to Financial Institutions.

(a) A manufacturing licensee may authorize the Department to provide information to a financial institution for purposes of facilitating the provision of financial services. The authorization shall be made in writing, through a form prescribed by the Department, which shall include the following information:

(1) The name of the licensed business for which the licensee is authorizing the release of information;

(2) The business's license number(s);

(3) The financial institution authorized to receive information;

(4) The name, phone number, email address, and signature of the owner submitting the authorization;

(5) The categories of information specified in subsection (b) that are authorized for release; and

(6) An acknowledgement that the authorization to release information includes information that is otherwise protected from disclosure, and waiving privilege and confidentiality is strictly for purposes of disclosure to the financial institution.

(b) After receipt of the authorization from a manufacturing licensee, the Department shall release the following information, as designated by the licensee, when requested by an authorized financial institution pursuant to section 17123.2 of this division:

(1) The license application(s), including renewal applications, excluding information required to be kept

confidential pursuant to Penal Code section 11105 and confidential personal information of individual owners of the licensed business;

(2) Information captured in the track and trace system established pursuant to Business and Professions Code section 26067, including, but not limited to, aggregated sales or transfer information, as applicable; and

(3) Documents issued to the licensee pursuant to disciplinary or enforcement proceedings.

(c) A licensee may withdraw the authorization to provide information to a financial institution at any time. The withdrawal shall be made in writing, through a form prescribed by the Department, and shall include the following information:

(1) The name of the licensed business for which the licensee is withdrawing the authorization of the release of information;

(2) The business's license number(s);

(3) The financial institution from which authorization to receive information is withdrawn; and

(4) The name, phone number, email address, and signature of the owner submitting the withdrawal.

NOTE: Authority cited: Section 26013, Business and Professions Code. Reference: Section 26260, Business and Professions Code.

§ 17123.2. Financial Institution Request for Manufacturing Licensee Information.

A financial institution as defined in Business and Professions Code section 26260(c)(3) may request information related to a manufacturing licensee for purposes of facilitating the provision of financial services for that licensee. The request shall be made in writing, through a form prescribed by the Department, which shall include the following information:

(a) The name of the financial institution;

(b) The name, phone number, email, and signature of the representative of the financial institution requesting information;

(c) The business name and license number of the licensee for which the financial institution is requesting information;

(d) The type of financial services for which the information is requested (including, but not limited to, establishment or maintenance of bank accounts, extending loans, and providing insurance) and whether the request is for consideration of a new service or maintenance of an existing service;

(e) The specific information requested as described in section 17123.1(b) if authorized by the licensee; and

(f) An acknowledgment that use of the information is limited to that which is necessary for the provision of financial services.

NOTE: Authority cited: Section 26013, Business and Professions Code. Reference: Section 26260, Business and Professions Code.

ARTICLE 2. SHARED-USE FACILITIES

§ 17124. Definitions.

For purposes of this article, the following definitions shall apply:

(a) "Common-use area" means any area of the manufacturer's registered shared-use facility, including equipment that is available for use by more than one licensed manufacturer, provided that the use of a common-use area is limited to one licensee at a time.

(b) "Designated area" means the area of the manufacturer's registered shared-use facility that is designated by the primary licensee for the sole and exclusive use of a Type S licensee, including storage of the Type S licensee's cannabis, cannabis concentrates, and cannabis products.

(c) "Primary licensee" means the Type 7, Type 6, or Type N licensee that has registered and been approved to operate its licensed premises as a shared-use facility.

(d) "Shared-use facility" means a manufacturing premises operated by a Type 7, Type 6, or Type N licensee in which Type S licensees are authorized to conduct manufacturing operations.

(e) "Use agreement" means a written agreement between a primary licensee and a Type S commercial cannabis business or licensee that specifies the designated area of the Type S licensee, the days and hours in which the Type S licensee is assigned to use the common-use area, any allocation of responsibility for compliance pursuant to section 17128, and an acknowledgement that the Type S licensee has sole and exclusive use of the common-use area during the Type S licensee's assigned time period.

NOTE: Authority cited: Sections 26013 and 26130, Business and Professions Code. Reference: Sections 26001, 26050, 26051.5 and 26130, Business and Professions Code.

§ 17126. Registration to Operate a Shared-Use Facility.

(a) No licensed manufacturer shall operate as a shared-use facility without prior approval by the Department.

(b) To register as a shared-use facility, a Type 7, Type 6, or Type N licensee shall submit the following to the Department through the online licensing system:

(1) A copy of the license, permit, or other authorization issued by the local jurisdiction that enables the licensee to operate as a shared-use facility. The Department shall contact the applicable local jurisdiction to confirm the validity of the authorization upon receipt of the application for registration. If the local jurisdiction does not respond within 10 calendar days, the Department shall consider the authorization valid.

(2) A registration form prescribed by the Department, which includes the following information:

(A) The proposed occupancy schedule that specifies the days and hours the common-use area will be available for use by Type S licensees and when the common-use area will be used by the primary licensee. The occupancy schedule shall allow for maintenance and sanitizing between uses by individual licensees.

(B) A diagram indicating:

(i) Each designated area for Type S licensee(s).

(ii) The common-use area, including identification of any shared equipment.

(c) The Department shall notify the Type 7, Type 6, or Type N licensee upon approval of the registration to operate as a shared-use facility. Notification shall be made through the online licensing system.

(d) At least one business day prior to a Type S licensee commencing manufacturing operations at a registered shared-use facility, the primary licensee shall provide written notification to the Department. The notification to the

Department shall include the Type S licensee's business name, contact person, contact phone number, and license number. The primary licensee shall also provide an updated occupancy schedule that includes the Type S licensee and an updated diagram that specifies the Type S licensee's designated area. Notification shall be provided by email or through the online licensing system.

(e) A primary licensee that wishes to discontinue operation as a shared-use facility may cancel its registration by providing written notice to the Department and each Type S licensee authorized to use the shared-use facility at least 30 calendar days prior to the effective date of the cancellation.

NOTE: Authority cited: Sections 26013 and 26130, Business and Professions Code. Reference: Sections 26051.5, 26055 and 26130, Business and Professions Code.

§ 17127. Shared-Use Facility Conditions for Operation.

(a) A primary licensee shall operate the shared-use facility in accordance with the conditions of operation specified in this section.

(b) Each Type S licensee shall be assigned a "designated area" that, at minimum:

(1) Is for exclusive use by the Type S licensee; and

(2) Provides an area for storage that is secure, fixed in place, locked with a commercial-grade lock, and accessible only to the Type S licensee for storage of that Type S licensee's cannabis, cannabis concentrates, and cannabis products.

(c) Any part of the premises used for manufacturing activities that is a common-use area shall be occupied by only one licensee at a time by restricting the time period that each licensee may use the common-use area. During the assigned time period, one licensee shall have sole and exclusive occupancy of the common-use area.

(d) The use of the shared-use facility shall be restricted to the primary licensee and the Type S licensees authorized by the Department to use the shared-use facility.

(e) Any cannabis product or other materials remaining after a Type S licensee ceases operation and discontinues use of its designated area shall be considered cannabis waste and disposed of by the primary licensee consistent with the requirements of the Act and this division.

(f) The shared-use facility shall meet all applicable requirements of the Act and this division.

(g) The occupancy schedule shall be prominently posted near the entrance to the shared-use facility.

(h) The primary licensee may conduct manufacturing activities as permitted under its Type 7, Type 6, or Type N license and may use the common-use area during its scheduled time period.

NOTE: Authority cited: Sections 26013 and 26130, Business and Professions Code. Reference: Sections 26011.5 and 26130, Business and Professions Code.

§ 17128. Shared-Use Facility Compliance Requirements.

(a) As part of the use agreement, the primary licensee and the Type S licensee(s) may allocate responsibility for providing and maintaining commonly used equipment and services, including, but not limited to, security systems, fire monitoring and protection services, and waste disposal services. However, the Department may take enforcement action against either the primary licensee or Type S licensee(s) regardless of the allocation of responsibility in the use agreement.

(b) A primary licensee or a Type S licensee is liable for any violation found at the shared-use facility during that licensee's scheduled occupancy or within that licensee's designated area. However, a violation of any provision of the Act or this division may be deemed a violation for which each Type S licensee and the primary licensee are responsible. In the event of a recall or embargo of a cannabis product produced at a shared-use facility, the Department, in its sole discretion, may include any or all cannabis products produced at the shared-use facility.

(c) The occupancy schedule and designated area for a Type S licensee shall not be altered without prior notification to the Department. Prior to making any changes to the occupancy schedule or the designated area, written notification that includes the intended changes shall be submitted by email or through the Department's online licensing system.

NOTE: Authority cited: Sections 26013 and 26130, Business and Professions Code. Reference: Sections 26011.5, 26055 and 26130, Business and Professions Code.

ARTICLE 3. SOLVENT USE AND SAFETY

§ 17202.1. General Requirements for Extraction and Post-Extraction Processing.

(a) A licensed manufacturer that uses a volatile solvent, a flammable liquid, or a solvent that creates an asphyxiant gas shall ensure that the solvent is used in accordance with the requirements of:

(1) Chapter 39 of the California Fire Code;

(2) Title 8, California Code of Regulations, sections 5416-5420, which includes ensuring adequate ventilation and controlling sources of ignition;

(3) All Division of Occupational Safety and Health (Cal/OSHA) regulations related to the processing, handling, and storage of the applicable solvent; and

(4) All fire, safety, and building code requirements related to the processing, handling, and storage of the applicable solvent or gas.

(b) No volatile solvent extraction or post-extraction processing operations or other closed-loop system operations shall occur in an area zoned as residential.

NOTE: Authority cited: Sections 26013 and 26130, Business and Professions Code. Reference: Sections 26011.5, 26105 and 26130, Business and Professions Code.

§ 17203. Permissible Extractions.

(a) Except as provided in subsection (b), cannabis extraction shall only be conducted using the following methods:

(1) Mechanical extraction;

(2) Chemical extraction using a nonvolatile solvent, as defined in section 15000(uu).

(3) Chemical extraction using CO2 gas in a professional closed-loop extraction system.

(4) Chemical extraction using a volatile solvent, as defined in section 15000(yyy), in a professional closed-loop extraction system; or

(5) Any other method authorized by the Department pursuant to subsection (b).

(b) To request authorization from the Department to conduct cannabis extraction using a method other than those specified in subsections (a)(1) through (4), the applicant or licensee shall submit a detailed description of the extraction method, including any documentation that validates the method and any safety procedures to be utilized to mitigate any risk to public or worker health and safety.

NOTE: Authority cited: Sections 26013 and 26130, Business and Professions Code. Reference: Sections 26011.5 and 26130, Business and Professions Code.

§ 17204. Solvent Requirements.

(a) Any solvents used for extraction or post-extraction processing shall meet the following minimum purity requirements:

(1) Hydrocarbon-based solvents shall be at least 99 percent purity.

(2) Nonhydrocarbon-based solvents shall be food-grade.

(3) CO2 gas used for extraction shall be food-grade.

(4) Ethanol shall be food-grade in accordance with 21 CFR, part 184, subpart B, section 184.1293.

(A) Solutions of ethanol may be used if the ethanol component is food-grade and it is combined with another food-grade solvent or a hydrocarbon-based solvent that meets the requirements of subsection (a)(1).

(B) Solutions of ethanol that include one or more volatile solvents that total 5% or less by volume of the total ethanol solution volume are considered nonvolatile solvents as defined in section 15000(uu).

(5) Water and ice shall be potable.

(6) Dry ice shall be food-grade.

(b) The licensed manufacturer shall maintain copies of the safety data sheets for any chemical solvents used and make these records readily available to employees and to the Department upon request.

(c) The licensed manufacturer shall maintain documentation evidencing the purity of any chemical solvents used and make these records readily available to employees and to the Department upon request.

NOTE: Authority cited: Sections 26013 and 26130, Business and Professions Code. Reference: Sections 26011.5, 26105 and 26130, Business and Professions Code.

§ 17205. Additional Requirements for Ethanol Operations.

A licensed manufacturer that uses ethanol in manufacturing operations for extractions or post-extraction processing shall receive approval for the facility and equipment from the local fire code official prior to commencing operations, if required by local ordinance.

NOTE: Authority cited: Sections 26013 and 26130, Business and Professions Code. Reference: Sections 26011.5 and 26130, Business and Professions Code.

§ 17206. Closed-Loop Extraction System Requirements.

(a) Chemical extractions using CO2; a volatile solvent; or chlorofluorocarbon, hydrocarbon, or other fluorinated gas shall be conducted in a professional closed-loop extraction system designed to recover the solvents that are certified in accordance with section 17206.1.

(b) The licensed manufacturer shall establish and implement procedures to ensure that the closed-loop extraction system is maintained in accordance with the equipment manufacturer specifications. The licensed manufacturer shall maintain logs documenting the date(s) of maintenance; description of the maintenance done, including any machine parts that were replaced; and the initials of the employee conducting the maintenance.

(c) The licensed manufacturer shall establish and implement procedures to ensure routine verification that the system is operating in accordance with equipment manufacturer specifications and continues to comply with fire, safety, and building code requirements. The licensed manufacturer shall conduct any verification recommended by the equipment manufacturer. The licensed manufacturer shall maintain logs documenting the date(s) of verification, description of the verification method, and the initials of the employee conducting the verification.

(d) A licensed manufacturer shall develop and implement written standard operating procedures, good manufacturing practices, and a training plan prior to using the closed-loop system. Any personnel using solvents or gases in a closed-loop system shall have direct access to applicable safety data sheets. Personnel shall be trained on how to use the system and handle and store solvents and gases safely prior to operating the system. The training shall be documented in accordance with section 17211.1.

(e) Professional closed-loop systems, other equipment used, the extraction operation, and facilities shall be approved for use by the local fire code official prior to commencing operation of the closed-loop system, if required by local ordinance. Licensed manufacturers shall provide documentation confirming compliance with this subsection to the Department upon request.

(f) The facility shall have a gas detection system that meets the requirements of title 24, California Code of Regulations, sections 3905.1-3905.2.

(g) All procedures and logs described in this section shall be in writing and made available to the Department upon request.

NOTE: Authority cited: Sections 26013 and 26130, Business and Professions Code. Reference: Sections 26011.5, 26105 and 26130, Business and Professions Code.

§ 17206.1. Certification of Closed-Loop Systems.

(a) The closed-loop system shall be commercially manufactured and bear a permanently affixed and visible serial number.

(b) After installation and before use of a closed-loop system, the licensed manufacturer shall have the closed-loop system certified by a California-licensed engineer that the system was commercially manufactured, safe for use with the intended solvent, and built and installed to codes of recognized and generally accepted good engineering practices. The certification document shall contain:

(1) The name, signature and stamp of the California-licensed professional engineer;

(2) The serial number of the extraction unit being certified;

(3) A list of the solvent(s) deemed safe for use with the equipment; and

(4) The address of the premises where the extraction unit was certified.

(c) The licensed manufacturer shall maintain the current certification document and make it available to the Department upon request.

(d) The closed-loop system shall be recertified if any of the following occur:

(1) The system is modified in a manner such that its operation no longer conforms to the original equipment manufacturer specifications, such as by adding or removing components that expand or reduce its capacity.

(2) The system is moved to a different premises.

(3) Five years have elapsed since the date of the certification.

NOTE: Authority cited: Sections 26013 and 26130, Business and Professions Code. Reference: Sections 26011.5, 26130 and 26132, Business and Professions Code.

ARTICLE 4. GOOD MANUFACTURING PRACTICES

§ 17207. Manufacturing Practices Definitions.

In addition to the definitions in section 26001 of the Act and section 15000 of this division, the following definitions shall govern the construction of this chapter:

(a) "Allergen cross-contact" means the unintentional incorporation of a food allergen into a cannabis product.

(b) "Component" means any substance or item intended for use in the manufacture of a cannabis product, including those substances or items that are not intended to appear in the finished cannabis product. "Component" includes cannabis, cannabis products used as ingredients, raw materials, other ingredients, and processing aids.

(c) "Contact surface" means any surface that contacts cannabis products and cannabis product components and those surfaces from which drainage, or other transfer, onto the cannabis product or cannabis product components, occurs during the normal course of operations. Examples of contact surfaces include containers, utensils, tables, and equipment.

(d) "Easily cleanable" means a characteristic of a surface that allows effective removal of soil, food residue, or other organic or inorganic materials by normal cleaning methods.

(e) "Environmental pathogen" means a pathogen capable of surviving and persisting within the manufacturing environment such that cannabis products may be contaminated and may result in illness if consumed or used without treatment to significantly minimize the environmental pathogen. Examples of environmental pathogens include Listeria monocytogenes and Salmonella spp. but do not include the spores of pathogenic spore-forming bacteria.

(f) "Hazard" means any biological, chemical, radiological, or physical agent that has the potential to cause illness or injury.

(g) "Holding" means storage of cannabis or cannabis products and includes activities performed incidental to storage of a cannabis product and activities performed as a practical necessity for the distribution of that cannabis product.

(h) "Microorganisms" means yeasts, molds, bacteria, viruses, protozoa, and microscopic parasites and includes species that are pathogens. The term "undesirable microorganisms" includes those microorganisms that are pathogens, that subject a cannabis product to decomposition, that indicate that a cannabis product is contaminated with filth, or that otherwise may cause a cannabis product to be adulterated.

(i) "Monitor" means to conduct a planned sequence of observations or measurements to assess whether preventive measures are operating as intended.

(j) "Pathogen" means a microorganism that can cause illness or injury.

(k) "Potable" means water that meets the requirements of Health and Safety Code section 113869.

(l) "Preventive measures" means those risk-based, reasonably appropriate procedures, practices, and processes that a person knowledgeable about the safe manufacturing, processing, packing, or holding of food would employ to significantly minimize or prevent the hazards identified pursuant to a product quality plan as specified in section 17214.

(m) "Processing aid" means any substance that is added to a cannabis product during manufacture but is removed in some manner from the cannabis product before it is packaged in its finished form. This includes substances that are converted into constituents normally present in the product, and do not significantly increase the amount of the constituent naturally found in the product. This also includes substances that are added to a product for their technical or functional effect in the processing but are present in the finished product at insignificant levels and do not have any technical or functional effect in that product.

(n) "Qualified individual" means a person who has the education, training, or experience (or a combination thereof) necessary to manufacture quality cannabis products as appropriate to the individual's assigned duties. A qualified individual may be, but is not required to be, an employee of the licensed manufacturer.

(o) "Quality control" means a planned and systematic operation or procedure for ensuring the quality of a cannabis product.

(p) "Quality control operation" means a planned and systematic procedure for taking all actions necessary to prevent cannabis product(s) from being adulterated or misbranded.

(q) "Quality control personnel" means any person, persons, or group designated by the licensed manufacturer to be responsible for quality control operations.

(r) "Raw material" means any unprocessed material in its raw or natural state that is intended to become part of the components of a cannabis product.

(s) "Sanitize" means to treat cleaned surfaces by a process that is effective in destroying vegetative cells of pathogens and substantially reducing numbers of other undesirable microorganisms, but without adversely affecting the product or its safety for the consumer.

(t) "Smooth" means any of the following:

> (1) A contact surface that is free of pits, pinholes, cracks, crevices, inclusions, rough edges, and other surface imperfections detectable by visual or tactile inspection.
>
> (2) A floor, wall, or ceiling having an even or level surface with no roughness or projections that render it difficult to clean.

(u) "Utensil" means an implement, tool, or container used in the storage, preparation, manufacture, or processing of cannabis and cannabis products. In addition to kitchenware, examples of utensils include, but are not limited to, gloves, screens, sieves, implements to create pre-rolls, buckets, and scissors.

(v) "Validate" means obtaining and evaluating scientific and technical evidence that a control measure, combination of control measures, or set of quality control procedures, when properly implemented, is capable of ensuring the quality of a cannabis product or effectively controlling an identified hazard.

(w) "Verification" means the application of methods, procedures, tests, or other evaluations, in addition to monitoring, to determine whether a control measure or combination of control measures is or has been operating as intended and to establish the validity of the quality control procedures.

(x) "Yield" means the quantity of a particular cannabis product expected to be produced at a given step of manufacture or packaging, as identified in the master manufacturing protocol. The expected yield is based upon the quantity of components or packaging to be used, in the absence of any loss or error in actual production. "Actual yield" means the quantity of a particular cannabis product that is actually produced at a given step of manufacture or packaging that is recorded in the batch production record.

NOTE: Authority cited: Sections 26013 and 26130, Business and Professions Code. Reference: Sections 26001 and 26130, Business and Professions Code.

§ 17208. Quality Control Program.

(a) A licensed manufacturer shall establish and implement a quality control program to ensure that cannabis products are not adulterated or misbranded. The quality control program shall describe how the licensee will comply with the following:

(1) Grounds, building, and manufacturing premises standards, as specified in section 17209;

(2) Equipment and utensil requirements, as specified in section 17210;

(3) Personnel procedures, as specified in section 17211;

(4) Cannabis product component procedures, as specified in section 17212; and

(5) Manufacturing processes and procedures, as specified in section 17213.

(b) The quality control program shall be under the supervision of one or more qualified individuals assigned responsibility for this function.

(c) For purposes of this article, for those requirements that are contained in the Health and Safety Code, use of the term "food" shall include cannabis, cannabis products, components, and contact surfaces.

NOTE: Authority cited: Sections 26013 and 26130, Business and Professions Code. Reference: Sections 26011.5 and 26039.6, Business and Professions Code.

§ 17209. Grounds, Building, and Manufacturing Premises.

(a) Exterior facility and grounds. A licensed manufacturer shall ensure the facility exterior and grounds under the licensed manufacturer's control meet the following minimum standards:

(1) Grounds shall be equipped with draining areas in order to prevent pooled or standing water;

(2) Weeds, grass, and vegetation shall be cut within the immediate vicinity of the cannabis manufacturing premises, litter and waste shall be removed, and equipment shall be stored in order to minimize the potential for the grounds to constitute an attractant, breeding place, or harborage for pests;

(3) Roads, yards, and parking lots shall be maintained so that these areas do not constitute a source of contamination in areas where cannabis products are handled or transported;

(4) Openings into the building (such as windows, exhaust fans, ventilation ducts, or plumbing vent pipes) shall be screened, sealed, or otherwise protected to minimize potential for pests to enter the building;

(5) Waste treatment and disposal systems shall be provided and maintained so as to prevent contamination in areas where cannabis products may be exposed to such a system's waste or waste by-products.

(6) A licensed manufacturer shall implement precautions within the premises, such as inspection or extermination, if the premises is bordered by grounds outside the licensed manufacturer's control that are not maintained in the manner described in subsections (1) through (5), in order to eliminate any pests, dirt, and filth that pose a source of cannabis product contamination. Any use of insecticide, rodenticide, or other pesticide within the premises shall meet the requirements of Health and Safety Code section 114254.

(b) Interior facility. A licensed manufacturer shall ensure construction, design, and maintenance of the interior of the manufacturing premises as follows:

(1) Walls, ceilings, and floors. Walls, ceilings, and floors shall be constructed of material that is smooth, nonporous, easily cleanable, corrosion-resistant, and suitable to the activity that will be conducted. Fixtures, ducts, and pipes shall not pose a source of drip or condensate that may contaminate cannabis, cannabis products, components, contact surfaces, or packaging material.

(2) Lighting. Interior facility lighting shall meet the requirements of the Health and Safety Code section 114252, subdivisions (a)(1) and (3), (b)(3) and (4), and (c). Interior facility lighting shall also meet the requirements for shatter-resistant lighting in Health and Safety Code section 114252.1. The requirements of Health and Safety Code section 114252.1(a), shall also apply to all areas where glass breakage may result in the contamination of exposed cannabis, cannabis products, components, contact surfaces, or packaging material.

(3) Plumbing system and fixtures.

(A) Water supply. Running water shall be supplied as required by Health and Safety Code section 114192 in all areas where required for the manufacturing of cannabis products; in all areas used for the cleaning of equipment, utensils, and packaging materials; and for employee sanitary facilities. Water that contacts cannabis, cannabis products, components, contact surfaces, or packaging materials shall be potable.

(B) Plumbing. Plumbing systems shall meet the requirements of Health and Safety Code section 114190.

(C) Sewage disposal. The sewage system shall be maintained and kept in good repair so that it does not pose a potential source of contamination of cannabis, cannabis products, components, contact surfaces, or packaging materials.

(D) Toilet facilities. A licensed manufacturer shall provide employees with access to toilet facilities that meet the requirements of Health and Safety Code section 114250. Toilet facilities shall be kept clean and shall not pose a potential source of contamination of cannabis, components, cannabis products, contact surfaces, or packaging materials.

(E) Hand-washing facilities. A licensed manufacturer shall provide hand-washing facilities that meet the requirements of Health and Safety Code sections 113953(a)-(d) and 113953.2.

(F) Waste disposal. A licensed manufacturer shall provide for waste disposal in accordance with Health and Safety Code sections 114244(a) and (c) and 114245.1. Cannabis waste shall be disposed of in accordance with section 17223.

(4) Ventilation. Ventilation systems shall meet the requirements of Health and Safety Code sections 114149 and 114149.3.

(5) Cleaning and maintenance. The premises, including any fixtures, and other physical facilities therein, shall be maintained in a clean and sanitary condition and kept in good repair so as to prevent cannabis products from becoming adulterated, and shall meet the requirements of Health and Safety Code section 114257.1.

(A) The premises shall have a janitorial facility that meets the requirements of Health and Safety Code section 114279(a).

(B) Cleaning equipment and supplies shall be stored in a manner that meets the requirements of Health and Safety Code section 114281.

(C) Poisonous or toxic materials such as cleaning compounds, sanitizing agents, and pesticide chemicals that are necessary for premises and equipment maintenance and operation shall be handled and stored in a manner that meets the requirements of Health and Safety Code sections 114254.1, 114254.2 and 114254.3.

NOTE: Authority cited: Sections 26013 and 26130, Business and Professions Code. Reference: Sections 26011.5 and

26039.6, Business and Professions Code.

§ 17210. Equipment and Utensils.

(a) Design and construction. Equipment and utensils shall meet the requirements of Health and Safety Code sections 114130.1, 114130.2, 114130.3, and 114130.4 and shall be used in accordance with their operating instructions to avoid the adulteration of cannabis products with lubricants, fuel, metal fragments, contaminated water, or any other contaminants.

(b) Installation. Equipment shall be installed so as to allow cleaning and maintenance of the equipment and of adjacent spaces. Equipment that is not easily moveable shall meet the requirements of Health and Safety Code section 114169.

(c) Cleaning, sanitizing, and maintenance. Equipment and utensils shall be maintained in a clean and sanitary condition and kept in good repair. The quality control program for cleaning, sanitizing, and maintenance of equipment and utensils shall include the following elements, at minimum:

(1) A detailed, written procedure for cleaning, sanitizing, and maintaining (including calibrating) equipment and utensils;

(2) A schedule for cleaning, sanitizing, and maintaining equipment and utensils;

(3) A log for documentation of the date and time of maintenance, cleaning, and sanitizing of equipment and utensils; and

(4) A procedure for storing cleaned and sanitized equipment and utensils in a manner to protect the equipment and utensils from contamination.

NOTE: Authority cited: Sections 26013 and 26130, Business and Professions Code. Reference: Sections 26011.5 and 26039.6, Business and Professions Code.

§ 17211. Manufacturing Personnel.

(a) Licensed manufacturers shall establish and implement procedures for personnel that include, at minimum:

(1) Disease control. Any individual who by medical examination or supervisory observation is shown to have, or appears to have, an illness specified in Health and Safety Code section 113949.2(a) or an open lesion (e.g., boil, sore, cut, rash, or infected wound), unless covered in accordance with the requirements of Health and Safety Code section 113949.2(b), shall be excluded from any manufacturing operations until their health condition is corrected. Personnel shall be instructed to report such health conditions to their supervisors.

(2) Cleanliness. All individuals working in direct contact with cannabis, cannabis products, components, contact surfaces, and packaging materials shall maintain personal cleanliness in order to protect against allergen cross-contact and contamination of cannabis products while on duty. The methods for maintaining personal cleanliness include:

(A) Wearing clean outer clothing to protect against allergen cross-contact and contamination of cannabis, cannabis products, components, contact surfaces, and packaging materials;

(B) Washing hands thoroughly in a hand-washing facility that meets the requirements of section 17209 before starting work, after each absence from a work station, at any time specified in Health and Safety Code section 113953.3, and at any time when the hands may have become soiled or contaminated;

(C) Removing all unsecured jewelry and other objects that might fall into cannabis, cannabis products, components, equipment, or containers. Hand jewelry that cannot be sanitized shall be removed during periods in which cannabis products are manipulated by hand. If such hand jewelry cannot be removed, it shall be covered by material that can be maintained in an intact, clean, and sanitary condition and that effectively protects against contamination by these objects of cannabis, cannabis products, components, contact surfaces, and packaging materials;

(D) Maintaining gloves used in cannabis product handling in an intact, clean, and sanitary condition;

(E) Wearing hair nets, caps, beard covers, or other hair restraints that are designed and worn to prevent hair contact with cannabis, cannabis products, components, contact surfaces, and packaging materials;

(F) Storing clothing and personal belongings in areas separate from those where cannabis products are exposed or where equipment or utensils are washed; and

(G) Confining the following activities to areas separate from those where cannabis products may be exposed or where equipment or utensils are washed: eating food, chewing gum, drinking beverages, and using tobacco.

(b) Nothing in this section prohibits a licensed manufacturer from establishing additional precautions to protect against allergen cross-contact and contamination of cannabis, cannabis products, components, contact surfaces, and packaging materials by microorganisms or foreign substances (e.g., perspiration, hair, cosmetics, tobacco, chemicals, and medicines applied to the skin).

(c) The procedures for manufacturing personnel shall be in writing and made available to the Department upon request.

NOTE: Authority cited: Sections 26013 and 26130, Business and Professions Code. Reference: Sections 26011.5 and 26039.6, Business and Professions Code.

§ 17211.1. Training Program.

(a) A manufacturing licensee shall establish and implement a training program to ensure that all personnel present at the premises are provided information and training that, at minimum, covers the following topics:

(1) Within 30 days of the start of employment:

(A) Health and safety hazards;

(B) Hazards presented by all solvents or chemicals used at the licensed premises as described in the safety data sheet for each solvent or chemical;

(C) Emergency response procedures;

(D) Security procedures;

(E) Record keeping requirements; and

(F) Training requirements.

(2) Prior to independently engaging in any cannabis manufacturing process:

(A) An overview of the cannabis manufacturing process and standard operating procedure(s);

(B) Quality control procedures;

(C) Product quality plans developed in accordance with section 17214;

(D) Proper and safe usage of equipment or machinery;

(E) Safe work practices applicable to an employee's job tasks, including appropriate use of any necessary safety or sanitary equipment;

(F) Cleaning and maintenance requirements;

(G) Emergency operations, including shutdown; and

(H) Any additional information reasonably related to an employee's job duties.

(3) Additionally, a manufacturing licensee that produces edible cannabis products shall ensure that all personnel who prepare, handle, or package edible products successfully complete a California food handler certificate course from an entity accredited by the American National Standards Institute (ANSI) within 90 days of commencing employment at the premises and again every three years during employment. A manufacturing licensee shall obtain documentation evidencing the fulfillment of this requirement;

(b) A manufacturing licensee shall ensure that all personnel receive annual refresher training to cover, at minimum, the topics listed in subsection (a). This annual refresher training must be completed within 12 months of the previous training completion date.

(c) A manufacturing licensee shall maintain a record of training containing, at minimum:

(1) A list of all personnel at the premises including, at minimum, name and job duties of each individual;

(2) Documentation of training topics and dates of training completion, including refresher training, for all personnel;

(3) The signatures of each individual and the licensee verifying receipt and understanding of each training or refresher training completed by the individual; and

(4) Any official documentation attesting to the successful completion of required training by personnel.

(d) A manufacturing licensee may assign responsibility for the training of individual personnel to supervisory personnel. Assigned supervisory personnel must have the education, training, or experience (or a combination thereof) necessary to ensure the production of quality cannabis products by all personnel. The assigned training personnel shall sign and date a document on an annual basis attesting that they received and understands all information that will be provided to personnel in the training program. This documentation shall be maintained as part of the record requirements in subsection (c).

NOTE: Authority cited: Sections 26013 and 26130, Business and Professions Code. Reference: Sections 26011.5, 26130 and 26160, Business and Professions Code.

§ 17212. Cannabis Product Components.

(a) In order to prevent adulteration of cannabis products, licensed manufacturers shall establish and implement written policies and procedures to ensure and maintain the quality of product components.

(b) Components are subject to the following minimum requirements:

(1) Components that are food must be obtained from a source that complies with federal and state food laws.

(2) Raw materials and other components shall be inspected upon intake to ensure that they are clean and suitable for manufacturing into cannabis products, and shall be stored under conditions that protect against allergen cross-contact and contamination and minimize deterioration.

(3) Raw materials shall be washed or cleaned as necessary to remove soil and other visible contaminants. Water

used for washing, rinsing, or conveying cannabis product ingredients shall be potable.

(4) Raw materials and other components shall not contain levels of microorganisms that render the cannabis product injurious to human health, or shall be pasteurized or otherwise treated during manufacturing so that they no longer contain levels of microorganisms that would cause the cannabis product to be adulterated.

(5) Raw materials and other components susceptible to contamination with aflatoxin or other natural toxins, pests, or extraneous material shall not exceed generally acceptable limits set by the U.S. Food and Drug Administration in the Defect Levels Handbook (Rev. February 2005), which is hereby incorporated by reference, before these raw materials or other ingredients are incorporated into cannabis products.

(6) Raw materials and other components shall be held in containers designed and constructed to protect against allergen cross-contact or contamination, and shall be held at a temperature and relative humidity and in a manner that prevents the cannabis products from becoming adulterated.

(7) Frozen raw materials and other components shall be kept frozen. If thawing is required prior to use, it shall be done in a manner that prevents the raw materials and other ingredients from becoming adulterated.

(8) Raw materials and other components that are food allergens shall be identified and held in a manner that prevents cross-contact with other raw materials or ingredients.

(c) Holding and storage of raw materials and other components shall meet the requirements of Health and Safety Code sections 114047(a) and (b), 114049, and 114051.

(d) The policies and procedures for components shall be in writing and made available to the Department upon request.

NOTE: Authority cited: Sections 26013 and 26130, Business and Professions Code. Reference: Sections 26011.5 and 26039.6, Business and Professions Code.

§ 17213. Manufacturing Procedures.

(a) A licensed manufacturer shall implement and maintain the following manufacturing procedures that ensure cannabis product quality:

(1) A product quality plan, as described in section 17214;

(2) Master manufacturing protocols, as described in section 17215, for each unique formulation of cannabis product manufactured to ensure only intended components are included and that the cannabis product is packaged and labeled in accordance with product specifications and this division; and

(3) Batch production records, as described in section 17216, to document the production process and, if needed, to verify that the established procedures, including the preventive measures and master manufacturing protocol, were implemented correctly.

(b) All manufacturing records and procedures shall be in writing and are subject to inspection by the Department, its inspectors and agents.

NOTE: Authority cited: Sections 26013 and 26130, Business and Professions Code. Reference: Sections 26011.5 and 26039.6, Business and Professions Code.

§ 17214. Product Quality Plan.

(a) A licensed manufacturer shall establish and implement a written product quality plan for each type of product manufactured at the premises. The product quality plan shall address the hazards associated with the premises or the manufacturing process that, if not properly mitigated, may cause the product to be adulterated or misbranded, or may cause the product to fail laboratory testing or quality assurance review.

(b) To create the product quality plan, the licensed manufacturer shall conduct a comprehensive assessment of the overall manufacturing process, as follows:

(1) Identify each step from component intake through transfer of product from the premises;

(2) Evaluate the potential risks associated with each step;

(3) Identify the preventive measures that shall be taken to mitigate the potential risks identified;

(4) Identify the methods to evaluate and monitor the effectiveness of the preventive measures; and

(5) Identify any action to take if a preventive measure was unsuccessful.

(c) The licensed manufacturer shall evaluate the following potential risks to cannabis product quality that could be introduced during manufacturing operations:

(1) Biological hazards, including microbiological hazards;

(2) Chemical hazards, including radiological hazards, pesticide contamination, solvent or other residue, natural toxins, decomposition, or allergens;

(3) Physical hazards, such as stone, glass, metal fragments, hair, or insects; and

(4) Process failures that may lead to product contamination, allergen cross-contact, packaging errors, labeling errors, or other errors affecting cannabis product quality.

(d) The licensed manufacturer shall identify and implement the preventive measure(s) necessary to mitigate each potential risk identified pursuant to subsection (c). Examples of preventive measures include, but are not limited to:

(1) Cleaning and sanitizing of equipment and utensils to mitigate against risk of microbiological hazards;

(2) Conducting in-house testing of raw cannabis to mitigate against the risk of pesticide contamination;

(3) Establishing an allergen control program to ensure that allergen cross-contact does not occur between product types; and

(4) Implementing procedures to ensure homogeneity of cannabinoids into a cannabis product to mitigate against the risk of a non-homogeneous product.

(e) The licensed manufacturer shall identify and implement methods to evaluate and monitor the effectiveness of the preventive measures in mitigating the potential risks identified in subsection (c). Methods for evaluation and monitoring of preventive measures include, but are not limited to, the following:

(1) Review of test results conducted to determine contamination such as pesticide residue;

(2) Maintaining and reviewing cleaning, sanitizing, or maintenance logs to verify such actions have been taken;

(3) Conducting environmental testing to determine if equipment or utensils are contaminated with pathogens; and

(4) Monitoring the temperature of raw materials that need to be held below 41 degrees Fahrenheit to prevent microbial contamination.

(f) The licensed manufacturer shall identify actions to be taken if the evaluation and monitoring of the preventive measure indicates that a risk was not properly mitigated. The corrective action shall be specific to the type of product under evaluation and the specific risk to be mitigated. Examples of corrective actions include, but are not limited to:

(1) Destruction of product components or finished cannabis product;

(2) Further manufacturing of cannabis extract to remove impurities; and

(3) Reworking the unfinished product to further homogenize the cannabinoids.

(g) The licensed manufacturer shall maintain the product quality plans and documentation of preventive measures, monitoring results, and corrective actions and make the records available to the Department upon the Department's request, including during the Department's onsite inspection of the premises. Nothing in this chapter requires the disclosure of product quality plans other than to the Department and its inspectors and agents. The licensed manufacturer may consider the product quality plan subject to trade secret protection.

NOTE: Authority cited: Sections 26013 and 26130, Business and Professions Code. Reference: Sections 26011.5 and 26039.6, Business and Professions Code.

§ 17215. Master Manufacturing Protocol.

(a) A licensed manufacturer shall establish and follow a written master manufacturing protocol for each unique formulation of cannabis product manufactured, and for each batch size, in order to mitigate the potential for adulteration through incorporation of incorrect amounts of cannabinoids, unintended ingredients, or hazards identified in the product quality plan; the potential for misbranding through incorporation of ingredients not identified on the label or mislabeling of the product; and to ensure uniformity in finished batches and across all batches produced.

(b) The master manufacturing protocol shall include:

(1) The name and intended cannabinoid concentration(s) of the cannabis product to be manufactured;

(2) A complete list of components to be used;

(3) The weight or measure of each component to be used. The master manufacturing protocol for any given product may include the ability to adjust the weight or measure of cannabinoid-containing ingredients in order to account for the variability of cannabinoid content in harvest batches;

(4) The identity and weight or measure of each ingredient that will be declared on the ingredients list of the cannabis product;

(5) The expected yield of the finished cannabis product, based upon the quantity of components or packaging to be used in the absence of any loss or error in actual production, and the maximum and minimum percentages of expected yield beyond which a deviation investigation of a batch will be necessary, material review will be conducted, and a decision on the disposition of the product will be made;

(6) A description of packaging and a representative label, or a cross-reference to the physical location of the actual or representative label;

(7) The expected number of packages and labels to be used, if the cannabis product will leave the manufacturing premises in final form and packaged and labeled as it will be sold at retail;

(8) Written instructions for each point, step, or stage in the manufacturing process; and

(9) Written instructions for any action to mitigate risk(s) identified in the product quality plan.

(c) Master manufacturing protocols shall be in writing and made available to the Department upon request.

(d) Nothing in this chapter requires disclosure of the master manufacturing protocol to any person other than the individuals conducting activities that utilize the protocol or to the Department and its inspectors and agents. The licensee may consider the master manufacturing protocol subject to trade secret protection.

NOTE: Authority cited: Sections 26013 and 26130, Business and Professions Code. Reference: Sections 26011.5 and 26039.6, Business and Professions Code.

§ 17216. Batch Production Record.

(a) A licensed manufacturer shall prepare a written batch production record every time a batch of a cannabis product is manufactured or a batch of cannabis or cannabis product is remediated. The batch production record shall accurately follow the appropriate master manufacturing protocol, and each step of the protocol shall be performed in the production of the batch.

(b) The batch production record shall document all the following information about each batch at the time the batch is produced or remediated:

(1) The licensee number or premises address of the facility at which the production occurred;

(2) The date each step of the master manufacturing protocol was performed and the initials of the employee performing each step;

(3) The identity and weight or measure of each component used in production of the batch;

(4) The specific equipment and processing lines used in producing or remediating the batch;

(5) A statement of the actual yield and the percentage difference from expected yield at appropriate phases of manufacturing as identified in the master manufacturing protocol;

(6) If the product quality plan identifies any monitoring needed to ensure product safety, the results of the monitoring action performed;

(7) An actual or representative label or other identification of the label to be used for the cannabis product;

(8) The actual quantity of the packages and labels used, and the difference from the expected quantity to be used, if the cannabis product will leave the manufacturing premises as a final form cannabis good;

(9) Documentation that quality control personnel:

(A) Reviewed the batch production record;

(B) Reviewed all required monitoring operation(s); and

(C) Either approved and released, or rejected, the finished cannabis product, including any remediated, repackaged or relabeled cannabis product;

(10) Documentation, at the time of performance, of any investigation identified in the product quality plan or master manufacturing protocol, including deviations from the expected yield or package and label count; and

(11) The UID and the batch or lot number of the finished batch of cannabis product and the UIDs of all cannabis or cannabis products used in the batch.

(c) The batch production record shall:

(1) Contain the actual values and observations obtained during monitoring and, as appropriate, during verification activities;

(2) Be accurate, indelible, and legible;

(3) Be created concurrently with performance of the activity documented; and

(4) Be as detailed as necessary to provide a history of work performed.

NOTE: Authority cited: Sections 26013 and 26130, Business and Professions Code. Reference: Sections 26011.5 and 26039.6, Business and Professions Code.

§ 17217. Standard Operating Procedures.

(a) A licensed manufacturer shall establish and maintain written standard operating procedures that are easily accessible to onsite personnel. The standard operating procedures shall, at minimum, include the following:

(1) Policies or procedures developed in accordance with the security plan required by section 15042.1;

(2) Emergency response procedures, including safety data sheets for any chemicals onsite;

(3) Policies and procedures developed in accordance with section 17206;

(4) Policies and procedures developed in accordance with this article;

(5) Procedures for complying with the track and trace requirements established in article 6 of chapter 1; and

(6) Cannabis waste management procedures in compliance with section 17223.

(b) Procedures shall be written in English but may be made available in other languages, as necessary for the licensee's personnel.

NOTE: Authority cited: Sections 26013 and 26130, Business and Professions Code. Reference: Sections 26011.5, 26130 and 26160, Business and Professions Code.

§ 17218. Inventory Control - Cannabis and Cannabis Products.

(a) A licensed manufacturer shall establish and implement a written inventory control plan capable of tracking the location and disposition of all cannabis and cannabis products at the licensed premises.

(b) A licensed manufacturer shall reconcile the on-hand inventory of cannabis and cannabis products at the licensed premises with the records in the track and trace system at least once every thirty (30) calendar days.

(c) If a licensed manufacturer finds a discrepancy between the on-hand inventory and the track and trace system, the licensee shall conduct an audit.

(d) If the inventory reconciliation conducted pursuant to subsection (b) or the audit conducted pursuant to subsection (c) reveals a discrepancy that is significant pursuant to section 15034, the licensed manufacturer shall notify the Department within 24 hours of the discovery. The result of inventory reconciliation and any audit shall be retained in the licensed manufacturer's records and shall be made available to the Department upon request.

(e) The licensed manufacturer shall maintain sales invoices and receipts for all batches of cannabis and cannabis products received at and transferred from its licensed premises. The licensed manufacturer shall prepare a sales invoice or receipt that meets the requirements of Business and Professions Code section 26161 prior to each sale or transport of cannabis products from the premises.

NOTE: Authority cited: Sections 26013 and 26130, Business and Professions Code. Reference: Sections 26011.5 and 26130, Business and Professions Code.

ARTICLE 5. SPECIAL MANUFACTURING

§ 17219. Juice Manufacturing.

Manufacturers of cannabis juice or cannabis-infused juice or beverages shall prepare and implement a written juice hazard analysis and critical control plan in accordance with the requirements of title 21, Code of Federal Regulations, Part 120, subpart A, section 120.8 and subpart B, section 120.24, (Rev. January 2001), which are hereby incorporated by reference. The hazard analysis and critical control plan shall be made available to the Department upon request.

NOTE: Authority cited: Sections 26013 and 26130, Business and Professions Code. Reference: Sections 26011.5 and 26039.6, Business and Professions Code.

§ 17220. Dried Meat Manufacturing.

Manufacturing of cannabis-infused dried meat products shall be conducted in accordance with the United States Department of Agriculture FSIS Compliance Guideline for Meat and Poultry Jerky Produced by Small and Very Small Establishments: 2014 Compliance Guideline (Rev. 2014), which is hereby incorporated by reference. Meat for manufacturing into dried meat products shall be acquired from a commercially-available source.

NOTE: Authority cited: Sections 26013 and 26130, Business and Professions Code. Reference: Sections 26011.5 and 26039.6, Business and Professions Code.

Chapter 9. Other Responsibilities

§ 17221. Weighing Devices and Weighmasters.

(a) A licensee shall use weighing devices approved, tested, and sealed in accordance with the requirements in Business and Professions Code, division 5, chapter 5 (commencing with section 12500) and its implementing regulations, and registered with the county sealer consistent with Business and Professions Code, division 5, chapter 2 (commencing with section 12240) and its implementing regulations whenever:

(1) Cannabis or cannabis product is bought or sold by weight or count;

(2) Cannabis or cannabis product is packaged for sale by weight or count;

(3) Cannabis or cannabis product is weighed or counted for entry into the track and trace system; and

(4) The weighing device is used for commercial purposes as defined in Business and Professions Code section 12500.

(b) Whenever the licensee is determining the weight, measure, or count of cannabis and cannabis products for the purposes specified in subsection (a), the weight, measure, or count shall be determined by a licensed weighmaster in compliance with the requirements of Business and Professions Code, division 5, chapter 7 (commencing with section 12700).

(c) A licensee shall obtain a weighmaster certificate that complies with the requirements of Business and Professions Code, division 5, chapter 7 (commencing with section 12700) whenever:

(1) Payment for the cannabis or cannabis product is dependent upon the quantity determined by the weighmaster; or

(2) Payment for service or processing of the cannabis or cannabis product is dependent upon the quantity determined by the weighmaster.

(d) The weighmaster certificate shall not be required when cannabis or cannabis products are weighed or counted for entry into the track and trace system.

(e) In any county in which a county sealer refuses or is not required to approve, register, test, and seal weighing devices used by a licensee, the licensee may have a service agency registered pursuant to Business and Professions Code, division 5, chapter 5.5 perform testing of a weighing device consistent with the requirements in title 4, California Code of Regulations, section 4070. The licensee shall keep a copy of the registered service agency's written inspection report attesting to the accuracy of the device for each device operated by the licensee.

NOTE: Authority cited: Sections 26013 and 26130, Business and Professions Code. Reference: Sections 26011.5 and 26060, Business and Professions Code.

§ 17223. Waste Management.

(a) A licensee shall dispose of all waste in accordance with the Public Resources Code and any other applicable state and local laws. It is the responsibility of the licensee to properly evaluate waste to determine if it should be designated and handled as a hazardous waste, as defined in Public Resources Code section 40141.

(b) A licensee shall establish and implement a written cannabis waste management plan that describes the method or methods by which the licensee will dispose of cannabis waste, as applicable to the licensee's activities. A licensee shall dispose of cannabis waste using only the following methods:

(1) On-premises composting of cannabis waste.

(2) Collection and processing of cannabis waste by a local agency, a waste hauler franchised or contracted by a local agency, or a private waste hauler permitted by a local agency in conjunction with a regular organic waste collection route.

(3) Self-haul cannabis waste to one or more of the following:

(A) A staffed, fully permitted solid waste landfill or transformation facility;

(B) A staffed, fully permitted composting facility or staffed composting operation;

(C) A staffed, fully permitted in-vessel digestion facility or staffed in-vessel digestion operation;

(D) A staffed, fully permitted transfer/processing facility or staffed transfer/processing operation;

(E) A staffed, fully permitted chip and grind operation or facility; or

(F) A recycling center as defined in title 14, California Code of Regulations, section 17402.5(d) that meets the following:

(i) The cannabis waste received shall contain at least ninety (90) percent inorganic material;

(ii) The inorganic portion of the cannabis waste is recycled into new, reused, or reconstituted products that meet the quality standards necessary to be used in the marketplace; and

(iii) The organic portion of the cannabis waste shall be sent to a facility or operation identified in subsections (b)(3)(A)-(E).

(4) Reintroduction of cannabis waste back into agricultural operation through on-premises organic waste recycling methods including, but not limited to, tilling directly into agricultural land and no-till farming.

(c) The licensee shall maintain any cannabis waste in a secured waste receptacle or secured area on the licensed premises until the time of disposal. Physical access to the receptacle or area shall be restricted to the licensee, employees of the licensee, the local agency, waste hauler franchised or contracted by the local agency, or private waste hauler permitted by the local agency only. Nothing in this subsection prohibits licensees from using a shared waste receptacle or area with other licensees, provided that the shared waste receptacle or area is secured and access is limited as required by this subsection.

(d) A licensee that disposes of waste through an entity described in subsection (b)(2) shall do all of the following:

(1) Maintain and make available to the Department upon request the business name, address, contact person, and contact phone number of the entity hauling the waste; and

(2) Obtain documentation from the entity hauling the waste that evidences subscription to a waste collection service.

(e) If a licensee is self-hauling cannabis waste as allowed by the local jurisdiction, the licensee shall be subject to all of the following requirements:

(1) Self-hauled cannabis waste shall only be transported by the licensee or its employees;

(2) Self-hauled cannabis waste shall only be transported to a facility specified in subsection (b)(3); and

(3) The licensee or its employee who transports the waste shall obtain for each delivery of cannabis waste a copy of a certified weight ticket or receipt from the solid waste facility.

(f) A batch of cannabis or cannabis products that is being disposed of because the batch has failed internal quality testing, quality assurance review by a distributor, or regulatory compliance testing shall comply with the following additional requirements:

(1) All cannabis or cannabis products in the batch shall be rendered unusable prior to disposal;

(2) Rendering of the cannabis or cannabis products shall be done under video surveillance, unless the rendering is performed by a licensee engaging in cultivation activities on a licensed premises authorized exclusively for cultivation activities or the cultivation area of a licensed microbusiness premises; and

(3) The reason for disposal and the disposition of the batch shall be noted in the track and trace system.

NOTE: Authority cited: Sections 26013 and 26130, Business and Professions Code. Reference: Sections 26011.5 and 26130, Business and Professions Code.

§ 17225. Product Complaints.

(a) A licensee shall review all product complaints made to the licensee to determine whether the complaints involve possible misbranding or adulteration of a cannabis good, and shall investigate the complaints to the extent practicable based on the information received and the records the licensee is required to maintain.

(b) For purposes of this section, "product complaint" means any written, electronic, or oral communication received by a licensee that contains any allegation expressing concern, for any reason, with the quality of a cannabis good. Examples of product complaints may include, but are not limited to: foul odor, caused illness or injury, foreign material in a cannabis product container, improper packaging, mislabeling, cannabis products that contain an incorrect concentration of cannabinoids, and cannabis products that contain an unidentified ingredient, or any form of contaminant.

(c) The licensee shall maintain written records for every product complaint received and any subsequent investigation. The records shall include:

(1) The name and description of the cannabis good;

(2) The batch number or UID of the cannabis good, if available;

(3) The date the complaint was received and the name, address, and telephone number of the complainant, if available;

(4) The nature of the complaint including, if known, how the product was used;

(5) The reply to the complainant, if any;

(6) The findings of the investigation or follow-up action taken when an investigation is performed;

(7) The basis for any determination not to conduct an investigation, if applicable; and

(8) The notification to the licensee that made the cannabis good, if applicable.

(d) The licensee shall conduct a recall, as specified in section 17226, when the investigation evidences adulteration or misbranding.

NOTE: Authority cited: Sections 26013 and 26130, Business and Professions Code. Reference: Sections 26011.5 and 26039.6, Business and Professions Code.

§ 17226. Voluntary Recalls.

(a) Licensees shall establish and implement written procedures for recalling cannabis goods that are determined to be misbranded or adulterated. The recall procedures shall be implemented upon discovery, or notification from the Department, that one or more batches of cannabis goods are adulterated or misbranded. These procedures shall include:

(1) Factors that necessitate a recall;

(2) Personnel responsible for implementing the recall procedures;

(3) Notification protocols, including:

(A) A mechanism to notify all customers that have, or could have, obtained the cannabis goods, including communication and outreach via media, as necessary and appropriate;

(B) A mechanism to notify any licensees that supplied or received the recalled cannabis goods; and

(C) Instructions to the general public and other licensees for the return or destruction of the recalled cannabis goods; and

(4) Procedures for the collection and destruction of any recalled cannabis goods. These procedures shall meet the following requirements:

(A) All recalled cannabis goods that are intended to be destroyed shall be quarantined for a minimum of 72 hours, unless a longer holding time is requested by the Department. The licensee shall affix to the recalled cannabis goods any bills of lading, shipping manifests, or other similar documents with the cannabis goods information and weight. The cannabis goods held in quarantine shall be subject to auditing by the Department.

(B) Following the quarantine period, the licensee shall render the recalled cannabis goods unusable and dispose of them in accordance with section 17223.

(b) In addition to the tracking requirements set forth in section 15049, a licensee shall use the track and trace system and onsite documentation to ensure that recalled cannabis goods intended for destruction are identified, weighed, and tracked while on the licensed premises and when disposed of in accordance with this section. For recalled cannabis goods, the licensee shall enter the following details into the track and trace system: the weight and count of the cannabis goods, reason for destruction, and date the quarantine period will begin.

(c) The licensee shall notify the Department of any recall within 24 hours of initiating the recall.

(d) A licensed manufacturer may submit a corrective action plan to the Department for recalled cannabis goods in accordance with section 17305. If the corrective action plan is not approved by the Department, the cannabis goods shall be destroyed pursuant to the procedures required by subsection (a)(4).

NOTE: Authority cited: Sections 26013 and 26130, Business and Professions Code. Reference: Sections 26039.1 and 26039.6, Business and Professions Code.

§ 17227. Mandatory Recalls.

(a) The Department may require licensees to conduct a recall of a cannabis good that is adulterated or misbranded in accordance with Business and Professions Code section 26039.1.

(b) The licensee shall conduct the mandatory recall in the same manner as a voluntary recall as provided in section 17226.

NOTE: Authority cited: Sections 26013 and 26130, Business and Professions Code. Reference: Sections 26039.1 and 26039.6, Business and Professions Code.

Chapter 10. Cannabis and Cannabis Products

ARTICLE 1. STANDARDS FOR MANUFACTURED CANNABIS PRODUCTS

§ 17300. Prohibited Products.

The following types of products shall not be sold as cannabis products:

(a) Alcoholic beverages, as defined in Business and Professions Code section 23004. This prohibition does not apply to tinctures that meet the requirements of section 17303.

(b) Any cannabis product containing any non-cannabinoid additive that would increase potency, toxicity, or addictive potential, or that would create an unsafe combination with other psychoactive substances including, but not limited to, nicotine.

(c) Any cannabis product that must be held at or below 41 degrees Fahrenheit to keep it safe for human consumption, including, but not limited to, cream- or custard-filled pies; pies or pastries consisting in whole or in part of milk or milk products, or eggs; and meat-filled pies or pastries. This prohibition shall not apply to juices or beverages that need to be held below 41 degrees Fahrenheit if the juice or beverage was processed in accordance with section 17219, or to infused butter manufactured as permitted by subsection (g).

(d) Any thermally-processed low-acid cannabis product packed in a hermetically sealed container that, if it did not contain cannabis, would be subject to the manufacturing requirements of title 21, Code of Federal Regulations, part 113.

(e) Any acidified cannabis product that, if it did not contain cannabis, would be subject to the manufacturing requirements of title 21, Code of Federal Regulations, part 114.

(f) Any juice that is not shelf-stable or that is not processed in accordance with section 17219.

(g) Dairy products of any kind, as prohibited by Business and Professions Code section 26001(u), except butter purchased from a licensed milk products plant or retail location that is subsequently infused or mixed with cannabis.

(h) Meat products other than dried meat products prepared in accordance with section 17220.

(i) Seafood products of any kind.

(j) Any product that is manufactured by application of cannabinoid concentrate or extract to commercially available candy or snack food items without further processing of the product. Commercially available candy or snack food items may be used as ingredients in a cannabis product, provided that they are used in a way that renders them unrecognizable as the commercially available items, and the label, including the ingredient list, does not reference the commercially available item.

(k) Any cannabis product that the Department determines, on a case-by-case basis, is attractive to children, as specified in section 17408.

(l) Any cannabis product that the Department determines, on a case-by-case basis, is easily confused with commercially available foods that do not contain cannabis.

(m) Any cannabis product in, or imprinted with the shape, either realistic or caricature, of a human being, animal, insect, or fruit.

(n) Any inhalable cannabis product that is delivered into the lungs through a metered-dose inhaler or dry-powder inhaler. Nothing in this section shall be interpreted to prohibit other dry-powder cannabis products or metered-dose vaporizers containing cannabis or cannabis oil.

(o) Any cannabis product that is administered to the eye or the nasal passages.

(p) Any cannabis product that is injected into the body by piercing the skin.

NOTE: Authority cited: Sections 26013 and 26130, Business and Professions Code. Reference: Sections 26011.5 and 26130, Business and Professions Code.

§ 17301. Additional Requirements for Edible Cannabis Products.

(a) Except for cannabis, cannabis products, or terpenes, no ingredient or component shall be used in the manufacture of an edible cannabis product unless that ingredient or component is permitted by the United States Food and Drug Administration for use in food or food manufacturing, as specified in Substances Added to Food in the United States, available at https://www.accessdata.fda.gov/scripts/fdcc/index.cfm?set=FoodSubstances or is Generally Recognized as Safe (GRAS) under sections 201(s) and 409 of the Federal Food, Drug, and Cosmetic Act (codified in 21 U.S.C. 321(s) and 21 U.S.C. 348).

(b) Edible cannabis products that consist of more than a single serving shall be marked or packaged in a manner such that a single serving is readily identifiable or measurable.

(c) An edible cannabis product consisting of multiple servings shall be homogenized so that each serving contains the same concentration of THC.

NOTE: Authority cited: Sections 26013 and 26130, Business and Professions Code. Reference: Sections 26011.5 and 26130, Business and Professions Code.

§ 17302. Additional Requirements for Topical Cannabis Products.

(a) Except for cannabis, cannabis concentrate, or terpenes, topical cannabis products shall only contain ingredients permitted for cosmetic manufacturing in accordance with title 21, Code of Federal Regulations, part 700, subpart B (section 700.11 et seq.) (Rev. March 2016), which is hereby incorporated by reference.

NOTE: Authority cited: Sections 26013 and 26130, Business and Professions Code. Reference: Section 26011.5, Business and Professions Code.

§ 17302.1. Additional Requirements for Tinctures.

(a) A tincture shall be no more than 2 fluid ounces and shall include a calibrated dropper or similar device for measuring a single serving.

(b) A tincture, defined at section 15000(rrr), may include ingredients other than cannabis extract and alcohol, vegetable oil, or glycerin provided that the primary ingredient by weight is alcohol, vegetable oil, or glycerin.

NOTE: Authority cited: Sections 26013 and 26130, Business and Professions Code. Reference: Section 26011.5, Business and Professions Code.

§ 17303. Orally Consumed Products Containing Alcohol.

(a) Any orally consumed product that contains more than 0.5% alcohol by volume as an ingredient, and is not otherwise an alcoholic beverage as defined in Business and Professions Code section 23004, shall be packaged in a container no larger than two (2) fluid ounces and shall include a calibrated dropper or other similar device capable of accurately measuring servings.

NOTE: Authority cited: Sections 26013 and 26130, Business and Professions Code. Reference: Section 26011.5, Business and Professions Code.

§ 17303.1. Additional Requirements for Inhaled Products.

(a) Cannabis products intended for inhalation shall only contain cannabis, cannabis concentrate, terpenes, rolling paper, leaf, pre-roll filter tips, or ingredients permitted by the United States Food and Drug Administration as an "inactive ingredient" for inhalation, as specified in the United States Food and Drug Administration Inactive Ingredients Database, available at https://www.fda.gov/drugs/drug-approvals-and-databases/inactive-ingredients-database-download.

NOTE: Authority cited: Sections 26013 and 26130, Business and Professions Code. Reference: Section 26011.5, Business and Professions Code.

ARTICLE 2. CANNABINOID CONCENTRATION LIMITS

§ 17304. THC Concentration Limits.

(a) An edible cannabis product shall not contain more than:

(1) 10 milligrams THC per serving; and

(2) 100 milligrams THC per package.

(b) Notwithstanding subsection (a), a package containing an edible product that is an orally dissolving product, such as sublingual lozenges or mouth strips, may contain up to 500 milligrams THC per package, if:

(1) The cannabis product consists of discrete servings of no more than 10 milligrams THC per piece;

(2) The cannabis product is labeled "FOR MEDICAL USE ONLY;" and

(3) The cannabis product is only available for sale to a medicinal-use patient.

(c) A topical cannabis product or a cannabis concentrate shall not contain more than 1,000 milligrams THC per package.

(d) Notwithstanding subsection (c), a topical cannabis product or a cannabis concentrate may contain more than 1,000 milligrams THC per package, but not more than 2,000 milligrams THC per package, if the product is labeled "FOR MEDICAL USE ONLY" and is only available for sale to a medicinal-use patient.

NOTE: Authority cited: Sections 26013 and 26130, Business and Professions Code. Reference: Sections 26011.5, 26120 and 26130, Business and Professions Code.

ARTICLE 3. FAILED PRODUCT BATCHES

§ 17305. Failed Product Batches.

(a) A finished cannabis product batch that fails any regulatory compliance laboratory testing requirement established in this division shall be destroyed unless:

(1) The cannabis product batch or harvest batch may be remediated by relabeling pursuant to subsection (d); or

(2) A corrective action plan for remediation is approved by the Department pursuant to subsection (e). The licensed manufacturer or microbusiness authorized to engage in manufacturing who submits a corrective action plan for remediation shall be the manufacturer that remediates the subject batch. The licensed manufacturer shall not receive the batch from the licensed distributor until the Department has approved the corrective action plan.

(b) Remediation of a failed product batch or the use of a harvest batch that has failed any regulatory compliance laboratory test shall comply with the requirements and procedures established by the Department in section 15306, in addition to the requirements of this article.

(c) Except as provided in subsections (d) and (f), edible cannabis products that fail regulatory compliance laboratory testing shall not be remediated and shall be destroyed. If any edible cannabis product that has failed regulatory compliance laboratory testing is remediated or otherwise mixed with another batch of cannabis product in violation of this section, such action shall render the final cannabis product adulterated, regardless of the defect level of the final cannabis product.

(d) A cannabis product batch that fails regulatory compliance laboratory testing for cannabinoid or terpenoid content may be remediated by relabeling the product with the correct information from the certificate of analysis for regulatory compliance, provided that the THC limits in section 17304 are met.

(e) Except as provided in subsection (d), a cannabis product batch or a harvest batch that fails regulatory compliance laboratory testing or quality assurance review shall not be remediated unless the Department has approved a corrective action plan submitted by the licensed manufacturer or microbusiness authorized to engage in manufacturing who will be performing the remediation. Edible cannabis products may only be remediated by relabeling pursuant to subsection (d) or repackaging as provided in subsection (f). Corrective action plans will be reviewed by the Department on a case-by-case basis. A corrective action plan shall be submitted to the Department at remediation@cannabis.ca.gov and contain the following:

(1) The licensed manufacturer's license number and legal business name;

(2) The licensed manufacturer's DBA, if any;

(3) The brand name of the product being remediated, the UID for the batch, and the size of the batch;

(4) The licensed manufacturer's premises address;

(5) The name, email address, and phone number of the licensed manufacturer's contact person for this remediation;

(6) A description of how the cannabis product or harvest batch will be remediated so that the cannabis product or harvest batch, or any product produced therefrom, will meet all regulatory compliance testing standards and quality assurance requirements; and

(7) Any additional information requested by the Department.

(f) Edible cannabis products that fail regulatory compliance testing because the per-package limit of THC has been exceeded may be remediated by repackaging under the following conditions:

(1) The Department has approved a corrective action plan for repackaging the product;

(2) The product batch is returned to the manufacturer who packaged the product;

(3) The product itself is not altered in any way; and

(4) The product is labeled to accurately state the contents.

(g) All remediation of harvest or product batches shall be documented in the batch production records. Remediated products, harvest batches, or products produced therefrom shall be transported to a licensed distributor and undergo regulatory compliance testing in accordance with chapters 2 and 6 and quality assurance review pursuant to sections 15307 and 15307.1 prior to being transported to a licensed retailer.

NOTE: Authority cited: Sections 26013 and 26130, Business and Professions Code. Reference: Section 26039.6, Business and Professions Code.

Chapter 11. Labeling and Packaging Requirements

ARTICLE 1. BULK CANNABIS OR CANNABIS PRODUCTS, IMMATURE PLANTS, AND SEEDS

§ 17398. Bulk Cannabis or Cannabis Products.

(a) For purposes of this section, "bulk cannabis or cannabis products" means cannabis or cannabis products transferred between licensees for the purpose of further processing and/or packaging.

(b) The packaging used to transport bulk cannabis or cannabis products shall protect the cannabis or cannabis products from contamination and shall not expose the cannabis or cannabis products to any toxic or harmful substance.

(c) Packages of bulk cannabis or cannabis products shall be labeled with the following:

(1) The type or common name of the cannabis or cannabis products contained therein;

(2) The UID assigned to the cannabis or cannabis products;

(3) The ingredients of the cannabis products, including a list of any allergens present as described in section 17406(a)(6); and

(4) The net weight or count of the cannabis or cannabis products.

NOTE: Authority cited: Sections 26013 and 26130, Business and Professions Code. Reference: Section 26120, Business and Professions Code.

§ 17399. Immature Plants.

(a) Immature plants to be sold at retail are not required to be placed in child-resistant or tamper-evident packaging prior to sale.

(b) Immature plants shall be labeled with the following:

(1) The legal business name, or any name listed on the license certificate, of the licensed nursery that cultivated the immature plant, and its contact number or website address;

(2) The strain name; and

(3) The statement: "This plant has not been tested in accordance with the Medicinal and Adult-Use Cannabis Regulation and Safety Act."

NOTE: Authority cited: Section 26013, Business and Professions Code. Reference: Sections 26070, 26100 and 26120, Business and Professions Code.

§ 17400. Seeds.

(a) Packages of seeds are not required to be placed in child-resistant packaging prior to sale.

(b) Packages of seeds to be sold at retail shall be labeled with the following:

(1) The legal business name, or any name listed on the license certificate, of the licensed nursery that cultivated the seeds, and its contact number or website address;

(2) The strain name(s);

(3) Either the weight or count of seeds in the package;

(4) The universal symbol described in section 17410; and

(5) The statement: "These seeds have not been tested in accordance with the Medicinal and Adult-Use Cannabis Regulation and Safety Act."

NOTE: Authority cited: Sections 26013 and 26130, Business and Professions Code. Reference: Section 26130, Business and Professions Code.

ARTICLE 2. CANNABIS PRODUCTS RELEASED FROM MANUFACTURING

§ 17401. Release to Distributor as Finished Product.

(a) Cannabis products shall not be transferred to a licensed distributor, or microbusiness authorized to engage in distribution, for regulatory compliance testing unless the cannabis products are in their final form and packaged and labeled for retail sale.

(b) Notwithstanding subsection (a), a product label may exclude labeling of cannabinoid content if the cannabinoid content is to be added to the label at the distribution premises after issuance of a Certificate of Analysis in accordance with section 17407.

NOTE: Authority cited: Sections 26013 and 26130, Business and Professions Code. Reference: Sections 26011.5 and 26130, Business and Professions Code.

ARTICLE 3. LABELING REQUIREMENTS

§ 17402. General Provisions.

(a) Any information required to be listed on a label shall be written in English.

(b) A label shall be unobstructed and conspicuous so that it can be read by the consumer.

(c) All required label information shall be located on the outside container or wrapper of the finished product to be sold at a retailer, or be easily legible through the outermost container or wrapper. If the immediate container holding the cannabis goods is separable from the outermost packaging, such as a container placed inside of a box, the immediate container shall be labeled with the universal symbol as described in section 17410.

NOTE: Authority cited: Sections 26013 and 26130, Business and Professions Code. Reference: Section 26120, Business and Professions Code.

§ 17403. Primary Panel Labeling Requirements: Nonmanufactured Cannabis Goods.

(a) The label for a package of nonmanufactured cannabis goods shall include a primary panel that includes the following information in a type size no smaller than 6 point and proportional to the size of the primary panel and container:

(1) The identity of the product;

(2) The net weight of cannabis in the package, listed in both metric and U.S. customary units; and

(3) The universal symbol described in section 17410.

(b) The label for a package of nonmanufactured cannabis goods shall include an informational label that includes the following information in a type size no smaller than 6 point and proportional to the size of the informational panel and container:

(1) The UID;

(2) The name of the licensed cultivator or licensee packaging the product (either the legal business name or the name listed on the license certificate) and that licensee's contact number or website address;

(3) The date of packaging for retail sale; and

(4) The following statement in bold print: "GOVERNMENT WARNING: THIS PACKAGE CONTAINS CANNABIS, A SCHEDULE I CONTROLLED SUBSTANCE. KEEP OUT OF REACH OF CHILDREN AND ANIMALS. CANNABIS MAY ONLY BE POSSESSED OR CONSUMED BY PERSONS 21 YEARS OF AGE OR OLDER UNLESS THE PERSON IS A QUALIFIED PATIENT. CANNABIS USE WHILE PREGNANT OR BREASTFEEDING MAY BE HARMFUL.

CONSUMPTION OF CANNABIS IMPAIRS YOUR ABILITY TO DRIVE AND OPERATE MACHINERY. PLEASE USE EXTREME CAUTION."

(c) Nothing in this section prohibits the inclusion of additional information on the primary panel, provided that the label does not violate the requirements of section 17408.

(d) The cannabinoid content for a package of nonmanufactured cannabis goods shall be labeled as specified in section 17407.

NOTE: Authority cited: Sections 26013 and 26130, Business and Professions Code. Reference: Section 26120, Business and Professions Code.

§ 17404. Primary Panel Labeling Requirements: Manufactured Cannabis Products.

(a) The label for a manufactured cannabis product shall include a primary panel that includes the following information in a type size no smaller than 6 point and proportional to the size of the primary panel and container:

(1) The identity of the product in a text size reasonably proportional to the most prominent printed matter on the panel;

(2) The universal symbol as described in section 17410; and

(3) The net weight or volume of the contents of the package, listed in both metric and U.S. customary units.

(b) Nothing in this section prohibits the inclusion of additional information on the primary panel, provided that the label does not violate the requirements of section 17408.

NOTE: Authority cited: Sections 26013 and 26130, Business and Professions Code. Reference: Section 26120, Business and Professions Code.

§ 17405. Additional Primary Panel Labeling Requirements: Edible Products.

(a) In addition to the requirements of section 17404, the primary panel of an edible cannabis product shall include the words "cannabis-infused" or "cannabis infused" immediately above the identity of the product in bold type and a text size larger than the text size used for the identity of the product.

NOTE: Authority cited: Sections 26013 and 26130, Business and Professions Code. Reference: Section 26120, Business and Professions Code.

§ 17406. Informational Panel Labeling Requirements.

(a) The label for a manufactured cannabis product shall include an informational panel that includes the following:

(1) The name of the licensed manufacturer (either the legal business name or the name listed on the license certificate) that manufactured the cannabis product and the manufacturer's contact number or website address;

(2) The date the cannabis product was packaged for retail sale;

(3) The following statement in bold print: "GOVERNMENT WARNING: THIS PRODUCT CONTAINS CANNABIS,

A SCHEDULE I CONTROLLED SUBSTANCE. KEEP OUT OF REACH OF CHILDREN AND ANIMALS. CANNABIS PRODUCTS MAY ONLY BE POSSESSED OR CONSUMED BY PERSONS 21 YEARS OF AGE OR OLDER UNLESS THE PERSON IS A QUALIFIED PATIENT. THE INTOXICATING EFFECTS OF CANNABIS PRODUCTS MAY BE DELAYED UP TO TWO HOURS. CANNABIS USE WHILE PREGNANT OR BREASTFEEDING MAY BE HARMFUL. CONSUMPTION OF CANNABIS PRODUCTS IMPAIRS YOUR ABILITY TO DRIVE AND OPERATE MACHINERY. PLEASE USE EXTREME CAUTION;"

(4) The statement: "FOR MEDICAL USE ONLY" if the package contains an amount of THC that exceeds the level allowed for adult-use cannabis goods, as specified in section 17304;

(5) A list of all product ingredients in descending order of predominance by weight or volume. If any product ingredient contains subingredients, the list shall either:

(A) Include the common name of the ingredient followed by a parenthetical listing of all ingredients in descending order by weight or volume; or

(B) List all subingredients as individual ingredients in descending order of predominance; however,

(C) This subsection shall not apply to flavoring, which shall instead comply with title 21, Code of Federal Regulations, Part 101.22 (Rev. Jan. 2009), hereby incorporated by reference;

(6) For cannabis products containing an ingredient, flavoring, coloring, or an incidental additive that bears or contains a major food allergen, the word "contains," followed by a list of the applicable major food allergens. The list shall conform with the requirements for food allergen labeling set forth in 21 U.S.C. § 343(w), paragraph (1)(A) or (1)(B);

(7) The names of any artificial colorings contained in the product;

(8) For edible cannabis products, the amount, in grams or milligrams, of sodium, sugar, carbohydrates, and total fat per serving;

(9) Instructions for use, such as the method of consumption or application, and any preparation necessary prior to use;

(10) The UID;

(11) The batch or lot number; and

(12) The statement: "KEEP REFRIGERATED" or "REFRIGERATE AFTER OPENING," as applicable, if the cannabis product is perishable or perishable after opening.

(b) The informational panel text shall be in a type size no smaller than 6 point and proportional to the size of the primary panel and container.

(c) Except for the information required by subsections (a)(1), (a)(10) and (a)(11), the requirements of subsection (a) may be fulfilled through the use of supplemental labeling, which may include, but is not limited to, a package insert, fold-out or booklet label, or a hanging tag.

(d) Cannabinoid content may be included on the informational panel. Cannabinoid content for manufactured cannabis products shall be labeled as specified in section 17407.

(e) Nothing in this section prohibits the inclusion of additional information on the informational panel provided that the label does not violate the requirements of section 17408.

NOTE: Authority cited: Sections 26013 and 26130, Business and Professions Code. Reference: Section 26120, Business and Professions Code.

§ 17407. Cannabinoid Content Labeling.

(a) Each package for retail sale of cannabis goods shall be labeled with the cannabinoid content on either the primary panel or an informational panel. For manufactured products, cannabinoid content may be included on the label prior to release to a distributor or it may be added to the label at the distribution premises after issuance of a regulatory compliance testing Certificate of Analysis for the batch as described in subsection (d).

(b) Cannabinoid content labeling shall include the following:

(1) For an edible product or a cannabis concentrate for which the manufacturer has established serving designations, THC and CBD content expressed in milligrams per serving and milligrams per package.

(2) For a topical cannabis product or a cannabis concentrate without serving designations, THC and CBD content expressed in milligrams per package.

(3) For nonmanufactured cannabis goods, Total THC content expressed as a percentage.

(4) Packages of infused pre-rolls shall be labeled with either:

(A) The cannabinoid content in milligrams; or

(B) The cannabinoid content of the dried flower expressed as a percentage and the added cannabinoid content in milligrams.

(c) Cannabis goods labeled prior to testing must include the items specified in subsection (b), as appropriate to the product. For THC or CBD concentration that is less than two (2) milligrams per serving or per package, the THC or CBD concentration may be stated as "<2 mg per serving" or "<2 mg per package."

(d) Cannabis goods labeled at the distribution premises after issuance of the Certificate of Analysis shall comply with the following:

(1) Each package of cannabis goods shall be labeled with the cannabinoid content as specified in subsection (b) that is indicated on the Certificate of Analysis, as well as any other cannabinoid that is five (5) percent or greater of the total cannabinoid content;

(2) Labeled cannabinoid content shall reflect the amount indicated on the Certificate of Analysis. The amount may be rounded to the nearest whole number, except that packages shall not be labeled with an amount greater than the allowable THC limits. If the THC or CBD content of a manufactured cannabis product is indicated on the Certificate of Analysis as "Not Detected" or "<LOQ," the cannabinoid content shall be labeled as "0 mg" or "<2 mg;"

(3) The cannabinoid content label shall be affixed to the outermost packaging of the cannabis goods and shall not obscure any other label information.

(e) Nothing in this section precludes the labeling of terpenes or additional cannabinoid content on the cannabis goods, provided that the information is verified by the Certificate of Analysis.

NOTE: Authority cited: Sections 26013 and 26130, Business and Professions Code. Reference: Section 26120, Business and Professions Code.

§ 17408. Labeling Restrictions.

(a) Cannabis goods labeling shall not contain any of the following:

(1) The name of a California city, county, or city and county, including any similar name that is likely to mislead consumers as to the origin of the cannabis contained therein, unless one hundred percent of the cannabis

contained therein was produced in that city, county, or city and county. For purposes of this subsection, a cannabis plant is considered to have been produced within a city, county, or city and county if it was cultivated within that boundary starting from the time the plant was no taller or wider than 18 inches.

(2) Content that is, or is designed to be, attractive to individuals under the age of 21, as specified in section 15040(a)(2) and (3).

(3) Any health-related statement that is untrue or misleading. Any health-related statement must be supported by the totality of publicly available scientific evidence (including evidence from well-designed studies conducted in a manner which is consistent with generally recognized scientific procedures and principles), and for which there is significant scientific agreement among experts qualified by scientific training and experience to evaluate such claims.

(4) If the product is an edible cannabis product, a picture of the product contained therein.

(5) Any information that is false or misleading. For purposes of this section, false and misleading information includes, but is not limited to:

(A) Any statement or indication that the cannabis or cannabis product is organic, unless the National Organic Program (section 6517 of the federal Organic Foods Production Act of 1990 (7 U.S.C. section 6501 et seq.)) authorizes organic designation and certification for cannabis and the cannabis or cannabis product meets the requirements for that designation and certification. This includes use of the word "organic" or variants in spelling such as "organix" on the labeling, except for use of the term "organic" in the ingredient statement on the informational panel of a cannabis product in compliance with the requirements of the programs established pursuant to Business and Professions Code section 26062.

(B) Any statement or indication that the cannabis or cannabis product is "OCal," "OCal certified," or made with "OCal cannabis," if the cannabis or cannabis product has not been cultivated, handled, processed, or manufactured in compliance with the requirements of the programs established pursuant to Business and Professions Code section 26062.

(6) Any statement or indication of an appellation of origin if the cannabis or cannabis product does not meet the requirements of the program established pursuant to Business and Professions Code section 26063.

NOTE: Authority cited: Sections 26013 and 26130, Business and Professions Code. Reference: Sections 26062.5, 26063, 26120, 26121 and 26154, Business and Professions Code.

§ 17409. Statement of Characteristic Anticipated Effects.

(a) A cannabis good may include information on the characteristic anticipated effects of the cannabis good if the licensee has substantiation that the information is truthful and not misleading. Such information may be located on the informational panel of the label or the supplemental labeling with the package. For purposes of this section, "characteristic anticipated effect" includes any physiological effect (a temporary effect on the body related to the consumption of cannabis goods) that is common to or expected from the particular cannabis strain, but excludes any claim of health benefits (i.e. claims of therapeutic action as a result of the consumption of cannabis goods).

NOTE: Authority cited: Sections 26013 and 26130, Business and Professions Code. Reference: Sections 26120 and 26130, Business and Professions Code.

§ 17410. Universal Symbol.

(a) The symbol established pursuant to Business and Professions Code section 26130 shall replicate the following in form:

(b) The symbol shall be black or white in color. The symbol shall be made conspicuous by printing the symbol on a contrasting color.

(c) The symbol shall be no smaller in height than one-half (0.5) inch except as allowed under subsection (d).

(d) A cannabis vape cartridge or integrated cannabis vaporizer shall bear a universal symbol in a size no smaller than one-quarter (0.25) inch wide by one-quarter (0.25) inch high that is engraved, printed, or affixed with a sticker.

(e) The symbol shall not be altered or cropped in any way other than to adjust the sizing for placement on the primary panel.

NOTE: Authority cited: Sections 26013 and 26130, Business and Professions Code. Reference: Sections 26120, 26121 and 26130, Business and Professions Code.

ARTICLE 4. PACKAGING

§ 17411. Packaging.

(a) A package used to contain a cannabis good shall comply with the following requirements:

(1) The package shall protect the cannabis good from contamination and shall not expose the good to any toxic or harmful substance.

(2) The package shall be tamper-evident, which means that the packaging is sealed so that the contents cannot be accessed without obvious destruction of the seal upon initial opening.

(3) If the cannabis good has more than one serving, the package shall be resealable.

(4) The package shall not imitate any package used for products typically marketed to children.

(5) If the cannabis good is an edible product, the package shall be opaque.

(6) Notwithstanding subsection (a)(5), cannabis beverages may be packaged in glass containers that are clear or any color.

(7) The package shall be child-resistant, as described in section 17412.

NOTE: Authority cited: Sections 26013 and 26130, Business and Professions Code. Reference: Sections 26120 and 26121, Business and Professions Code.

§ 17412. Child-Resistant Packaging Requirements.

(a) A package containing cannabis or cannabis products transferred to a distributor for retail sale shall be child-resistant, as follows:

(1) The package for an edible product, an orally consumed concentrate, or a suppository shall be child-resistant for the life of the product. A package that contains more than a single serving is not required to be child-resistant if each individual serving is packaged in child-resistant packaging.

(2) Cannabis or a cannabis product intended to be inhaled or a cannabis product that is applied topically may utilize packaging that is child-resistant only until first opened, if the package is labeled with the statement: "This package is not child-resistant after opening."

(b) The following packages are considered child-resistant for purposes of this article:

(1) Any package that has been certified as child-resistant under the requirements of the Poison Prevention Packaging Act of 1970 Regulations (16 C.F.R. § 1700.15(b)(1)) (Rev. July 1995), which is hereby incorporated by reference.

(2) A bottle sealed with a pry-off, metal crown, cork-style bottle cap, provided that the bottle contains only a single serving.

(3) Plastic packaging that is at least four (4) mils thick and heat-sealed without an easy-open tab, dimple, corner, or flap, provided that the package contains a cannabis product described in subsection (a)(2) or a cannabis product that is only a single serving.

NOTE: Authority cited: Sections 26013 and 26130, Business and Professions Code. Reference: Sections 26011.5, 26120 and 26121, Business and Professions Code.

§ 17500. Record Keeping Requirements. [Repealed]

Note: Authority cited: Sections 26012, 26013 and 26130, Business and Professions Code. Reference: Sections 26011.5 and 26160, Business and Professions Code.

Chapter 12. Enforcement

ARTICLE 1. AUTHORITY

§ 17800. Right of Access.

(a) The Department and its authorized representatives, for purposes of inspection, investigation, review, or audit, shall have full and immediate access to:

(1) Enter any premises licensed by the Department.

(2) Inspect and test any vehicle or equipment possessed by, in control of, or used by a licensee or their agents and employees for the purpose of conducting commercial cannabis activity.

(3) Test any cannabis goods or cannabis-related materials or products possessed by, in control of, or used by a licensee or their agents and employees for the purpose of conducting commercial cannabis activity.

(4) Copy any materials, books, or records of any licensee or their agents and employees.

(b) Failure to cooperate with and participate in any Department investigation pending against the licensee may result in a licensing violation subject to discipline. This subsection shall not be construed to deprive a licensee of any privilege guaranteed by the Fifth Amendment to the Constitution of the United States, or any other constitutional or statutory privileges. This subsection shall not be construed to require a licensee to cooperate with a request that would require the licensee to waive any constitutional or statutory privilege or to comply with a request for information or other matters within an unreasonable period of time in light of the time constraints of the licensee's business. Any constitutional or statutory privilege exercised by the licensee shall not be used against the licensee in a regulatory or disciplinary proceeding against the licensee.

(c) Prior notice of an inspection, investigation, review, or audit is not required.

(d) Any inspection, investigation, review, or audit of a licensed premises shall be conducted anytime the licensee is exercising privileges under the license, or as otherwise agreed to by the Department and the licensee or its agents, employees, or representatives.

(e) If the licensed premises is not accessible because access is only available by going through another licensed premises and the licensee occupying the other licensed premises denies the Department access, the licensees shall both be held responsible and subject to discipline.

NOTE: Authority cited: Section 26013, Business and Professions Code. Reference: Sections 26013, 26015 and 26160, Business and Professions Code; and Section 11181, Government Code.

ARTICLE 2. COMPLIANCE AND ENFORCEMENT ACTIONS

§ 17801. Notice to Comply.

(a) The Department may issue a Notice to Comply to a licensee for violation(s) of the Act or this division discovered during an investigation or audit or observed during an inspection.

(b) The Notice to Comply shall be in writing and describe the nature and facts of each violation, including a reference to the statute or regulation violated, and may indicate the manner in which the licensee must correct the violation(s) to achieve compliance.

(c) The Department may serve the Notice to Comply personally, by email, or by mail to the licensee or an employee, agent, or person delegated by the licensee to accept notice.

(d) The licensee shall sign and return the Notice to Comply and describe how compliance was achieved within 30 calendar days after the date of personal service or the date of emailing or mailing of the notice or a different date specified by the Department. The Department may also require the licensee to provide a plan for review and approval by the Department on a case-by-case basis.

(e) Failure to correct the violation(s) in the Notice to Comply may result in disciplinary action.

NOTE: Authority cited: Section 26013, Business and Professions Code; Reference: Sections 26012 and 26018, Business and Professions Code.

§ 17801.1. Notice of Violation.

(a) Until October 1, 2021, the Department may issue a Notice of Violation to a licensee for violation(s) of the Act or this division that shall inform the licensee of:

(1) The violation(s) alleged;

(2) The proposed fine amount; and

(3) The licensee's right to request a hearing pursuant to subsection (b).

(b) Within 30 calendar days after issuance by the Department, a licensee may appeal a Notice of Violation by submitting a written request for an informal hearing by mail to the Department of Cannabis Control, Legal Affairs Division, 2920 Kilgore Road, Rancho Cordova, CA 95670, or by email to appeals@cannabis.ca.gov. The request shall include the following:

(1) The licensee's name, mailing address, and daytime phone number;

(2) The license number issued by the Department;

(3) A copy of the Notice of Violation; and

(4) A clear and concise statement of the basis of the appeal.

(c) If the licensee fails to submit a timely request for hearing pursuant to subsection (b), the Notice of Violation is not appealable and the Department may proceed upon the noticed violation(s) without a hearing.

(d) A hearing requested to appeal a Notice of Violation will be scheduled and conducted in accordance with chapter 5 (commencing with section 11500) of part 1 of division 3 of the Government Code.

(e) For all written requests for a hearing submitted by licensees and received by the Department prior to October 1, 2021, with hearings scheduled to take place on or after October 1, 2021, the following will occur:

(1) Informal hearing proceedings noticed prior to October 1, 2021, shall be converted to adjudicative proceedings under chapter 5 (commencing with section 11500) of part 1 of division 3 of the Government Code.

(2) Any scheduled informal hearings will be vacated, and a new hearing date, location and time will be noticed by the Department.

NOTE: Authority cited: Section 26013, Business and Professions Code. Reference: Sections 26012, 26031 and 26031.5, Business and Professions Code.

§ 17801.5. Embargo of Cannabis or Cannabis Products.

(a) The Department may embargo cannabis or cannabis products to prevent their sale, disposal, or removal from the location when the Department has probable cause to believe the cannabis or cannabis products are adulterated or misbranded or the sale would otherwise be in violation of the Act or this division.

(b) To embargo cannabis or cannabis products, the Department shall:

(1) Provide initial notice to the licensee or product owner that the cannabis or cannabis products are subject to embargo and the reason for the embargo. Initial notice may be oral or written and may be provided in person or by telephone, mail, facsimile transmission, email, or other electronic means;

(2) Affix a tag or marking to the cannabis or cannabis products, or component thereof, subject to embargo; and

(3) Provide an inventory of the embargoed items to the licensee or product owner.

(c) The Department shall provide a supplemental written notice to the licensee or product owner of the embargoed items that includes the following:

(1) The factual and legal bases for the embargo;

(2) A description of the cannabis or cannabis products under embargo;

(3) A request for a written plan to address the items under embargo and the issues(s) that resulted in the embargo;

(4) A summary of the proceedings for condemnation in accordance with chapter 5 (commencing with section 11500) of part 1 of division 3 of title 2 of the Government Code;

(5) Notification that the embargoed items cannot be removed from embargo, sold, or disposed of without

authorization of the Department or a court; and

(6) The penalty for violation of the embargo.

(d) The licensee or product owner may submit a written plan to the Department that describes how the licensee or product owner will address the items under embargo and the issue(s) that resulted in the embargo.

(1) If the Department determines that the plan will resolve the issue(s) that resulted in the embargo, and that all of the provisions of the Act and this division can be complied with, the Department will approve the plan and supervise the completion of the plan.

(2) If the Department cannot approve the plan, or the Department does not receive a response from the licensee within seven (7) calendar days after providing the notice described in subsection (c), the Department may initiate condemnation proceedings in accordance with Business and Professions Code section 26039.3(f).

(e) A licensee or product owner or their authorized representative may agree in writing to the voluntary condemnation and destruction of the cannabis and cannabis products subject to embargo. Destruction and disposal of the cannabis or cannabis products shall be at the licensee or product owner's expense and shall be conducted with the approval of and under the supervision of the Department.

(f) A licensee or product owner shall not remove the tag or marking from cannabis or cannabis products under embargo. A licensee or product owner shall not undertake corrective action or destruction of the items under embargo unless the Department has provided written approval and removed the embargo tag.

(g) A licensee or product owner shall not remove from embargo, sell, or dispose of any cannabis or cannabis products under embargo without written permission of the Department or a court. Each item removed, sold, or disposed of without written permission of the Department or a court constitutes a separate violation of the Act.

(h) A licensed cultivator or a microbusiness authorized to engage in cultivation may request permission to continue cultivation or harvesting of cannabis under embargo. The request shall be made to the Department in writing at compliance@cannabis.ca.gov and shall specify the cultivation or harvesting activities in which the licensee requests to engage. The Department may, in its sole discretion, authorize and impose conditions on the continued cultivation or harvesting of the cannabis under embargo.

(i) Cannabis and cannabis products found, cultivated, processed, produced, or manufactured at an unlicensed location, or derived from an unlicensed source, cannot be corrected and shall be destroyed.

NOTE: Authority cited: Section 26013, Business and Professions Code. Reference: Section 26039.3, Business and Professions Code.

§ 17802. Citations; Orders of Abatement; Administrative Fines.

(a) The Department may issue citations containing orders of abatement and fines against a licensee, or an unlicensed person, for any acts or omissions that are in violation of any provision of the Act or this division, or any another California laws applicable to cannabis licensees including, but not limited to, state labor law.

(b) The Department may issue a citation under this section to a licensee for a violation of a term or condition contained in a decision placing that licensee on probation.

(c) Each citation may contain either order(s) of abatement, monetary fine(s), or both, and shall:

(1) Be in writing and describe with particularity the nature of the violation, including a reference to the statute or regulation determined to have been violated;

(2) Fix a reasonable time for abatement of the violation if the citation contains an order of abatement;

(3) Assess an administrative fine of up to $5,000 per violation, per day, by a licensee and up to $30,000 per violation, per day, by an unlicensed person if the citation contains a fine;

(4) Be served personally or by certified mail; and

(5) Inform the licensee or person that they may request an informal conference, or contest the citation, or both, pursuant to section 17803.

(d) Fines issued with a citation must be paid within 30 calendar days after service of the citation, unless the fine is contested. If a citation is not appealed and the fine is not paid, the full amount of the assessed fine shall be added to the fee for renewal of the license. A license shall not be renewed without payment of the renewal fee and fine.

(e) The amount of any fine assessed by the Department under this section shall take into consideration the factors listed in Business and Professions Code section 26031.5(a)(1)-(3).

(f) Nothing in this section shall be deemed to prevent the Department from filing an accusation to suspend or revoke a license where grounds for such suspension or revocation exist.

NOTE: Authority cited: Section 26013, Business and Professions Code. Reference: Sections 26012, 26030 and 26031.5, Business and Professions Code.

§ 17803. Contesting Citations.

(a) A cited licensee or person may, within 30 calendar days after service of the citation, contest the citation by submitting to the Department a written request for a hearing, conducted in accordance with chapter 5 (commencing with section 11500) of part 1 of division 3 of the Government Code. If a hearing is not requested, it is waived and payment of a fine will not constitute an admission of the violation charged.

(b) In addition to requesting a hearing provided for in subsection (a), the cited licensee or person may, within 15 calendar days after service of the citation, submit a written request for an informal conference with the Department regarding the acts or omissions charged in the citation.

(c) The Department shall, within 15 calendar days after receipt of the written request, hold an informal conference with the cited licensee or person and/or their legal counsel or authorized representative.

(d) At the conclusion of the informal conference, the Department may affirm, modify, or dismiss the citation, including any fines levied or orders of abatement issued. A written decision stating the reasons for the decision shall be mailed to the cited licensee or person and their legal counsel, if any, within 15 calendar days after the date of the informal conference. This decision shall be deemed to be a final order with regard to the citation issued, including the levied fine and the order of abatement, if any.

(e) If the citation is dismissed, any request for a hearing shall be deemed withdrawn. If the citation is affirmed or modified, the cited licensee or person may either withdraw the request for a hearing or proceed with the administrative hearing process.

(f) If the citation, including any fines levied or orders of abatement issued, is modified, the citation originally issued shall be considered withdrawn and new citation issued. If a hearing is requested for the subsequent citation, it shall be requested within 30 calendar days after issuance of the citation.

NOTE: Authority cited: Section 26013, Business and Professions Code. Reference: Sections 26012, 26016 and 26031.5, Business and Professions Code.

§ 17804. Citation Compliance.

(a) If a citation with an order of abatement is issued, the time to abate or correct a violation as provided for in the order of abatement may be extended for good cause. If a cited licensee or person who has been issued an order of abatement is unable to complete the correction within the time set forth in the citation because of conditions beyond their control after the exercise of reasonable diligence, the cited licensee or person may request an extension of time from the Department in which to complete the correction. The request must be in writing and made within the time set forth for abatement.

(b) When a citation is not contested, or if it is contested and the cited licensee or person does not prevail, failure to abate the violation within the time allowed or pay a fine that was imposed shall constitute a separate violation.

(c) Failure to timely comply with an order of abatement or pay a fine that was imposed may result in further action being taken by the Department, including, but not limited to, suspension or revocation of a license, or further administrative or civil proceedings.

NOTE: Authority cited: Section 26013, Business and Professions Code. Reference: Sections 26012 and 26031.5, Business and Professions Code.

§ 17805. Minor Decoys.

(a) Peace officers may use a person under 21 years of age to attempt to purchase cannabis goods, for the purposes of enforcing the Act and to apprehend licensees, employees, or agents of licensees who sell cannabis goods to minors. For purposes of this section, a "minor" is a person under 21 years of age.

(b) The following minimum standards shall apply to the use of a minor decoy:

(1) At the time of the operation, the decoy shall be less than 20 years of age.

(2) A decoy shall either carry identification showing the decoy's correct date of birth or carry no identification. A decoy who carries identification shall present it upon request to any seller of cannabis goods.

(3) A decoy shall truthfully answer any questions about their age.

(4) Following any completed sale, but not later than the time a citation, if any, is issued, the peace officer directing the decoy shall make a reasonable attempt to enter the licensed premises or respond to the location where the licensee is located and have the minor decoy who purchased cannabis goods identify the alleged seller of the cannabis goods.

NOTE: Authority cited: Sections 26013 and 26140, Business and Professions Code. Reference: Section 26140, Business and Professions Code.

§ 17806. Attire and Conduct.

(a) No licensee shall allow the following:

(b) Employment or use of any person in the sale or service of cannabis goods in or upon the licensed premises while such person is unclothed or in such attire, costume, or clothing as to expose to view any portion of the breast below the top of the areola or of any portion of the pubic hair, anus, cleft of the buttocks, vulva, or genitals.

(c) Employment or use of the services of any host or other person to mingle with the patrons while such host or other person is unclothed or in such attire, costume, or clothing as described in subsection (a).

(d) Encouraging or permitting any person on the licensed premises to touch, caress, or fondle the breasts, buttocks, anus, or genitals of any other person.

(e) Permitting any employee or person to wear or use any device or covering, exposed to view, which simulates the breast, genitals, anus, pubic hair, or any portion thereof.

NOTE: Authority cited: Section 26013, Business and Professions Code. Reference: Section 26011.5, Business and Professions Code.

§ 17807. Entertainers and Conduct.

(a) Live entertainment is permitted on a licensed premises, except that no licensee shall permit any person to perform acts of or acts that simulate:

(1) Sexual intercourse, masturbation, sodomy, bestiality, oral copulation, flagellation, or any sexual acts that are prohibited by law.

(2) Touching, caressing, or fondling of the breast, buttocks, anus, or genitals.

(3) Displaying of the buttocks, breasts, pubic hair, anus, vulva, or genitals.

(b) No licensee shall permit any person to use artificial devices or inanimate objects to depict any of the prohibited activities described in this section.

(c) No licensee shall permit any person to remain in or upon the licensed premises who exposes to public view any portion of their breast, buttocks, genitals, or anus.

NOTE: Authority cited: Section 26013, Business and Professions Code. Reference: Section 26011.5, Business and Professions Code.

ARTICLE 3. DISCIPLINARY ACTIONS

§ 17808. Additional Grounds for Discipline.

The following include, but are not limited to, additional grounds that constitute a basis for disciplinary action:

(a) Failure to pay a fine imposed by the Department or agreed to by the licensee.

(b) Failure to take reasonable steps to correct objectionable conditions on the licensed premises, including the immediately adjacent area that is owned, leased, or rented by the licensee, that constitute a nuisance, within a reasonable time after receipt of notice to make those corrections, under Penal Code section 373a.

(c) Failure to take reasonable steps to correct objectionable conditions that occur during operating hours on any public sidewalk abutting a licensed premises and constitute a nuisance, within a reasonable time after receipt of notice to correct those conditions from the Department. This subsection shall apply to a licensee only upon written notice to the licensee from the Department. The Department shall issue this written notice upon its own determination, or upon a request from the local law enforcement agency in whose jurisdiction the licensed premises is located, that is supported by substantial evidence that persistent objectionable conditions are occurring on the public sidewalk abutting the licensed premises. For purposes of this subsection:

(1) "Any public sidewalk abutting a licensed premises" means the publicly owned, pedestrian-traveled way, not more than 20 feet from the licensed premises, that is located between a licensed premises, including any immediately adjacent area that is owned, leased, or rented by the licensee, and a public street.

(2) "Objectionable conditions that constitute a nuisance" means disturbance of the peace, public intoxication, drinking alcoholic beverages in public, smoking or ingesting cannabis or cannabis products in public,

harassment of passersby, gambling, prostitution, loitering, public urination, lewd conduct, drug trafficking, or excessive loud noise.

(3) "Reasonable steps" means all of the following:

(A) Calling the local law enforcement agency. Timely calls to the local law enforcement agency that are placed by the licensee or their agents or employees shall not be construed by the Department as evidence of objectionable conditions that constitute a nuisance.

(B) Requesting that those persons engaging in activities causing objectionable conditions to cease those activities, unless the licensee or their agents or employees feel that their personal safety would be threatened in making that request.

(C) Making good faith efforts to remove items that facilitate loitering, such as furniture, except those structures approved or permitted by the local jurisdiction. The licensee shall not be liable for the removal of those items that facilitate loitering.

(4) When determining what constitutes "reasonable steps," the Department shall consider site configuration constraints related to the unique circumstances of the nature of the business.

(5) Even after correcting the objectionable conditions that constitute a nuisance, the licensee has a continuing obligation to meet the requirements of subsections (b) and (c), and failure to do so shall constitute grounds for disciplinary action.

(d) Knowingly permitting the illegal sale, or negotiations for the illegal sale, of controlled substances or dangerous drugs upon the licensed premises. Successive sales, or negotiations for sales, over any continuous period of time shall be deemed evidence of permission. As used in this section, "controlled substances" has the same meaning as in Health and Safety Code section 11007, and "dangerous drugs" has the same meaning as in Business and Professions Code section 4022.

(e) If the licensee has employed or permitted any person to solicit or encourage others, directly or indirectly, to buy that person's cannabis goods in the licensed premises under any commission, percentage, salary, or other profit-sharing plan, scheme, or conspiracy.

NOTE: Authority cited: Section 26013, Business and Professions Code. Reference: Sections 26011.5, 26012, 26030 and 26031, Business and Professions Code.

§ 17809. Disciplinary Actions.

(a) When an accusation recommending disciplinary action against a licensee has been filed pursuant to Business and Professions Code section 26031, the accusation shall be served on the licensee in accordance with Government Code section 11505.

(b) A hearing shall be conducted in accordance with the provisions of chapter 5 (commencing with section 11500) of part 1 of division 3 of title 2 of the Government Code to determine if cause exists to take action against the licensee. At the hearing, the Department shall have all of the powers granted by the statutes cited above and by the Business and Professions Code.

(c) If a hearing on an accusation against a licensee results in a finding that the licensee has committed any of the acts or omissions constituting grounds for disciplinary action, the Department may order the license revoked, suspended outright for a specified period of time, or suspended on probationary restriction for a specified period of time, including terms and conditions of probation the Department considers appropriate on the basis of its findings, impose a fine, or any combination thereof. The Department may also issue other lawful orders it considers appropriate on the basis of its findings.

(d) An accusation may be terminated by written stipulation at any time prior to the conclusion of the hearing on the accusation. If a licensee submits a proposed stipulation to the Department for its consideration and the Department subsequently declines to accept the proposed stipulation, the Department shall not thereafter be disqualified from hearing evidence on the accusation and taking action thereon as authorized in this section.

NOTE: Authority cited: Section 26013, Business and Professions Code. Reference: Sections 26012, 26031 and 26034, Business and Professions Code.

§ 17810. Interim Suspension.

(a) Pursuant to Business and Professions Code section 494, the Department may petition for an interim order to suspend any license or impose licensing restrictions upon any licensee if:

(1) The licensee has engaged in acts or omissions constituting a violation of the Business and Professions Code or this division, or been convicted of a crime substantially related to the licensed activity, and

(2) Permitting the licensee to continue to engage in the licensed activity would endanger the public health, safety, or welfare.

(b) An interim order for suspension or restrictions may be issued with notice, as follows:

(1) The Department shall provide the licensee with at least 15 days' notice of the hearing on the petition for an interim order.

(2) The notice shall include all documents submitted in support of the petition.

(c) An interim order for suspension or restrictions may be issued without notice to the licensee if it appears from the Department's petition and supporting documents that serious injury would result to the public before the matter could be heard on notice.

(1) The licensee shall be entitled to a hearing on the petition within 20 days after issuance of the initial interim order.

(2) Notice of the hearing shall be provided to the licensee by the Department within two days after issuance of the initial interim order.

(3) The licensee shall receive all documents in support of the petition.

(d) The Department shall file an accusation, pursuant to chapter 5 (commencing with section 11500) of part 1 of division 3 of title 2 of the Government Code, within 15 calendar days after issuance of the interim order.

NOTE: Authority cited: Section 26013, Business and Professions Code; Reference: Sections 494, 26011.5, 26012 and 26031, Business and Professions Code.

§ 17813. Enforcement Costs.

(a) In any order in resolution of a disciplinary proceeding for suspension or revocation of a license, the Department may request the administrative law judge to direct a licensee found to have committed a violation or violations of the Act or this division to pay a sum not to exceed the reasonable costs of the investigation and enforcement of the case.

(b) A certified copy of the actual costs, or a good faith estimate of costs where actual costs are not available, signed by the Department's designated representative shall be prima facie evidence of reasonable costs of investigation and prosecution of the case. The costs shall include the amount of investigative and enforcement costs up to the date of the hearing, including, but not limited to, charges imposed by the Attorney General.

(c) The administrative law judge shall make a proposed finding of the amount of reasonable costs of investigation and prosecution of the case when requested pursuant to subsection (a). The Department may reduce or eliminate the cost award, or remand to the administrative law judge where the proposed decision fails to make a finding on costs requested pursuant to subsection (a).

(d) Where an order for recovery of costs is made and timely payment is not made as directed in the decision, the Department may enforce the order for repayment in any appropriate court. This right of enforcement shall be in addition to any other rights the Department may have to recover costs.

(e) In any action for recovery of costs, proof of the decision shall be conclusive proof of the validity of the order of payment and the terms for payment.

(f) Except as provided in subsection (g), the Department shall not renew or reinstate any license of a licensee who has failed to pay all of the costs ordered under this division.

(g) Notwithstanding subsection (f), the Department may, in its discretion, conditionally renew or reinstate for a maximum of one year the license of any licensee who demonstrates financial hardship and enters into a formal agreement with the Department for reimbursement within that one-year period for the unpaid costs.

(h) Nothing in this section shall preclude the Department from including recovery of the costs of investigation and enforcement of a case in any stipulated settlement.

NOTE: Authority cited: Section 26013, Business and Professions Code. Reference: Sections 125.3, 26012 and 26031, Business and Professions Code.

§ 17814. Disciplinary Guidelines.

In reaching a decision on a disciplinary action under the Act and the Administrative Procedure Act (Govt. Code section 11400 et seq.), the Department shall consider the disciplinary guidelines entitled "Department of Cannabis Control Disciplinary Guidelines for All Commercial Cannabis Licenses Amended July 2022," which are hereby incorporated by reference. Deviation from these guidelines and orders, including the standard terms of probation, is appropriate where the Department in its sole discretion determines that the facts of the particular case warrant such a deviation (e.g., the presence of mitigating factors, the age of the case, or evidentiary problems).

NOTE: Authority cited: Section 26013, Business and Professions Code. Reference: Sections 26012 and 26031, Business and Professions Code.

ARTICLE 4. EMERGENCY DECISION AND ORDERS

§ 17815. Emergency Decision and Order.

(a) The Department may issue an emergency decision and order for temporary, interim relief to prevent or avoid immediate danger to the public health, safety, or welfare. Such circumstances include, but are not limited to, the following:

(1) The Department has information that cannabis goods at a licensee's premises have a reasonable probability of causing serious adverse health consequences or death.

(2) To prevent the sale, transfer, or transport of contaminated or illegal cannabis goods in possession of a licensee.

(3) The Department observes or has information that conditions at a licensee's premises exist that present an

immediate risk to worker or public health and safety.

(4) To prevent illegal diversion of cannabis goods, or other criminal activity at a licensee's premises.

(5) To prevent the destruction of evidence related to illegal activity or violations of the Act.

(6) To prevent misrepresentation to the public, such as selling untested cannabis goods, providing inaccurate information about the cannabis goods or cannabis goods that have been obtained from an unlicensed person.

(b) Temporary, interim relief may include a suspension or administrative hold by one or more of the following:

(1) An order temporarily suspending a license.

(2) An order to segregate or isolate specific cannabis goods.

(3) An order prohibiting the movement of cannabis goods to or from the premises.

(4) An order prohibiting the sale of specific cannabis goods.

(5) An order prohibiting the destruction of specific cannabis goods.

(c) The emergency decision and order issued by the Department shall include a brief explanation of the factual and legal bases of the emergency decision that justify the Department's determination that emergency action is necessary, and the specific actions ordered. The emergency decision and order shall be effective when issued or as otherwise provided by the decision and order.

(d) To issue an administrative hold that prohibits activity related to specified cannabis goods, the Department shall comply with the following:

(1) Provide notice of the administrative hold that includes a description of the cannabis goods subject to the administrative hold.

(2) Following notice, the Department shall identify the cannabis goods subject to the administrative hold in the track and trace system.

(e) A licensee subject to an administrative hold shall comply with the following:

(1) Within 24 hours after receipt of notice of the administrative hold, physically segregate all designated cannabis goods in a limited-access area of the licensed premises. The licensee shall ensure that all cannabis goods subject to the administrative hold are safeguarded and preserved in a manner that prevents tampering, degradation, or contamination.

(2) While the administrative hold is in effect, the licensee shall not sell, donate, transfer, transport, gift, or destroy the cannabis goods subject to the hold.

(3) A microbusiness licensee subject to an administrative hold may continue to cultivate any cannabis subject to an administrative hold. If the cannabis subject to the hold must be harvested, the licensee shall place the harvested cannabis into separate batches.

(4) A licensee may voluntarily surrender cannabis goods that are subject to an administrative hold. The licensee shall identify the cannabis goods being voluntarily surrendered in the track and trace system. Voluntary surrender shall not be construed to waive the right to a hearing or any associated rights.

(f) To issue a temporary suspension, the Department shall specify in the order that the licensee shall immediately cease conducting all commercial cannabis activities under its license, unless otherwise specified in the order.

(g) A microbusiness licensee subject to a temporary suspension may continue to cultivate cannabis at the licensed premises only as prescribed by the Department in the order. If the order permits the cannabis to be harvested, the licensee shall place the harvested cannabis into separate batches.

(h) The emergency decision and order for temporary, interim relief shall be issued in accordance with the following procedures:

(1) The Department shall give notice of the emergency decision and order and an opportunity to be heard to the licensee prior to the issuance, or effective date, of the emergency decision and order, if practicable.

(2) Notice and hearing under this section may be oral or written and may be provided by telephone, personal service, mail, facsimile transmission, electronic mail, or other electronic means, as the circumstances permit.

(3) Notice may be given to the licensee, any person meeting the definition of owner for the license, or to a manager or other personnel at the licensed premises.

(4) Upon receipt of the notice, the licensee may request a hearing within three (3) business days by submitting a written request for hearing to the Department through electronic mail, facsimile transmission, or other means. The hearing shall commence within five (5) business days after receipt of the written request for hearing, unless a later time is agreed upon by the Department and the licensee.

(5) The hearing may be conducted in the same manner as an informal conference under section 17803; however, the timeframes provided in section 17803 shall not apply to a hearing under this section. Pre-hearing discovery or cross-examination of witnesses is not required under this section.

(6) The emergency decision and order shall be affirmed, modified, or set aside as determined appropriate by the Department within five (5) business days after the hearing.

(i) Within ten (10) calendar days after the issuance or effective date of the emergency decision and order for temporary, interim relief, the Department shall commence adjudicative proceedings in accordance with chapter 5 (commencing with section 11500) of part 1 of division 3 of title 2 of the Government Code to resolve the underlying issues giving rise to the temporary, interim relief.

(j) After formal proceedings are held pursuant to subsection (i), a licensee aggrieved by a final decision of the Department may appeal the decision to the Cannabis Control Appeals Panel pursuant to section 26043 of the Act.

(k) Notwithstanding administrative proceedings commenced pursuant to subsection (i), the licensee may obtain judicial review of the emergency decision and order pursuant to section 1094.5 of the Code of Civil Procedure in the manner provided in section 11460.80 of the Government Code without exhaustion of administrative remedies.

(l) The Department's authority provided by this section may be used in addition to any civil, criminal, or other administrative remedies available to the Department.

NOTE: Authority cited: Section 26013, Business and Professions Code. Reference: Section 26012, Business and Professions Code; and Sections 11460.10, 11460.20, 11460.30, 11460.40, 11460.50, 11460.60, 11460.70 and 11460.80, Government Code.

ARTICLE 5. POSTING NOTICES OF SUSPENSION AND REVOCATION

§ 17816. Posting of Notice of Suspension.

(a) A licensee whose license has been suspended shall conspicuously and continuously display a notice on the exterior of the licensee's premises for the duration of the suspension.

(b) The notice shall be 11 inches in length and 8.5 inches in width. The notice shall read:

NOTICE OF SUSPENSION

The Department of Cannabis Control License(s) Issued For This

Premises Has Been

Suspended For Violation of State Law

(c) Advertising or posting signs to the effect that the licensed premises has been closed or that business has been suspended for any reason other than the reason provided in the decision suspending the license, shall be deemed a violation of this section.

(d) Failure to display the notice as required in this section or removal of the notice prior to the expiration of the suspension shall be a violation of this section and may result in additional disciplinary action.

(e) A licensee shall notify the Department by submitting the Licensee Notification and Request Form, Notifications and Requests Regarding Regulatory Compliance, DCC-LIC-028 (New 2/22), incorporated herein by reference, within 24 hours of discovering that the notice under subsection (b) has been removed or damaged to an extent that makes the notice illegible.

NOTE: Authority cited: Section 26013, Business and Professions Code. Reference: Sections 26011.5 and 26012, Business and Professions Code.

§ 17817. Posting of Notice of Revocation.

(a) A person whose license has been revoked shall conspicuously display a notice on the exterior of the premises indicating that the license has been revoked. The notice shall remain continuously on the premises for at least 15 calendar days.

(b) The notice shall be 11 inches in length and 8.5 inches in width. The notice shall read:

NOTICE OF REVOCATION

The Department of Cannabis Control License(s) Issued For This

Premises Has Been

Revoked For Violation of State Law

(c) Advertising or posting signs to the effect that the premises has been closed, or that business has been suspended for any reason other than the reason provided in the decision revoking the license, shall be deemed a violation of this section.

(d) If the Department revokes a license at a licensed premises that has one or more licenses at the location that will remain active after the revocation, the revocation notice shall remain posted for a period of at least 15 calendar days.

(e) Failure to display the notice for the time required in this section shall be a violation of this section and may result in additional disciplinary action.

(f) A person whose license has been revoked shall notify the Department by submitting the Licensee Notification and Request Form, Notifications and Requests Regarding Regulatory Compliance, DCC-LIC-028 (New 2/22), incorporated herein by reference, within 24 hours of discovering that the notice under subsection (b) has been removed or damaged to an extent that makes the notice illegible.

NOTE: Authority cited: Section 26013, Business and Professions Code. Reference: Sections 26011.5 and 26012, Business and Professions Code.

Chapter 13. Other Provisions

ARTICLE 1. RESEARCH FUNDING

§ 17900. Eligibility.

(a) Only public universities in California shall be eligible to be selected to receive funds disbursed pursuant to Revenue and Taxation Code section 34019(b).

(b) Subject to available funding, the amounts to be disbursed to the university or universities will not exceed the sum of ten million dollars ($10,000,000) for each fiscal year, ending with the 2028-2029 fiscal year.

NOTE: Authority cited: Section 26013, Business and Professions Code. Reference: Section 34019, Revenue and Taxation Code.

§ 17901. Request for Proposals.

(a) A Request for Proposal (RFP) is the document issued by the Department to notifiy all eligible fund recipients of the following, at a minimum:

> (1) The funding available for research related to the Act or this division;
>
> (2) Disbursement of funds to eligible applicants through a review and selection process, including the criteria that will be used for review and selection;
>
> (3) The specified timeframes for the proposal review and selection process, including the deadline for submission of proposals;
>
> (4) Proposal requirements, including necessary documentation;
>
> (5) Any priorities or restrictions imposed upon the use of the funds;
>
> (6) The governing statutes and regulations; and
>
> (7) The name, address, and telephone number of a contact person within the Department who can provide further information regarding the process for submission of proposals.

NOTE: Authority cited: Section 26013, Business and Professions Code. Reference: Section 34019, Revenue and Taxation Code.

§ 17902. Selection Process and Criteria.

(a) The selection process shall involve eligible proposals timely received by the Department, in response to an applicable RFP, or similar notice.

(b) The Department will consider only one proposal per applicant for a given research project. Applicants may submit more than one proposal if the proposals are for separate and distinct research projects or activities.

(c) The Department will make a selection for funding based on criteria including, but not limited to:

> (1) The extent to which the proposed project is designed to achieve objectives specified in Revenue and Taxation Code section 34019(b).
>
> (2) The extent to which the proposed project is designed to achieve measurable outcomes, and the clarity of the measures for success, including, for research-based objectives, the scientific and technical merit of the

proposed project as evaluated by relevant experts.

(3) The extent to which the proposed project is feasible, demonstrated by:

(A) A timeline for project completion, including readiness; and

(B) Budget detail.

(4) Qualifications of the staff who will be assigned to or working on the proposed project.

(5) Any other criteria to determine the proposed project's efficacy in evaluating the implementation and effect of the Act.

(d) Applicants selected for funding will be notified of the selection and amount of funding in writing.

(e) The Department's selection decision is final and not subject to appeal.

NOTE: Authority cited: Section 26013, Business and Professions Code. Reference: Section 34019, Revenue and Taxation Code.

§ 17903. Release of Funds.

(a) The Department shall not cause funds to be disbursed until the recipient has executed a Grant Agreement and any other required documents.

(b) Selected recipients shall receive a single disbursement of funds for the duration of the research project.

(c) Funds released to the recipient that will be used for the purchase of any equipment related to the research project shall, at a minimum, meet the following conditions:

(1) Prior to the purchase of any equipment, the recipient shall obtain written approval from the Department.

(2) Receipts or other documentation for the purchase of any equipment shall be provided to the Department immediately upon purchase and request and retained pursuant to section 17904.

(d) Any funds that are not used prior to the completion of the research project shall be forfeited.

NOTE: Authority cited: Section 26013, Business and Professions Code. Reference: Section 34019, Revenue and Taxation Code.

§ 17904. Reports to the Department.

(a) The recipient of funds shall provide regular performance reports to the Department in the following manner, unless otherwise specified in the Grant Agreement:

(1) At monthly intervals for research projects with an estimated completion time not exceeding one year.

(2) At quarterly intervals for research projects with an estimated completion time exceeding one year.

(b) Performance reports shall include, at a minimum:

(1) A detailed, estimated time schedule of completion for the research project;

(2) A description of any measurable outcomes, results achieved, or other completed objectives of the research project;

(3) A description of remaining work to be completed;

(4) A summary of expenditures of the funds and statement of whether the research project is meeting the proposed budget. If not, the reasons for any discrepancies and a list of actions that will be taken to ensure completion of the research project; and

(5) Any changes to the information provided in the proposal, including, but not limited to, change in staff.

NOTE: Authority cited: Section 26013, Business and Professions Code. Reference: Section 34019, Revenue and Taxation Code.

§ 17905. Research Records.

Recipients shall retain all research and financial data necessary to substantiate the purposes for which the funds were spent for the duration of the funding, and for a period of seven years after completion of the research project. Recipients shall provide this documentation to the Department upon request.

NOTE: Authority cited: Section 26013, Business and Professions Code. Reference: Section 26160, Business and Professions Code; and Section 34019, Revenue and Taxation Code.

Title 14. Natural Resources

DIVISION 1. FISH AND GAME COMMISSION - DEPARTMENT OF FISH AND GAME

SUBDIVISION 3. GENERAL REGULATIONS

Chapter 3. Miscellaneous

§ 722. General Lake or Streambed Alteration Agreement for Activities Related to Cannabis Cultivation.

(a) Purpose.

(1) This regulation constitutes a general lake or streambed alteration agreement under Section 1617 of the Fish and Game Code, referred to herein as the "General Agreement."

(2) This General Agreement applies only to the construction, Reconstruction, maintenance, or repair of Stream Crossings, in the form of a bridge, culvert, or rock ford, and Water Diversions on non-finfish rivers, streams, and lakes that are used or will be used for the purpose of Cannabis Cultivation, each a "Covered Activity."

(b) Requirements. An Entity shall be authorized under this General Agreement to conduct a Covered Activity only if all of the following occur:

(1) The Eligibility Criteria in subsection (d) are met.

(2) The Entity notifies the department and pays a fee or fees in accordance with subsection (f).

(3) The Entity receives notice from the department that the Covered Activity is authorized under this General Agreement.

(4) The Entity complies with all applicable measures and requirements in subsections (h)-(k).

(c) Definitions. The following definitions apply to this section:

(1) "Authorized Activity" means a Covered Activity an Entity is authorized to conduct under this General Agreement after notice by the department.

(2) "Biological Resources Assessment" means a survey and biological resource report of the Project Site by a Biologist. In preparing a Biological Resources Assessment, the Biologist shall do the following:

(A) Identify the presence or potential presence of any Species of Greatest Conservation Need and finfish and their habitat, and invasive species, relying on the U.S. Department of Agriculture's Ecoregion Classification system; California's Vegetation Classification and Mapping Program macrogroups (based on the National Vegetation Classification System) at https://www.wildlife.ca.gov/Data/VegCAMP; the U.S. Geological Survey's Hydrologic Classification hydrologic unit code 8 at http://datagateway.nrcs.usda.gov; the U.S. Fish and Wildlife Service's Information for Planning and Consultation at https://ecos.fws.gov/ipac/; and the National Marine Fisheries Service's California Species List Tools at: http://www.westcoast.fisheries. noaa.gov/maps_data/california_species_list_tools.html.

(3) "Biologist" means a person who meets the following minimum qualifications:

(A) Possesses a degree in biological or natural resources, or a closely related scientific discipline, from an accredited university.

(B) Is familiar with Species of Greatest Conservation Need, their home ranges compared to the Project Site, and their local ecology.

(C) Has experience analyzing project impacts on Species of Greatest Conservation Need and their habitat.

(D) Is familiar with invasive species prevention and eradication.

(4) "Bladder" means a flexible container designed to store water.

(5) "Cannabis Cultivation" means any activity involving the planting, growing, harvesting, drying, curing, grading, or trimming of cannabis.

(6) "Covered Activity" means the construction, Reconstruction, maintenance, or repair of a Stream Crossing or Water Diversion that is used or will be used for the purpose of Cannabis Cultivation for which the Entity is seeking authorization under this General Agreement.

(7) "Design Plan" means a detailed description of the site-specific design for the construction or Reconstruction of a Stream Crossing or reservoir prescribed by a Licensed Professional that includes drawings, sizing methods, component details, and construction notes that give specific directions on the construction methods that will be employed for the work.

(8) "Entity" means "entity" as defined in Section 1601, subdivision (d), of the Fish and Game Code.

(9) "Finfish" means any species of bony fish. Finfish do not include mollusks, crustaceans, amphibians, or invertebrates.

(10) "Finfish stream or lake" means any stream or lake where finfish are always or seasonally present.

(11) Fish means "fish" as defined in Section 45 of the Fish and Game Code.

(12) "Licensed Professional" means a person licensed under the Professional Engineer Act (Bus. & Prof. Code, §§ 6700-6799), the Geologist and Geophysicist Act (Bus. & Prof. Code, §§ 7800-7887), the Professional Land Surveyors' Act (Bus. & Prof. Code, §§ 8700-8805), or the Professional Foresters Law (Pub. Resources Code, §§ 750-783) or a licensed professional hydrologist.

(13) “Listed or Fully Protected Species” means any native plant species listed as rare under the Native Plant Protection Act (Fish & G. Code, § 1900 et seq. ; Cal. Code Regs., tit. 14, § 670.2); any species that is listed or is a candidate for listing under the California Endangered Species Act (Fish & G. Code, § 2080 et seq. ; Cal. Code Regs., tit. 14, §§ 670.2, 670.5); or any fully protected species (Fish & G. Code, §§ 3511, 4700, 5050, 5515).

(14) “Permittee” means an Entity who has obtained authorization from the department to conduct a Covered Activity under this General Agreement.

(15) “Project Site” means the location of the Covered Activity and the surrounding area.

(16) “Property” means the property on which the Project Site is located as identified by an Assessor’s Parcel Number.

(17) “Property Diagram” means a diagram to scale of the Property that identifies the following with locations also provided as coordinates in either latitude and longitude or the California Coordinate System:

(A) The location and size of all existing stream crossings, water diversions, water diversion infrastructure, and water storage facilities of any type on the Property.

(B) The location of the Project Site on the Property.

(C) Each river, stream, lake, and other waters on the Property, including springs.

(D) Sources of water used on the Property and the location of all points of diversion, including pumps and wells.

(E) Water distribution systems.

(F) The Assessor’s Parcel Number for the Property.

(18) “Reconstruction” means the major repair or complete replacement of an existing Stream Crossing or Water Diversion where any new structure:

(A) Will be located on the same site as the structure replaced or repaired and will have substantially the same purpose as the structure replaced or repaired.

(B) Will minimize or avoid direct and indirect adverse impacts on fish and wildlife resources compared to the existing structure.

(19) “River” includes stream.

(20) “Species of Greatest Conservation Need” means “Species of Greatest Conservation Need” that are listed in Appendix C of the California State Wildlife Action Plan 2015 Update, Volume II (https://www.wildlife.ca.gov/SWAP) or meet the definition of “endangered” or “rare” in Section 15380.

(21) “Stream” means any stream or river, including streams or rivers that are dry for periods of time.

(22) “Stream Crossing” means a bridge, culvert, or rock ford in or over a stream or river, and all fill material within the crossing prism.

(23) “Take” means “take” as defined in Section 86 of the Fish and Game Code.

(24) “Water Diversion” means the act of diverting surface flow or hydrologically connected subsurface flow for use or storage. “Water diversion” includes all infrastructure used to divert (e.g., rock dams, excavation pools in fast-moving water, and wells) or store such flow.

(25) “Water Storage Facility” means an artificial water storage facility comprised of a bladder, reservoir, or storage tank.

(26) "Waters of the State" means "state waters" as defined in Section 89.1 of the Fish and Game Code.

(d) Eligibility Criteria. This General Agreement shall apply to a Covered Activity when the Entity certifies to the department all of the following:

(1) Each activity for which the Entity is notifying the department under subsection (f) is a Covered Activity.

(2) Each Covered Activity included in the notification under subsection (f) meets the applicable Design Criteria in subsection (e).

(3) The Covered Activity will not occur on or in a finfish stream or lake.

(4) The Covered Activity will not result in take of a Listed or Fully Protected Species.

(5) The Covered Activity is not the subject of a complaint or order by the department under Section 12025 of the Fish and Game Code, a complaint filed by a city attorney, District Attorney, the Attorney General, or an order by a court.

(6) If the Entity is seeking authorization under this General Agreement in response to a notice of violation by the department, the authorization will address each violation alleged in the notice.

(7) The Entity will meet the applicable measures and requirements in subsections (h)-(k).

(e) Design Criteria.

(1) Bridge.

(A) Comprised of a single span structure across a stream with all abutments located outside the top of the stream banks.

(B) Minimally conveys a 100-year peak storm flow with one foot of freeboard.

(C) Does not prevent, impede, or tend to prevent or impede the passing of fish up and downstream.

(D) The tops of any abutment footings are below the calculated scour depth.

(2) Culvert.

(A) Comprised of a single pipe.

(B) Sized to minimally convey a 100-year peak storm flow or designed to withstand a 100-year peak storm flow.

(C) Aligned within the channel and otherwise engineered, installed, and maintained to prevent washout and erosion of the streambed, stream banks, and fill.

(D) Embedded below the natural channel grade to facilitate substrate deposition on the culvert floor. Where physical conditions preclude embedment (e.g., channels composed of bedrock or large boulders), the maximum slope of the culvert must be 0.5 percent with no hydraulic drop at the outlet.

(E) Extended lengthwise completely beyond the toe of fill.

(F) Set to the natural stream grade of the stream reach, if feasible based on the composition of the affected streambed.

(G) Inlets, outlets (including the outfall area), and fill faces are armored using rock where stream flow, road runoff, or rainfall is likely to cause erosion.

(H) Open bottom culverts are placed on footings excavated below the calculated scour depth.

(I) Corrugated metal pipe is used in areas of high to very high fire hazard as indicated by CAL FIRE Fire Hazard Severity Zone Maps.

(J) Does not prevent, impede, or tend to prevent or impede the passing of fish up and downstream.

(3) Rock ford.

(A) Located in a stable stream reach with a coarse gravel and cobble streambed.

(B) Oriented perpendicular to flow and designed to maintain the range of surface flows that occur in the stream.

(C) Constructed using rock that can withstand streambed and bank erosion by the expected range of flow velocities.

(D) Does not contain concrete or asphalt in any form.

(E) Does not prevent, impede, or tend to prevent or impede the passing of fish up and downstream.

(4) Water Diversion.

(A) Water diverted at each place or point of diversion does not exceed an instantaneous diversion rate of 10 gallons per minute and shall bypass a minimum 50 percent of the surface flow past the point of diversion, as estimated based on visually observing surface water flow at least daily.

(B) Water Diversion intakes, including intakes for water trucks, are fitted with a commercially available water pump strainer designed for use in aquatic environments that is securely attached to the intake.

(C) All infrastructure used to intercept surface flow, such as rock dams, does not prevent, impede, or tend to prevent or impede the passing of fish up and downstream.

(D) Water diverted to storage for cannabis cultivation does not exceed five acre-feet per year and is stored in a Water Storage Facility ("WSF") that meets the following criteria:

1. Located off-stream and outside the active 100-year floodplain.

2. Is not used to store or mix chemicals.

3. If the WSF is a reservoir:

a. Artificially constructed, off-stream water body not exceeding five acre-feet of storage, designed by a Licensed Professional.

b. No hydrologic connectivity to upstream surface waters.

c. The overflow outlet is designed and located to prevent erosion in case of overtopping.

d. Constructed and operated in a manner that enables wildlife to exit the waterbody.

4. If the WSF is a bladder, the WSF includes a secondary containment structure that will contain 110 percent of water volume in case of bladder failure and will enable wildlife to escape the structure.

5. If the WSF is a tank:

a. Enclosed (i.e., no open top).

b. Made of rigid material, such as metal or high-density polyethylene, designed to hold water.

c. Piping includes backflow prevention devices to minimize backflow and cross contamination, for example, from mixing tanks.

(f) Notification and Fee Requirements. To seek authorization to conduct a Covered Activity under this General Agreement, the Entity must go to the website for the department's Lake and Streambed Alteration Program at: https://www.wildlife.ca.gov/Conservation/LSA and follow the links and instructions to apply for authorization. To apply for authorization, the Entity must provide the information specified in subsection (f)(1) ("Notification"), make the certifications described in subsection (f)(2) ("Certifications"), and when applicable, pay the fee(s) as specified in subsection (f)(3) below.

(1) Information. The Entity must provide to the department the information described below for each Covered Activity for the purpose of seeking authorization to conduct the Covered Activity under this General Agreement.

(A) The name, mailing address, telephone and fax numbers, and email address of the following individuals:

1. The Entity.

2. The Entity's designated representative or contact person, if applicable.

3. The Property owner if different from the Entity.

4. The Biologist who prepared the Biological Resources Assessment.

5. The Licensed Professional who prepared the Design Plan, if a Design Plan is required.

(B) Information for the purpose of calculating the total fee, including the cost of each Covered Activity and the fee for each.

(C) Whether the Covered Activity is the subject of a notice of violation by the department; a complaint or order by the department under Section 12025 of the Fish and Game Code; a complaint by a city attorney, District Attorney, or the Attorney General; or an order or notice by a court or agency other than the department, and information regarding the notice, complaint, or order.

(D) Location of the Project Site, including the address or description of the location with reference to the nearest city or town; the county; driving directions from a major road or highway; the name of the stream or lake in or near where the Covered Activity will occur; the watercourse or waterbody to which the stream or lake is tributary; the USGS 7.5 Minute Quad Map Name, the Township, Range, Section, 1/4 Section, and Meridian; coordinates, such as latitude/longitude and UTM; and the Assessor's Parcel Number for the Property the Project Site is located on.

(E) The type of Covered Activity (i.e., bridge, culvert, rock ford, or water diversion).

(F) A description of the Covered Activity.

(G) Information to confirm the Covered Activity meets the Eligibility and Design Criteria in subsections (d) and (e) and to confirm the Entity is able to and will meet the applicable measures and requirements in subsections (h)-(k).

(H) Information regarding any temporary or annual license the California Department of Food and Agriculture has issued to the Entity, or that the Entity has applied or will apply for, that authorizes or would authorize the Cannabis Cultivation the Covered Activity relates to.

(I) Whether the Covered Activity would be a new activity or is an existing activity.

(J) Information regarding the Entity's Water Diversion.

(2) Certifications. The Entity must certify the following:

(A) The Entity has in its possession the following documents:

1. A Biological Resources Assessment.

2. A Design Plan for the construction or Reconstruction of each Stream Crossing or reservoir.

3. A Property Diagram.

(B) The Covered Activity and Entity meet the Eligibility Criteria in subsection (d), relying in part on the Biological Resources Assessment and, where applicable, the Design Plan.

(3) Fees.

(A) The Entity must pay a fee in the amount the Entity would need to pay for a Standard Agreement for a term of five years or less, as specified in the department's fee schedule for lake and streambed alteration agreements in Section 699.5, subsection (b).

(B) The Entity must also pay a remediation fee specified in Section 699.5, subsection (i), if applicable.

(4) A Notification made to the department under this subsection may include more than one Covered Activity.

(g) Authorization. Upon receipt of the Notification, Certifications, and applicable fee(s) specified in subsection (f), the department shall authorize the Covered Activity or Activities described in the Notification by providing notice to the Entity.

(h) Administrative Measures.

(1) Documentation at Project Site. Permittee shall make the following documents available to all persons conducting the Authorized Activity at the Project Site on behalf of Permittee, including, but not limited to, contractors, subcontractors, inspectors, and monitors, and shall present these documents to any department or other governmental agency employee upon the employee's request:

(A) The department's authorization under subsection (g) and the information provided by the Entity to the department pursuant to subsection (f)(1).

(B) Any approval by a local, state, or federal agency that relates to the Authorized Activity, including a temporary or annual cannabis cultivation license issued by the California Department of Food and Agriculture.

(C) Biological Resources Assessment.

(D) Any Design Plan.

(E) Property Diagram.

(F) Each survey, plan, and report described in subsections (i), (j), and (k).

(2) Document Submittal. Permittee shall electronically submit to the department a copy of the Biological Resources Assessment, Design Plan, and Property Diagram within 90 days of receiving authorization from the department under subsection (g). The documents shall be submitted to the department through the website for the department's Lake and Streambed Alteration Program at: https://www.wildlife.ca.gov/ Conservation/LSA.

(3) Notice to Cease Authorized Activity. Permittee shall cease an Authorized Activity if the department notifies Permittee in writing that the activity is adversely affecting fish and wildlife resources. This includes, but is not limited to, information made available to the department that indicates that bypass flows or diversion rates under this General Agreement are not keeping aquatic life downstream in good condition or avoiding take of Listed or Fully Protected Species.

(4) Take. This General Agreement does not authorize take of a Listed or Fully Protected Species, and

compliance with this General Agreement does not ensure that take will be avoided in all circumstances. Permittee remains responsible for complying with all provisions in the Fish and Game Code that pertain to take of Listed and Fully Protected Species, including Sections 2080 et seq., 3503, 3503.5, 3511, 3513, 4700, 5050, and 5515.

(5) Access to Project Site. Permittee shall allow department employees access to the Project Site to inspect or monitor any Authorized Activity. Inspection and monitoring shall be conducted between the standard business hours of 8:00 a.m. and 5:00 p.m. (Pacific Standard Time) or at other reasonable times as mutually agreed to by the department and the Permittee. Prior notice of inspection is not required.

(i) General Measures to Protect Fish and Wildlife Resources.

(1) Work Periods. Permittee may only conduct work on or within the bed, bank, or channel of a stream or lake from June 15 to October 15.

(2) Work in Dry Weather Only. Permittee shall cease the Authorized Activity when the National Weather Service ("NWS") 72-hour weather forecast indicates a 30 percent chance or higher of precipitation. Permittee shall implement all necessary erosion control measures prior to the onset of precipitation and remove construction equipment and materials if precipitation is likely. Work activity halted due to precipitation may resume when the NWS 72-hour weather forecast indicates less than a 30 percent chance of precipitation. No Authorized Activity shall occur during a dry-out period of 24 hours after wet weather. Permittee shall provide documentation of weather forecasts upon the department's request.

(3) Wildlife.

(A) Leave Wildlife Unharmed. If any wildlife is encountered during the Authorized Activity, Permittee shall not disturb the wildlife and shall allow wildlife to leave the work site unharmed.

(B) Habitat Elements. Permittee shall take measures to minimize disturbance to aquatic and riparian habitat elements such as pools and structures including large wood or vegetation that overhangs the channel.

(C) Check for Wildlife. Every day, prior to beginning any construction work, Permittee shall visually check all sections of pipe/construction materials and associated work equipment for the presence of wildlife sheltering in them. Alternatively, the ends of any pipes may be capped while stored on site to prevent wildlife from entering.

(D) Escape Ramp in Trench. At the end of each workday, Permittee shall place an escape ramp at each end of any open trench to allow wildlife that may have become entrapped in the trench to escape. The ramp may be constructed of dirt, wood planking, or other suitable material and shall be placed at an angle no greater than 30 degrees.

(E) Nest/Den Surveys. If construction, grading, vegetation removal, or other Authorized Activity is scheduled between February 1 and August 31, a Biologist shall conduct a focused survey for nests and dens of birds and mammals within seven days prior to beginning the Authorized Activity. If a nest or den is found, Permittee shall consult with the department before commencing the Authorized Activity. Any time there is a lapse in the Authorized Activity of seven days or longer, a Biologist shall conduct another focused survey.

(F) Active Nest/Den Buffers. If a nest or den is found during any survey, the Biologist shall establish a protective buffer and ensure appropriate action is taken to avoid or minimize impacts on the birds or mammals while the nest or den is occupied, during the Authorized Activity.

1. The buffer distance must be site-specific and adequate to protect normal animal behavior to prevent reproductive failure or nest/den abandonment, as determined by the Biologist. To meet this objective, the Biologist shall determine the buffer distance after the Biologist conducts field

investigations that evaluate the apparent distress of the animal(s) in the presence of people or equipment at various distances.

2. Abnormal nesting or denning behaviors that might cause reproductive harm include, but are not limited to, defensive movements, flights, or vocalizations directed towards work personnel, standing up from a brooding position, and moving or flying away from the nest or den. The Biologist shall have authority to order cessation of the Authorized Activity if the nesting animal exhibits abnormal behavior that could cause reproductive failure (i.e., nest or den abandonment and loss of eggs or young) until an appropriate buffer is established.

(4) Vegetation.

(A) Minimum Vegetation Removal. Permittee shall limit the disturbance or removal of native vegetation to the minimum necessary to achieve design guidelines and standards for the Authorized Activity. Permittee shall take precautions to avoid damage to vegetation outside the work area.

(B) Plant Species of Greatest Conservation Need. If the Biologist finds at the Project Site a population of any plant designated as a Species of Greatest Conservation Need, or determines the plant may be present, based, for example, on habitat types or other cues, the Biologist shall establish a protective buffer and ensure appropriate action is taken to avoid or minimize impacts on the plants during the Authorized Activity.

1. The buffer distance must be site-specific and adequate to protect the plants, as determined by the Biologist.

(5) Temporary Dewatering and Flow Bypass.

(A) When the Authorized Activity occurs in a flowing stream, Permittee shall divert the stream flow around or through the work area during the Authorized Activity.

(B) Sufficient Flow Downstream. Permittee shall allow sufficient flow at all times to pass downstream for purposes of maintaining aquatic life.

(C) Minimize Turbidity, Siltation, and Pollution. Permittee shall use only clean, non-erodible materials, such as rock or sandbags that do not contain soil or fine sediment, to construct any temporary stream flow bypass. Permittee shall divert stream flow around the work site in a manner that minimizes turbidity, siltation, and pollution, and does not result in erosion or scour downstream of the diversion.

(D) Remove any Materials upon Completion. Permittee shall remove all materials used for the temporary stream flow bypass after the Authorized Activity is completed.

(E) Restore Natural Flow. Permittee shall restore the natural stream flow pattern immediately upon completion of the Authorized Activity.

(6) Herbicide and Pesticide Use.

(A) Avoid Waters of the State. Permittee shall not use chemical herbicides or pesticides, including chemical rodenticides, that are deleterious to fish, plant life, mammals, or bird life, where they may pass into the waters of the state.

(B) No Chemical Rodenticides. Permittee shall not treat areas considered suitable habitat for Species of Greatest Conservation Need or areas with suspected occupied nesting or denning habitats with chemical rodenticides at the Project Site.

(7) Erosion Control and Pollution.

(A) Erosion Control. Permittee shall use erosion control measures throughout all work phases where sediment runoff threatens to enter a stream, lake, or other Waters of the State.

(B) Seed and Mulch. Upon completion of construction operations and/or the onset of wet weather, Permittee shall stabilize exposed soil areas within the work area by applying mulch and seed. Permittee shall restore all exposed or disturbed areas and access points within the stream and riparian zone by applying local native and weed-free erosion control grass seeds. Locally native wildflower and/or shrub seeds may also be included in the seed mix. Permittee shall mulch restored areas using at least two to four inches of weed-free clean straw or similar biodegradable mulch over the seeded area. Alternately, Permittee may cover seeding with jute netting, coconut fiber blanket, or similar non-synthetic monofilament netting erosion control blanket.

(C) Erosion and Sediment Barriers. Permittee shall monitor and maintain all erosion and sediment barriers in good operating condition throughout the work period and the following rainy season, defined herein to mean October 15 through June 15. Maintenance includes, but is not limited to, removal of accumulated sediment and/or replacement of damaged sediment fencing, coir logs, coir rolls, and/or straw bale dikes. If the sediment barrier fails to retain sediment, Permittee shall employ corrective measures, and notify the department immediately.

(D) Fill Material. Fill materials placed in the stream channel shall be adequate to withstand high stream flow and shall consist of clean, non-erodible, silt-free material. All fill material shall be free from any substance or material deleterious to fish and wildlife (e.g., corrosive, combustible, noxious, or reactive materials). Permittee shall not use asphalt, rebar, or concrete as fill material.

(E) Prohibition on Use of Monofilament Netting. To minimize the risk of ensnaring and strangling wildlife, Permittee shall not use any erosion control materials that contain synthetic (e.g., plastic or nylon) monofilament netting, including photo- or bio-degradable plastic netting. Geotextiles, fiber rolls, and other erosion control measures shall be made of loose-weave mesh, such as jute, hemp, coconut (coir) fiber, or other products without welded weaves.

(F) Site Maintenance. Permittee shall be responsible for site maintenance including, but not limited to, re-establishing erosion control to minimize surface erosion and ensuring drainage structures and altered streambeds and banks remain sufficiently armored and/or stable.

(G) Removal, Storage, and Disposal of Fill, Spoil Piles, and Debris. Permittee shall remove all excavated fill, spoil piles, and debris from any stream, lake, or other Waters of the State and place it in stable upland locations where it cannot discharge into such waters, or dispose of it according to state and local laws and ordinances.

(H) Cover Spoil Piles. Permittee shall have readily available erosion control materials such as wattles, natural fiber mats, or plastic sheeting, to cover and contain exposed spoil piles and exposed areas in order to prevent sediment from moving into a stream or lake. Permittee shall apply and secure these materials prior to rain events to prevent loose soils from entering a stream, lake, or other Waters of the State.

(I) Stockpiled Materials. Permittee shall not stockpile or store any building materials and/or construction materials where they may be washed or percolate into a stream, lake, or other Waters of the State, or where they may adversely affect stream habitat or aquatic or riparian vegetation.

(J) No Dumping. Permittee shall not deposit, permit to pass into, or place where it can pass into a stream, lake, or other Waters of the State any material deleterious to fish and wildlife, or abandon, dispose of, or throw away within 150 feet of a stream, lake, or other Waters of the State any cans, bottles, garbage, motor vehicle or parts thereof, rubbish, litter, refuse, waste, debris, or the viscera or carcass of any dead mammal, or the carcass of any dead bird.

(K) Debris Removal. Permittee shall pick up all debris and waste daily, and shall dispose of it according to local and state law.

(L) Wash Water. Permittee shall not allow water containing mud, sediment, or other pollutants from equipment washing or other activities to enter a stream, lake, or other Waters of the State.

(M) Staging and Storage. Permittee shall not stage or store any equipment, materials, fuels, lubricants, solvents, or hazardous or toxic materials where they may enter a stream or lake, or where they have potential to enter a stream, lake, or other Waters of the State (e.g., through storm water runoff or percolation). Equipment shall be positioned over drip pans. Stationary heavy equipment shall have suitable containment to handle a catastrophic spill/leak.

(N) Equipment Maintenance and Fueling. Permittee shall not conduct any maintenance activity or refuel equipment in any location where the petroleum products or other pollutants may enter a stream, lake, or other Waters of the State.

(8) Hazardous Materials and Spills.

(A) Toxic Materials. Permittee shall store any hazardous or toxic materials that could be deleterious to aquatic life in accordance with all applicable federal, state, and local laws and ordinances.

(B) Hazardous Substances. Permittee shall prevent raw cement/concrete or washings thereof, asphalt, paint or other coating material, oil or other petroleum products, or any other substance that could be hazardous to aquatic life from contaminating the soil or entering a stream or lake. Permittee shall immediately remove any of these materials placed within, or where they may enter, a stream or lake or other Waters of the State.

(C) Cleanup and Containment. In the case of a spill, Permittee shall immediately notify the California Office of Emergency Services State Warning Center at 1-800-852-7550 and immediately initiate clean-up activities. The local department Regional Office shall be notified of clean-up procedures.

(9) Invasive Species Control. Permittee shall conduct the Authorized Activity in a manner that prevents the introduction, transfer, and spread of invasive species from one work site or waterbody to another by following the requirements below.

(A) Decontamination of Work Equipment. Permittee shall inspect and decontaminate all tools, waders, boots, and other work-related equipment that will enter water prior to entering and exiting the work site and/or between each use in different waterbodies to avoid the introduction and transfer of organisms between waterbodies. Permittee shall decontaminate project gear and equipment using one of three methods: 1) drying; 2) hot water soak; or 3) freezing, as appropriate to the type of gear or equipment. For all methods, Permittee shall begin the decontamination process by thoroughly scrubbing equipment, paying close attention to small crevices such as bootlaces, seams, and net corners, with a stiff-bristled brush to remove all organisms. To decontaminate by drying, Permittee shall allow equipment to dry thoroughly (i.e., until there is a complete absence of water), preferably in the sun, and keep the equipment dry for a minimum of 48 hours. To decontaminate using a hot water soak, Permittee shall immerse equipment in 140oF or hotter water and soak, completely submerged, for a minimum of five minutes. To decontaminate by freezing, Permittee shall place equipment in a freezer 32oF or colder for a minimum of eight hours. Repeat decontamination is required only if the equipment or clothing is removed from the Project Site, used within a different waterbody, and returned to the Project Site or different waterbody.

(B) Decontamination of Larger Vehicles. Permittee shall decontaminate vehicles and other Covered Activity-related equipment too large to immerse in a hot water bath by pressure washing with hot water at a minimum temperature of 140oF at the point of contact or 155oF at the nozzle. Following the hot water wash, Permittee shall drain water and dry all vehicles and other large equipment as thoroughly as possible.

(C) Decontamination Sites. Permittee shall perform decontamination of vehicles, tools, waders and boots, and other project-related equipment in a designated location where runoff can be contained and not allowed to pass into a stream, lake, or other Waters of the State, or other sensitive habitat areas.

(j) Specific Measures to Protect Fish and Wildlife Resources.

(1) All Stream Crossings.

(A) Road Approaches. Permittee shall maintain Stream Crossings to minimize erosion and sediment delivery to the stream, lake, or other Waters of the State. Permittee shall ensure road approaches are hydrologically disconnected to the maximum extent feasible to prevent sediment from entering the crossing site, including when a Stream Crossing is being constructed or reconstructed.

(B) Vegetation Management. Permittee shall limit vegetation management (e.g., trimming, pruning, or limbing) and removal for the purpose of Stream Crossing maintenance to the use of hand tools. Vegetation management shall not include treatment with herbicides.

(C) Time Period for Reconstruction. Reconstruction must be completed within one calendar year from the date the department authorizes the Covered Activity under this General Agreement, unless the department extends the one-year time period at its sole discretion.

(2) Bridges.

(A) Concrete Abutments - Primary Containment. Permittee shall install the necessary containment structures for concrete bridge abutments to control the placement of wet concrete and to prevent it from entering into the bed, bank, or channel outside of these structures.

(B) Concrete Abutments - Secondary Containment. Permittee shall install a secondary containment structure between the primary containment structures to prevent wet concrete from entering into the stream upon failure or leak of the primary structures.

(C) Concrete Abutments - Designated Monitor. Permittee shall designate a monitor to inspect containment structures and ensure there is no failure of containment structures when pouring or working with wet concrete placed for bridge abutments.

(D) Concrete Washout. Permittee shall ensure that concrete washout occurs in a designated and appropriately prepared area outside the active 100-year floodplain. Permittee shall not allow wash water or debris to enter the stream or riparian area. Permittee shall inspect concrete washout facilities daily and after rain to check for leaks and damage to linings and sidewalls caused by construction activities.

(3) Culverts.

(A) Concrete. Permittee shall ensure poured concrete is excluded from the wetted channel for a period of at least 30 days. Permittee shall not allow runoff from the concrete to enter a stream and shall ensure it is disposed of properly.

(B) Concrete Sealant. Permittee may apply sealants to the poured concrete surface where it may be difficult to exclude water flow for a long period. If sealant is used, Permittee shall exclude water from the site until the sealant is dry.

(C) Culvert Maintenance. Permittee shall maintain culverts and keep them clear of debris. Such work shall maintain culvert location design and materials. Maintenance does not include replacement.

(4) Water Diversions.

(A) Season of Diversion. After October 31, 2018, Permittee shall confine the period of diversion to December 15 through March 31.

(B) Water Storage and Control. Permittee shall cease all water diversion at the point of diversion when WSFs are filled to capacity. Water shall not leak, overflow, or overtop WSFs at any time. Permittee shall regularly inspect all WSFs and infrastructure used to divert water to storage and use and repair any leaks.

(C) Diversion Intakes. Permittee shall plug, cap, block (e.g., with a shut-off valve), or remove all intakes at the end of each diversion season.

(D) Underground Water Diversion Infrastructure. Infrastructure installed in the streambed (e.g., cistern or spring box) shall not exceed 10 percent of the active channel width and shall not be located in the deepest portion of the channel. The depth of the intake shall be no greater than one foot below the streambed.

(E) Diversion Maintenance. Permittee shall inspect, maintain, and clean intake strainers and bypass structures as necessary to ensure proper operation for the protection of non-finfish and wildlife.

(F) Bypass Flow. Permittee shall ensure that Permittee's diversion facility passes sufficient flow at all times to keep fish below the facility in good condition. If at any time the diversion rate identified in subsection (e)(4)(A) cannot be maintained, Permittee shall cease diversion and all natural flow shall be allowed to bypass the point of diversion.

(G) Diversion Materials. Permittee shall not use or construct the diversion structure with materials deleterious to fish or wildlife, including, but not limited to, particle board, plastic sheeting, bentonite, pressure treated lumber, creosote, concrete, or asphalt.

(H) Diversion Monitoring. Permittee shall install and maintain an adequate measuring device for measuring the instantaneous and cumulative rate of diversion. The device shall be installed within the flow of diverted water. Permittee shall maintain records of diversion with:

1. The date and time diversion occurred, and

2. The amount of water used per day for cannabis cultivation separated out from the amount of water used for other irrigation purposes and other uses of water (e.g., domestic use or fire protection).

3. Permittee shall make available for review at the request of the department the daily diversion records required by the State Water Resources Control Board (Board) in Attachment A to the Board's Cannabis Cultivation Policy (October 17, 2017), No. 84, pages 40-41 (see Cal. Code Regs., tit. 23, § 2925).

(I) Invasive Species Management for Reservoirs. Permittee shall implement an invasive species management plan prepared by a Biologist for any existing or proposed reservoir. The plan shall include, at a minimum, an annual survey for invasive aquatic species. The Biologist, if appropriate, shall implement eradication measures if invasive aquatic species are identified as part of the survey.

(J) No Stocking. Stocking of fish, wildlife, or plant of any kind, in any Waters of the State, including reservoirs, shall be prohibited without written permission from the department pursuant to Section 6400 of the Fish and Game Code.

(k) Reporting Requirements. Permittee shall submit the reports described below in electronic form to the department through the website for the department's Lake and Streambed Alteration Program at: https://www.wildlife.ca.gov/Conservation/LSA.

(1) Project Completion Report. Permittee shall submit to the department a Project Completion Report for any Authorized Activity that includes construction within 30 days of completing the activity. The report shall include the following:

(A) The beginning and ending dates of the Authorized Activity.

(B) Before and after photographs. Photographs shall include the staging area, access area, and stream facing upstream, downstream, and perpendicular.

(2) Water Diversion and Use Reports. For each Water Diversion, Permittee shall submit to the department a copy of each report Permittee must submit to the Board, in accordance with Sections 910-938 of Title 23 of the California Code of Regulations, on the same date Permittee submits the report to the Board while the Water Diversion is authorized under this General Agreement.

(3) California Natural Diversity Database Observations. Permittee shall submit all observations of Species of Greatest Conservation Need to the department's California Natural Diversity Database at: https://www.wildlife.ca.gov/Data/CNDDB/Submitting-Data.

(l) Liability. Permittee shall be solely liable for any violations of the measures and requirements herein that apply to the Authorized Activity, whether committed by Permittee or any person acting on behalf of Permittee, including its officers, employees, representatives, agents, or contractors and subcontractors, to complete or conduct the Authorized Activity.

(m) Suspension and Revocation.

(1) The department may suspend or revoke in its entirety the department's authorization of a Permittee's Covered Activity if the department determines that:

(A) Permittee or any person acting on behalf of Permittee, including its officers, employees, representatives, agents, or contractors and subcontractors, is not acting in compliance with this General Agreement. Noncompliance may include, but is not limited to, failure of Permittee to implement the Authorized Activity as prescribed in this General Agreement, or

(B) The Authorized Activity was not eligible under the General Agreement.

(2) Nothing herein precludes the department from pursuing an enforcement action against Permittee instead of, or in addition to, suspending or revoking the department's authorization of a Permittee's Covered Activity.

(n) Period of Authorization.

(1) Authorization of a Covered Activity under this General Agreement shall expire five years after the date the department authorizes the activity under subsection (g), unless the department extends the period of authorization prior to expiration.

(2) Upon expiration of the department's authorization, Permittee shall be responsible for complying with Section 1602 of the Fish and Game Code before continuing the activity.

Note: Authority cited: Section 1617, Fish and Game Code. Reference: Sections 1602 and 1617, Fish and Game Code.

Title 16. Professional and Vocational Regulations

DIVISION 42. BUREAU OF CANNABIS CONTROL [RENUMBERED]

Change without regulatory effect renumbering and amending title 16, division 42 (chapters 1-8, sections 5000-5905) to new title 4, division 19 (chapters 1-8, sections 15000-15905), including repealer of section 5016.

DIVISION 43. CANNABIS CONTROL APPEALS PANEL

ARTICLE 1. GENERAL

§ 6000. Definitions.

For purposes of this division:

(a) "Appellant" means any person who files an appeal with the Panel.

(b) "Days" means calendar days, unless otherwise stated.

(c) "Executive Director" means the executive director of the Panel.

(d) "Licensing authority" means a state agency responsible for the issuance, renewal, or reinstatement of a license, or a state agency authorized to take disciplinary action against a licensee, as defined in Business and Professions Code section 26001(aa).

(e) "Panel" means the Cannabis Control Appeals Panel of California.

(1) Any reference to the Panel's "Sacramento office" means 801 Capitol Mall, Suite 601, Sacramento, CA 95814.

(f) "Party" means the licensing authority, the appellant, and any person, other than an officer or an employee of the licensing authority in his official capacity, who has been allowed to appear in the proceeding before the licensing authority.

(g) Unless otherwise stated, the words "appellant" or "party" include the attorney of such person.

Note: Authority cited: Section 26042, Business and Professions Code. Reference: Sections 26042 and 26043, Business and Professions Code.

§ 6001. Time and Date Calculations.

(a) The time provided by this division within which any act must be performed shall be computed by excluding the first day and including the last day, unless it is a Saturday, Sunday, or holiday, in which case the last day shall also be excluded.

Note: Authority cited: Section 26042, Business and Professions Code. Reference: Sections 26042 and 26043, Business and Professions Code.

§ 6002. Notices to Authorized Agents.

(a) Whenever the Notice of Appeal indicates that a party is represented by an attorney or other authorized agent, such attorney or agent shall be entitled to a copy of all notices and decisions to which the party would be entitled.

Note: Authority cited: Section 26042, Business and Professions Code. Reference: Sections 26042 and 26043, Business and Professions Code.

ARTICLE 2. FILING OF APPEAL

§ 6003. Timing and Contents of Notice of Appeal.

(a) Any person aggrieved by the decision of a licensing authority as described in Business and Professions Code section 26043(a) may appeal the licensing authority's written decision to the Panel as follows:

(1) The appellant shall complete and submit the CCAP Form 6003, Notice of Appeal (New 04/18), which is hereby incorporated by reference, to the Panel at its Sacramento office or by scanning and emailing the completed form to the Panel at appeals@ccap.ca.gov.

(2) The Notice of Appeal must be received by the Panel within 30 days after the last day on which reconsideration of the underlying decision of the licensing authority can be requested pursuant to Government Code section 11521.

(A) Failure to submit the Notice of Appeal to the Panel within the time set forth in this subsection may result in dismissal of the appeal pursuant to section 6011.

(3) The appellant shall also serve a copy of the completed Notice of Appeal upon all parties to the proceeding. Such service shall be made by delivering or mailing a copy of the Notice of Appeal to each party, and proof of service shall be submitted to the Panel at the same time the Notice of Appeal is submitted pursuant to subsection (a)(1). The parties may stipulate in writing to provide service to one another via electronic mail, and such service shall be indicated on the proof of service.

Note: Authority cited: Section 26042, Business and Professions Code. Reference: Sections 26042 and 26043, Business and Professions Code.

ARTICLE 3. RECORD ON APPEAL

§ 6004. Submitting the Record.

(a) From the date the Notice of Appeal is submitted to the Panel, the appellant shall have 60 days to obtain the complete underlying administrative record from the Office of Administrative Hearings, pursuant to title 1, CCR, section 1038, or if an informal or emergency hearing was conducted by the licensing agency pursuant to Government Code section 11445.10, obtain the complete underlying administrative record from the licensing agency, and submit the original hardcopy and one electronic version to the Panel at its Sacramento office. Failure to submit a complete administrative record within the time set forth in this subsection may result in dismissal of the matter pursuant to section 6011.

(1) Notwithstanding the foregoing, if all parties to the appeal so stipulate in writing, and the Panel approves, the appellant may submit only those parts of the administrative record relevant to the issue being appealed. In such event, the Panel may still require submission of the complete administrative record at any time during the appeal.

(b) If the underlying administrative hearing was recorded by means other than transcription, the appellant shall arrange to have a certified copy transcribed prior to submission of the administrative record to the Panel. The complete transcript shall be included with the administrative record at the time of submission to the Panel in accordance with subsection (a).

(c) The appellant shall also serve a copy of the complete administrative record upon all parties to the proceeding. Such service shall be made by delivering or mailing a copy of the administrative record to each party or by electronic service in accordance with section 6005, and proof of service shall be submitted to the Panel at the same time the administrative record is submitted pursuant to subsection (a).

(d) An appellant may, for good cause, request an extension of the 60-day limit set forth in subsection (a). Such extensions shall be granted or denied by the Panel in its discretion, or the Panel may delegate this authority to its executive director. Alternatively, all parties may stipulate in writing to one extension of up to 20 days, which shall be granted by the Panel, or its executive director if so authorized, upon notice to the Panel of the stipulation.

Note: Authority cited: Section 26042, Business and Professions Code. Reference: Sections 26042 and 26043, Business and Professions Code.

ARTICLE 4. FILING BRIEFS

§ 6005. Service and Filing by Electronic Mail.

(a) Upon submission of a Notice of Appeal to the Panel, the appellant shall also submit a completed CCAP Form 6005, Certification of Email Address (New 04/18), which is hereby incorporated by reference, to the Panel at its Sacramento office or by scanning and emailing the completed form to the Panel at appeals@ccap.ca.gov.

(b) Within 30 days after receipt of service of the Notice of Appeal, all other parties to the appeal shall complete and submit CCAP Form 6005, Certification of Email Address (New 04/18), to the Panel at its Sacramento office or by scanning and emailing the completed form to the Panel at appeals@ccap.ca.gov. At the same time, each party shall also serve a copy of their completed CCAP Form 6005, Certification of Email Address (New 04/18), on all other parties to the appeal, including the appellant.

(c) Once all parties to the appeal have submitted their CCAP Form 6005, Certification of Email Address (New 04/18), to the Panel, they may use each party's official email address, if one is provided, for service of correspondence, notices, pleadings, or any other documentation in connection with the appeal, unless a stipulation to the contrary is agreed to.

(d) The Panel and its executive director may use each party's official email address, if one is provided, to send documents, notices, decisions, or any other correspondence to the party.

(e) Any party to an appeal that has submitted its CCAP Form 6005, Certification of Email Address (New 04/18), in accordance with subsection (a) or (b) may subsequently submit notices, pleadings, or any other documentation in connection with the appeal by electronic mail to the Panel at appeals@ccap.ca.gov unless instructed otherwise by the Panel or its executive director.

Note: Authority cited: Section 26042, Business and Professions Code. Reference: Sections 26042 and 26043, Business and Professions Code.

§ 6006. Filing of Briefs by Parties.

(a) The appellant may file an opening brief, the respondent may file an opposition brief, and the appellant may thereafter file a reply brief.

(b) All briefs shall be typewritten or printed upon paper 8 1/2 x 11 inches in size, and all copies must be legible. Only one side of the paper shall be used, and the margins shall be at least one inch on all sides of the page. The lines shall be double spaced. Headings shall be capitalized. An original of each brief shall contain a certification that copies have been served upon or mailed to each party or their attorney or agent. Parties may serve one another by electronic mail in compliance with section 6005.

(c) Briefs shall comply with the following length restrictions; however, the page limitations set forth in this subsection do not include exhibits, appendices, tables of contents, or cover or title pages:

(1) Opening briefs shall be no more than 20 pages in length.

(2) Opposition briefs shall be no more than 20 pages in length.

(3) Reply briefs shall be no more than 10 pages in length.

(d) Any party to the appeal may file a motion in accordance with section 6010 to request a waiver of the page length restrictions in subsection (c). The motion shall be submitted to the Panel and served on all other parties at least ten days before the moving party's brief is due as set forth in subsection (e) of this section. An opposition to the motion may be submitted to the Panel and served on all other parties within five days of the initial motion's service on the opposing party. The matter will be decided by the Panel without hearing.

(e) The opening brief shall be submitted to the Panel and served on all parties to the appeal within 30 days of the date the administrative record is served on the Panel and other parties pursuant to section 6004. Any opposition brief shall be submitted to the Panel and served on all parties within 15 days after the opening brief is served on the Panel and other parties. Any reply brief shall be submitted to the Panel and served on all parties within seven days after the opposition brief is served on the Panel and other parties. Any party to the appeal may file a motion in accordance with section 6010 to request an extension of time within which to file a brief. Motions may only be granted by the Panel upon a showing of good cause.

Note: Authority cited: Section 26042, Business and Professions Code. Reference: Sections 26042 and 26043, Business and Professions Code.

ARTICLE 5. HEARINGS

§ 6007. Optional Hearing.

(a) After all briefs have been submitted to the Panel pursuant to section 6006, the Panel shall make a preliminary decision in the appeal based on the record. Once the Panel has reached its preliminary decision, the executive director shall notify all parties that the Panel is ready to enter its final order in accordance with section 6016. Each party shall have 20 days from the date they are served with the notice to submit a written request for a hearing to the Panel.

(b) Notwithstanding subsection (a), the Panel may direct for a hearing to be conducted on the appeal even if no party requests a hearing.

(c) If requested by a party or directed by the Panel, a hearing date and location shall be set by the Panel's executive director and a notice shall be sent to all parties.

(d) After a date and location have been set for hearing by the executive director, requests by any party for a continuance and/or location change may be granted by the Panel only upon a showing of good cause. The Panel may delegate its authority to decide requests for continuances and location changes to its executive director.

(1) A party seeking a continuance or location change shall stipulate to an alternative date or location for the hearing with all other parties to the appeal, and then coordinate with the executive director to reschedule the date or location if the Panel's schedule and docket permits. If the other party or parties will not stipulate to an alternative date or location, the requesting party can submit a motion to the Panel requesting an alternative date or location in accordance with section 6010. The other party or parties may submit an opposition to the motion to the Panel within five days of receipt of the initial motion.

Note: Authority cited: Section 26042, Business and Professions Code. Reference: Sections 26042 and 26043, Business and Professions Code.

§ 6008. Oral Argument.

(a) In the event that a hearing for the appeal or a motion is scheduled, and unless otherwise directed by the Panel:

(1) A party shall be allowed a maximum of 20 minutes for oral argument;

(2) Not more than one person on a side may be heard;

(3) The appellant, or moving party, shall have the right to present an opening statement and closing statement; however, both statements shall count towards the 20-minute total limit.

(4) No evidence, other than what is contained in the administrative record, shall be referenced by any party.

(5) Panel members may ask questions of any party at the conclusion of oral argument. Panel member questions and party responses will not count towards the 20-minute time limit.

Note: Authority cited: Section 26042, Business and Professions Code. Reference: Sections 26042 and 26043, Business and Professions Code.

ARTICLE 6. NEWLY DISCOVERED EVIDENCE

§ 6009. Nature of Evidence and Showing.

(a) A party may file a motion to remand the case back to the licensing authority in accordance with Business and Professions Code section 26044 on the grounds that there is relevant evidence which, in the exercise of reasonable diligence, could not have been produced at the underlying hearing. In support of the motion, the party shall submit the following in the form of a declaration or affidavit:

(1) The substance of the newly discovered evidence;

(2) Its relevancy and the part of the record to which it pertains;

(3) Names of witnesses to be produced, if any, and their expected testimony;

(4) The nature of any exhibits to be introduced, if any; and

(5) A detailed statement of the reasons why such evidence could not, with due diligence, have been discovered and produced at the underlying hearing. Merely cumulative evidence shall not constitute a valid ground for remand.

Note: Authority cited: Section 26042, Business and Professions Code. Reference: Sections 26042, 26043 and 26044, Business and Professions Code.

ARTICLE 7. MOTIONS

§ 6010. Motions.

(a) All motions referenced in this division shall be prepared and submitted as follows:

(1) A motion shall follow the formatting requirements set forth in section 6006(b).

(2) A motion shall be no more than 10 pages in length unless accompanied by a declaration showing good cause for additional pages, but in no case shall be more than 15 pages in length.

(3) A motion submitted to the Panel shall include proof of service that the motion was served on all parties to the appeal.

(b) Any party opposing a motion may submit their written opposition to the Panel within five days of receipt of service of the initial motion. The opposition shall follow the same requirements described in subsections (a)(1) through (3).

(c) The Panel's executive director shall set a date and location for a hearing on the motion and send notice of the hearing to all parties to the appeal within 20 days of the deadline to submit the opposition described in subsection (b). Notwithstanding the foregoing, at any time after receiving the motion and opposition, the Panel may elect to rule on the motion without holding a hearing.

Note: Authority cited: Section 26042, Business and Professions Code. Reference: Sections 26042 and 26043, Business and Professions Code.

ARTICLE 8. DISMISSAL OF APPEAL

§ 6011. Dismissal of Appeal.

(a) The Panel may issue an order dismissing an appeal of the decision of the licensing authority:

(1) Upon appellant submitting to the Panel a request to dismiss the appeal;

(2) Upon motion of a party, or upon the Panel's own notice to the parties, that appellant has failed to perfect their appeal by failing to timely submit the Notice of Appeal or the administrative record to the Panel as set forth in sections 6003 and 6004;

(3) Upon certification by the licensing authority that reconsideration has been granted in the case after the Notice of Appeal has been submitted, and dismissal on this ground shall be without prejudice to the submission of a subsequent appeal in the same case; or

(4) Upon a motion by the licensing authority or other party, or upon the Panel's own notice to the parties, where sufficient cause exists for dismissal. In such an instance, the Panel's decision shall set forth with specificity the sufficient cause for the dismissal.

Note: Authority cited: Section 26042, Business and Professions Code. Reference: Sections 26042, 26043 and 26044, Business and Professions Code.

ARTICLE 9. PANEL MEMBERS

§ 6012. Disqualification of Panel Members.

(a) A Panel member shall disqualify himself or herself and withdraw from any case in which the member cannot accord a fair and impartial hearing. Any party may request the disqualification of any member by filing an affidavit with the Panel before the submission of the case, stating with particularity the grounds upon which it is claimed that a fair and impartial appeal cannot be accorded by the Panel member. The issue raised by the request shall be determined by the other members of the Panel. No member of the Panel shall withdraw voluntarily from any hearing, or be subject to disqualification, if this would prevent the Panel from acting in the particular case.

(b) An affidavit submitted to the Panel pursuant to this section shall become a part of the record.

Note: Authority cited: Section 26042, Business and Professions Code. Reference: Sections 26042 and 26043, Business and Professions Code.

§ 6013. Attendance of Panel Members.

(a) If a Panel member cannot attend a hearing where there will be oral argument, the remaining members of the Panel shall select one other member to recuse from the hearing in order to maintain an odd number of members, unless to do so would prevent the Panel from acting in a particular case.

Note: Authority cited: Section 26042, Business and Professions Code. Reference: Sections 26042 and 26043, Business and Professions Code.

ARTICLE 10. STAYS AND SETTLEMENTS

§ 6014. Stay.

(a) In any appeal where the underlying decision of a licensing authority is denial of a license renewal, or cancelation, suspension, or revocation of a license, and upon a motion from the appellant made pursuant to section 6010, the Panel may stay the effect of the underlying decision until the Panel enters its final order.

(b) Notwithstanding subsection (a), the Panel may only grant a stay upon a motion by the appellant demonstrating that:

(1) there is a substantial likelihood that the appellant will prevail in the appeal;

(2) the appellant will experience immediate and irreparable harm if the stay is not granted; and

(3) the stay is not detrimental to the health and welfare of the public.

Note: Authority cited: Section 26042, Business and Professions Code. Reference: Sections 26042 and 26043, Business and Professions Code.

§ 6015. Settlements.

(a) Whenever any matter is pending before the Panel, and the parties to the matter agree upon a settlement, the Panel shall, upon the stipulation by the parties that such an agreement has been reached, dismiss the matter.

Note: Authority cited: Section 26042, Business and Professions Code. Reference: Sections 26042 and 26043, Business and Professions Code.

ARTICLE 11. ORDERS

§ 6016. Time Limit for Entry of Order.

(a) In all cases, the Panel shall enter its order within 90 days after the hearing on the merits is held in accordance with section 6007. If no hearing is conducted, then the Panel shall enter its order within 90 days of the executive director's notice to the parties that the Panel has reached a preliminary decision in accordance with section 6007(a).

Note: Authority cited: Section 26042, Business and Professions Code. Reference: Sections 26042 and 26043, Business and Professions Code.

§ 6017. Form of Order.

(a) Each order of the Panel on appeal from a decision of a licensing authority shall be in writing and shall be filed by delivering copies to the parties personally or by mailing copies to them by certified mail or electronic mail pursuant to section 6005. Each order shall become final upon being filed as provided herein, and there shall be no reconsideration or rehearing by the Panel.

Note: Authority cited: Section 26042, Business and Professions Code. Reference: Sections 26042 and 26043, Business and Professions Code.

ARTICLE 12. EX PARTE COMMUNICATIONS

§ 6018. Ex Parte Communications.

(a) While an appeal is pending there shall be no communication, direct or indirect, regarding any issue in the proceeding, to the Panel from any party to the appeal without notice and opportunity for all parties to participate in the communication.

(b) Nothing in this section precludes a communication made on the record at a hearing.

(c) Notwithstanding subsection (a), the following communications are permissible:

(1) Communications that are required for disposition of an ex parte matter specifically authorized by statute.

(2) Communications concerning a matter of procedure or practice that is not in controversy.

Note: Authority cited: Section 26042, Business and Professions Code. Reference: Sections 26042 and 26043, Business and Professions Code.

ARTICLE 13. CONFLICT OF INTEREST CODE PROVISIONS

§ 6020. General Provisions.

The Political Reform Act (Government Code Section 81000, et seq.) requires state and local government agencies to adopt and promulgate conflict of interest codes. The Fair Political Practices Commission has adopted a regulation (2 California Code of Regulations Section 18730) that contains the terms of a standard conflict of interest code, which can be incorporated by reference in an agency's code. After public notice and hearing, the standard code may be amended by the Fair Political Practices Commission to conform to amendments in the Political Reform Act. Therefore, the terms of 2 California Code of Regulations Section 18730 and any amendments to it duly adopted by the Fair Political Practices Commission are hereby incorporated by reference. This regulation and the attached Appendix, designating positions and establishing disclosure categories, shall constitute the conflict of interest code of the Cannabis Control Appeals Panel (Panel).

Panel members and the Executive Director must file their statements of economic interests electronically with the Fair Political Practices Commission. All other individuals holding designated positions must file their statements with the Panel. All statements must be made available for public inspection and reproduction under Government Code Section 81008.

16 CCR Appendix

Designated Positions and Disclosure Categories

Position Title	Assigned Categories
Panel Member	1, 2
Executive Officer	1, 2
Attorney (all levels)	1, 2
Associate Governmental Program Analyst	2

Category 1:

Individuals holding a designated position assigned to this category must report all interests in real property located in California as well as investments and business positions in business entities and sources of income (including receipt of gifts, loans and travel payments) if the business entity or source of income is any of the following:

- An applicant for, or current holder of, a cannabis license of any type; or
- The holder of a cannabis license of any type at any time within the preceding four years.

Category 2:

Individuals holding a designated position assigned to this category must report investments and business positions in business entities and sources of income (including receipt of gifts, loans and travel payments) if the business entity or source provides leased facilities, products, equipment, vehicles, machinery or services (including training or consulting services) of the type utilized by the Panel.

Note: Authority cited: Section 87300, Government Code. Reference: Sections 87300 and 87302, Government Code; and Title 2 Code of Regulations Section 18730.

Title 17. Public Health

DIVISION 1. STATE DEPARTMENT OF HEALTH SERVICES

Chapter 13. Manufactured Cannabis Safety [Renumbered]

Change without regulatory effect renumbering and amending title 17, division 1, chapter 13 (subchapters 1-7, sections 40100-40601) to new title 4, division 19 (chapters 10-15, sections 17000-17510), including repealer of section 40156.

Title 18. Public Revenues

DIVISION 2. CALIFORNIA DEPARTMENT OF TAX AND FEE ADMINISTRATION - BUSINESS TAXES

Chapter 8.7. Cannabis Tax Regulations

§ 3700. Cannabis Excise and Cultivation Taxes.

(a) Definitions. For purposes of this chapter (Cannabis Tax Regulations, commencing with Regulation 3700), the definitions of terms in part 14.5, Cannabis Tax, (commencing with section 34010) of division 2 of the Revenue and Taxation Code shall apply and the following terms are defined or further defined below.

(1) "California Cannabis Track-and-Trace system" means the system all persons licensed pursuant to division 10 (commencing with section 26000) of the Business and Professions Code are required to use to record the inventory and movement of cannabis and cannabis products through the commercial cannabis supply chain.

(2) "Cannabis accessories" shall have the same meaning as set forth in section 11018.2 of the Health and Safety Code.

(3) "Cannabis flowers" means the flowers of the plant Cannabis sativa L. that have been harvested, dried, trimmed or untrimmed, and cured, and prior to any processing whereby the plant material is transformed into a concentrate, including, but not limited to, concentrated cannabis, or an edible or topical product containing cannabis or concentrated cannabis and other ingredients. The term "cannabis flowers" excludes leaves and stems removed from the cannabis flowers prior to the cannabis flowers being transferred or sold.

(4) "Cannabis leaves" means all parts of the plant Cannabis sativa L. other than cannabis flowers that are sold or consumed.

(5) "Cultivator" means all persons required to be licensed to cultivate cannabis pursuant to division 10 (commencing with section 26000) of the Business and Professions Code, including a microbusiness that cultivates cannabis as set forth in paragraph (3) of subdivision (a) of section 26070 of the Business and Professions Code.

(6) "Distributor" means a person required to be licensed as a distributor pursuant to division 10 (commencing with section 26000) of the Business and Professions Code, including a microbusiness that acts as a licensed distributor as set forth in paragraph (3) of subdivision (a) of section 26070 of the Business and Professions Code.

(7) "Fresh cannabis plant" means the flowers, leaves, or a combination of adjoined flowers, leaves, stems, and stalk from the plant Cannabis sativa L. that is either cut off just above the roots, or otherwise removed from the plant. To be considered "fresh cannabis plant," the flowers, leaves, or combination of adjoined flowers, leaves, stems, and stalk must be weighed within two hours of the plant being harvested and without any artificial drying such as increasing the ambient temperature of the room or any other form of drying, or curing and must be entered into the California Cannabis Track-and-Trace system, manifested, and invoiced as "fresh cannabis plant." If the California Cannabis Track-and-Trace system is not available, or a licensee is not required to record activity, the paper manifest or invoice shall indicate "fresh cannabis plant" is being sold or transferred.

(8) "Manufacturer" means a person required to be licensed as a manufacturer pursuant to division 10 (commencing with section 26000) of the Business and Professions Code, including a microbusiness that acts as a licensed manufacturer as set forth in paragraph (3) of subdivision (a) of section 26070 of the Business and Professions Code.

(9) "Ounce" means 28.35 grams.

(10) "Plant waste" means waste of the plant Cannabis sativa L. that is managed pursuant to the cannabis waste management provisions of chapter 1, division 8 of title 3 of the California Code of Regulations.

(11) "Wholesale cost" means:

(A) Prior to January 1, 2020, the amount paid by the cannabis retailer for the cannabis or cannabis products, including transportation charges. Discounts and trade allowances must be added back when determining wholesale cost. For purposes of this subdivision, "discounts or trade allowances" are price reductions, or allowances of any kind, whether stated or unstated, and include, without limitation, any price reduction applied to a supplier's price list. The discounts may be for prompt payment, payment in cash, bulk purchases, related-party transactions, or "preferredcustomer" status.

(B) On and after January 1, 2020, the amount paid by the cannabis retailer for the cannabis or cannabis products, including transportation charges.

(b) Collection of Cultivation Tax When Testing Requirement is Waived. For purposes of the cultivation tax imposed on all harvested cannabis that enters the commercial market pursuant to section 34012 of the Revenue and Taxation Code, when the testing requirement is waived pursuant to subdivision (1) of section 26070 of the Business and Professions Code, a distributor shall collect the cultivation tax from cultivators when cannabis is transferred or sold to the distributor.

(c) Cultivation Tax. For transactions made on and after January 1, 2018, the rate of the cultivation tax applies as follows:

(1) Per dry-weight ounce of cannabis flowers, and at a proportionate rate for any other quantity.

(2) Per dry-weight ounce of cannabis leaves, and at a proportionate rate for any other quantity.

(3) Per ounce of fresh cannabis plant, and at a proportionate rate for any other quantity.

(d) Cultivation Tax Invoicing Requirements. A cultivator is liable for the cultivation tax imposed pursuant to section 34012 of the Revenue and Taxation Code. A cultivator's liability for the cultivation tax is not extinguished until the cultivation tax has been paid to the State, except as otherwise provided in subdivision (h) of Revenue and Taxation Code section 34012.

(1) The distributor shall provide to the cultivator, or to the manufacturer if the cannabis was first sold or transferred to a manufacturer, an invoice, receipt, or similar document that identifies the licensee receiving the product, the originating cultivator, associated unique identifier of the cannabis, the amount of cultivation tax, and the weight and category of the cannabis. The weight and category of the cannabis identified on the invoice shall equal the weight and category of the cannabis entered into the California Cannabis Track-and-Trace system.

(2) The manufacturer shall provide to the cultivator when a cultivator sells or transfers cannabis to a manufacturer, an invoice, receipt, or similar document that identifies the licensee receiving the product, the originating cultivator, the associated unique identifier of the cannabis, the amount of cultivation tax, and the weight and category of the cannabis. The weight and category of the cannabis identified on the invoice shall equal the weight and category of the cannabis entered into the California Cannabis Track-and-Trace system.

(3) The manufacturer shall include on the invoice, receipt, or similar document to the distributor or the next party in the transaction, the associated weight and category of the cannabis used to produce the cannabis products. This associated cultivation tax and the weight and category of the cannabis used to produce a cannabis product shall follow the cannabis product from one party to the next until it reaches a distributor for quality assurance review, as described in section 26110 of the Business and Professions Code.

(e) Remittance of Cultivation Tax. A distributor who conducts the required quality assurance review before the cannabis or cannabis products can be sold or transferred to a cannabis retailer pursuant to section 5307, of chapter

2, division 42 of title 16 of the California Code of Regulations, is responsible for the remittance of the cultivation tax based on the weight and category of the cannabis that enters the commercial market.

(f) Cannabis Removed from a Cultivator's Premises is Presumed Sold.

(1) Unless the contrary is established, it shall be presumed that all cannabis removed from the cultivator's premises, except for plant waste, is sold and thereby taxable pursuant to section 34012 of the Revenue and Taxation Code.

(2) The presumption in subdivision (f)(1) may be rebutted by a preponderance of the evidence demonstrating that the cannabis was removed for purposes other than for entry into the commercial market. Reasons for which cannabis may be removed and not subject to tax on that removal include, but are not limited to, the following:

(A) Fire,

(B) Flood,

(C) Pest control,

(D) Processing by a cultivator, such as trimming, drying, curing, grading, packaging, or labeling,

(E) Storage prior to the completion of, and compliance with, the quality assurance review and testing, as required by Business and Professions Code section 26110, and

(F) Testing.

(g) Receipts for Cannabis Excise Tax Paid to Cannabis Retailers. A purchaser of cannabis or cannabis products is liable for the cannabis excise tax imposed pursuant to section 34011 of the Revenue and Taxation Code. A purchaser's liability for the cannabis excise tax is not extinguished until the cannabis excise tax has been paid to the State, except as otherwise provided in subdivision (g)(2).

(1) Each cannabis retailer is required to provide a purchaser of cannabis or cannabis products with an invoice, receipt, or other document that includes a statement that reads: "The cannabis excise taxes are included in the total amount of this invoice."

(2) An invoice, receipt, or other document with the required statement set forth in subdivision (g)(1) obtained from the cannabis retailer is sufficient to relieve the purchaser of the cannabis excise tax imposed on the purchase of the cannabis or cannabis products.

(3) A cannabis retailer may separately state a charge for the cannabis excise tax when the cannabis or cannabis products are sold to a purchaser and the separately stated charge shall be equal to the cannabis excise tax required to be paid to a distributor pursuant to section 34011 of the Revenue and Taxation Code.

(h) Excess Cannabis Excise Tax Collected by a Cannabis Retailer.

(1) Definition. When an amount represented by a cannabis retailer to a customer as constituting cannabis excise tax is computed upon an amount that is not taxable or is in excess of the taxable amount and is actually paid by the customer to the cannabis retailer, the amount so paid is excess cannabis excise tax collected. Excess cannabis excise tax is charged when tax is computed on a transaction which is not subject to cannabis excise tax, when cannabis excise tax is computed on an amount in excess of the amount subject to cannabis excise tax, when cannabis excise tax is computed using a tax rate higher than the rate imposed by law, and when mathematical or clerical errors result in an overstatement of the cannabis excise tax on an invoice, receipt, or similar document.

(2) Procedure Upon the Determination of Excess Cannabis Excise Tax Collected. Whenever the Department determines that a person has collected excess cannabis excise tax, the person will be afforded an opportunity to

refund the excess cannabis excise tax collection to the customers from whom they were collected.

(3) Evidence Sufficient to Establish that Excess Cannabis Excise Tax Amounts Have Been or Will Be Returned to the Customer.

(A) If a person already has refunded to each customer amounts collected as excess cannabis excise tax due, this may be evidenced by any type of record that can be verified by audit such as:

1. Receipts or cancelled checks.

2. Books of account showing that credit has been allowed the customer as an offset against an existing indebtedness owed by the customer to the person.

(B) If a person has not already made excess cannabis excise tax refunds to each customer but desires to do so rather than incur an obligation to the state, the person must:

1. Inform in writing each customer from whom an excess cannabis excise tax amount was collected that the excess cannabis excise tax amount collected will be refunded to the customer or that, at the customer's option, the customer will be credited with such amount, and

2. The person must obtain and retain for verification by the Department an acknowledgement from the customer that the customer has received notice of the amount of indebtedness of the person to the customer.

(C) In the event a cannabis retailer is unable to make such refunds to a customer, the cannabis retailer shall remit the excess cannabis excise tax to a distributor pursuant to paragraph 4 of this subdivision.

(4) Cannabis Retailer's Remittance of Excess Cannabis Excise Tax to a Distributor.

(A) Once a cannabis retailer determines that it has collected excess cannabis excise tax and is unable to make a refund to the customer, and has not previously paid the excess cannabis excise tax to a distributor, the cannabis retailer shall remit the excess cannabis excise tax to a distributor licensed pursuant to division 10 (commencing with section 26000) of the Business and Professions Code.

(B) Upon a cannabis retailer's remittance of the excess cannabis excise tax to a distributor, as set forth in subdivision (h)(4)(A), a distributor shall provide the cannabis retailer with an invoice, receipt, or other similar document that contains all of the following:

1. Date of execution of the invoice, receipt, or other similar document,

2. Name of the distributor,

3. Name of the cannabis retailer,

4. The amount of excess cannabis excise tax,

5. The number of the seller's permit held by the cannabis retailer, and

6. The number of the seller's permit held by the distributor. If the distributor is not required to hold a seller's permit because the distributor makes no sales, the distributor must include a statement to that effect on the receipt in lieu of a seller's permit number.

(5) Distributor's Reporting and Remittance of the Excess Cannabis Excise Tax. A distributor shall report and remit the excess cannabis excise tax collected from the cannabis retailer pursuant to subdivision (h)(4) with the distributor's first return subsequent to receiving the excess cannabis excise tax from the cannabis retailer.

(6) The excess cannabis excise tax provisions in subdivisions (h)(1) through (5) are superseded by the provisions in Regulation 3703 and no longer operative on and after January 30, 2023.

(i) Cannabis or Cannabis Products Sold with Cannabis Accessories. A cannabis excise tax shall be imposed upon purchasers of cannabis or cannabis products sold in this state at the rate of 15 percent of the average market price of any retail sale by a cannabis retailer. Unless as otherwise provided below, the cannabis excise tax does not apply to cannabis accessories.

(1) When cannabis or cannabis products are sold or transferred with cannabis accessories (e.g., vape cartridges) to a cannabis retailer, and a distributor separately states the price of the cannabis or cannabis products from the cannabis accessories, the cannabis excise tax applies to the average market price of the cannabis or cannabis products, and not to the separately stated charge for the cannabis accessories.

(A) A distributor that makes a sales price segregation must maintain supporting documentation used to establish the individual cost of the cannabis or cannabis products and the cannabis accessories.

(B) Charges will be regarded as separately stated only if they are separately set forth in the invoice, receipt, or other document issued to the purchaser contemporaneously with the sale. The fact that the charges can be computed from other records will not suffice as a separate statement.

(2) When cannabis or cannabis products are sold or transferred with cannabis accessories (e.g., vape cartridges) to a cannabis retailer, and a distributor does not separately state the sales price of the cannabis or cannabis products from the cannabis accessories, the cost of the cannabis accessories shall be included in the average market price to which the cannabis excise tax applies.

(j) Reporting the Cannabis Excise Tax. A distributor shall report and remit the cannabis excise tax due with the return for the quarterly period in which the distributor sells or transfers the cannabis or cannabis products to a cannabis retailer.

(1) A person that holds both a cannabis retailer license and a distributor license, or a microbusiness that is authorized to act as a distributor, is subject to the same cannabis excise tax collection and reporting requirements as a person that holds only a distributor license.

(2) A distributor that sells or transfers cannabis or cannabis products to another distributor is not responsible for collecting the cannabis excise tax from the other distributor.

(3) Transactions between two distributors shall document that no cannabis excise tax was collected or remitted on the invoice between the two distributors. Documentation shall identify the selling distributor, the selling distributor's license number, the purchasing distributor, and the purchasing distributor's license number. When the transaction is between a distributor and a microbusiness acting as a distributor, the documentation shall indicate that the microbusiness is acting as a distributor.

(4) The distributor or microbusiness that sells or transfers cannabis or cannabis products to a cannabis retailer is responsible for collecting the cannabis excise tax from the cannabis retailer based on the average market price of the cannabis or cannabis products supplied to the cannabis retailer.

(k) Penalties.

(1) Penalty for Unpaid Taxes. In addition to any other penalty imposed pursuant to the Fee Collection Procedures Law (commencing with section 55001 of the Revenue and Taxation Code) or any other penalty provided by law, a penalty of 50 percent of the amount of the unpaid cannabis excise tax or cannabis cultivation tax shall be added to the cannabis excise tax and cultivation tax not paid in whole or in part within the time required pursuant to sections 34015 and 55041.1 of the Revenue and Taxation Code.

(2) Relief from Penalty for Reasonable Cause. If the Department finds that a person's failure to make a payment of the cannabis excise tax or cannabis cultivation tax is due to reasonable cause and circumstances beyond the person's control, and occurred notwithstanding the exercise of ordinary care and the absence of willful neglect, the person may be relieved of the penalty provided by subdivision (k)(1) for such failure. Any person seeking to be relieved of the penalty shall file with the Department a statement under penalty of perjury setting forth the

facts upon which the claim for relief is based.

Note: Authority cited: Section 15570.40(b), Government Code; and Section 34013, Revenue and Taxation Code. Reference: Sections 34010, 34011, 34012, 34013, 34015, 55041.1 and 55044, Revenue and Taxation Code; Section 11018.2, Health and Safety Code; and Section 15570.40(b), Government Code.

§ 3701. Collection and Remittance of the Cannabis Excise Tax (Repealed).

§ 3702. California Cannabis Track and Trace.

A distributor or cannabis retailer that is required to record commercial cannabis activity in the California Cannabis Track-and-Trace system pursuant to the Medicinal and Adult-Use Cannabis Regulation and Safety Act (commencing with section 26000 of the Business and Professions Code), shall enter into the California Cannabis Track-and-Trace system specified information as follows:

(1) Wholesale Cost. When cannabis or cannabis products are sold or transferred to a cannabis retailer in an arm's length transaction, the distributor and cannabis retailer shall enter the cannabis retailer's wholesale cost of the cannabis or cannabis products.

(2) Retail Selling Price. When cannabis or cannabis products are sold in a retail sale, the cannabis retailer shall enter the retail selling price of the cannabis or cannabis products.

Note: Authority cited: Section 34013, Revenue and Taxation Code. Reference: Sections 34011 and 34015, Revenue and Taxation Code; and Section 26067, Business and Professions Code.

§ 3703. Excess Cannabis Tax.

(a) Excess Cannabis Tax. For purposes of this regulation, "excess cannabis tax" means any amount:

(1) A cannabis retailer collected from a purchaser under the representation by the cannabis retailer that it was cannabis excise tax, which was computed upon an amount that is not subject to cannabis excise tax or was in excess of the amount of cannabis excise tax required to be collected from the purchaser.

(2) A distributor collected from a cannabis retailer under the representation by the distributor that it was cannabis excise tax, which was computed upon an amount that is not subject to cannabis excise tax or was in excess of the amount of cannabis excise tax required to be collected from the cannabis retailer.

(3) A distributor or manufacturer collected from a cultivator under the representation by the distributor or manufacturer that it was cultivation tax, which was computed upon an amount that is not subject to cultivation tax or was in excess of the amount of cultivation tax required to be collected from the cultivator.

(4) A distributor or manufacturer collected from a cultivator under the representation by the distributor or manufacturer that it was cultivation tax, which was computed upon harvested cannabis or harvested cannabis used to make cannabis products that did not enter the commercial market on or before June 30, 2022.

(b) Debt for Unreturned Excess Cannabis Tax. Any amount of excess cannabis tax that is not returned to the purchaser, cannabis retailer, or cultivator that paid it constitutes a debt owed to this state.

(c) Procedures for Cannabis Retailers. When a cannabis retailer ascertains that they have collected excess cannabis tax from a purchaser that has not been paid to the state, they should refund the excess cannabis tax to the purchaser that paid it. If the cannabis retailer is unable or chooses not to refund the excess cannabis tax to the purchaser that paid it, then they shall report and remit it to the Department, unless it was remitted to a distributor pursuant to Regulation 3700 prior to January 30, 2023.

(d) Procedures for Distributors and Manufacturers.

(1) When a manufacturer ascertains that they collected excess cannabis tax from a cultivator that has not been paid to the state, they should refund the excess cannabis tax to the cultivator that paid it. If the manufacturer is unable or chooses not to refund the excess cannabis tax to the cultivator that paid it, then they shall notify the Department so it can collect the excess cannabis tax from the manufacturer, unless the excess cannabis tax was transferred to a distributor to report and remit to the Department pursuant to Regulation 3700 prior to January 30, 2023.

(2) When a distributor ascertains that they collected excess cannabis tax from a cultivator or cannabis retailer that has not been paid to the state, they should refund the excess cannabis tax to the cultivator or cannabis retailer that paid it. If the distributor is unable or chooses not to refund the excess cannabis tax to the cultivator or cannabis retailer that paid it, then they shall notify the Department so it can collect the excess cannabis tax from the distributor, unless the distributor remitted the excess cannabis tax to the Department on or before January 31, 2023.

(e) Determination for Excess Cannabis Tax. When the Department ascertains that a cannabis retailer, distributor, or manufacturer has collected excess cannabis tax that has not been paid to the state, they will be afforded an opportunity to establish that it has been or will be refunded to the purchaser, cannabis retailer, or cultivator that paid it. If the cannabis retailer, distributor, or manufacturer fails or refuses to refund the excess cannabis tax, the Department will issue a notice of determination for the amount of the excess cannabis tax not previously refunded or paid to the state.

(1) A cannabis retailer, distributor, or manufacturer that disagrees with any item included in a notice of determination for excess cannabis tax may file a petition for redetermination with the Department within 30 days from the date that the notice of determination was mailed in accordance with the procedures in article 2a of chapter 1 of division 5 (commencing with section 35005) of title 18 of the California Code of Regulations. If a petition for redetermination is not filed within the 30-day period, the amount determined to be due becomes final and collectible at the expiration of that period.

(2) A timely filed petition for redetermination shall be acknowledged and reviewed in accordance with articles 2a and 8 of chapter 1 of division 5 (commencing with section 35005) of title 18 of the California Code of Regulations, and the amount determined to be due becomes final and collectible 30 days after the Department's final decision on the petition was mailed.

(f) Evidence to Establish that Excess Cannabis Tax Has Been or Will be Refunded.

(1) A person may establish that excess cannabis tax was refunded to a purchaser, cannabis retailer, or cultivator by providing any type of record showing the refund that can be verified by audit, such as a receipt, cancelled check, or books of account showing that credit has been allowed the purchaser, cannabis retailer, or cultivator as an offset against an existing indebtedness owed to the person making the refund.

(2) To establish that excess cannabis tax will be refunded to a purchaser, cannabis retailer, or cultivator, the person must:

(A) Inform the purchaser, cannabis retailer, or cultivator in writing that the excess cannabis tax will be refunded to the purchaser, cannabis retailer, or cultivator or that, at their option, they will be credited with such amount as an offset against an existing indebtedness owed to the person making the refund; and

(B) Obtain and retain for verification by the Department an acknowledgement from the purchaser, cannabis retailer, or cultivator that they received notice of the amount of indebtedness of the person to the purchaser, cannabis retailer, or cultivator.

(g) Records. A cannabis retailer, distributor, or manufacturer shall maintain and make available for examination on request by the Department or its authorized representatives all records necessary to determine whether it owes excess cannabis tax to the state. Such records include, but are not limited to:

(1) Books of account;

(2) Receipts, invoices, cash register tapes, and other documents of original entry supporting the entries in the books of account; and

(3) Schedules or working papers used in connection with the preparation of tax returns and reports.

Note: Authority cited: Section 34013, Revenue and Taxation Code. Reference: Sections 34011, 34012, 34012.3, 34012.5, 34013 and 34015, Revenue and Taxation Code.

§ 3800. Cannabis Excise Tax and Cannabis Retailer Excise Tax Permit.

(a) Definitions. For purposes of this regulation, the following terms have the following meanings:

(1) "Business information" means information the Department deems necessary to determine if a person is required to obtain a cannabis retailer excise tax permit from the Department, determine if the person is required to remit the cannabis excise tax it collects by electronic funds transfer, assign the person a reporting period, and determine how to obtain access to the person's books and records. Such information includes, but is not limited to, the name of the person's business, the addresses of the person's business locations, the date the person's business started or will start, the business's business activities, the business's projected revenue, and the name and contact information of at least one individual the Department may contact to obtain access to the business's books and records.

(2) "Contact information" means information the Department deems necessary to contact and communicate with a person applying for a cannabis retailer excise tax permit and with that person's authorized representative(s). Such information includes, but is not limited to, a current mailing address, email address, and telephone number.

(3) "Department" means the California Department of Tax and Fee Administration.

(4) "Identifying information" means information the Department deems necessary to specifically identify a person applying for a cannabis retailer excise tax permit. Such information includes the person's name, the person's type (e.g., individual, partnership, limited liability company, corporation, etc.), and the person's Federal Employer Identification Number, and may also include, but is not limited to, the person's driver's license number or other government-issued identification card number or entity number issued by the California Secretary of State.

(5) "Ownership information" means information the Department deems necessary to identify the owners of an entity or business. Such information includes, but is not limited to, the owners' names and contact information.

(6) "Representative information" means information the Department deems necessary to verify that the individual who submitted an application for a cannabis retailer excise tax permit is the person applying for a cannabis retailer excise tax permit or is authorized to submit the application on behalf of the person applying for a cannabis retailer excise tax permit. Such information includes, but is not limited to, the individual's name, title, and contact information.

(b) A cannabis excise tax is imposed upon purchasers of cannabis or cannabis products sold at retail in this state on and after January 1, 2023, pursuant to Revenue and Taxation Code section 34011.2. The tax is 15 percent of the cannabis retailer's gross receipts from the retail sale of the cannabis and cannabis products to the purchaser on and after January 1, 2023, and the cannabis retailer is responsible for collecting the cannabis excise tax from the purchaser and remitting that tax to the Department.

(c) On and after January 1, 2023, a person must have a cannabis retailer excise tax permit issued by the Department to engage in business as a cannabis retailer.

(d) To obtain a cannabis retailer excise tax permit, a person shall complete and submit an application for a cannabis retailer excise tax permit through the Department's online services portal via its website at www.cdtfa.ca.gov. Every application for a cannabis retailer excise tax permit shall provide the applicant's identifying information, contact information, business information, ownership information, and representative information.

Note: Authority cited: Section 34013, Revenue and Taxation Code. Reference: Sections 34011.2, 34014, 34015 and 55302, Revenue and Taxation Code.

§ 3805. Cannabis Excise Tax Credit.

(a) A cannabis retailer may claim a credit on their cannabis tax return for the cannabis excise tax amount the cannabis retailer paid to a distributor, pursuant to Revenue and Taxation Code section 34011, on cannabis or cannabis products the distributor sold or transferred to the cannabis retailer prior to January 1, 2023, and the cannabis retailer sold to a purchaser on or after January 1, 2023, in a retail sale subject to cannabis excise tax, pursuant to Revenue and Taxation Code section 34011.2.

(1) The credit must be taken on the cannabis retailer's cannabis tax return filed for the period in which the retail sale of the cannabis or cannabis products occurred. If the credit is not taken on the proper return, the cannabis retailer may file a claim for refund for the amount for which they could have claimed a timely credit.

(2) A cannabis retailer may not claim a credit or refund under this regulation for any amount that a distributor refunded to the retailer.

(b) To support a cannabis excise tax credit or refund, the cannabis retailer shall maintain records, such as invoices, receipts, and other similar documents, that can be verified by audit of:

(1) The retail sale of the cannabis or cannabis products to the purchaser on or after January 1, 2023, including the associated unique identifier for the cannabis or cannabis products sold to the purchaser.

(2) The cannabis excise tax paid to the distributor on the cannabis or cannabis products sold to the purchaser, including:

(A) The distributor's name and Department of Cannabis Control license number;

(B) The date the distributor sold or transferred the cannabis or cannabis products to the cannabis retailer;

(C) The amount of cannabis excise tax the cannabis retailer paid to the distributor on the cannabis or cannabis products sold to the purchaser; and

(D) The associated unique identifier for the cannabis or cannabis products on which the cannabis excise tax was paid to the distributor.

Note: Authority cited: Section 34013, Revenue and Taxation Code. Reference: Sections 34011.01 and 55302, Revenue and Taxation Code.

§ 3810. Vendor Compensation.

(a) Definitions. For purposes of this regulation, the following definitions shall apply:

(1) "Cannabis excise tax" means the cannabis excise tax imposed by section 34011.2 of the Revenue and Taxation Code.

(2) "Department" means the California Department of Tax and Fee Administration.

(3) "Fee waiver" means a retailer license fee waiver or retailer license renewal fee waiver provided pursuant to section 26249 of the Business and Professions Code and implementing regulations.

(4) "Licensed cannabis retailer" means a cannabis retailer, as defined in section 34010 of the Revenue and Taxation Code, that has obtained a retailer license.

(5) "Licensed retail premises" means the physical location from which commercial cannabis activities are authorized to be conducted under a retailer license.

(6) "Retailer license" means a license issued by the Department of Cannabis Control pursuant to division 10 (commencing with section 26000) of the Business and Professions Code authorizing a cannabis retailer to engage in the retail sale of cannabis or cannabis products to customers.

(b) Requirements to Retain Vendor Compensation. A licensed cannabis retailer may retain vendor compensation in an amount equal to 20 percent of the cannabis excise taxes imposed on their retail sales of cannabis or cannabis products authorized under their retailer license for one licensed retail premises, during the periods prescribed by subdivision (d), if the licensed cannabis retailer has received:

(1) Approval from the Department of Cannabis Control for a fee waiver that applies to the issuance or renewal of that retailer license; and

(2) A notice from the Department described in subdivision (c)(4) approving the licensed cannabis retailer to retain vendor compensation from the cannabis excise taxes imposed on their retail sales of cannabis or cannabis products authorized under that retailer license.

(c) Vendor Compensation Application.

(1) A licensed cannabis retailer must request approval to retain vendor compensation by submitting a completed Vendor Compensation Application to the Department through the Department's online services portal via its website at www.cdtfa.ca.gov.

(2) Every Vendor Compensation Application shall include the following:

(A) The name under which the cannabis retailer transacts or intends to transact business;

(B) The addresses of each licensed premises at which the licensed cannabis retailer is authorized to engage in retail sales of cannabis or cannabis products, and identification of the licensed premises where commercial cannabis activities are authorized to be conducted under the retailer license for which the Department of Cannabis Control approved the licensed cannabis retailer's fee waiver;

(C) The number of the licensed cannabis retailer's cannabis tax permit issued pursuant to part 14.5 (commencing with section 34010) of division 2 of the Revenue and Taxation Code;

(D) The issuance and expiration dates and number of the retailer license of the licensed cannabis retailer for which the Department of Cannabis Control approved the licensed cannabis retailer's fee waiver;

(E) The date the Department of Cannabis Control approved the licensed cannabis retailer's fee waiver;

(F) The number of the licensed cannabis retailer's seller's permit issued pursuant to article 2 (commencing with section 6066), chapter 2, part 1, division 2 of the Revenue and Taxation Code; and

(G) The contact information for the individual completing the application, including the individual's first and last name, telephone number, and email address.

(3) Each completed Vendor Compensation Application shall also be submitted with the following:

(A) A copy of the Department of Cannabis Control approved fee waiver issued to the licensed cannabis retailer; and

(B) A copy of the retailer license of the licensed cannabis retailer for which the Department of Cannabis Control approved the licensed cannabis retailer's fee waiver.

(4) The Department will notify the licensed cannabis retailer in writing as to whether they are approved to retain vendor compensation. If they are approved, the Department will also specify the quarterly periods for which they are approved to retain vendor compensation, as provided in subdivision (b), from the cannabis excise taxes imposed on their retail sales of cannabis or cannabis products authorized under their retailer license referred to in subdivision (b).

(d) Retention Periods.

(1) An approval to retain vendor compensation is effective on the first day of the calendar quarter commencing after the date the Department issued the notice approving a licensed cannabis retailer's Vendor Compensation Application and is valid for that calendar quarter. For example, if the Department issues the notice approving a licensed cannabis retailer's Vendor Compensation Application on February 22, 2023, then the cannabis retailer's approval is effective April 1, 2023, and the cannabis retailer is approved to retain vendor compensation, as provided in subdivision (b), from the cannabis excise taxes they are required to report to the Department for the second calendar quarter of 2023.

(2) In general, an approval to retain vendor compensation shall remain valid for four consecutive calendar quarters beginning with the first calendar quarter commencing after the date the Department issued the notice approving the licensed cannabis retailer's Vendor Compensation Application and shall expire at the end of that one-year period. For example, if the Department issues the notice approving a licensed cannabis retailer's Vendor Compensation Application on February 22, 2023, then the cannabis retailer is approved to retain vendor compensation, as provided in subdivision (b), from the cannabis excise taxes they are required to report to the Department for the second, third, and fourth calendar quarters of 2023, and first calendar quarter of 2024, unless the approval to retain vendor compensation expires earlier under subdivision (d)(3).

(3) Unless an approval to retain vendor compensation would expire earlier pursuant to subdivision (d)(2), it shall expire on the last day of the calendar quarter commencing after the date the Department of Cannabis Control first notifies the Department that the cannabis retailer is no longer eligible for a fee waiver, pursuant to subdivision (a)(5) of section 34011.1 of the Revenue and Taxation Code, by either:

(A) Updating a database maintained by the Department of Cannabis Control and accessible to the Department to reflect that the cannabis retailer has become ineligible for a fee waiver; or

(B) Otherwise providing information to the Department reflecting that the cannabis retailer has become ineligible for a fee waiver at the Department's request and for purposes of verifying a cannabis retailer's eligibility to retain vendor compensation. For example, if the Department of Cannabis Control first notifies the Department on March 20, 2024, that a cannabis retailer has become ineligible for a fee waiver, the cannabis retailer's approval to retain vendor compensation expires at the end of the second quarter on June 30, 2024, unless the approval to retain vendor compensation already expired under subdivision (d)(2).

(4) A licensed cannabis retailer may not retain vendor compensation from the cannabis excise taxes required

to be reported to the Department for any period commencing after the date their approval to retain vendor compensation expires.

(e) License Limitation. An approval to retain vendor compensation issued under this regulation only approves a licensed cannabis retailer to retain vendor compensation from cannabis excise taxes imposed on their retail sales of cannabis or cannabis products authorized under their retailer license referred to in subdivision (b), including retail sales authorized under that retailer license after it was renewed. An approval to retain vendor compensation does not approve a licensed cannabis retailer to retain vendor compensation from cannabis excise taxes imposed on any other retail sales. Such retail sales include, but are not limited to, retail sales made after their retailer license referred to in subdivision (b) expired and before that retailer license was renewed, made after that retailer license was revoked, or made under any other retailer license, including a new retailer license for the same premises.

(f) New Application Requirement. If a licensed cannabis retailer's approval to retain vendor compensation has expired or their retailer license referred to in subdivision (b) has expired and not been renewed or has been revoked, the licensed cannabis retailer must submit a new Vendor Compensation Application to the Department as provided in subdivision (c) along with:

(1) A copy of the current Department of Cannabis Control approved fee waiver issued to the licensed cannabis retailer; and

(2) A copy of the current retailer license of the licensed cannabis retailer for which the Department of Cannabis Control approved the licensed cannabis retailer's fee waiver.

(g) Claiming Vendor Compensation.

(1) If approved, a licensed cannabis retailer shall report the amount of vendor compensation retained from the cannabis excise taxes imposed on their retail sales of cannabis or cannabis products, pursuant to subdivision (b), as a credit on their Cannabis Retailer Excise Tax Return for the corresponding reporting period in which they made the retail sales of cannabis or cannabis products.

(2) If a licensed cannabis retailer remits any amount of cannabis excise tax to the Department that they were eligible to retain under this regulation, then the licensed cannabis retailer must file a timely claim for refund to obtain a refund for that amount.

(h) Expiration. A licensed cannabis retailer shall not retain vendor compensation from cannabis excise taxes imposed on retail sales of cannabis or cannabis products made after December 31, 2025.

Note: Authority cited: Section 34013, Revenue and Taxation Code. Reference: Sections 34010, 34011.1 and 34011.2, Revenue and Taxation Code.

Title 23. Waters

DIVISION 3. STATE WATER RESOURCES CONTROL BOARD AND REGIONAL WATER QUALITY CONTROL BOARDS

Chapter 5. Fees.

§ 1068. Fees for Small Domestic, Livestock Stockpond and Small

Irrigation Use Restrictions.

(a) A person who registers an appropriation of water for small domestic or livestock stockpond use pursuant to Water Code section 1228.3 shall pay to the board a non-refundable registration fee of $250.

(b) Each holder of a registration for small domestic or livestock stockpond use issued pursuant to Water Code section 1228.5 shall pay to the board an annual fee in each year after the registration was first registered as follows:

(1) In fiscal year 2018-19, $50.

(2) In fiscal year 2019-20, $75.

(3) In fiscal year 2020-21, $100.

(4) For a small domestic use registration held by a low-income resident for purposes of providing water for human consumption, cooking and sanitary purposes, the annual fee shall be reduced by 20 percent.

(5) For purposes of this section, a low-income resident is: (A) someone whose household income is 200 percent or less of federal poverty level; or (B) someone who is enrolled in a qualified public assistance program.

(6) Any holder of a small domestic use registration who submits adequate substantiation of eligibility for the annual fee reduction pursuant to paragraph (4), above, during fiscal year 2018-19, shall receive a credit on their fiscal year 2019-20 bill in the amount of any overpayment.

(7) For any holder of a small domestic use registration who submits adequate substantiation of eligibility for the annual fee reduction pursuant to paragraph (4), above, after fiscal year 2018-19, the reduction shall take effect in the subsequent fiscal year.

(8) For livestock stockpond use, the maximum annual fee for a single primary owner holding 5 or more registrations shall be as follows:

(A) In fiscal year 2018-19, $250.

(B) In fiscal year 2019-20, $375.

(C) In fiscal year 2020-21, $500.

(c) A person who registers an appropriation of water for small irrigation use other than for irrigation use for cannabis shall pay to the board a non-refundable registration fee of $750.

(d) A person who registers an appropriation of water for small irrigation use other than for irrigation use for cannabis shall pay to the board an annual fee of $100 in each year after the registration was first registered.

(e) A person who registers an appropriation of water for small irrigation use pursuant to Water Code section 1228.3, for which cannabis cultivation is an intended use and for which no onstream reservoir will be constructed or used, shall pay to the board a non-refundable annual fee of $750.

(f) A person who registers an appropriation of water for small irrigation use for cannabis that involves construction or use of an onstream reservoir shall pay a non-refundable filing fee of $4,750.

(g) A person who registers an appropriation of water for small irrigation use for cannabis that involves construction or use of an onstream reservoir shall pay an annual fee of $1,000 in each year after the year in which they pay the filing fee identified in subdivision (f).

(h) A person who registers both an appropriation of water for small irrigation use other than for cannabis use and an appropriation of water for small irrigation use for cannabis that use the same diversion shall receive a 50 percent discount on the fees required pursuant to subdivisions (c) and (d).

(i) A person who, following submittal of a small irrigation use registration for cannabis, claims to divert from a fully-contained spring shall include with the filing of a report intended to demonstrate the diversion is from a fully-contained spring a filing fee of $4,000.

Note: Authority cited: Sections 1058 and 1530, Water Code. Reference: Sections 1228.3, 1228.5 and 1525, Water Code.

§ 1070.5. Statements of Water Diversion and Use for Cannabis Cultivation.

(a) A person who files a statement of water diversion and use pursuant to division 2, part 5.1 (commencing with section 5100) of the Water Code that reports water was used for cannabis cultivation, shall pay to the board a filing fee of $200.

Note: Authority cited: Sections 1058 and 1530, Water Code. Reference: Sections 1525 and 5101, Water Code.

Chapter 9. Waste Discharge Reports and Requirements.

§ 2200.7. Annual Fee Schedule for Cannabis Cultivation.

a) Annual fees for dischargers covered under Statewide General Waste Discharge Requirements for Discharges of Waste Associated with Cannabis Cultivation shall be as follows:

(1) Tier 1 - Dischargers that have a disturbed area greater than 2,000 square feet and less than one acre:

Risk Designation	Annual Fee
Low Risk	$690
Moderate Risk	$1,890
High Risk	$4,890

(2) Tier 2 - Dischargers that have a disturbed area equal to or greater than one acre:

Risk Designation	Annual Fee
Low Risk	$1,090
Moderate Risk	$3,090
High Risk	$8,090

Dishcarges that have a disturbed area equal to or greater than two acres shall pay the applicable surcharge below to a maximum surcharge fee of $20,565:

Acres	Per Acre Surcharge
2-50	$185
51-100	$100
101+	$50

(3) Waiver of Waste Discharge Requirements - Dischargers with indoor cultivation sites that meet the requirements for a waiver of waste discharge requirements or conditionally exempt outdoor sites:

Discharge Type	Application Fee	Annual Fee
Waste Hauler	$690	$690
Municial Sewer	$690	$185
Condititionally Exempt Outdoor Site	$690	$185

Note: Authority cited: Sections 185 and 1058, Water Code. Reference: Sections 13260 and 13269, Water Code.

Chapter 22. State Policy for Water Quality Control.

§ 2925. Cannabis Cultivation Policy - Principles and Guidelines for Cannabis Cultivation.

On October 17, 2017, the State Water Resources Control Board adopted Resolution No. 2017- 0063, adopting the Cannabis Cultivation Policy - Principles and Guidelines for Cannabis Cultivation (Cannabis Policy).

The Cannabis Policy establishes principles and guidelines (requirements) for cannabis cultivation activities to protect water quality and instream flows. The purpose of the Cannabis Policy is to ensure that the diversion of water and discharge of waste associated with cannabis cultivation does not have a negative impact on water quality, aquatic habitat, riparian habitat, wetlands, and springs. The Cannabis Policy applies to the following cannabis cultivation activities throughout California:

- Commercial Recreational
- Commercial Medical
- Personal Use Medical

The Cannabis Policy does not apply to recreational cannabis cultivation for personal use, which is limited to six plants under the Adult Use of Marijuana Act (Proposition 64, approved by voters in November 2016).[1]

---

1 Recreational cannabis cultivation for personal use as defined in Health and Safety Code section 11362.1(a)(3) and section 11362.2.

On February 5, 2019, the State Water Resources Control Board adopted Resolution No. 2019-0007, adopting updates to the Cannabis Policy. The updates were focused on requirements related to tribal buffers, indoor cultivation sites, onstream reservoirs, and winterization requirements. The Cannabis Policy and all updates to the Cannabis Policy were adopted in accordance with California Water Code Section 13149.

Part 3: Charts of California Cannabis License Types

Cultivation Licenses

License Type	License Name	Other Info
1	Specialty Outdoor	5,000 sq. ft. or less, or up to 50 mature plants on noncontiguous plots
1A	Specialty Indoor	501 – 5,000 sq. ft.
1B	Specialty Mixed-Light	2,501 – 5000 sq. ft.
1C	Specialty Cottage	Outdoor site - up to 25 mature plants or 2,500 sq. ft. or less Indoor - 500 sq. ft. or less Mixed-light - 2,500 sq. ft. or less of total canopy
2	Small Outdoor	5,001 – 10,000 sq. ft.
2A	Small Indoor	5,001 – 10,000 sq. ft.
2B	Small Mixed-Light	5,001 – 10,000 sq. ft.
3	Medium Outdoor	10,001 sq. ft. – 1 acre
3A	Medium Indoor	10,001 – 22,000 sq. ft.
3B	Medium Mixed-Light	10,001 – 22,000 sq. ft.
4	Nursery	Cultivation of clones, immature plants, seeds, and other agricultural products used specifically for propagation
5	Large Outdoor	Greater than 1 acre
5A	Large Indoor	Greater than 22,000 sq. ft.
5B	Large Mixed-Light	Greater than 22,000 sq. ft.
PROCESSOR	Processor	Conducts only trimming, drying, curing, grading, packaging, and labeling

Manufacturer Licenses

License Type	License Name	Other Info
6	Non-Volatile Manufacturing	Mechanical methods or non-volatile solvents; May also do what Type N, Type P, and Type S may do
7	Volatile Manufacturing	Volatile solvents; May also do what Type 6, Type N, Type P, and Type S may do
N	Infusion	Infusions; May also do what Type P and Type S may do
P	Packaging & Labeling	Manufacturers that only package and label
S	Shared-Use Manufacturer	Must use a designated shared-use facility

Additional Licenses

License Type	License Name	Other Info
8	Testing Laboratory	Laboratory testing; Must be independent
9	Non-Storefront Retail	Retail sales; Delivery-only
10	Retail	Retail sales on premises; Can deliver with local permit
11	Distributor	"Tax collector"; Need Distributor or Type 13 to move product
12	Microbusiness	Must engage in at least 3 of the following 4: Cultivation, Manufacturing, Distribution, and Retail Sale
13	Transport-Only Distribution	Need this or Type 11 to move product; Different fee schedule if only doing self-transport
14	Event Organizer	Needed to host cannabis events
EVENT	Temporary Cannabis Event	Separate licenses needed for each event; Local approval needed

Index

A

B

C

D

E

F

G

H

I

L

M

N

O

P

R

S

T

TAXES

V

W

www.ingramcontent.com/pod-product-compliance
Lightning Source LLC
LaVergne TN
LVHW081948200926
848484LV00009B/2523